Microsoft® Access 2002

Illustrated Complete

Lisa Friedrichsen

Australia • Canada • Mexico • Singapore • Spain • United Kingdom • United States

Microsoft Access 2002 - Illustrated Complete

Lisa Friedrichsen

Managing Editor:
Nicole Jones Pinard

Production Editor:
Catherine DiMassa

QA Manuscript Reviewers:
John Freitas, Ashlee Welz, Alex White, Harris Bierhoff, Serge Palladino, Holly Schabowski, Jeff Schwartz, Marianne Broughey

Product Manager:
Emily Heberlein

Developmental Editors:
Rachel Biheller Bunin, Lisa Ruffolo

Text Designer:
Joseph Lee, Black Fish Design

Associate Product Manager:
Emeline Elliott

Editorial Assistant:
Christina Kling Garrett

Composition House:
GEX Publishing Services

Printed in the United States of America

2 3 4 5 6 7 8 9 BM 05 04 03 02

For more information, contact Course Technology, 25 Thomson Place, Boston, Massachusetts, 02210.

Or find us on the World Wide Web at: www.course.com

ISBN 0-619-04508-6

The Illustrated Series Vision

Teaching and writing about computer applications can be extremely rewarding and challenging. How do we engage students and keep their interest? How do we teach them skills that they can easily apply on the job? As we set out to write this book, our goals were to develop a textbook that:

- works for a beginning student
- provides varied, flexible and meaningful exercises and projects to reinforce the skills
- serves as a reference tool
- makes your job as an educator easier, by providing resources above and beyond the textbook to help you teach your course

Our popular, streamlined format is based on advice from instructional designers and customers. This flexible design presents each lesson on a two-page spread, with step-by-step instructions on the left, and screen illustrations on the right. This signature style, coupled with high-caliber content, provides a comprehensive yet manageable introduction to Microsoft Access 2002—it is a teaching package for the instructor and a learning experience for the student.

ACKNOWLEDGMENTS

This Access book is dedicated to my students, and all who are using this book to teach and learn about Access. Thank you. Also, thank you to all of the professionals who helped me create this book.

Thanks to the reviewers who provided feedback and ideas to us, especially Stephanie Hazen and Dr. Dominic Ligori.

Lisa Friedrichsen
and the Illustrated Team

Preface

Welcome to *Microsoft Access 2002–Illustrated Complete.* Each lesson in the book contains elements pictured to the right in the sample two-page spread.

► How is the book organized?

Two units on Windows 2000 introduce students to basic operating system skills. The book is then organized into 16 units on Access, covering creating and using tables, queries, forms, and reports, through advanced database skills including creating data access pages, macros & modules, and managing database objects.

► What kinds of assignments are included in the book? At what level of difficulty?

The lesson assignments use MediaLoft, a fictional chain of bookstore cafés, as the case study. The assignments on the blue pages at the end of each unit increase in difficulty. Project files and case studies, with many international examples, provide a great variety of interesting and relevant business applications for skills. Assignments include:

- **Concepts Reviews** include multiple choice, matching, and screen identification questions.
- **Skills Reviews** provide additional hands-on, step-by-step reinforcement.
- **Independent Challenges** are case projects requiring critical thinking and application of the skills learned in the unit. The Independent Challenges increase in difficulty, with the first Independent Challenge in each unit being the easiest (most step-by-step with detailed instructions). Independent Challenges 2 and 3 become increasingly open-ended, requiring more independent thinking and problem solving.
- **E-Quest Independent Challenges** are case projects with a Web focus. E-Quests require the use of the World Wide Web to conduct research to complete the project.
- **Visual Workshops** show a completed file and require that the file be created without any step-by-step guidance, involving problem solving and an independent application of the unit skills.

Each 2-page spread focuses on a single skill.

Concise text that introduces the basic principles in the lesson and integrates the brief case study (indicated by the paintbrush icon).

Access 2002

Understanding Sorting, Filtering, and Finding

The records of a datasheet are automatically sorted according to the data in the primary key field. Often, however, you may want to view or print records in an entirely different sort order, or you may want to display a subset of the records, such as those within the same music category or those below a certain retail price. Access makes it easy to sort, find data, and filter a datasheet by using buttons on the Table Datasheet toolbar, summarized in Table B-2. Kelsey studies the sort, find, and filter features to better learn how to find and retrieve information.

Details

- **Sorting** refers to reorganizing the records in either ascending or descending order based on the contents of a field. In ascending order, Text fields sort from A to Z, Number and Currency fields from the lowest to the highest value, and Date/Time fields from the oldest date to the date furthest into the future. In Figure B-9 the Music Inventory table has been sorted in ascending order on the Artist field. Notice that in a Text field, numbers sort before letters.
- **Filtering** means temporarily isolating a subset of records, as shown in Figure B-10. For example, by using a filter, you can produce a listing of all music with the value "Rock" in the Category field. To redisplay all of the records in the datasheet, click the Remove Filter button. The filtered subset can be formatted and printed just like the entire datasheet.
- **Finding** refers to locating a specific piece of data, such as "Amy." The Find and Replace dialog box is shown in Figure B-11. The options in this dialog box are summarized below.
  - **Find What:** Provides a text box for your search criteria. The search criteria might be Amy, Beatles, or Capitol Records.
  - **Look In:** Determines whether Access looks for the search criteria in the current field or in the entire datasheet.
  - **Match:** Determines whether the search criteria must exactly match the contents of the whole field, any part of the field, or the start of the field.
  - **Search:** Allows you to search the entire datasheet (All) or just those records before (Up) or after (Down) the current record.
  - **Match Case:** Determines whether the search criteria is case sensitive (e.g., NH vs. Nh vs. nh).
  - **Search Fields As Formatted:** Determines whether the search criteria is compared to the actual value of the field or the formatted appearance of the value (e.g., 10 vs. $10.00).
  - **Replace tab:** Provides a Replace With text box for you to specify replacement text. For example, you can find every occurrence of CD and replace it with Compact Disc.

QuickTip

If you close a datasheet without saving the layout changes, the records return to the original sort order based on the values in the primary key field. If you close a datasheet and save layout changes, the last sort order will be saved.

Using wildcards

Wildcards are symbols you use as substitutes for characters to locate data that matches your Find criteria. Access uses these wildcards: the asterisk (*) represents any group of characters, the question mark (?) stands for any single character, and the pound sign (#) stands for a single number digit. For example, to find any word beginning with S, type s* in the Find What text box.

► ACCESS B-10 USING TABLES AND QUERIES

Hints as well as troubleshooting advice, right where you need it – next to the step itself.

Clues to Use boxes provide concise information that either expands on the major lesson skill or describes an independent task that in some way relates to the major lesson skill.

Every lesson features large, full-color representations of what the screen should look like as students complete the numbered steps.

FIGURE B-9: Music Inventory datasheet sorted by Artist

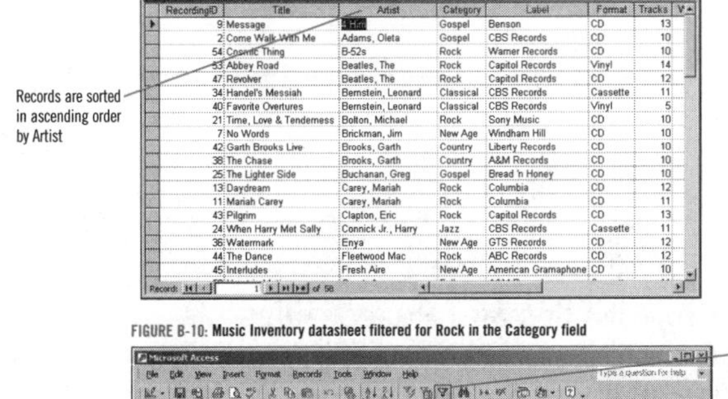

FIGURE B-10: Music Inventory datasheet filtered for Rock in the Category field

Sort Ascending button

Sort Descending button

Selection criteria = Rock

Field description text

Apply Filter or Remove Filter button

Filter By Form button

Filter By Selection button

Number of records in filtered subset

FIGURE B-11: Find and Replace dialog box

Search criteria

Look In field

Search direction

Search criteria must match whole field

TABLE B-2: Sort, Filter, and Find buttons

name	button	purpose
Sort Ascending		Sorts records based on the selected field in ascending order (0 to 9, A to Z)
Sort Descending		Sorts records based on the selected field in descending order (Z to A, 9 to 0)
Filter By Selection		Filters records based on selected data and hides records that do not match
Filter By Form		Filters records based on more than one selection criteria by using the Filter By Form window
Apply Filter or Remove Filter		Applies or removes the filter
Find		Searches for a string of characters in the current field or all fields

Access 2002

USING TABLES AND QUERIES ACCESS B-11

Quickly accessible summaries of key terms, toolbar buttons, or keyboard alternatives connected with the lesson material. Students can refer easily to this information when working on their own projects at a later time.

The pages are numbered according to unit. B indicates the unit, 11 indicates the page.

► What online content solutions are available to accompany this book?

Visit www.course.com for more information on our online content for Illustrated titles. Options include:

MyCourse.com

Need a quick, simple tool to help you manage your course? Try MyCourse.com, the easiest to use, most flexible syllabus and content management tool available. MyCourse.com offers you brand new content, including Topic Reviews, Extra Case Projects, and Quizzes, to accompany this book.

WebCT

Course Technology and WebCT have partnered to provide you with the highest quality online resources and Web-based tools for your class. Course Technology offers content for this book to help you create your WebCT class, such as a suggested Syllabus, Lecture Notes, Practice Test questions, and more.

Blackboard

Course Technology and Blackboard have also partnered to provide you with the highest quality online resources and Web-based tools for your class. Course Technology offers content for this book to help you create your Blackboard class, such as a suggested Syllabus, Lecture Notes, Practice Test questions, and more.

► Is this book MOUS Certified?

Microsoft Access 2002 – Illustrated Complete covers the Core and Expert objectives for Access and has received certification approval as courseware for the MOUS program. See the inside front cover for more information on MOUS certification.

The first page of each unit includes MOUS symbols to indicate which skills covered in the unit are MOUS skills. A grid in the back of the book lists all the exam objectives and cross-references them with the lessons and exercises.

Instructor Resources

The Instructor's Resource Kit (IRK) CD is Course Technology's way of putting the resources and information needed to teach and learn effectively into your hands. All the components are available on the IRK (pictured below), and many of the resources can be downloaded from www.course.com.

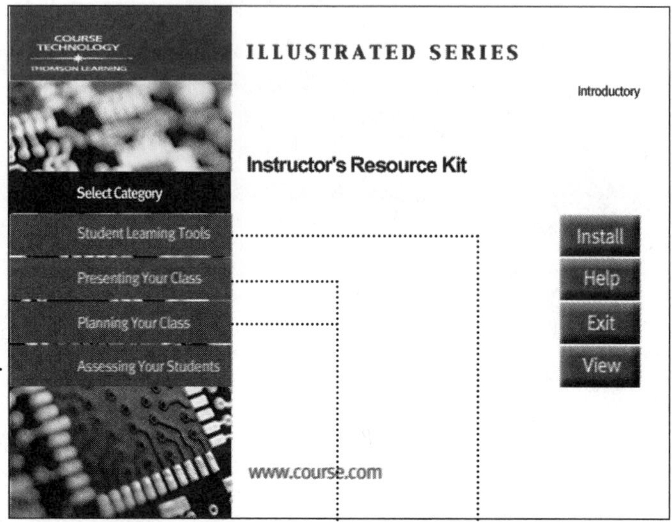

ASSESSING YOUR STUDENTS

Solution Files

Solution Files are Project Files completed with comprehensive sample answers. Use these files to evaluate your students' work. Or, distribute electronically or in hard copy so students can verify their own work.

ExamView

ExamView is a powerful testing software package that allows you to create and administer printed, computer (LAN-based), and Internet exams. ExamView includes hundreds of questions that correspond to the topics covered in this text, enabling students to generate detailed study guides that include page references for further review. The computer-based and Internet testing components allow students to take exams at their computers, and also save you time by grading each exam automatically.

PRESENTING YOUR CLASS

Figure Files

Figure Files contain all the figures from the book in .jpg format. Use the figure files to create transparency masters or in a PowerPoint presentation.

STUDENT TOOLS

Project Files and Project Files List

To complete most of the units in this book, your students will need **Project Files**. Put them on a file server for students to copy. The Project Files are available on the Instructor's Resource Kit CD-ROM, the Review Pack, and can also be downloaded from www.course.com.

Instruct students to use the **Project Files List** at the end of the book. This list gives instructions on copying and organizing files.

PLANNING YOUR CLASS

Instructor's Manual

Available as an electronic file, the Instructor's Manual is quality-assurance tested and includes unit overviews, detailed lecture topics for each unit with teaching tips, comprehensive sample solutions to all lessons and end-of-unit material, and extra Independent Challenges. The Instructor's Manual is available on the Instructor's Resource Kit CD-ROM, or you can download it from www.course.com.

Sample Syllabus

Prepare and customize your course easily using this sample course outline (available on the Instructor's Resource Kit CD-ROM).

SAM, Skills Assessment Manager for Microsoft Office XP

SAM is the most powerful Office XP assessment and reporting tool that will help you gain a true understanding of your students' proficiency in Microsoft Word, Excel, Access, and PowerPoint 2002. (Available separately from the IRK CD.)

TOM, Training Online Manager for Microsoft Office XP

TOM is Course Technology's MOUS-approved training tool for Microsoft Office XP. Available via the World Wide Web and CD-ROM, TOM allows students to actively learn Office XP concepts and skills by delivering realistic practice through both guided and self-directed simulated instruction.

Brief Contents

Contents

Windows 2002

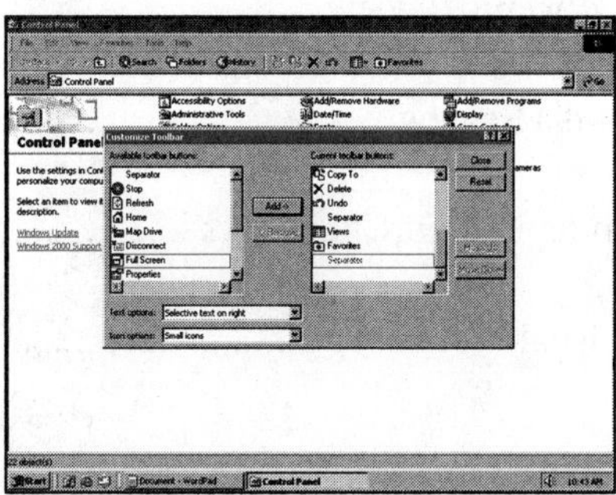

Contents

Working with Programs, Files, and Folders WINDOWS B-1

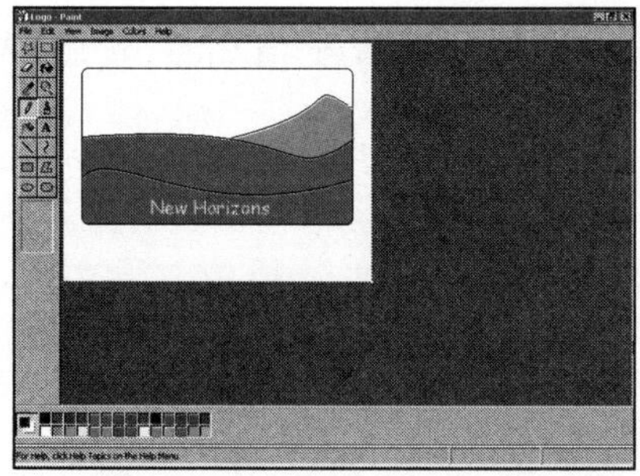

Access 2002

Getting Started with Access 2002

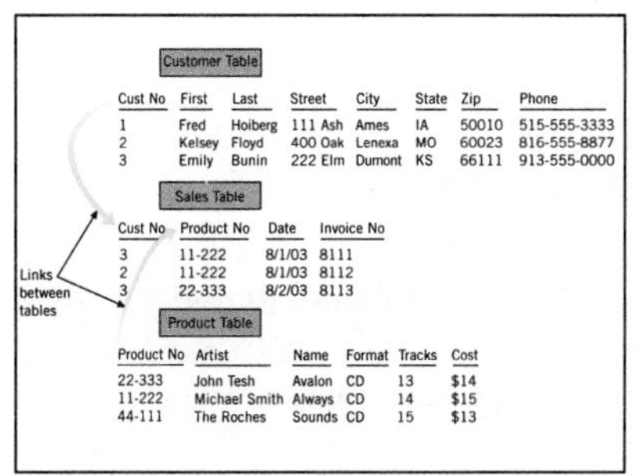

Customer Table

Cust No	First	Last	Street	City	State	Zip	Phone
1	Fred	Hoiberg	111 Ash	Ames	IA	50010	515-555-3333
2	Kelsey	Floyd	400 Oak	Lenexa	MO	60023	816-555-8877
3	Emily	Bunin	222 Elm	Dumont	KS	66111	913-555-0000

Sales Table

Cust No	Product No	Date	Invoice No
3	11-222	8/1/03	8111
2	11-222	8/1/03	8112
3	22-333	8/2/03	8113

Product Table

Product No	Artist	Name	Format	Tracks	Cost
22-333	John Tesh	Avalon	CD	13	$14
11-222	Michael Smith	Always	CD	14	$15
44-111	The Roches	Sounds	CD	15	$13

Contents

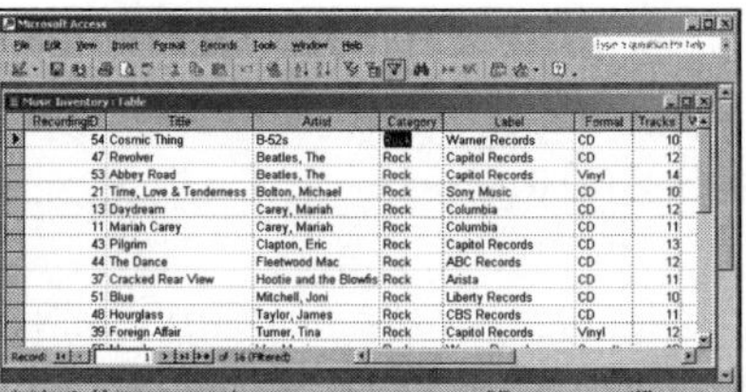

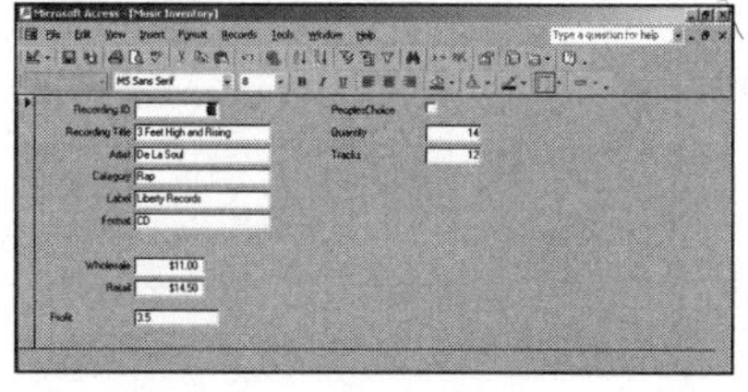

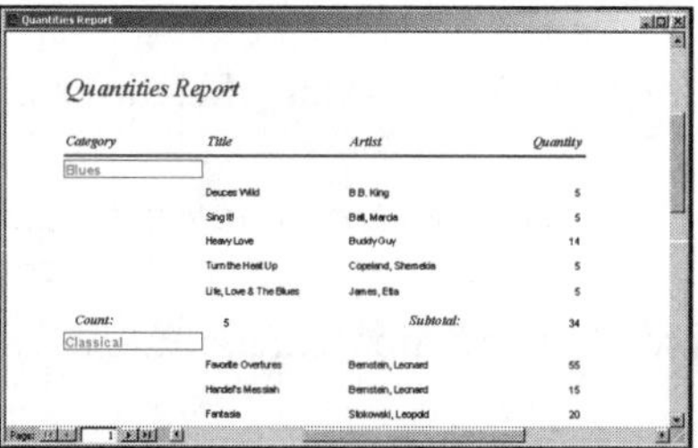

Quantities Report
Category
Title
Artist
Quantity

Contents

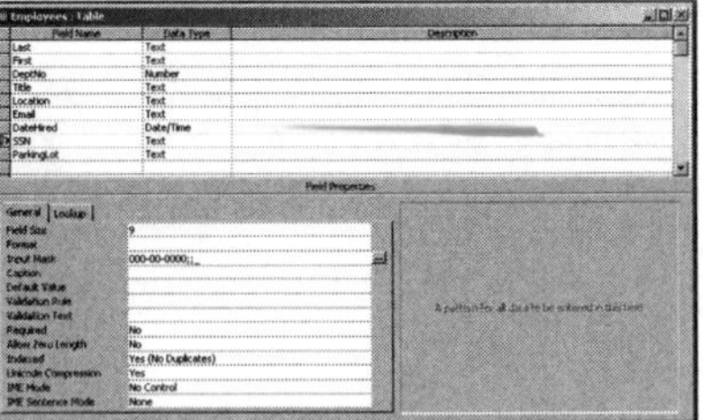

Creating Multiple Table Queries ACCESS F-1

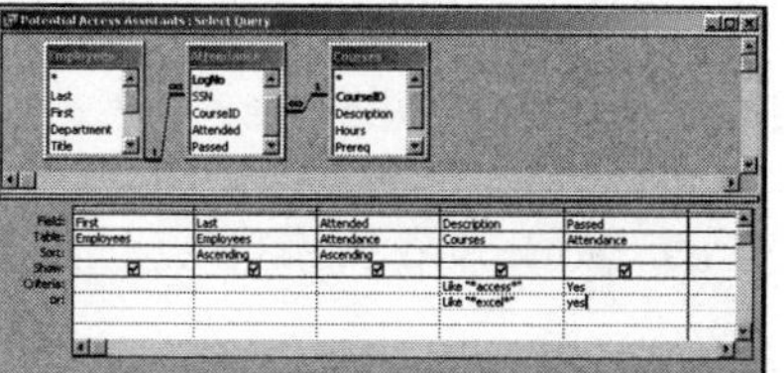

Developing Forms and Subforms ACCESS G-1

Contents

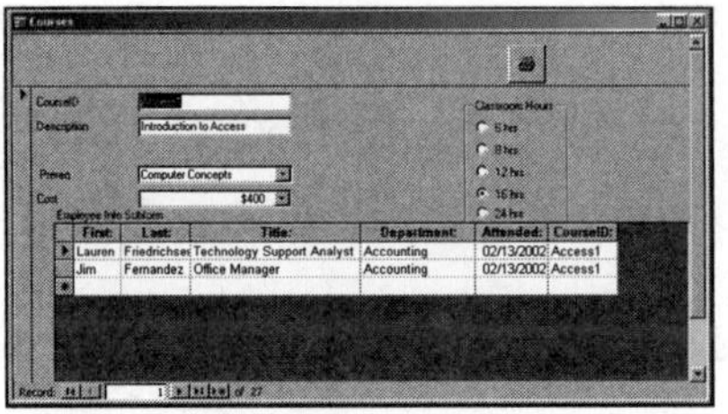

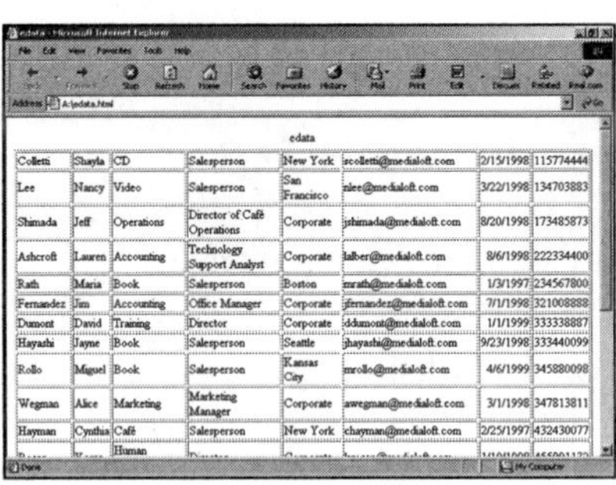

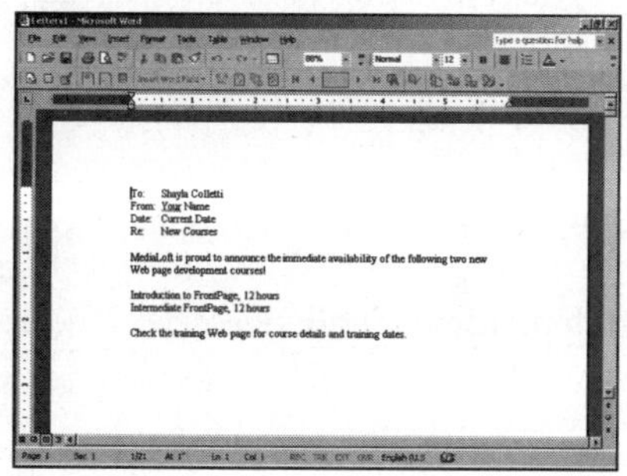

Contents

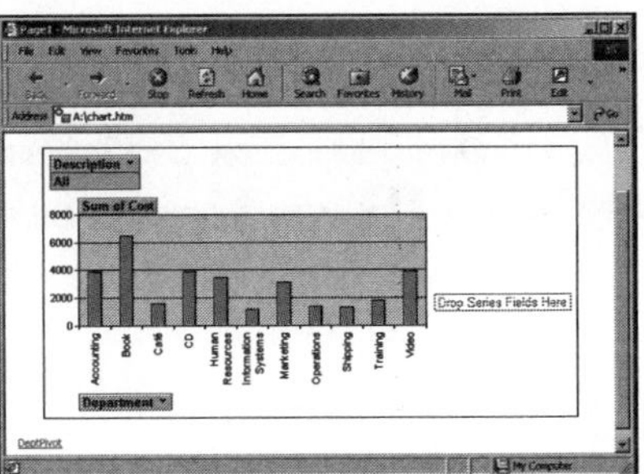

Page1 - Microsoft Internet Explorer
File Edit View Favorites Tools Help
Back Forward Stop Refresh Home Search Favorites History Mail Print Edit
Address A:\chart.htm
Go
Description
All
Sum of Cost
8000
6000
4000
2000
0
Accounting
Book
Café
CD
Human Resources
Information Systems
Marketing
Operations
Shipping
Training
Video
Drop Series Fields Here
Department
DeptPivot
My Computer

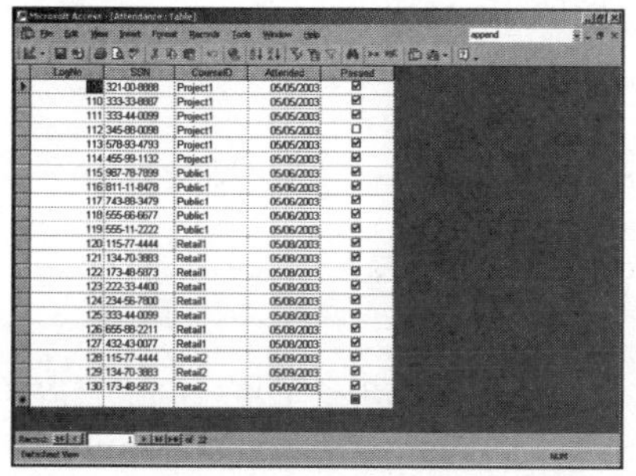

Creating Advanced Forms and Reports

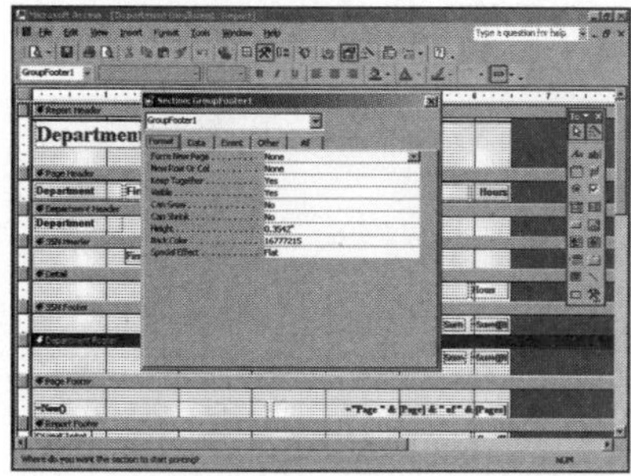

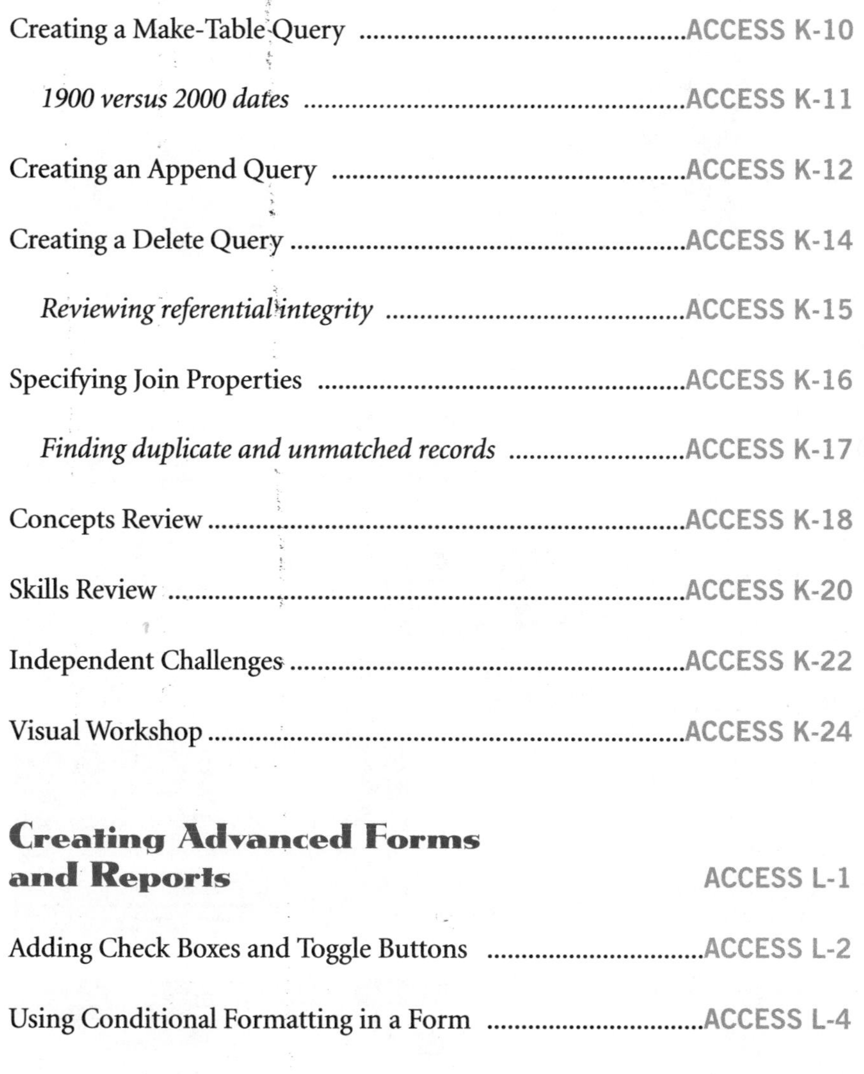

Contents

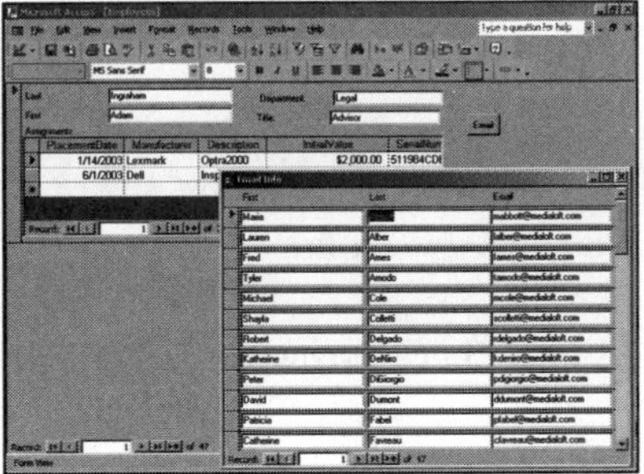

Creating Macros

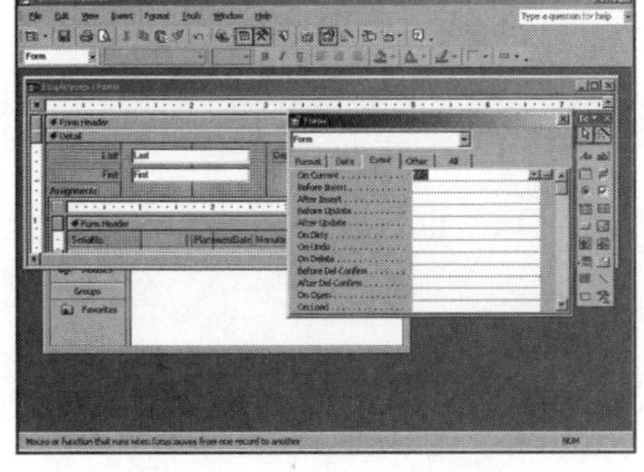

Creating Modules

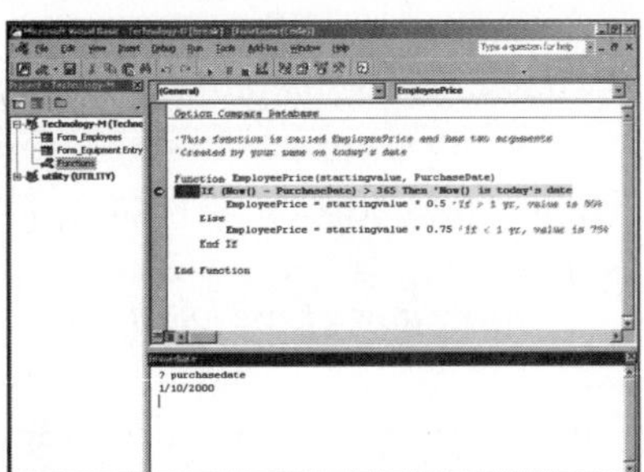

Contents

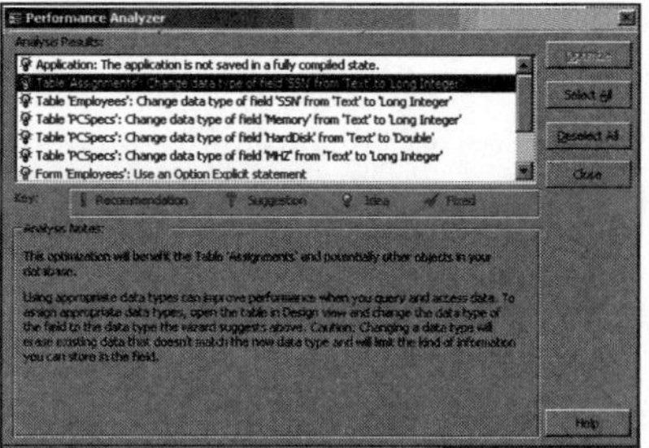

Performance Analyzer
Application: The application is not saved in a fully compiled state.
Table 'Employees': Change data type of field 'SSN' from 'Text' to 'Long Integer'
Table 'PCSpecs': Change data type of field 'Memory' from 'Text' to 'Long Integer'
Table 'PCSpecs': Change data type of field 'HardDisk' from 'Text' to 'Double'
Table 'PCSpecs': Change data type of field 'MHZ' from 'Text' to 'Long Integer'
Form 'Employees': Use an Option Explicit statement
Close

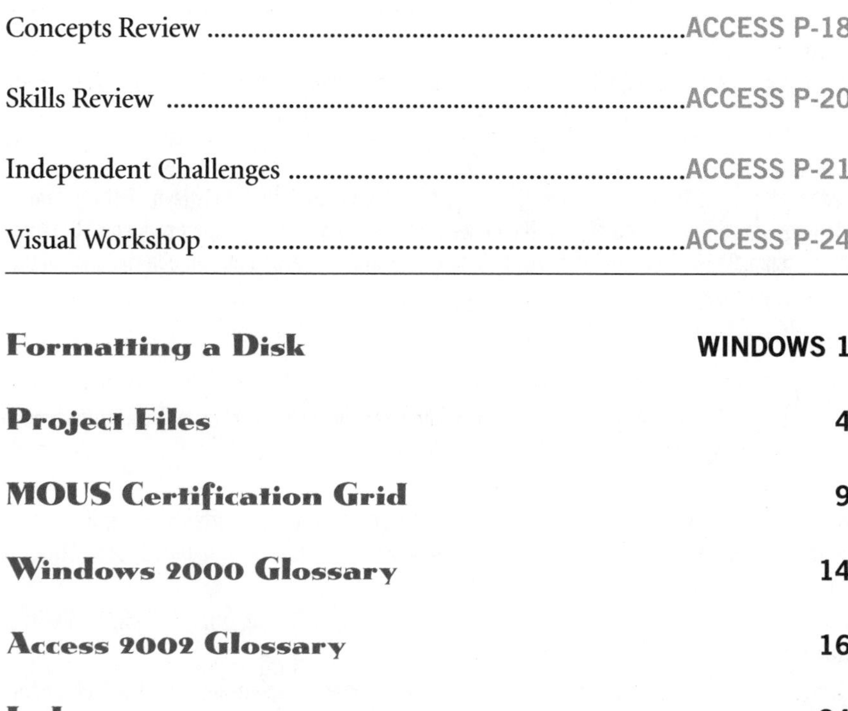

Read This Before You Begin

Software Information and Required Installation

This book was written and tested using Microsoft Office XP - Professional Edition, with a typical installation on Microsoft Windows 2000, with Internet Explorer 5.0 or higher.

What are Project Files?

To complete many of the units in this book, you need to use Project Files. You begin with a Project File so you don't have to type in all the information you need in the database. Your instructor will either provide you with a copy of the Project Files or ask you to make your own copy. Detailed instructions on how to organize your files, as well as a complete listing of all the files you'll need and will create, can be found in the back of the book (look for the yellow pages) in the Project Files List.

Why is my screen different from the book?

1. Your Desktop components and some dialog box options might be different if you are using an operating system other than Windows 2000.
2. Depending on your computer hardware capabilities and the Windows Display settings on your computer, you may notice the following differences:
   - Your screen may look larger or smaller because of your screen resolution (the height and width of your screen)
   - The colors of the title bar in your screen may be a solid blue
3. Depending on your Office settings, your toolbars may display on a single row and your menus may display with a shortened list of frequently used commands. Office menus and toolbars can modify themselves to your working style by displaying only the most frequently used buttons and menu commands.

To view buttons not currently displayed, click a Toolbar Options button at the end of either the Standard or Formatting toolbar. To view the full list of menu commands, click the double arrow at the bottom of the menu.

This book assumes you are displaying toolbars on two rows and full menus. To view, modify or reset the toolbar and menu options, click Tools on the menu bar, then click Customize, and select the option best suited for your working style.

Important Information if you are using floppy disks

Compact on Close?

If you are storing your Access databases on floppy disks, you should NOT use the Compact on Close option (available from the Tools menu). While the Compact on Close feature works well if your database is stored on your hard drive or on another large storage device, it can cause problems if your database is stored on a floppy when the size of your database is greater than the available free space on the floppy. Here's why: When you close a database with the Compact on Close feature turned on, the process creates a temporary file that is just as large as the original database file. In a successful compact process, this temporary file is deleted after the compact procedure is completed. But if there is not enough available space on your floppy to create this temporary file, the compact process never finishes, which means that your original database is never closed properly. And if you do not close an Access database properly before attempting to use it again, you can easily corrupt it beyond repair. *Therefore, if you use floppies to complete these exercises, please follow the guidelines on how to organize your databases on floppies in the **Project Files List** so that you do not run out of room on a floppy. Also, please **do not use the Compact on Close feature for databases stored on floppies**.*

Closing a Database Properly

It is extremely important to close your databases properly before copying, moving, e-mailing the database file, or before ejecting the Project Files floppy disk from the disk drive. Access database files are inherently multi-user, which means that multiple people can work on the same database file at the same time. To accomplish this capability, Access creates temporary files to keep track of which record you are working on while the database is open. These temporary files must be closed properly before you attempt to copy, move, or e-mail the database. They must also be closed before you eject a floppy that contains the database. If these temporary files do not get closed properly, the database can easily be corrupted beyond repair. Fortunately, Access closes these temporary files automatically when you close the Access application window. So to be sure that you have properly closed a database that is stored on a floppy, *close not only the database window, but also **close the Access application window** before copying, moving, or e-mailing a database file, as well as before ejecting a floppy that stores the database.*

2000 vs. 2002 File Format

New databases created in Access 2002 default to an Access 2000 file format. That's why "Access 2000 file format" is shown in the database window title bar for the figures in this book. This also means that Access databases now support seamless backward compatibility with the prior version of Access like other products in the Microsoft Office suite such as Word and Excel. But while the Project Files for this book could be opened and used in Access 2000, the figures in this book represent the Access 2002 application, use the Access 2002 menus and toolbars, and highlight the new features of Access 2002, including new task panes, new quick keystrokes, PivotTables, and improved dynamic Web pages.

Windows 2000

Getting Started with Windows 2000

Objectives

- Start Windows and view the Active Desktop
- Use the mouse
- Start a program
- Move and resize windows
- Use menus, keyboard shortcuts, and toolbars
- Use dialog boxes
- Use scroll bars
- Use Windows Help
- Close a program and shut down Windows

Microsoft Windows 2000 is an **operating system**, a computer **program**, or set of instructions, that controls how the computer carries out basic tasks such as displaying information on your computer screen and running programs. Windows 2000 helps you save and organize the results of your work as **files**, which are electronic collections of data. Windows 2000 also coordinates the flow of information among the programs, printers, storage devices, and other components of your computer system, as well as among other computers on a network. When you work with Windows 2000, you will notice many **icons**, small pictures intended to be meaningful symbols of the items they represent. You will also notice rectangular-shaped work areas known as **windows**, thus the name of the operating system. These icons, windows, and various other words and symbols create what is referred to as a **graphical user interface** (**GUI**, pronounced "gooey"), through which you interact with the computer. This unit introduces you to basic skills that you can use in all Windows programs.

Windows 2000

Starting Windows and Viewing the Active Desktop

When you turn on your computer, Windows 2000 automatically starts and the Active Desktop appears. The **Active Desktop**, shown in Figure A-1, is where you organize all the information and tools you need to accomplish your computer tasks. You can access, store, share, and explore information seamlessly, whether it resides on your computer, a network, or the **Internet**, a worldwide collection of over 40 million computers linked together to share information. The desktop is called "active" because it offers an interactive link between your computer and the Internet, so that Internet content displayed on your desktop, such as stock prices or weather information, is always up to date. When you start Windows for the first time, the desktop appears with the **default** settings, those preset by the operating system. For example, the default color of the desktop is blue. If any of the default settings have been changed on your computer, your desktop will look different than the one in the figures, but you should be able to locate all the items you need. The bar at the bottom of your screen is called the **taskbar**, which shows what programs are currently running. You use the Start menu, accessed by clicking the **Start button** at the left end of the taskbar, to perform such tasks as starting programs, finding and opening files, and accessing Windows Help. The **Quick Launch toolbar** is next to the Start button; it contains several buttons you can click to start Internet-related programs quickly, and another that you can click to show the desktop when it is not currently visible. Table A-1 identifies the icons and other elements you see on your desktop. If Windows 2000 is not currently running, follow the steps below to start it now.

Trouble?

If you don't know your password, see your instructor or technical support person.

1. **Turn on your computer and monitor**
   You might see a "Please select the operating system to start" prompt. Don't worry about selecting one of the options; Microsoft Windows 2000 Professional automatically starts after 30 seconds. When Windows starts and the desktop appears, you may see a Log On to Windows dialog box. If so, continue to Step 2. If not, view Figure A-1, then continue on to the next lesson.

Trouble?

If the Getting Started with Windows 2000 dialog box opens, move your mouse pointer over the Exit button in the lower-right corner of the dialog box and press the left mouse button once to close the dialog box.

2. **Enter the correct user name, type your password, then press [Enter]**
   Once the password is accepted, the Windows desktop appears on your screen. See Figure A-1.

Accessing the Internet from the Active Desktop

Windows 2000 provides a seamless connection between your desktop and the Internet with Internet Explorer. Internet Explorer is an example of a **browser,** a program designed to access the **World Wide Web** (also known as the **WWW**, or simply the **Web**). Internet Explorer is integrated with the Windows 2000 operating system. You can access it by clicking its icon on the desktop or on the Quick Launch toolbar. You can access Web pages, and place Web content such as weather or stock updates on the desktop for instant viewing. This information is updated automatically whenever you connect to the Internet, making your desktop truly active. You can also communicate electronically with other Internet users, using the Windows e-mail and newsreader program, Outlook Express.

FIGURE A-1: Windows Active Desktop

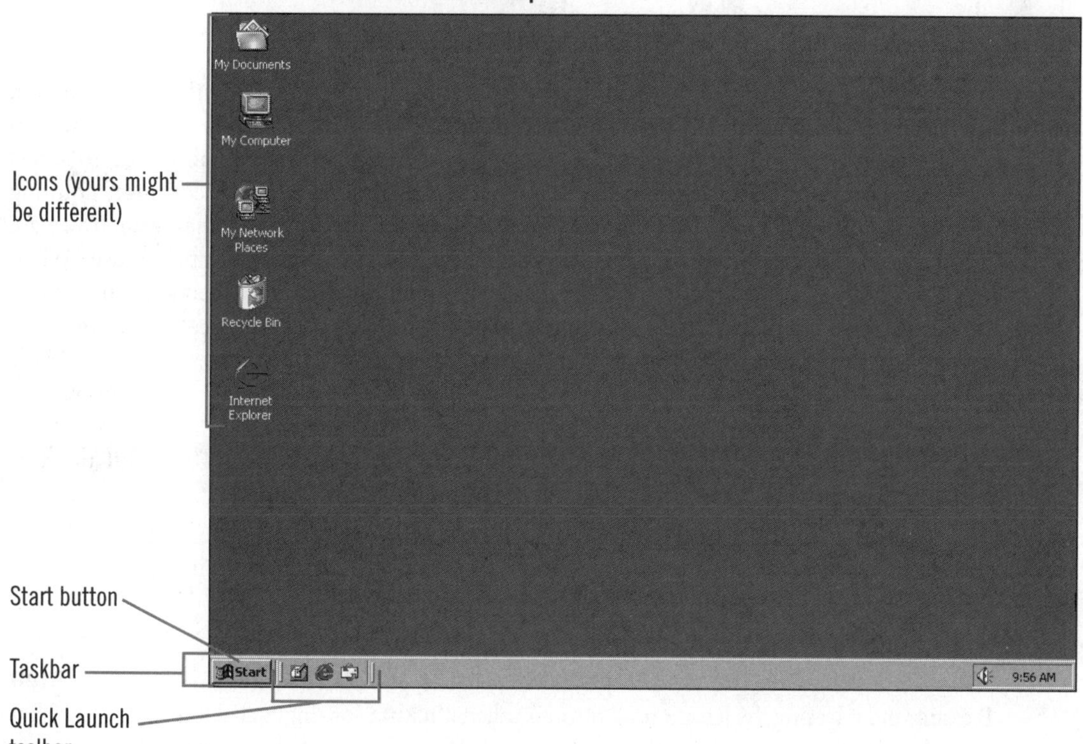

TABLE A-1: Elements of the Windows desktop

desktop element	icon	allows you to
My Documents folder		Store programs, documents, graphics, or other files
My Computer		Work with different disk drives and printers on your computer
My Network Places		Open files and folders on other computers and install network printers
Recycle Bin		Delete and restore files
Internet Explorer		Start Internet Explorer to access the Internet
Connect to the Internet		Set up Internet access
Start button	Start	Start programs, open documents, search for files, and more
Taskbar		Start programs and switch among open programs
Quick Launch toolbar		Start Internet Explorer, start Outlook Express, and display the desktop

Windows 2000

Using the Mouse

A **mouse** is a hand-held **input or pointing device** that you use to interact with your computer. Input or pointing devices come in many shapes and sizes; some, like a mouse, are directly attached to your computer with a cable; others function like a TV remote control and allow you to access your computer without being right next to it. Figure A-2 shows examples of common pointing devices. Because the most common pointing device is a mouse, this book uses that term. If you are using a different pointing device, substitute that device whenever you see the term "mouse." When you move the mouse, the **mouse pointer** on the screen moves in the same direction. The **mouse buttons** are used to select icons and commands, which is how you communicate with the computer. Table A-2 shows some common mouse pointer shapes that indicate different activities. Table A-3 lists the five basic mouse actions. Begin by experimenting with the mouse now.

1. **Locate the mouse pointer on the desktop, then move the mouse across your desk or mousepad**
   Watch how the mouse pointer moves on the desktop in response to your movements; practice moving the mouse pointer in circles, then back and forth in straight lines.
2. **Position the mouse pointer over the My Computer icon**
   Positioning the mouse pointer over an item is called **pointing**.
3. **With the pointer over the My Computer icon, press and release the left mouse button**
   Pressing and releasing the left mouse button is called **clicking** (or single-clicking, to distinguish it from double-clicking, which you'll do in Step 7). When you position the mouse pointer over an icon or any item and click, you select that item. When an item is **selected**, it is **highlighted** (shaded differently from other items), and the next action you take will be performed on that item.
4. **With the My computer icon selected, press and hold down the left mouse button, then move the mouse down and to the right and release the mouse button**
   The icon becomes dimmed and moves with the mouse pointer; this is called **dragging**, which you do to move icons and other Windows elements. When you release the mouse button, the item is positioned at the new location.
5. **Position the mouse pointer over the My Computer icon, then press and release the right mouse button**
   Clicking the right mouse button is known as **right-clicking**. Right-clicking an item on the desktop produces a **pop-up menu**, as shown in Figure A-3. This menu lists the commands most commonly used for the item you have clicked. A **command** is a directive that provides access to a program's features.
6. **Click anywhere outside the menu to close the pop-up menu**
7. **Position the mouse pointer over the My Computer icon, then quickly press and release the left mouse button twice**
   Clicking the mouse button twice quickly is known as **double-clicking**, which, in this case, opens the My Computer window. The **My Computer** window contains additional icons that represent the drives and system components that are installed on your computer.
8. **Click the Close button in the upper-right corner of the My Computer window**

Trouble?

If the My Computer window opens during this step, your mouse isn't set with the Windows 2000 default mouse settings. See your instructor or technical support person for assistance. This book assumes your computer is set to all Windows 2000 default settings.

QuickTip

When a step tells you to "click," use the left mouse button. If it says "right-click," use the right mouse button.

TABLE A-2: Common mouse pointer shapes

shape	used to
(arrow)	Select items, choose commands, start programs, and work in programs
(I-beam)	Position mouse pointer for editing or inserting text; called the insertion point
(hourglass)	Indicate Windows is busy processing a command
↔	Change the size of a window; appears when mouse pointer is on the border of a window
(hand)	Select and open Web-based data

FIGURE A-2: Common pointing devices

FIGURE A-3: Displaying a pop-up menu

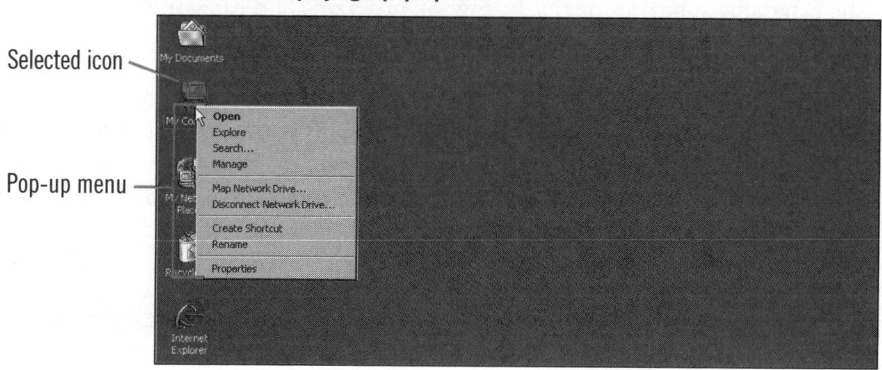

More about the mouse: Classic style and Internet style

Because Windows 2000 integrates the use of the Internet with its other functions, it allows you to extend the way you click in a Web browser program on the Internet to the way you click in other computer programs. With the default Windows 2000 settings, you click an item to select it and double-click an item to open it. In a Web browser program, however, you point to an item to select it and single-click to open it. Windows 2000 gives you two choices for clicking: with the **Classic style**, you double-click to open items, and with the **Internet style**, you single-click to open items. To switch between styles, double-click the My Computer Icon (or click if you are currently using the Internet style), click Tools on the menu bar, click Folder Options, click the General tab if necessary, click the Single-click to Open an Item option or the Double-click to Open an Item option in the Click items as follows section, and then click OK.

TABLE A-3: Basic mouse techniques

technique	what to do
Pointing	Move the mouse to position the mouse pointer over an item on the desktop
Clicking	Press and release the left mouse button
Double-clicking	Press and release the left mouse button twice quickly
Dragging	Point to an item, press and hold the left mouse button, move the mouse to a new location, then release the mouse button
Right-clicking	Point to an item, then press and release the right mouse button

Starting a Program

Clicking the Start button on the taskbar opens the Start menu, which lists submenus for a variety of tasks described in Table A-4. As you become familiar with Windows, you might want to customize the Start menu to include additional items that you use most often. Windows 2000 comes with several built-in programs, called **accessories**. Although not as feature-rich as many programs sold separately, Windows accessories are useful for completing basic tasks. In this lesson, you start a Windows accessory called **WordPad**, which is a word-processing program you can use to create and edit simple documents.

1. Click the **Start button** on the taskbar
   The Start menu opens.
2. Point to **Programs**
   The Programs submenu opens, listing the programs and categories for programs installed on your computer. WordPad is in the category called Accessories.
3. Point to **Accessories**
   The Accessories menu, shown in Figure A-4, contains several programs to help you complete common tasks. You want to start WordPad. If you do not see WordPad, rest the mouse pointer over the double arrows at the bottom of Programs submenu and wait. The full menu will open after a few seconds.
4. Click **WordPad**
   WordPad opens with a blank document window open, as shown in Figure A-5. Don't worry if your window does not fill the screen; you'll learn how to maximize it in the next lesson. Note that a **program button** appears on the taskbar and is highlighted, indicating that WordPad is open.

QuickTip

Windows 2000 features personalized menus, which list only the commands you've most recently used. Whenever you want to view other commands available on the menu, rest the mouse pointer over the double arrows at the bottom of the menu.

TABLE A-4: Start menu categories

category	description
Windows Update	Connects to a Microsoft Web site and updates your Windows 2000 files as necessary
Programs	Displays a menu of programs included on the Start menu
Documents	Displays a menu of the most recently opened and recently saved documents
Settings	Displays a menu of tools for selecting settings for your system
Search	Locates programs, files, folders, people, or computers on your computer network, or finds information and people on the Internet
Help	Provides Windows Help information by topic, alphabetical index, or search criteria
Run	Opens a program or file based on a location and filename that you type or select
Shut Down	Provides options to log off, shut down, or restart the computer

FIGURE A-4: Cascading menus

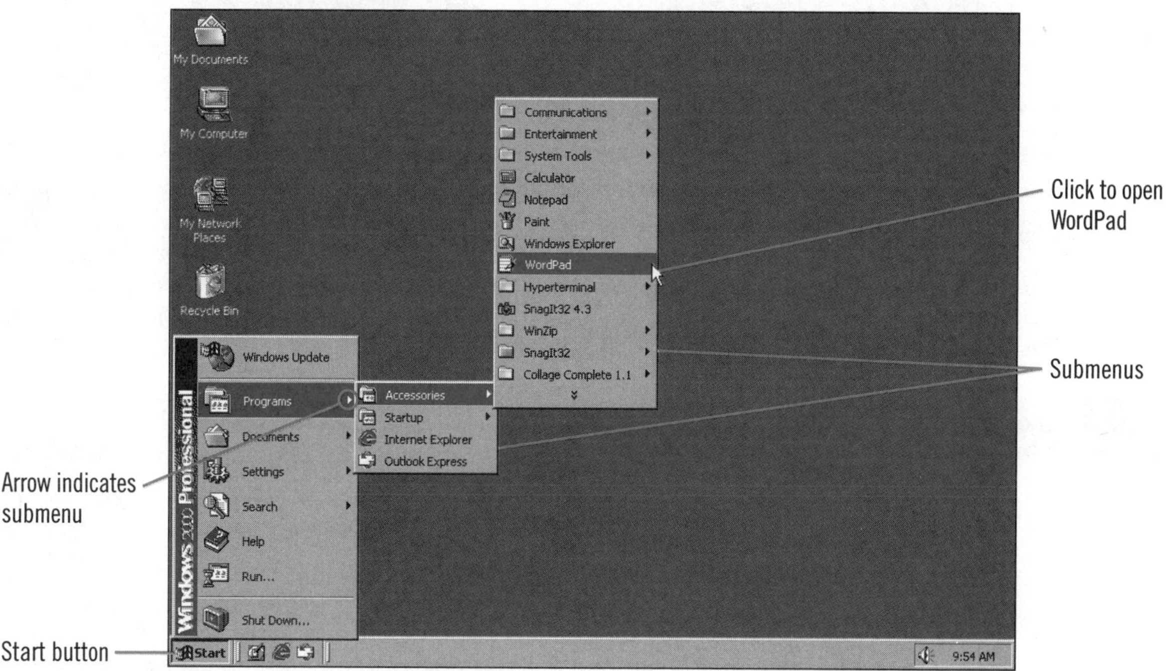

FIGURE A-5: WordPad program window

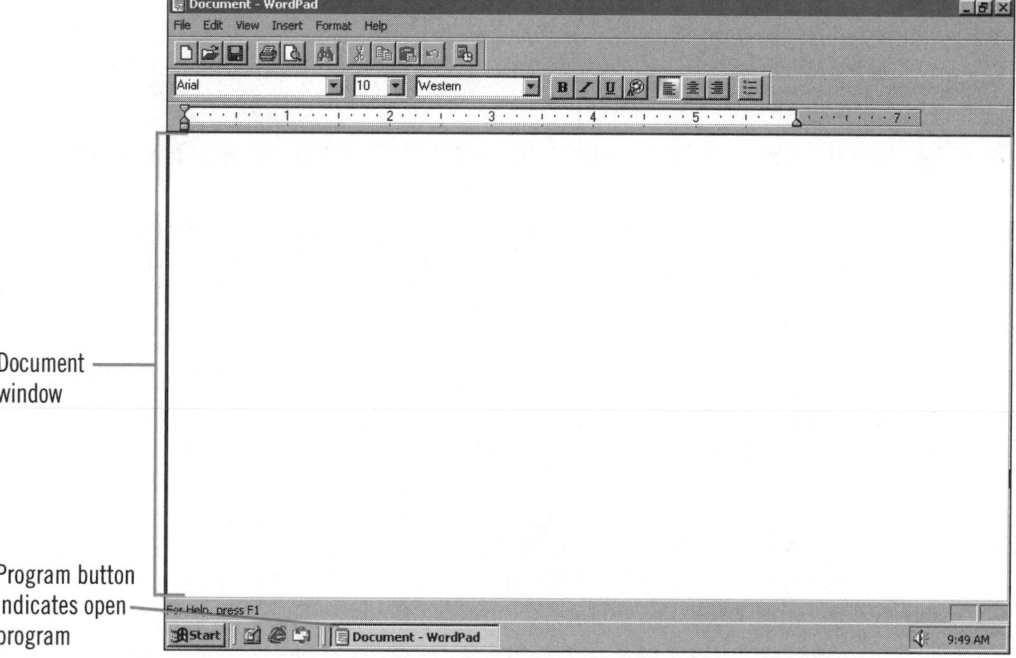

The Startup Folder

You can specify one or more programs to open each time you start Windows 2000 by placing shortcuts in the Startup Folder. This might be useful if you know you will be working in the same programs first thing every day. To place a program in the Startup Folder, click the Start button, point to Settings, then click Taskbar & Start Menu. Click the Advanced tab of the Taskbar and Start Menu Properties dialog box, click Advanced, and then, in the Start Menu folder, locate the shortcut to the program you want to specify, and drag it to the Startup folder.

Windows 2000

Moving and Resizing Windows

One of the powerful features of Windows is the ability to open more than one window or program at once. This means, however, that the desktop can get cluttered with the various programs and files you are using. You can keep your desktop organized by changing the size of a window or moving it. You can do this by clicking the sizing buttons in the upper-right corner of any window and dragging a corner or border of any window that does not completely fill the screen. Practice sizing and moving the WordPad window now.

Steps

1. If the WordPad window does not already fill the screen, click the **Maximize button** in the WordPad window
   When a window is **maximized**, it takes up the whole screen.

2. Click the **Restore button** in the WordPad window
   To **restore** a window is to return it to its previous size, as shown in Figure A-6. The Restore button only appears when a window is maximized.

3. Position the pointer on the right edge of the WordPad window until the pointer changes to ↔, then drag the border to the right
   The width of the window increases. You can size the height or width of a window by dragging any of the four sides individually.

4. Position the pointer in the lower-right corner of the WordPad window until the pointer changes to ↘, as shown in Figure A-6, then drag down and to the right
   The height and width of the window increase proportionally when you drag a corner instead of a side. You can also position a restored window wherever you wish on the desktop by dragging its title bar. The **title bar** is the area along the top of the window that displays the file name and program used to create it.

5. Drag the **title bar** on the WordPad window up and to the left, as shown in Figure A-6
   The window is repositioned on the desktop. At times, you might wish to close a program window, yet keep the program running and easily accessible. You can accomplish this by minimizing a window.

6. In the WordPad window, click the **Minimize button**
   When you **minimize** a window, it shrinks to a program button on the taskbar, as shown in Figure A-7. WordPad is still running, but it is out of your way.

7. Click the **WordPad program button** on the taskbar to reopen the window
   The WordPad program window reopens.

8. Click the **Maximize button** in the upper-right corner of the WordPad window
   The window fills the screen.

QuickTip

You can resize windows by dragging any corner. You can also drag any border to make the window taller, shorter, wider, or narrower.

QuickTip

If you have more than one window open and you want to quickly access something on the desktop, you can click the Show Desktop button on the Quick Launch toolbar. All open windows are minimized so the desktop is visible.

FIGURE A-6: Restored program window

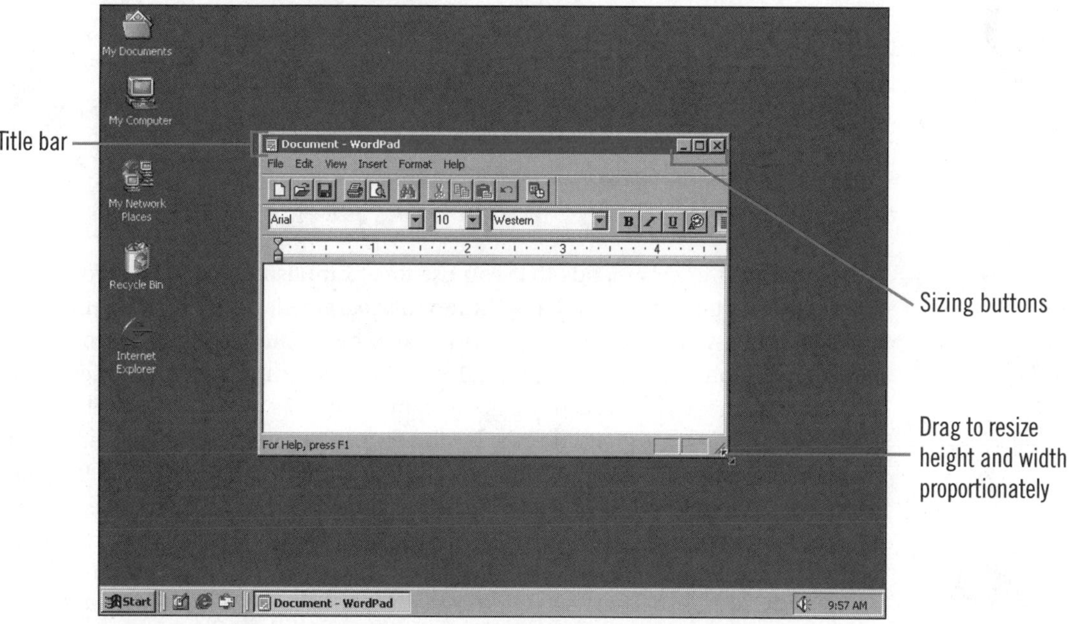

FIGURE A-7: Minimized program window

More about sizing windows

Keep in mind that many programs contain two sets of sizing buttons: one that controls the program window itself and another that controls the window for the file with which you are working. The program sizing buttons are located in the title bar and the file sizing buttons are located below them. See Figure A-8. When you minimize a file window within a program, the file window is reduced to an icon in the lower-left corner of the program window, but the size of the program window remains intact.

FIGURE A-8: Program and file sizing buttons

Program window sizing buttons

File window sizing buttons

Windows 2000

Using Menus, Keyboard Shortcuts, and Toolbars

A **menu** is a list of commands that you use to accomplish certain tasks. You've already used the Start menu to start WordPad. Each Windows program also has its own set of menus, which are located on the **menu bar** under the title bar. The menus organize commands into groups of related operations. See Table A-5 for a description of items on a typical menu. **Toolbar buttons** offer another method for executing menu commands; instead of clicking the menu and then the menu command, you simply click the button for the command. A **toolbar** is a set of buttons usually positioned below the menu bar in a Windows program. In Windows 2000, you can customize a toolbar by adding buttons to or removing buttons from toolbars to suit your preferences. You will open the Control Panel, then use a menu and toolbar button to change how the contents of the window appear, and then add and remove a toolbar button.

QuickTip

You now have two windows open: WordPad and the Control Panel. The Control Panel is the active window (or active program) because it is the one with which you are currently working. WordPad is inactive because it is open but you are not working with it. Working with more than one window at a time is called multitasking.

1. **Click the Start button on the taskbar, point to Settings, then click Control Panel**
   The Control Panel window opens over the WordPad window. The **Control Panel** contains icons for various programs that allow you to specify how your computer looks and performs.
2. **Click View on the menu bar**
   The View menu appears, listing the View commands, as shown in Figure A-9. On a menu, a **check mark** identifies a feature that is currently enabled or "on." To disable or turn "off" the feature, you click the command again to remove the check mark. A **bullet mark** can also indicate that an option is enabled. To disable a bulleted option, you must select another option in its place.
3. **Click Small Icons**
   The icons are now smaller than they were before, taking up less room in the window.
4. **Press [Alt][V] to open the View menu, then press [T] to execute the Toolbars command**
   The View menu appears again, and then the Toolbars submenu appears, with checkmarks next to the commands that are currently selected. You opened these menus using the keyboard. Notice that a letter in each command on the View menu is underlined. These are **keyboard navigation indicators**, indicating that you can press the underlined letter, known as a **keyboard shortcut**, instead of clicking to execute the command.
5. **Press [C] to execute the Customize command**
   The Customize Toolbar dialog box opens. A dialog box is a window in which you make specifications for how you want a task performed; you'll learn more about working in a dialog box shortly. In the Customize Toolbar dialog box, you can add toolbar buttons to the current toolbar, or remove buttons already on the toolbar. The list on the right shows which buttons are currently on the toolbar, and the list on the left shows which buttons are available to add.
6. **Click the Favorites button in the Available toolbar buttons section, then click the Add button**
   As shown in Figure A-10, the Favorites button is added to the Standard toolbar of the Control Panel window.
7. **Click Favorites in the Current toolbar buttons section, click the Remove button, then click Close on the Customize Toolbar dialog box**
   The Favorites button disappears from the Standard toolbar, and the Customize Toolbar dialog box closes.
8. **On the Control Panel toolbar, click the Views button list arrow**
   Some toolbar buttons have an arrow, which indicates the button contains several choices. Clicking the button shows the choices.
9. **In the list of View choices, click Details**
   The Details view includes a description of each program in the Control Panel.

QuickTip

When you rest the pointer over a button without clicking, a Screentip appears, telling you the name of the button.

FIGURE A-9: **Opening a menu**

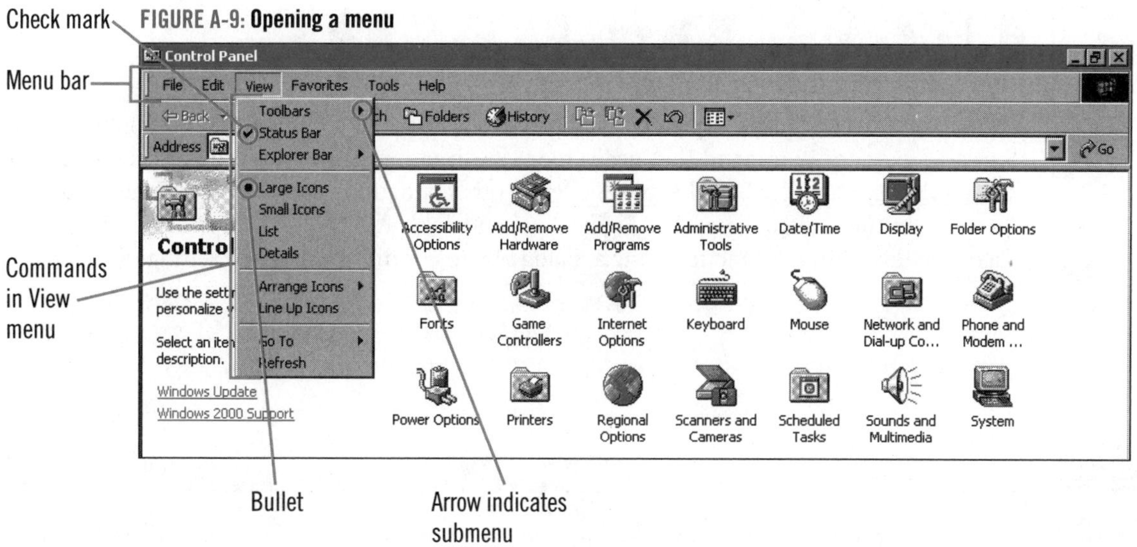

FIGURE A-10: **Customize Toolbar dialog box**

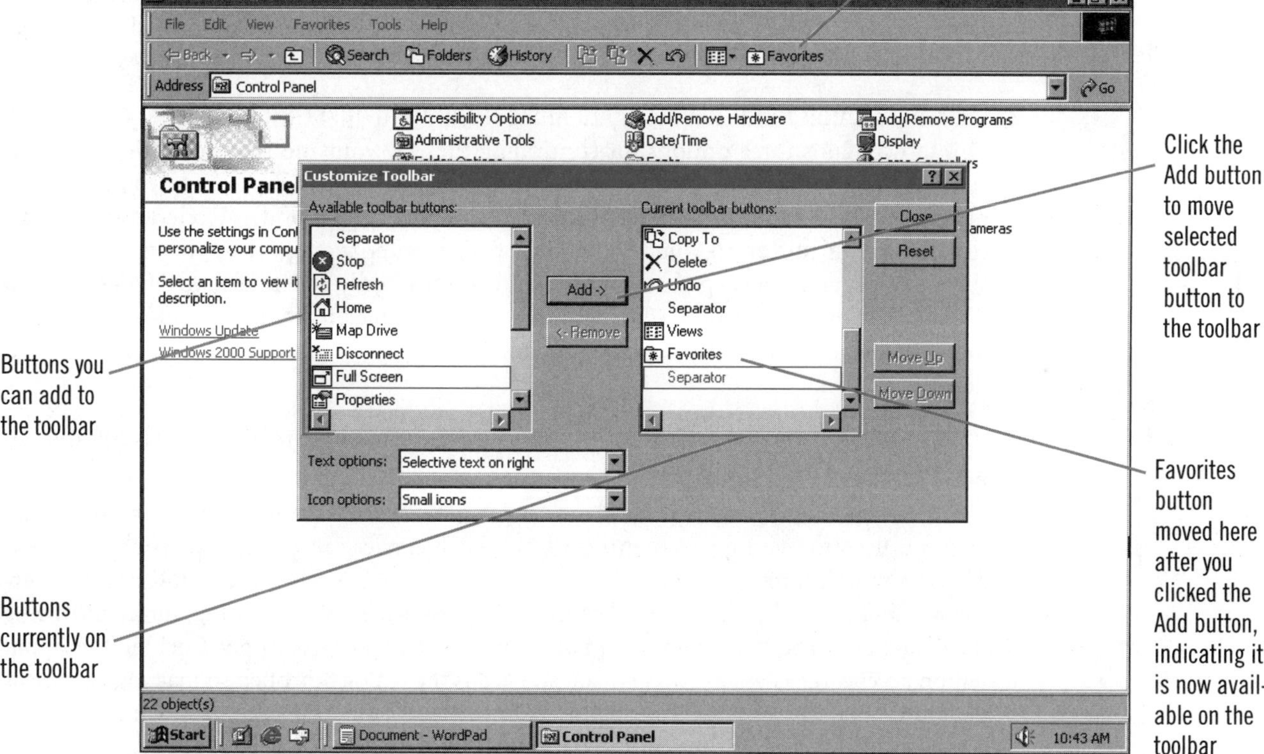

TABLE A-5: **Typical items on a menu**

item	description	example
Dimmed command	Indicates the menu command is not currently available	Undo Ctrl+Z
Ellipsis	Opens a dialog box that allows you to select different or additional options	Save As...
Triangle	Opens a cascading menu containing an additional list of commands	Zoom ▸
Keyboard shortcut	Executes a command using the keyboard instead of the mouse	Paste Ctrl+V
Underlined letter	Indicates the letter to press for the keyboard shortcut	Print Preview

Using Dialog Boxes

A **dialog box** is a window that opens when you choose a menu command that is followed by an ellipsis (…), or any command that needs more information before the program can carry out the command you selected. Dialog boxes open in other situations as well, such as when you open a program in the Control Panel. See Figure A-11 and Table A-6 for some of the typical elements of a dialog box. Practice using a dialog box to control your mouse settings.

Trouble?

If you can't see the Mouse icon, resize the Control Panel window.

1. In the Control Panel window, double-click the **Mouse icon**

   The Mouse Properties dialog box opens, as shown in Figure A-12. **Properties** are characteristics of a specific computer element (in this case, the mouse) that you can customize. The options in this dialog box allow you to control the way the mouse buttons are configured, select the types of pointers that appear, choose the speed of the mouse movement on the screen, and specify what type of mouse you are using. **Tabs** at the top of the dialog box separate these options into related categories.

2. Click the **Motion tab** if necessary to make it the front-most tab

   This tab contains three options for controlling the way your mouse moves. Under Speed, you can set how fast the pointer moves on the screen in relation to how you move the mouse. You drag a **slider** to specify how fast the pointer moves. Under Acceleration, you can click an **option button** to adjust how much your pointer accelerates as you move it faster. When choosing among option buttons, you can select only one at a time. Under Snap to default, there is a **check box**, which is a toggle for turning a feature on or off—in this case, for setting whether or not you want your mouse pointer to move to the default button in dialog boxes.

3. Under Speed, drag the **slider** all the way to the left for Slow, then move the mouse pointer across your screen

   Notice how slowly the mouse pointer moves. After you select the options you want in a dialog box, you need to select a **command button**, which carries out the options you've selected. The two most common command buttons are OK and Cancel. Clicking OK accepts your changes and closes the dialog box; clicking Cancel leaves the original settings intact and closes the dialog box. The third command button in this dialog box is Apply. Clicking the Apply button accepts the changes you've made and keeps the dialog box open so that you can select additional options. Because you might share this computer with others, it's important to return the dialog box options back to the original settings.

QuickTip

You can also use the keyboard to carry out commands in a dialog box. Pressing [Enter] is the same as clicking OK; pressing [Esc] is the same as clicking Cancel.

4. Click **Cancel**

   The original settings remain intact and the dialog box closes.

FIGURE A-11: Elements of a typical dialog box

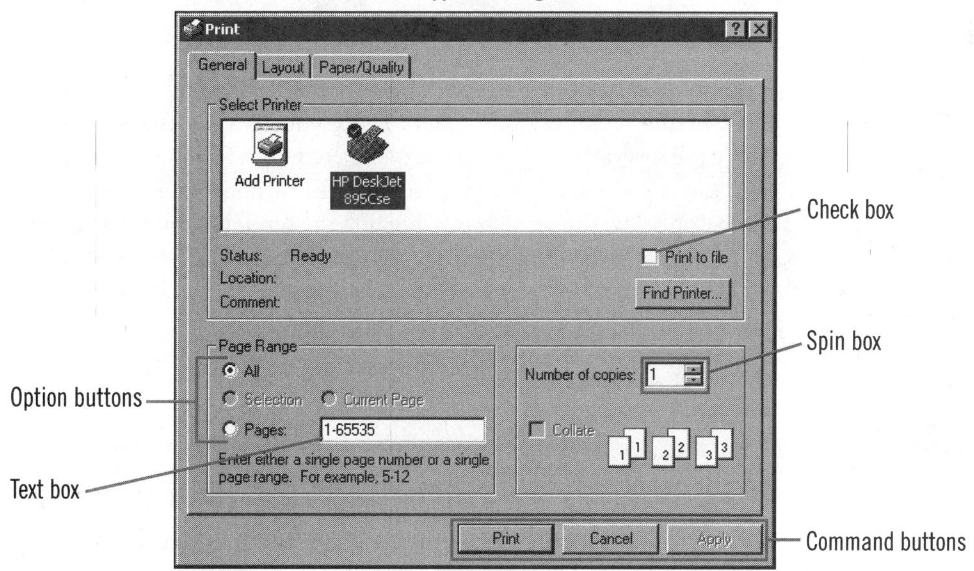

FIGURE A-12: Mouse Properties dialog box

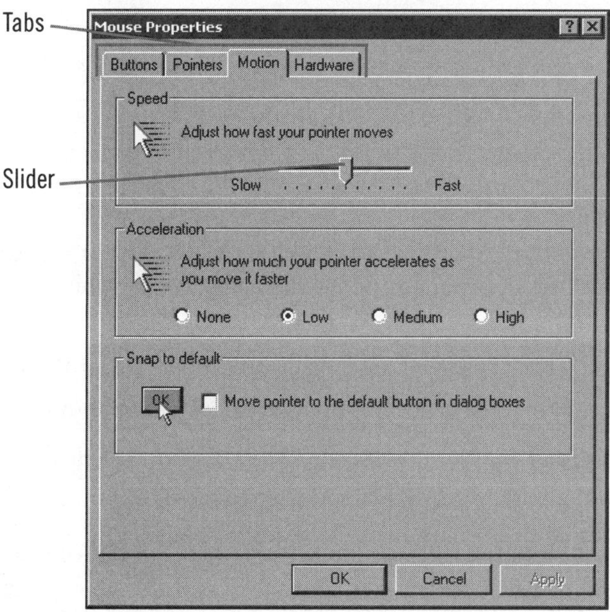

TABLE A-6: Typical items in a dialog box

item	description	item	description
Check box	A box that turns an option on (when the box is checked) and off (when it is unchecked)	**List box**	A box containing a list of items; to choose an item, click the list arrow, then click the desired item
Text box	A box in which you type text	**Spin box**	A box with two arrows and a text box; allows you to scroll in numerical increments or type a number
Option button	A small circle that you click to select a single dialog box option; you cannot check more than one option button in a list	**Slider**	A shape that you drag to set the degree to which an option is in effect
Command button	A rectangular button in a dialog box with the name of the command on it	**Tab**	A place in a dialog box where related commands and options are organized

Windows 2000

Using Scroll Bars

When you cannot see all of the items available in a window, scroll bars appear on the right and/or bottom edges of the window. **Scroll bars** allow you to view the additional contents of the window. There are several ways you can scroll in a window. When you need to scroll only a short distance, you can use the scroll arrows. To scroll the window in larger increments, click in the scroll bar above or below the scroll box. Dragging the scroll box moves you quickly to a new part of the window. See Table A-7 for a summary of the different ways to use scroll bars. With the Control Panel window in Details view, you can use the scroll bars to view all of the items in this window.

Steps

1. **In the Control Panel window, drag the lower-right corner of the dialog box up toward the upper-left corner until the scroll bars appear, as shown in Figure A-13**
   Scroll bars appear only when the window is not large enough to include all the information. After you resize the dialog box, they appear along the bottom and right side of the dialog box. You may have to size your window smaller than the one in the figure for your scroll bars to appear.
2. **Click the down scroll arrow, as shown in Figure A-13**
   Clicking this arrow moves the view down one line.
3. **Click the up scroll arrow in the vertical scroll bar**
   Clicking this arrow moves the view up one line.
4. **Click anywhere in the area below the scroll box in the vertical scroll bar**
   The view moves down one window's height. Similarly, you can click in the scroll bar above the scroll box to move up one window's height.
5. **Drag the scroll box all the way down to the bottom of the vertical scrollbar**
   The view now includes the items that appear at the very bottom of the window.
6. **Drag the scroll box all the way up to the top of the vertical scroll bar**
   This view shows the items that appear at the top of the window.
7. **Click the area to the right of the scroll box in the horizontal scroll bar**
   The far right edge of the window comes into view. The horizontal scroll bar works the same as the vertical scroll bar.
8. **Click the area to the left of the scroll box in the horizontal scroll bar**
   You should return the Control Panel to its original settings.
9. **Maximize the Control Panel window, click the Views button list arrow on the Control Panel toolbar, then click Large Icons**

QuickTip

The size of the scroll box changes to reflect how much information does not fit in the window. A larger scroll box indicates that a relatively small amount of the window's contents is not currently visible; you need to scroll only a short distance to see the remaining items. A smaller scroll box indicates that a relatively large amount of information is currently not visible.

FIGURE A-13: Scroll bars

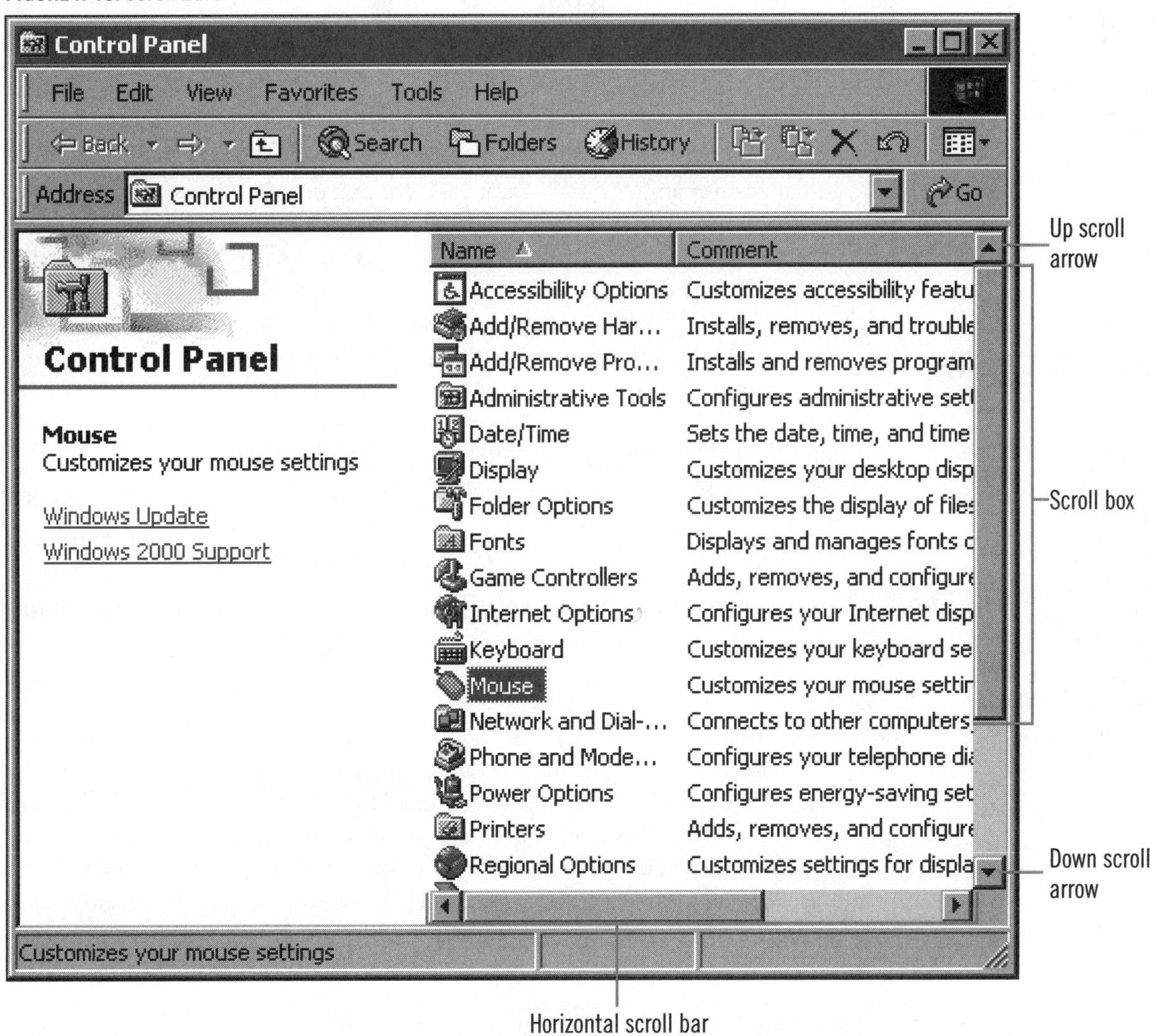

TABLE A-7: Using scroll bars in a window

to	do this
Move down one line	Click the down arrow at the bottom of the vertical scroll bar
Move up one line	Click the up arrow at the top of the vertical scroll bar
Move down one window height	Click in the area below the scroll box in the vertical scroll bar
Move up one window height	Click in the area above the scroll box in the vertical scroll bar
Move up a large distance in the window	Drag the scroll box up in the vertical scroll bar
Move down a large distance in the window	Drag the scroll box down in the vertical scroll bar
Move a short distance side-to-side in a window	Click the left or right arrows in the horizontal scroll bar
Move to the right one window width	Click in the area to the right of the scroll box in the horizontal scroll bar
Move to the left one window width	Click in the area to the left of the scroll box in the horizontal scroll bar
Move left or right a large distance in the window	Drag the scroll box in the horizontal scroll bar

Windows 2000

Using Windows Help

When you have a question about how to do something in Windows 2000, you can usually find the answer with a few clicks of your mouse. **Windows Help** works like a book stored on your computer, with a table of contents and an index to make finding information easier. Help provides guidance on many Windows features, including detailed steps for completing procedures, definitions of terms, lists of related topics, and search capabilities. You can browse or search for information in the Help window, or you can connect to a Microsoft Web site on the Internet for the latest technical support on Windows 2000. You can also access **context-sensitive help**, help specifically related to what you are doing, using a variety of methods such as right-clicking an object or using the question mark button in a dialog box. In this lesson, you get Help on starting a program. You also get information on the taskbar.

Steps

1. **Click the Start button on the taskbar, then click Help**

   The Windows Help window opens with the Contents tab in front, as shown in Figure A-14. The Contents tab provides you with a list of Help categories. Each category contains two or more topics that you can see by clicking the book or the category next to it.

2. **Click the Contents tab if it isn't the front-most tab, click Working with Programs, then view the Help categories that are displayed**

   The Help window contains a selection of topics related to working with programs.

3. **Click Start a Program**

   Help information for this topic appears in the right pane, as shown in Figure A-15. **Panes** divide a window into two or more sections. At the bottom of the text in the right pane, you can click Related Topics to view a list of topics that may also be of interest to you. Some Help topics also allow you to view additional information about important words; these words are underlined, indicating that you can click them to display a pop-up window with the additional information.

4. **Click the underlined word taskbar, read the definition, then press [Enter] or click anywhere outside the pop-up window to close it**

5. **In the left pane, click the Index tab**

   The Index tab provides an alphabetical list of all the available Help topics, like an index at the end of a book. You can type a topic in the text box at the top of the pane. As you type, the list of topics automatically scrolls to try to match the word or phrase you type. You can also scroll down to the topic. In either case, the topic appears in the right pane.

6. **In the left pane, click the Search tab**

   You can use the Search tab to locate a Help topic using keywords. You enter a word or phrase in the text box and click List Topics; a list of matching topics appears below the text box. To view a topic, double-click it or select the topic, then click Display.

7. **In the left pane, click the Favorites tab**

   You can add the To Start a Program topic, or any other displayed topic, to the Favorites tab of the Help window by simply clicking the Favorites tab, then clicking the Add button.

8. **Click the Web Help button on the toolbar**

   Information on the Web site for Windows 2000 Help appears in the right pane (a **Web site** is a document or related documents that contain highlighted words, phrases, and graphics that link to other sites on the Internet). To access online support or information, click one of the available options.

9. **Click the Close button in the upper-right corner of the Windows Help window**

   The Help window closes.

QuickTip

Click the Glossary category on the Contents tab to access definitions for hundreds of computer terms.

QuickTip

To get help on a specific Windows program, click Help on the program's menu bar.

FIGURE A-14: Windows Help window

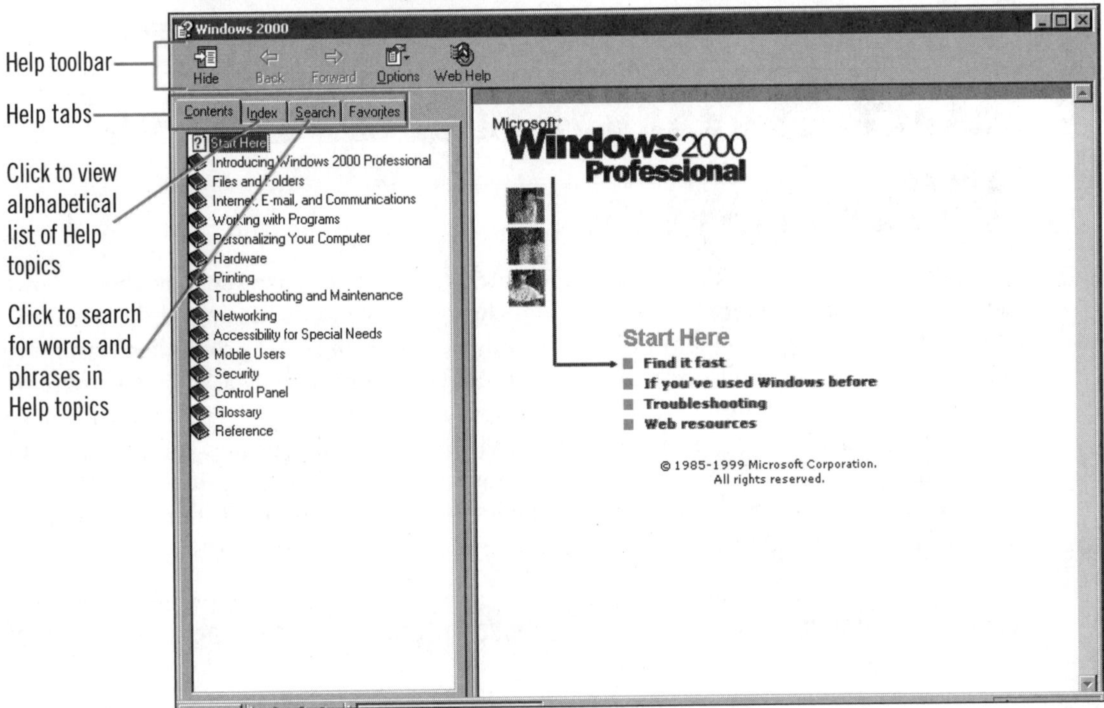

FIGURE A-15: Viewing a Help topic

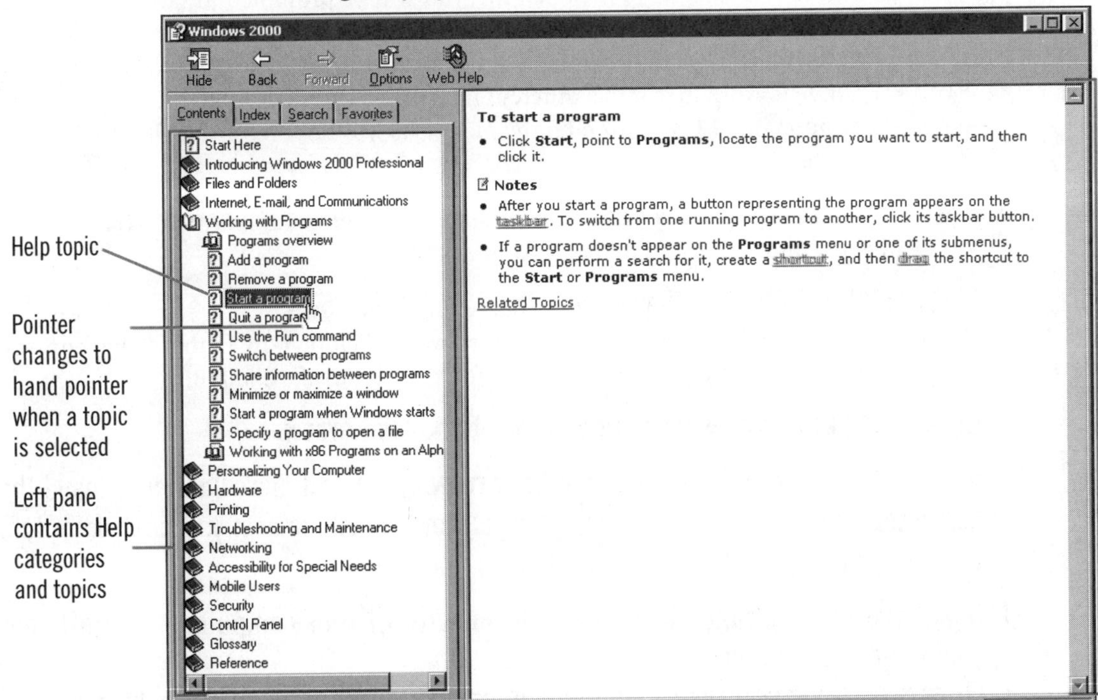

Context-sensitive help

To receive help in a dialog box, click the Help button in the upper-right corner of the dialog box; the mouse pointer changes to ?. Click the Help pointer on the item for which you need additional information. A pop-up window provides a brief explanation of the selected feature. You can also right-click the button on an item in a dialog box, then click the What's This? button to view the Help explanation.

Closing a Program and Shutting Down Windows

When you are finished working on your computer, you need to make sure you shut it down properly. This involves several steps: saving and closing all open files, closing all the open programs and windows, shutting down Windows, and finally, turning off the computer. If you turn off the computer while Windows is running, you could lose important data. To **close** programs, you can click the Close button in the window's upper-right corner or click File on the menu bar and choose either Close or Exit. To shut down Windows after all your files and programs are closed, click Shut Down from the Start menu, then select the desired option from the Shut Down dialog box, shown in Figure A-16. See Table A-8 for a description of shut down options. Close all your open files, windows, and programs, then exit Windows.

1. **In the Control Panel window, click the Close button in the upper-right corner of the window**
   The Control Panel window closes.

2. **Click File on the WordPad menu bar, then click Exit**
   If you have made any changes to the open file, you will be prompted to save your changes before the program quits. Some programs also give you the option of choosing the Close command on the File menu in order to close the active file but leave the program open, so you can continue to work in it with a different file. Also, if there is a second set of sizing buttons in the window, the Close button on the menu bar will close the active file only, leaving the program open for continued use.

3. **If you see a message asking you to save changes to the document, click No**
   WordPad closes and you return to the desktop.

4. **Click the Start Button on the taskbar, then click Shut Down**
   The Shut Down Windows dialog box opens, as shown in Figure A-16. In this dialog box, you have the option to log off, shut down the computer, or restart the computer.

5. **Click the What do you want the computer to do? list arrow**

6. **If you are working in a lab, click the list arrow again and click Cancel to leave the computer running; if you are working on your own machine or if your instructor told you to shut down Windows, click Shut down, then click OK**

7. **If you see the message "It is now safe to turn off your computer," turn off your computer and monitor**
   On some computers, the power shuts off automatically, so you may not see this message.

QuickTip

Complete the remaining steps to shut down Windows and your computer only if you have been told to do so by your instructor or technical support person.

FIGURE A-16: Shut Down Windows dialog box

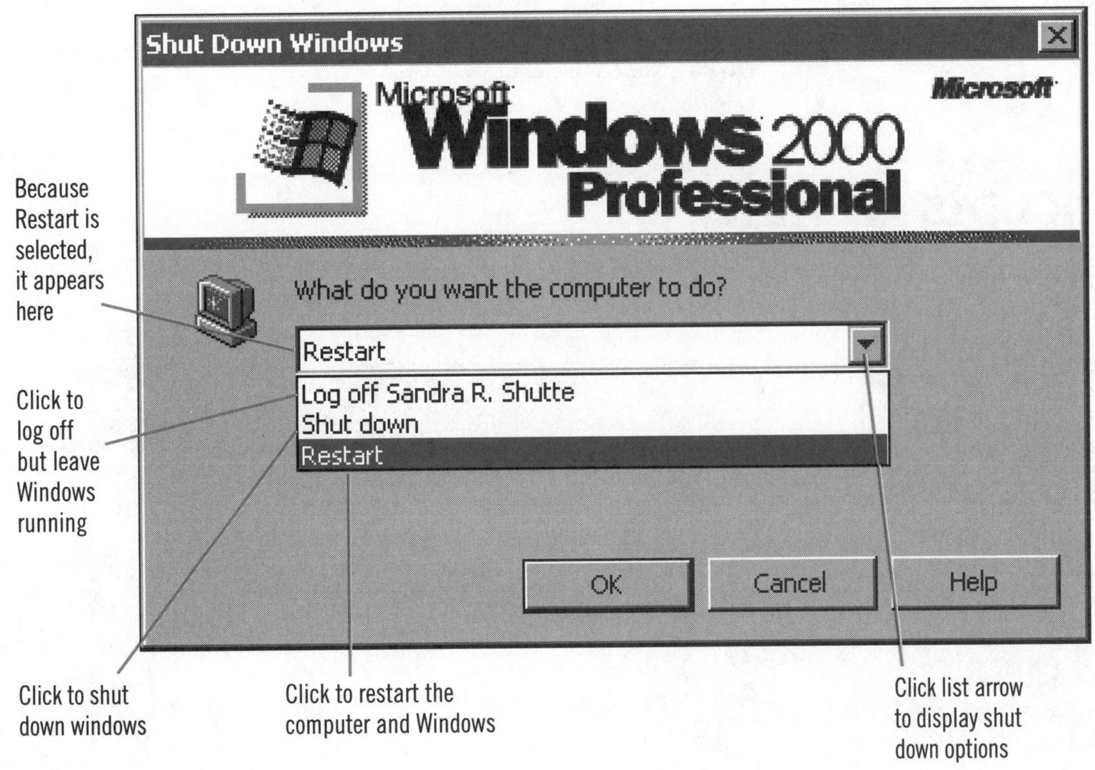

The Log Off command

To change users on the same computer quickly, you can choose the Log Off command from the Shut Down Windows dialog box. When you choose this command, the current user is logged off and Windows 2000 shuts down and automatically restarts, stopping at the point where you need to enter a password. When the new user enters a user name and password, Windows restarts and the desktop appears as usual.

TABLE A-8: Shut down options

shut down option	function	when to use it
Shut down	Prepares the computer to be turned off	When you are finished working with Windows and you want to shut off your computer
Restart	Restarts the computer and reloads Windows	When you want to restart the computer and begin working with Windows again (your programs might have frozen or stopped working)
Log off	Ends your session, then reloads Windows for another user	When you want to end your session but leave the computer running for another user

Practice

▶ Concepts Review

Identify each of the items labeled in Figure A-17.

FIGURE A-17

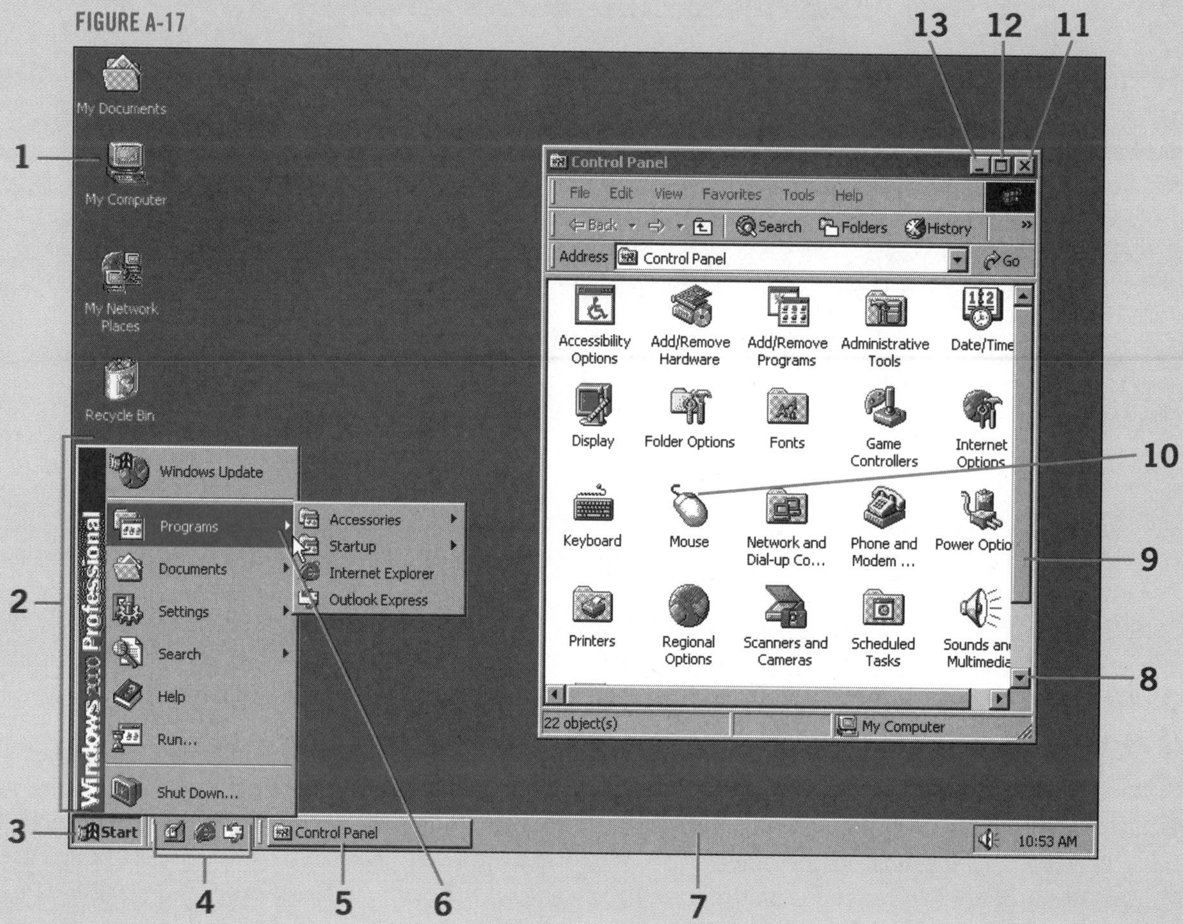

Match each of the statements with the term it describes.

14. Shrinks a window to a button on the taskbar
15. Shows the name of the window or program
16. The taskbar item you first click to start a program
17. Requests more information that you supply before carrying out command
18. Shows the Start button, Quick Launch toolbar, and any currently open programs
19. An input device that lets you point to and make selections
20. Graphic representation of program

a. Taskbar
b. Dialog box
c. Start button
d. Mouse
e. Title bar
f. Minimize button
g. Icon

Select the best answer from the list of choices.

21. The acronym GUI stands for
- **a.** Grayed user information.
- **b.** Group user icons.
- **c.** Graphical user interface.
- **d.** Group user interconnect.

22. Which of the following is NOT provided by Windows 2000?
- **a.** The ability to organize files
- **b.** Instructions to coordinate the flow of information among the programs, files, printers, storage devices, and other components of your computer system
- **c.** Programs that allow you to specify the operation of the mouse
- **d.** Spell checker for your documents

23. All of the following are examples of using a mouse, EXCEPT
- **a.** clicking the Maximize button.
- **b.** pressing [Enter].
- **c.** double-clicking to start a program.
- **d.** dragging the My Computer icon.

24. The term for moving an item to a new location on the desktop is
- **a.** pointing.
- **b.** clicking.
- **c.** dragging.
- **d.** restoring.

25. The Maximize button is used to
- **a.** return a window to its previous size.
- **b.** expand a window to fill the computer screen.
- **c.** scroll slowly through a window.
- **d.** run programs from the Start menu.

26. What appears if a window contains more information than can be viewed in the window?
- **a.** Program icon
- **b.** Cascading menu
- **c.** Scroll bars
- **d.** Check boxes

27. A window is active when
- **a.** you can only see its program button on the taskbar.
- **b.** its title bar is dimmed.
- **c.** it is open and you are currently using it.
- **d.** it is listed in the Programs submenu.

28. You can exit Windows by
- **a.** double-clicking the Control Panel application.
- **b.** double-clicking the Program Manager control menu box.
- **c.** clicking File, then clicking Exit.
- **d.** selecting the Shut Down command from the Start menu.

Skills Review

1. Start Windows and view the Active Desktop.
- **a.** Turn on the computer, if necessary.
- **b.** After Windows starts, identify as many items on the desktop as you can, without referring to the lesson material.
- **c.** Compare your results to Figure A-1.

2. Use the mouse.
- **a.** Double-click the Recycle Bin icon.
- **b.** Drag the Recycle Bin window to the upper-right corner of the desktop.
- **c.** Right-click the title bar of the Recycle Bin, then click Close.

3. Start a program.
- **a.** Click the Start button on the taskbar, then point to Programs.
- **b.** Point to Accessories, then click Calculator (rest your pointer on the double arrows to display more menu commands if necessary).
- **c.** Minimize the Calculator window.

4. Move and resize windows.
- **a.** Drag the Recycle Bin icon to the bottom of the desktop.
- **b.** Double-click the My Computer icon to open the My Computer window.
- **c.** Maximize the window, if it is not already maximized.

   d. Restore the window to its previous size.
   e. Resize the window until you see the vertical scroll bar.
   f. Minimize the My Computer window.
   g. Drag the Recycle Bin back to the top of the desktop.

5. **Use menus, keyboard shortcuts, and toolbars.**
   a. Click the Start button on the taskbar, point to Settings, then click Control Panel.
   b. Click View on the menu bar, point to Toolbars, then click Standard Buttons to deselect the option and hide the toolbar.
   c. Redisplay the toolbar.
   d. Press [Alt][V] to display the View menu, then press [L] to view the Control Panel as a list.
   e. Note the change, then use keyboard shortcuts to change the view back.
   f. Click the Up One Level button to view My Computer.
   g. Click the Back button to return to the Control Panel.
   h. Click View, click Toolbars, then click Customize.
   i. Add a button to the toolbar, remove it, then close the Customize the Toolbar dialog box.
   j. Click the Restore button on the Control panel window.

6. **Use dialog boxes.**
   a. Double-click the Display icon, then click the Screen Saver tab.
   b. Click the Screen Saver list arrow, click any screen saver in the list, then view it in the Preview box above the list.
   c. Click the Effects tab.
   d. In the Visual effects section, click the Use large icons check box to select it, then click Apply.
   e. Note the change in the icons on the desktop and in the Control Panel window.
   f. Click the Use large icons check box to deselect it, click the Screen Saver tab, return the screen saver to its original setting, then click Apply.
   g. Click the Close button in the Display Properties dialog box, but leave the Control Panel open.

7. **Use scroll bars.**
   a. Click View on the Control Panel toolbar, then click Details.
   b. Resize the Control Panel window, if necessary, so that both scroll bars are visible.
   c. Drag the vertical scroll box down all the way.
   d. Click anywhere in the area above the vertical scroll box.
   e. Click the down scroll arrow until the scroll box is back at the bottom of the scroll bar.
   f. Drag the horizontal scroll box so you can read the descriptions for the icons.

8. **Get Help.**
   a. Click the Start button on the taskbar, then click Help.
   b. Click the Contents tab, then click Introducing Windows 2000 Professional.
   c. Click Tips for New Users, click the Use the Personalized Menus feature, then click Overview of Personalized Menus.
   d. Read the topic contents, then click Related Topics.

9. **Close a program and shut down Windows.**
   a. Click the Close button to close the Help topic window.
   b. Click File on the menu bar, then click Close to close the Control Panel window.
   c. Click the Calculator program button on the taskbar to restore the window.
   d. Click the Close button in the Calculator window to close the Calculator program.
   e. Click the My Computer program button on the taskbar, then click the Close button to close the window.
   f. If you are instructed to do so, shut down your computer.

Independent Challenges

1. Windows 2000 has an extensive help system. In this independent challenge, you will use Help to learn about more Windows 2000 features and explore the help that's available on the Internet.

a. Open Windows Help and locate help topics on adjusting the double-click speed of your mouse and displaying Web content on your desktop.

If you have a printer, print a Help topic for each subject. If you do not have a printer, write a summary of each topic.

b. Follow these steps below to access help on the Internet. If you don't have Internet access, you can't do this step.

i. Click the Web Help button on the toolbar.

ii. Click the link Windows 2000 home page. A browser opens and prompts you to connect to the Internet if you are not already connected.

iii. Write a summary of what you find.

iv. Click the Close button in the title bar of your browser, then disconnect from the Internet and close Windows Help.

2. You may need to change the format of the clock and date on your computer. For example, if you work with international clients it might be easier to show the time in military (24-hour) time and the date with the day before the month. You can also change the actual time and date on your computer, to accomodate such things as time zone changes.

a. Open the Control Panel window, then double-click the Regional Options icon.

b. Click the Time tab to change the time to show a 24-hour clock rather than a 12-hour clock.

c. Click the Date tab to change the Short date format to show the date, followed by the month, followed by the year (e.g., 30/3/01).

d. Change the time to one hour later using the Date/Time icon in the Control Panel window.

e. Return the settings to the original time and format, then close all open windows.

3. Calculator is a Windows program on the Accessories menu that you can use for calculations you need to perform while using the computer. Follow these guidelines to explore the Calculator and the Help that comes with it:

a. Start the Calculator from the Accessories menu.

b. Click Help on the menu bar, then click Help Topics. The Calculator Help window opens, showing several help topics.

c. View the help topic on how to perform simple calculations, then print it if you have a printer connected.

d. Open the Perform a scientific calculation category, then view the definition of a number system.

e. Determine how many months you have to work to earn an additional week of vacation if you work for a company that provides one additional day of paid vacation for every 560 hours you work. (*Hint:* Divide 560 by the number of hours you work per month.)

f. Close all open windows.

4. You can customize many Windows features to suit your needs and preferences. One way you do this is to change the appearance of the taskbar on the desktop. In this challenge, try the guidelines described to explore the different ways you can customize the appearance of the taskbar.

a. Position the pointer over the top border of the taskbar. When the pointer changes shape, drag up an inch.

b. Resize the taskbar back to its original size.

c. Click the Start button on the taskbar, point to Settings, then click Taskbar & Start Menu.

d. In the upper-right corner of the General tab, click the Help button, then click the first check box to view the pop-up window describing it. Repeat this for each check box.

e. Click each check box and observe the effect in the preview area. (*Note:* Do not click OK.)

f. Click Cancel.

► Visual Workshop

Use the skills you have learned in this unit to customize your desktop so it looks like the one in Figure A-18. Make sure you include the following:

- Calculator program minimized
- Vertical scroll bar in Control Panel window
- Large icons view in Control Panel window
- Rearranged icons on desktop; your icons may be different (*Hint:* If the icons *snap* back to where they were, they are set to be automatically arranged. Right-click a blank area of the desktop, point to Arrange Icons, then click Auto Arrange to deselect this option.)

Use the Print Screen key to make a copy of the screen, then print it from the Paint program. (To print from the Paint program, click the Start button on the taskbar, point to Programs, point to Accessories, then click Paint; in the Paint program window, click Edit on the menu bar, then click Paste; click Yes to fit the image on the bitmap, click the Print button on the toolbar, then click Print in the Print dialog box. See your instructor or technical support person for assistance.)

When you have completed this exercise, be sure to return your settings and desktop back to their original arrangement.

FIGURE A-18

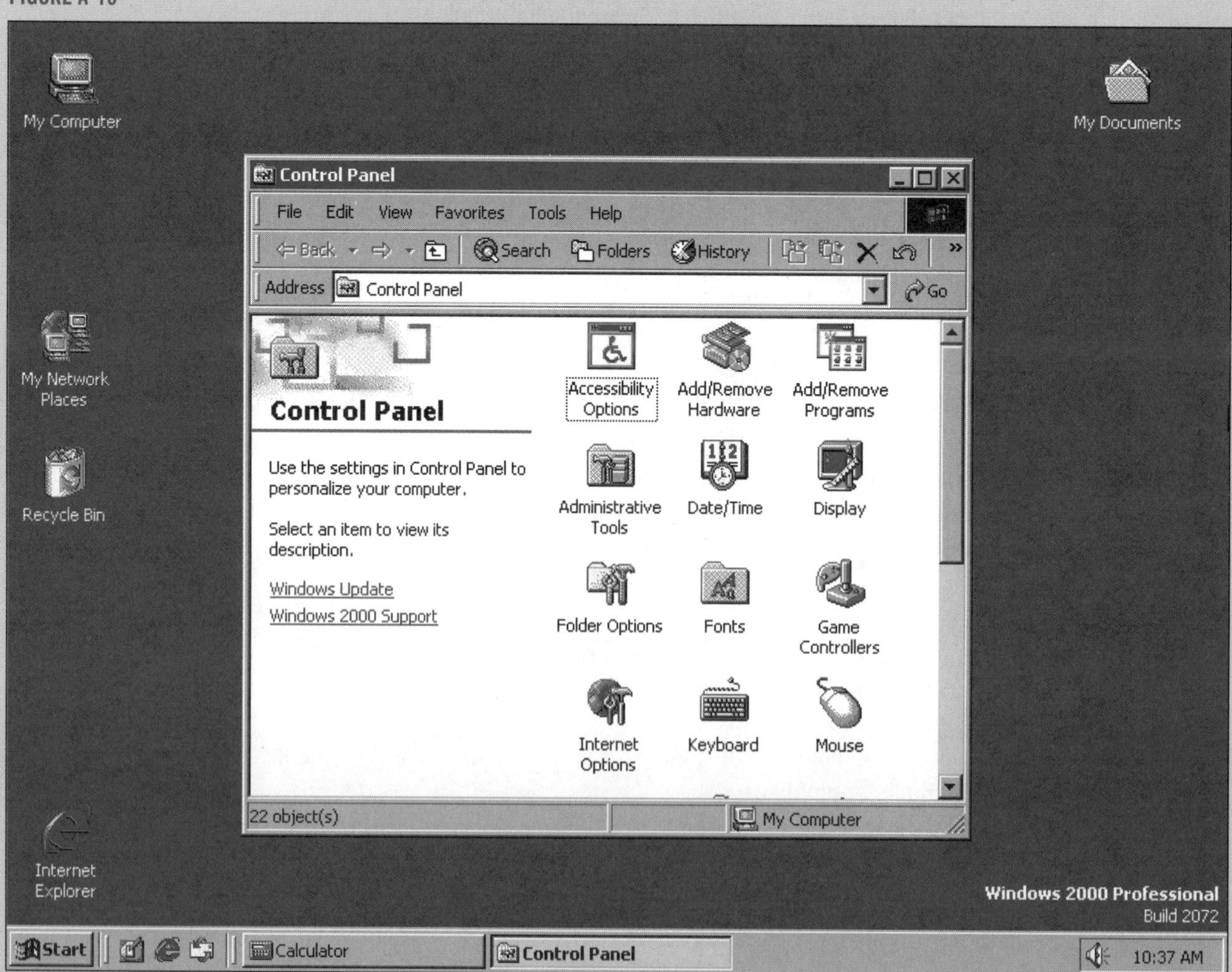

Working with Programs, Files, and Folders

Objectives

- Create and save a WordPad document
- Open, edit, and save an existing Paint file
- Work with multiple programs
- Understand file management
- View files and create folders with My Computer
- Move and copy files with My Computer
- Manage files with Windows Explorer
- Delete and restore files
- Create a shortcut on the desktop

Most of your work on a computer involves using programs to create files. For example, you might use WordPad to create a resumé or Microsoft Excel to create a budget. The resumé and the budget are examples of **files**, electronic collections of data that you create and save on a disk. In this unit, you learn how to work with files and the programs you use to create them. You create new files, open and edit an existing file, and use the Clipboard to copy and paste data from one file to another. You also explore the file management features of Windows 2000, using My Computer and Windows Explorer. Finally, you learn how to work more efficiently by managing files directly on your desktop.

Windows 2000

Creating and Saving a WordPad Document

As with most programs, when you start WordPad a new, blank **document** (or file) opens. To create a new file, such as a memo, you simply begin typing. Your work is automatically stored in your computer's **random access memory (RAM)** until you turn off your computer, at which point anything stored in the computer's RAM is erased. To store your work permanently, you must save your work as a file on a disk. You can save files either on an internal **hard disk**, which is built into your computer, usually the C: drive, or on a removable 3.5" or 5.25" **floppy disk**, which you insert into a drive on your computer, usually the A: or B: drive. Before you can save a file on a floppy disk, the disk must be formatted. (See the Appendix, "Formatting a Disk," or your instructor or technical support person for more information.) When you name a file, you can use up to 255 characters including spaces and punctuation in the File Name box, using either upper- or lowercase letters. In this lesson, you start WordPad and create a file that contains the text shown in Figure B-1. Then you save the file to Project Disk 1.

Trouble?

If you make a mistake, press [Backspace] to delete the character to the left of the insertion point.

QuickTip

Double-click to select a word or triple-click to select a paragraph.

Trouble?

This unit assumes that the Project Disk is in the A: drive. If not, substitute the correct drive any time you are instructed to use the 3½ Floppy (A:) drive. See your instructor or technical support person for help.

1. Click the **Start button** on the taskbar, point to **Programs**, point to **Accessories**, click **WordPad**, then click the **Maximize button** if the window does not fill your screen
   The WordPad program window opens with a new, blank document in the document window. The blinking **insertion point** indicates where the text you type will appear.
2. Type **Memo**, then press **[Enter]**
   Pressing [Enter] inserts a new line and moves the insertion point to the next line.
3. Press **[Enter]** again, then type the remaining text shown in Figure B-1, pressing **[Enter]** at the end of each line
   Now that the text is entered, you can format it. **Formatting** changes the appearance of text to make it more readable or attractive.
4. Click to the left of the word **Memo**, drag the mouse to the right to highlight the word, then release the mouse button
   The text is now **selected** and any action you make will be performed on the text.
5. Click the **Center button** on the Formatting toolbar, then click the **Bold button** on the Formatting toolbar
   The text is centered and bold.
6. Click the **Font Size list arrow** 10, then click **16** in the list
   A **font** is a particular shape and size of type. The text is enlarged to 16 point. One **point** is 1/72 of an inch in height. Now that your memo is complete, you are ready to save it to your Project Disk.
7. Click **File** on the menu bar, then click **Save As**
   The Save As dialog box opens, as shown in Figure B-2. In this dialog box, you specify where you want your file saved and also give your document a name.
8. Click the **Save in list arrow**, and then click **3½ Floppy (A:)**, or whichever drive contains your Project Disk 1
   The drive containing your Project Disk is now active, meaning that any files currently on the disk appear in the list of folders and files and that the file you save now will be saved on the disk in this drive.
9. Click the **text** in the File name text box, type **Memo**, then click **Save**
   Your memo is now saved as a WordPad file with the name "Memo" on your Project Disk. Notice that the WordPad title bar contains the name of the file.

FIGURE B-1: **Text to enter in WordPad**

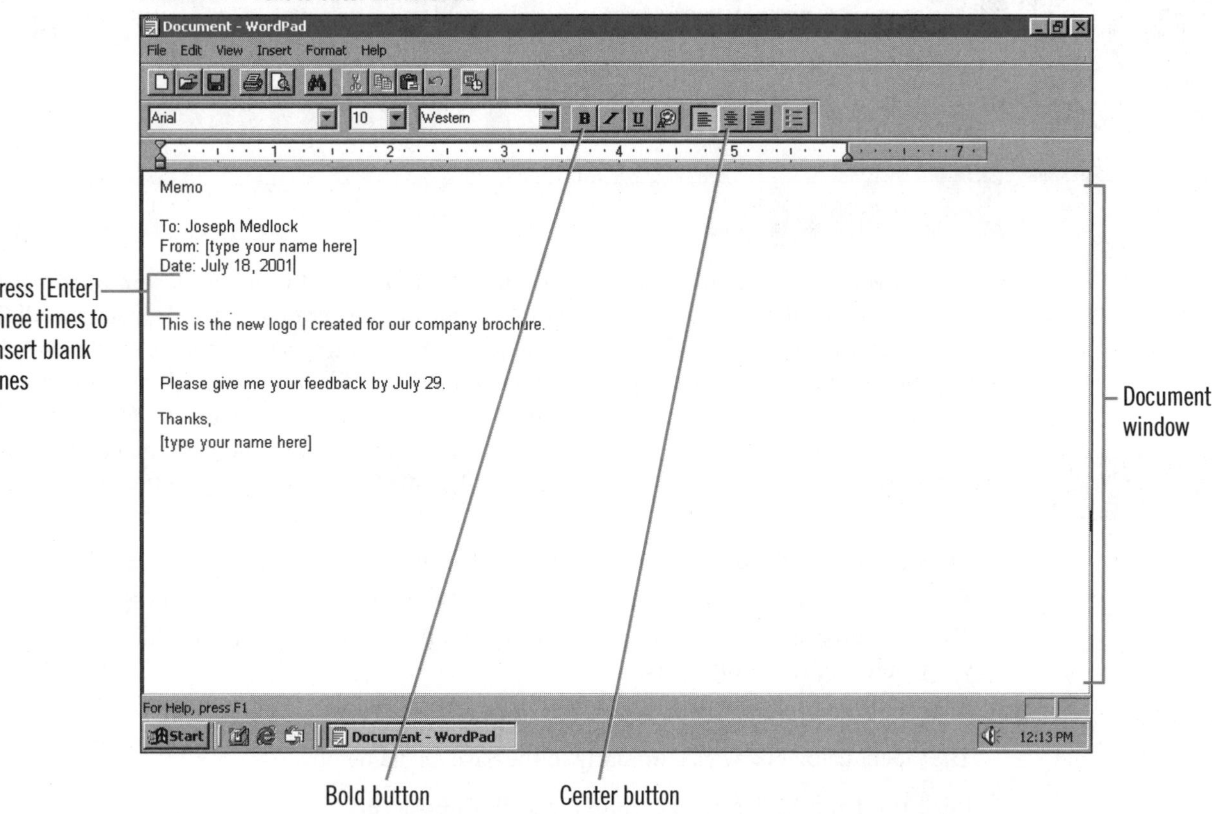

FIGURE B-2: **Save As dialog box**

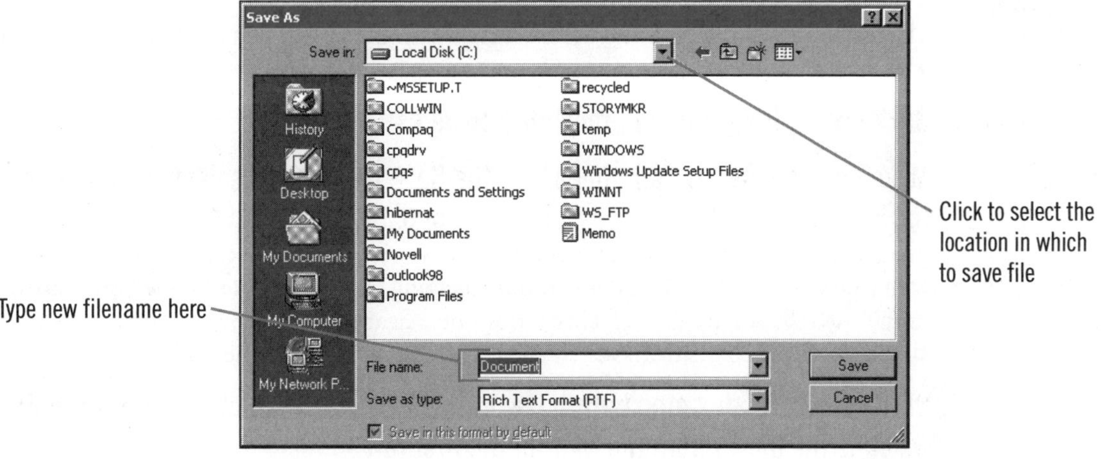

Creating a new document

When you want to create a new document in WordPad once the program is already open and another document is active, you can click the New button on the Standard toolbar. A dialog box opens from which you can choose to create a new Rich Text, Word 6, Text, or Unicode Text document. **Rich Text** documents, the WordPad default document format, can include text formatting and tabs, and be available for use in a variety of other word-processing programs; **Word 6** documents can be opened, edited, and enhanced in Microsoft Word version 6.0 or later without conversion; **Text** documents can be used in numerous other programs because they contain no formatting; and **Unicode Text** documents can contain text from any of the world's writing systems, such as Roman, Greek, and Chinese. You select one of the options by clicking it, and then clicking OK.

Windows 2000

Opening, Editing, and Saving an Existing Paint File

Sometimes you create files from scratch, but often you may want to use a file you or someone else has already created; to do so, you need to **open** the file. Once you open a file, you can **edit** it, or make changes to it, such as adding or deleting text. After editing a file, you can save it with the same filename, which means that you no longer will have the file in its original form, or you can save it with a different filename, so that the original file remains unchanged. In this lesson, you use **Paint**, a drawing program that comes with Windows 2000, to open a file, edit it by changing a color, then save the file with a new filename to leave the original file unchanged.

Steps

1. Click the **Start button** on the taskbar, point to **Programs**, point to **Accessories**, click **Paint**, then click the **Maximize button** if the window doesn't fill the screen
   The Paint program opens with a blank work area. If you wanted to create a file from scratch, you would begin working now.
2. Click **File** on the menu bar, then click **Open**
   The Open dialog box works similarly to the Save As dialog box.
3. Click the **Look in list arrow**, then click **3½ Floppy (A:)**
   The Paint files on your Project Disk 1 are listed in the Open dialog box, as shown in Figure B-3.
4. Click **Win B-1** in the list of files, and then click **Open**
   The Open dialog box closes and the file named Win B-1 opens. Before you make any changes to a file, you should save it with a new filename, so that the original file is unchanged.
5. Click **File** on the menu bar, then click **Save As**
6. Make sure **3½ Floppy (A:)** appears in the Save in text box, select the text **Win B-1** in the File name text box if necessary, type **Logo**, then click **Save**
   The Logo file appears in the Paint window, as shown in Figure B-4. Because you saved the file with a new name, you can edit it without changing the original file. You will now use buttons in the **Tool Box**, a toolbar of illustration tools available in Windows Paint, and the **Color Box**, a palette of colors from which you can choose, to modify the graphic.
7. Click the **Fill With Color button** in the Tool Box, then click the **Blue color box**, which is the fourth from the right in the first row
   Notice how clicking a button in the Tool Box changes the mouse pointer. Now when you click an area in the image, it will be filled with the color you selected in the Color Box. See Table B-1 for a description of the tools in the Tool Box.
8. Move the pointer into the **white area that represents the sky** until the pointer changes to , then click
   The sky is now blue.
9. Click **File** on the menu bar, then click **Save**
   The change you made is saved to disk.

QuickTip

You can also open a file by double-clicking it in the Open dialog box.

FIGURE B-3: Open dialog box

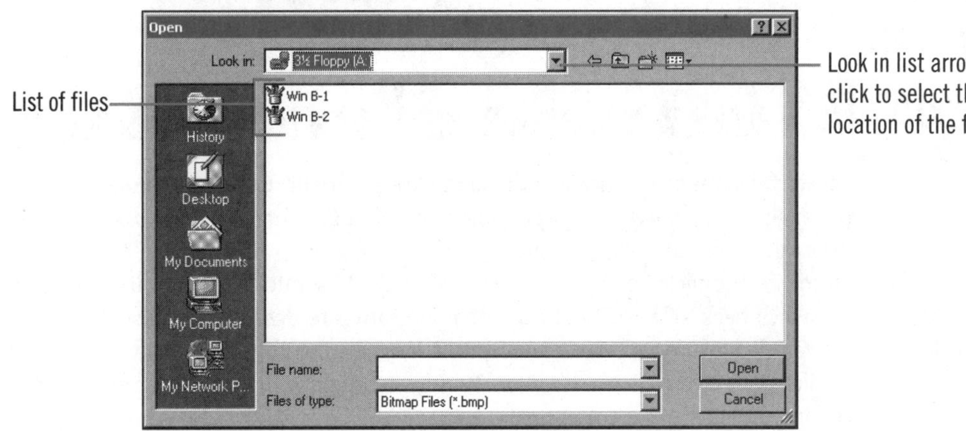

FIGURE B-4: Paint file saved with new filename

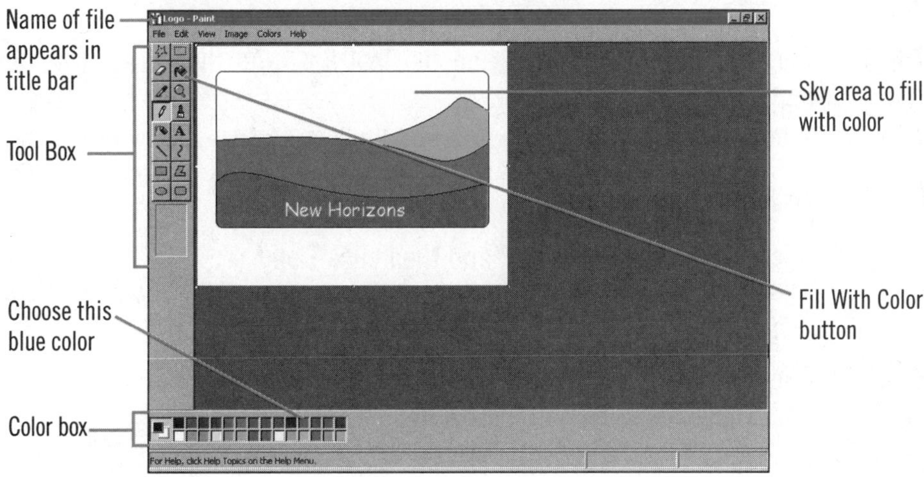

TABLE B-1: Paint Tool Box buttons

tool	description	tool	description
Free-Form Select button	Selects a free-form section of the picture to move, copy, or edit	Airbrush button	Produces a circular spray of dots
Select button	Selects a rectangular section of the picture to move, copy, or edit	Text button	Inserts text into the picture
Eraser button	Erases a portion of the picture using the selected eraser size and foreground color	Line button	Draws a straight line with the selected width and foreground color
Fill With Color button	Fills closed shape or area with the current drawing color	Curve button	Draws a wavy line with the selected width and foreground color
Pick Color button	Picks up a color off the picture to use for drawing	Rectangle button	Draws a rectangle with the selected fill style; also used to draw squares by holding down [Shift] while drawing
Magnifier button	Changes the magnification; lists magnifications under the toolbar	Polygon button	Draws polygons from connected straight-line segments
Pencil button	Draws a free-form line one pixel wide	Ellipse button	Draws an ellipse with the selected fill style; also used to draw circles by holding down [Shift] while drawing
Brush button	Draws using a brush with the selected shape and size	Rounded Rectangle button	Draws rectangles with rounded corners using the selected fill style; also used to draw rounded squares by holding down [Shift] while drawing

Windows 2000

Working with Multiple Programs

A powerful feature of Windows is its capability to run more than one program at a time. For example, you might be working with a document in WordPad and want to search the Internet to find the answer to a question. You can start your browser, a program designed to access information on the Internet, without closing WordPad. When you find the information, you can leave your browser open and switch back to WordPad. Each open program is represented by a program button on the taskbar that you click to switch between programs. You can also copy data from one file to another, (whether the files were created with the same Windows program or not), using the **Clipboard**, a temporary area in your computer's memory, and the Cut, Copy, and Paste commands. See Table B-2 for a description of these commands. In this lesson, you copy the logo graphic you worked with in the previous lesson into the memo you created in WordPad.

Trouble?

If some parts of the image or text are outside the dotted rectangle, click anywhere outside the image, then select the image again, making sure you include everything.

QuickTip

To switch between programs using the keyboard, press and hold down [Alt], press [Tab] until the program you want is selected, then release [Alt].

1. **Click the Select button on the Tool Box, and then drag a rectangle around the entire graphic**
   When you release the mouse button, the dotted rectangle surrounds the selected area, as shown in Figure B-5. Make sure the entire image is inside the rectangle. The next action you take affects the entire selection.
2. **Click Edit on the menu bar, and then click Copy**
   The logo is copied to the Clipboard. When you **copy** an object onto the Clipboard, the object remains in its original location and is also available to be pasted into another location.
3. **Click the WordPad program button on the taskbar**
   WordPad becomes the active program.
4. **Click in the first line below the line that ends "for our company brochure."**
   The insertion point indicates where the logo will be pasted.
5. **Click the Paste button on the WordPad toolbar**
   The contents of the Clipboard, in this case the logo, are pasted into the WordPad file, as shown in Figure B-6.
6. **Click the Save button on the toolbar**
   The Memo file is saved with the logo inserted.
7. **Click the WordPad Close button**
   Your WordPad document and the WordPad program close. Paint is now the active program.
8. **Click the Paint Close button; if you are prompted to save changes, click Yes**
   Your Paint document and the Paint program close. You return to the desktop.

TABLE B-2: Overview of cutting, copying and pasting

Toolbar button	function	keyboard shortcut
Cut	Removes selected information from a file and places it on the Clipboard	[Ctrl][X]
Copy	Places a copy of selected information on the Clipboard, leaving the file intact	[Ctrl][C]
Paste	Inserts whatever is currently on the Clipboard into another location within the same file, or in a different file	[Ctrl][V]

FIGURE B-5: Selecting the logo to copy and paste into the Memo file

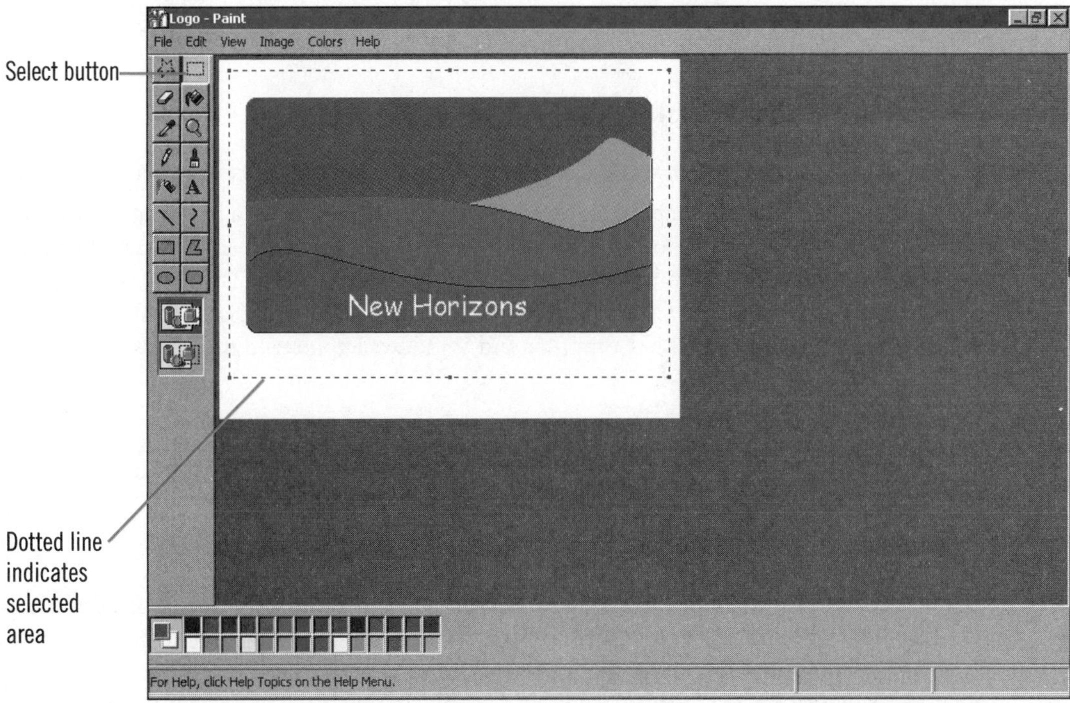

FIGURE B-6: Memo with pasted logo

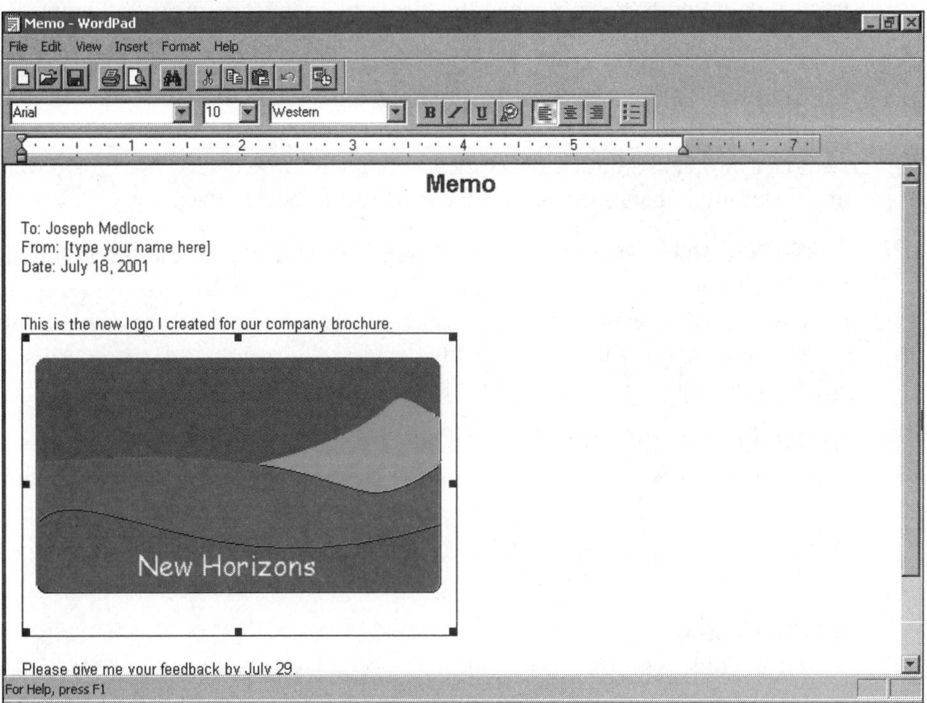

Understanding File Management

After you have created and saved numerous files using various programs, **file management**, the process of organizing and keeping track of all of your files, can be a challenge. Fortunately, Windows 2000 provides tools to keep everything organized so you can easily locate the files you need, move files to new locations, and delete files you no longer need. There are two main tools for managing your files: My Computer and Windows Explorer.  In this lesson, you preview the ways you can use My Computer and Windows Explorer to manage your files.

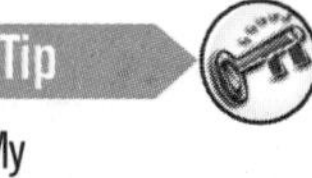

Windows 2000 gives you the ability to:

Create folders in which you can save your files

Folders are areas on a floppy disk or hard disk in which you can store files. For example, you might create a folder for your documents and another folder for your graphic files. Folders can also contain additional folders, which creates a more complex structure of folders and files, called a **file hierarchy**. See Figure B-7 for an example of how files can be organized.

QuickTip

To browse My Computer using multiple windows, click Tools on the menu bar, and then click Folder Options. In the Folder Options dialog box, click the General tab, and then under Browse Folders, click the Open each folder in its own window option button. Each time you open a new folder, a new window opens, leaving the previous folder's window open so that you can view both at the same time.

Examine and organize the hierarchy of files and folders

You can use either My Computer or Windows Explorer to see the overall structure of your files and folders. By examining your file hierarchy with these tools, you can better organize the contents of your computer and adjust the hierarchy to meet your needs. Figures B-8 and B-9 illustrate how My Computer and Windows Explorer list folders and files.

Copy, move, and rename files and folders

If you decide that a file belongs in a different folder, you can move it to another folder. You can also rename a file if you decide a different name is more descriptive. If you want to keep a copy of a file in more than one folder, you can copy it to new folders.

Delete files and folders you no longer need, as well as restore files you delete accidentally

Deleting files and folders you are sure you don't need frees up disk space and keeps your file hierarchy more organized. The **Recycle Bin**, a space on your computer's hard disk that stores deleted files, allows you to restore files you deleted by accident. To free up disk space, you should occasionally empty the Recycle Bin by deleting the files permanently from your hard drive.

Locate files quickly with the Windows 2000 Search feature

As you create more files and folders, you may forget where you placed a certain file or you may forget what name you used when you saved a file. With Search, you can locate files by providing only partial names or other factors, such as the file type (for example, a WordPad document or a Paint graphic) or the date the file was created or modified.

Use shortcuts

If a file or folder you use often is located several levels down in your file hierarchy (in a folder within a folder, within a folder), it might take you several steps to access it. To save time accessing the files and programs you use frequently, you can create shortcuts to them. A **shortcut** is a link that gives you quick access to a particular file, folder, or program.

FIGURE B-7: Sample file hierarchy

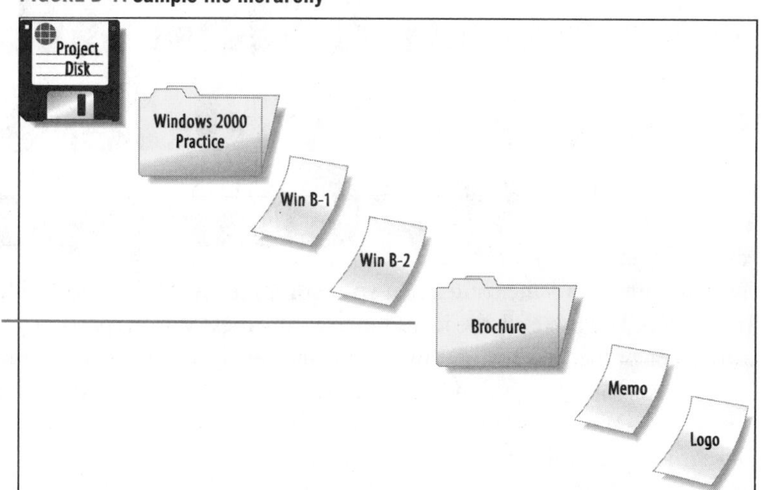

In this hierarchy, Brochure folder is a subfolder of Windows 2000 Practice folder

FIGURE B-8: Brochure folder shown in My Computer

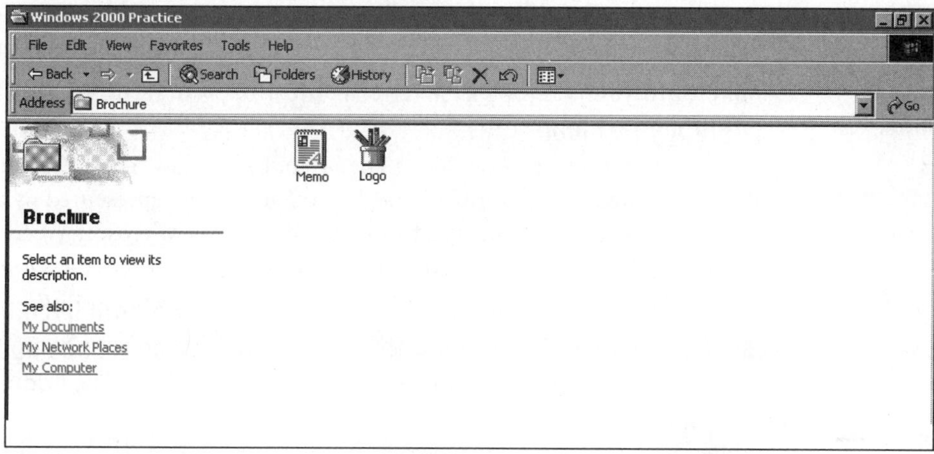

FIGURE B-9: Brochure folder shown in Windows Explorer

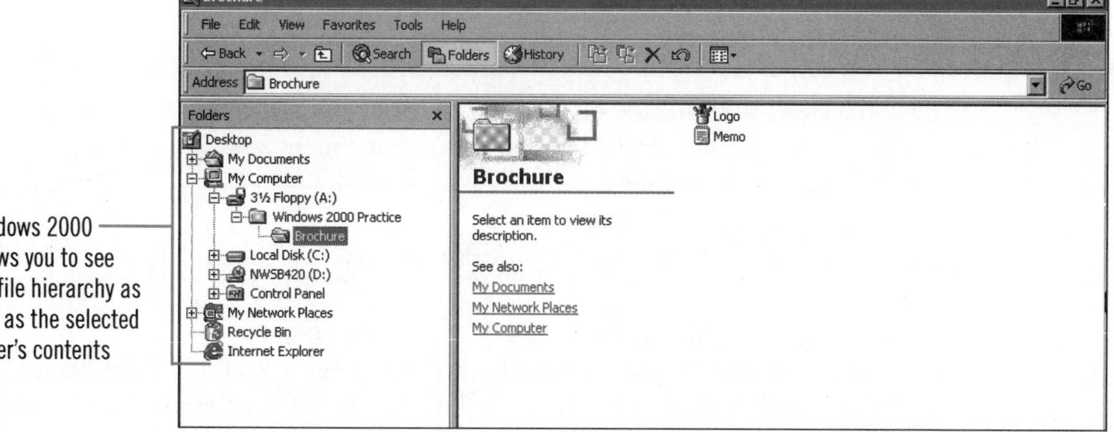

Windows 2000 allows you to see the file hierarchy as well as the selected folder's contents

Windows 2000

Viewing Files and Creating Folders with My Computer

My Computer shows the contents of your computer, including files, folders, programs, disk drives, and printers. You can click the icons representing these various parts of your computer to view their contents or properties. You can manage your files using the My Computer menu bar and toolbar. See Table B-3 for a description of the toolbar buttons. In this lesson, you begin by using My Computer to move around in your computer's file hierarchy, then you create two new folders on your Project Disk 1 for the files you created.

Trouble?

If you do not see the toolbar, click View on the menu bar, point to Toolbars, and then click Standard Buttons. If you do not see the Address Bar, click View, point to Toolbar, and then click Address Bar.

Trouble?

This book assumes that your hard drive is the C: drive. If yours differs, substitute the appropriate drive for the C: drive wherever it is referenced. See your instructor or technical support person for assistance.

QuickTip

To rename a folder, click the folder to select it, click the folder name so it is surrounded by a rectangle, type the new folder name, then press [Enter].

1. Double-click the **My Computer icon** on your desktop, then click the **Maximize button** if the My Computer window does not fill the screen
   My Computer opens and displays the contents of your computer, as shown in Figure B-10. Your window may contain icons for different folders, drives, and printers.
2. Make sure your Project Disk 1 is in the floppy disk drive, then double-click the **3½ Floppy (A:) icon**
   The contents of your Project Disk 1 appear in the window. These are the project files and the files you created using WordPad and Paint. Each file is represented by an icon, which indicates the program that was used to create the file. If Microsoft Word is installed on your computer, the Word icon appears for the WordPad files; if not, the WordPad icon appears.
3. Click the **Address list arrow** on the Address Bar, as shown in Figure B-10, then click **Local Disk (C:)** or the letter for the main hard drive on your computer
   The window changes to show the contents of your hard drive. The **Address Bar** allows you to open and view a drive, folder, or even a Web page. You can also type in the Address Bar to go to a different drive, folder, or Web page. For example, typing "C:\" will display drive C:; typing "E:\Personal Letters" will display the Personal Letters folder on the E: drive, and typing "http://www.microsoft.com" opens Microsoft's Web site if your computer is connected to the Internet.
4. Click the **Back button** on the toolbar
   The Back button displays the previous location, in this case, your Project Disk.
5. Click the **Views button** on the toolbar, then click **Details**
   Details view shows not only the files and folders, but also the sizes of the files, the types of files, folders, or drives and the date the files were last modified.
6. Click , then click **Thumbnails**
   This view offers less information but provides a preview of graphics and a clear view of the contents of the disk.
7. Click **File** on the menu bar, point to **New**, then click **Folder**
   A new folder is created on your Project Disk 1, as shown in Figure B-11. The folder is called "New Folder" by default. It is selected and ready to be renamed. You can also create a new folder by right-clicking in the blank area of the My Computer window, clicking New, then clicking Folder.
8. Type **Windows 2000 Practice**, then press **[Enter]**
   Choosing descriptive names for your folders helps you remember their contents.
9. Double-click the **Windows 2000 Practice folder**, repeat Step 7 to create a new folder in the Windows 2000 Practice folder, type **Brochure** for the folder name, then press **[Enter]**
10. Click the **Up button** to return to your Project Disk 1

FIGURE B-10: My Computer window

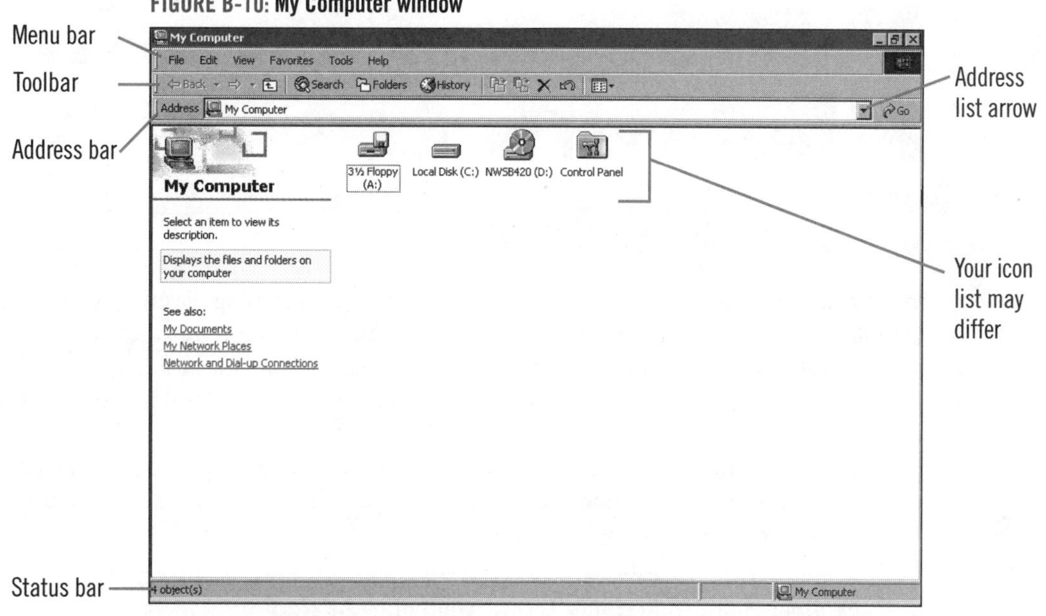

FIGURE B-11: Creating a new folder

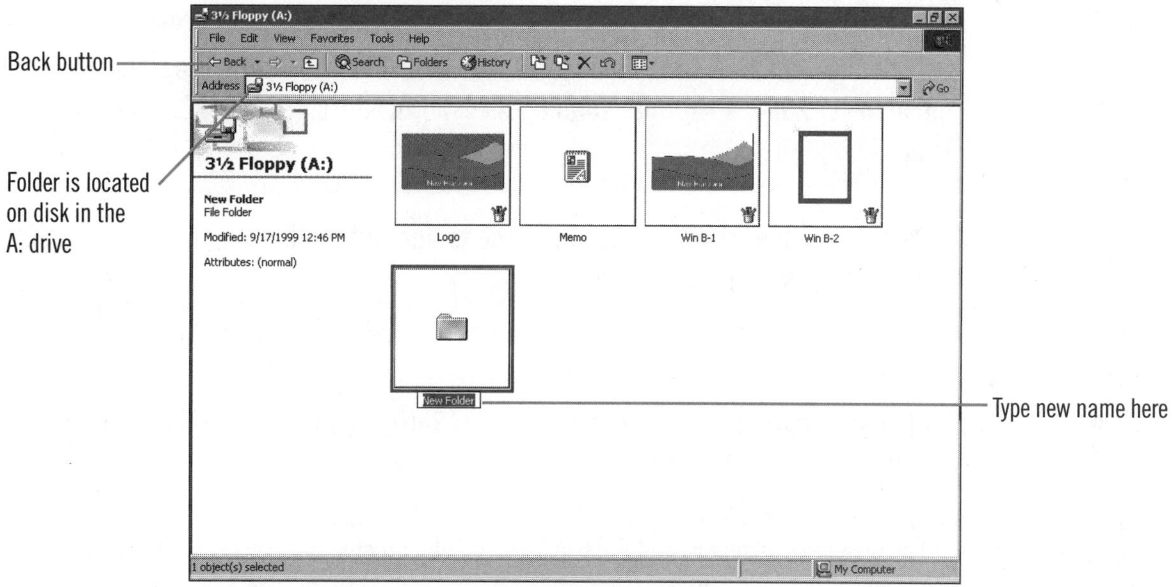

TABLE B-3: Buttons on the My Computer toolbar

button	function
	Moves back to the previous location you have already visited
	Moves forward to the previous location you have already visited
	Moves up one level in the file hierarchy
	Opens the Browse For Folder dialog box, to move the selected file to a new location
	Opens the Browse For Folder dialog box, to copy the selected file to a new location
	Undoes the most recent My Computer operation
	Deletes a folder or file permanently
	Lists the contents of My Computer using different views

Windows 2000

Moving and Copying Files with My Computer

You can move a file or folder from one location to another using a variety of methods in My Computer or Windows Explorer. If the file or folder and the location to which you want to move it are both visible on the desktop, you can simply drag the item from one location to the other. You can also use the cut, copy, and paste commands on the Edit menu or the corresponding buttons on the toolbar. Finally you can right-click the file or folder and choose the Send to command to "send" it to another location—most often a floppy disk for **backing up** files. Backup copies are made in case you have computer trouble, which may cause you to lose files. In this lesson, you move your files into the folder you created in the last lesson.

Steps

1. Click **View**, point to **Arrange Icons**, then click **by Name**
   In this view, folders are listed first in alphabetical order, followed by files, also in alphabetical order.
2. Click the **Win B-1 file**, hold down the mouse button and drag the file onto the **Windows 2000 Practice folder**, as shown in Figure B-12, then release the mouse button
   Win B-1 is moved into the Windows 2000 Practice folder.
3. Double-click the **Windows 2000 Practice folder** and confirm that it contains the Win B-1 file as well as the Brochure folder
4. Click the **Up button** on the My Computer toolbar, as shown in Figure B-12
   You return to your Project Disk. The Up button shows the next level up in the folder hierarchy.
5. Click the **Logo file**, press and hold down **[Shift]**, then click the **Memo file**
   Both files are selected. Table B-4 describes methods for selecting multiple objects.
6. Click the **Move To button** on the 3½ Floppy (A:) toolbar
   The filenames turn gray, and the Browse For Folder dialog box opens, as shown in Figure B-13.
7. Click the **plus sign** next to My Computer if you do not see 3½ Floppy (A:) listed, double-click the **3½ Floppy (A:) drive**, double-click the **Windows 2000 Practice folder**, double-click the **Brochure folder**, then click **OK**
   The two files are moved to the Brochure folder. Only the Windows 2000 Practice folder and the Win B-2 file remain.
8. Click the **Close button** in the 3½ Floppy (A:) window

QuickTip

It is easy to confuse the Back button with the Up button. The Back button returns you to the last location you visited, no matter where it is in your folder hierarchy. The Up button displays the next level up in the folder hierarchy, no matter where you last visited.

FIGURE B-12: Dragging a file from one folder to another

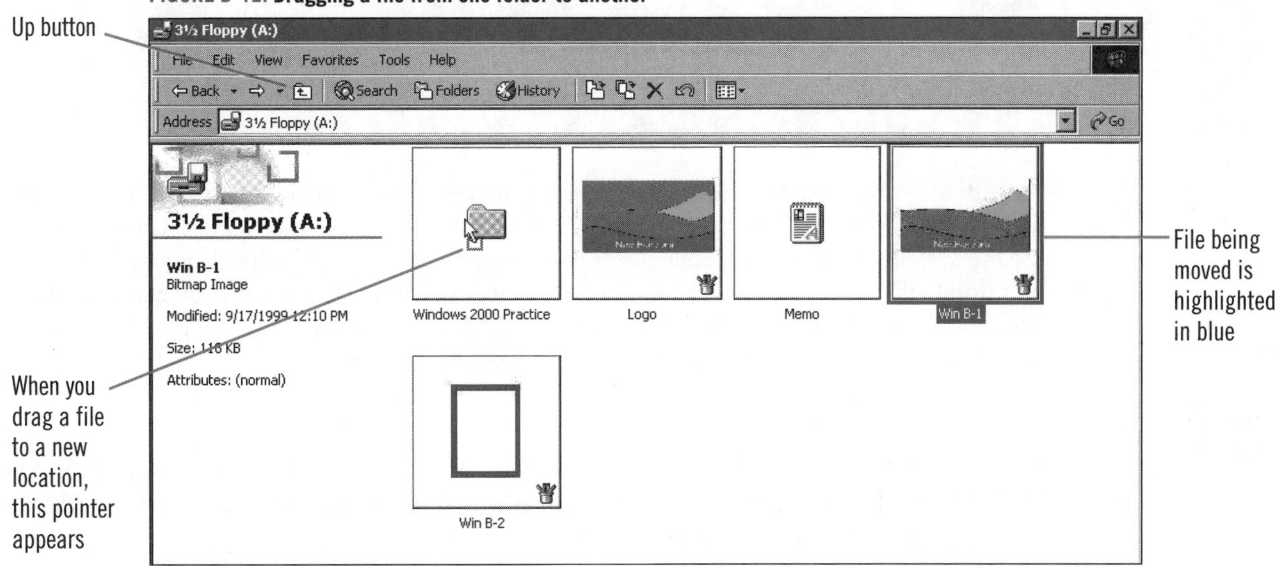

FIGURE B-13: Moving files

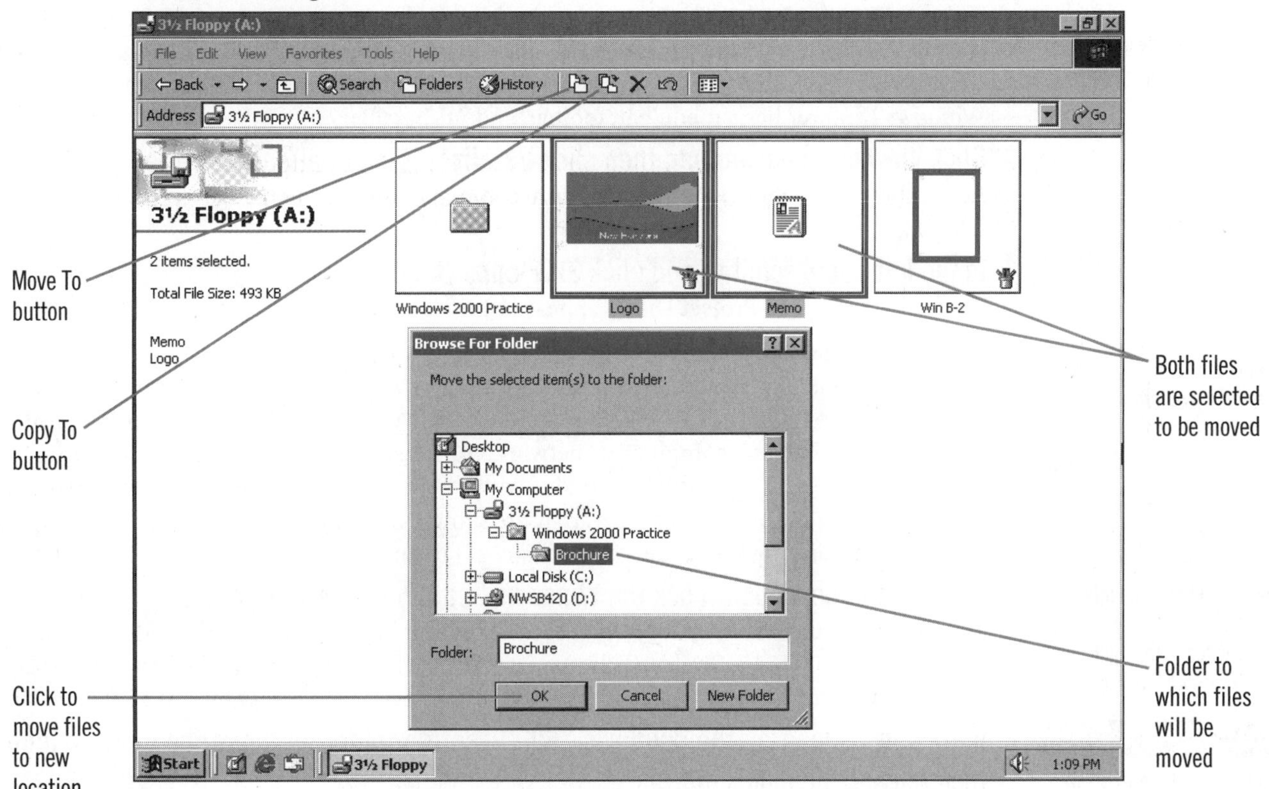

TABLE B-4: Techniques for selecting multiple files and folders

to select	do this
Individual objects not grouped together	Click the first object you want to select, then press and hold down [Ctrl] as you click each additional object you want to add to the selection
Objects grouped together	Click the first object you want to select, then press and hold down [Shift] as you click the last object in the list of objects you want to select; all the objects listed between the first and last objects are selected

Managing Files with Windows Explorer

As with My Computer, you can use Windows Explorer to copy, move, delete, and rename files and folders. However, **Windows Explorer** is more powerful than My Computer: it allows you to see the overall structure of the contents of your computer or network, (the file hierarchy), while you work with individual files and folders within that structure. This means you can work with more than one computer, folder, or file at once. In this lesson, you copy a folder from your Project Disk 1 onto the hard drive and then rename the folder.

Steps

1. **Click the Start button, point to Programs, point to Accessories, click Windows Explorer, then click the Maximize button if the Windows Explorer window doesn't already fill the screen**

   Windows Explorer opens, as shown in Figure B-14. The window is divided into two areas called **panes**. The left pane, called the **Explorer Bar**, displays the drives and folders on your computer in a hierarchy. The right pane displays the contents of whatever drive or folder is currently selected in the left pane. Each pane has its own set of scroll bars, so that changing what you can see in one pane won't affect what you can see in the other. Like My Computer, Windows Explorer has a menu bar, toolbar, and Address Bar.

Trouble? If you do not see the toolbar, click View on the menu bar, point to Toolbars, then click Standard Buttons. If you do not see the Address Bar, click View, point to Toolbars, then click Address Bar.

2. **Click View on the menu bar, then click Details if it is not already selected**

   Remember that a bullet point next to a command on the menu bar indicates that it's selected.

3. **In the left pane, scroll to and click 3½ Floppy (A:)**

   The contents of your Project Disk 1 appear in the right pane.

Trouble? If you cannot see the A: drive, you may have to click the plus sign (+) next to My Computer to view the available drives on your computer.

4. **In the left pane, click the plus sign (+) next to 3½ Floppy (A:)**

   You can click the plus sign (+) or minus sign (-) next to any item in the left pane to show or hide the different levels of the file hierarchy, so that you don't always have to look at the entire structure of your computer or network. A plus sign (+) next to a computer, drive, or folder indicates there are additional folders within that object. A minus sign (-) indicates that all the folders of the next level of hierarchy are shown. Clicking the + displays (or "expands") the next level; clicking the – hides (or "collapses") them.

QuickTip When neither a + nor a – appears next to an icon, it means that the item does not have any folders in it, although it may have files, which you can see listed in the right pane by clicking the icon.

5. **In the left pane, double-click the Windows 2000 Practice folder**

   The contents of the Windows 2000 Practice folder appear in the right pane of Windows Explorer, as shown in Figure B-15. Double-clicking an item in the left pane that has a + next to it displays its contents in the right pane and also expands the next level in the hierarchy in the left pane.

6. **In the left pane, drag the Windows 2000 Practice folder on top of the C: drive icon, then release the mouse button**

   When you drag files or folders to a different drive, they are copied rather than moved. The Windows 2000 Practice folder and the files in it are copied to the hard disk.

Trouble? If you are working in a lab setting, you may not be able to add items to your hard drive. Skip Steps 6, 7, and 8 if you are unable to complete them.

7. **In the left pane, click the C: drive icon**

   The Windows 2000 Practice folder should now appear in the list of folders in the right pane. You may have to scroll to see it. Now you should rename the folder so you can distinguish the original folder from the copy.

8. **Right-click the Windows 2000 Practice folder in the right pane, click Rename in the pop-up menu, type Practice Copy, then press [Enter]**

QuickTip You can also rename a selected file by pressing [F2], or using the Rename command on the File menu.

FIGURE B-14: Windows Explorer window

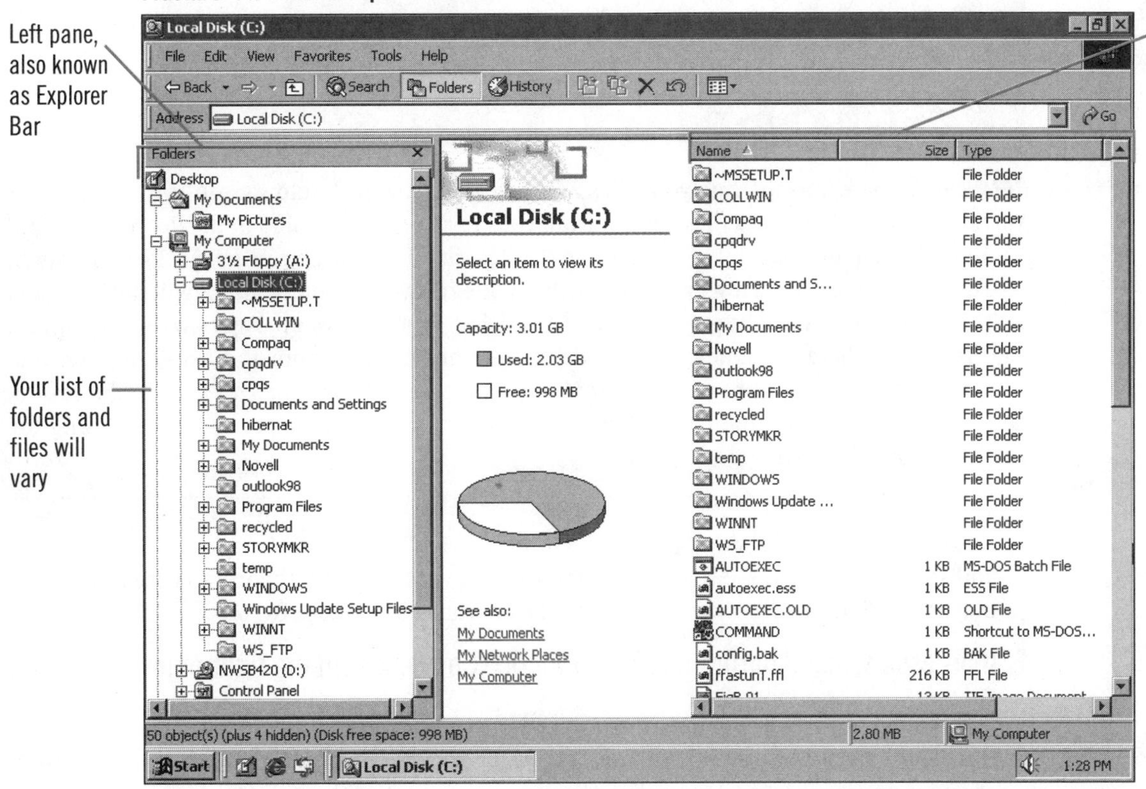

FIGURE B-15: Contents of Windows 2000 Practice folder

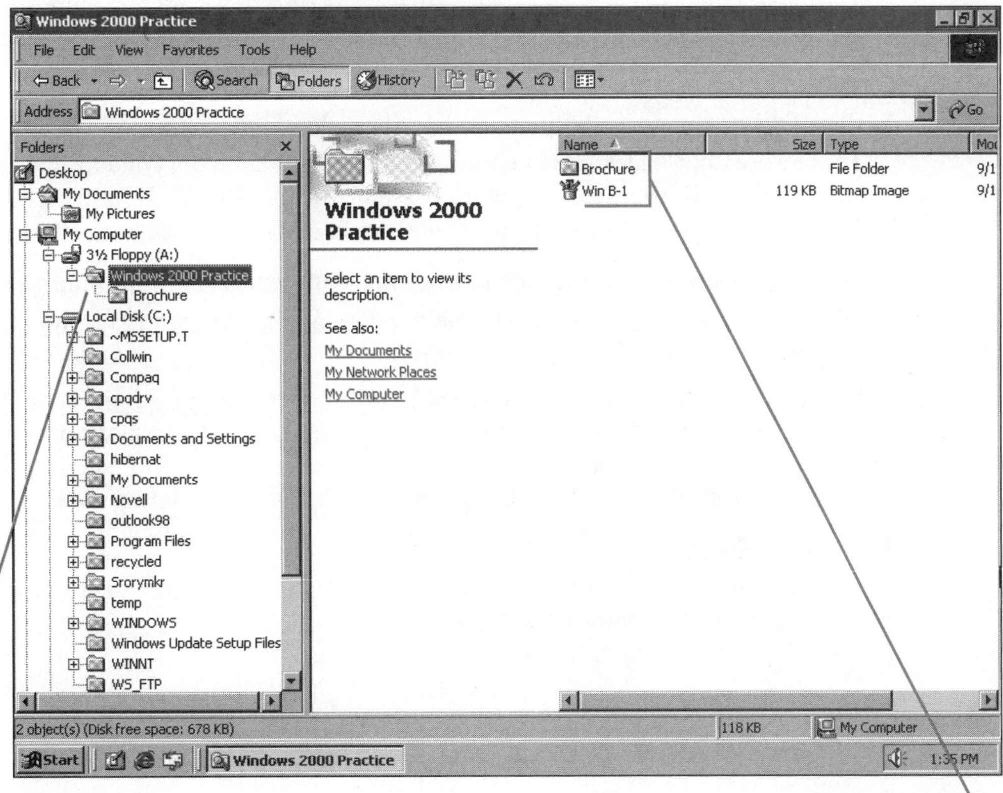

Windows 2000

Deleting and Restoring Files

To save disk space and manage your files more effectively, you should **delete** (or remove) files you no longer need. Because files deleted from your hard drive are stored in the Recycle Bin until you remove them permanently by emptying the Recycle Bin, you can restore any files you might have deleted accidentally. However, if you delete a file from your floppy disk it will not be stored in the Recycle Bin—it will be permanently deleted. See Table B-5 for an overview of deleting and restoring files. There are many ways to delete files and folders from the My Computer and Windows Explorer windows, as well as from the Windows 2000 desktop. In this lesson, you delete a file by dragging it to the Recycle Bin, restore it, and delete a folder by using the Delete command in Windows Explorer.

Steps

1. Click the **Restore button** on the Windows Explorer title bar
   You should be able to see the Recycle Bin icon on your desktop. If you can't see it, resize or move the Windows Explorer window until it is visible. See Figure B-16.
2. If necessary, scroll until you see the Practice Copy folder in the right pane of Windows Explorer
3. Drag the **Practice Copy folder** from the right pane to the **Recycle Bin** on the desktop, as shown in Figure B-16, then click **Yes** to confirm the deletion if necessary
   The folder no longer appears in Windows Explorer because you have moved it to the Recycle Bin.
4. Double-click the **Recycle Bin icon** on the desktop
   The Recycle Bin window opens, as shown in Figure B-17. Depending on the number of files already deleted on your computer, your window might look different. Use the scroll bar if you can't see the files.
5. Click **Edit** on the Recycle Bin menu bar, then click **Undo Delete**
   The Practice Copy folder is restored and should now appear in the Windows Explorer window. You might need to minimize your Recycle Bin window if it blocks your view of Windows Explorer, and you might need to scroll to the bottom of the right pane to find the restored folder.
6. Click the **Practice Copy folder** in the right pane, click the **Delete button** on the Windows Explorer toolbar (resize the window as necessary to see the button), then click **Yes**
   When you are sure you no longer need files you've moved into the Recycle Bin, you can empty the Recycle Bin. You won't do this now, in case you are working on a computer that you share with other people. But, when you're working on your own machine, simply right-click the Recycle Bin icon, then click Empty Recycle Bin in the pop-up menu.
7. Close the Recycle Bin
   If you minimized the Recycle Bin in Step 4, click its program button to open the Recycle Bin window, and then click the Close button.

QuickTip

If you are unable to delete the file, it might be because your Recycle Bin is full, or too small, or the properties have been changed so that files are not stored in the Recycle Bin but are deleted instead. See your instructor or technical support person for assistance.

FIGURE B-16: Dragging a folder to delete it

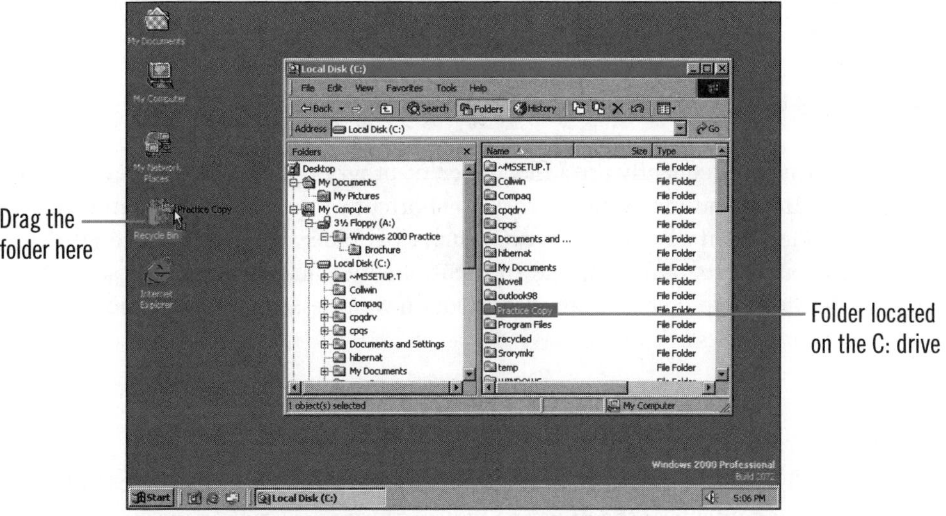

FIGURE B-17: Recycle Bin window

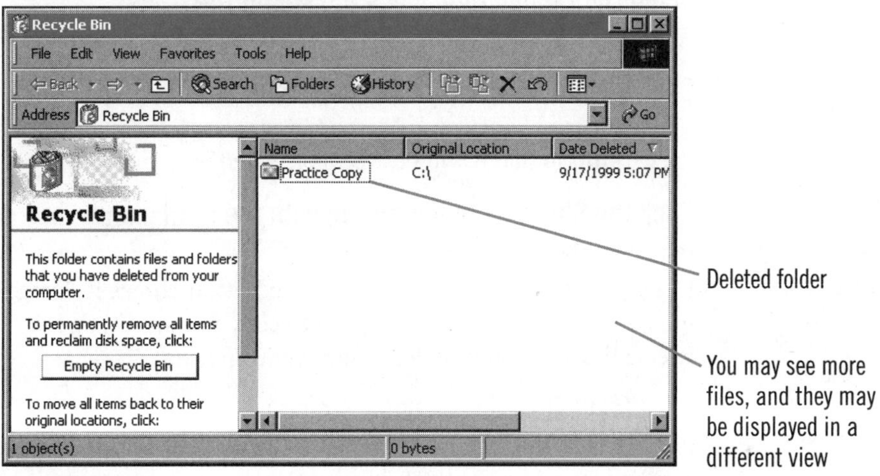

TABLE B-5: Methods for deleting and restoring files

ways to delete a file	ways to restore a file from the Recycle Bin
Select the file, then click the Delete button on the toolbar	Click the Undo button on the toolbar
Select the file, then press [Delete]	Select the file, click File, then click Restore
Right-click the file, then click Delete on the pop-up menu	Right-click the file, then click Restore
Drag the file to the Recycle Bin	Drag the file from the Recycle Bin to any other location

Customizing your Recycle Bin

You can set your Recycle Bin according to how you like to delete and restore files. For example, if you do not want files to go to the Recycle Bin but rather want them to be immediately and permanently deleted, right-click the Recycle Bin, click Properties, then click the Do Not Move Files to the Recycle Bin check box. If you find that the Recycle Bin fills up too fast and you are not ready to delete the files permanently, you can increase the amount of disk space devoted to the Recycle Bin by moving the Maximum Size of Recycle Bin slider to the right. This, of course, reduces the amount of disk space you have available for other things. Also, you can choose not to have the Confirm File Delete dialog box open when you send files to the Recycle Bin. See your instructor or technical support person before changing any of the Recycle Bin settings.

Windows 2000

Creating a Shortcut on the Desktop

When you frequently use a file, folder, or program that is located several levels down in the file hierarchy, you may want to create a shortcut to the object. You can place the shortcut on the desktop or in any other location, such as a folder, that you find convenient. To open the file, folder, or program using the shortcut, double-click the icon. In this lesson, you use Windows Explorer to create a shortcut on your desktop to the Memo file.

Steps

1. In the left pane of the Windows Explorer window, click the **Brochure folder**
   The contents of the Brochure folder appear in the right pane.
2. In the right pane, right-click the **Memo file**
   A pop-up menu appears, as shown in Figure B-18.
3. Click **Create Shortcut** in the pop-up menu
   The file named Shortcut to Memo file appears in the right pane. Now you need to move it to the desktop so that it will be accessible whenever you need it.

Trouble?

Make sure to use the right mouse button in Step 4. If you used the left mouse button by accident, right-click the Shortcut to Memo file in the right pane of Windows Explorer, click Delete, and repeat Step 4.

4. Click the **Shortcut to Memo file** with the right-mouse button, then drag the **shortcut** to an empty area of the desktop
   Dragging an icon using the left mouse button copies it. Dragging an icon using the right mouse button gives you the option to copy it, move it, or create a shortcut to it. When you release the mouse button a pop-up menu appears.
5. Click **Move Here** in the pop-up menu
   A shortcut to the Memo file now appears on the desktop, as shown in Figure B-19. You might have to move or resize the Windows Explorer window to see it.
6. Double-click the **Shortcut to Memo file icon**
   WordPad starts and the Memo file opens (if you have Microsoft Word installed on your computer, it will start and open the file instead). Using a shortcut eliminates the many steps involved in starting a program and locating and opening a file.
7. Click the **Close button** in the WordPad or Word title bar
   Now you should delete the shortcut icon in case you are working in a lab and share the computer with others.

QuickTip

Deleting a shortcut deletes only the link; it does not delete the original file or folder to which it points.

8. On the desktop, click the **Shortcut to Memo file**, press **[Delete]**, then click **Yes** to confirm the deletion
   The shortcut is removed from the desktop and is now in the Recycle Bin.
9. Close all windows, then shut down Windows

FIGURE B-18: **Creating a shortcut**

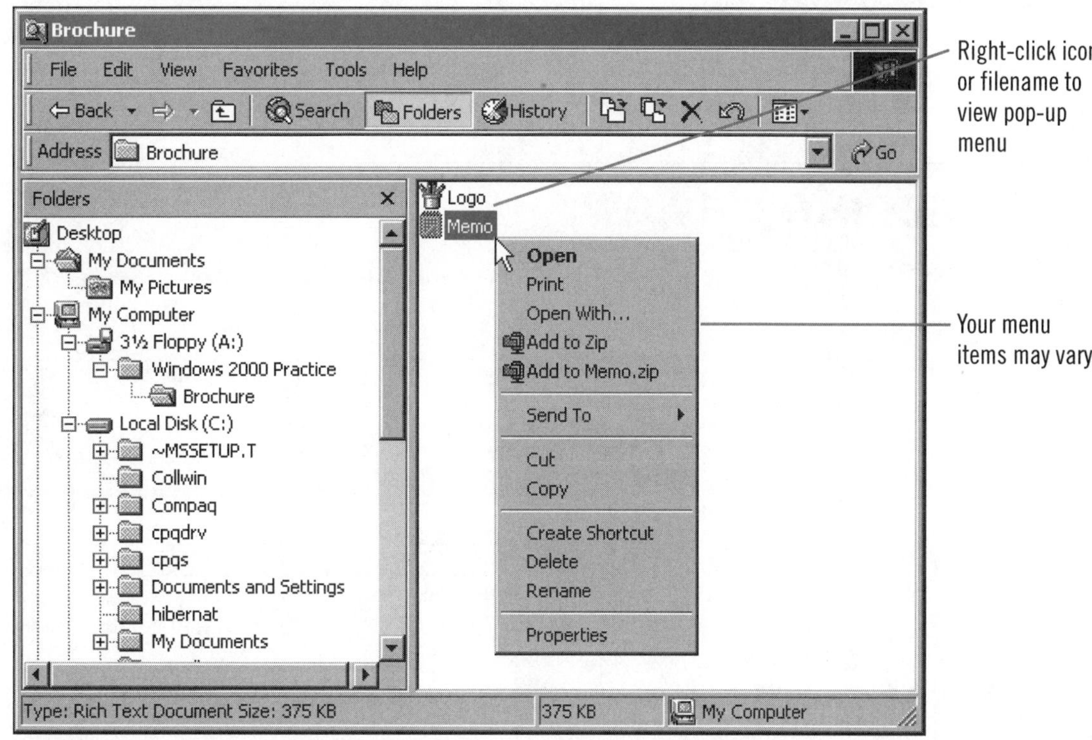

FIGURE B-19: **Shortcut on desktop**

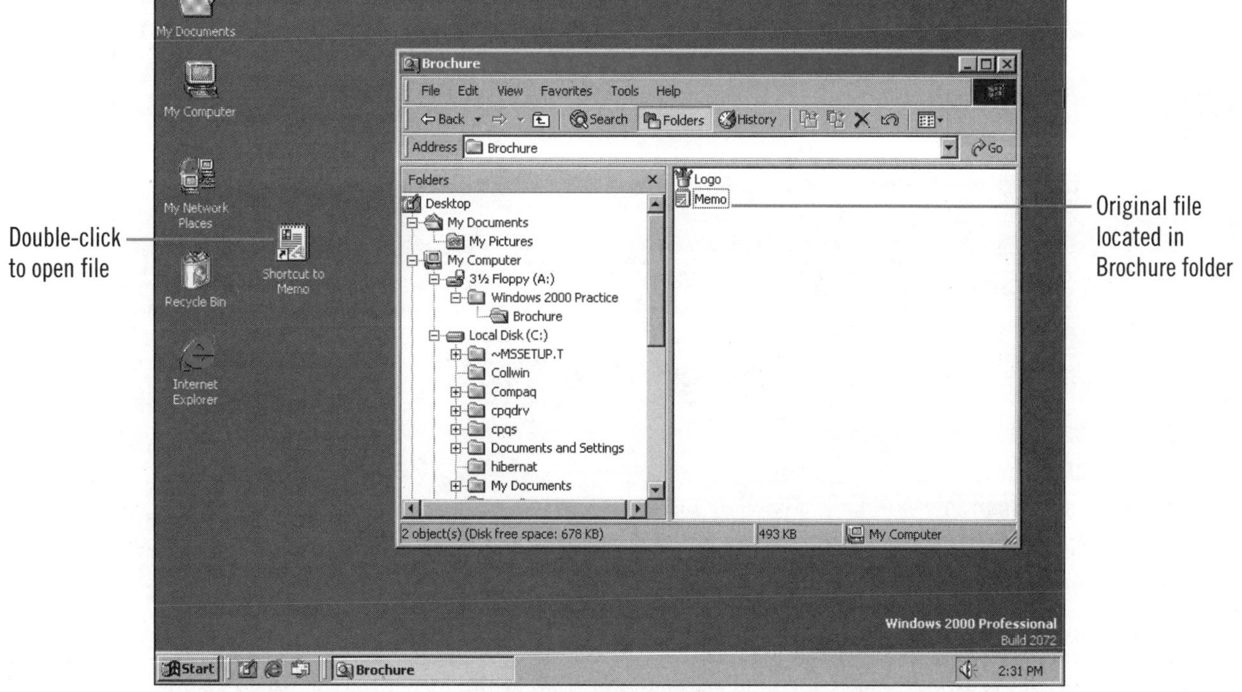

Adding shortcuts to the Start menu

If you do not want your desktop to get cluttered with icons but you would still like easy access to certain files, programs, and folders, you can create a shortcut on the Start menu. Drag the file, program, or folder that you want to add to the Start menu from the Windows Explorer window to the Start button. The file, program, or folder will appear on the first level of the Start menu.

Practice

► Concepts Review

Label each of the elements of the Windows Explorer window shown in Figure B-20.

FIGURE B-20

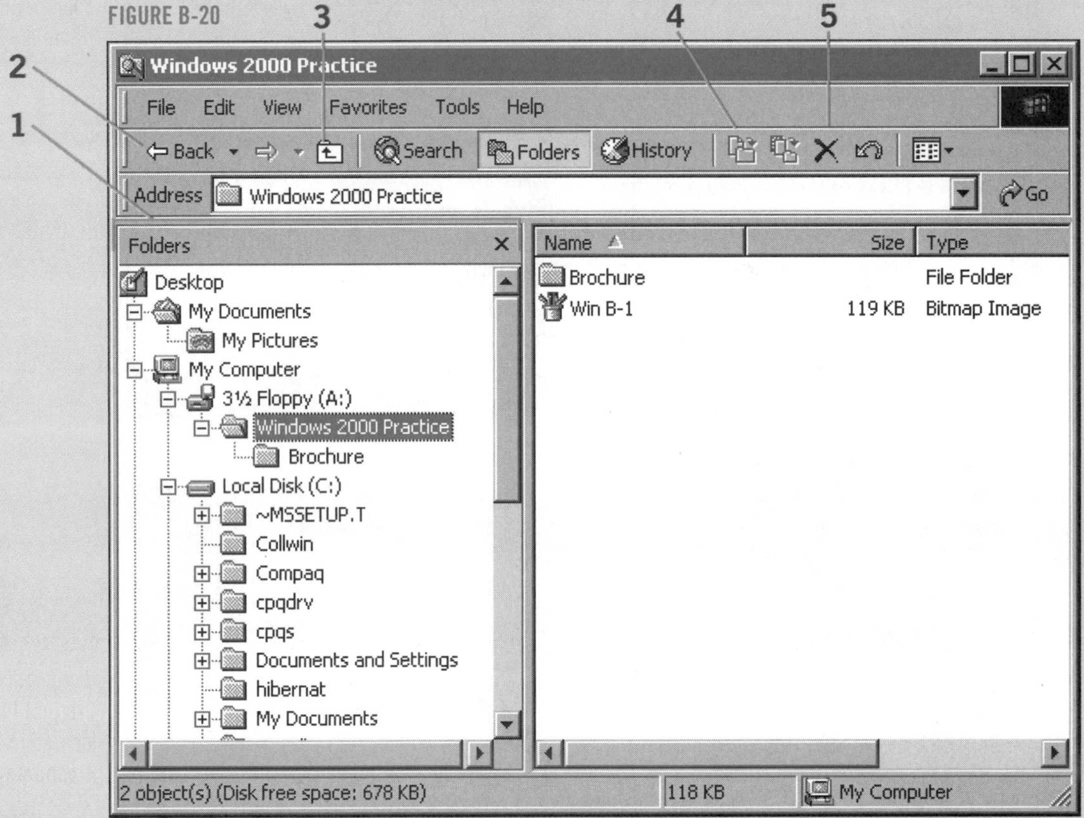

Match each of the statements with the term it describes.

6. Electronic collections of data
7. Your computer's temporary storage area
8. Temporary location of information you wish to paste into another program
9. Storage areas on your hard drive for files, folders, and programs
10. Structure of files and folders

a. RAM
b. Folders
c. Files
d. File hierarchy
e. Clipboard

Select the best answer from the list of choices.

11. To prepare a floppy disk to save your files, you must first do which of the following?
- **a.** Copy work files to the disk
- **b.** Format the disk
- **c.** Erase all the files that might be on the disk
- **d.** Place the files on the Clipboard

12. You can use My Computer to
- **a.** create a drawing of your computer.
- **b.** view the contents of a folder.
- **c.** change the appearance of your desktop.
- **d.** add text to a WordPad file.

13. Which of the following best describes WordPad?
- **a.** A program for organizing files
- **b.** A program for performing financial analysis
- **c.** A program for creating basic text documents
- **d.** A program for creating graphics

14. Which of the following is NOT a way to move files from one folder to another?
- **a.** Open the file and use the Save As command to save the file in a new location
- **b.** In My Computer or the Windows Explorer, drag the selected file to the new folder
- **c.** Use the Move To button on the Standard toolbar in the My Computer or the Windows Explorer window
- **d.** Use the [Ctrl][X] and [Ctrl][V] keyboard shortcuts while in the My Computer or the Windows Explorer window

15. In which of the following can you view the hierarchy of drives, folders, and files in a split pane window?
- **a.** Windows Explorer
- **b.** Programs
- **c.** My Computer
- **d.** WordPad

16. To restore files that you have sent to the Recycle Bin,
- **a.** click File, then click Empty Recycle Bin.
- **b.** click Edit, then click Undo Delete.
- **c.** click File, then click Undo.
- **d.** You cannot retrieve files sent to the Recycle Bin.

17. To select files that are not grouped together, select the first file, then
- **a.** press [Shift] while selecting the second file.
- **b.** press [Alt] while selecting the second file.
- **c.** press [Ctrl] while selecting the second file.
- **d.** click on the second file.

18. Pressing [Backspace]
- **a.** deletes the character to the right of the cursor.
- **b.** deletes the character to the left of the cursor.
- **c.** moves the insertion point one character to the right.
- **d.** deletes all text to the left of the cursor.

19. The size of a font is measured in
- **a.** centimeters.
- **b.** points.
- **c.** places.
- **d.** millimeters.

20. The Back button on the My Computer toolbar
- **a.** starts the last program you used.
- **b.** displays the next level of the file hierarchy.
- **c.** backs up the currently selected file.
- **d.** displays the last location you visited.

Skills Review

Use Project Disk 2 to complete the exercises in this section.

1. Create and save a WordPad file.
- **a.** Start Windows, then start WordPad.
- **b.** Type **My Drawing Ability**.
- **c.** Press [Enter] three times.
- **d.** Save the document as *Drawing Ability* to your Project Disk 2.

2. Open, edit, and save an existing Paint file.
- **a.** Start Paint and open the file Win B-2 on your Project Disk 2.
- **b.** Inside the picture frame, use the ellipses tool to create a circle filled with purple and then use the rectangle tool to place a square filled with yellow inside the circle.
- **c.** Save the picture as *First Unique Art* to your Project Disk 2.

3. Work with multiple programs.
- **a.** Select the entire graphic and copy it to the Clipboard, then switch to WordPad.
- **b.** Place the insertion point in the last blank line, paste the graphic into your document, then deselect the graphic.
- **c.** Save the changes to your WordPad document.
- **d.** Switch to Paint.
- **e.** Using the Fill With Color button, change the color of a filled area of your graphic.
- **f.** Save the revised graphic with the new name *Second Unique Art* to Project Disk 2.
- **g.** Select the entire graphic and copy it to the Clipboard.
- **h.** Switch to WordPad, move the insertion point to the line below the graphic by clicking below the graphic and press [Enter], type **This is another version of my graphic.** below the first picture, then press [Enter].

i. Paste the second graphic under the text you just typed.
j. Save the changed WordPad document as *Two Drawing Examples* to your Project Disk 2.
k. Exit Paint and WordPad.

4. **View files and create folders with My Computer.**
   a. Open My Computer.
   b. Double-click the drive that contains your Project Disk 2.
   c. Create a new folder on your Project Disk 2 by clicking File, New, then Folder, and name the new folder *Review.*
   d. Open the folder to display its contents (it is empty).
   e. Use the Address Bar to view your hard drive, usually (C:).
   f. Create a folder on the hard drive called *Temporary*, then use the Back button to view the Review folder.
   g. Create two new folders in it, one named *Documents* and the other named *Artwork.*
   h. Click the Forward button as many times as necessary to move up in the file hierarchy and view the contents of the hard drive.
   i. Change the view to Details.

5. **Move and copy files with My Computer.**
   a. Use the Address Bar to view your Project Disk 2.
   b. Use the [Shift] key to select *First Unique Art* and *Second Unique Art*, then cut and paste them into the Artwork folder.
   c. Use the Back button as many times as necessary to view the contents of Project Disk 2.
   d. Select the two WordPad files, *Drawing Ability* and *Two Drawing Examples*, then move them into the Review folder.
   e. Open the Review folder, select the two WordPad files again, then drag them into the Documents folder.

6. **Manage files with Windows Explorer.**
   a. Open Windows Explorer and view the contents of the Artwork folder in the right pane.
   b. Select the two Paint files.
   c. Drag the two Paint files from the Artwork folder to the Temporary folder on the hard drive to copy them.
   d. View the contents of the Documents folder in the right pane.
   e. Select the two WordPad files.
   f. Repeat Step c to copy the files to the Temporary folder on the hard drive.
   g. View the contents of the Temporary folder in the right pane to verify that the four files are there.

7. **Delete and restore files and folders.**
   a. Resize the Windows Explorer window so you can see the Recycle Bin icon on the desktop, then scroll in Windows Explorer so you can see the Temporary folder in the left pane.
   b. Delete the Temporary folder from the hard drive by dragging it to the Recycle Bin.
   c. Click Yes if necessary to confirm the deletion.
   d. Open the Recycle Bin, restore the Temporary folder and its files to your hard disk, and then close the Recycle Bin. (*Note:* If your Recycle Bin is empty, your computer is set to automatically delete items in the Recycle Bin.)
   e. Delete the Temporary folder again by pressing [Delete]. Click Yes if necessary to confirm the deletion.

8. **Create a shortcut on the desktop.**
   a. Use the left pane of Windows Explorer to locate the Windows folder on your hard drive. Select the folder to view its contents in the right pane. (*Note:* If you are in a lab setting, you may not have access to the Windows folder.)
   b. In the right pane, scroll through the list of objects until you see a file called Explorer.
   c. Drag the Explorer file with the right mouse button to the desktop to create a shortcut.
   d. Close Windows Explorer.
   e. Double-click the new shortcut to make sure it starts Windows Explorer. Then close Windows Explorer again.
   f. Delete the shortcut for Windows Explorer and exit Windows.

► Independent Challenges

If you are doing all of the Independent Challenges, you may need to use additional floppy disks. Label the first new disk Project Disk 3, and the next Project Disk 4.

1. You have decided to start a bakery business and you want to use Windows 2000 to organize the files for the business.

- **a.** Create two new folders on your Project Disk 3, one named *Advertising* and one named *Customers*.
- **b.** Use WordPad to create a letter inviting new customers to the open house for the new bakery, then save it as *Open House Letter* and place it in the Customers folder.
- **c.** Use WordPad to create a list of five tasks that need to get done before the business opens (such as purchasing equipment, decorating the interior, and ordering supplies), then save it as *Business Plan* to your Project Disk 3, but don't place it in a folder.
- **d.** Use Paint to create a simple logo for the bakery, save it as *Bakery Logo*, and then place it in the Advertising folder.
- **e.** Print the file Bakery Logo, then delete it from your Project Disk 3.

2. On your computer's hard drive, create a folder called *IC2*. Follow the guidelines listed here to create the file hierarchy shown in Figure B-21.

FIGURE B-21

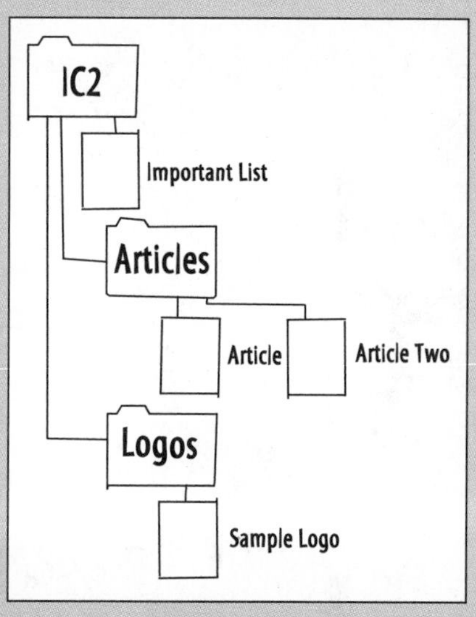

- **a.** Start WordPad, create a new file that contains a list. Save the file as *To Do List* to your Project Disk 3 (Project Disk 4 if you are out of space on Project Disk 3).
- **b.** Start My Computer and copy the Open House Letter file on your Project Disk 3 to the IC2 folder. Rename the file *Article*.
- **c.** Copy the Memo file again to the IC2 folder on your hard drive and rename the second copy of the file *Article Two*.
- **d.** Use My Computer to copy any Paint file to the IC2 folder and rename the file *Sample Logo*, then delete the Sample Logo file.
- **e.** Copy the To Do List from your Project Disk 3 to the IC2 folder and rename the file *Important List*.
- **f.** Move the files into the folders shown in Figure B-21.
- **g.** Copy the IC2 folder to your Project Disk 3. Then delete the IC2 folder on your hard drive. Using the Recycle Bin, restore the file called IC2. To remove all your work on the hard drive, delete this folder again.

3. With Windows 2000, you can access the Web from My Computer and Windows Explorer, allowing you to search for information located not only on your computer or network, but also on any computer on the Internet.

- **a.** Start Windows Explorer, then click in the Address Bar so the current location (probably your hard drive) is selected, type **www.microsoft.com**, then press [Enter].
- **b.** Connect to the Internet if necessary. The Microsoft Web page appears in the right pane of Windows Explorer.
- **c.** Click in the Address Bar, then type **www.course.com**, press [Enter], and then wait a moment while the Course Technology Web page opens.
- **d.** Make sure your Project Disk is in the floppy disk drive, then click 3½ Floppy (A:) in the left pane.
- **e.** Click the Back button list arrow, then click Welcome to Microsoft's Homepage.
- **f.** Capture a picture of your desktop by pressing [Print Screen] located on the upper-right side of your keyboard. (This stores the picture on the Clipboard.) Open the Paint program, paste the contents of the Clipboard into the drawing window, then print it.
- **g.** Close Paint without saving your changes.
- **h.** Close Windows Explorer and disconnect from the Internet.

4. Create a shortcut to the drive that contains your Project Disk 3. Then capture a picture of your desktop showing the new shortcut by pressing [Print Screen], located on the upper-right side of your keyboard. The picture is stored temporarily on the Clipboard. Then open the Paint program and paste the contents of the Clipboard into the drawing window. Click No when asked to enlarge the Bitmap. Print the screen, close Paint without saving your changes, then delete the shortcut when you are finished.

► Visual Workshop

Recreate the screen shown in Figure B-22, which contains the Brochure window in My Computer, two shortcuts on the desktop, and two open files. Press [Print Screen] to make a copy of the screen, (a copy of the screen is placed on the Clipboard), open Paint, click Paste to paste the screen picture into Paint, then print the Paint file.

FIGURE B-22

Access 2002

Getting
Started with Access 2002

Objectives

- Define database software
- Learn database terminology
- Start Access and open a database
- MOUS View the database window
- MOUS Navigate records
- MOUS Enter records
- MOUS Edit records
- Preview and print a datasheet
- Get Help and exit Access

In this unit, you will learn the purpose, advantages, and terminology of Microsoft Access 2002, a database software program. You will learn how to use the different elements of the Access window and how to get help. You'll learn how to navigate through a database, enter and update data, and preview and print data. Kelsey Lang is a Marketing Manager at MediaLoft, a nationwide chain of bookstore cafés that sells books, music, and videos. Recently, MediaLoft switched to Access for storing and maintaining customer information. Kelsey will use Access to maintain this valuable information for MediaLoft.

Access 2002

Defining Database Software

Microsoft Access 2002 is a database software program that runs on Windows. **Database software** is used to manage data that can be organized into lists of related information, such as customers, products, vendors, employees, projects, or sales. Many small companies record customer, inventory, and sales information in a spreadsheet program such as Microsoft Excel. While this electronic format is more productive than using a paper-based system, Excel still lacks many of the database advantages provided by Access. Refer to Table A-1 for a comparison of the two programs. Kelsey reviews the advantages of database software over manual systems.

The advantages of using Access include:

- **Data entry is faster and easier**
  Before inexpensive microcomputers, small businesses used manual paper systems, as illustrated in Figure A-1, such as index cards, to record each customer, sale, and inventory item. Using an electronic database such as Access, you can create on-screen data entry forms that make managing a database easier, more accurate, and more efficient than manual systems.

- **Information retrieval is faster and easier**
  Retrieving information in a manual system is tedious because the information has to be physically handled, sorted, and stored. Also, one error in filing can cause serious retrieval problems later. With Access you can quickly find, display, and print information about customers, sales, or inventory.

- **Information can be viewed and sorted in multiple ways**
  A manual system allows you to sort information in only one order, unless the information is duplicated for a second arrangement. In such a system, complete customer and product information is recorded for each sale. This can easily compromise data accuracy. Access allows you to view or sort the information from one or more subjects simultaneously. For example, you might want to find all the customers who purchased a particular product, or find all the products purchased by a particular customer. A change made to the data in one view of Access is automatically updated in every other view or report.

- **Information is more secure**
  Paper can be torn, misplaced, and stolen. There is no password required to read a paper document. A flood or fire can destroy the single copy of information in a manual system. If information is stored in an Access database file, you can back up an Access database file on a regular basis and store the file at an offsite location. You can also protect data with a password so only those users with appropriate security clearances can view or manipulate it.

- **Information can be shared among several users**
  An index card system is limited to those users who have physical access to it. If one user keeps a card for an extended period of time, then others cannot use or update that information. Access databases are inherently multiuser. More than one person can be entering, updating, and using the data at the same time.

- **Duplicate data entry is minimized**
  A paper-based system requires that you record the customer and product information for each sale twice—once on the customer index card and once on the inventory index card. With Access, you only need to enter each piece of information once. Figure A-2 shows a possible structure for an Access database that records sales.

FIGURE A-1: Using a manual system to organize sales data

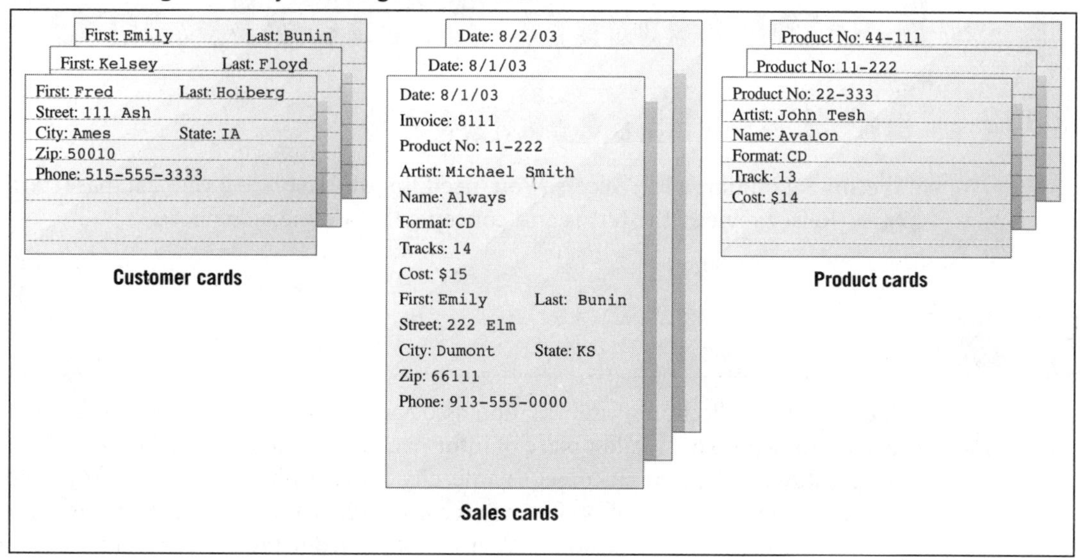

FIGURE A-2: Using Access, an electronic relational database, to organize sales data

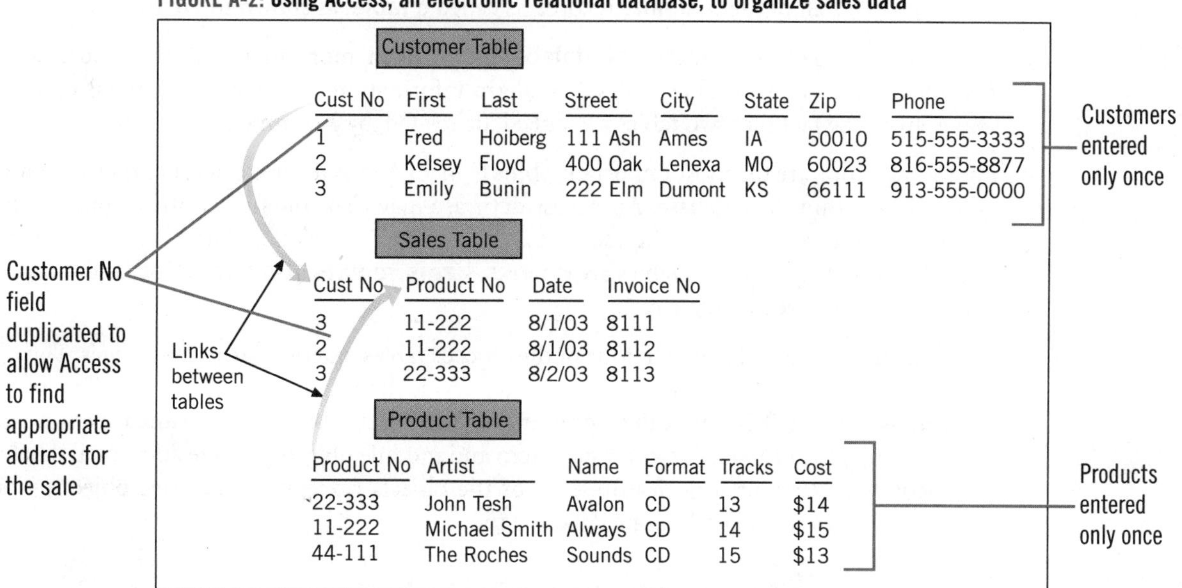

TABLE A-1: Comparing Excel to Access

feature	Excel	Access
Layout	Provides a natural tabular layout for easy data entry	Provides a natural tabular layout as well as customized data entry screens
Storage	Limited to approximately 65,000 records per sheet	Able to store any number of records up to two gigabytes
Linked tables	Manages single lists of information	Allows links between lists of information to reduce data redundancy
Reporting	Limited to the current spreadsheet arrangement of data	Able to create and save multiple report presentations of data
Security	Limited to file and password security options such as marking the file "read-only" or protecting a range of cells	Each user can be given access to only the records and fields they need
Multiuser capabilities	Does not easily allow multiple users to simultaneously enter and update data	Naturally allows multiple users to simultaneously enter and update data
Data entry screens	Provides limited data entry screens	Provides the ability to create extensive data entry screens called forms

Access 2002

Learning Database Terminology

To become familiar with Access, you need to understand basic database terminology. Kelsey reviews the terms and concepts that define a database.

Details

- A **database** is a collection of information associated with a topic (for example, sales of products to customers). The smallest piece of information in a database is called a **field**, or category of information, such as the customer's name, city, state, or phone number. A **key field** is a field that contains unique information for each record, such as a social security number for a person or a customer number for a customer. A group of related fields, such as all of the demographic information for one customer, is called a **record**. In Access, a collection of records for a single subject, such as all of the customer records, is called a **table**, as shown in Figure A-3.
- An Access database is a **relational database**, in which more than one table, such as the Customer, Sales, and Product tables, can share information. The term "relational database" comes from the fact that two tables are linked, or related, by a common field.
- Tables, therefore, are the most important **objects** in an Access database because they contain all of the data within the database. An Access database may also contain six other objects. These other objects serve to increase the usefulness and value of the relational data. The other objects in an Access database besides tables are **queries**, **forms**, **reports**, **pages**, **macros**, and **modules**. They are summarized in Table A-2.
- Data can be entered and edited in four of the objects: tables, queries, forms, and pages. The relationship between tables, queries, forms, and reports is shown in Figure A-4. Regardless of how the data is entered, it is physically stored in a table object. Data can be printed from a table, query, form, page, or report object. The macro and module objects provide additional database productivity and automation features. All of the objects (except for the page objects, which create Web pages) are stored in one database file.

TABLE A-2: Access objects and their purpose

object	purpose
Table	Contains all of the raw data within the database in a spreadsheet-like view; tables can be linked with a common field to share information and therefore minimize data redundancy
Query	Provides a spreadsheet-like view of the data similar to tables, but a query can be designed to provide the user with a subset of fields or records from one or more tables; queries are created when a user has a question about the data in the database
Form	Provides an easy-to-use data entry screen, which generally shows only one record at a time
Report	Provides a professional printout of data that may contain enhancements such as headers, footers, and calculations on groups of records
Page	Creates dynamic Web pages which interact with an Access database; also called Data Access Page
Macro	Stores a set of keystrokes or commands, such as the commands to print several reports or to display a toolbar when a form opens
Module	Stores Visual Basic for Applications programming code that extends the functions and automated processes of Access

FIGURE A-3: Tables contain fields and records

Customer Table

Cust No	First	Last	Street	City	State	Zip	Phone
1	Fred	Hoiberg	111 Ash	Ames	IA	50010	515-555-3333
2	Kelsey	Floyd	400 Oak	Lenexa	MO	60023	816-555-8877
3	Emily	Bunin	222 Elm	Dumont	KS	66111	913-555-0000

Sales Table

Cust No	Product No	Date	Invoice No
3	11-222	8/1/03	8111
2	11-222	8/1/03	8112
3	22-333	8/2/03	8113

Product Table

Product No	Artist	Name	Format	Tracks	Cost
22-333	John Tesh	Avalon	CD	13	$14
11-222	Michael Smith	Always	CD	14	$15
44-111	The Roches	Sounds	CD	15	$13

FIGURE A-4: The relationship between Access objects

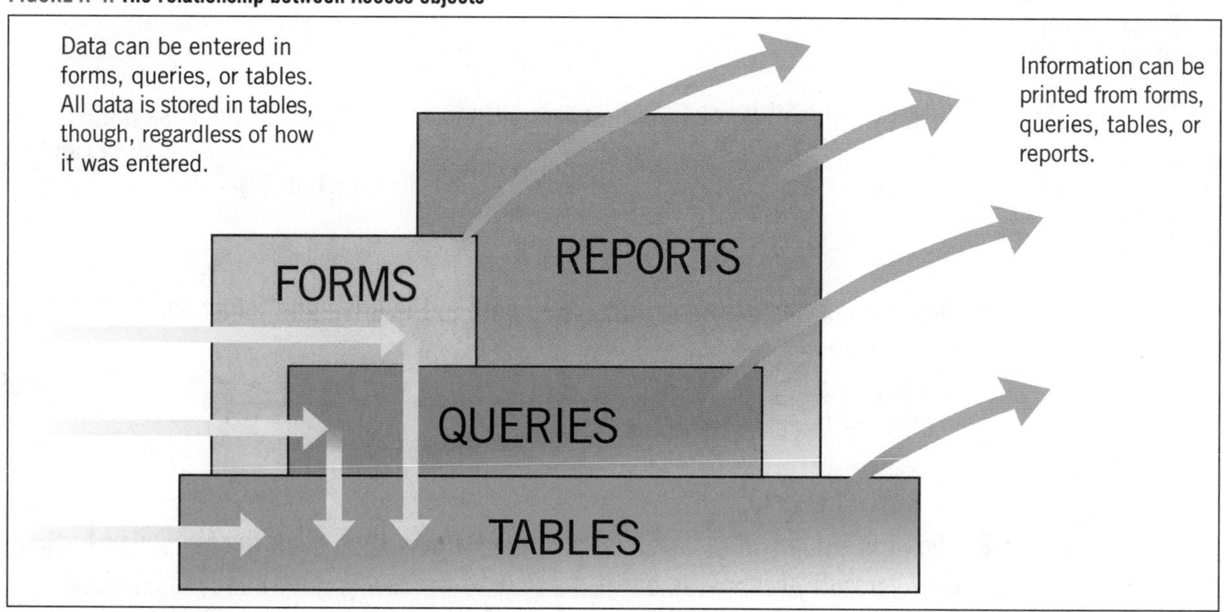

Access 2002

Starting Access 2002 and Opening a Database

You can start Access by clicking the Access icon on the Windows desktop or on the Microsoft Office shortcut bar. Since not all computers will provide a shortcut icon on the desktop or display the Office shortcut bar, you can always find Access by clicking the Start button on the taskbar, pointing to Programs, and then choosing Access from the Programs menu. You can open a database from within Access or by finding the database file on the desktop, in My Computer, or in Windows Explorer, and then opening it. Kelsey starts Access and opens the MediaLoft-A database.

Steps

1. Click the **Start button** on the taskbar
   The Start button is the first item on the taskbar, and is usually located in the lower-left corner of your screen. You can use the Start menu to start any program on your computer.

2. Point to **Programs**
   Access is generally located on the Programs menu. All the programs stored on your computer can be found on the Programs menu.

3. Click **Microsoft Access**
   Access opens and displays a task pane on the right, from which you can open an existing file or create a new database.

4. Click the **Files** or **More files** link in the Open a file section of the task pane
   The Open dialog box opens, as shown in Figure A-5. Depending on the databases and folders stored on your computer, your dialog box may look slightly different.

5. Click the **Look in list arrow**, then navigate to the drive and folder where your Project Files are stored
   When you have navigated to the correct folder, a list of the Microsoft Access database files in that folder appears in the Open dialog box.

6. Click the **MediaLoft-A** database file, click **Open**, then click the **Maximize button** on the Microsoft Access title bar if the Access window is not already maximized
   The MediaLoft-A database opens as shown in Figure A-6.

Trouble?

If Microsoft Access is not located on the Programs menu, look for it within program group menus such as the Microsoft Office group.

Trouble?

If the task pane does not appear on the right side of your screen, click File on the menu bar, then click New.

FIGURE A-5: Open dialog box

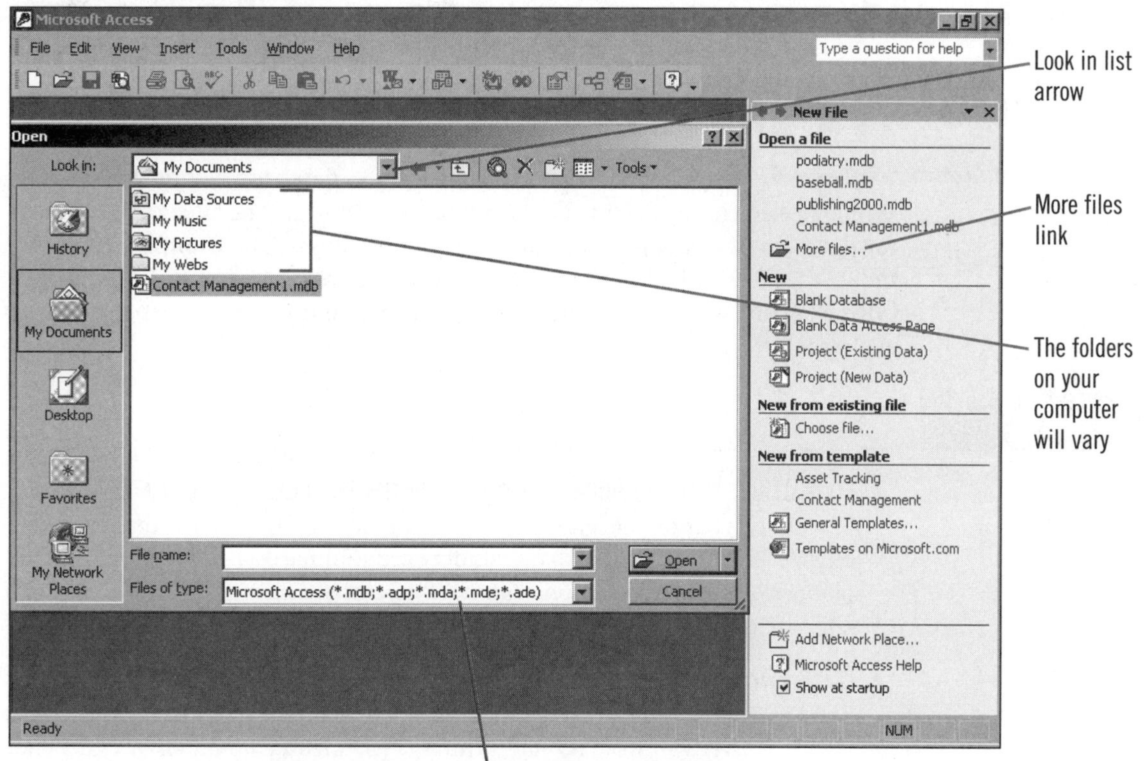

FIGURE A-6: MediaLoft-A database

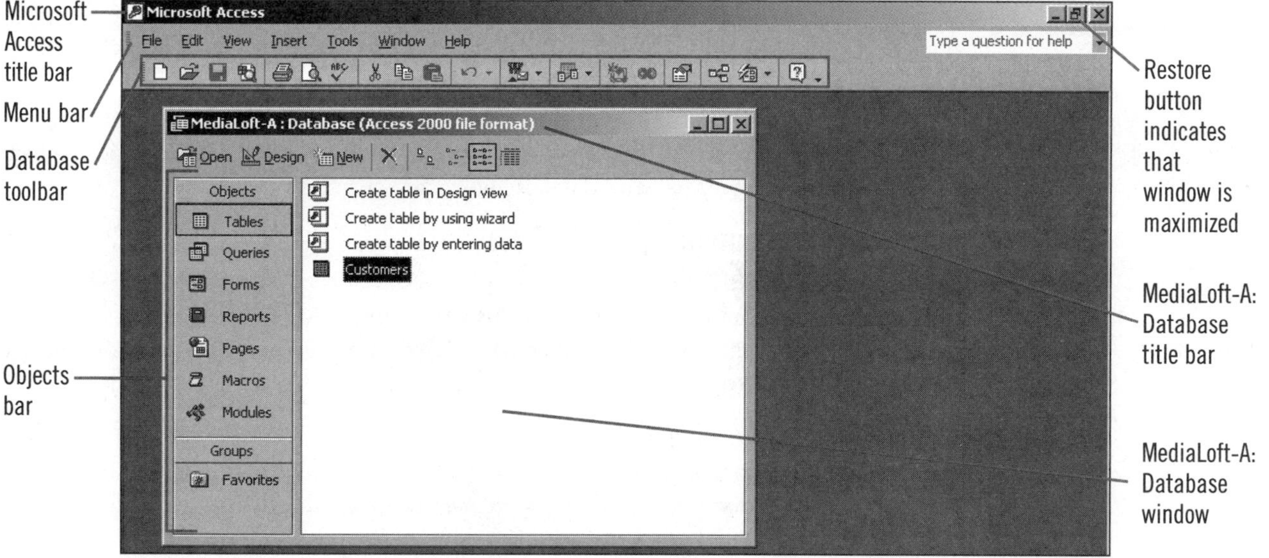

Personalized toolbars and menus in Access 2002

All of the applications within Office 2002 support personalized toolbars and personalized menus to some extent. "Personalized" means that the toolbars and menus modify themselves to reflect those features that you most commonly use. To view, modify, or reset the toolbar and menu options, click Tools on the menu bar, and then click Customize. On the Options tab you can reset the personalized usage data, eliminate the delay when displaying full menus, and change other toolbar button characteristics.

Viewing the Database Window

When you start Access and open a database, the **database window** displays such common Windows elements as the title bar, menu bar, and toolbar. The **Objects bar** displays the buttons for the seven Access objects as well as the group buttons. The **Groups** area displays other commonly used files and folders, such as the Favorites folder. Clicking the **Objects button** or **Groups button** on the Objects bar alternatively expands and collapses that section. Kelsey explores the MediaLoft-A database.

1. **Look at each of the Access window elements shown in Figure A-7**
   The Objects bar on the left side of the database window displays the seven object types. The other elements of the database window are summarized in Table A-3. Because the Tables object is selected, the buttons you need to create a new table or to work with the existing table are displayed in the MediaLoft-A Database window.
2. **Click File on the menu bar**
   The File menu contains commands for opening a new or existing database, saving a database in a variety of formats, and printing. The menu commands vary depending on which window or database object is currently in use.
3. **Point to Edit on the menu bar, point to View, point to Insert, point to Tools, point to Window, point to Help, move the pointer off the menu, then press [Esc] twice**
   All menus close when you press [Esc]. Pressing [Esc] a second time deselects the menu bar.

QuickTip

Double-click a menu option to quickly display the full menu.

4. **Point to the New button on the Database toolbar**
   Pointing to a toolbar button causes a descriptive **ScreenTip** to automatically appear, providing a short description of the button. The buttons on the toolbars represent the most commonly used Access features. Toolbar buttons change just as menu options change depending on which window and database object are currently in use.
5. **Point to the Open button on the Database toolbar, then point to the Save button on the Database toolbar**
   Sometimes toolbar buttons or menu options are dimmed, which means they are not currently available. For example, the Paste button is dimmed because there is nothing on the Clipboard ready to be pasted.
6. **Click Queries on the Objects bar**
   The query object window provides ways to create a new query, and displays the names of previously created queries as shown in Figure A-8. There are three existing query objects displayed within the MediaLoft-A Database window.
7. **Click Forms on the Objects bar, then click Reports on the Objects bar**
   The MediaLoft-A database contains the Customers table, three queries, one form, and three reports.

Viewing objects

You can change the way you view the objects in the database window by clicking the last four buttons on the database window toolbar. You can view the objects as Large Icons, Small Icons, in a List (default view), and with Details. The Details view shows a description of the object, as well as the date the object was last modified and the date it was originally created.

FIGURE A-7: MediaLoft-A database screen elements

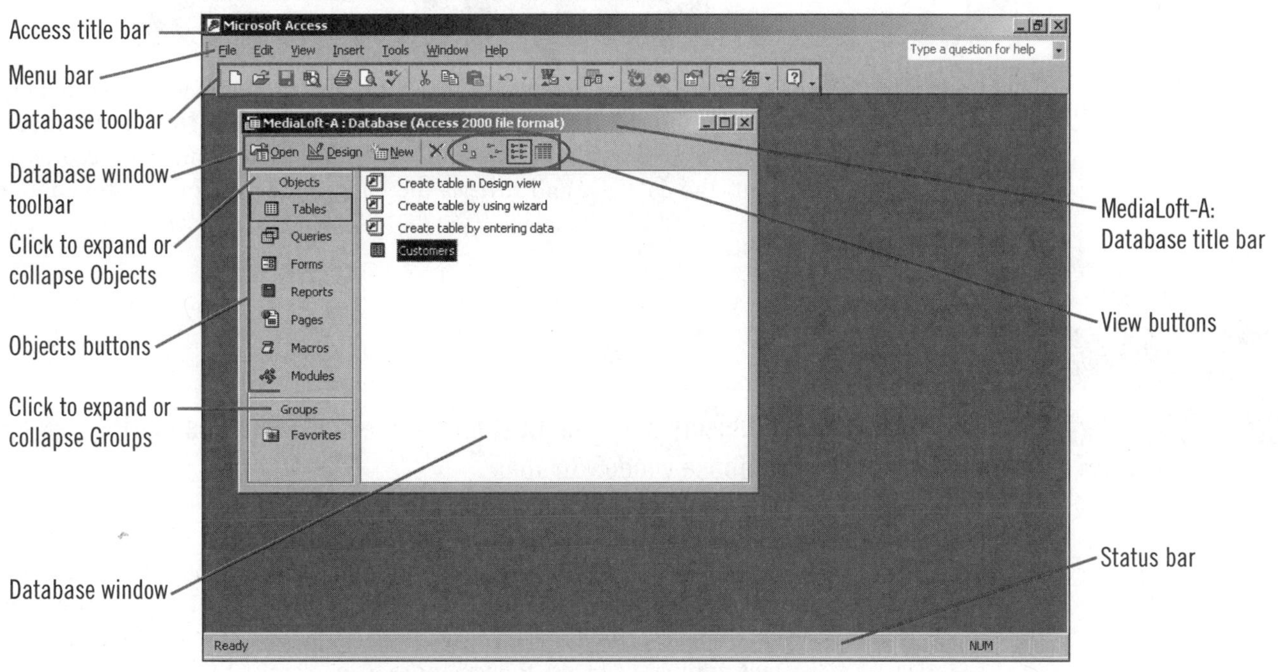

FIGURE A-8: MediaLoft-A query objects

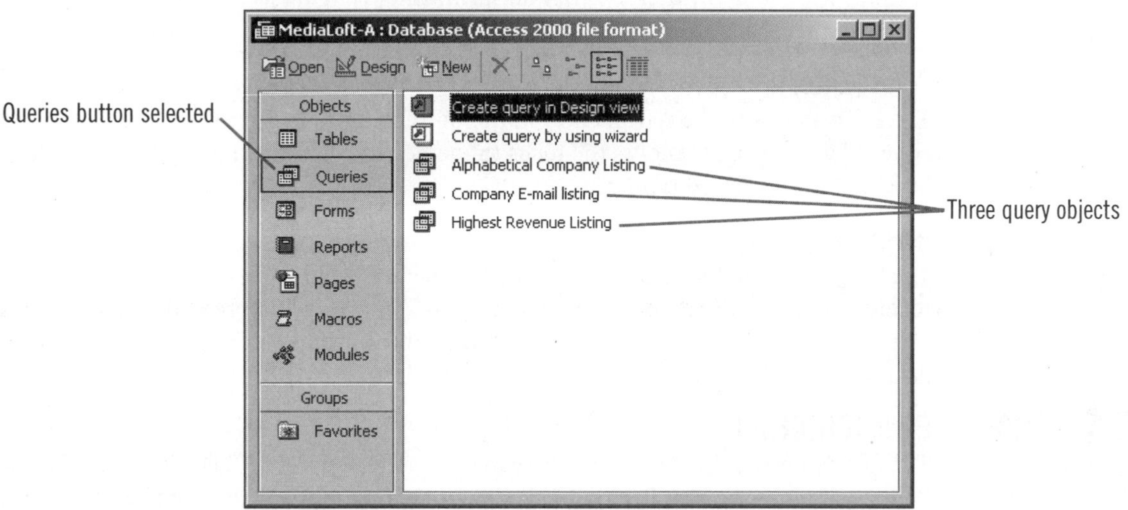

TABLE A-3: Elements of the database window

element	description
Database toolbar	Contains buttons for commonly performed tasks that affect the entire database (e.g., New, Open, or Relationships) or are common to all database objects (e.g., Print, Copy, or Spelling)
Database window	Allows you to work with the individual objects and groups stored within the database
Menu bar	Contains menus options appropriate for the current view of the database
Objects buttons	Objects buttons on the Objects bar display a list of each type of database object
Database window toolbar	Contains buttons used to open, modify, create, delete, or view objects
Status bar	Displays messages regarding the current database operation
Title bar	Contains the program name or filename of the active database

Navigating Records

Your ability to navigate the fields and records of a database is fundamental to your productivity and success with the database. You can navigate through the information in **Navigation mode** in the table's **datasheet**, a spreadsheet-like grid that displays fields as columns and records as rows. Kelsey opens the database and reviews the table containing information about MediaLoft's customers.

QuickTip

You can also double-click an object to open it.

1. **Click Tables on the Objects bar, click Customers, then click the Open button on the MediaLoft-A Database window toolbar**

   The datasheet for the Customers table opens, as shown in Figure A-9. The datasheet contains 27 customer records with 13 fields of information for each record. **Field names** are listed at the top of each column. The number of the selected record in the datasheet is displayed in the **Specific Record box** (also called the **record number box**) at the bottom of the datasheet window. Depending on the size of your monitor and your screen area settings, you may see a different number of fields. To view more fields, scroll to the right.

2. **Press [Tab] to move to Sprint**

   Sprint is selected in the first record. The Sprint entry is in the second field, named Company, of the first record.

3. **Press [Enter]**

   The focus moves to the Aaron entry in the third column, in the field named First. Pressing either [Tab] or [Enter] moves the focus to the next field. **Focus** refers to which field would be edited if you started typing.

4. **Press [↓]**

   The focus moves to the Jacob entry in the field named First of the second record. The **current record symbol** in the **record selector box** also identifies which record you are navigating. The Next Record and Previous Record **navigation buttons** in the lower-left corner of the datasheet can also be used to navigate the datasheet.

Trouble?

If [Ctrl][End] doesn't move the focus to the last field of the last record, you are probably working in Edit mode. Press [Tab] to return to Navigation mode, and then press [Ctrl][End].

5. **Press [Ctrl][End]**

   The focus moves to the $6,790.33 entry in the last field, named YTDSales, of the last record. You can also use the Last Record navigation button to move to the last record.

6. **Press [Ctrl][Home]**

   The focus moves to the 1 entry in the field named ID of the first record. You can also use the First Record navigation button to move to the first record. A complete listing of navigation keystrokes to move the focus between fields and records is shown in Table A-4.

Changing to Edit mode

If you click a field with the mouse pointer instead of pressing [Tab] or [Enter] to navigate through the datasheet, you change from **Navigation mode** to Edit mode. In **Edit mode**, Access assumes that you are trying to make changes to that particular field value, so keystrokes such as [Ctrl][End], [Ctrl][Home], [→] and [←] move the insertion point *within* the field. To return to Navigation mode, press [Tab] or [Enter] (thus moving the focus to the next field), or press [↑] or [↓] (thus moving the focus to a different record).

FIGURE A-9: **Customers datasheet**

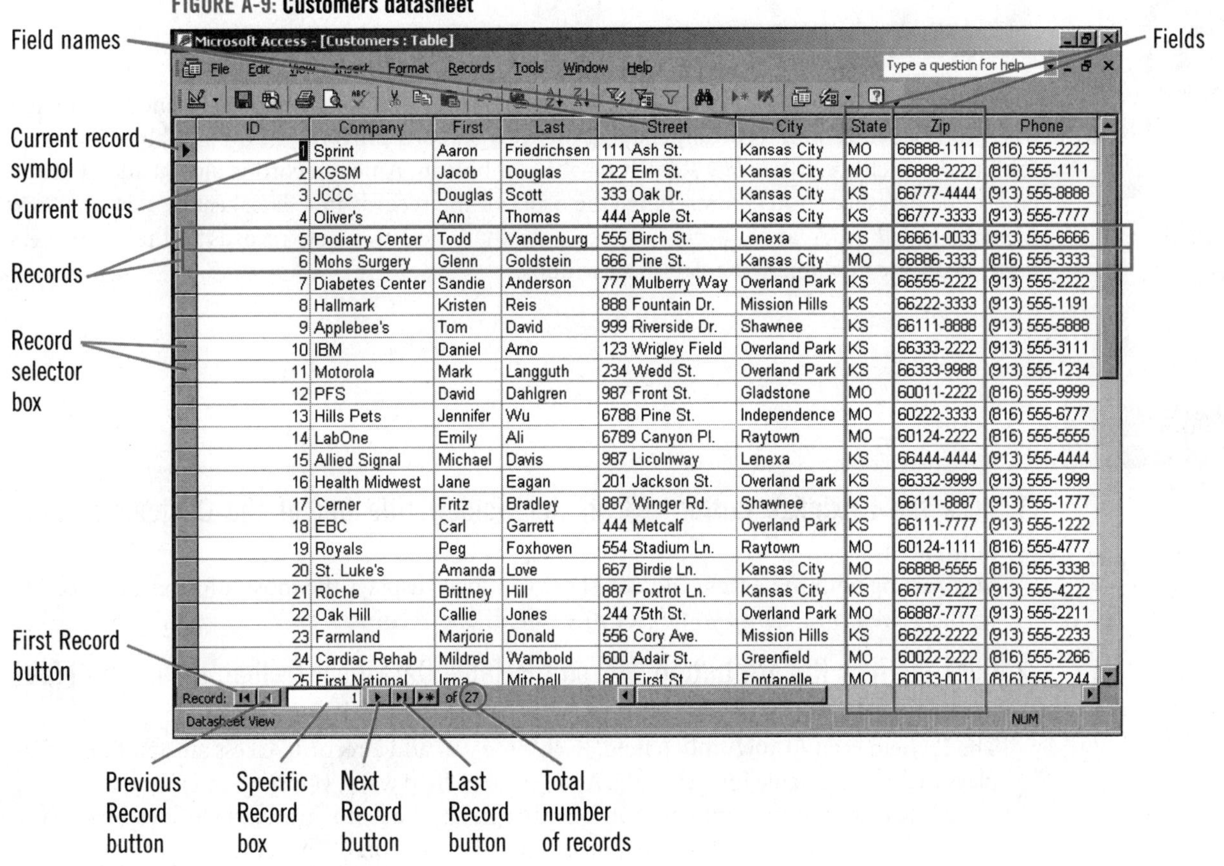

TABLE A-4: **Navigation mode keyboard shortcuts**

shortcut key	to move to the
[Tab], [Enter] or [→]	Next field of the current record
[Shift][Tab] or [←]	Previous field of the current record
[Home]	First field of the current record
[End]	Last field of the current record
[Ctrl][Home]	First field of the first record
[Ctrl][End]	Last field of the last record
[↑]	Current field of the previous record
[↓]	Current field of the next record
[Ctrl][↑]	Current field of the first record
[Ctrl][↓]	Current field of the last record
[F5]	Specific record entered in the Specific Record box

Entering Records

The ability to add records into a database is a critical task that is usually performed on a daily basis. You can add a new record by clicking the **New Record button** on the Table Datasheet toolbar or by clicking the New Record navigation button. A new record is always added at the end of the datasheet. You can rearrange the order of the records in a datasheet by sorting them, which you will learn later. Kelsey is ready to add two new records in the Customers table. First, she maximizes the datasheet window.

Steps

1. Click the **Maximize button** in the window title bar of the Customers Table datasheet
   Maximizing both the Access and datasheet windows displays the most information possible on the screen, and allows you to see more fields and records.

2. Click the **New Record button** on the Table Datasheet toolbar, then press **[Tab]** to move through the ID field and into the Company field
   The ID field is an **AutoNumber** field. Each time you add a record, Access automatically displays the next available integer in the AutoNumber field when you start entering data in that record. You cannot type into an AutoNumber field. The AutoNumber field logs how many records have been added to the datasheet since the creation of the table. It does not tell you how many records are currently in the table because Access will not reuse an AutoNumber value that was assigned to a record that has been deleted.

3. Type **CIO**, press **[Tab]**, type **Taylor**, press **[Tab]**, type **McKinsey**, press **[Tab]**, type **420 Locust St.**, press **[Tab]**, type **Lenexa**, press **[Tab]**, type **KS**, press **[Tab]**, type **66111-8899**, press **[Tab]**, type **9135551189**, press **[Tab]**, type **9135551889**, press **[Tab]**, type **9/6/69**, press **[Tab]**, type **taylor@cio.com**, press **[Tab]**, type **5433.22**, then press **[Enter]**
   The value of 28 was automatically entered in the ID field for this record. Notice that the Navigation buttons indicate that you are now working on record 29 of 29.

4. Enter the new record for Cooper Michaels shown below

in field:	type:	in field:	type:
ID	**[Tab]**	Zip	**65555-4444**
Company	**Four Winds**	Phone	**913-555-2289**
First	**Cooper**	Fax	**913-555-2889**
Last	**Michaels**	Birthdate	**8/20/68**
Street	**500 Sunset Blvd.**	Email	**coop@4winds.com**
City	**Manhattan**	YTDSales	**5998.33**
State	**KS**		

5. Press **[Tab]**, then compare your updated datasheet with Figure A-10
   You should have 29 records. You can confirm that you have 29 records by using the navigation buttons.

FIGURE A-10: Customers table with two new records

Microsoft Access - [Customers : Table]

File Edit View Insert Format Records Tools Window Help — Type a question for help

ID	Company	First	Last	Street	City	State	Zip	Phone
7	Diabetes Center	Sandie	Anderson	777 Mulberry Way	Overland Park	KS	66555-2222	(913) 555-2222
8	Hallmark	Kristen	Reis	888 Fountain Dr.	Mission Hills	KS	66222-3333	(913) 555-1191
9	Applebee's	Tom	David	999 Riverside Dr.	Shawnee	KS	66111-8888	(913) 555-5888
10	IBM	Daniel	Arno	123 Wrigley Field	Overland Park	KS	66333-2222	(913) 555-3111
11	Motorola	Mark	Langguth	234 Wedd St.	Overland Park	KS	66333-9988	(913) 555-1234
12	PFS	David	Dahlgren	987 Front St.	Gladstone	MO	60011-2222	(816) 555-9999
13	Hills Pets	Jennifer	Wu	6788 Pine St.	Independence	MO	60222-3333	(816) 555-6777
14	LabOne	Emily	Ali	6789 Canyon Pl.	Raytown	MO	60124-2222	(816) 555-5555
15	Allied Signal	Michael	Davis	987 Licolnway	Lenexa	KS	66444-4444	(913) 555-4444
16	Health Midwest	Jane	Eagan	201 Jackson St.	Overland Park	KS	66332-9999	(913) 555-1999
17	Cerner	Fritz	Bradley	887 Winger Rd.	Shawnee	KS	66111-8887	(913) 555-1777
18	EBC	Carl	Garrett	444 Metcalf	Overland Park	KS	66111-7777	(913) 555-1222
19	Royals	Peg	Foxhoven	554 Stadium Ln.	Raytown	MO	60124-1111	(816) 555-4777
20	St. Luke's	Amanda	Love	667 Birdie Ln.	Kansas City	MO	66888-5555	(816) 555-3338
21	Roche	Brittney	Hill	887 Foxtrot Ln.	Kansas City	KS	66777-2222	(913) 555-4222
22	Oak Hill	Callie	Jones	244 75th St.	Overland Park	MO	66887-7777	(913) 555-2211
23	Farmland	Marjorie	Donald	556 Cory Ave.	Mission Hills	KS	66222-2222	(913) 555-2233
24	Cardiac Rehab	Mildred	Wambold	600 Adair St.	Greenfield	MO	60022-2222	(816) 555-2266
25	First National	Irma	Mitchell	800 First St.	Fontanelle	MO	60033-0011	(816) 555-2244
26	IKON	Ralph	Gregory	500 Maple St.	Adair	MO	60044-0022	(816) 555-2288
27	St. Thomas	Frances	Gustaphson	400 Russel Ln.	Casey	MO	60055-0055	(816) 555-5556
28	CIO	Taylor	McKinsey	420 Locust St.	Lenexa	KS	66111-8899	(913) 555-1189
29	Four Winds	Cooper	Michaels	500 Sunset Blvd.	Manhattan	KS	65555-4444	(913) 555-2289
(AutoNumber)								

Record: 30 of 30

Datasheet View — NUM

Table datasheet toolbar

Both windows are maximized

New Record button

Two new records

New Record button

Moving datasheet columns

You can reorganize the fields in a datasheet by dragging the field name left or right. Figure A-11 shows how the mouse pointer changes to ⇱ as the Email field is moved to the left. The black vertical line between the Fax and Birthdate fields represents the new location for the field you are moving. Release the mouse button when you have appropriately positioned the field.

FIGURE A-11: Moving a field

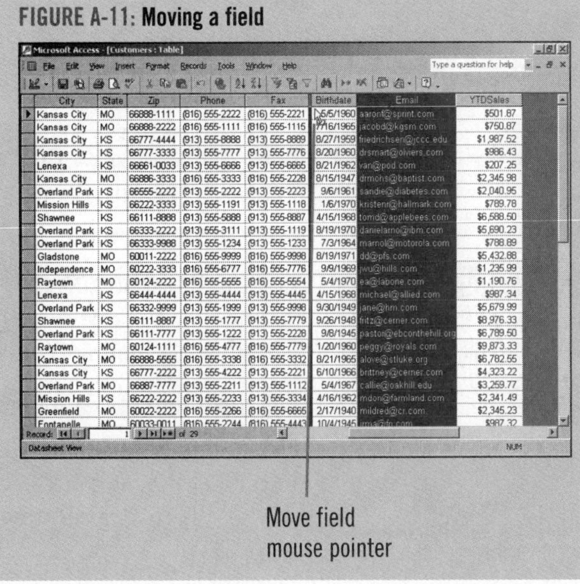

Access 2002

Editing Records

Updating existing information is another important daily task. To change the contents of an existing record, click the field you want to change, then type the new information. You can delete unwanted data by clicking the field and using the [Backspace] or [Delete] keys to delete text to the left or right of the insertion point. Other data entry keystrokes are summarized in Table A-5. Kelsey needs to make some corrections to the datasheet of the Customers table. She starts by correcting an error in the Street field of the first record.

Steps

1. Press **[Ctrl][Home]** to move to the first record, click to the right of **111 Ash St.** in the Street field, press **[Backspace]** three times to delete **St.**, then type **Dr.**
   When you are editing a record, the **edit record symbol**, which looks like a small pencil, appears in the record selector box to the left of the current record, as shown in Figure A-12.
2. Click to the right of **Hallmark** in the Company field in record 8, press **[Spacebar]**, type **Cards**, then press [↓] to move to the next record
   You do not need to explicitly save new records or changes to existing records because Access saves the new data as soon as you move to another record or close the datasheet.
3. Click **Shawnee** in the City field for record 17, then press **[Ctrl][']**
   The entry changes from "Shawnee" to "Overland Park." Pressing [Ctrl]['] inserts the data from the same field in the previous record.
4. Click to the left of **EBC** in the Company field for record 18, press **[Delete]** to remove the **E**, press **[Tab]** to move to the next field, then type **Doug**
   "EBC" becomes "BC" in the Company field, and "Doug" replaces "Carl" in the First field. Notice the edit record symbol in the record selector box to the left of record 18. Since you are still editing this record, you can undo the changes using the [Esc] key.
5. Press **[Esc]**
   The Doug entry changes back to Carl. Pressing [Esc] once removes the current field's editing changes.
6. Press **[Esc]** again
   Pressing [Esc] a second time removes all changes made to the record you are currently editing. The Company entry is restored to EBC. The ability to use [Esc] in Edit mode to remove data entry changes is dependent on whether or not you are still editing the record (as evidenced by the edit record symbol to the left of the record). Once you move to another record, the changes are saved, and you return to Navigation mode. In Navigation mode you can no longer use [Esc] to remove editing changes, but you can click the **Undo button** on the Table Database toolbar to undo the last change you made.
7. Press [↓] to move to **Peg** in the First field of record 19, type **Peggy**, then press [↓] to move to record 20
   Since you are no longer editing record 19, [Esc] has no effect on the last change.
8. Click the **Undo button** on the Table Datasheet toolbar
   You undo the last edit and Peggy is changed back to Peg. Some areas of Access allow you to undo multiple actions, but a datasheet allows you to undo only your last action.
9. Click anywhere in the **Allied Signal (ID 15)** record, click the **Delete Record button** on the Table Datasheet toolbar, then click **Yes**
   The message warns that you cannot undo a record deletion operation. Notice that the Undo button is dimmed, indicating that it cannot be used at this time.

QuickTip

The ScreenTip for the Undo button displays the action you can undo.

FIGURE A-12: Editing records

Microsoft Access - [Customers : Table]

File Edit View Insert Format Records Tools Window Help — Type a question for help

Print Preview button

Edit symbol

ID	Company	First	Last	Street	City	State	Zip	Phone
1	Sprint	Aaron	Friedrichsen	111 Ash Dr.	Kansas City	MO	66888-1111	(816) 555-2222
2	KGSM	Jacob	Douglas	222 Elm St.	Kansas City	MO	66888-2222	(816) 555-1111
3	JCCC	Douglas	Scott	333 Oak Dr.	Kansas City	KS	66777-4444	(913) 555-8888
4	Oliver's	Ann	Thomas	444 Apple St.	Kansas City	KS	66777-3333	(913) 555-7777
5	Podiatry Center	Todd	Vandenburg	555 Birch St.	Lenexa	KS	66661-0033	(913) 555-6666
6	Mohs Surgery	Glenn	Goldstein	666 Pine St.	Kansas City	MO	66886-3333	(816) 555-3333
7	Diabetes Center	Sandie	Anderson	777 Mulberry Way	Overland Park	KS	66555-2222	(913) 555-2222
8	Hallmark	Kristen	Reis	888 Fountain Dr.	Mission Hills	KS	66222-3333	(913) 555-1191
9	Applebee's	Tom	David	999 Riverside Dr.	Shawnee	KS	66111-8888	(913) 555-5888
10	IBM	Daniel	Arno	123 Wrigley Field	Overland Park	KS	66333-2222	(913) 555-3111
11	Motorola	Mark	Langguth	234 Wedd St.	Overland Park	KS	66333-9988	(913) 555-1234
12	PFS	David	Dahlgren	987 Front St.	Gladstone	MO	60011-2222	(816) 555-9999
13	Hills Pets	Jennifer	Wu	6788 Pine St.	Independence	MO	60222-3333	(816) 555-6777
14	LabOne	Emily	Ali	6789 Canyon Pl.	Raytown	MO	60124-2222	(816) 555-5555
15	Allied Signal	Michael	Davis	987 Licolnway	Lenexa	KS	66444-4444	(913) 555-4444
16	Health Midwest	Jane	Eagan	201 Jackson St.	Overland Park	KS	66332-9999	(913) 555-1999
17	Cerner	Fritz	Bradley	887 Winger Rd.	Shawnee	KS	66111-8887	(913) 555-1777
18	EBC	Carl	Garrett	444 Metcalf	Overland Park	KS	66111-7777	(913) 555-1222
19	Royals	Peg	Foxhoven	554 Stadium Ln.	Raytown	MO	60124-1111	(816) 555-4777
20	St. Luke's	Amanda	Love	667 Birdie Ln.	Kansas City	MO	66888-5555	(816) 555-3338
21	Roche	Brittney	Hill	887 Foxtrot Ln.	Kansas City	KS	66777-2222	(913) 555-4222
22	Oak Hill	Callie	Jones	244 75th St.	Overland Park	MO	66887-7777	(913) 555-2211
23	Farmland	Marjorie	Donald	556 Cory Ave.	Mission Hills	KS	66222-2222	(913) 555-2233
24	Cardiac Rehab	Mildred	Wambold	600 Adair St.	Greenfield	MO	60022-2222	(816) 555-2266
25	First National	Irma	Mitchell	800 First St.	Fontanelle	MO	60033-0011	(816) 555-2244

Record: 1 of 29

Datasheet View — NUM

Insertion point

TABLE A-5: Edit mode keyboard shortcuts

editing keystroke	action
[Backspace]	Deletes one character to the left of the insertion point
[Delete]	Deletes one character to the right of the insertion point
[F2]	Switches between Edit and Navigation mode
[Esc]	Undoes the change to the current field
[Esc][Esc]	Undoes all changes to the current record
[F7]	Starts the spell check feature
[Ctrl][']	Inserts the value from the same field in the previous record into the current field
[Ctrl][;]	Inserts the current date in a Date field

Resizing datasheet columns

You can resize the width of a field in a datasheet by dragging the thin black line that separates the field names to the left or right. The mouse pointer changes to ✛ as you make the field wider or narrower. Release the mouse button when you have resized the field. To adjust the column width to accommodate the widest entry in the field, double-click the thin black line that separates the field names.

Access 2002

Previewing and Printing a Datasheet

After entering and editing the records in a table, you can print the datasheet to obtain a hard copy of it. Before printing the datasheet, you should preview it to see how it will look when printed. Often you will want to make adjustments to margins and page orientation. Kelsey is ready to preview and print the datasheet.

Steps

QuickTip

If you want your name to appear on the printout, enter it as a new record in the datasheet before printing.

1. Click the **Print Preview button** on the Table Database toolbar
   The datasheet appears as a miniature page in the Print Preview window, as shown in Figure A-14. The Print Preview toolbar provides options for printing, viewing more than one page, and sending the information to Word or Excel.

2. Click the pointer on the top of the datasheet
   By magnifying this view of the datasheet, you can see Customers, the name of the table, in the center of the header. Today's date is positioned in the right section of the header.

3. Scroll down to view the bottom of the page
   The word "Page" and the current page number are positioned in the center of the footer.

4. Click the **Two Pages button** on the Print Preview toolbar
   The navigation buttons in the lower-left corner are dimmed, indicating that the entire printout fits on two pages. To make further changes, use the Page Setup dialog box.

5. Click **File** on the menu bar, then click **Page Setup**
   The Page Setup dialog box opens, as shown in Figure A-15. This dialog box provides options for changing margins, removing the headings (the header and footer), and changing page orientation from portrait (default) to landscape by using the Page tab.

6. Double-click **1** in the Top text box, type **2**, then click **OK**
   The modified datasheet appears in the Print Preview window.

7. Click the **Print button** on the Print Preview toolbar, then click the **Close button**
   The datasheet appears on the screen.

Hiding fields

Sometimes you may not want all the fields of a datasheet to appear on the printout. To temporarily hide a field, click anywhere in the field, click Format on the menu bar, and then click Hide Columns. To redisplay the column, click Format, then click Unhide Columns. The Unhide Columns dialog box, shown in Figure A-13, opens. The unchecked boxes indicate which columns are currently hidden.

FIGURE A-13: Unhide Columns dialog box

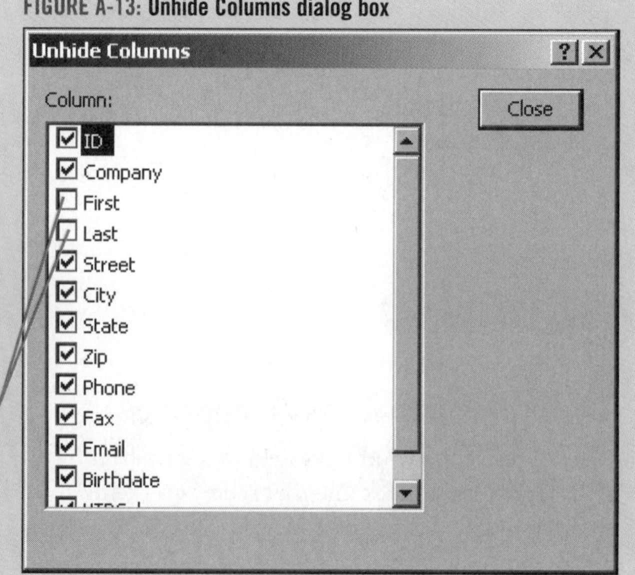

FIGURE A-14: Datasheet in print preview (portrait orientation)

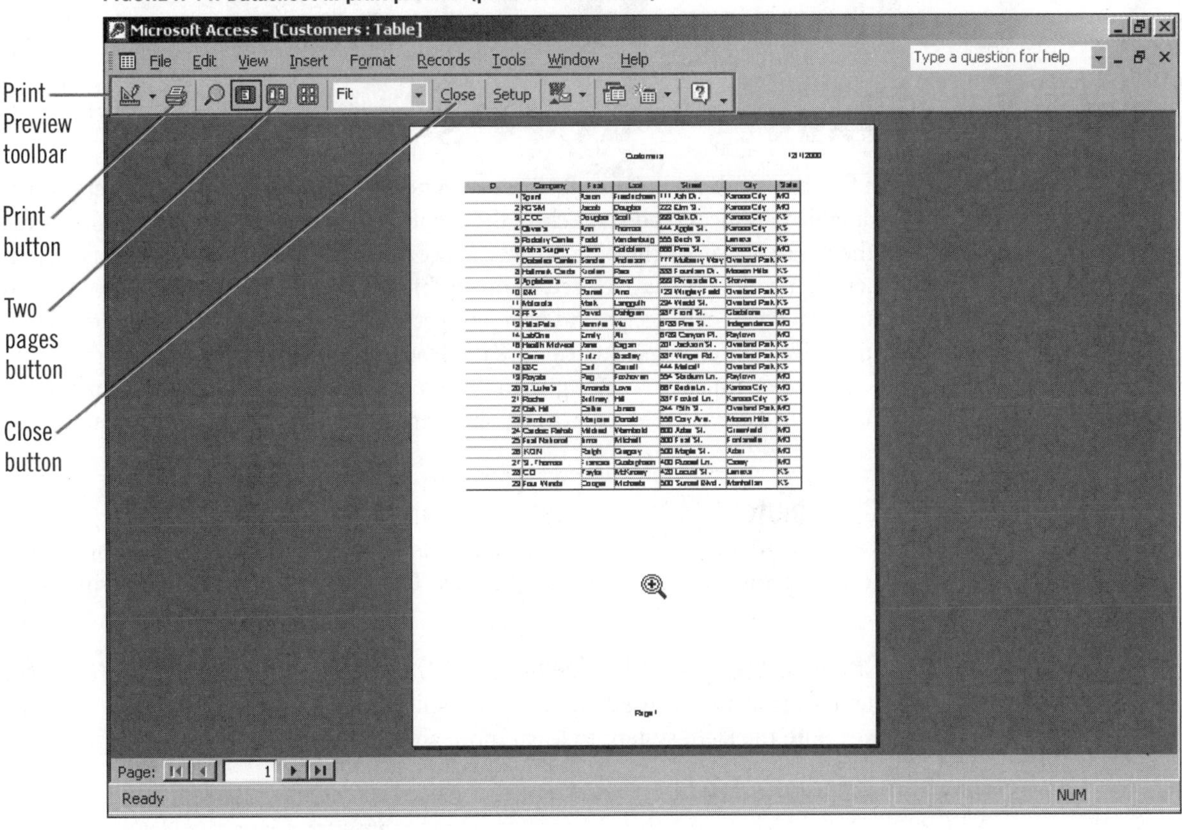

FIGURE A-15: Page Setup dialog box

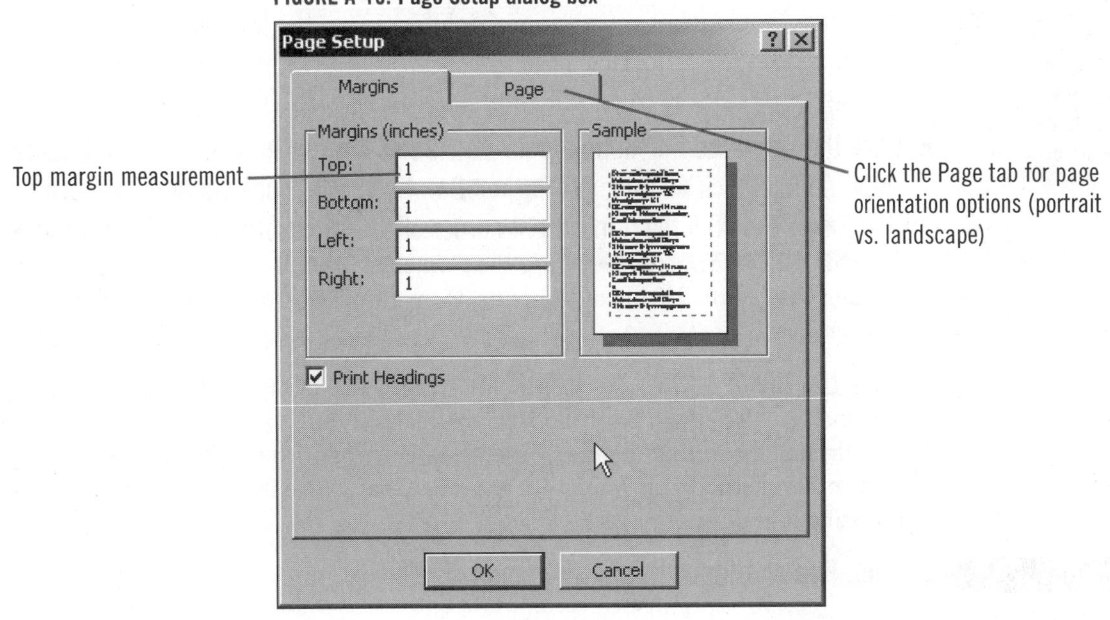

Access 2002

Getting Help and Exiting Access

When you have finished working in your database, you need to close the object you were working in, such as a table datasheet, and then close the database. To close a table, click File on the menu bar and then click Close, or click the object's Close button located in the upper-right corner of the menu bar. Once you have closed all open objects, you can exit the program. As with most programs, if you try to exit Access and have not yet saved changes to open objects, Access will prompt you to save your changes. You can use the Help system to learn more about the program. Kelsey has finished working with Access for now, so she closes the Customers table and MediaLoft-A database. Before exiting, she learns more about the Help system, and then exits Access.

Steps

1. Click the **Close button** for the Customers datasheet
   If you make any structural changes to the datasheet such as moving, resizing, or hiding columns, you are prompted to save those changes. The MediaLoft-A database window is now active.
2. Click the **Close button** for the MediaLoft-A Database, as shown in Figure A-16
   The MediaLoft-A database is closed, but Access is still running, so you could open another database or explore the Help system to learn more about Access.
3. Click the **Ask a question box**, type **naming fields**, then press [**Enter**]
   A list of potential Help topics that relate to your entry appears. Using the Help text box is similar to initiating keyword searches via the Office Assistant or using the Answer Wizard. Help menu options and terminology are further explained in Table A-6.
4. Click **About renaming a field in a table**
   The Help manual opens to the specific page that explains how to rename an existing field in a table. **Glossary terms** are shown as blue hyperlinks. Clicking a blue hyperlink displays a definition for that word in green text.
5. Click the **Show All** link in the upper-right corner of the Microsoft Access Help window
   An expanded view of the Help page with all subcategories and definitions appears as shown in Figure A-17. The Show All link now becomes the Hide All link.
6. Click the **Contents tab**, double-click **Microsoft Access Help**, double-click **Working with Data**, double-click **Adding, Editing, or Deleting Data**, click **Delete a record**, then click the **Show All** link in the upper-right corner of the Microsoft Access Help window
   Searching for information by using the Contents tab is similar to locating information by starting with a broad Table of Contents, then continuing to narrow the subject matter into smaller areas.
7. Click the **Close button** for the Microsoft Access Help window
   Whether you prefer to browse the Help manual by typing key words into the Ask a question box, drilling down through the Contents, interacting with the Office Assistant, or through some other method, it is important to realize that you're using the same Help system, but accessing it in different ways.
8. Click **File** on the menu bar, then click **Exit**

Trouble?

If you do not see the Contents, Answer Wizard, and Index tabs to the left of the Help window, click the Show Help button on the Help toolbar.

QuickTip

If your Project Files are stored on a floppy disk, do not remove your floppy disk from drive A until you have completely exited Access.

FIGURE A-16: Closing a database

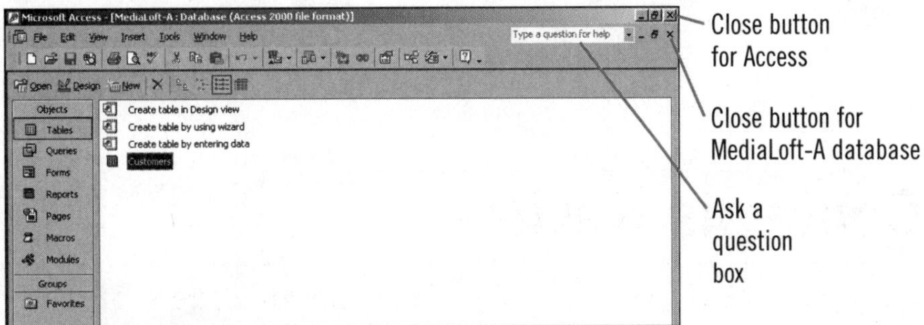

FIGURE A-17: Microsoft Access Help window

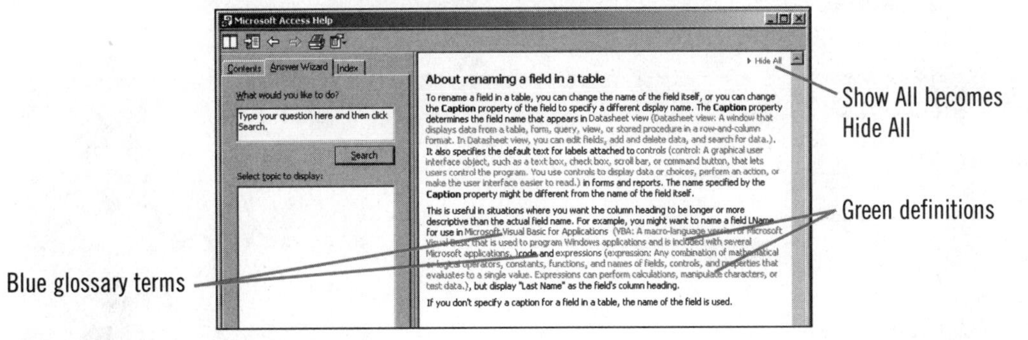

TABLE A-6: Help menu options

Help menu option	description
Microsoft Access Help	Opens the Office Assistant which prompts you for a keyword search of the Help manual
Show the Office Assistant	Presents the **Office Assistant**, an automated character that provides tips and interactive prompts while you are working
Hide the Office Assistant	Temporarily closes the Office Assistant for the working session
What's This	Changes the mouse pointer to ↖?. Click an area, icon, or menu option using this special mouse pointer to get a short description of that item.
Office on the Web	If you are connected to the Web, provides additional Microsoft information and support articles stored at the Microsoft Web site
Sample Databases	Provides easy access to the sample databases installed with Access 2002
Detect and Repair	Analyzes a database for possible data corruption and attempts to repair problems
About Microsoft Access	Provides the version and product ID of Access

Compact on Close

The Compact on Close option found on the General tab of the Options dialog box compacts and repairs your database each time you close it. To open the Options dialog box, click Tools on the menu bar, and then click Options. While the Compact on Close feature works extremely well if your database is stored on your hard drive or on another large storage device, it can cause problems if your Project File is stored on a floppy disk. The Compact on Close process creates a temporary file that is just as large as the original database file. This temporary file is used during the compaction process, and is deleted after the procedure successfully finishes. Therefore, if your database file grows larger than half of the available storage space on your floppy disk, the Compact on Close process will not be able to create the necessary temporary file or successfully compact the database. Such an error might result in a harmless error message or, in the worst case, a corrupt database.

Practice

► Concepts Review

Label each element of the Access window shown in Figure A-18.

FIGURE A-18

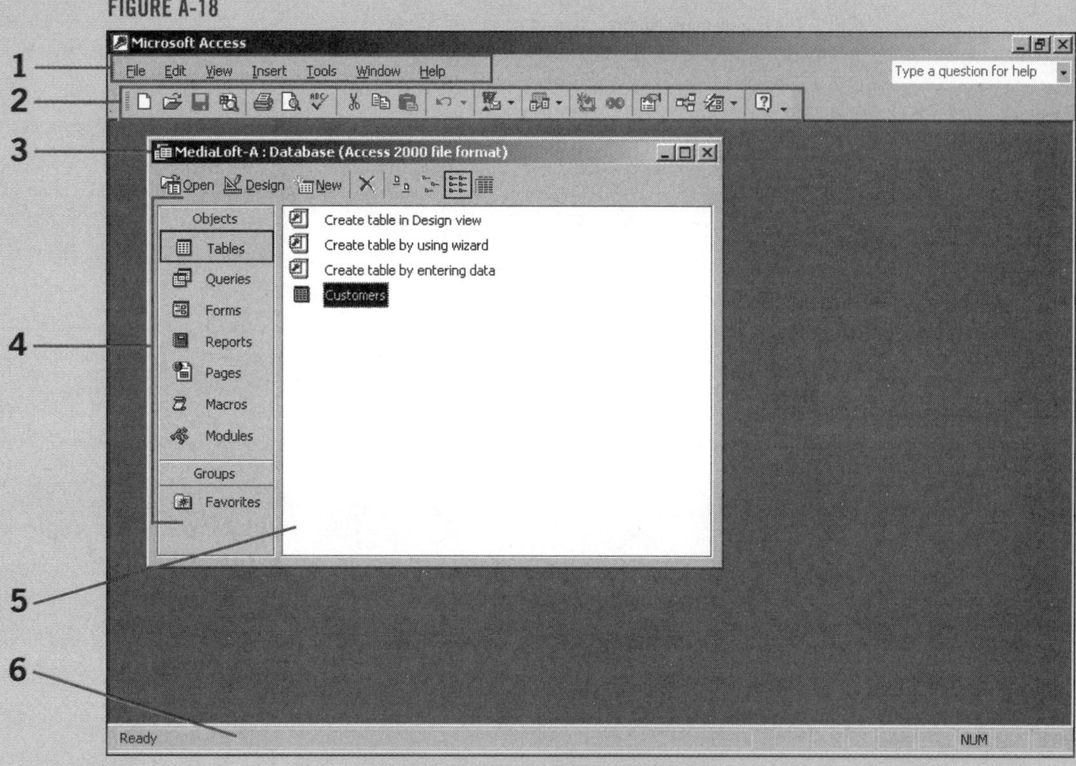

Match each term with the statement that describes it.

7. Objects
8. Table
9. Record
10. Field
11. Datasheet

a. A group of related fields, such as all of the demographic information for one customer
b. A collection of records for a single subject, such as all the customer records
c. A category of information in a table, such as a customer's name, city, or state
d. A spreadsheet-like grid that displays fields as columns and records as rows
e. Seven types of these are contained in an Access database and are used to enter, enhance, and use the data within the database

Select the best answer from the list of choices.

12. Which of the following is NOT a typical benefit of relational databases?

a. Easier data entry
b. Faster information retrieval
c. Minimized duplicate data entry
d. Automatic trend analysis

13. Which of the following is NOT an advantage of managing data with a relational database versus a spreadsheet?

a. Doesn't require planning before data is entered
b. Allows links between lists of information
c. Provides greater security
d. Allows multiple users to enter data simultaneously

14. The object that holds all of the data within an Access database is the:

a. Query.
b. Table.
c. Form.
d. Report.

15. The object that provides an easy-to-use data entry screen is the:

a. Table.
b. Query.
c. Form.
d. Report.

16. What displays messages regarding the current database operation?

a. Status bar
b. Title bar
c. Database toolbar
d. Object tabs

Skills Review

1. Define database software.

a. Identify five disadvantages of using a noncomputerized system to organize database information.
b. Identify five advantages of managing database information in Access versus using a spreadsheet.

2. Learn database terminology.

a. Explain the relationship between a field, a record, a table, and a database.
b. Identify the seven objects of an Access database, and explain the main purpose of each.
c. Which object of an Access database is most important? Why?

3. Start Access and open a database.

a. Click the Start button, point to Programs, then click Microsoft Access.
b. Open the **Recycle-A** database from the drive and location where your Project Files are stored.
c. Identify the following items. (*Hint*: To create a printout of any screen, press [Print Screen] to capture an image of the screen to the Windows clipboard, start any word-processing program, then click the Paste button. Print the document that now contains a picture of the opening database window, and identify the elements on the printout.)

- Database toolbar
- Recycle-A database window
- Menu bar
- Object buttons
- Objects bar
- Status bar

4. View the database window.

a. Maximize both the Access window and the Recycle-A database window.
b. Click each of the Object buttons, then write down the object names of each type that exist in the Recycle-A database.

5. Navigate records.

a. Open the Clubs table.
b. Press [Tab] or [Enter] to move through the fields of the first record.
c. Press [Shift][Tab] to move backward through the fields of the first record.
d. Press [Ctrl][End] to move to the last field of the last record.
e. Press [Ctrl][Home] to move to the first field of the first record.
f. Click the Last Record navigation button to quickly move to the Oak Hill Patriots record.

6. **Enter records.**
   a. In the Clubs table, click the New Record button, then add the following two records:

Name	Street	City	State	Zip	Phone	FName	LName	Club Number
EBC Angels	10100 Metcalf	Overland Park	KS	66001	555-7711	Steve	Grigsby	8
Friends of the Zoo	111 Holmes	Kansas City	MO	65001	555-8811	Jim	Wheeler	9

   b. Move the Club Number field from the last column of the datasheet to the first column.

7. **Edit records.**
   a. In the Clubs table, change the Name field in the first record from Jaycees to **JC Club**.
   b. Change the Name field in the second record from Boy Scouts #1 to **Oxford Cub Scouts**.
   c. Change the LName field in the fifth record from Perry to **Griffiths**.
   d. Enter your name and unique information as a new record using **99** as the Club Number.
   e. Delete the record for Club Number 8.

8. **Preview and print a datasheet.**
   a. Preview the Clubs table datasheet.
   b. Use the Page Setup option on the File menu to change the page orientation from portrait to landscape.
   c. Print the Clubs table datasheet.

9. **Get Help and exit Access.**
   a. Close the Clubs table object, saving the changes.
   b. Close the Recycle-A database, but leave Access running.
   c. Search for the Help topics by entering the keyword **subdatasheet** into the Ask a question box. Click the link for the About subdatasheets option.
   d. Click the Show All link to display all of the glossary terms, then click the Print button on the Help window toolbar to print that page.
   e. Close the Microsoft Access Help window.
   f. Exit Access.

► Independent Challenge 1

Ten examples of database tables are given below. For each example, write a brief answer for the following.

a. What field names would you expect to find in each table?
b. Provide an example of two possible records for each table.

- Telephone directory
- College course offerings
- Restaurant menu
- Cookbook
- Movie listing
- Encyclopedia
- Shopping catalog
- Corporate inventory
- Party guest list
- Members of the House of Representatives

 Independent Challenge 2

You are working with several civic groups to coordinate a community-wide cleanup effort. You have started a database called Recycle-A that tracks the clubs, their trash deposits, and the trash centers that are participating.

a. Start Access.

b. Open the **Recycle-A** database from the location where your Project Files are stored, then write down the number of records and fields in each of the tables.

c. Open the datasheet for the Centers table. An expand button appears as a small plus sign to the left of the Name field for each record. Click the expand button to the left of each of the records in the Centers datasheet. A subdatasheet for each Center will appear. Count the records in each subdatasheet. How many records are in the subdatasheets, and what does this tell you about the relationship between the Centers and Deposits tables?

d. Close the Centers table, and then open the datasheet for the Clubs table. Click the expand button to the left of each of the Club records and count the records in each subdatasheet. How many records are in the subdatasheets, and what does this tell you about the relationship between the Clubs and Deposits tables?

e. Close the Clubs table, then exit Access.

 Independent Challenge 3

You are working with several civic groups to coordinate a community-wide cleanup effort. You have started a database called Recycle-A that tracks the clubs, their trash deposits, and the trash centers that are participating.

a. Start Access and open the **Recycle-A** database from the location where your Project Files are stored.

b. Add the following records to the Clubs table:

Club Number	Name	Street	City	State	Zip	Phone	FName	LName
10	Take Pride	222 Lincoln Way	Olathe	KS	66001	555-2211	David	Reis
11	Cub Scouts #321	333 Ward Pkwy.	Kansas City	MO	65002	555-8800	Jacob	Langguth

c. Edit the following records in the Clubs table. The Street field has changed for Club Number 6 and the Phone and FName fields have changed for Club Number 7.

Club Number	Name	Street	City	State	Zip	Phone	FName	LName
6	Girl Scouts #1	55 Oak Terrace	Shawnee	KS	68777	555-4444	Jonathan	Bacon
7	Oak Hill Patriots	888 Switzer	Overland Park	KS	66444	555-9988	Cynthia	Ralston

d. If you haven't entered a record containing your own information, enter this record using **99** as the Club Number.

e. Print the datasheet.

f. Close the Clubs table, close the Recycle-A database, then exit Access.

Independent Challenge 4

The World Wide Web can be used to research information about almost any topic. In this exercise, you'll go to Microsoft's Web site for Access, and explore what's new about Access 2002.

a. Connect to the Internet, and use your browser to go to the www.microsoft.com/access Web page.

b. Web sites change often, but there will probably be a link that provides a tour of Access 2002, or an introduction to Access 2002. Click that link and follow the tour or introduction. Based on what you learned, describe two new things that you discovered about Access 2002.

c. Go back to the www.microsoft.com/access or www.microsoft.com/office Web page, then click the appropriate hyperlinks to find out how Office XP suites are organized. You might find this information within a pricing or ordering link. Find the Web page that describes what is included in the various Office XP suites and print it. On the printout, identify which suites include Access.

Visual Workshop

Open the **Recycle-A** database from the drive and folder where your Project Files are stored, then open the Centers table datasheet. Modify the records in the existing Centers table to reflect the changes shown in Figure A-19. The Street field for the first record has changed, the ContactLast field for the first three records have changed, and two new records have been added. Also, enter a new record using your name as the contact with **99** as the Center Number. Print the datasheet, close the Centers table, close the Recycle-A database, then exit Access.

FIGURE A-19

Centers : Table

Center Nu	Name	Street	City	State	Zip	Phone	ContactFirst	ContactLast	Hazardous
1	Trash 'R Us	989 Main St.	Lenexa	KS	61111	555-7777	Ben	Garrett	☑
2	You Deliver	12345 College	Overland Park	KS	63444	555-2222	Jerry	Welch	☑
3	County Landfill	12444 Pflumm	Lenexa	KS	64222	555-4422	Jerry	Anderson	☐
4	Cans and Stuff	543 Holmes	Kansas City	MO	60011	555-2347	Gretchen	Pratt	☐
5	We Love Trash	589 Oak St.	Kansas City	KS	60022	555-3456	Mitchell	Arno	☑
*									

Record: 1 of 5

Access 2002

Unit B

Using

Tables and Queries

Objectives

- Plan a database
- MOUS Create a table
- MOUS Modify a table
- MOUS Format a datasheet
- Understand sorting, filtering, and finding
- MOUS Sort records and find data
- MOUS Filter records
- MOUS Create a query
- MOUS Modify a query

Now that you are familiar with some of the basic Access terminology and features, you are ready to plan and build your own database. Your first task is to create the tables that store the data. Once the tables are created and the data is entered, you can use several techniques for finding specific information in the database, including sorting, filtering, and building queries. Kelsey Lang, a marketing manager at MediaLoft, wants to build and maintain a database containing information about MediaLoft's products. The information in the database will be useful when Kelsey provides information for future sales promotions.

Planning a Database

The most important object in a database is the table object. Tables store the **raw data**, the individual pieces of information stored in the fields in the database. When you design a table, you identify the fields of information the table will contain and the type of data to be stored in each field. Some databases contain multiple tables linked together. Kelsey plans her database containing information about MediaLoft's products.

In planning a database it is important to:

- **Determine the purpose of the database and give it a meaningful name**
  The database will store information about MediaLoft's music products. You decide to name the database MediaLoft, and name the first table Music Inventory.
- **Determine what reports you want the database to produce**
  You want to be able to print inventory reports that list the products by artist, type of product (CD, cassette, minidisk), quantity in stock, and price. These pieces of information will become the fields in the Music Inventory table.
- **Collect the raw data that will be stored in the database**
  The raw data for MediaLoft's products might be stored on index cards, in paper reports, and in other electronic formats, such as word processing documents, spreadsheets, or accounting system files. You can use Access to import data from many other electronic sources, which greatly increases the efficiency of your data entry.
- **Sketch the structure of each table, including field names and data types**
  Using the data you collected, identify the field name and data type for each field in each table as shown in Figure B-1. The **data type** determines what type of information you can enter in a field. For example, a field with a Currency data type does *not* accept text. Properly defining the data type for each field helps you maintain data consistency and accuracy. Table B-1 lists the data types available within Access.

Choosing between the Text and Number data type

When assigning data types, avoid choosing the Number data type for a telephone or zip code field. Although these fields generally contain numbers, they should still be Text data types. Consider the following: You may want to enter 1-800-BUY-BOOK in a telephone number field. This would not be possible if the field is designated as a Number data type. Also, when you sort the fields, you want them to sort alphabetically, like Text fields. For example, with the zip codes 60011 and 50011-8888, if the zip code field is designated as a Number data type, the zip codes would be interpreted incorrectly as the values 60,011 and 500,118,888, and sorted in that order, too.

FIGURE B-1: **Music Inventory fields and data types**

Field Name	Data Type
RecordingID	AutoNumber
RecordingTitle	Text
RecordingArtist	Text
MusicCategory	Text
RecordingLabel	Text
Format	Text
NumberofTracks	Number
PurchasePrice	Currency
RetailPrice	Currency
Notes	Memo

TABLE B-1: **Data types**

data type	description of data	size
Text	Text information or combinations of text and numbers, such as a street address, name, or phone number	Up to 255 characters
Memo	Lengthy text such as comments or notes	Up to 65,536 characters
Number	Numeric information used in calculations, such as quantities	Several sizes available to store numbers with varying degrees of precision
Date/Time	Dates and times	Size controlled by Access to accommodate dates and times across thousands of years (for example, 1/1/1850 and 1/1/2150 are valid dates)
Currency	Monetary values	Size controlled by Access; accommodates up to 15 digits to the left of the decimal point and four digits to the right
AutoNumber	Integers assigned by Access to sequentially order each record added to a table	Size controlled by Access
Yes/No	Only one of two values stored (Yes/No, On/Off, True/False)	Size controlled by Access
OLE Object	Objects and files linked or embedded (OLE) that are created in other programs, such as pictures, sound clips, documents or spreadsheets	Up to one gigabyte
Hyperlink	Web addresses	Size controlled by Access
Lookup Wizard	Invokes a wizard that helps link the current table to another table or list through the current field.	Size controlled through the choices made in the Lookup Wizard

Creating a Table

After you plan the structure of the table, your next step is to create the actual database file. This file will eventually contain the table and all of the other objects within the database file such as queries, forms, and reports. When you create a database, you start by naming it, and then you can build the first table object and enter data. Access offers several methods for creating the database and the first table. For example, you can import a table from another data source such as a spreadsheet, or use the Access **Table Wizard** to create a table from scratch. The Table Wizard provides interactive help to create the field names and data types for each field. Kelsey is ready to create the MediaLoft database. She uses the Table Wizard to create the Music Inventory table.

Steps

Trouble?

If the task pane does not appear in the Access window, click File on the menu bar, then click New.

1. Start Access, click the **Blank Database link** in the New section of the task pane as shown in Figure B-2

   The File New Database dialog box opens.

2. Type **MediaLoft** in the File name text box, click the **Save in list arrow**, navigate to the drive and folder where your Project Files are stored, then click **Create**

   The MediaLoft database file is created and saved where your Project Files are stored. There are many ways to create the first table in the database, but the Table Wizard offers an efficient and easy way to get started.

Trouble?

If the Create table by using wizard option does not appear in the database window, click Tools on the menu bar, then click Options. On the View tab, make sure that the New object shortcuts check box is selected, then click OK.

3. Double-click **Create table by using wizard** in the MediaLoft Database window

   The Table Wizard dialog box opens, as shown in Figure B-3. The Table Wizard offers 25 business and 20 personal sample tables from which you can select sample fields. The Recordings sample table in the Personal database category most closely matches the fields you want to include in the Music Inventory table.

4. Click the **Personal option button**, scroll down and click **Recordings** in the Sample Tables list box, then click the **Select All Fields button** >>

   At this point, you can change the suggested field names to better match your needs.

5. Click **RecordingArtistID** in the Fields in my new table list box, click **Rename Field**, type **RecordingArtist** in the Rename field text box, then click **OK**

6. Click **Next**

   The second Table Wizard dialog box allows you to name the table and determine if Access should set the **primary key**, a special field that contains unique information for each record in a table.

Trouble?

If you are viewing an empty datasheet, click the Design View button on the Table Datasheet toolbar.

7. Type **Music Inventory**, make sure the **Yes, set a primary key for me option button** is selected, click **Next**, click the **Modify the table design option button**, then click **Finish**

   The table opens in Design View, shown in Figure B-4, which allows you to add, delete, or modify the fields in the table. The **key symbol** indicates that the RecordingID field has been designated as the primary key field.

FIGURE B-2: New File task pane

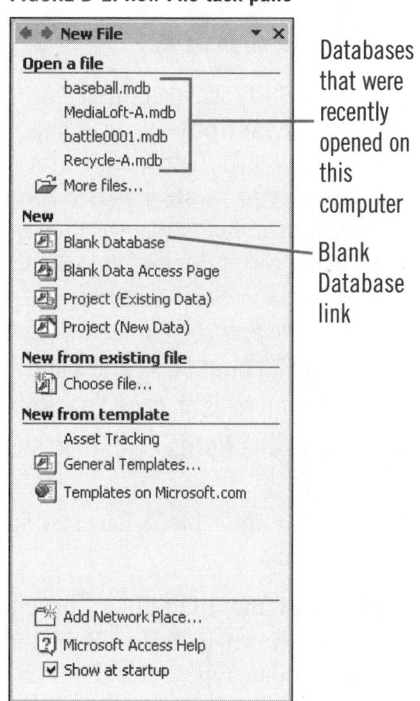

FIGURE B-3: Table Wizard

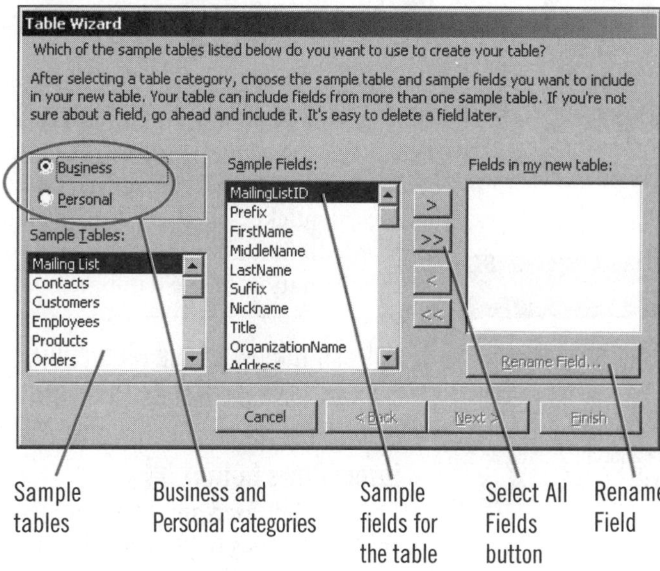

FIGURE B-4: Music Inventory table in Design view

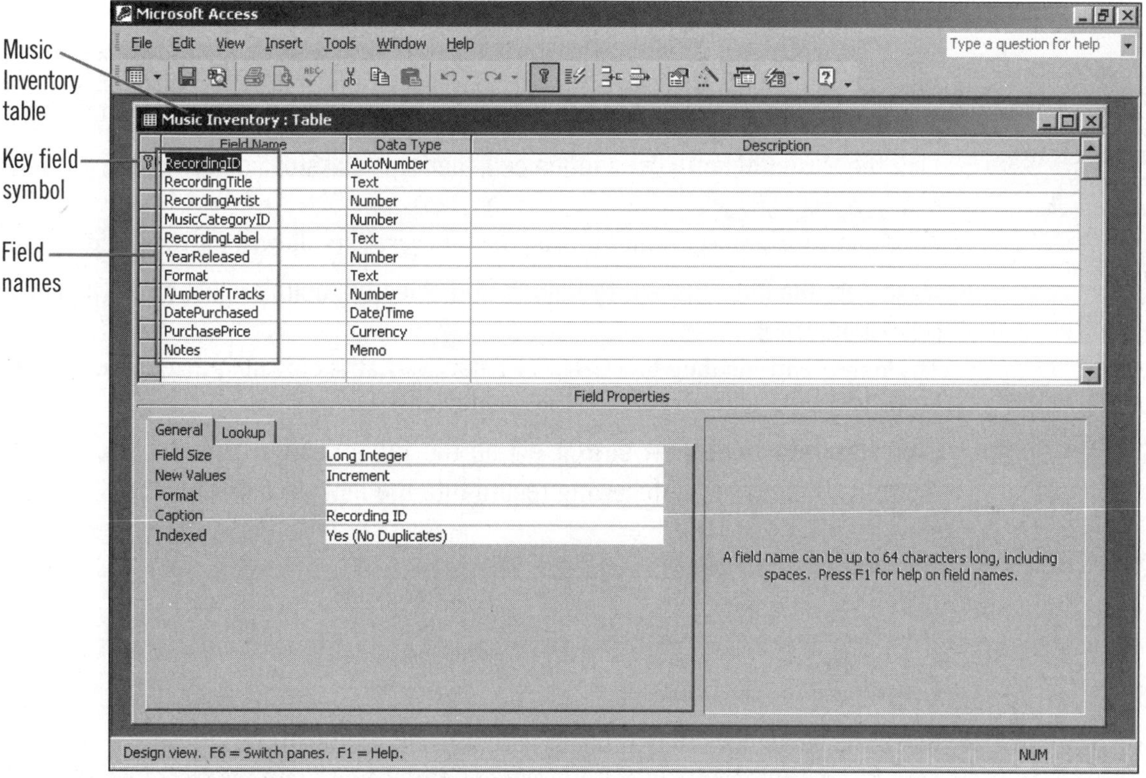

Access 2002

Modifying a Table

Each database object has a **Design View** in which you can modify its structure. The Design View of a table allows you to add or delete fields, add **field descriptions**, or change other field properties. Field **properties** are additional characteristics of a field such as its size or default value. Using the Table Wizard, Kelsey was able to create a Music Inventory table very quickly. Now in Design View she further modifies the fields to meet her specific needs. MediaLoft doesn't track purchase dates or release dates, but it does need to store retail price information in the database.

Steps

QuickTip
Deleting a field from a table deletes any data stored in that field for all records in the table!

1. In Design View of the Music Inventory table, click **DatePurchased** in the Field Name column, click the **Delete Rows button** on the Table Design toolbar, click **YearReleased** in the Field Name column, click to delete the field, click the **Notes** field, then click the **Insert Rows button**
   The Year Released and Date Purchased fields are deleted from the table. A new row appears above the Notes field in which you can enter a new field name.

QuickTip
You can also choose a data type by pressing its first letter such as C for Currency.

2. Type **RetailPrice**, press **[Tab]**, click the **Data Type list arrow**, then click **Currency**
   The new field is added to the Music Inventory table, as shown in Figure B-5. Both the RecordingArtist and MusicCategoryID fields have a Number data type, but it should be Text.
3. Click the **Number** Data Type for the RecordingArtist field, click the **Data Type list arrow**, click **Text**, click the **Number** Data Type for the MusicCategoryID field, click the **Data Type list arrow**, then click **Text**
   Now, descriptive words can be entered in these fields rather than just numbers. You must work in the Design View of a table to make structural changes to fields such as changing the data type.
4. Click to the right of **MusicCategoryID**, press **[Backspace]** twice to delete ID, then click the **Save button** on the Table Design toolbar
   Field names can include any combination of letters, numbers and spaces, up to 64 characters long. The only special characters that are not allowed include the period (.), exclamation point (!), accent grave (`), and square brackets [ ]. Field descriptions are optional, but help to further describe the field.

QuickTip
The Field Description entry appears in the status bar when that field has the focus in Datasheet View.

5. Click the **MusicCategory Description cell**, then type **classical, country, folk, gospel, jazz, new age, rap, or rock**
   The **Field Size** property limits the number of characters allowed for each field.
6. Make sure the **MusicCategory** field is still selected, double-click **50** in the Field Size cell, then type **9**
   The longest entry in the MusicCategory field, classical, is only nine characters. The finished Music Inventory table Design View should look like Figure B-6.

QuickTip
The Datasheet View button becomes the Design View button when working in Datasheet View.

7. Click the **Datasheet View button** on the Table Design toolbar, click **Yes** to save the table, then type the following record into the new datasheet:

in field:	type:	in field:	type:
Recording ID	[Tab]	Format	CD
Recording Title	No Words	Number of Tracks	12
RecordingArtist	Brickman, Jim	Purchase Price	10
Music Category ID	New Age	RetailPrice	13
Recording Label	Windham Hill	Notes	[Tab]

8. Close the Music Inventory table, then close the MediaLoft database
   Data is saved automatically, so you were not prompted to save the record when you closed the datasheet.

FIGURE B-5: Music Inventory table with new RetailPrice field

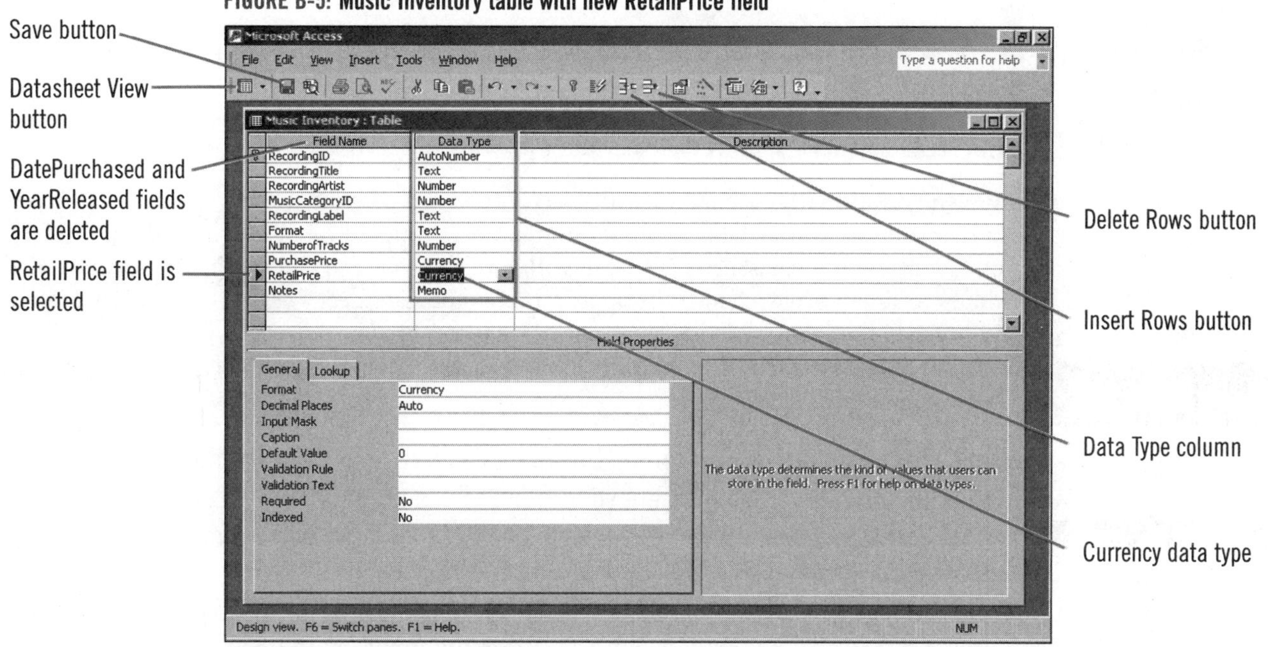

FIGURE B-6: Modifying field properties

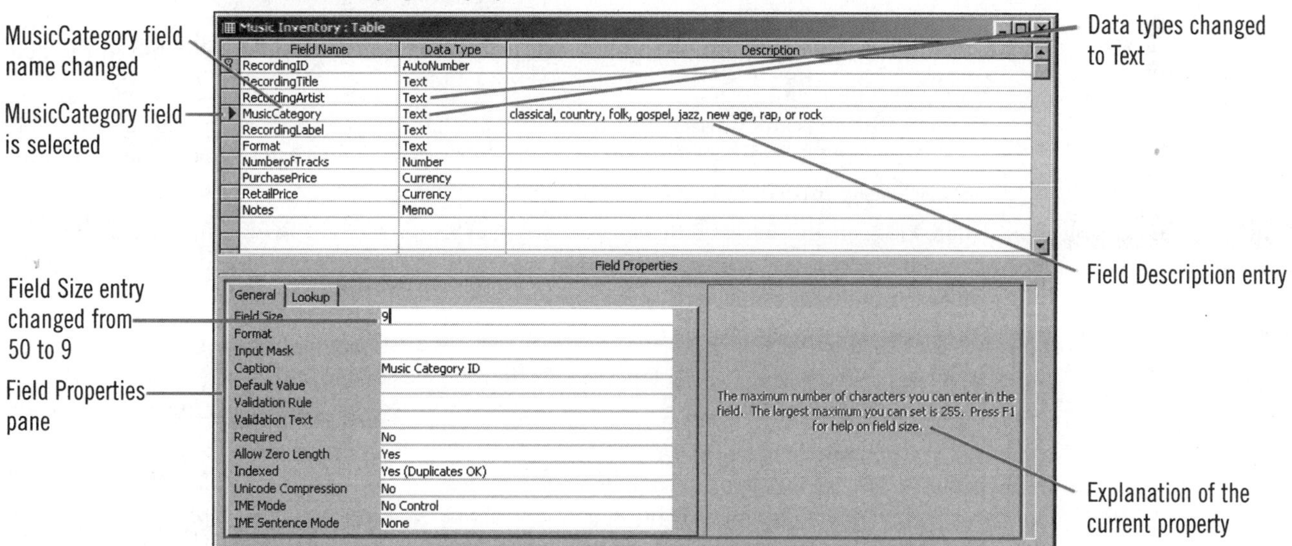

Learning about field properties

Properties are the characteristics that define the field. Two properties are required for every field: Field Name and Data Type. Many other properties, such as Field Size, Format, Caption, and Default Value are defined in the Field Properties pane found in the Design View of the table. As you add more property entries, you are generally restricting the amount or type of data that can be entered in the field, which in turn increases data entry accuracy. For example, you might change the Field Size property for a State field to 2 in order to eliminate an incorrect entry such as FLL. The Field Properties change depending on the data type of the selected field. For example, there would be no Field Size property for a Birth Date field, because Access controls the size of fields with a Date/Time data type. The **Caption** property is used to override the field name with an easy-to-read caption on datasheets, forms, and reports. Database designers often insist on field names without spaces because they are easier to reference in other Access objects. Yet database *users* would rather view field names with spaces when entering data. That's why the tables created by the wizards have field names without spaces, but display more readable captions on the datasheet.

Access 2002

Formatting a Datasheet

Although you primarily use the report object to create professional printouts from an Access database, you can print a datasheet too. Although you cannot create custom headings or insert graphic images on a datasheet as you can with a report, you can change the fonts, colors, and gridlines to dramatically change the appearance of the datasheet. Kelsey has entered some information about MediaLoft's music products into the Music Inventory table of the MediaLoft-B database. Now she will print the Music Inventory datasheet after formatting it with a new font and gridline color.

Steps

1. Click the **Open button** on the Database toolbar, select the **MediaLoft-B** database from the drive and folder where your Project Files are stored, then click **Open**
2. Click the **Music Inventory** table in the MediaLoft-B database window, then click the **Open button** on the database window toolbar
   The Music Inventory table on the Database window toolbar contains 58 records, as shown in Figure B-7. Formatting options for a datasheet are found on the Format menu or on the Formatting (Datasheet) toolbar. When you format a datasheet, every record in the datasheet is formatted the same way.
3. Click **Format** on the menu bar, click **Font**, scroll and click **Comic Sans MS** in the Font list, then click **OK**
   Comic Sans MS is an informal font that simulates handwritten text, but is still very readable. By default, the Formatting (Datasheet) toolbar does not appear in Datasheet View, but toolbars are easily turned on and off using the View menu.
4. Click **View** on the menu bar, point to **Toolbars**, then click **Formatting (Datasheet)**.
   The Formatting (Datasheet) toolbar contains the most common formatting options for changing the font, colors, and gridlines of the datasheet.
5. Click the **Line/Border Color button list arrow**, click the **red** box, click the **Gridlines button list arrow**, then click the **Gridlines: Horizontal** box
   In addition to formatting changes, you may wish to change the page setup options before you print a datasheet.
6. Select **Cook, Jesse** in the Artist field of the first record, type your last name, your first name, click **File** on the menu bar, click **Page Setup**, click the **Page tab**, click the **Landscape option button**, then click **OK**
   Your name is in the Artist field of the first record to uniquely identify your printout.
7. Click the **Print Preview button** on the Table Datasheet toolbar, click the **Next Page button** in the Print Preview Navigation buttons to view page 2, then click the **Print button**
   The First Page and Previous Page buttons will be dimmed if you are viewing the first page of the datasheet. The Next Page and Last Page buttons will be dimmed if you are viewing the last page of the datasheet. By default, the table name and current date print in the datasheet header, and the page number prints in the datasheet footer as shown in Figure B-8.
8. Click the **Close button** for the preview window, click **No** when asked to save the changes to the layout of the table, double-click the **Music Inventory** table to reopen the datasheet, then study the first record
   The font and gridline formatting changes were *not* saved when you answered No to the question about saving changes to the layout. Your name entry in the Artist field of the first record *was* automatically saved by Access. Remember, all data entries and data edits are automatically saved as you move between records or close a datasheet.

QuickTip

You can also double-click an object to open it.

QuickTip

Right-click any toolbar to open a shortcut menu of available toolbars. A check mark appears next to displayed toolbars.

QuickTip

You can click the Setup button Setup on the Print Preview toolbar to open the Page Setup dialog box to modify margins and paper orientation.

FIGURE B-7: Music Inventory table datasheet

Music Inventory : Table

RecordingID	Title	Artist	Category	Label	Format	Tracks	W
1	Gravity	Cook, Jesse	New Age	Columbia	CD	15	
2	Come Walk With Me	Adams, Oleta	Gospel	CBS Records	CD	10	
3	Greatest Hits	Winans, BeBe & CeC	Gospel	Benson	Vinyl	9	
4	Tribute	Yanni	New Age	MCA	CD	10	
5	World Café	Tree Frogs	Rap	New Stuff	CD	12	
6	Relationships	Winans, BeBe & CeC	Gospel	Capitol	CD	14	
7	No Words	Brickman, Jim	New Age	Windham Hill	CD	10	
8	God's Property	Nu Nation	Rap	B-Rite Music	Cassette	13	
9	Message	4 Him	Gospel	Benson	CD	13	
10	Sacred Road	Lantz, David	New Age	Narada	Cassette	12	
11	Mariah Carey	Carey, Mariah	Rock	Columbia	CD	11	
12	Ironman Triathlon	Tesh, John	New Age	GTS Records	Cassette	9	
13	Daydream	Carey, Mariah	Rock	Columbia	CD	12	
14	Heartsounds	Lantz, David	New Age	Narada	CD	14	
15	The Roches	Roches, The	Folk	Warner Bros. Records	Cassette	10	
16	Can We Go Home Now	Roches, The	Folk	Ryko	CD	11	
17	Live at the Red Rocks	Tesh, John	New Age	GTS Records	CD	16	
18	I'll Lead You Home	Smith, Michael	Gospel	Reunion	CD	14	
19	Winter Song	Tesh, John	New Age	GTS Records	CD	12	
20	December	Winston, George	New Age	Windham	CD	12	
21	Time, Love & Tenderness	Bolton, Michael	Rock	Sony Music	CD	10	

Record: 1 of 58

58 total records

FIGURE B-8: Previewing the formatted datasheet

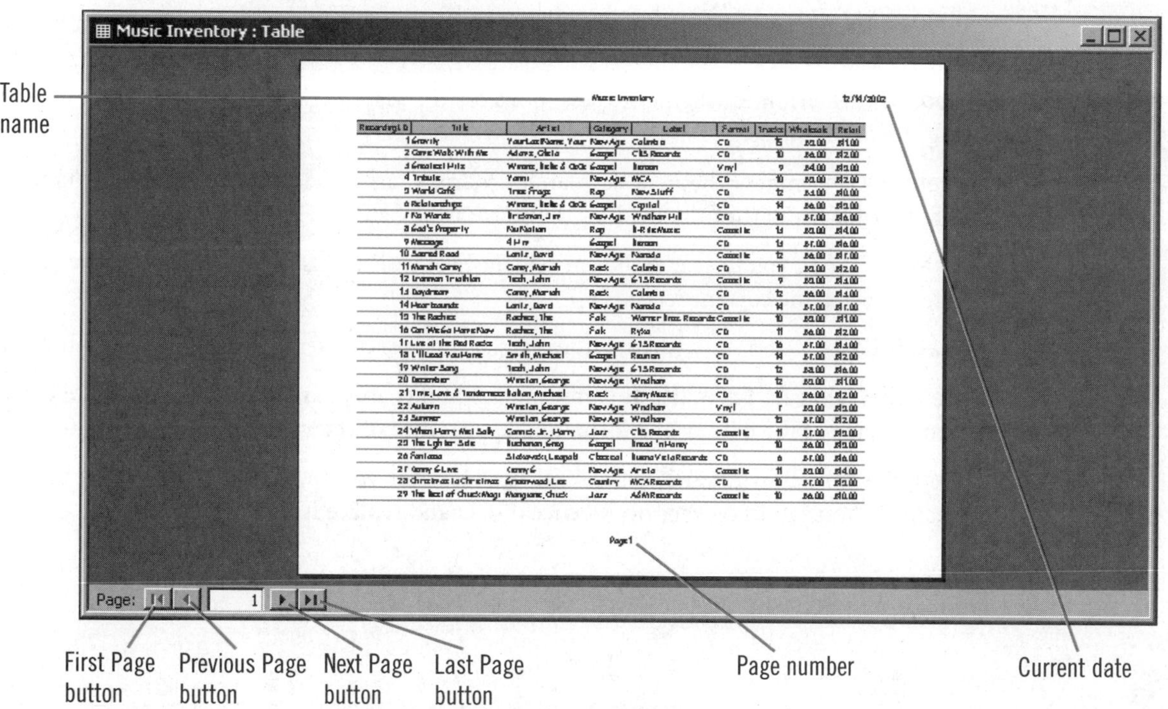

Access 2002

Access 2002

Understanding Sorting, Filtering, and Finding

The records of a datasheet are automatically sorted according to the data in the primary key field. Often, however, you may want to view or print records in an entirely different sort order, or you may want to display a subset of the records, such as those within the same music category or those below a certain retail price. Access makes it easy to sort, find data, and filter a datasheet by using buttons on the Table Datasheet toolbar, summarized in Table B-2. Kelsey studies the sort, find, and filter features to better learn how to find and retrieve information.

Details

- **Sorting** refers to reorganizing the records in either ascending or descending order based on the contents of a field. In ascending order, Text fields sort from A to Z, Number and Currency fields from the lowest to the highest value, and Date/Time fields from the oldest date to the date furthest into the future. In Figure B-9 the Music Inventory table has been sorted in ascending order on the Artist field. Notice that in a Text field, numbers sort before letters.
- **Filtering** means temporarily isolating a subset of records, as shown in Figure B-10. For example, by using a filter, you can produce a listing of all music with the value "Rock" in the Category field. To redisplay all of the records in the datasheet, click the Remove Filter button. The filtered subset can be formatted and printed just like the entire datasheet.
- **Finding** refers to locating a specific piece of data, such as "Amy." The Find and Replace dialog box is shown in Figure B-11. The options in this dialog box are summarized below.
    - **Find What:** Provides a text box for your search criteria. The search criteria might be Amy, Beatles, or Capitol Records.
    - **Look In:** Determines whether Access looks for the search criteria in the current field or in the entire datasheet.
    - **Match:** Determines whether the search criteria must exactly match the contents of the whole field, any part of the field, or the start of the field.
    - **Search:** Allows you to search the entire datasheet (All) or just those records before (Up) or after (Down) the current record.
    - **Match Case:** Determines whether the search criteria is case sensitive (e.g., NH vs. Nh vs. nh).
    - **Search Fields As Formatted:** Determines whether the search criteria is compared to the actual value of the field or the formatted appearance of the value (e.g., 10 vs. $10.00).
    - **Replace tab:** Provides a Replace With text box for you to specify replacement text. For example, you can find every occurrence of CD and replace it with Compact Disc.

Using wildcards

Wildcards are symbols you use as substitutes for characters to locate data that matches your Find criteria. Access uses these wildcards: the **asterisk (*)** represents any group of characters, the **question mark (?)** stands for any single character, and the **pound sign (#)** stands for a single number digit. For example, to find any word beginning with S, type s* in the Find What text box.

FIGURE B-9: **Music Inventory datasheet sorted by Artist**

Music Inventory : Table

RecordingID	Title	Artist	Category	Label	Format	Tracks
9	Message	4 Him	Gospel	Benson	CD	13
2	Come Walk With Me	Adams, Oleta	Gospel	CBS Records	CD	10
54	Cosmic Thing	B-52s	Rock	Warner Records	CD	10
53	Abbey Road	Beatles, The	Rock	Capitol Records	Vinyl	14
47	Revolver	Beatles, The	Rock	Capitol Records	CD	12
34	Handel's Messiah	Bernstein, Leonard	Classical	CBS Records	Cassette	11
40	Favorite Overtures	Bernstein, Leonard	Classical	CBS Records	Vinyl	5
21	Time, Love & Tenderness	Bolton, Michael	Rock	Sony Music	CD	10
7	No Words	Brickman, Jim	New Age	Windham Hill	CD	10
42	Garth Brooks Live	Brooks, Garth	Country	Liberty Records	CD	10
38	The Chase	Brooks, Garth	Country	A&M Records	CD	10
25	The Lighter Side	Buchanan, Greg	Gospel	Bread 'n Honey	CD	10
13	Daydream	Carey, Mariah	Rock	Columbia	CD	12
11	Mariah Carey	Carey, Mariah	Rock	Columbia	CD	11
43	Pilgrim	Clapton, Eric	Rock	Capitol Records	CD	13
24	When Harry Met Sally	Connick Jr., Harry	Jazz	CBS Records	Cassette	11
36	Watermark	Enya	New Age	GTS Records	CD	12
44	The Dance	Fleetwood Mac	Rock	ABC Records	CD	12
45	Interludes	Fresh Aire	New Age	American Gramaphone	CD	10

Record: 1 of 58

Records are sorted in ascending order by Artist

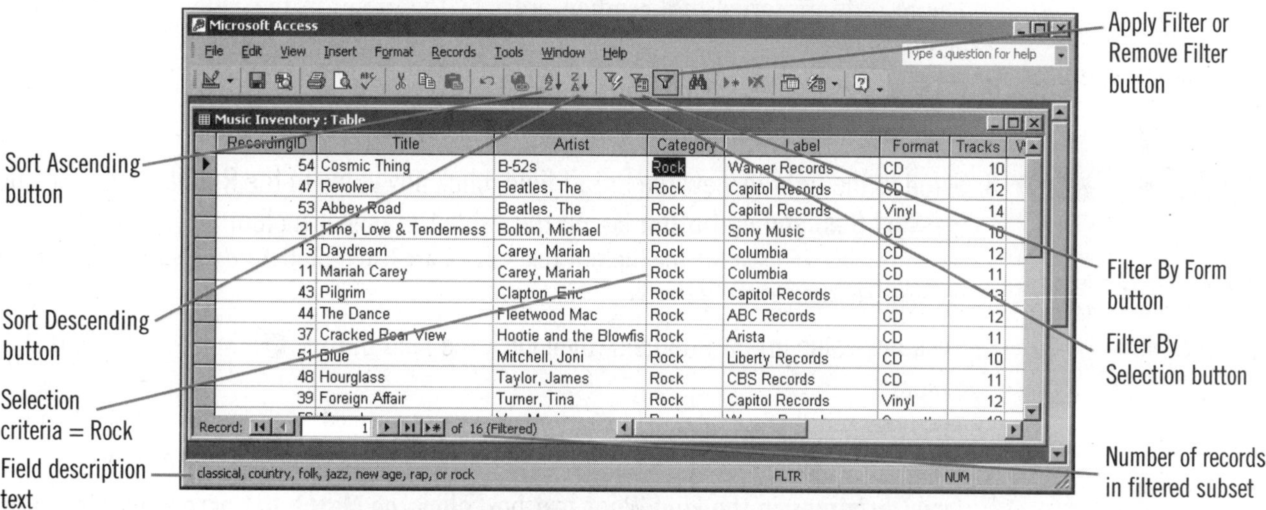

RecordingID	Title	Artist	Category	Label	Format	Tracks
54	Cosmic Thing	B-52s	Rock	Warner Records	CD	10
47	Revolver	Beatles, The	Rock	Capitol Records	CD	12
53	Abbey Road	Beatles, The	Rock	Capitol Records	Vinyl	14
21	Time, Love & Tenderness	Bolton, Michael	Rock	Sony Music	CD	10
13	Daydream	Carey, Mariah	Rock	Columbia	CD	12
11	Mariah Carey	Carey, Mariah	Rock	Columbia	CD	11
43	Pilgrim	Clapton, Eric	Rock	Capitol Records	CD	13
44	The Dance	Fleetwood Mac	Rock	ABC Records	CD	12
37	Cracked Rear View	Hootie and the Blowfis	Rock	Arista	CD	11
51	Blue	Mitchell, Joni	Rock	Liberty Records	CD	10
48	Hourglass	Taylor, James	Rock	CBS Records	CD	11
39	Foreign Affair	Turner, Tina	Rock	Capitol Records	Vinyl	12

FIGURE B-10: **Music Inventory datasheet filtered for Rock in the Category field**

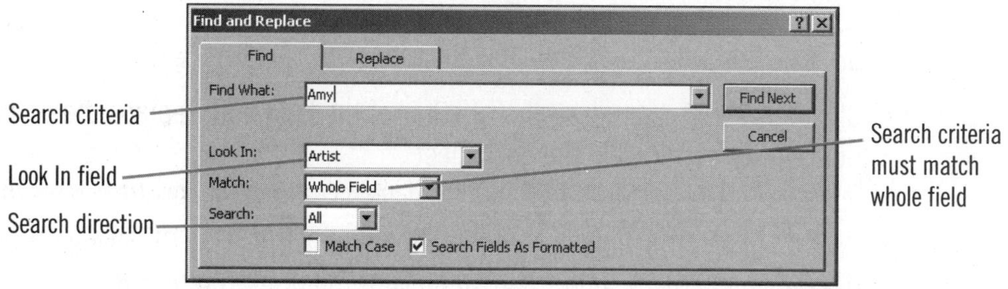

FIGURE B-11: **Find and Replace dialog box**

TABLE B-2: **Sort, Filter, and Find buttons**

name	button	purpose
Sort Ascending		Sorts records based on the selected field in ascending order (0 to 9, A to Z)
Sort Descending		Sorts records based on the selected field in descending order (Z to A, 9 to 0)
Filter By Selection		Filters records based on selected data and hides records that do not match
Filter By Form		Filters records based on more than one selection criteria by using the Filter By Form window
Apply Filter or Remove Filter		Applies or removes the filter
Find		Searches for a string of characters in the current field or all fields

Access 2002

Access 2002

Sorting Records and Finding Data

The sort and find features are powerful tools that help you work more efficiently whether you are working with data in a datasheet or viewing it through a form. Kelsey needs to create several different printouts of the Music Inventory datasheet to satisfy various departments. The marketing department wants the records sorted by Title and by Artist. The accounting department wants the records sorted from the highest retail price to the lowest.

Steps

1. In the Music Inventory datasheet, click any value in the Title field, then click the **Sort Ascending button** on the Table Datasheet toolbar
   The records are sorted in ascending order by the values in the Title field, as shown in Figure B-12.
2. Click **any cell** in the Artist field, then click
   The records are sorted in ascending order by the values in the Artist field.
3. Scroll to the right to view the Retail field, click any value in the Retail field, then click the **Sort Descending button** on the Table Datasheet toolbar
   The products that sell for the highest retail price are listed first. Access also lets you find all records based on search criteria.
4. Click any value in the Title field, then click the **Find button** on the Table Datasheet toolbar
   The Find and Replace dialog box opens with Title selected as the Look In field. You have been asked to find the titles that may be hot sellers during the Christmas season.
5. Type **Christmas** in the Find What text box, click the **Match list arrow**, then click **Any Part of Field**, as shown in Figure B-13
   "Christmas" is the search criteria. Access will find all occurrences of the word Christmas in the Title field, whether it is the first, middle, or last part of the title.
6. Click **Find Next**, then drag the title bar of the Find and Replace dialog box up and to the right to better view the datasheet
   If you started the search at the top of the datasheet, A Family Christmas is the first title found.
7. Click **Find Next** to find the next occurrence of the word Christmas, then click **Find Next** as many times as it takes to move through all the records
   When no more occurrences of the search criteria Christmas are found, Access provides a dialog box that tells you that no more matching records can be found.
8. Click **OK** when prompted that Access has finished searching the records, then click **Cancel** to close the Find and Replace dialog box

QuickTip

If you close a datasheet without saving the layout changes, the records return to the original sort order based on the values in the primary key field. If you close a datasheet and save layout changes, the last sort order will be saved.

FIGURE B-12: Music Inventory datasheet sorted by Title

Music Inventory : Table

RecordingID	Title	Artist	Category	Label	Format	Tracks
55	A Christmas Album	Grant, Amy	Folk	Reunion Records	CD	11
46	A Family Christmas	Tesh, John	New Age	GTS Records	CD	14
32	A Winter's Solstice	Windham Hill Artists	New Age	Windham	CD	10
53	Abbey Road	Beatles, The	Rock	Capitol Records	Vinyl	14
22	Autumn	Winston, George	New Age	Windham	Vinyl	7
51	Blue	Mitchell, Joni	Rock	Liberty Records	CD	10
16	Can We Go Home Now	Roches, The	Folk	Ryko	CD	11
35	Christmas	Mannheim Steamroller	New Age	Sony Music	CD	11
28	Christmas to Christmas	Greenwood, Lee	Country	MCA Records	CD	10
31	Closeup	Sandborn, David	Jazz	MCA Records	Cassette	10
2	Come Walk With Me	Adams, Oleta	Gospel	CBS Records	CD	10
54	Cosmic Thing	B-52s	Rock	Warner Records	CD	10
37	Cracked Rear View	Hootie and the Blowfis	Rock	Arista	CD	11
13	Daydream	Carey, Mariah	Rock	Columbia	CD	12
52	Decade	Young, Neil	Rock	A&M Records	CD	10
20	December	Winston, George	New Age	Windham	CD	12
26	Fantasia	Stokowski, Leopold	Classical	Buena Vista Records	CD	6
40	Favorite Overtures	Bernstein, Leonard	Classical	CBS Records	Vinyl	5
39	Foreign Affair	Turner, Tina	Rock	Capitol Records	Vinyl	12
42	Garth Brooks Live	Brooks, Garth	Country	Liberty Records	CD	10
8	God's Property	Nu Nation	Rap	B-Rite Music	Cassette	13

Record: 1 of 58

Records are sorted ascending by Title

FIGURE B-13: Enter Christmas as the search criteria for the Title field

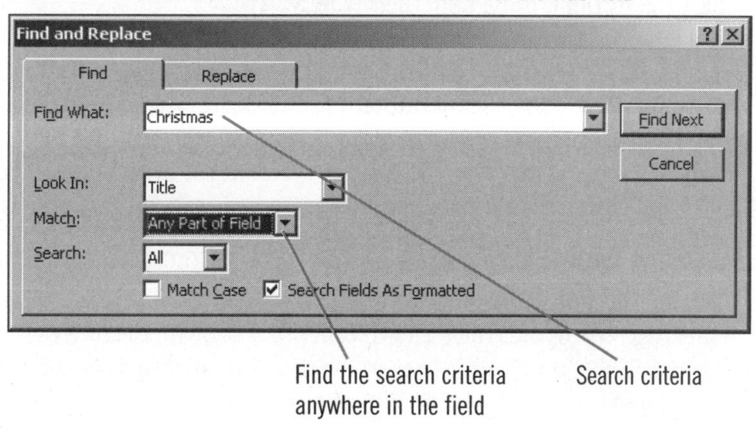

Find the search criteria anywhere in the field

Search criteria

Using more than one sort field

The telephone book sorts records by last name (**primary sort field**) and when ties occur on the last name (for example, two Smiths), the telephone book further sorts the records by first name (**secondary sort field**). Access allows you to sort by more than one field using the query object, which you will learn more about later in this unit. Queries allow you to use more than one sort field by specifying sort criteria in Query Design View.

Access 2002

Access 2002

Filtering Records

Filtering the datasheet temporarily displays only those records that match criteria. **Criteria** are rules or limiting conditions you set. For example, you may want to show only those records where the Category field is equal to Rap, or where the PurchasePrice field is less than $10. Once you have filtered a datasheet or form to display a subset of records, you can still sort the records and find data just as if you were working with all of the records. The accounting department asked Kelsey for a listing of cassettes with a retail price of $15 or more. Kelsey uses the datasheet filter buttons to fulfill this request.

Steps

1. **In the Music Inventory datasheet, click the RecordingID field, click the Sort Ascending button on the Table Datasheet toolbar, click any occurrence of Cassette in the Format field, then click the Filter By Selection button on the Table Datasheet toolbar**
   Twelve records are selected, as shown in Figure B-14. Filter By Selection is a fast and easy way to filter the records for an exact match (in this case, where the Format field value is *equal to* Cassette). To filter for comparative data and to specify more complex criteria including **comparison operators** (for example, where PurchasePrice is *equal to or greater than* $15), you must use the Filter By Form feature. See Table B-3 for more information on comparison operators.

QuickTip
If criteria become lengthy, you can widen a column to display the entire criteria entry just as you can widen columns in a datasheet. If you need to clear previous criteria, click the Clear Grid button.

2. **Click the Filter By Form button on the Table Datasheet toolbar, scroll to the right to click the Retail criteria cell, then type >=15**
   The Filter By Form window is shown in Figure B-15. The previous Filter By Selection criteria, Cassette in the Format field, is still in the grid. Access distinguishes between text and numeric entries by placing quotation marks around text entries. Filter By Form is more powerful than Filter By Selection because it allows you to enter criteria for more than one field at a time so that *both* criteria must be true in order for the record to be shown in the resulting datasheet.

3. **Click the Apply Filter button on the Filter/Sort toolbar, then scroll to the right to display the Retail field**
   Only two records are true for both criteria, as shown in Figure B-16. The Record Navigation buttons in the lower-left corner of the datasheet display how many records were chosen for the filtered subset. The Apply Filter button becomes the Remove Filter button after a filter is applied.

QuickTip
Be sure to remove existing filters before you apply a new filter or you will end up filtering a subset of records versus the entire datasheet.

4. **Click the Remove Filter button on the Table Datasheet toolbar**
   The datasheet redisplays all 58 records.

5. **Click any value in the Label field, click , click A&M Records in the Label field if it is not already selected, then click**
   Using sort and filter skills, you quickly found the five records that met the A&M Records criteria.

6. **Close the datasheet, then click Yes if prompted to save the changes to the Music Inventory table**
   Saving a table layout saves the last sort order, but filters are always removed when you close a datasheet, regardless of whether you save the changes to the layout.

FIGURE B-14: Music Inventory datasheet filtered for Cassette in the Format field

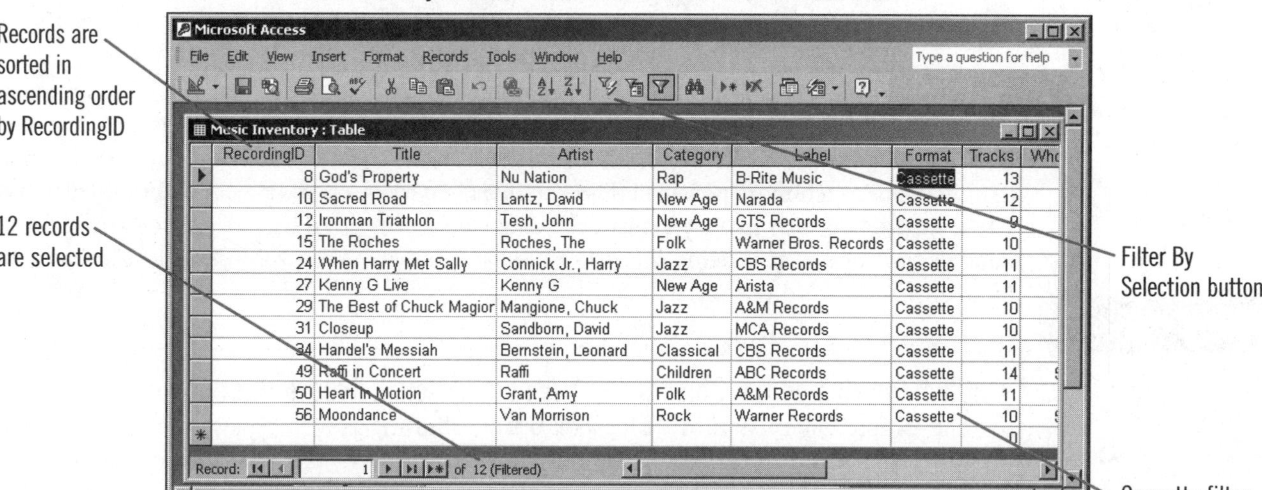

FIGURE B-15: Filter By Form grid

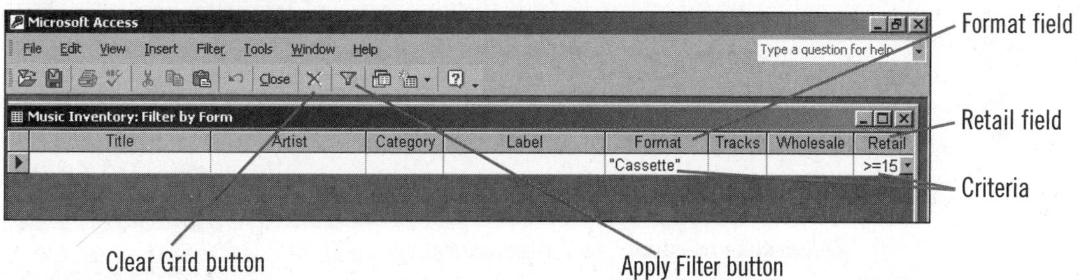

FIGURE B-16: Two records matched Filter By Form criteria

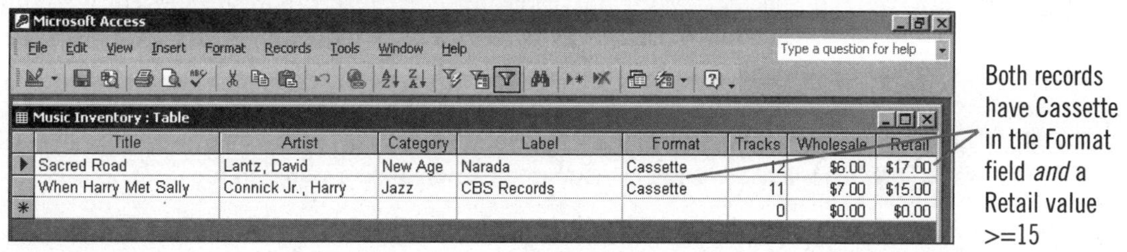

TABLE B-3: Comparison operators

operator	description	expression	meaning
>	Greater than	>500	Numbers greater than 500
>=	Greater than or equal to	>=500	Numbers greater than or equal to 500
<	Less than	<"Braveheart"	Names from A to Braveheart, but not Braveheart
<=	Less than or equal to	<="Bridgewater"	Names from A through, and including, Bridgewater
<>	Not equal to	<>"Cyclone"	Any name except for Cyclone

Searching for blank fields

Is Null and Is Not Null are two other types of common criteria. Is Null criteria will find all records where no entry has been made in the field. Is Not Null will find all records where there is any entry in the field, even if the entry is 0. Primary key fields cannot have a null entry.

Access 2002

Creating a Query

A **query** is a database object that creates a datasheet of specified fields and records from one or more tables. It displays the answer to a question about the data in your database. You can edit, navigate, sort, find, and filter a query's datasheet just like a table's datasheet. A query is similar to a filter, but much more powerful. For example, a query is a saved object within the database whereas a **filter** is a temporary view of the data whose criteria is discarded when you close the datasheet or form that is being filtered. Table B-4 compares the two. Kelsey uses the Simple Query Wizard to build a query.

Steps

1. **Click Queries on the Objects bar, then double-click Create query by using wizard**
   The Simple Query Wizard dialog box opens, allowing you to choose the table or query which contains the fields you want to display in the query. You select the fields in the order that you want them to appear on the final query datasheet.

QuickTip
You can double-click a field to move it from the Available Fields list to the Selected Fields list.

2. **Click Category in the Available Fields list, click the Select Single Field button >, click Title, click >, click Artist, click >, click Tracks, then click >**
   The Simple Query Wizard dialog box should look like Figure B-17. The fields shown in the Available Fields list are determined by what table or query is selected in the Tables/Queries list.

3. **Click Next, click Next to accept the Detail option, then click Finish to accept the suggested query title and to view the data**
   The Music Inventory Query's datasheet opens with all 58 records, but with only the four fields that you requested in the query wizard, as shown in Figure B-18. You can use a query datasheet to edit or add information.

4. **Double-click 10 in the Tracks cell for record 7, No Words, then type 11**
   The Specific Record box indicates what record you are currently editing. Editing data through a query datasheet changes the data in the underlying table just as if you were working directly in the table's datasheet. A query does *not* produce a duplicate set of data, but rather, displays the original table data in a new arrangement. A query is sometimes called a **logical view** of the data. Any data additions, deletions, or editions you make through a query datasheet are actually made to the original data stored in the table object.

5. **Click the Design View button on the Query Datasheet toolbar**
   The **Query Design View** opens, showing you a **field list** for the Music Inventory table in the upper portion of the window, and the fields you have requested for this query in the **query design grid** in the lower portion of the window.

QuickTip
Criteria is not case sensitive so country and Country produce the same results.

6. **Click the Criteria cell for the Category field, then type country as shown in Figure B-19**
   Query Design View is used to add, delete, or change the order of fields, sort the records, or add criteria to limit the number of records shown in the resulting datasheet. Any change made in Query Design View is saved with the query object.

7. **Click the Datasheet View button on the Query Design toolbar**
   The resulting datasheet has four records that match the country criteria in the Category field. To save this query with a more descriptive name than the one currently displayed in the query title bar, use the Save As command on the File menu.

8. **Click File on the menu bar, click Save As, type Country Music in the Save Query 'Music Inventory Query' To text box, click OK, then close the query datasheet**
   Both the original Music Inventory Query and the modified Country Music queries are saved in this database. You can double-click a query to reopen the datasheet in the same way as you can open the datasheet of a table.

FIGURE B-17: Simple Query Wizard dialog box

Music Inventory table is chosen

Fields in the Music Inventory table

Select Single Field button

Fields for this query

FIGURE B-18: Music Inventory Query datasheet

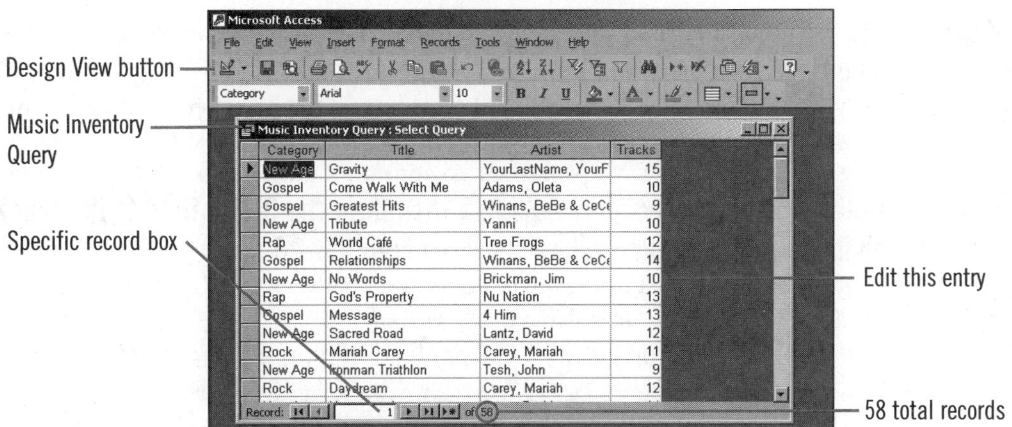

FIGURE B-19: Query Design View

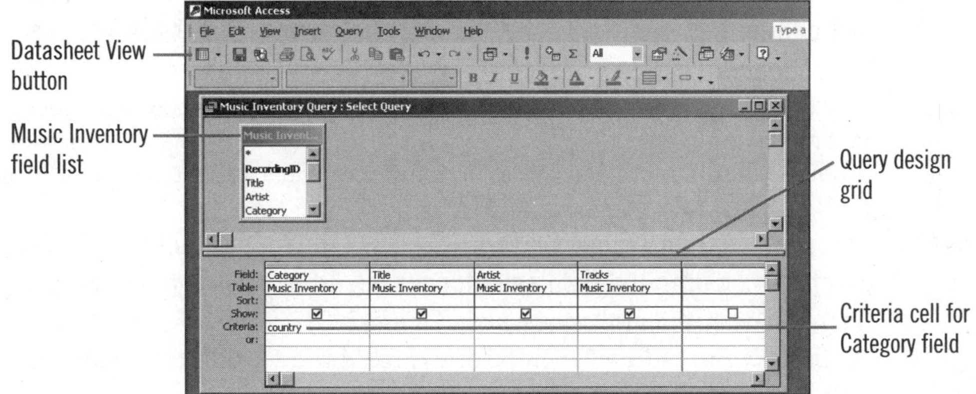

TABLE B-4: Queries vs. filters

Characteristics	filters	queries
Are saved as an object in the database	No	Yes
Can be used to select a subset of records in a datasheet	Yes	Yes
Can be used to select a subset of fields in a datasheet	No	Yes
Its resulting datasheet can be used to enter and edit data	Yes	Yes
Its resulting datasheet can be used to sort, filter, and find records	Yes	Yes
Is commonly used as the source of data for a form or report	No	Yes
Can calculate sums, averages, counts, and other types of summary statistics across records	No	Yes
Can be used to create calculated fields	No	Yes

Modifying a Query

Whether an existing query is created through the use of a wizard or built from scratch in Query Design View, to modify the query you work in Query Design View in the same way you modify existing tables by working in Table Design View. Query Design View is where you employ powerful query features such as defining complex criteria, defining multiple sort orders, and building calculated fields. Kelsey wants to modify the Country Music query in a variety of ways. She uses Query Design View to make the changes and then she prints the resulting datasheet.

Steps

QuickTip

Right-click an object and click Design View from the shortcut menu to open it in this view.

Trouble?

If the field list in the upper portion of Query Design View is not visible, use the Query Design scroll bars to move to the top and left part of the window.

Trouble?

Click the field selector for a field to select it, release the mouse button, then drag the field selector for the chosen field. A thin, black, vertical bar will indicate where the field will be positioned as you drag it.

1. Click the **Country Music query** in the MediaLoft-B Database window, then click the **Design button** on the database window toolbar
   Query Design View opens, displaying the current fields and criteria for the Country Music query. To add fields to the query, you drag the fields from the field list to the position in the query design grid where you want them to appear on the datasheet.
2. Scroll in the Music Inventory field list, then drag the **Retail field** to the **Tracks Field cell** in the query design grid as shown in Figure B-20
   The Retail field is added to the query design grid between the Artist and Tracks fields. You can also delete fields in the existing query grid.
3. Click the **field selector** for the Category field, then press the **Delete** key
   Deleting a field from Query Design View does not have any affect on the data stored in the underlying table. Deleting a field from a query means that this field will not be displayed on the datasheet for this query.
4. Click the **Sort cell** for the Title field, click the **Sort list arrow**, click **Ascending**, click the **Sort cell** for the Artist field, click the **Sort list arrow**, click **Ascending**, then click the **Datasheet View button** on the Query Design toolbar to view the resulting datasheet
   Since sort orders are evaluated in a left-to-right order and there are no duplicate values in the primary sort order (Title), the secondary sort order (Artist) is never used to further determine the order of the records. To change the primary and secondary sort orders for a query, use Query Design View.
5. Click on the Query Datasheet toolbar, click the **field selector** for the Artist field to select it, then drag the **field selector** for the Artist field to the first column position in the query design grid as shown in Figure B-21
   The primary sort order will now be determined by the Artist field, and the secondary sort order by the Title field.
6. Click to view the resulting datasheet
   Study records 4 and 5, which contain the same Artist value, "Beatles, The." Note that the records are further sorted by the values in the Title field. You can specify as many sort orders as you desire in Query Design View, but they are always evaluated in a left-to-right order. You can also add multiple criteria values in Query Design View.
7. Click , click the first **Criteria cell** for the Retail field, type **>=15**, click the first **Criteria cell** for the Tracks field, type **>=12**, then click to view the resulting datasheet as shown in Figure B-22
   Twelve records are selected that matched both criteria. The query design grid row into which query criteria is entered is extremely important. Criteria entered on the same row must *both* be true for the record to be selected. Criteria entered on different rows are evaluated separately, and a record need only be true for *one* row of criteria in order to be selected for the resulting datasheet.
8. Click the **Print button** on the Query Datasheet toolbar, close the datasheet without saving changes, close the MediaLoft-B database, then exit Access

FIGURE B-20: Retail field added to query grid

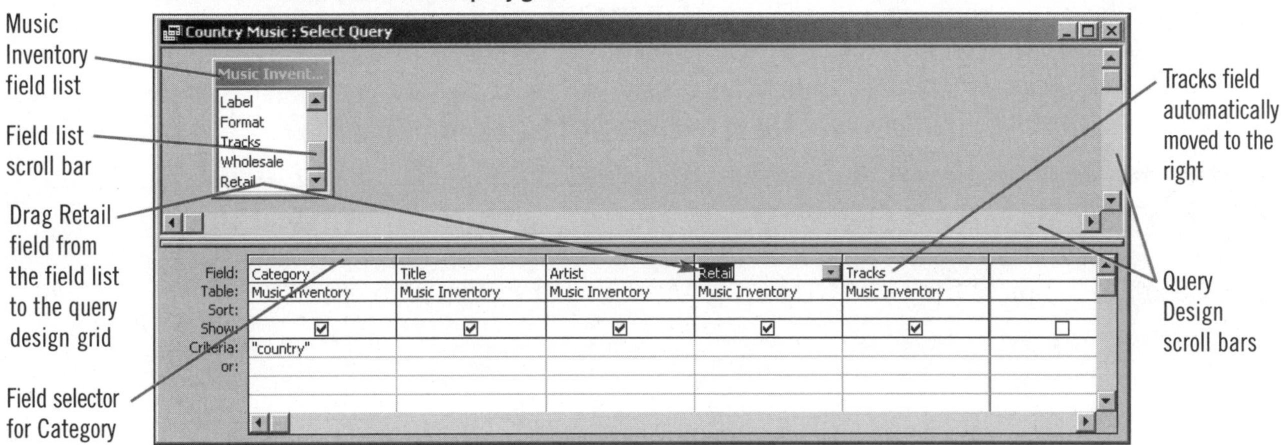

FIGURE B-21: Sorting records using the Artist and Category fields

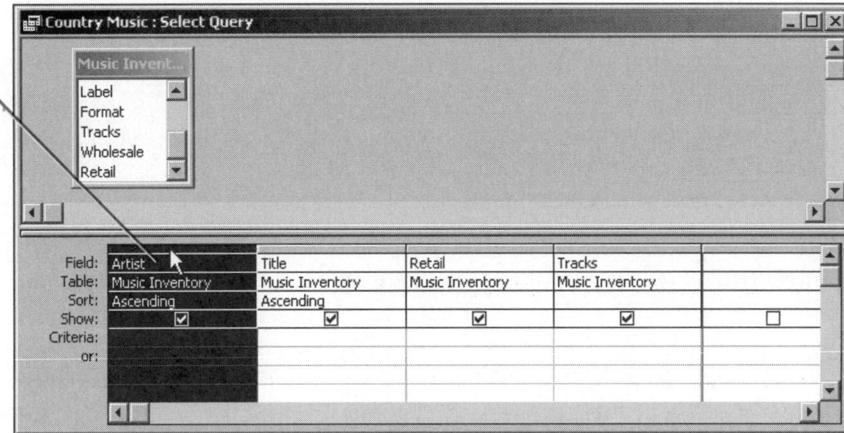

FIGURE B-22: The final datasheet

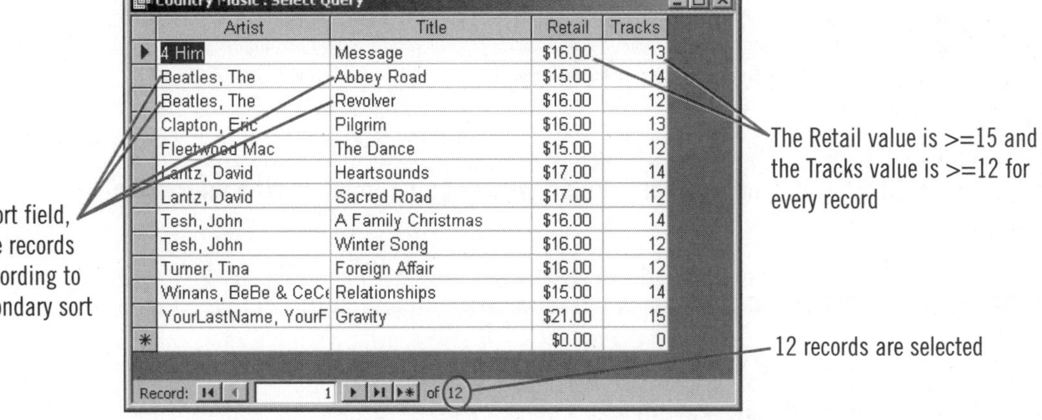

Country Music : Select Query

Artist	Title	Retail	Tracks
4 Him	Message	$16.00	13
Beatles, The	Abbey Road	$15.00	14
Beatles, The	Revolver	$16.00	12
Clapton, Eric	Pilgrim	$16.00	13
Fleetwood Mac	The Dance	$15.00	12
Lantz, David	Heartsounds	$17.00	14
Lantz, David	Sacred Road	$17.00	12
Tesh, John	A Family Christmas	$16.00	14
Tesh, John	Winter Song	$16.00	12
Turner, Tina	Foreign Affair	$16.00	12
Winans, BeBe & CeCe	Relationships	$15.00	14
YourLastName, YourF	Gravity	$21.00	15
*		$0.00	0

Record: 1 of 12

Understanding And and Or criteria

Criteria placed on different rows of the query design grid are **Or criteria**. In other words, a record may be true for *either* row of criteria in order for it to be displayed on the resulting datasheet. Placing additional criteria in the *same* row, however, creates **And criteria**. Records must meet the criteria for *all* of the criteria on one row in order to be chosen for that datasheet. As you add additional rows of criteria (Or criteria) to the query design grid, you increase the number of records displayed on the resulting datasheet because the record needs to be true for the criteria in only *one* of the rows in order to be displayed on the datasheet for that query.

Access 2002

Practice

▶ Concepts Review

Label each element of the Select Query window shown in Figure B-23.

FIGURE B-23

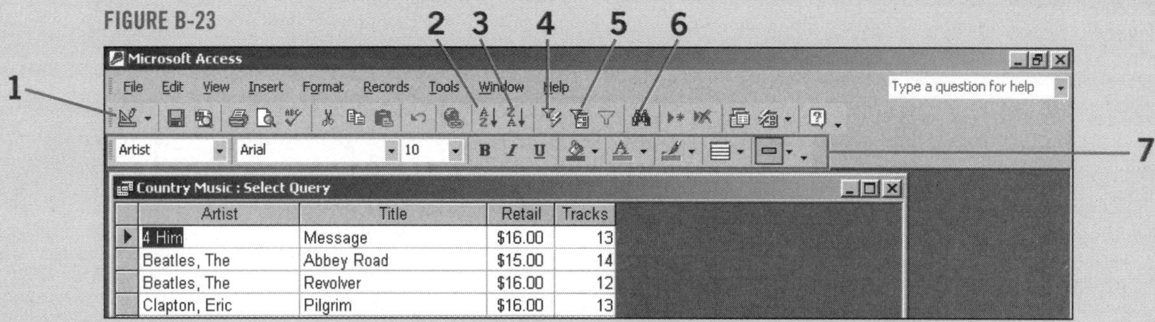

Match each term with the statement that describes it.

8. Primary key	a. Determines what type of data can be stored in each field
9. Table Wizard	b. Provides interactive help to create the field names and data types for each field in a new table
10. Filter	c. A database object that creates a datasheet of specified fields and records from one or more tables
11. Data type	d. A field that contains unique information for each record
12. Query	e. Creates a temporary subset of records

Select the best answer from the list of choices.

13. Which data type would be best for a field that was going to store birth dates?

- **a.** Text
- **b.** Number
- **c.** AutoNumber
- **d.** Date/Time

14. Which data type would be best for a field that was going to store Web addresses?

- **a.** Text
- **b.** Memo
- **c.** OLE
- **d.** Hyperlink

15. Which data type would be best for a field that was going to store telephone numbers?

- **a.** Text
- **b.** Number
- **c.** OLE
- **d.** Hyperlink

16. Each of the following is true about a filter, *except*:

- **a.** It creates a temporary datasheet of records that match criteria.
- **b.** The resulting datasheet can be sorted.
- **c.** The resulting datasheet includes all fields in the table.
- **d.** A filter is automatically saved as an object in the database.

17. Sorting refers to:

- **a.** Reorganizing the records in either ascending or descending order.
- **b.** Selecting a subset of fields and/or records to view as a datasheet from one or more tables.
- **c.** Displaying only those records that meet certain criteria.
- **d.** Using Or and And criteria in the query design grid.

► Skills Review

1. **Plan a database.**
   a. Plan a database that will contain the names and addresses of physicians. You might use a telephone book to gather information.
   b. On paper, sketch the Table Design view of a table that will hold this information. Write the field names in one column and the data types for each field in the second column.
2. **Create a table.**
   a. Start Access and use the Blank Access database option to create a database. Save the file as **Doctors** in the drive and folder where your Project Files are stored.
   b. Use the Table Wizard to create a new table. Use the Contacts sample table found in the Business database category.
   c. Choose each of the sample fields in the following order: ContactID, FirstName, LastName, Address, City, StateOrProvince, PostalCode, Title.
   d. Rename the StateOrProvince field as **State**.
   e. Name the table **Addresses**, and allow Access to set the primary key field.
   f. Click the Modify the table design option button in the last Table Wizard dialog box, then click Finish.
3. **Modify a table.**
   a. In the first available blank row (after the Title field), add a new field called **PhoneNumber** with a Text data type.
   b. Change the Field Size property of the State field from 20 to **2**.
   c. Insert a field named **Suite** with a Text data type between the Address and City fields.
   d. Add the description **M.D. or D.O.** to the Title field.
   e. Save the Addresses table, display the Addresses datasheet, and enter one record using your own information in the name fields. Remember that the ContactID field is specified with an AutoNumber data type that automatically increments the value in that field when you start making an entry in any other field.
   f. Use the Page Setup dialog box to change the Page Orientation to Landscape. Preview the datasheet. If it doesn't fit on one page, return to the datasheet and resize the columns until the record previews on a single page, and then print that page.
   g. Close the Doctors database.
4. **Format a datasheet.**
   a. Open the **Doctors-B** database from the drive and folder where your Project Files are stored. Open the Doctor Addresses table datasheet.
   b. Change the font of the datasheet to Arial Narrow, and the font size to 9.
   c. Change the gridline color to black, and remove the vertical gridlines.
   d. Change the Page Orientation to Landscape and all of the margins to 0.5". Preview the datasheet (it should fit on one page), then print and close it without saving the formatting changes.
5. **Understand sorting, filtering, and finding.**
   a. On a sheet of paper, identify three ways that you might want to sort an address list, such as the Doctor Addresses datasheet. Be sure to specify both the field you would sort on and the sort order (ascending or descending).
   b. On a sheet of paper, identify three ways that you might want to filter an address list, such as the Doctor Addresses datasheet. Be sure to specify both the field you would filter on and the criteria that you would use.
6. **Sort records and find data.**
   a. Open the Doctor Addresses datasheet, sort the records in ascending order on the Last field, then list the first two last names on paper.
   b. Sort the Doctor Addresses records in descending order on the Zip field, then list the first two doctors on paper.
   c. Find the records in which the Address1 field contains Baltimore in any part of the field. How many records did you find?
   d. Find the records where the Zip field contains **64012**. How many records did you find?

7. **Filter records.**
   a. In the Doctor Addresses datasheet, filter the records for all physicians with the Title **D.O.** Print this datasheet with narrow margins and in landscape orientation so that it fits on one page.
   b. In the Doctor Addresses datasheet, filter the records for all physicians with **M.D.** in the Title field and **64012** in the Zip field, then print this datasheet with narrow margins and in landscape orientation so that it fits on one page.
   c. Close the Doctor Addresses datasheet, and save the layout changes.
8. **Create a query.**
   a. Use the Query Wizard to create a new query based on the Doctor Addresses table with the following fields: First, Last, City, State, Zip.
   b. Name the query **Doctors in Missouri**, then view the datasheet.
   c. In Query Design View, add the criteria **MO** to the State field, then view the datasheet.
   d. Change Mark Garver's last name to **Garvey**.
   e. Change Samuel Harley's first and last name to your first and last name, then save the query.
9. **Modify a query.**
   a. Modify the Doctors in Missouri query to include only those doctors in Kansas City, Missouri. Be sure that the criteria is in the same row so that both criteria must be true for the record to be displayed.
   b. Save the query with the name **Doctors in Kansas City Missouri**. Print the query results, then close the query datasheet.
   c. Modify the Doctors in Kansas City Missouri query so that the records are sorted in ascending order on the last name, then add the DoctorNumber field as the first field in the datasheet.
   d. Print and save the sorted datasheet for that query, then close the datasheet.
   e. Close the Doctors-B database then exit Access.

► Independent Challenge 1

You want to start a database to track your personal video collection.

a. Start Access and create a new database called **Movies** in the drive and folder where your Project Files are located.
b. Using the Table Wizard, create a table based on the Video Collection sample table in the Personal category with the following fields: MovieTitle, YearReleased, Rating, Length, DateAcquired, PurchasePrice.
c. Rename the YearReleased field as **Year** and the PurchasePrice field as **Purchase**.
d. Accept the default name **Video Collection** for the table and allow Access to set a primary key field.
e. Modify the Video Collection table in Design View with the following changes:
   - Delete the Rating Field.
   - Change the Length field to a Number data type.
   - Change the DateAcquired field name to **DatePurchased**.
   - Add a field between Year and Length called **PersonalRating** with a Number data type.
   - In the Description of the PersonalRating field, enter: **My personal rating on a scale from 1 (bad) to 10 (great)**.
   - Add a field between PersonalRating and Length fields called **Rated** with a Text data type.
   - In the Description of the Rated field, enter: **G**, **PG**, **PG-13**, **R**.
   - Change the Field Size property of the Rated field to **5**.
f. Save the Video Collection table, and then open it in Datasheet View.
g. Enter five records with sample data from videos you own or movies you've seen, print the datasheet, close the Video Collection table, close the Movies database, then exit Access.

► Independent Challenge 2

You work for a marketing company that sells medical supplies to doctors' offices.

a. Start Access and open the **Doctors-B** database from the drive and folder where your Project Files are located, then open the Doctors Addresses table datasheet.
b. Filter the records to find all those physicians who live in **Grandview**, modify column widths so that all data is visible, edit William Baker's last name to your last name, change the paper orientation to landscape, preview, then print the datasheet.
c. Sort the filtered records by last name, change the cell color to silver (use the Fill/Back Color button on the Formatting toolbar or the Background Color list found in the Datasheet Formatting dialog box), change the font style to bold, then print the datasheet.
d. Close the Doctors Addresses datasheet without saving the changes.
e. Using the Query Wizard, create a query with the following fields: First, Last, Phone.
f. Name the query **Telephone Query**. Sort the records in ascending order by last name, then print the datasheet. Close the query without saving the changes.
g. In Query Design View of the Telephone Query, delete the First field, then add the Title field between the existing Last and Phone fields. Add an ascending sort order to the Phone field. Save, view, and print the datasheet.
h. In Query Design View of the Telephone Query, add the State field to the fourth column. Add criteria so that only those records where there is no entry in the State field are displayed on the resulting datasheet. (*Hint*: Use **Is Null** criteria for the State cell.)
i. View the datasheet, and then change Sanderson's last name to your last name. Print and close the Telephone Query without saving the changes. Close the Doctors-B database, then exit Access.

► Independent Challenge 3

You want to create a database to keep track of your personal contacts.

a. Start Access and create a new database called **People** in the drive and folder where your Project Files are located.
b. Using the Table Wizard, create a table based on the Addresses sample table in the Personal category with the following fields: FirstName, LastName, SpouseName, Address, City, StateOrProvince, PostalCode, EmailAddress, HomePhone, Birthdate.
c. Name the table **Contact Info**, allow Access to set the primary key field, and choose the Enter data directly into the table option in the last Table Wizard dialog box.
d. Enter at least five records into the table, making sure that two people have the same last name. Use your name for one of the records. Note that the Contact InfoID field has an AutoNumber data type.
e. Sort the records in ascending order by last name, then save and close the Contact Info datasheet.
f. Using the Query Wizard, create a query with the following fields from the Contact Info table in this order: LastName, FirstName, Birthdate. Name the query **Birthday List**.
g. In Query Design View, sort the records in ascending order by LastName and then by FirstName.
h. Save the query as **Sorted Birthday List**, then view the query. Change the Birthdate value to **1/6/71** for your record.
i. Modify the datasheet by making font and color changes, print it, then close it without saving it.
j. Open the datasheet for the Contact Info table and observe the Birthdate value for your record. On a piece of paper, explain why the 1/6/71 value appears in the datasheet for the table when you made the edit in the Sorted Birthday List query.
k. Explain why the 1/6/71 value was saved even though you closed the query without saving the layout changes.
l. Close the Contact Info table, close the People database, then exit Access.

Independent Challenge 4

You are on the staff of an economic development team whose goal is to encourage tourism in the Baltic Sea region. You have created an Access database called Baltic-B to track important fields of information on the countries in that region, and will use the Internet to find information about the area.

a. Start Access and open the **Baltic-B** database from the drive and folder where your Project Files are located.

b. Open the Countries table datasheet, then click the expand button to the left of Norway as well as to the left of Oslo using Figure B-24 as a guide.

c. This arrangement of data shows you how events are tracked by city, and how cities are tracked by country in the Baltic-B database.

d. Connect to the Internet, and then go to www.yahoo.com, www.ask.com, or any general search engine to conduct some research for your database. Your goal is to enter at least one city record (the country's capital city) for each country. Be sure to enter the Population data for that particular city, rather than for the entire country. You can enter the data by expanding the country record subdatasheets as shown for Norway in Figure B-24, or by entering the records directly into the Cities datasheet.

e. Return to the search engine, and research upcoming tourist events for Oslo, Norway. Enter three more events for Oslo into the database. You can enter the data into the Event subdatasheet shown in Figure B-24, or enter the records directly into the Events datasheet by opening the Events table datasheet. If you enter the records into the Events datasheet, remember that the CityID field value for Oslo is 1.

f. Open the Countries datasheet, expand all records so that all of the cities for each country as well as all of the events for Oslo appear. Print the expanded datasheet.

g. Close the Countries datasheet, close the Baltic-B database, then exit Access.

FIGURE B-24

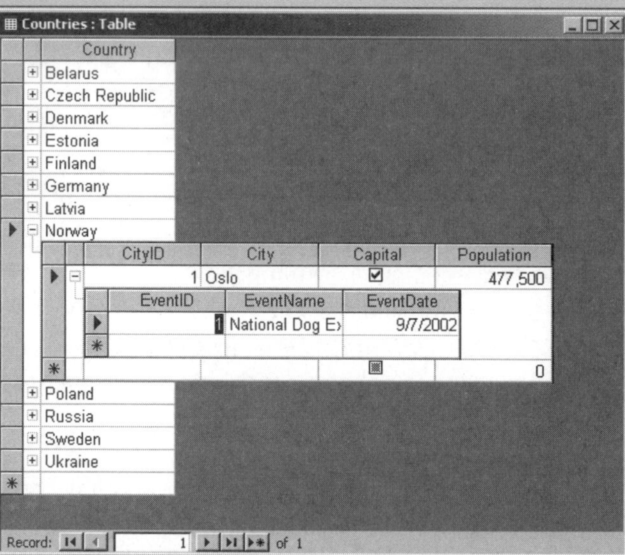

Visual Workshop

Open the **MediaLoft-B** database from the drive and folder where your Project Files are located. Create a query based on the Music Inventory table that displays the datasheet shown in Figure B-25. Notice that only the Jazz category is displayed and that the records are sorted in a descending order on the Retail field. Change the Title of the first record to include your last name, then print the datasheet. Save the query as **Jazz Selections** in the MediaLoft-B database.

FIGURE B-25

Jazz Selections : Select Query

Category	Retail	Artist	Title	Tracks
Jazz	$15.00	Connick Jr., Harry	When Harry Met Sally	11
Jazz	$13.00	Sandborn, David	Closeup	10
Jazz	$10.00	Mangione, Chuck	The Best of Chuck Mangione	10
	$0.00			0

Record: 1 of 3

Access 2002

Using Forms

Objectives

- ► Plan a form
- MOUS ► Create a form
- MOUS ► Move and resize controls
- MOUS ► Modify labels
- MOUS ► Modify text boxes
- MOUS ► Modify tab order
- MOUS ► Enter and edit records
- MOUS ► Insert an image

A **form** is an Access database object that allows you to present information in a format that makes the task of entering and editing data quick and easy. Forms are the primary object used to find, enter, and edit data. Although the datasheet view of a table or query can be used to navigate, enter, and edit data, all of the fields for one record are sometimes not visible unless you scroll left or right. A form solves that problem by allowing you to design the layout of fields on the screen, and typically displays the data for only one record at a time. A form also supports graphical elements such as pictures, buttons, and tabs, which make the form's arrangement of data easy to understand and use. Fellow employees are excited about the MediaLoft music inventory database. They have asked Kelsey Lang to create a form to make it easier to access, enter, and update inventory data.

Access 2002

Planning a Form

Properly organized and well-designed forms make a tremendous difference in the productivity of the end user. Since forms are the primary object used to enter and edit data, time spent planning a form is time well spent. Forms are often built to match a **source document** (for example, an employment application or a medical history form) to facilitate fast and accurate data entry. Now, however, it is becoming more common to type data directly into the database rather than first recording it on paper. Therefore, form design considerations, such as clearly labeled fields and appropriate formatting, are extremely important. Other form design considerations include how the user tabs from field to field, and what type of **control** is used to display the data. See Table C-1 for more information on form controls. Kelsey considers the following form design considerations when planning her Music Inventory form.

Details

- **Determine the overall purpose of the form**
  Interview the users to determine how the form will be used. Name your form with its specific purpose such as "Music Inventory Entry Form" rather than a generic name such as "Music."

- **Determine the underlying record source**
  The **record source** is defined by either a table or query object. The record source determines the data that the form will display.

- **Gather the source documents used to design your form**
  It's a good idea to sketch the form by hand, making sure that you list every element, including fields, text, and graphics that you want the form to display.

- **Determine the best type of control to use for each item on the form**
  Figures C-1 and C-2 show examples of several controls. **Bound controls** display data from the underlying record source and are also used to edit and enter data. **Unbound controls** do not change from record to record and exist only to clarify and enhance the appearance of the form.

TABLE C-1: Form Controls

name	used to:	bound or unbound
Label	Provide consistent descriptive text as you navigate from record to record; the label is the most common type of unbound control	Unbound
Text box	Display, edit, or enter data for each record from an underlying record source; the text box is the most common type of bound control	Bound
List box	Display a list of possible data entries	Bound
Combo box	Display a list of possible data entries for a field, and also provide a text box for an entry from the keyboard; a combination of the list box and text box controls	Bound
Tab control	Create a three-dimensional aspect to a form	Unbound
Check box	Display "yes" or "no" answers for a field; if the box is checked, it means "yes"	Bound
Toggle button	Display "yes" or "no" answers for a field; if the button is pressed, it means "yes"	Bound
Option button	Display a choice for a field	Bound
Option group	Display and organize choices (usually presented as option buttons) for a field	Bound
Bound object frame	Display OLE (Object Linking and Embedding) data, such as a picture	Bound
Unbound object frame	Display a picture or clip art image that doesn't change from record to record	Unbound
Line and Rectangle	Draw lines and rectangles on the form	Unbound
Command button	Provide an easy way to initiate a command or run a macro	Unbound

FIGURE C-1: Form controls

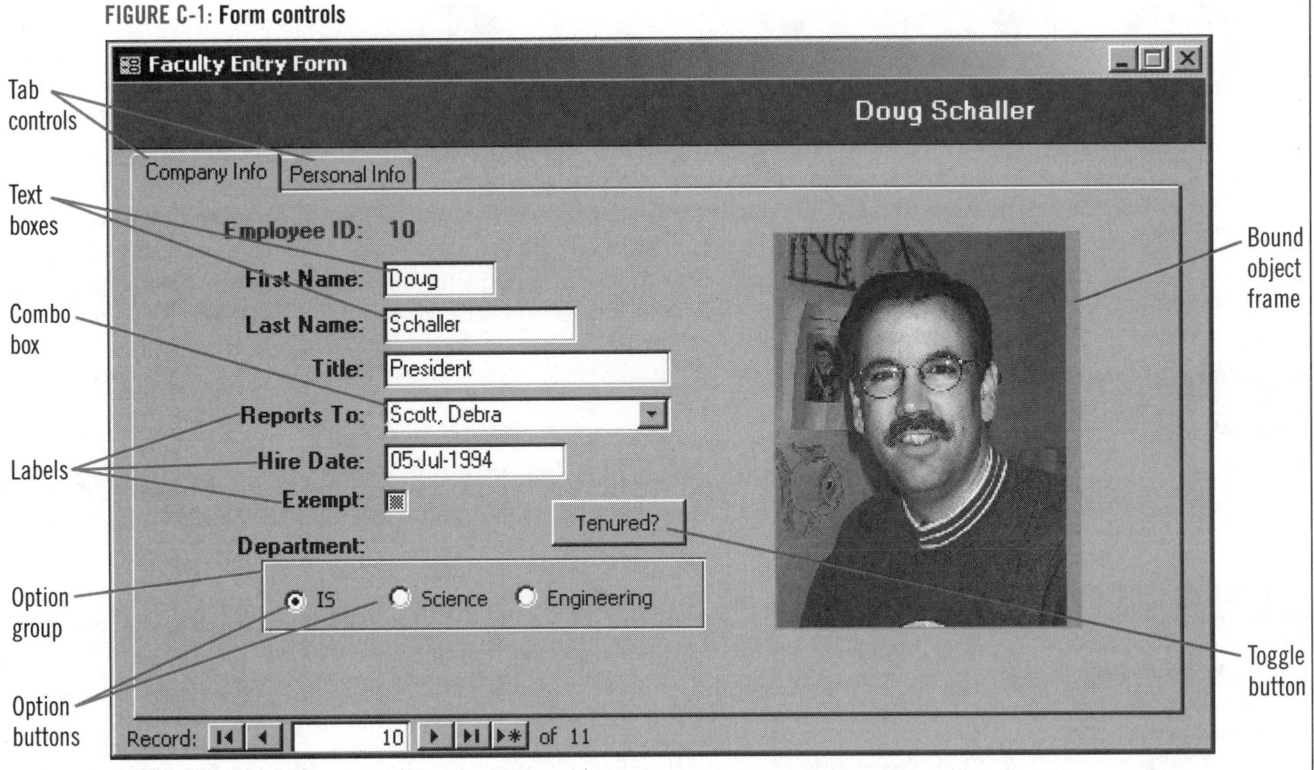

FIGURE C-2: Form controls

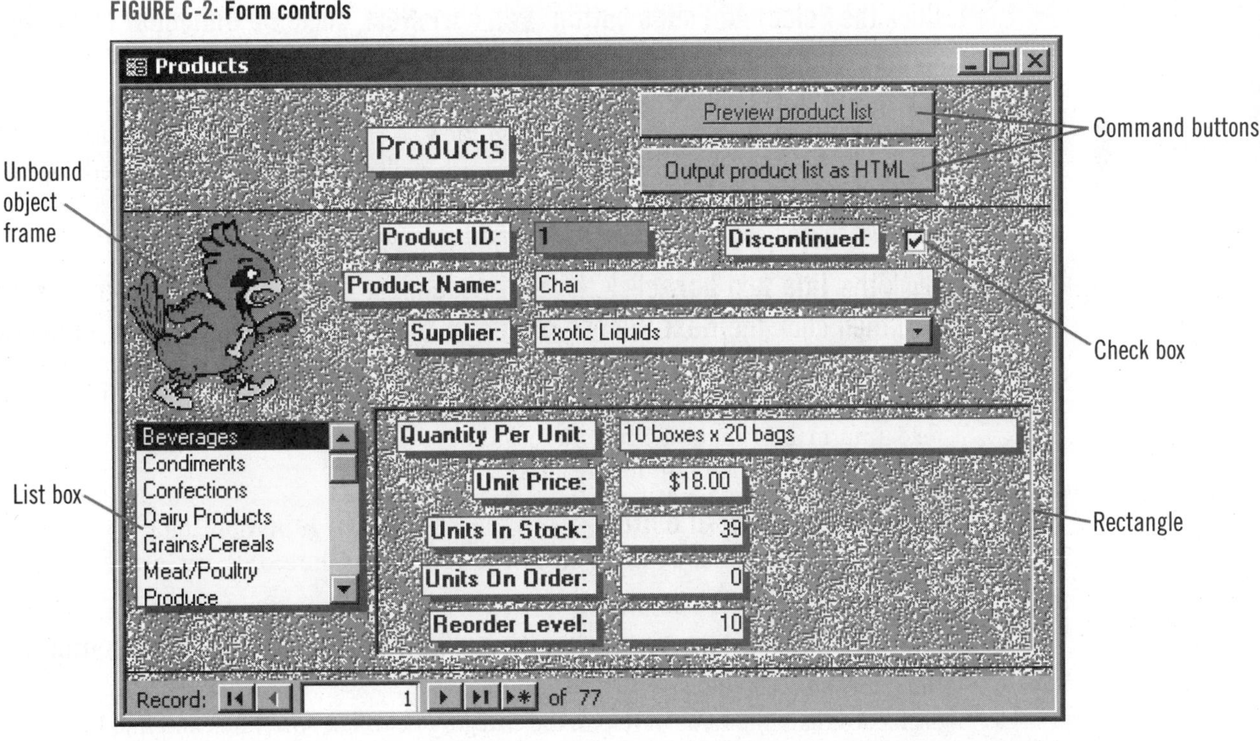

Access 2002

Creating a Form

There are many ways to create a form. You can create a form from scratch using **Form Design View**, or you can use the **Form Wizard** to provide guided steps for the form development process. The Form Wizard prompts you to select the record source for the form, choose an overall layout, choose a style, and title the form. The Form Wizard is an easy way to create an initial version of a form. Table C-2 summarizes the ways to create a form. No matter what technique is used to create a form, you use Form Design View to modify an existing form object. Kelsey made some notes on how she'd like the final Music Inventory form arranged. Now she uses the Form Wizard to get started.

Steps

QuickTip

You can also double-click the Create form by using wizard option in the database window to start the Form Wizard.

1. Start Access, click the **More files** link in the New File task pane, then open the **MediaLoft-C** database from the drive and folder where your New File Project Files are located
2. Click **Forms** on the Objects bar in the MediaLoft-C Database window, then click the **New button** on the database window toolbar
   The New Form dialog box opens, presenting the various techniques used to create a new form.
3. Click **Form Wizard** in the New Form dialog box, click the **Choose the table or query where the object's data comes from list arrow**, click **Music Inventory**, then click **OK**
   The Music Inventory table will serve as the record source for this form. If this database contained multiple tables or queries, these additional objects would have been presented as well as the Music Inventory table.
4. Click the **Select All Fields button** >>, click **Next**, click the **Columnar layout option button**, click **Next**, click the **Standard** style, click **Next**, then click **Finish** to accept the title and to open the form to view or enter information
   The Music Inventory form opens in **Form View**, as shown in Figure C-3. Descriptive labels appear in the first column, and text boxes that display data from the underlying record source appear in the second column. A check box control displays the Yes/No data in the PeoplesChoice field. You can enter, edit, find, sort, and filter records using a form.
5. Click the **Title text box**, click the **Sort Ascending button** on the Form View toolbar, then click the **Next Record button** in the Record Navigation buttons four times to move to the fifth record
   Abbey Road is the fifth record when the records are sorted in ascending order by the Title field. Information about the current record number and total number of records appears in the Record Navigation buttons area.
6. Click the **Last Record button** in the Record Navigation buttons
   World Café by the Tree Frogs is the last record when the records are sorted in ascending order by the Title field.
7. Click **Rap** in the Category text box, then click the **Filter By Selection button** on the Form View toolbar
   Six records have the value of Rap in the Category field. The sort, filter, and find buttons work the same way in a form as they do in a datasheet.
8. Close the Music Inventory form
   The last sort order is automatically saved when you close a form. Filters are automatically removed when you close a form just as they are for a datasheet.

FIGURE C-3: Music Inventory form

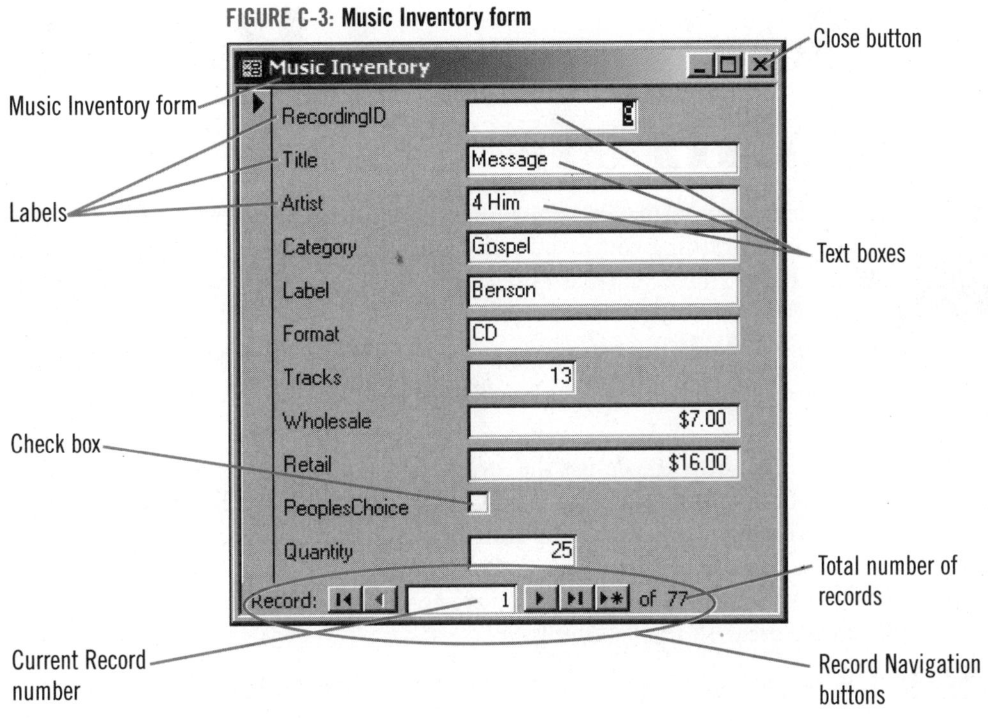

Access 2002

TABLE C-2: Form creation techniques

technique	description
Design View	Provides a layout screen in which the form developer has complete control over the data, layout, and formatting choices that will be displayed by the form. Since Form Design View is the most powerful and flexible technique used to create a form, it is also the most complex. Form Design View is also used to modify all existing forms, regardless of how they were created.
Form Wizard	Provides a guided series of steps to create a form. Prompts for record source, layout, style, and title.
AutoForm	Instantly creates a form that displays all the fields in the chosen record source. There are five different AutoForm options (Columnar, Tabular, Datasheet, PivotTable, and PivotChart) that correspond to five different form layouts in the New Form dialog box.
Chart Wizard	Provides a guided series of steps to create a graphical arrangement of data in the form of a business chart such as a bar, column, line, or pie chart that is placed on a form.
PivotTable Wizard	Provides a guided series of steps to create a summarized arrangement of data in a PivotTable View of a form. Fields used for the column and row headings determine how the data is grouped and summarized.

Using the AutoForm button

You can quickly create a form by clicking a table or query object in the Database window, then clicking the New Object: AutoForm button on the Database toolbar. The New Object: AutoForm button offers no prompts or dialog boxes; it instantly creates a columnar form that displays all the fields in the selected table or query.

Access 2002

Moving and Resizing Controls

After you create a form, you can work in Form Design View to modify the size, location, and appearance of existing controls. Form Design View also allows you to add or delete controls. Kelsey moves and resizes the controls on the form to improve the layout.

Trouble?

Be sure you open the Design View of the Music Inventory form and not the Music Inventory table.

1. Click the **Music Inventory form**, click the **Design button** on the database window toolbar, then click the **Maximize button** for the form
   Maximizing the form makes it easier to modify the form. In Form Design View, several elements that help you design the form may automatically appear. The **Toolbox toolbar** contains buttons that allow you to add controls to the form. The **field list** contains the fields in the record source. The vertical and horizontal rulers help you position controls on the form. These items are shown in Figure C-4. You work with the Toolbox and field list when you add or change existing controls. If you are not working with the Toolbox or the field list you can toggle them off to unclutter your screen.

QuickTip

Press [F8] to open the field list.

2. If the Toolbox toolbar is visible, click the **Toolbox button** on the Form Design toolbar to toggle it off, and if the field list is visible, click the **Field List button** on the Form Design toolbar to toggle it off
   Before moving, resizing, deleting, or changing a control in any way, you must select it.
3. Click the **PeoplesChoice check box**
   Sizing handles appear in the corners and on the edges of selected controls. When you work with controls, the mouse pointer shape is very important. Pointer shapes are summarized in Table C-3.

QuickTip

If you make a mistake, click the Undo button and try again. In Form Design View, you can undo up to 20 actions.

4. Point to the selected **PeoplesChoice check box** so that the pointer changes to, then drag the control so that it is positioned to the right of the RecordingID text box and the right edge of the check box is at the **4.5 inch** mark on the horizontal ruler
   The form will automatically widen to accommodate the new position for the check box. Also, when you move a bound control, such as a text box or check box, the accompanying unbound label moves with it. The field name for the selected control appears in the **Object list box**.

QuickTip

If you undo too many actions, click Edit on the menu bar, then click Redo.

5. Select and move the **Quantity** and **Tracks text boxes** using the pointer to match their final locations as shown in Figure C-5
   Moving a text box automatically moves its associated label. If you want to move only the text box or only the label, you would use the mouse pointer. Resizing controls also improves the design of the form.

QuickTip

You can move controls one **pixel** (picture element) at a time by pressing [Ctrl] and an arrow key. You can resize controls one pixel at a time by pressing [Shift] and an arrow key.

6. Click the **Retail text box**, use the ↔ pointer to drag the middle-right edge sizing handle left to the **2 inch** mark on the horizontal ruler, click the **Wholesale text box**, then use the ↔ pointer to drag the middle-right edge sizing handle left to the **2 inch** mark
   Moving and resizing controls requires great concentration and mouse control. Don't worry if your screen doesn't *precisely* match the figure, but *do* make sure that you understand how to use the move and resize mouse pointers used in Form Design View. Precision and accuracy naturally develop with practice, but even experienced form designers regularly rely on the Undo button.
7. Click the **Form View button** on the Form Design toolbar to view the final form as shown in Figure C-6

FIGURE C-4: Design View of the Music Inventory form

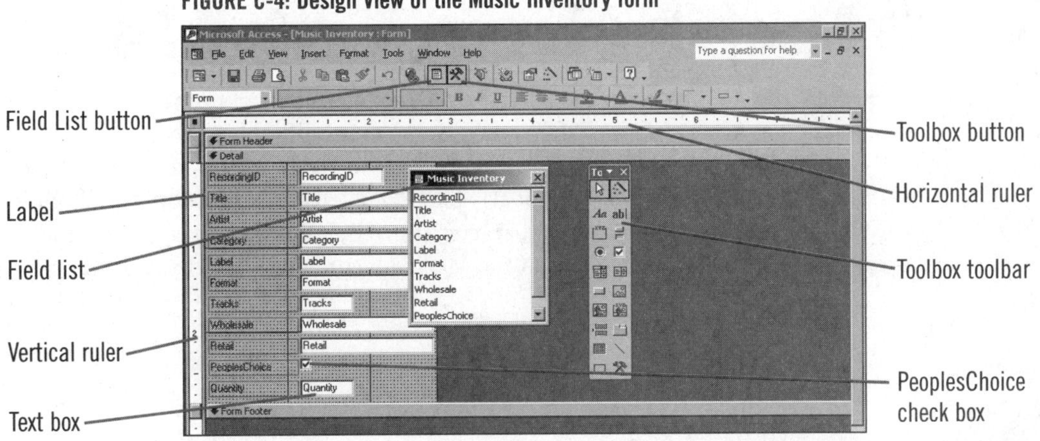

FIGURE C-5: Controls have been moved

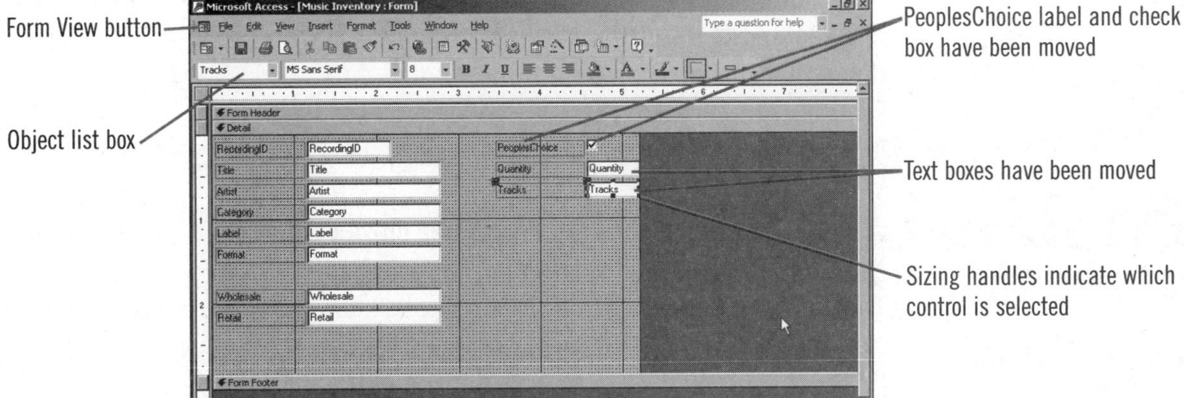

FIGURE C-6: Reorganized Music Inventory form

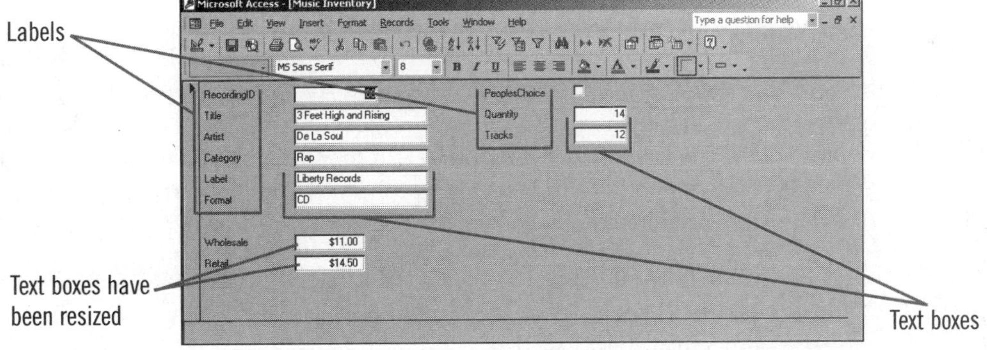

TABLE C-3: Form Design View mouse pointer shapes

shape	when does this shape appear?	action
	When you point to any unselected control on the form (the default mouse pointer)	Single-clicking with this mouse pointer *selects* a control
	When you point to the edge of a selected control (but not when you are pointing to a sizing handle)	Dragging this mouse pointer moves all selected controls
	When you point to the larger sizing handle in the upper-left corner of a selected control	Dragging this mouse pointer *moves only the single control* where the pointer is currently positioned, not other controls that may also be selected
	When you point to any sizing handle (except the larger one in the upper-left corner)	Dragging this mouse pointer *resizes* the control

Access 2002

Modifying Labels

When you create a form with the Form Wizard, it places a label to the left of each text box that displays the name of the field. Often, you'll want to modify those labels to be more descriptive or user-friendly. You can modify a label control by directly editing it in Form Design View, or you can make the change in the property sheet of the label. The **property sheet** is a comprehensive listing of all **properties** (characteristics) that have been specified for that control.  Kelsey modifies the labels of the Music Inventory form to be more descriptive.

Steps

1. **Click the Design View button on the Form View toolbar, click the RecordingID label to select it, click between the g and I in the RecordingID label, then press [Spacebar] to insert a space**

   Directly editing labels in Form Design View is tricky because you must single-click the label to select it, then precisely click where you want to edit it. If you double-click the label, you will open its property sheet.

2. **Click the Title label, click the Properties button on the Form Design toolbar, then click the Format tab, as shown in Figure C-7**

   The **Caption** property controls the text displayed by the label control. The property can be found on either the Format or the All tabs. The All tab presents a complete list of all the properties for a control.

3. **Click to the left of Title in the Caption property, type Recording, press [Spacebar], then click to toggle the property sheet off**

   Don't be overwhelmed by the number of properties available for each control on the form. Over time, you may want to learn about most of these properties, but in the beginning you'll be able to make the vast majority of the property changes through menu and toolbar options rather than by accessing the property sheet itself. For example, you may wish to right-align the labels in the first column so that they are closer to their respective text boxes. You could directly modify the Text Align property in the property sheet for each label, or make the same property changes using the Formatting (Form/Report) toolbar.

4. **Click the Recording ID label, then click the Align Right button on the Formatting (Form/Report) toolbar**

   The Recording ID label caption is now much closer to its associated text box. See Table C-4 for a list of techniques to quickly select several controls so that you can apply alignment and formatting changes to more than one control simultaneously.

5. **Click the 0.5 inch mark on the horizontal ruler to select the first column of controls as shown in Figure C-8, then click**

   All the labels in the first column are right-aligned.

6. **Click the Save button on the Form Design toolbar, then click the Form View button on the Form Design toolbar to view the changes in Form View**

Trouble?

Be sure to modify the Title *label* control and not the Title *text box* control. Text box controls do not have a Caption property.

QuickTip

To discard all changes that you have made to a form or report in Design View and return to the last saved version of the object, click File on the menu bar, then click Revert.

FIGURE C-7: Examining the property sheet for a label

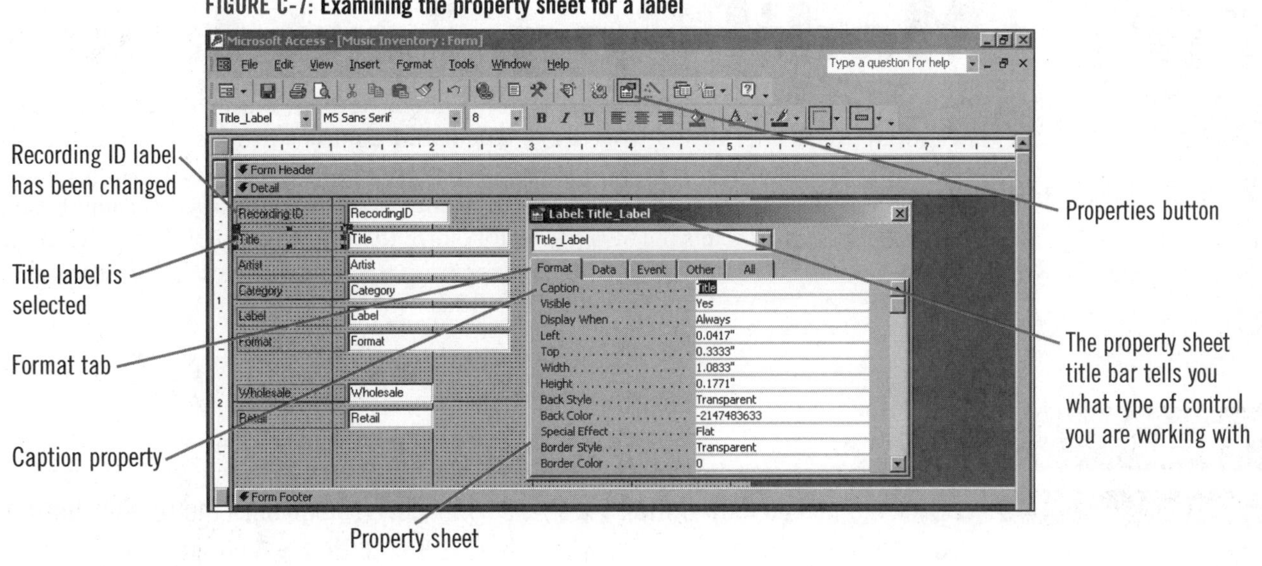

FIGURE C-8: Selecting several labels at the same time

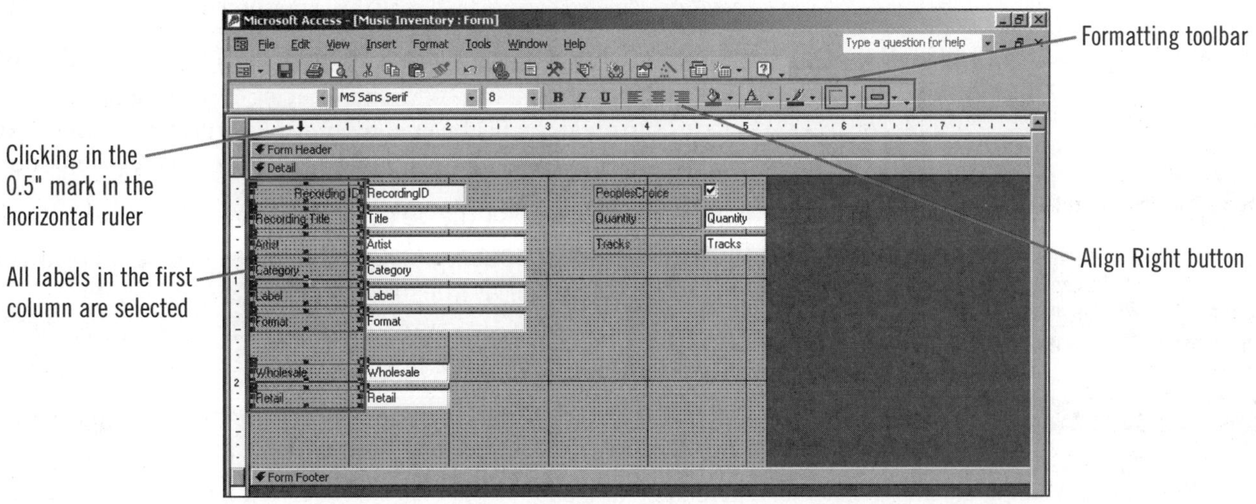

Access 2002

TABLE C-4: Selecting more than one control

technique	description
Click, [Shift]+click	Click a control, then press and hold [Shift] while clicking other controls; each one is selected
Drag a selection box	Drag a selection box (an outline box you create by dragging the pointer in Form Design View); every control that is in or is touched by the edges of the box is selected
Click in the ruler	Click in either the horizontal or vertical ruler to select all controls that intersect the selection line
Drag in the ruler	Drag through either the horizontal or vertical ruler to select all controls that intersect the selection line as it is dragged through the ruler

Modifying Text Boxes

Text boxes are generally used to display data from underlying fields and are therefore *bound* to that field. A text box control may also serve as a **calculated control** when it stores an **expression**, a combination of symbols that calculates a result. Sample expressions include calculating the current page number, determining the current date, calculating a grade point average, or manipulating text values. Kelsey wants the Music Inventory form to calculate the profit for each record. She creates a calculated control by entering an expression within a text box to find the difference between the values in the Retail and Wholesale fields.

Steps

QuickTip

The Toolbox toolbar may be floating or docked on the edge of your screen. Drag the title bar of a floating toolbar to move it to a convenient location.

1. Click the **Design View button** on the Form View toolbar, click the **Toolbox button** on the Form View toolbar, then click the **Text Box button** on the Toolbox toolbar
   The mouse pointer changes to .
2. Click just below the **Retail text box** on the form, then use to move the new text box and label control into the position shown in Figure C-9
   Adding a new text box automatically added a new label with the default caption Text22:. The number in the default caption depends on how many controls you have previously added to the form. You can create the calculated control by typing the expression directly in the text box.
3. Click **Unbound** in the new text box, type **=[Retail]-[Wholesale]**, then press **[Enter]**
   All expressions start with an equal sign (=). When referencing a field name within an expression, square brackets surround the field name. You must type the field name exactly as it appears in the Table Design View, but you do not need to worry about capitalization.

Trouble?

If your calculated control did not work, return to Design View, click the calculated control, press [Delete], then repeat steps 1 through 4.

4. Click the **Text22: label** to select it, click the **Text22: label** again to edit it, double-click **Text22**, type **Profit** as the new caption, press **[Enter]**, then click the **Form View button** to view the changes as shown in Figure C-10
   The Profit for the first record is calculated as $3.50 and displays as 3.5. Property changes such as applying a Currency format can be made in Form View.

QuickTip

Press [F4] to open the property sheet.

5. Click **3.5** in the Profit text box, click **View** on the menu bar, then click **Properties**
   Monetary values such as the calculated Profit field should be right-aligned and display with a dollar sign and two digits to the right of the decimal point.
6. Click the **Format tab** in the Text Box property sheet if not already selected, click the **Format property list arrow**, click **Currency**, scroll through the property sheet to display the **Text Align property**, click the **Text Align property list arrow**, then click **Right**
   A short description of the selected property appears in the status bar. Some changes to a form, such as moving, deleting, or adding controls, can only be accomplished in Form Design View.
7. Click , click to toggle off the property sheet, use to switch the position of the **Retail and Wholesale text boxes**, move and align the **Profit label** under the Wholesale label, resize the **Profit text box** to be the same size as the Wholesale text box, then click
   The final form is shown in Figure C-11.

FIGURE C-9: Adding a text box

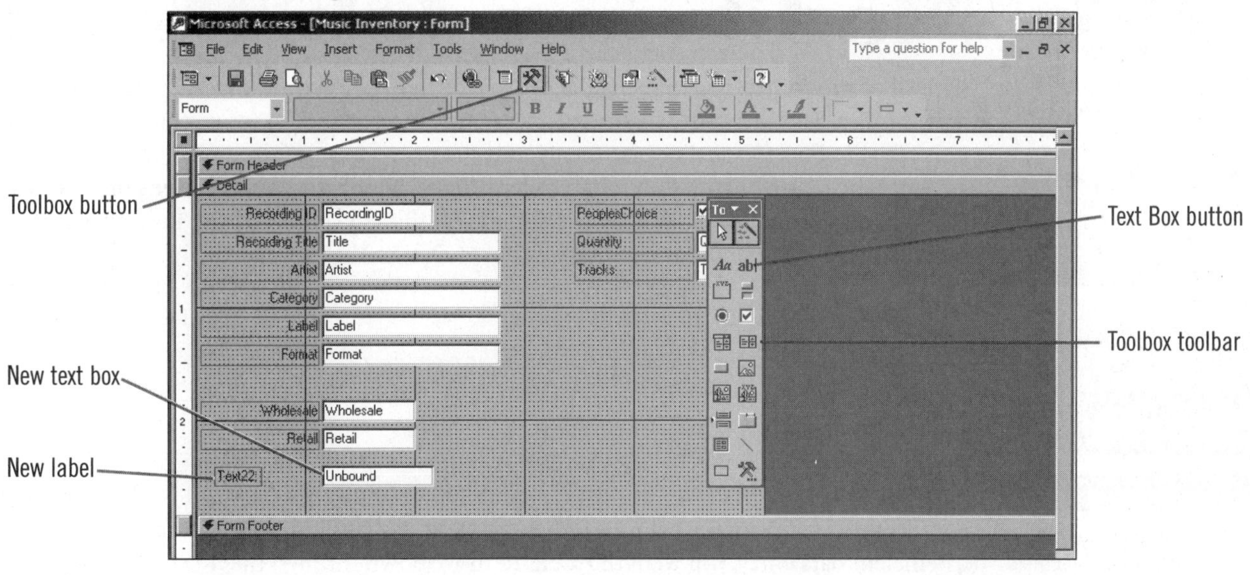

FIGURE C-10: Displaying a calculation

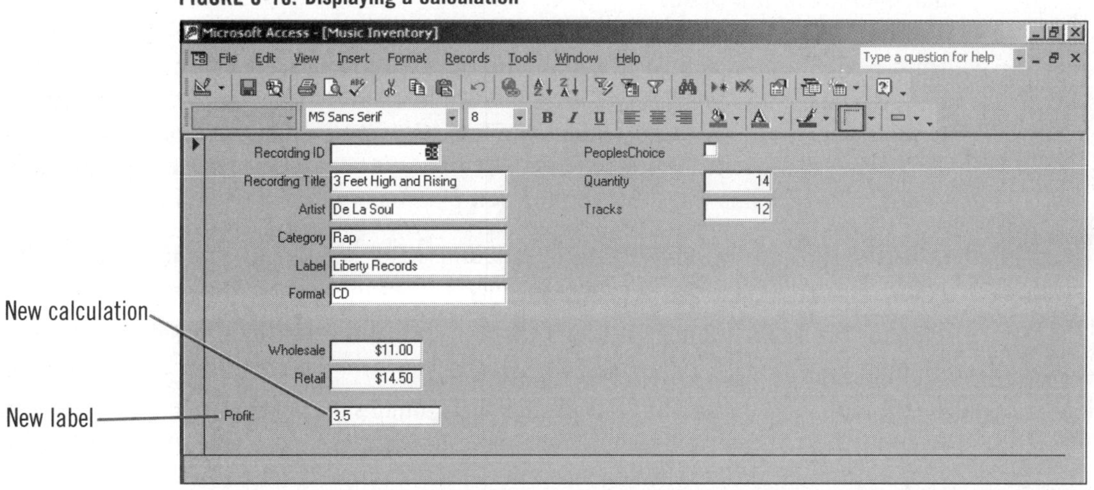

FIGURE C-11: Updated Music Inventory form

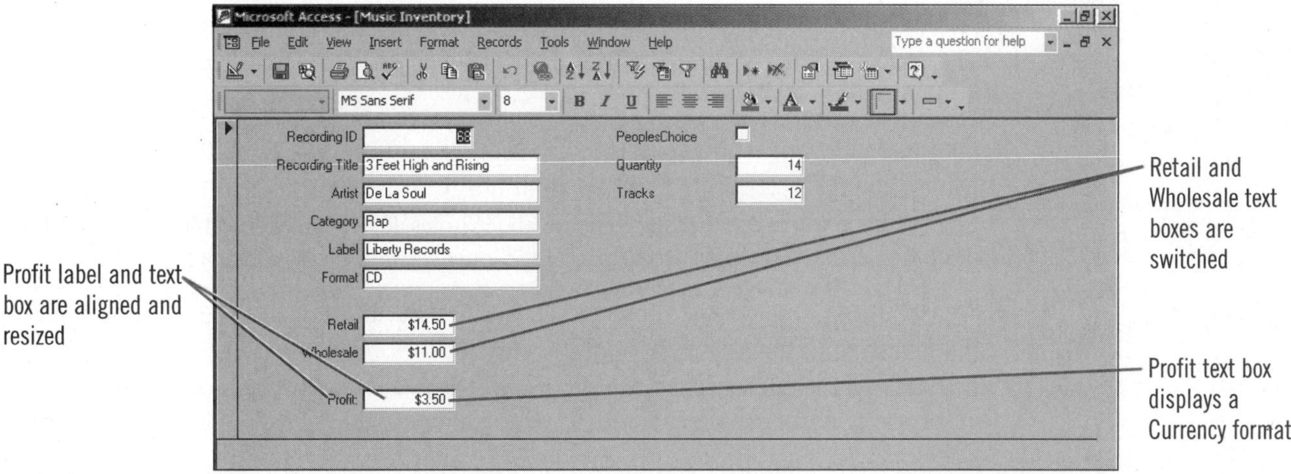

Access 2002

Access 2002

Modifying Tab Order

Once all of the controls have been added, moved, and resized on the form, you'll want to check the tab order. The **tab order** is the order in which the **focus** (the active control) moves as you press [Tab] in Form View. Because the form is the primary object by which users will view, edit, and enter data, careful attention to tab order is essential to maintain the user's productivity and satisfaction with the form. Kelsey checks the tab order of the Music Inventory form, then changes the tab order as necessary in Form Design View.

QuickTip

You can also press [Enter] to move the focus from field to field in a form.

QuickTip

Click the Auto Order button in the Tab Order dialog box to automatically set a left-to-right, top-to-bottom tab order for the current arrangement of controls on the form.

QuickTip

In Form Design View, press [Ctrl][.] to switch to Form view. In Form View, press [Ctrl][,] to switch to Form Design View.

1. **Press [Tab] 11 times watching the focus move through the bound controls of the form**
   Currently, focus moves back and forth between the left and right columns of controls. For efficient data entry, you want the focus to move down through the first column of text boxes before moving to the second column.

2. **Click the Design View button on the Form View toolbar, click View on the menu bar, then click Tab Order**
   The Tab Order dialog box allows you to change the tab order of controls in three sections: Form Header, Detail, and Form Footer. You can expand these sections in Form Design View by dragging the bottom edge of a section down to open it. Right now, all of the controls are positioned in the form's Detail section. See Table C-5 for more information on form sections. To change tab sequence, drag the **row selector**, positioned to the left of the field name, up or down. A black line will show you the new placement of the field in the list.

3. **Click the Retail row selector in the Custom Order list, drag it up and position it just below Format, click the Wholesale row selector, drag it under Retail, click the Tracks row selector, drag it under Quantity, click the Text22 row selector, then drag it under Wholesale, as shown in Figure C-12**
   Text22 represents the name of the text box that contains the profit calculation. If you wanted to give it a more descriptive name, you could have changed its Name property. The **Name property** for a text box is analogous to the Caption property for a label.

4. **Click OK in the Tab Order dialog box, click the Save button, then click the Form View button on the Form Design toolbar**
   Although nothing visibly changes on the form, the tab order is different.

5. **Press [Enter] 11 times to move through the fields of the form with the new tab order**
   The focus now moves through all of the text boxes of the first column, and then moves through the second column.

6. **Continue pressing [Enter] until you reach the Retail value of the second record (which should be $15.00), type 16, then press [Enter]**
   Changing the value in either the Retail or the Wholesale fields will automatically recalculate the value in the Profit field. Recording ID 55 now shows a profit of $6.00.

7. **Press [Enter] to move the focus to the Profit field, attempt to type 77, and observe the message in the status bar**
   Even though the calculated control can receive the focus, its value cannot be directly edited in Form view. As the message indicates, its value is bound to the expression [Retail]-[Wholesale].

FIGURE C-12: Tab Order dialog box

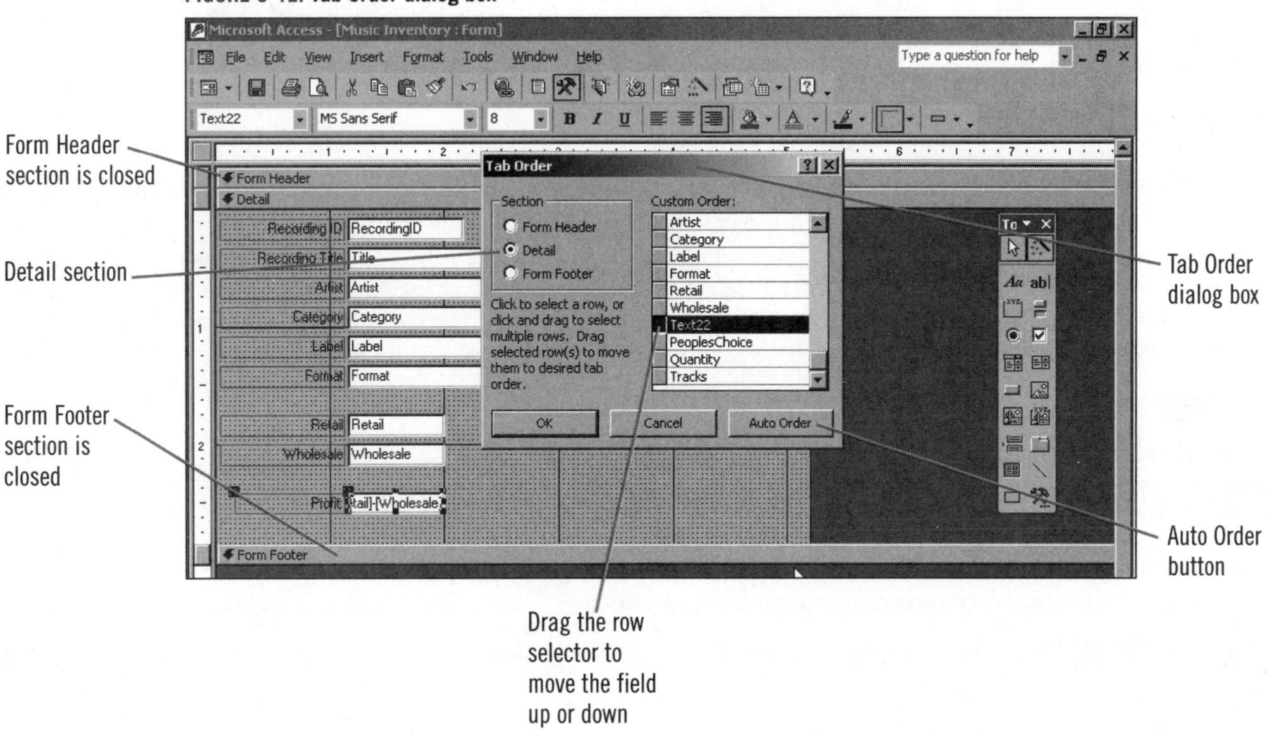

TABLE C-5: Form sections

section	description
Form Header	Controls placed in the Form Header section print only once at the top of the printout; by default, this section is closed in Form Design View
Detail	Controls placed in the Detail section display in Form View and print once for every record in the underlying table or query object; all controls created by the Form Wizard are placed in this section
Form Footer	Controls placed in the Form Footer section print only once at the end of the printout; by default, this section is closed in Form Design View

Access 2002

Entering and Editing Records

The most important reasons for using a form are to find, enter, or edit records in the underlying record source. You can also print a form, but printing all records in a form layout often produces a very long printout because of the vertical orientation of the fields. Kelsey uses the Music Inventory form to add a new record to the Music Inventory table. Then she prints only the new record.

Steps

QuickTip
A New Record button is also located on the Navigation buttons.

QuickTip
To enter a check in a check box press [Spacebar].

Trouble?
Don't click the Print button on the Form View toolbar unless you want *all* of the records to print.

QuickTip
As the confirmation message indicates, you cannot undo the deletion of a record.

1. Click the **New Record button** on the Form View toolbar
   A new, blank record is displayed. The Recording ID field is an AutoNumber field that will automatically increment when you begin to enter data. The Specific Record box indicates the current record number.
2. Press **[Tab]** to move the focus to the **Recording Title text box**, type **Your Name Dancers** to insert your name in the record, then enter the rest of the information shown in Figure C-13
   The Profit text box shows the calculated result of $6.00. The new record is stored as record 78 in the Music Inventory table.
3. Click **File** on the menu bar, click **Print** to open the Print dialog box, click the **Selected Record(s) option button** in the Print Range section, then click **OK**
   Forms are also often used to find, edit, or delete existing records in the database.
4. Click the **Recording Title text box**, click the **Find button** on the Form View toolbar to open the Find and Replace dialog box, type **Mermaid Avenue** in the Find What text box, then click **Find Next**
   Record 46 appears behind the Find and Replace dialog box, as shown in Figure C-14.
5. Click **Cancel** in the Find and Replace dialog box, click the **Delete Record button** on the Form View toolbar, then click **Yes** to confirm the deletion
   Forms are also a great way to filter the records to a specific subset of information.
6. Click **Gospel** in the Category text box, click the **Filter By Form button** on the Form View toolbar, click the **Category list arrow**, click **Gospel**, click the **Or tab** in the lower-left corner of the Filter By Form window, click the **Category list arrow**, click **Children**, then click the **Apply Filter button** on the Filter/Sort toolbar
   Eight records were found that matched the Gospel or Children criteria in the Category field.
7. Click the **Print Preview button** on the Form View toolbar, then click the **Last Page button** in the Navigation buttons
   Previewing the records helps to determine how many pages the printout would be. Since about three records print on a page, your printout is three pages long.
8. Click the **Close button** on the Print Preview toolbar, then click the **Remove Filter button** on the Form View toolbar so that all 77 records in the Music Inventory table are redisplayed

FIGURE C-13: Entering a new record into a form

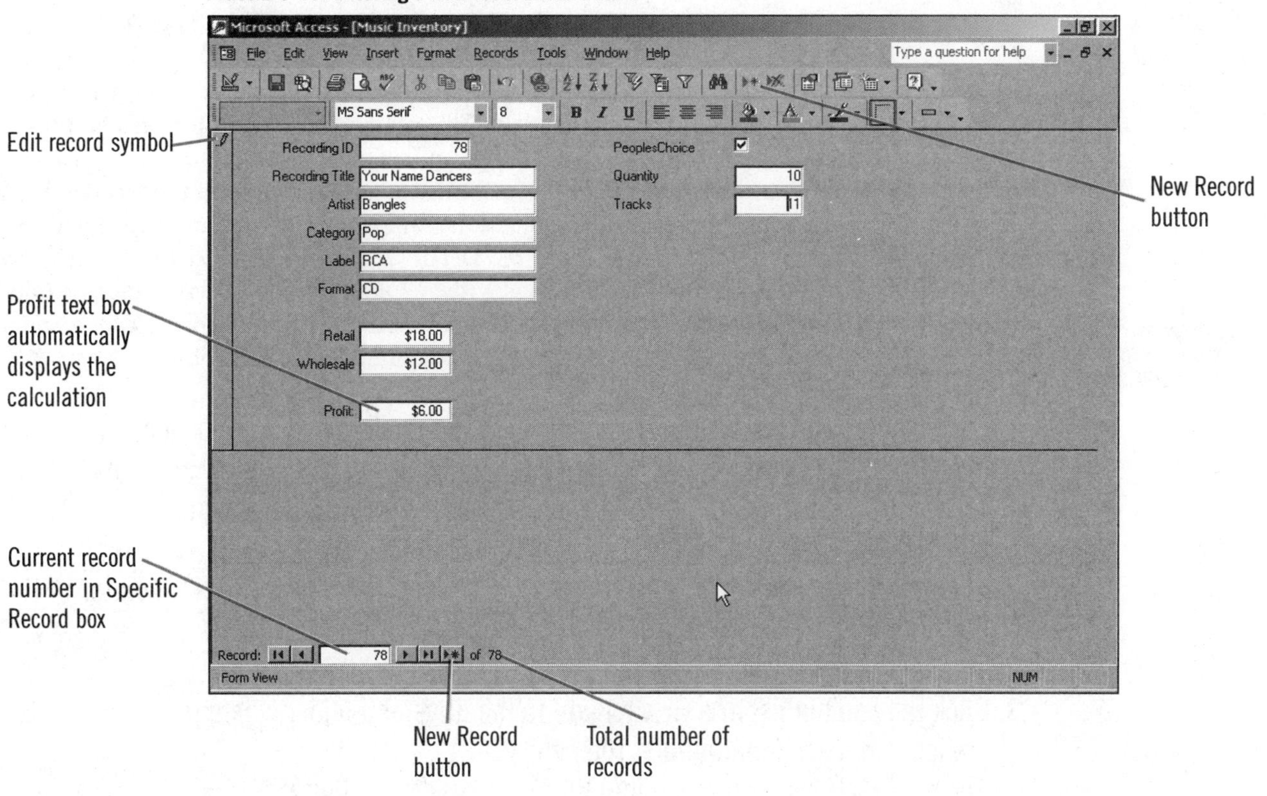

FIGURE C-14: Finding data using a form

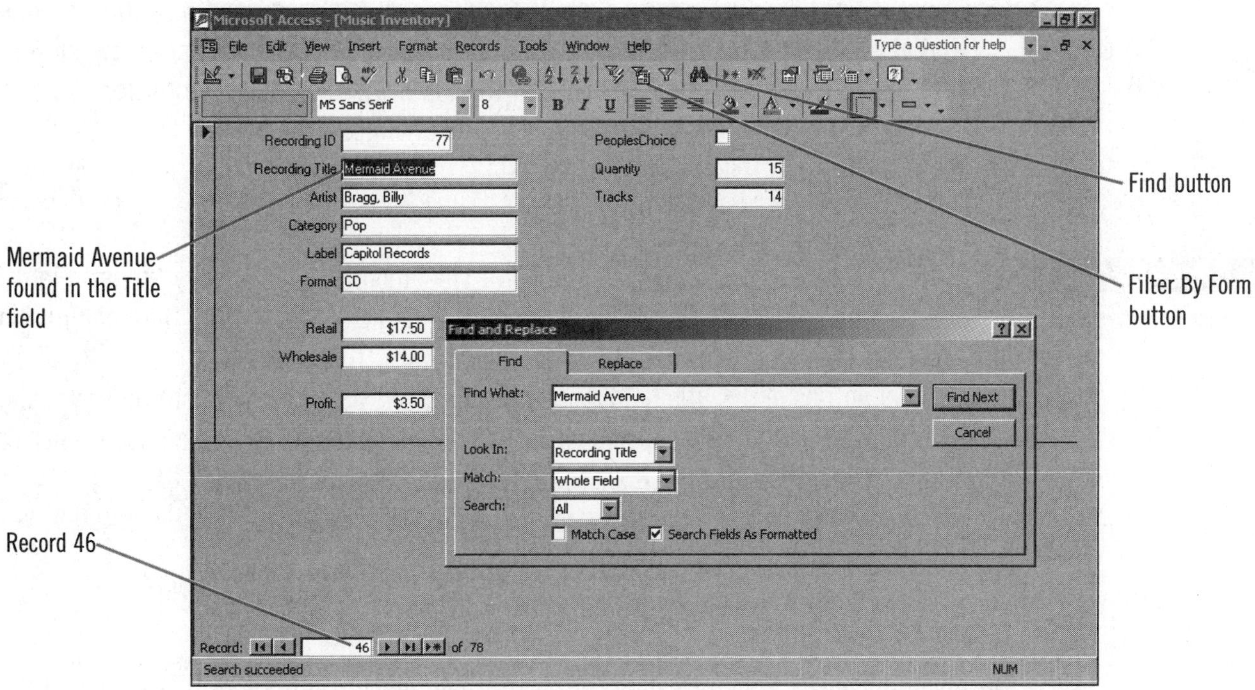

Access 2002

Access 2002

Inserting an Image

Graphic images, such as pictures, a logo, or clip art, can add style and professionalism to a form. Images are added to a form as either bound or unbound controls. The form section in which they are placed is also significant. For example, if you add an **unbound image** such as a company logo to the Form Header section, the image will appear at the top of the form in Form View as well as at the top of a printout. If you add the same unbound image to the Detail section, it would appear multiple times because the Detail section is reproduced once for every record. **Bound images** are tied to a field defined with an OLE Object data type and store multimedia data such as pictures or sound clips. Kelsey adds the MediaLoft logo and a descriptive title to the Form Header section using an unbound image control.

Steps 1 2 3 4

1. Click the **Design View button** on the Form View toolbar, place the pointer on the bottom edge of the **Form Header section** so that the pointer changes to ✛, then drag the bottom of the Form Header section to the **1 inch** mark on the vertical ruler
   The Form Header section is open.
2. Click the **Image button** on the Toolbox toolbar, then click the pointer in the **Form Header section** at the **1 inch** mark on the horizontal ruler
   The Insert Picture dialog box opens.
3. Click the **Look in list arrow**, navigate to the drive and folder where your Project Files are located, click **Smallmedia**, then click **OK**
   The MediaLoft logo is inserted into the Form Header, as shown in Figure C-15. Placing a title in the Form Header section adds a finishing touch to the form.
4. Click the **Label button** on the Toolbox toolbar, click the +A pointer to the right of the **MediaLoft logo** in the Form Header section, type **MediaLoft Music**, then press **[Enter]**
   Labels can be formatted to enhance the appearance on the form.
5. Click the **Font Size list arrow**, click **24**, double-click a **sizing handle** so that the label **MediaLoft Music** is completely displayed, click the **Font/Fore Color list arrow**, click the dark blue box (second from the right on the top row), click the **Save button**, then click the **Form View button** to observe the changes, as shown in Figure C-16
   You can spell check the records to correct any errors. The Spelling dialog box has options to ignore all values in a particular field, ignore a single occurrence of a word, ignore all occurrences of a word, plus other options.
6. Click the **Spelling button** on the Form View toolbar, click **Ignore 'Artist' Field** in the Spelling dialog box as shown in Figure C-17, click **Ignore All** in the Spelling dialog box to skip all occurrences of Ryko, click **Ignore 'Title' Field** to ignore Closeup and all other entries in the Title field, click **Ignore All** to skip all occurrences of Arista, click **Ignore All** to skip all occurrences of Narada, click **Ignore All** to skip all occurrences of Gramaphone, click **Change** to change Recrds to Records, then click **OK**
   To add an entry such as Ryko to the custom dictionary, you would click the Add button in the Spelling dialog box.
7. Find and print the record for RecordingID 78, which displays Your Name Dancers in the Recording Title
8. Close the Music Inventory form, close the MediaLoft-C database, then exit Access

QuickTip

[F7] is the quick keystroke to open the Spelling dialog box.

FIGURE C-15: Adding an image to the Form Header section

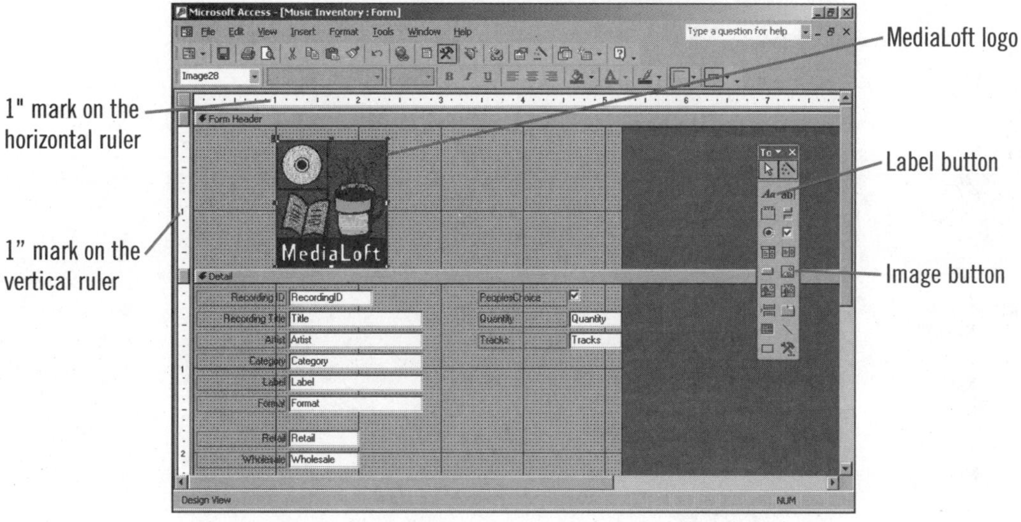

FIGURE C-16: The final Music Inventory form

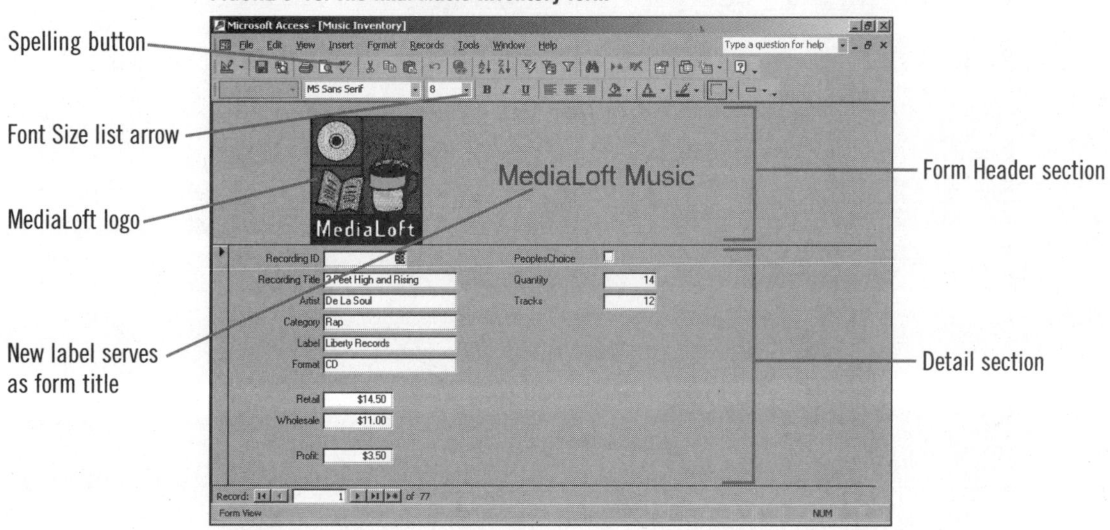

FIGURE-C-17: Spelling dialog box

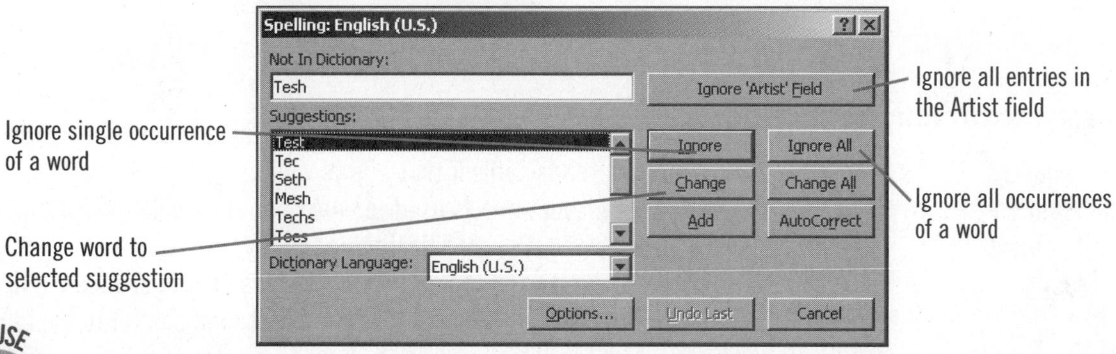

CLUES TO USE

Using the Custom Dictionary

The **custom dictionary** is a supplemental dictionary to which you add words that are spelled correctly, such as proper names, but which are not already stored in the default Access dictionary. Since the custom dictionary file is used across all Office applications on a particular computer, do not add words to it unless you are the only user of that computer.

Access 2002

Practice

▶ Concepts Review

Label each element of Form View shown in Figure C-18.

FIGURE C-18

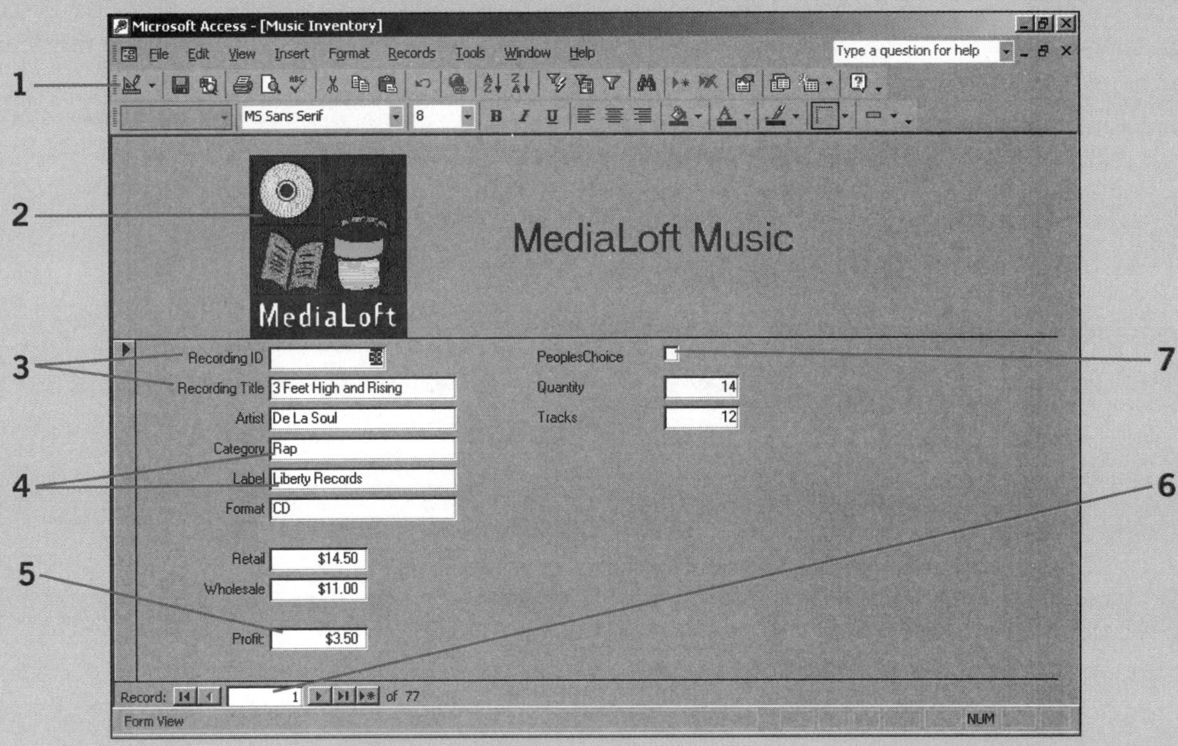

Match each term with the statement that describes it.

8. Sizing handles
9. Detail section
10. Bound control
11. Tab order
12. Form
13. Calculated control

a. An Access database object that allows you to arrange the fields of a record in any layout and is used to enter, edit, and delete records
b. Used on a form to display data from a field
c. Squares that appear in the corners and edges of the selected control
d. The way in which the focus moves from one bound control to the next
e. Uses a text box and an expression to display an answer
f. Controls placed here print once for every record in the underlying table or query object

Practice

Select the best answer from the list of choices.

14. Every element on a form is called a:
- **a.** Property.
- **b.** Control.
- **c.** Piece.
- **d.** Handle.

15. The mouse pointer that is used to resize a control is:
- **a.**
- **b.** 
- **c.**
- **d.**

16. The most common bound control is the:
- **a.** Label.
- **b.** Text box.
- **c.** Combo box.
- **d.** Check box.

17. The most common unbound control is the:
- **a.** Label.
- **b.** Text box.
- **c.** Combo box.
- **d.** Image.

18. The ____________ View is used to move or resize form controls.
- **a.** Form
- **b.** Datasheet
- **c.** Print Preview
- **d.** Design

19. The ____________ control is commonly used to display data on a form from a field with a Yes/No data type.
- **a.** Text box
- **b.** Label
- **c.** Check box
- **d.** Combo box

20. The ____________ dictionary is a supplemental dictionary to which you add words that are spelled correctly, such as proper names.
- **a.** Custom
- **b.** Caption
- **c.** Name
- **d.** User

Skills Review

1. **Plan a form.**
   a. Plan a form to use for entering business contacts by looking at several business cards.
   b. Write down the organization of the fields on the form.
   c. Determine what type of control you will use for each bound field.
   d. Identify the labels you would like to display on the form.
2. **Create a form.**
   a. Start Access and open the **Membership-C** database from the drive and folder where your Project Files are located.
   b. Click the Forms button in the Membership-C Database window, then double-click the Create form by using wizard option.
   c. Base the form on the CONTACTS table, and include all of the fields.
   d. Use a Columnar layout, a Standard style, and title the form **Contact Entry Form**.
   e. Display the form in Form View.
3. **Move and resize controls.**
   a. Open and maximize the Design View window for the Contact Entry Form.
   b. Move the LNAME text box and corresponding label to the right of the FNAME text box.
   c. Move the DUESOWED and DUESPAID text boxes and corresponding labels to the right of the address controls.
   d. Resize the PHONE and ZIP text boxes to be the same size as the CITY text box.
   e. Move the PHONE text box and corresponding label between the FNAME and COMPANY controls. The resulting form should look similar to Figure C-19.

FIGURE C-19

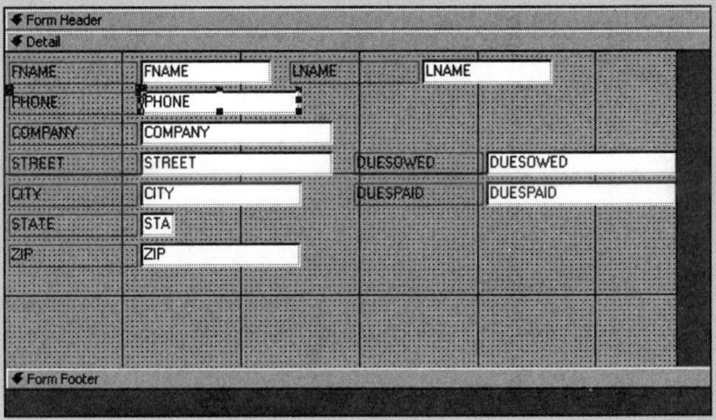

4. **Modify labels.**
   a. Right-align all of the labels. Be careful to right-align the labels, and not the text boxes.
   b. Edit the caption of the FNAME label to **FIRST NAME**, the LNAME label to **LAST NAME**, the DUESOWED label to **DUES OWED**, and the DUESPAID label to **DUES PAID**.
5. **Modify text boxes.**
   a. Add a new text box below the DUESPAID text box.
   b. Type the expression **=[DUESOWED]-[DUESPAID]** in the new unbound text box. (*Hint:* Remember that you must use the *exact field names* as defined in Table Design View in a calculated expression.)
   c. In the property sheet for the new calculated control, change the Format property to Currency.
   d. Right-align the new calculated control.
   e. Change the accompanying label from Text20: to **BALANCE**.
   f. Move and resize the new calculated control and label so that it is aligned beneath the DUESOWED and DUES-PAID controls.
6. **Modify tab order.**
   a. Change the Tab order so that pressing [Tab] moves the focus through the text boxes in the following order: FNAME, LNAME, PHONE, COMPANY, STREET, CITY, STATE, ZIP, DUESOWED, DUESPAID, Text20 (the calculated control).
   b. Save your changes, open the form in Form View, then test the new tab order.

7. **Enter and edit records.**
   a. Use the Contact Entry Form to enter the following new records:

	FIRST NAME	LAST NAME	PHONE	COMPANY	STREET
Record 1	Jane	Eagan	555-1166	Cummins Construction	1515 Maple St.
Record 2	Connie	Sinclaire	555-2277	Motorola	1010 Green St.

	CITY	STATE	ZIP	DUES OWED	DUES PAID
1 con't.	Fontanelle	KS	50033	$50.00	$25.00
2 con't.	Bridgewater	KS	50022	$50.00	$50.00

   b. Find the Connie Sinclaire record, enter your last name in the COMPANY text box, then print that record.
   c. Find the Lois Goode record, enter **IBM** in the COMPANY text box, change Barnes in the STREET field to **your last name**, then print that record.
   d. Filter for all records with a ZIP entry of 64145. How many records did you find? Write the answer on the back of the previous printout.
   e. Sort the filtered 64145 zip code records in ascending order by LAST NAME, change the street name for this record to **your last name**, then print this record.
8. **Insert an image.**
   a. In Form Design View, expand the Form Header section to the 1" mark on the vertical ruler.
   b. Use the Image control to insert the **Hand.bmp** file in the left side of the Form Header. (*Note:* The Hand.bmp file is on the drive and folder where your Project Files are located.)
   c. Centered and below the graphic file, add the label **MEMBERSHIP INFORMATION** in a 24-point font. Be sure to resize the label so that all of the text is visible.
   d. Below the MEMBERSHIP INFORMATION label, add your name as a label.
   e. View the form in Form View, then spell check the records.
   f. Sort the records in descending order based on the COMPANY values. Print only the first record.
   g. Save and close the form, close the database, then exit Access.

Independent Challenge 1

As the office manager of a cardiology clinic, you need to create a data entry form for new patients.

a. Start Access, open the **Clinic-C** database from the drive and folder where your Project Files are located.
b. Using the Form Wizard, create a form that includes all the fields in the Demographics table, using the Columnar layout and Standard style. Title the form **Patient Entry Form**.
c. In Form Design View, move the DOB, Gender, Ins Code, and Entry Date controls to a second column to the right of the existing column. DOB should be next to Last Name.
d. Switch the positions of the State and ZIP controls.

FIGURE C-20

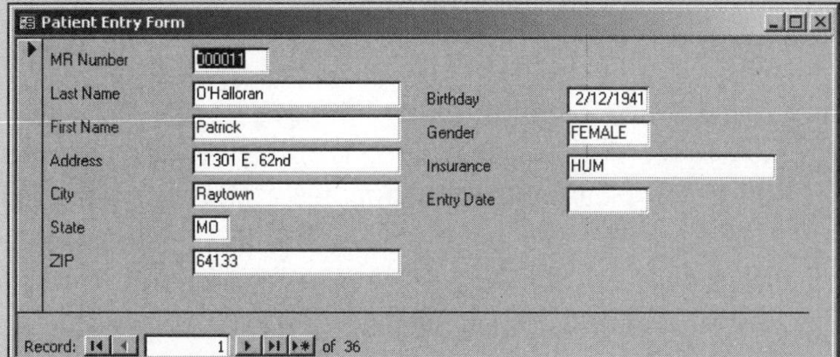

- **e.** Modify the Medical Record Number label to **MR Number**, the Address 1 label to **Address**, the DOB label to **Birthday**, and the Ins Code label to **Insurance**. Be sure to modify the labels, not the text boxes. The final organization of the form is shown in Figure C-20.
- **f.** Change the tab order so that State is before Zip.
- **g.** Use the newly created form to add a record using your own personal information. Enter **2002** for the MR Number, **BCBS** for the Insurance, and **2/1/02** for the Entry Date.
- **h.** Print only the new record that you just added.
- **i.** Save and close the Patient Entry Form, close the Clinic-C database, then exit Access.

► Independent Challenge 2

As office manager of a cardiology clinic, you want to build a form that quickly calculates a height-to-weight ratio value based on information in the Outcomes Data table.

- **a.** Start Access, then open the **Clinic-C** database from the drive and folder where your Project Files are located.
- **b.** Using the Form Wizard, create a form based on the Outcomes Data table with only the following fields: MR#, Height, and Weight.
- **c.** Use the Columnar layout and Standard style, and name the form **Height to Weight Ratio Form**.
- **d.** In Design View, use the Text Box button to add a text box and accompanying label below the Weight text box.
- **e.** Enter the expression **=[Height]/[Weight]** in the unbound text box.
- **f.** Modify the calculated expression's label from Text6: to **Ratio**.
- **g.** Resize the Ratio label so that it is closer to the calculated expression control, then right-align all of the labels.
- **h.** Change the format property of the calculated control to Fixed.
- **i.** Open the Form Header section about 0.5", then add a label to that section with your name as the caption.
- **j.** Save and view the form, then print the form for the record with the MR Number of 006494.
- **k.** Sort the records in descending order by Height, change the value in the Weight field to **200**, then print this record.
- **l.** Close the Height to Weight Ratio Form, close the Clinic-C database, then exit Access.

► Independent Challenge 3

As office manager of a cardiology clinic, you want to build a form to enter new insurance information.

- **a.** Open the **Clinic-C** database from the drive and folder where your Project Files are located.
- **b.** Using the Form Wizard, create a form based on the Insurance Company Information table, and include all of the fields.
- **c.** Use the Columnar layout, Standard style, and accept **Insurance Company Information** as the title.
- **d.** Edit the Caption of the Insurance Company Name label to **Insurance Company**. Be sure to modify the Insurance Company Name label, not the text box.
- **e.** Resize the State text box so that it is the same size as the City text box.
- **f.** Expand the Form Header section, then add the graphic image **Medical.bmp** to the left side of the Form Header section. The Medical.bmp file is in the drive and folder where your Project Files are located.
- **g.** Add a label **Insurance Entry Form** and another for **your name** to the right of the medical clip art in the Form Header section.
- **h.** Increase the size of the Insurance Entry Form label to 18 points. Resize the label to display the entire caption.
- **i.** Switch to Form View, then find the record for the Cigna Insurance Company. Change Sherman in the City field to your last name, then print this record.
- **j.** Filter for all records with a State entry of KS. How many records did you find? Write the answer on the back of the previous printout.
- **k.** Save and close the Insurance Company Information Form, close the Clinic-C database, then exit Access.

Independent Challenge 4

You are on the staff of an economic development team whose goal is to encourage tourism in the Baltic Sea region. You have created an Access database called Baltic-C to track important fields of information for the countries in that region, and will use the Internet to find information about the area and enter it into existing forms.

a. Start Access and open the **Baltic-C** database from the drive and folder where your Project Files are located.

b. Connect to the Internet, then go to www.about.com, www.alltheweb.com, or any general search engine to conduct research for your database. Your goal is to find information for at least one new city record for each country.

c. Open the Countries form. You can enter the data you found on the Internet for each city by using the City fields shown in Figure C-21. This arrangement of data organizes cities within countries using a main form/subform arrangement. The main form contains a single text box tied to the Country field. The subform presents a datasheet of four City fields. Be sure to enter the Population data for that particular city, rather than for the entire country. CityID is an AutoNumber field, so it will automatically increment as you enter the City, Capital, and Population data.

FIGURE C-21

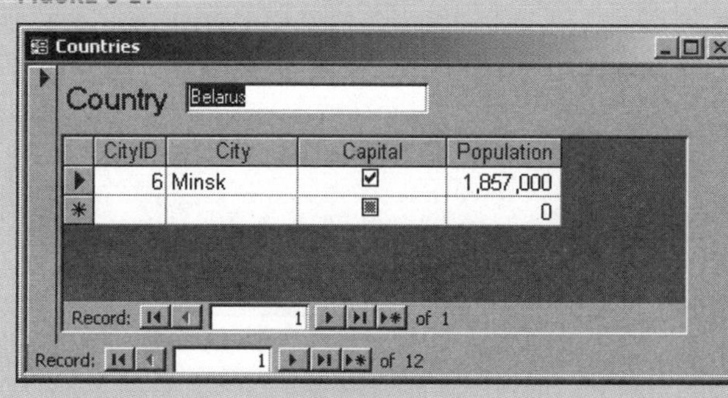

d. Close the Countries form, then open the Countries table datasheet. Click all of the expand buttons to the left of each of the Country records to show the city records that you just entered through the Countries form, then print the expanded datasheet. Close the Countries table.

e. Open the Cities form and find the Olso, Norway record shown in Figure C-22. This form shows another main form/subform arrangement. The main form contains fields that describe the city, whereas the subform contains a datasheet with fields that describe the events for that city.

FIGURE C-22

f. Return to the search engine, and research upcoming tourist events for Copenhagen, Denmark.

g. In the Cities form, find the Copenhagen record, then enter three events for Copenhagen. EventID is an AutoNumber field, so it will automatically increment as you enter the EventName and EventDate information.

h. Print the Copenhagen record, close the Cities form, close the Baltic-C database, then exit Access.

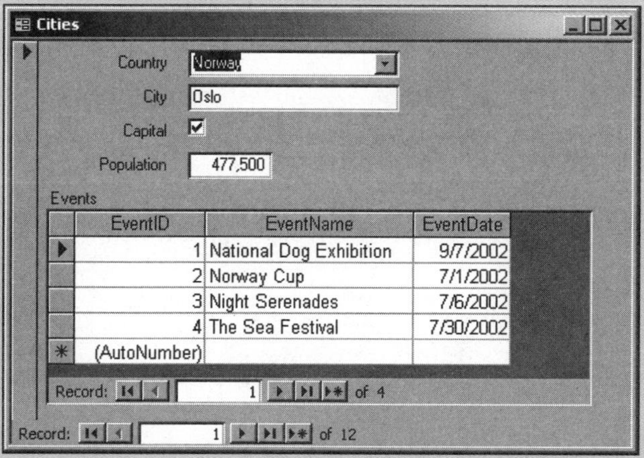

▶ Visual Workshop

Open the **Clinic-C** database, then use the Form Wizard to create the form based on the Demographics table, as shown in Figure C-23. Notice that the label **Patient Form** is 24 points and has been placed in the Form Header section. The clip art, Medstaff.bmp, can be found in the drive and folder where your Project Files are located. The image has been placed on the right side of the Detail section, and many controls were moved and resized. Also notice that the labels are right-aligned. To change the background color of the Detail section to white, double-click the Detail section bar in Form Design View, then modify the Back Color property on the Format tab of the property sheet to **16777215**, the value that corresponds to white. Enter your own name and gender for the first record, then print it.

FIGURE C-23

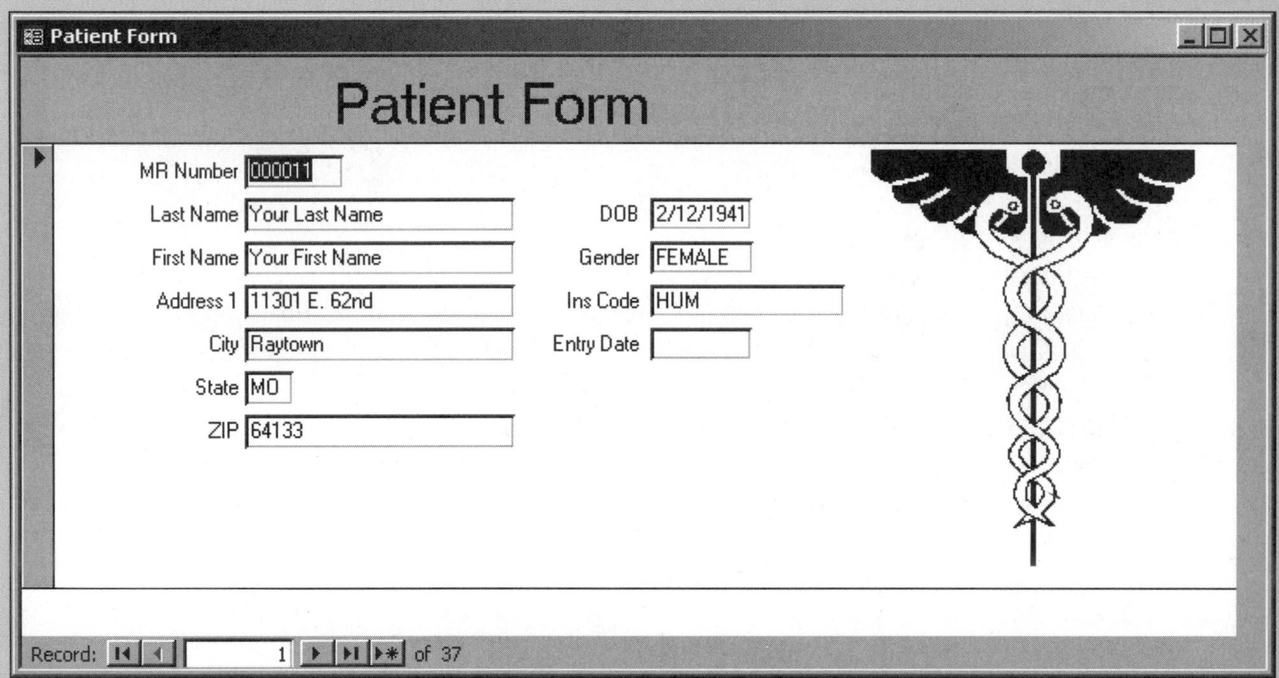

Access 2002

Unit D

Using Reports

Objectives

- MOUS ► Plan a report
- MOUS ► Create a report
- MOUS ► Group records
- MOUS ► Change the sort order
- MOUS ► Add a calculation
- MOUS ► Align controls
- MOUS ► Format controls
- ► Create mailing labels

A **report** is an Access object used to create professional printouts. The record source for an Access report is either a table or a query object. A report is created using commands and tools similar to those used to create a form. Although you can print a datasheet or form, reports are the primary object used to create professional printouts because reports provide many more printing options. For example, a report may include formatting embellishments such as multiple fonts and colors, extra graphical elements such as clip art and lines, and multiple headers and footers. Reports are also very powerful analysis tools. A report can calculate subtotals, averages, counts, or other statistics for groups of records. You cannot enter or edit data through a report. Kelsey Lang, a marketing manager at MediaLoft, wants to produce some reports to distribute to MediaLoft employees.

Access 2002

Planning a Report

Hard copy reports are often the primary tool used to communicate database information at meetings, with clients or customers, or with top executives. Time spent planning your report not only increases your productivity but also ensures that the report meets its intended objectives. Creating a report is similar to creating a form, and you work with bound, unbound, and calculated controls in Report Design View just as you do in Form Design View. Reports, however, have more sections than forms. The report **section** determines how often and where controls placed within that section print in the final report. See Table D-1 for more information on report sections.

Kelsey has been asked to provide several reports on a regular basis to the MediaLoft executives. Her first report summarizes inventory quantities within each music category.

Kelsey uses the following guidelines to plan her report:

- **Identify a meaningful title for the report**
  The title should clearly identify the purpose of the report and be meaningful to those who will be reading the report. The title is created with a label control placed in the Report Header section.
- **Determine the information (the fields and records) that the report will show**
  You can base a report on a table, but usually you create a query to gather the specific fields from the one or more tables upon which the report is based. If you base the report on a query, you are also able to set criteria within the query to limit the number of records displayed by the report.
- **Determine how the fields should be organized on the report**
  Most reports display fields in a horizontal layout across the page, but you can arrange them any way you want. Just as in forms, bound text box controls are used on a report to display the data stored in the underlying fields. These text boxes are generally placed in the report **Detail** section. The Detail section of a report is always visible in Report Design View.
- **Determine how the records should be sorted and/or grouped within the report**
  In an Access report, **grouping** means to sort records in a particular order *plus* provide a section before the group of records called the Group Header section and a section after the group of records called the Group Footer section. The **Group Header** section contains controls that introduce the upcoming group of records. The **Group Footer** section holds controls that calculate statistics such as subtotals for the preceding group of records.
  The ability to group records is extremely powerful. For example, you might group the records of an address report by the State field. Since State is the grouping field, you would be able to add the State Header and State Footer sections to the report. In the State Header section you might add a text box bound to the State field that displays the name of the state before listing the Detail records for that state. In the State Footer section you might add a text box that contains an expression to count the number of records within each state. You might want to further sort the records by the City field, so that the Detail records printed for each state would be listed in ascending order based on the value of the City field.
  Group Header and Footer sections are opened by specifying a Yes value to these field properties in the Sorting and Grouping dialog box, opened by clicking the Sorting and Grouping button on the Report Design toolbar.
- **Identify any other descriptive information that should be placed at the beginning or end of the report, or at the top or bottom of each page**
  You will use the **Report Header**, **Report Footer**, **Page Header**, and **Page Footer** sections to add information that you wish to print on every page, or at the beginning or end of the report. For example, you might add a text box that contains an expression to display the current date in the Page Header section, or you might add a text box that contains an expression to display the current page number in the Page Footer section. The Report Header and Report Footer sections of a report can be opened using the Report Header/Footer option on the View menu in Report Design View.
  Kelsey sketched her first report as shown in Figure D-1.

FIGURE D-1: Sketch of the Quantities Report

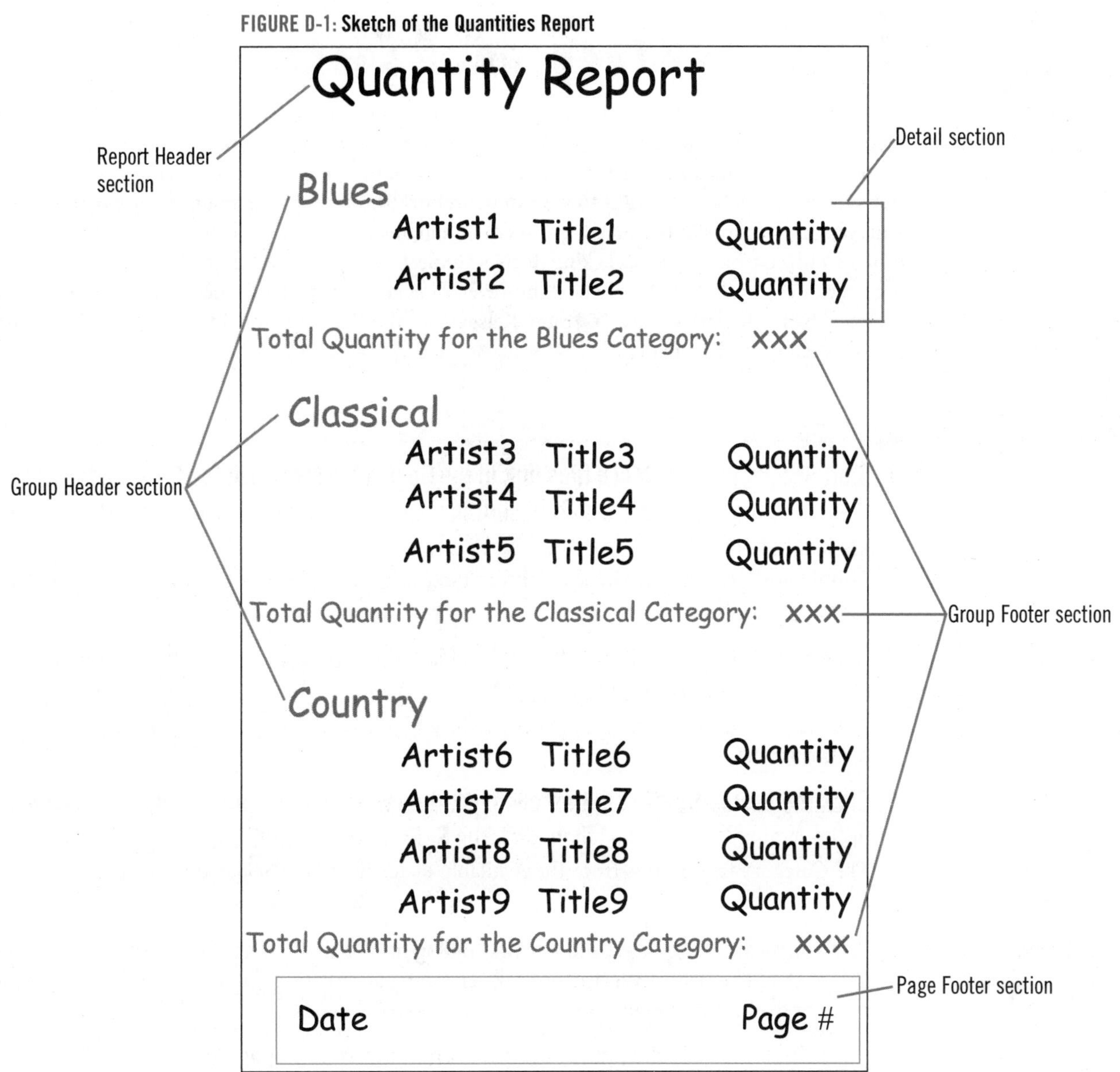

Access 2002

TABLE D-1: Report sections

section	where does this section print?	which controls are most commonly placed in this section?
Report Header	At the top of the first page of the report	Label controls containing the report title; can also include clip art, a logo image, or a line separating the title from the rest of the report
Page Header	At the top of every page (but below the Report Header on page one)	Text box controls containing a page number or date expression
Group Header	Before every group of records	Text box control for the field by which the records are grouped
Detail	Once for every record	Text box controls for the rest of the fields in the recordset (the table or query upon which the report is built)
Group Footer	After every group of records	Text box controls containing calculated expressions, such as subtotals or counts, for the records in that group
Page Footer	At the bottom of every page	Text box controls containing a page number or date expression
Report Footer	At the end of the entire report	Text box controls containing expressions such as grand totals or counts that calculate a value for all of the records in the report

Creating a Report

You can create reports in Access in Report Design View, or you can use the Report Wizard to help you get started. The **Report Wizard** asks questions that guide you through the initial development of the report, similar to the Form Wizard. Your responses to the Report Wizard questions specify the fields you want to view in the report, the style and layout of the report, and how you want the records to be sorted, grouped, and analyzed. Another way to quickly create a report is by selecting a table or query, clicking the New Object list arrow on the Database toolbar, and then clicking AutoReport. AutoReport, however, does not give you a chance to review the options provided by the Report Wizard. Kelsey uses the Report Wizard to create the Quantities Report she planned on paper.

Steps

1. Start Access, click the **More files link** in the Open a file section of the New File task pane, then open the **MediaLoft-D** database from the drive and folder where your Project Files are located
   This database contains a Music Inventory table and a query object from which you will base your reports.
2. Click **Reports** on the Objects bar in the MediaLoft-D database window, then double-click **Create report by using wizard**
   The Report Wizard dialog box opens. The Selection Quantities query has the fields you need for this report.
3. Click the **Tables/Queries list arrow**, click **Query: Selection Quantities**, click **Category** in the Available Fields list, then click the **Select Single Field button** >
   The Category field moves from the Available Fields list to the Selected Fields list.
4. Double-click **Title**, double-click **Artist**, then double-click **Quantity**
   The four fields are selected and the first dialog box of the Report Wizard should look like Figure D-2. The Report Wizard also asks grouping and sorting questions that determine the order and amount of detail provided on the report.
5. Click **Next**, click **Next** to move past the grouping levels question, click the **first sort order list arrow** in the Report Wizard dialog box, then click **Category**
   You can use the Report Wizard to specify up to four sort fields in either an ascending or descending sort order for each field.
6. Click **Next**, click **Next** to accept the **Tabular** layout and **Portrait** orientation, click **Corporate** for the style, click **Next**, type **Quantities Report** for the report title, verify that the **Preview the report option button** is selected, then click **Finish**
   The Quantities Report opens in Print Preview, as shown in Figure D-3. It is very similar to the sketch created earlier. Notice that the records are sorted by the Category field.

Trouble?

If you did not select the fields in the correct order, click the Remove Single Field button < to move fields from the Selected Fields list back to the Available Fields list.

Trouble?

Click Back to review previous dialog boxes within a wizard.

FIGURE D-2: **Report Wizard dialog box**

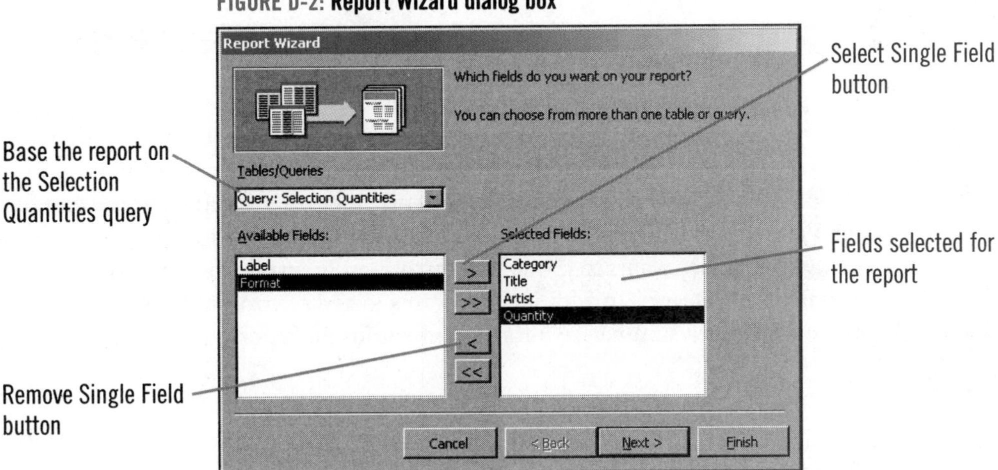

FIGURE D-3: **Quantities Report in Print Preview**

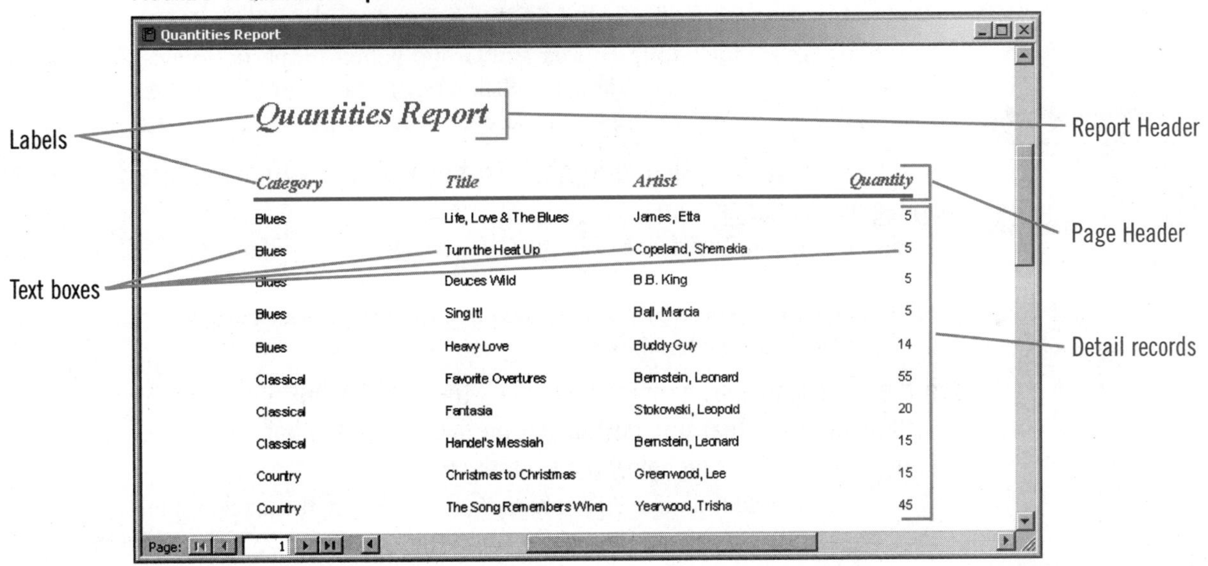

Why reports should be based on queries

Although you can use the first dialog box of the Report Wizard to select fields from different tables without first creating a query to collect those fields into one object, it is not recommended. If you later decide that you want to add more fields to the report or limit the number of records in the table, you will find it very easy to add fields or criteria to an underlying query object to meet these new needs. To accomplish this same task without using an intermediary query object requires that you change the Record Source property of the report itself, which most users find more difficult than working with a query.

Access 2002

Access 2002

Grouping Records

Grouping refers to sorting records on a report *in addition to* providing an area above and below the group of records in which additional controls can be placed. These two special sections of the report are called the Group Header and Group Footer. You can create groups on a report through the Report Wizard, or you can change an existing report's grouping and sorting fields in Report Design View. Just as with forms, you make all structural changes to a report in the object's Design View. Kelsey wants to group the Quantities Report by the Category field instead of simply sorting it by Category. In addition, she wants to add controls to the Group Header and Group Footer to clarify and summarize information within the report.

Steps

1. Click the **Design View button** on the Print Preview toolbar to switch to Report Design View

   Report Design View shows you the sections of the report as well as the controls within each section. It is difficult to visually distinguish labels and text boxes in Report Design View, but you can always open the property sheet and view its title bar to determine the type of control you're working with. Report Design View is where you change grouping and sorting fields.

2. Click the **Sorting and Grouping button** on the Report Design toolbar, click the **Group Header text box**, click the **Group Header list arrow**, click **Yes**, click the **Group Footer text box**, click the **Group Footer list arrow**, then click **Yes**

   Specifying Yes for the Group Header and Group Footer properties opens those sections of the report in Report Design View. The dialog box is shown in Figure D-4.

Trouble?

Be careful to drag the Category text box in the Detail section rather than the Category label in the Page Header section.

3. Click to close the Sorting and Grouping dialog box, click the **Category text box** in the Detail section, then drag the **text box** with the pointer straight up into the Category Header section

   By placing the Category text box in the Category Header, it will print once for each new category value rather than once for each record. You can add a calculated control to subtotal each category of records by placing a text box in the Category Footer section, and entering an expression into the text box.

4. If the Toolbox toolbar is not visible, click the **Toolbox button** on the Report Design toolbar, click the **Text Box button** on the Toolbox toolbar, then click in the **Category Footer section** directly below the Quantity text box

   Your screen should look like Figure D-5. You can modify the label and text box controls in the Category Footer section to describe and define the Quantity field subtotal.

Trouble?

If you double-click the label itself (versus Text13), you will open the control's property sheet.

5. Click the **Text13: label** in the Category Footer section to select it, double-click **Text13**, type **Subtotal**, then press **[Enter]**

6. Click the **unbound text box control** in the Category Footer section to select it, click **Unbound** within the text box control to edit it, type **=sum([Quantity])**, then press **Enter**

   The expression that calculates the sum of the Quantity field is now in the text box control. Calculated expressions start with an equal sign. When entering an expression, the field name is not case sensitive, but it must be surrounded by square brackets and match the field name as defined in Table Design View.

7. Click the **Print Preview button** on the Report Design toolbar

   Since the Category text box was moved to the Category Header section, it prints only once per group of records as shown in Figure D-6. Each group of records is followed by a Group Footer that includes the Subtotal label as well as a calculated field that subtotals the Quantity field for that group of records.

8. Click the **Close button** on the Print Preview toolbar, click to toggle off the Toolbox, click the **Save button**, then close the Quantities Report

FIGURE D-4: Sorting and Grouping dialog box

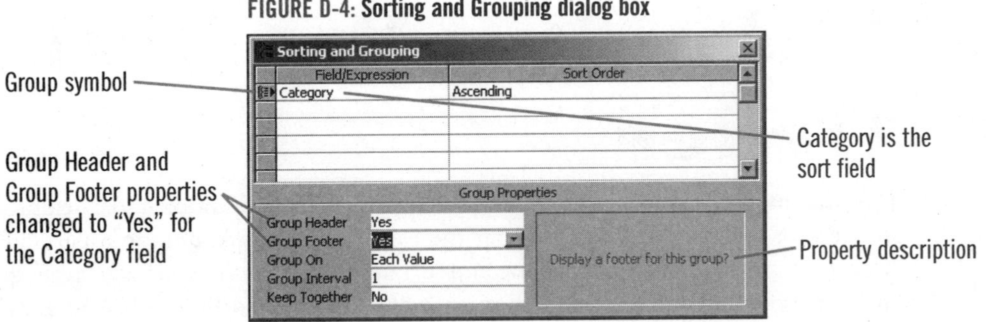

FIGURE D-5: Quantities Report in Report Design View

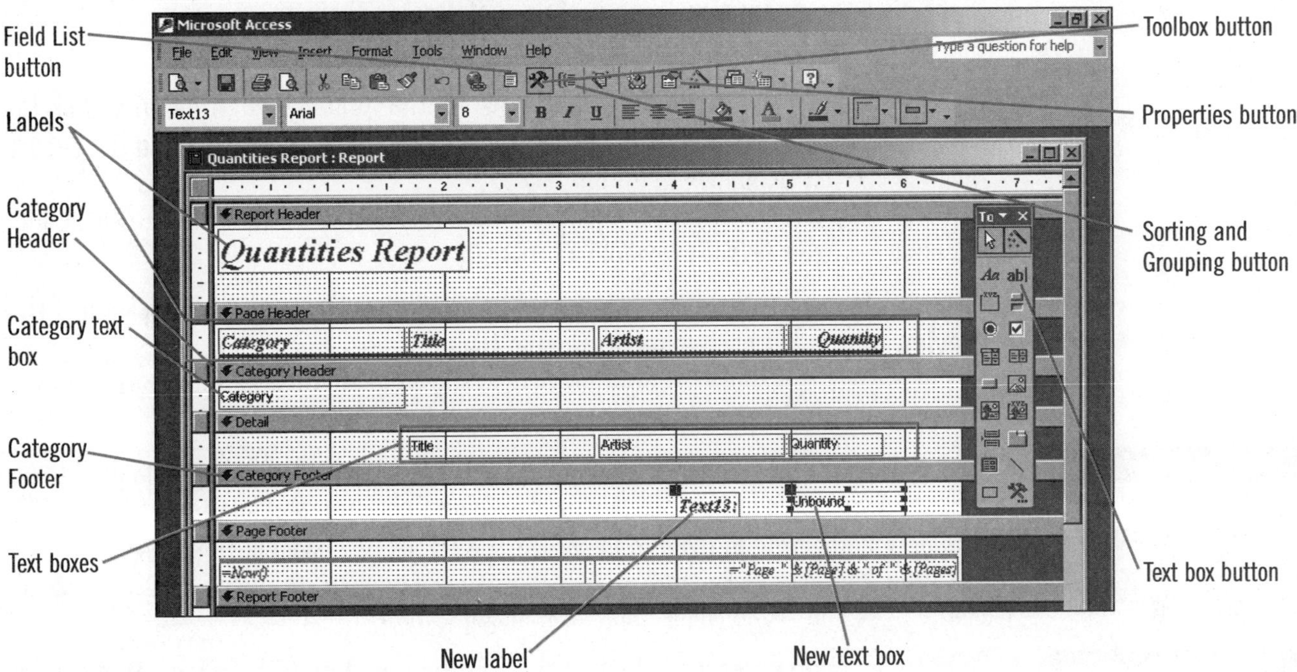

FIGURE D-6: The Quantities Report grouped by the Category field

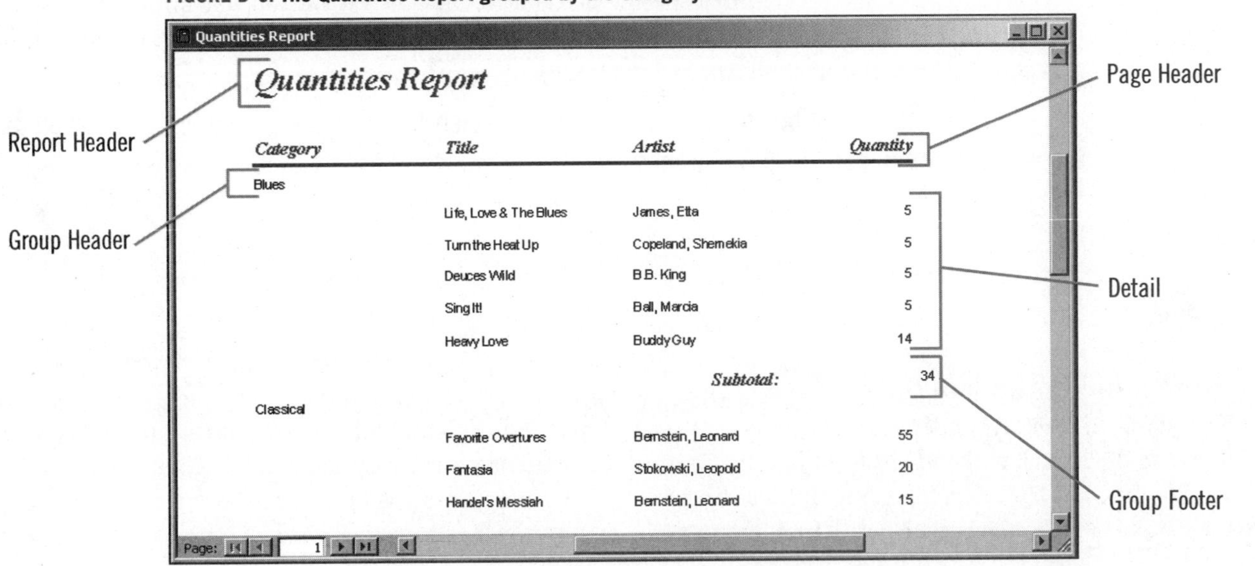

Access 2002

Access 2002

Changing the Sort Order

The grouping field acts as a primary sort field. You can define additional sort fields too. When you sort records within a group, you order the Detail records according to a particular field. The Report Wizard prompts you for group and sort information at the time you create the report, but you can also group and sort an existing report by using the Sorting and Grouping dialog box in Report Design View. Kelsey wants to modify the Quantities Report so that the Detail records are sorted by the Artist field within the Category group.

Steps

1. Right-click the **Quantities Report**, then click **Design View**
   The Quantities Report opens in Design View.
2. Click the **Sorting and Grouping button** on the Report Design toolbar, click the **Field/Expression text box** in the second row, click the **Field/Expression list arrow**, then click **Artist** as shown in Figure D-7
   Both the Group Header and Group Footer Group property values are set to No, which indicates that the Artist field is providing a sort order only.
3. Click to toggle the Sorting and Grouping dialog box off, then click the **Print Preview button** on the Report Design toolbar
   Part of the report is shown in Print Preview, as shown in Figure D-8. You can use the buttons on the Print Preview toolbar to view more of the report.

QuickTip
The grid will expand to 4 × 5 pages if you keep dragging to expand it.

4. Click the **One Page button** on the Print Preview toolbar to view one miniature page, click the **Two Pages button** to view two pages, click the **Multiple Pages button**, then drag to the right in the grid to show **1 × 4 Pages** as shown in Figure D-9
   The Print Preview window displays the four pages of the report. You can click the **Zoom pointers** and to change the zoom magnification.

QuickTip
You can also type a number into the Fit text box to zoom at a specific percent.

5. Point to the **last subtotal** on the last page of the report with the pointer, click to read the number **92** in the last subtotal of the report, then click again to view all four pages of the report in the Preview window
   To zoom the preview to a specific percentage, click the **Fit button list arrow** Fit on the Print Preview toolbar, then click a percentage. The **Fit** option automatically adjusts the preview to display all pages in the report.
6. Click the **Close button** Close on the Print Preview toolbar, then click the **Save button** on the Report Design toolbar

Adding a field to a report

To add a field from the underlying table or query object to the report, click the Field List button on the Report Design toolbar, then drag the field from the field list to the appropriate position on the report. This action creates both a label control that displays the field name and a bound text box control that displays the value of the field on the resulting report.

FIGURE D-7: Specifying a sort order

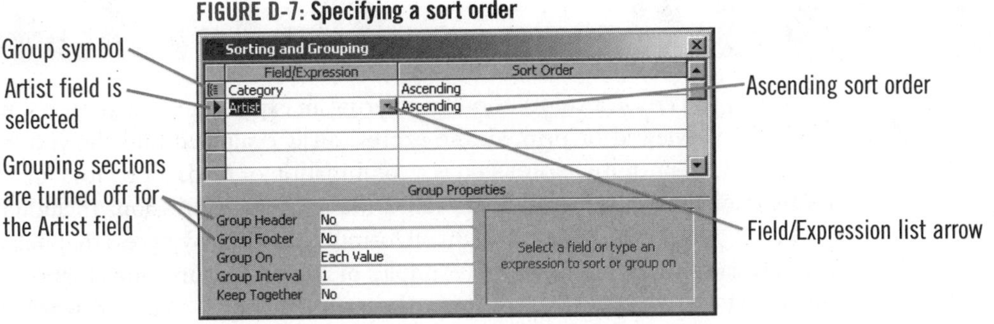

FIGURE D-8: The Quantities Report sorted by Artist

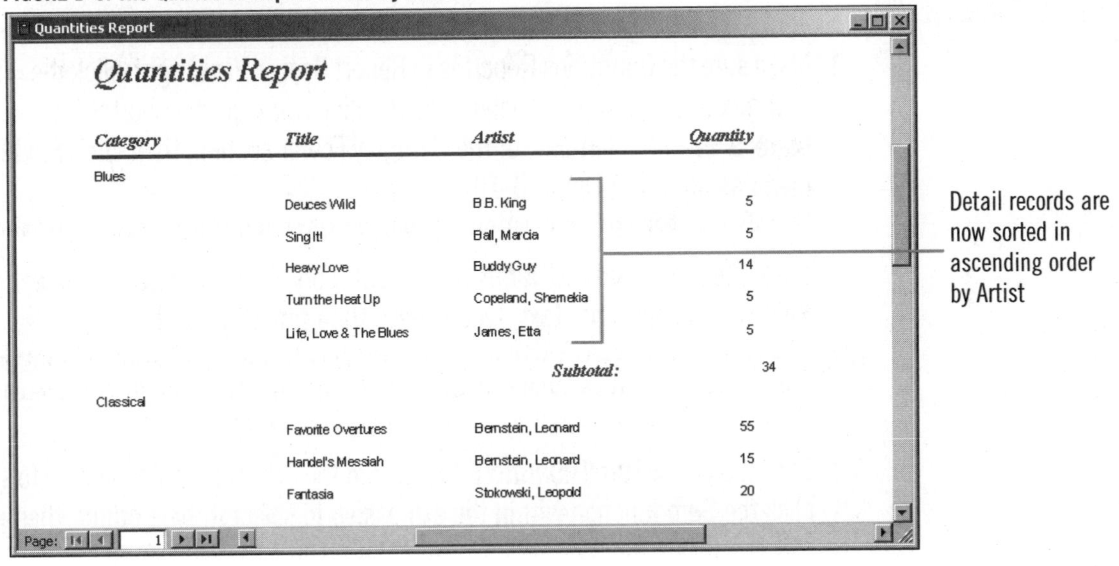

FIGURE D-9: Print Preview

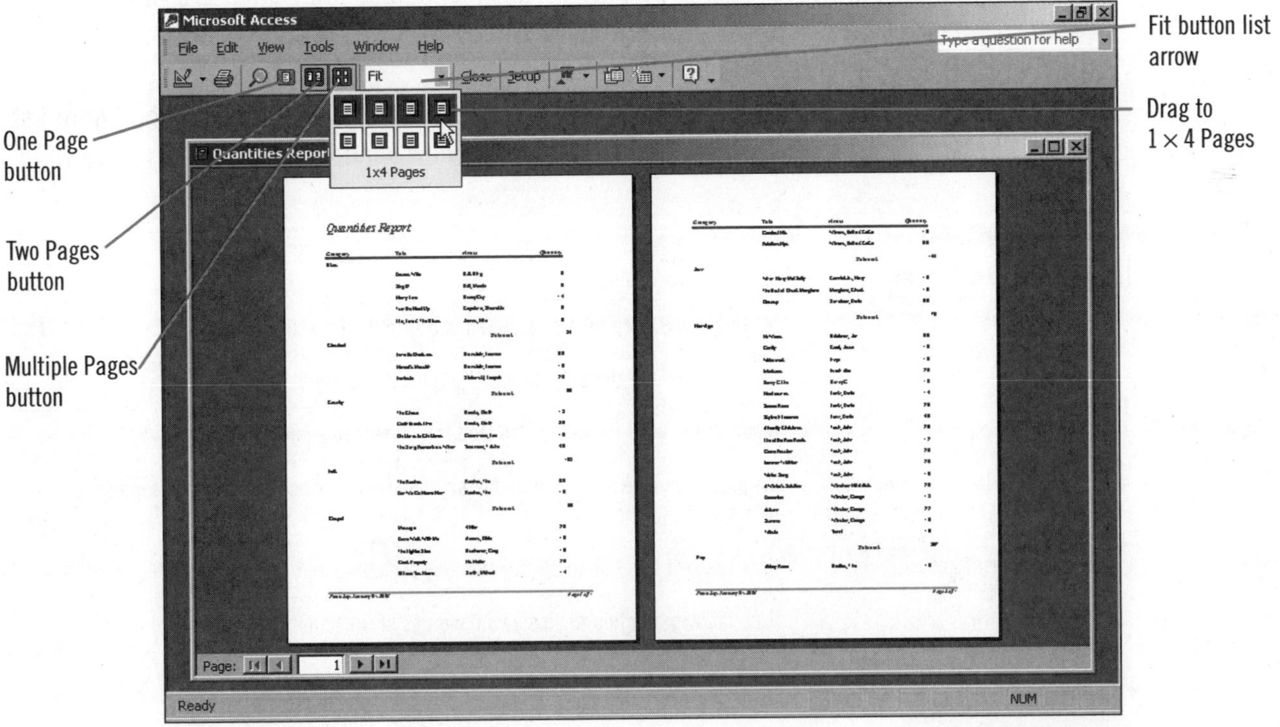

Access 2002

Access 2002

Adding a Calculation

In a report, you create a **calculation** by entering an expression into an unbound text box. When a report is previewed or printed, the expression is evaluated and the resulting calculation is placed on the report. An **expression** is a combination of fields, operators (such as +, –, / and *), and functions that result in a single value. Many times, expressions include functions such as SUM or COUNT. A **function** is a built-in formula provided by Access that helps you quickly create a calculation. See Table D-2 for examples of common expressions that use Access functions. Notice that every calculated expression starts with an equal sign, and when it uses a function, the arguments for the function are placed in parentheses. **Arguments** are the pieces of information that the function needs to create the final answer. Kelsey adds another calculation to the Quantities Report that counts the number of records within each music category.

Steps

1. **Make sure the Quantities Report is in Report Design View, right-click the =Sum([Quantity]) text box in the Category Footer section, click Copy on the shortcut menu, right-click in a blank area in the left part of the Category Footer section, then click Paste on the shortcut menu as shown in Figure D-10**
   Modifying a copy of the existing calculated expression control saves time and reduces errors.
2. **Click the new Subtotal label in the Category Footer section to select it, double-click Subtotal to select the text, type count, then press [Enter]**
   The label is only descriptive text. The text box to the right of the Count label will contain the expression that calculates the count. Right now, however, it still calculates a sum of the Quantity values instead of a count of Quantity values.
3. **Click the new =Sum([Quantity]) text box in the Category Footer section to select it, double-click the Sum function within the expression to select it, type count, then press [Enter]**
   The expression now counts the number of records in each group.
4. **Click the Save button on the Report Design toolbar**
   When you save a report object, you are saving the report definition, not the data displayed by the report. The data that the report displays was automatically saved as it was previously entered into the database. Once a report object is saved, it will always show the most up-to-date data when you preview or print the report.
5. **Click the Print Preview button on the Report Design toolbar, click the Zoom list arrow 100%, click 100%, then scroll the Preview window as shown in Figure D-11**

TABLE D-2: Common Access expressions

category	sample expression	description
Arithmetic	=[Price]*1.05	Multiplies the Price field by 1.05 (adds 5% to the Price field)
Arithmetic	=[Subtotal]+[Shipping]	Adds the value of the Subtotal field to the value of the Shipping field
Page Number	="Page "&[Page]	Displays the word Page, a space, and the current page number
Text	=[FirstName]& " "&[LastName]	Displays the value of the FirstName and LastName fields in one control separated by a space
Text	=Left([ProductNumber],2)	Uses the **Left** function to display the first two characters in the ProductNumber field
Aggregate	=Avg([Freight])	Uses the **Avg** function to display an average of the values in the Freight field
Date	=Date()	Uses the **Date** function to display the current date in the form of mm-dd-yy

FIGURE D-10: Copying and pasting a calculated control

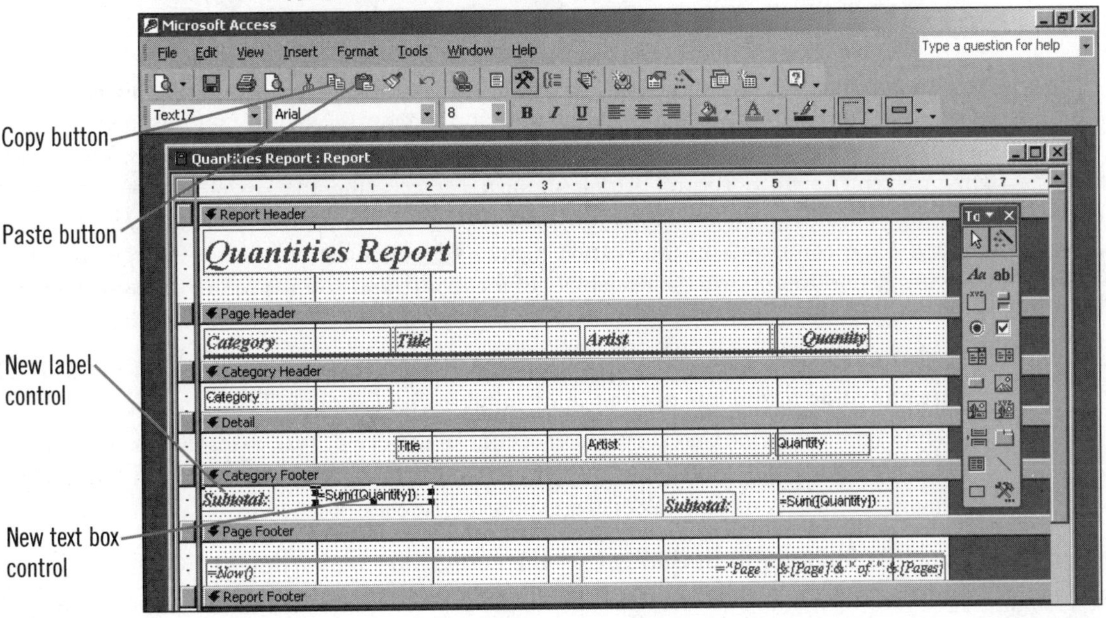

FIGURE D-11: Previewing the Count calculated control

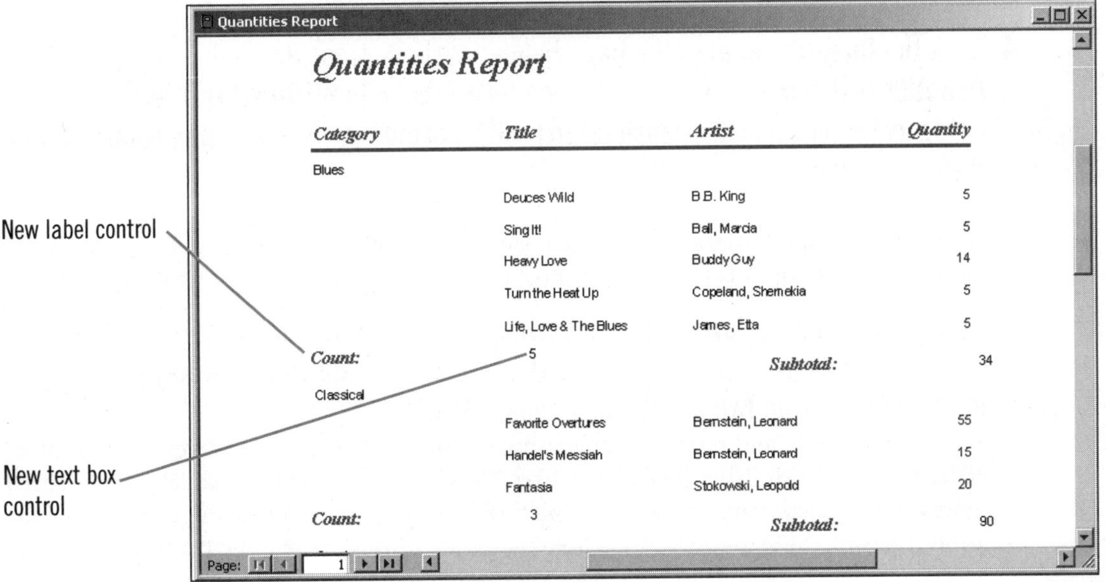

Using the Office Clipboard

The Office Clipboard lets you copy and paste multiple items within or between the Microsoft Office applications. To view the Clipboard task pane, click Edit on the menu bar, then click Clipboard. The Clipboard can collect up to 24 items, and you can paste any of these items at any time. Click the Options button within the Office Clipboard task pane to set Clipboard characteristics such as when it will automatically appear.

Access 2002

Access 2002

Aligning Controls

Once the information that you want to present has been added to the appropriate section of a report, you may also want to rearrange the data on the report. Aligning controls in columns and rows makes the information easier to read. There are several **alignment** commands. You can left-, right-, or center-align a control *within its own border* using the Alignment buttons on the Formatting (Form/Report) toolbar, or you can align the edges of controls *with respect to one another* using the Align command on the Format menu. Kelsey aligns several controls on the Quantities Report to improve the readability of the report, and give it a more professional look.

1. Click the **Design View button** on the Print Preview toolbar, then click in the **vertical ruler** to the left of the Count label in the Category Footer section
   All four controls in the Category Footer section are selected. Text boxes that display numeric fields are right-aligned by default. The label and text box that you added in the Category Footer section that display calculated expressions are left-aligned by default.
2. Click the **Align Right button** on the Formatting (Form/Report) toolbar
   Your screen should look like Figure D-12. Now the information displayed by these controls is right-aligned within the border of that control.
3. With the four controls still selected, click **Format** on the menu bar, point to **Align**, then click **Bottom**
   The bottom edges of the four controls are now aligned with respect to one another. You can also align the right or left edges of controls in different sections.
4. Click the **Quantity label** in the Page Header section, press and hold **[Shift]**, click the **Quantity text box** in the Detail section, click the **=Sum([Quantity])** text box in the Category Footer section, release **[Shift]**, click **Format** on the menu bar, point to **Align**, then click **Right**
   The right edges of the Quantity label, Quantity text box, and Quantity calculated controls are aligned. With the edges at the same position and the information right-aligned within the controls, the controls form a perfect column on the final report.
5. Click the **blue line** below the labels between the Artist and and Quantity Fields in the Page Header section, press and hold **[Ctrl]**, press the **Down Arrow key [↓]** twice to move the line down two pixels, then release **[Ctrl]**
   You can also move and resize controls using the mouse, but precise movements are often easier to accomplish using quick keystrokes. Pressing the arrow keys while holding [Ctrl] moves the selected control one pixel (picture element) at a time in the direction of the arrow. Pressing the arrow keys while holding [Shift] resizes the selected control.
6. With the blue line still selected, press and hold **[Shift]**, then press the **Right Arrow key [→]** as many times as necessary to extend the line to the right edge of the Quantity label
   The extended line better defines the sections on the page.
7. Click the **Save button**, click the **Print Preview button**, then scroll and zoom so that your report looks similar to Figure D-13

Trouble?

If you make a mistake, click the Undo button.

QuickTip

Try not to expand the right edge of a report or your printout will be wider than one sheet of paper.

FIGURE D-12: **Working with the alignment buttons**

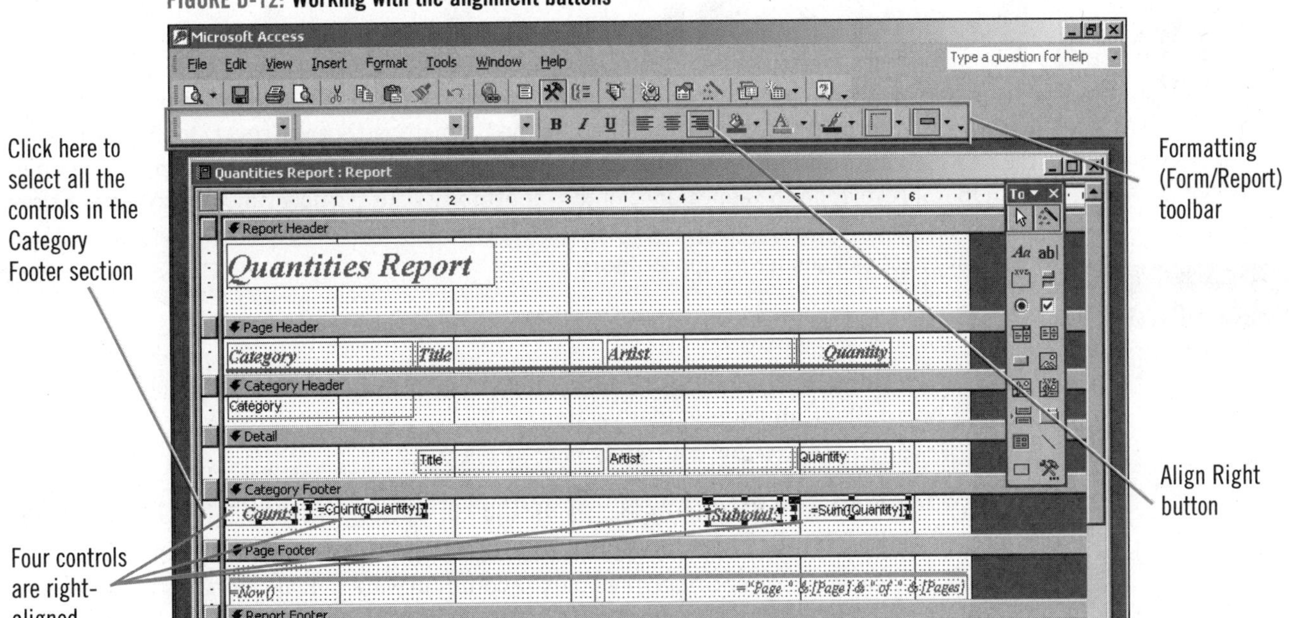

FIGURE D-13: **Controls are aligned**

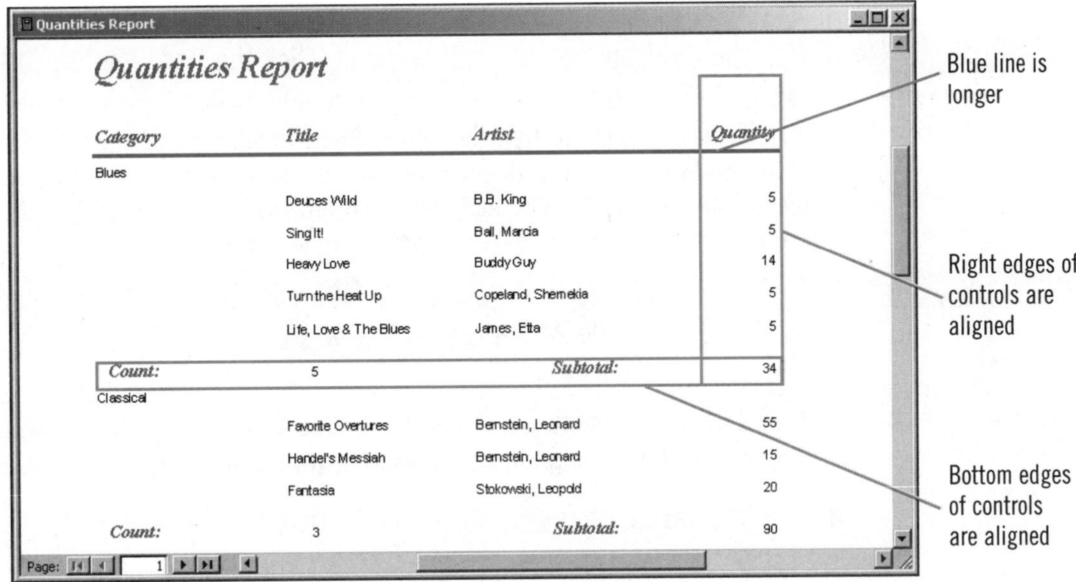

Access 2002

Formatting Controls

Formatting refers to enhancing the appearance of the information. Table D-3 lists several of the most popular formatting commands found on the Formatting (Form/Report) toolbar. Although the Report Wizard automatically applies many formatting embellishments to a report, you often want to improve upon the appearance of the report to fit your particular needs. Kelsey doesn't feel that the music category information is prominent on the report, so she wants to format that control to change its appearance.

Steps

1. Click the **Design View button** on the Print Preview toolbar, then click the **Category text box** in the Category Header section
   Before you can format any control, it must be selected.
2. Click the **Font Size list arrow** on the Formatting (Form/Report) toolbar, click **11**, then click the **Bold button** on the Formatting (Form/Report) toolbar
   Increasing the font size and applying bold are common ways to make information more visible on a report. You can also change the colors of the control.
3. With the Category text box still selected, click the **Font/Fore Color list arrow**, then click the **red box** (third row, first column on the left) as shown in Figure D-14
   Many buttons on the Formatting (Form/Report) toolbar include a list arrow that you can click to reveal a list of formatting choices. When you click the color list arrow, a palette of available colors is displayed.
4. With the Category text box still selected, click the **Fill/Back Color list arrow**, then click the **light gray box** (fourth row, last column on the right)
   Be careful about relying too heavily on color formatting. Background shades often become solid black boxes when printed on a black-and-white printer or fax machine. Fortunately, Access allows you to undo up to your 20 most recent actions in Report Design View.
5. With the Category text box still selected, click the **Undo button** on the Report Design toolbar to remove the background color, click to remove the font color, click **Edit** on the menu bar, then click **Redo Property Setting** to redo the font color
   If you undo more actions than desired, use the Redo command on the Edit menu to redo the last undone action. The Redo menu command changes depending on the last undone action, and it can be used to redo up to 20 undone actions.
6. Click the **Line/Border Color list arrow**, click the **blue box** (second row, sixth column), then click the **Print Preview button**
   The screen should look like Figure D-15.
7. Click **File** on the menu bar, click **Print**, type **1** in the From text box, type **1** in the To text box, click **OK**, then click the **Close button** on the Print Preview toolbar
8. Click the **Save button**, then close the Quantities Report

QuickTip

When the color on the Fill/Back Color, Font/Fore Color, or Line/Border button displays the color you want, you simply click the button to apply that color.

QuickTip

The quick keystroke for Undo is [CTRL][Z]. The quick keystroke for Redo is [CTRL][Y].

QuickTip

If you want your name on the printout, switch to Report Design view and add your name as a label to the Page Header section.

FIGURE D-14: Working with color formats

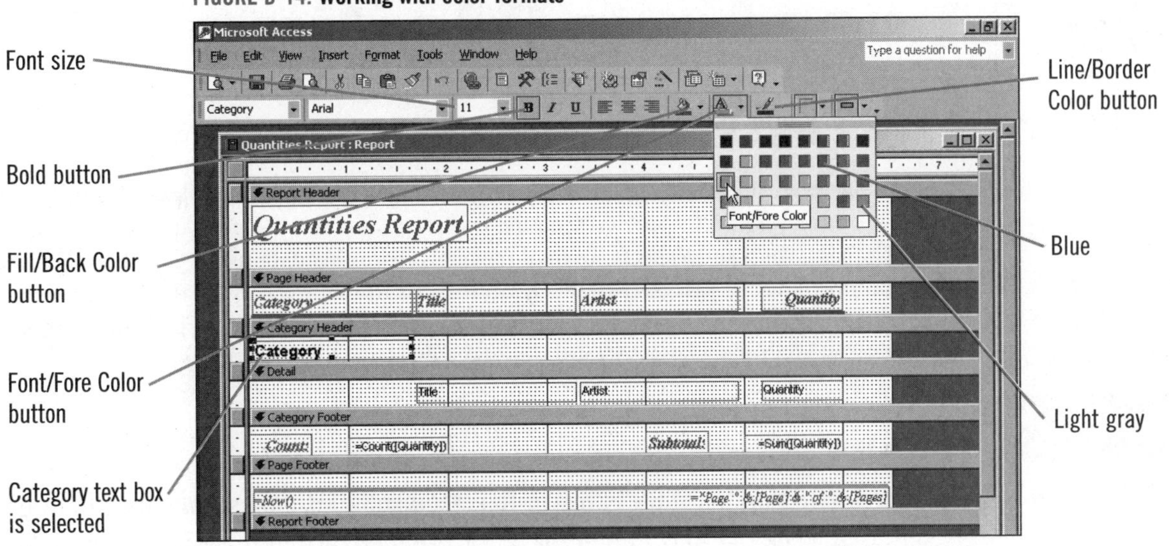

FIGURE D-15: Formatted Quantities Report

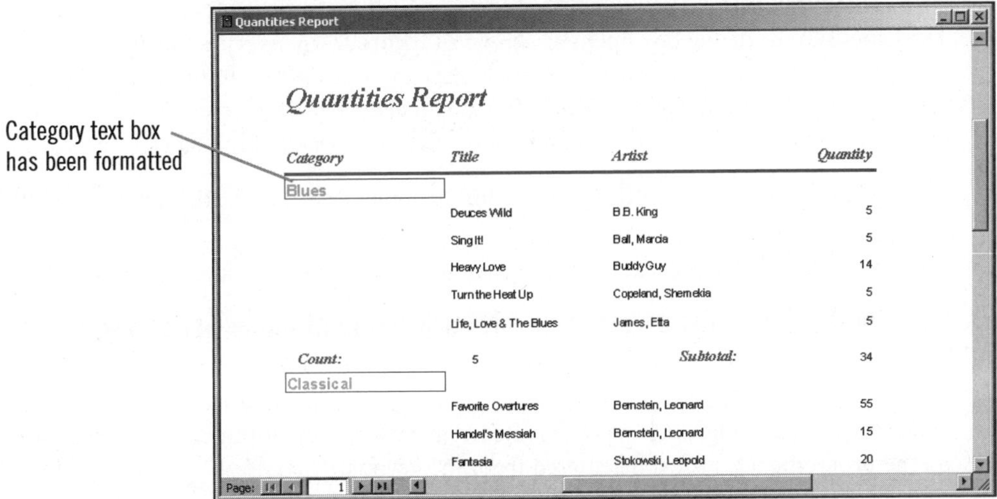

TABLE D-3: Useful formatting commands

button	button name	description
	Bold	Toggles bold on or off for the selected control(s)
	Italic	Toggles italics on or off for the selected control(s)
	Underline	Toggles underline on or off for the selected control(s)
	Align Left	Left-aligns the selected control(s) within its own border
	Center	Center-aligns the selected control(s) within its own border
	Align Right	Right-aligns the selected control(s) within its own border
	Fill/Back Color	Changes the background color of the selected control(s)
	Font/Fore Color	Changes the text color of the selected control(s)
	Line/Border Color	Changes the border color of the selected control(s)
	Line/Border Width	Changes the style of the border of the selected control(s)
	Special Effect	Changes the special visual effect of the selected control(s)

Access 2002

Creating Mailing Labels

Mailing Labels are used for many business purposes such as identifying folders in a filing cabinet, labeling products for sale, or providing addresses for mass mailings. Once you enter data into your Access database, you can easily create mailing labels from this data using the **Label Wizard** that creates a report object. Kelsey has been asked to create labels for the display cases in the MediaLoft stores with the Artist and Title fields only. The labels are to be printed in alphabetical order by Artist and then by Title. Kelsey uses the Label Wizard to get started.

Steps

1. Click **Reports** on the Objects bar in the MediaLoft-D database window (if not already selected), click the **New button**, click **Label Wizard** in the New Report dialog box, click the **Choose the table or query where the object's data comes from list arrow**, click **Music Inventory**, then click **OK**
   The Label Wizard dialog box opens as shown in Figure D-16. Avery is the default manufacturer, and produces a wide variety of labels measured in both millimeters and inches, but many other international label manufacturers can also be chosen. Avery 5160 labels are one of the most popular sizes in the United States, and are measured in inches.
2. Click the **English** option button (if not already selected), scroll and click **5160** in the Product number list, then click **Next**
   The next wizard dialog box allows you to change the font, font size, and other text attributes.
3. Click the **Font size list arrow**, click **11**, click the **Font name list arrow**, scroll and click **Comic Sans MS**, then click **Next**
   The next wizard dialog box asks you to set up the **prototype label**, a sample format upon which the final mailing labels will be created. Any text, spaces, or punctuation that you want on the prototype label must be entered from the keyboard.
4. Double-click **Artist**, press **[Enter]**, then double-click **Title**
   Your screen should look like Figure D-17.
5. Click **Next**, double-click **Artist** for the primary sort field, then double-click **Title** for the secondary sort field
   Artist is specified as the primary sort field and Title as the secondary sort field so that the labels will be printed in ascending order based on the value in the Artist field, with records from the same artist further sorted in ascending order by the value in the Title field.
6. Click **Next**, type **Artist-Title Labels** to name the report, click **Finish**, click **OK** if prompted about the size of the columns, then click the **Zoom pointer** to see a full page of labels
   The labels should look like Figure D-18.
7. Click the **Close button** Close on the Print Preview toolbar, then click the **Save button**
8. Click **File** on the menu bar, then click **Exit** to exit Access

Trouble?

If your fields are on the same line, you did not press [Enter] after each line. Select and delete the fields, then redo Step 4.

FIGURE D-16: Label Wizard

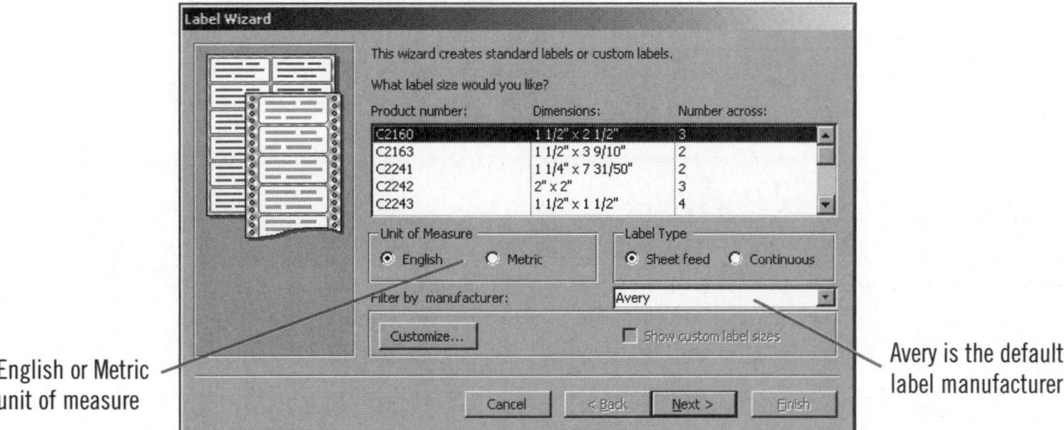

FIGURE D-17: The prototype label

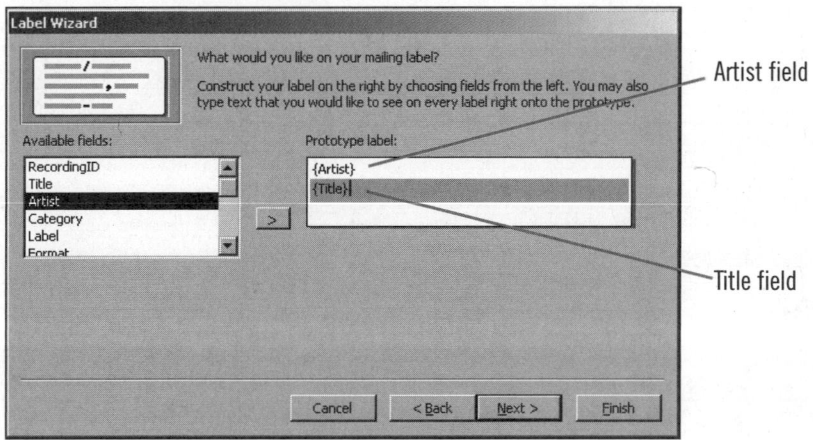

FIGURE D-18: The Artist-Title Labels report

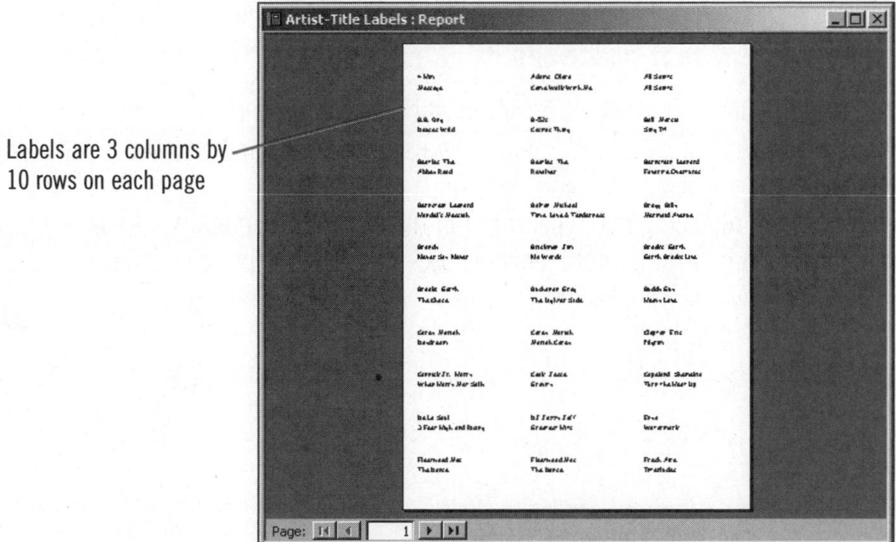

Access 2002

Practice

► Concepts Review

Label each element of the Report Design View window shown in Figure D-19.

FIGURE D-19

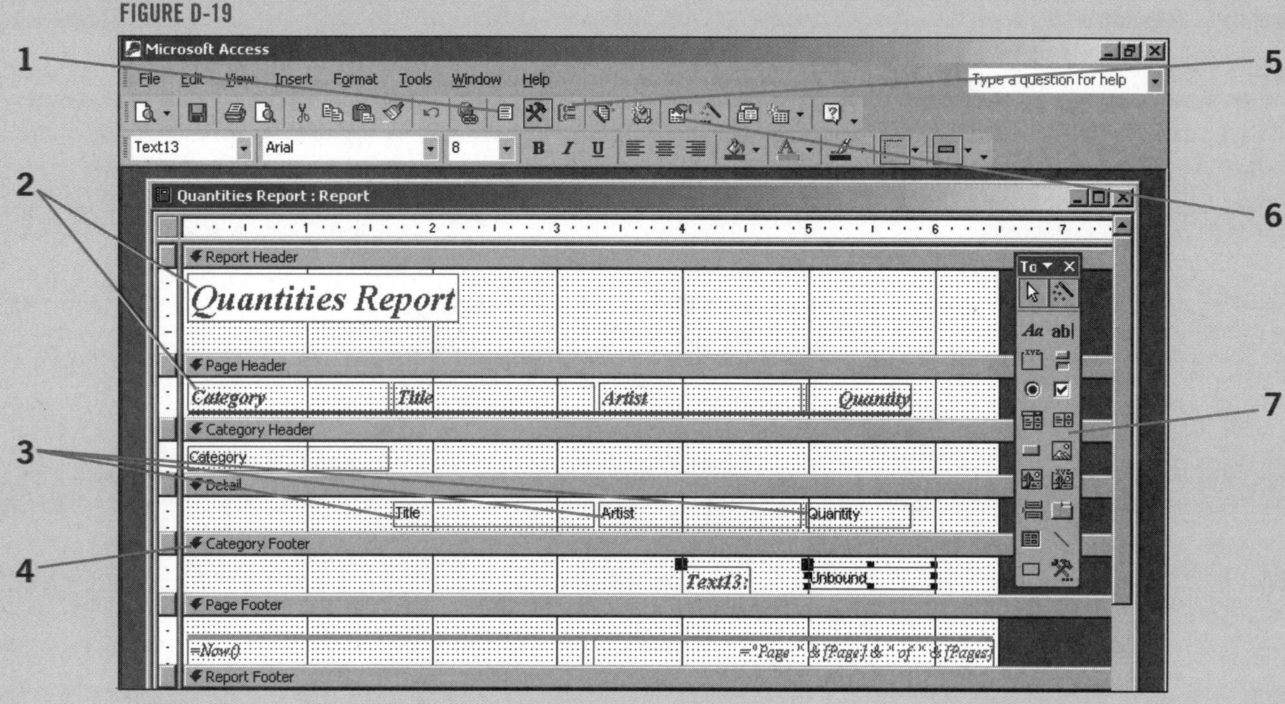

Match each term with the statement that describes it.

8. **Function**
9. **Section**
10. **Detail section**
11. **Report**
12. **Formatting**
13. **Grouping**

a. Determines where a control will display on the report
b. Sorting records *plus* providing a section before and after the group of records
c. Access object used to create paper printouts
d. Enhancing the appearance of the way information displays in the report
e. A built-in formula provided by Access that helps you quickly create a calculated expression
f. Prints once for every record

Select the best answer from the list of choices.

14. Press and hold which key to select more than one control in Report Design View?
- **a.** [Ctrl]
- **b.** [Alt]
- **c.** [Shift]
- **d.** [Tab]

15. Which type of control is most commonly placed in the Detail section?
- **a.** Label
- **b.** Text box
- **c.** Combo box
- **d.** List box

16. Which type of control is most commonly placed in the Page Header section?
- **a.** Label
- **b.** Combo box
- **c.** Command button
- **d.** Bound image

17. A calculated expression is most often placed in which report section?
- **a.** Report Header
- **b.** Detail
- **c.** Formulas
- **d.** Group Footer

18. Which of the following would be the appropriate expression to count the number of records using the FirstName field?
- **a.** =Count(FirstName)
- **b.** =Count[FirstName]
- **c.** =Count{FirstName}
- **d.** =Count([FirstName])

19. To align the edges of several controls with respect to one another, you use the alignment commands on the:
- **a.** Formatting toolbar.
- **b.** Standard toolbar.
- **c.** Print Preview toolbar.
- **d.** Format menu.

20. To display the Clipboard task pane, you would choose the Office Clipboard from which menu?
- **a.** Format
- **b.** Edit
- **c.** View
- **d.** Tools

Skills Review

1. **Plan a report.**
   a. Plan a report to use for tracking job opportunities as if you were looking for a new job. To gather the raw data for your report, find a newspaper or Web site with job listings in your area of interest.
   b. Identify the Report Header, Group Header, and Detail sections of the report by using sample data based on the following information:
      - The title of the report should be **Job Opportunity Report**.
      - The records should be grouped by the Job Title field. For example, if you are interested in working with computers, job titles might be Database Specialist or Computer Analyst. Include at least two job title groupings in your sample report.
      - The Detail section should include information on the company, contact person, and telephone number for each job opportunity.
2. **Create a report.**
   a. Start Access and open the **Club-D** database from the drive and folder where your Project Files are located.
   b. Use the Report Wizard to create a report based on the CONTACTS table.
   c. Include the following fields in the following order for the report: STATUS, FNAME, LNAME, DUESOWED, DUESPAID
   d. Do not add any grouping or sorting fields.
   e. Use the Tabular layout and Portrait orientation.
   f. Use a Bold style and title the report **Contact Status Report**.
   g. Preview the first page of the new report.
3. **Group records.**
   a. In Report Design View, open the Sorting and Grouping dialog box, and group the report by the STATUS field in ascending order. Open both the Group Header and Group Footer sections for the STATUS field, then close the Sorting and Grouping dialog box.
   b. Move the STATUS text box in the Detail section up to the left edge of the STATUS Header section.
   c. Preview the first page of the new report.
4. **Change the sort order.**
   a. In Report Design View, open the Sorting and Grouping dialog box, then add LNAME as a sort field in ascending order immediately below the STATUS field.
   b. Close the Sorting and Grouping dialog box, then preview the first page of the new report.
5. **Add a calculation.**
   a. In Report Design View, add a text box control in the STATUS Footer section directly below the DUESOWED text box that is in the Detail section.
   b. Delete the accompanying label to the left of the unbound text box.
   c. Add another text box control in the STATUS Footer section directly below the DUESPAID text box in the Detail section.
   d. Delete the accompanying label to the left of the new unbound text box.
   e. Modify the unbound text boxes added to the STATUS Footer section so that they subtotal the DUESOWED and DUESPAID fields, respectively. The calculated expressions will be **=Sum([DUESOWED])** and **=Sum([DUESPAID])**.
   f. Add your name as a label to the Report Header section.
   g. Preview both pages of the report, then print both pages of the report.
6. **Align controls.**
   a. In Report Design View, right-align the new calculated controls in the STATUS Footer section.
   b. Select the DUESOWED text box in the Detail section, and the =Sum([DUESOWED]) calculated expression in the STATUS Footer section, then right-align the controls with respect to one another.

c. Select the DUESPAID text box in the Detail section, and the =Sum([DUESPAID]) calculated expression in the STATUS Footer section, then right-align the controls with respect to one another.
d. Select the two calculated controls in the STATUS Footer section, then align the bottoms of the controls with respect to one another.

7. **Format controls.**
   a. Select the two calculated controls in the STATUS Footer section, click the Properties button, then change the Format property on the Format tab to Currency. Close the property sheet.
   b. Select the STATUS text box in the STATUS Header section, change the font size to 12 points, bold and italicize the control, then change the Fill/Back color to bright yellow. The Report Design View should look like Figure D-20.

FIGURE D-20

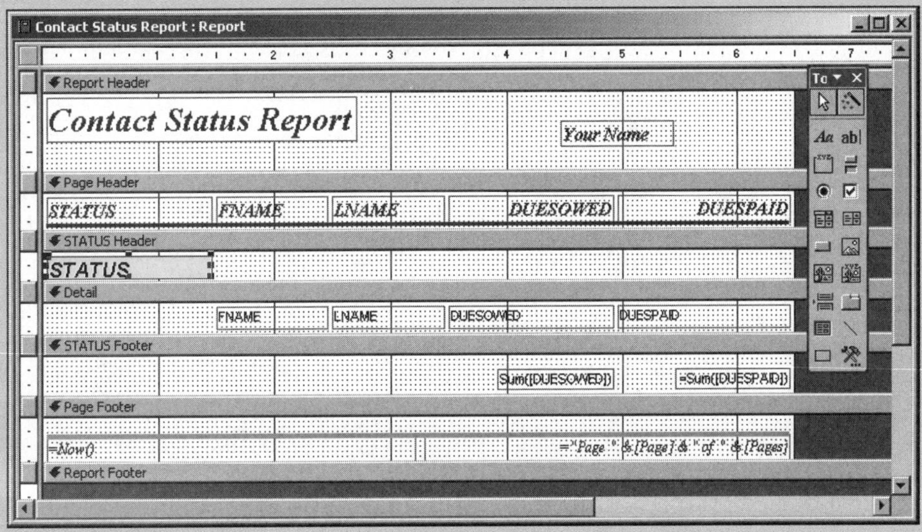

   c. Save, preview, print, then close the report.

8. **Create mailing labels.**
   a. Use the Label Wizard and the CONTACTS table to create mailing labels using Avery metric labels.
   b. The text should be formatted with an Arial 10 point font, Light (font weight), black (text color), with the product number L7668, and with no italic or underline attributes.
   c. Organize the prototype label as follows:
      FNAME LNAME
      COMPANY
      STREET
      CITY, STATE ZIP
      You have to enter spaces between the FNAME and LNAME fields as well as between the CITY, STATE, and ZIP fields. Also, you have to type a comma after the CITY field.
   d. Sort the labels by the ZIP field.
   e. Save and name the report **Mailing Labels**, then view the report.
   f. Close the Club-D database then exit Access.

Independent Challenge 1

You have been hired to create a report for a physical therapy clinic.

a. Start Access then open the **Therapy-D** database from the drive and folder where your Project Files are located.
b. Use the Report Wizard to create a report using all of the fields from the Location Financial Query.
c. View your data by Survey, group by Street, sort by PatientLast, click the Summary Options button, then sum both the AmountSent and AmountRecorded fields.
d. Use the Stepped layout, Portrait orientation, and Soft Gray style.
e. Name the report **Location Financial Report**.
f. Modify the AmountSent and AmountRecorded labels in the Page Header section to **Sent** and **Recorded**, respectively.
g. Change the font/fore color of the labels in the Page Header section to bright blue.
h. Widen the Street text box in the Street Header section to twice its current size, and change the border color to bright blue.
i. Add your name as a label to the Report Header section.
j. Save, then print the report.
k. Close the Therapy-D database then exit Access.

Independent Challenge 2

You have been hired to create a report for a physical therapy clinic.

a. Start Access and open the **Therapy-D** database from the drive and folder where your Project Files are located.
b. Use the Report Wizard to create a report using all of the fields from the Therapist Satisfaction Query except for the Initials and First fields.
c. View the data by Survey. Do not add any grouping levels and do not add any sorting levels.
d. Use the Tabular layout, Portrait orientation, and Casual style.
e. Title the report **Therapist Satisfaction Report**, then view the report.
f. In Report Design View, add your name as a label in the Report Header section, then print the report.
g. Group the report by Last, and open both the Group Header and Group Footer sections for the Last field.
h. Use the Sorting and Grouping dialog box to further sort the records by PatientLast. Close the Sorting and Grouping dialog box.
i. Move the Last text box from the Detail section up into the Last Header section.
j. Remove bold from all of the labels in the Page Header section, then widen the title label in the Report Header section to make sure all of the text appears when previewed.
k. Using the Text Box button on the Toolbar, add two text boxes in the Last Footer section. Place them directly below the Courtesy and Knowledge text boxes that are in the Detail section. Delete the labels that accompany the new text boxes.
l. Insert an expression into the new unbound text boxes to create the calculated controls **=Avg([Courtesy])** and **=Avg([Knowledge])**, respectively.
m. Resize the new calculated controls so that they are the same size as the Courtesy and Knowledge text boxes in the Detail section.
n. Use the property sheet for the two new calculated controls to change the Format property on the Format tab to Fixed.
o. Right-align the two new calculated controls within their own borders. Also, align the right edge of the =Avg([Courtesy]) and the Courtesy text boxes with respect to each other. Right-align the edges of the =Avg([Knowledge]) and Knowledge text boxes with respect to each other.
p. Align the top edges of the new calculated controls with respect to each other.

q. If the report is wider than 6.5" wide, drag the right edge of the report to the left so that the final report is no wider than 6.5".
r. Save, then preview the report. The report should look like Figure D-21.
s. Print the report, close the Therapy-D database, then exit Access.

FIGURE D-21

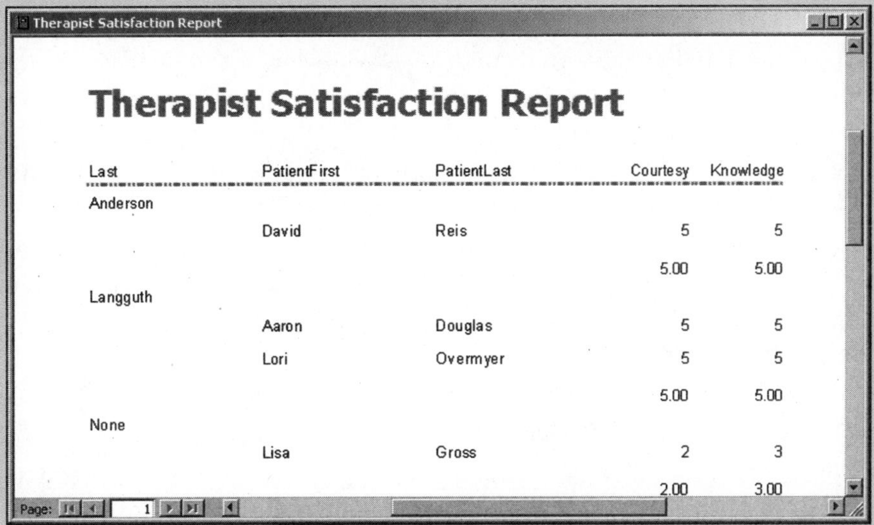
Therapist Satisfaction Report

Therapist Satisfaction Report

Last	PatientFirst	PatientLast	Courtesy	Knowledge
Anderson				
	David	Reis	5	5
			5.00	5.00
Langguth				
	Aaron	Douglas	5	5
	Lori	Overmyer	5	5
			5.00	5.00
None				
	Lisa	Gross	2	3
			2.00	3.00

► Independent Challenge 3

Use the knowledge and skills that you have acquired about Access to create an attractive report that includes information about colleges and universities that offer programs in computer science. Create a database containing this information, and then design a report that displays the data. Gather information from libraries, friends, and the Web to enter into the database.

a. Start Access then create a new database called **Colleges** in the drive and folder where your Project Files are located. Include any fields you feel are important, but make sure you include the institution's name, state, and whether it is a four- or two-year school.
b. Find information on schools that offer programs in computer science. If you are using the Web, use any available search engines.
c. Compile a list of at least five institutions, and enter the five records into a table named **Computer Science Schools**.
d. Create a report that includes all the fields in the table **Computer Science Schools**, and group by the field that contains the information on whether the college is a four- or two-year school.
e. Sort the records by the state, then by the institution's name.
f. Use an appropriate style and title for your report. Insert your initials at the end of the report title.
g. Save, preview, then print the report.
h. Close the Colleges database, then exit Access.

Independent Challenge 4

You are on the staff of an economic development team whose goal is to encourage tourism in the Baltic Sea region. You have created an Access database called Baltic-D to track important fields of information for the countries in that region. You have been using the Internet to find information about events and demographics in the area and entering that information into the database using existing forms. You need to create and then print reports to present to the team.

a. Start Access and open the **Baltic-D** database from the drive and folder where your Project Files are located.
b. Connect to the Internet, then go to www.google.com, www.lycos.com, or another search engine to conduct research for your database. Your goal is to find three upcoming events for Helsinki, Finland, and to print the Web pages.
c. Open the Cities form, find the Helsinki record, and enter three events for Helsinki into the Events fields. EventID is an AutoNumber field, so it will automatically increment as you enter the EventName and EventDate information.
d. Use the Report Wizard to create a report based on the Baltic Area Festivals query. Use all of the fields. View the data by Cities, do not add any more grouping levels, and sort the records in ascending order by EventDate.
e. Use a Stepped layout, a Portrait orientation, and a Corporate style.
f. Title the report **Baltic Area Events**.
g. Switch to Report Design View to apply additional formatting embellishments as desired.
h. Add your name as a label to the Report Header section.
i. Save, print, then close the report. Exit Access.

Visual Workshop

Open the **Club-D** database from the drive and folder where your Project Files are located to create the report based on the CONTACTS table. The report is shown in Figure D-22. The Report Wizard, Stepped Layout, and the Corporate style were used to create this report. Note that the records are grouped by the CITY field and sorted within each group by the LNAME field. A calculated control that counts the number of records is displayed in the City Footer. Add a label with your name to the Report Header section, then save and print the report.

FIGURE D-22

Membership by City — *Your Name*

CITY	LNAME	FNAME	PHONE
Belton			
	Duman	Mary Jane	555-8844
	Hubert	Holly	555-6004
	Mayberry	Mitch	555-0401
Count: 3			
Kansas City			
	Alman	Jill	555-6931
	Bouchart	Bob	555-3081
	Collins	Christine	555-3602
	Diverman	Barbara	555-0401

Access 2002

Modifying

a Database Structure

Objectives

- MOUS ▶ Examine relational databases
- MOUS ▶ Plan related tables and lookups
- MOUS ▶ Create related tables
- MOUS ▶ Define Text fields
- MOUS ▶ Define Number and Currency fields
- MOUS ▶ Define Date/Time and Yes/No fields
- MOUS ▶ Define field validation properties
- MOUS ▶ Create one-to-many relationships
- MOUS ▶ Create lookups

In this unit, you will add new tables to an existing database and link them in one-to-many relationships to create a relational database. You will also modify several field properties to format and validate data. Fred Ames, the new coordinator of training at MediaLoft, has created an Access database to track the courses attended by MediaLoft employees. Courses include hands-on computer classes, business seminars, and self-improvement workshops. The database consists of multiple tables. Fred will link them together to create a relational database.

Access 2002

Examining Relational Databases

A **relational database** is a collection of related tables that share information. The purpose of a relational database is to satisfy dynamic information management needs and to eliminate duplicate data entry wherever possible. MediaLoft employees have tried to track course attendance using a single Access table called Attendance Log, as shown in Figure E-1. Fred sees a data redundancy problem because there are multiple occurrences of the same employee and same course information. He knows that redundant data in one table is a major clue that the database needs to be redesigned. Therefore, Fred studies the principles of relational database design.

- **A relational database is based on multiple tables of data, and each table should be based on only one subject**

  Right now the Attendance Log table in the Training database contains three subjects: courses, attendance, and employees. Therefore, you have to duplicate several fields of information such as the employee's name every time an employee attends a course. Redundant data in one table causes extra data entry work, a higher rate of data inconsistencies and errors, and larger physical storage requirements. Moreover, it limits the user's ability to search for, analyze, and report on the data. These problems can be minimized or eliminated by implementing a properly designed relational database.

- **Each record in a table should be uniquely identified with a primary key field or key field combination**

  A **primary key field** is a field that contains unique information for each record. An Employee Identification or Social Security Number field often serves this purpose in an Employees table. Although using the employee's last name as the primary key field might accommodate a small database, it is a poor choice because it does not accommodate the situation in which two employees have the same last name. The primary key field is also often called the **key field**.

- **Tables in the same database should be related, or linked, through a common field in a one-to-many relationship**

  To tie the information from one table to another, a field must be common to each table. This common field will be the primary key field in one of the tables, creating the "one" side of the relationship and the **foreign key field** in the other table creating the "many" side of the relationship. The primary key field contains a unique entry for each record, but the foreign key field contains the same value "many" times to create a **one-to-many relationship** between the tables. Table E-1 shows common examples of one-to-many relationships between two database tables.

TABLE E-1: One-to-many relationships

table on "one" side of relationship	table on "many" side of relationship	linking field	description
Products	Sales	ProductID	A ProductID field must have a unique entry in a Products table, but will be listed many times in a Sales table as multiple copies of that item are sold
Customers	Sales	CustomerID	A CustomerID field must have a unique entry in a Customers table, but will be listed many times in a Sales table as multiple sales are recorded for the same customer
Employees	Promotions	EmployeeID	An EmployeeID field must have a unique entry in an Employees table, but will be listed many times in a Promotions table as the employee is promoted over time

FIGURE E-1: Attendance Log as a single table

CourseID	Description	Hours	Prereq	Cost	Last	First	Department	Attended	Passed
Comp1	Computer Fundamentals	12		$200	Colletti	Shayla	CD	01/30/2002	☑
Excel1	Introduction to Excel	12	Comp1	$200	Colletti	Shayla	CD	02/13/2002	☑
Excel2	Intermediate Excel	12	Excel1	$200	Colletti	Shayla	CD	03/07/2002	☑
ExcelLab	Excel Case Problems	12	Excel2	$200	Colletti	Shayla	CD	03/15/2002	☐
Internet1	Internet Fundamentals	12	Comp1	$200	Colletti	Shayla	CD	03/07/2002	☑
Netscape1	Introduction to Netscape	12	Internet1	$200	Colletti	Shayla	CD	04/05/2002	☑
Outlook1	Introduction to Outlook	12	Comp1	$200	Colletti	Shayla	CD	04/02/2002	☑
Retail1	Introduction to Retailing	16		$100	Colletti	Shayla	CD	05/08/2002	☑
Retail2	Store Management	16	Retail1	$100	Colletti	Shayla	CD	05/09/2002	☑
Word2	Intermediate Word	12	Word1	$200	Colletti	Shayla	CD	02/14/2002	☑
Word1	Introduction to Word	12	Comp1	$200	Colletti	Shayla	CD	01/19/2002	☑
Comp1	Computer Fundamentals	12		$200	Lee	Nancy	Video	01/30/2002	☑
Access1	Introduction to Access	12	Comp1	$200	Lee	Nancy	Video	02/13/2002	☑
Internet1	Internet Fundamentals	12	Comp1	$200	Lee	Nancy	Video	03/07/2002	☑
Netscape1	Introduction to Netscape	12	Internet1	$200	Lee	Nancy	Video	04/05/2002	☑
Outlook1	Introduction to Outlook	12	Comp1	$200	Lee	Nancy	Video	04/02/2002	☑
PP1	Introduction to PowerPoint	12	Comp1	$200	Lee	Nancy	Video	04/08/2002	☑
Retail1	Introduction to Retailing	16		$100	Lee	Nancy	Video	05/08/2002	☑
Retail2	Store Management	16	Retail1	$100	Lee	Nancy	Video	05/09/2002	☑
Word2	Intermediate Word	12	Word1	$200	Lee	Nancy	Video	02/14/2002	☑
Word1	Introduction to Word	12	Comp1	$200	Lee	Nancy	Video	01/19/2002	☑
Comp1	Computer Fundamentals	12		$200	Shimada	Jeff	Operations	01/30/2002	☑
Excel1	Introduction to Excel	12	Comp1	$200	Shimada	Jeff	Operations	02/13/2002	☑
Excel2	Intermediate Excel	12	Excel1	$200	Shimada	Jeff	Operations	03/07/2002	☑
Internet1	Internet Fundamentals	12	Comp1	$200	Shimada	Jeff	Operations	03/07/2002	☑

Course fields

Attendance fields

Employee fields

Many-to-many relationships

As you are designing your database, you may find that two tables have a many-to-many relationship. To join them, you must establish a third table called a junction table, which creates separate one-to-many relationships with the two original tables. For example, the Customers and Products tables usually have a many-to-many relationship. One customer can purchase many products and one product can be sold to many customers. To implement a connection between the Customers and Products tables in an Access database, you would build a junction table between them, perhaps called the Sales table. Using the Sales table, you would establish one-to-many relationships with the original two tables. Figure E-2 shows how the Sales table would connect the original Customers and Products tables.

FIGURE E-2: Using a junction table

Relationships

Customers: CustomerNo, CustomerName, ContactFirst, ContactLast, Street, City, State, Zip, Phone

Sales: SaleNo, SaleDate, CustomerNo, ProductID

Products: ProductID, Description, UnitCost, UnitPrice

Customers table

Products table

Sales table

One-to-many relationship for Products and Sales tables

Foreign key fields

One-to-many relationship for Customers and Sales tables

Access 2002

Planning Related Tables and Lookups

Careful planning is crucial to successful relational database design. When a database is not planned carefully before it is created, several common database problems occur. These problems range from simple issues such as confusing field names, to complex issues such as improper table structures that limit the flexibility and reliability of information in the database. The most common symptom of an inappropriately designed database is the existence of excessively duplicated data, such as the same customer's name entered in multiple records in the Customers table. Duplicated data is not only prone to error and inefficient to enter, but also limits the query and reporting capabilities of the overall database. A well-designed database minimizes redundant data. After studying the concepts of relational database design, Fred is ready to redesign MediaLoft's Training database. He follows these steps to move from a single table of data to the powerful relational database capabilities provided by Access.

► **List all of the fields of data that need to be tracked**
Typically, these fields are already present in existing tables or paper reports. Still, it is a good idea to document each field in order to examine all fields at the same time.

► **Group fields together in subject matter tables**
The new MediaLoft training database will track courses attended by employees. It will contain three core tables: Courses, Employees, and Attendance. It will also contain one lookup table: Departments.

► **Identify primary key fields that exist in tables**
Each table should include a key field or key field combination in order to uniquely identify each record. Fred will create a SSN field in the Employees table, a CourseID field in the Courses table, and an automatically incrementing (AutoNumber data type) LogID field in the Attendance table to handle this requirement. DeptNo is the primary key field for the Departments table.

► **Link the tables with a one-to-many relationship via a common field**
By adding an SSN field to the Attendance table, Fred creates a common field in both the Employees and Attendance tables that can serve as the link between them. Similarly, by adding a CourseID field to the Attendance table, Fred creates a common field in both the Attendance and Courses tables that can serve as the link. For a valid one-to-many relationship, the linking field must be designated as the primary key field in the "one" side of the one-to-many relationship.

► **Create lookups**
Lookups are reference tables or lists that are used to populate the values of a field. Lookups are established by adding Lookup properties to the field for which you want the lookup behavior to occur. Foreign key fields are good lookup candidates because the data that they contain would often be easier to understand if accompanied by descriptive text. For example, in the MediaLoft-E database the Employees table contains the foreign key field DeptNo that stores numeric department codes. Fred decides to apply Lookup properties to the DeptNo field to look up and display the descriptive DeptName values from the Departments table rather than the less informative departmental numeric code which is physically stored in the DeptNo field. Another common application for Lookup properties exists when a field has a limited set of possible values. The ParkingLot field in the Employees table has only three valid entries: Red, Blue, and Green. Fred uses the Lookup properties of the ParkingLot field to create a value list to store these choices. Fields that contain Lookup properties are called **lookup fields**. Table E-2 summarizes the fields with Lookup properties for the MediaLoft database. The final relationships, fields, and tables for Fred's redesigned relational database are shown in Figure E-3.

FIGURE E-3: One-to-many relationships

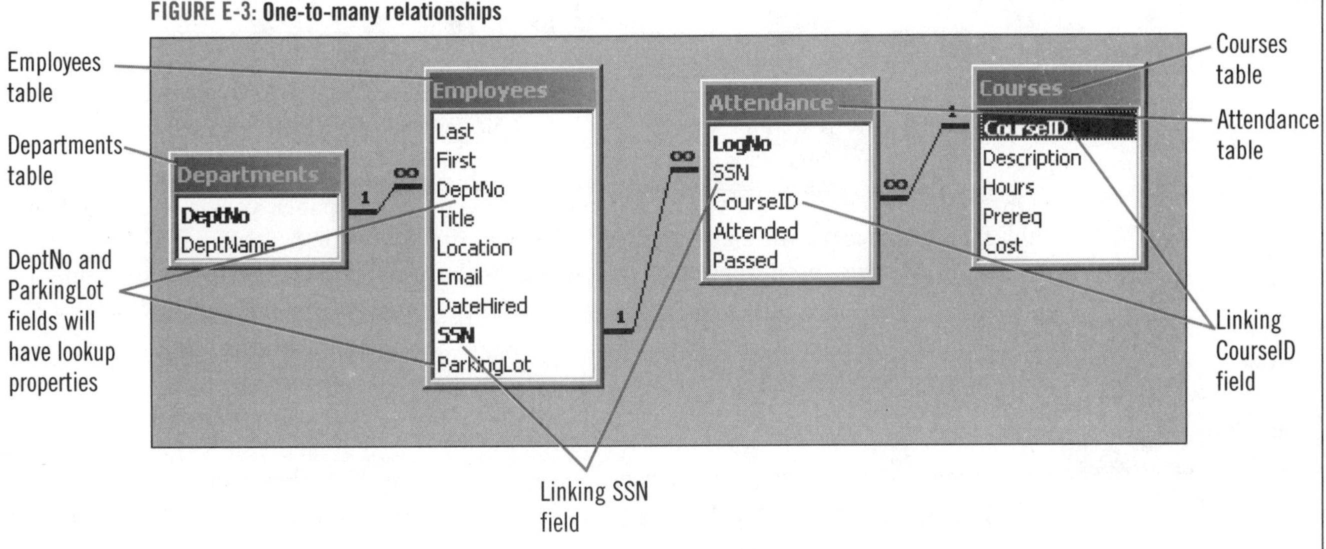

TABLE E-2: Lookup fields

lookup field	table that contains the lookup field	values displayed by the lookup field	where values displayed by the lookup field are stored
DeptNo	Employees	Accounting, Human Resources, Information Systems, Marketing, Operations, Shipping, Training, Book, Café, CD, Video	In the DeptName field of the Departments table
ParkingLot	Employees	Red, Green, Blue	In the Row Source lookup property of the ParkingLot field

Identifying key field combinations

Identifying a single primary key field may be difficult in some tables. Consider, for instance, a table that records employee promotions over time and contains the three fields of EmployeeNumber, Date, and PayRate. None of the fields could individually serve as a valid key field because none are restricted to unique data. The values in the EmployeeNumber and Date fields considered together, however, could serve as a valid **key field combination** because an employee can only be promoted once on any given date.

Creating Related Tables

Once you have developed a valid relational database design on paper, you are ready to define the tables in Access. All characteristics of a table including field names, data types, field descriptions, field properties, lookup properties, and primary key field designations are defined in **Table Design View.** Using the new database design, Fred creates the Attendance table.

Steps

QuickTip

When specifying field data types, you can type the first letter of the data type; for example, type a for AutoNumber, d for Date/Time, or c for Currency.

1. **Start Access, then open the Training-E database from the drive and folder where your Project Files are located**
   The Courses, Employees, and Departments tables already exist in the database.
2. **Click Tables on the Objects Bar (if it is not already selected), then click the New Table button in the Training-E database window**
   The New Table dialog box opens. You define fields for a new table in Table Design View.
3. **Click Design View in the New Table dialog box, then click OK**
   Field names should be as short as possible, but long enough to be descriptive. The field name entered in Table Design View is used as the default name for the field in all later queries, forms, reports, and Web pages.
4. **Type LogNo, press [Enter], click the Data Type list arrow, click AutoNumber, then press [Enter] twice to move to the next row**
   The LogNo field will contain a unique number used to identify each record in the Attendance table (each occurrence of an employee taking a course). The AutoNumber data type, which automatically sequences each new record with the next available integer, works well for this field.
5. **Type the other field names, data types, and descriptions as shown in Figure E-4**
   Field descriptions entered in Table Design View are optional. In Table Datasheet View, the description entry appears in the status bar, and therefore provides further clarification about the data. The descriptions for SSN and CourseID fields are used to clarify the role of these foreign key fields. You are not required to use the same field name for the primary and foreign key fields, but doing so makes it easier to understand the one-to-many relationship.
6. **Click LogNo in the Field Name column, then click the Primary Key button on the Table Design toolbar**
   A **key symbol** appears to the left of LogNo to indicate that this field is defined as the primary key field for this table.
7. **Click the Save button on the Table Design toolbar, type Attendance in the Table Name text box, click OK, then close the table**
   The Attendance table is now displayed as a table object in the Training-E database window.

FIGURE E-4: Design View for the Attendance table

Primary Key button

LogNo will be the primary key field

Field Name	Data Type	Description
LogNo	AutoNumber	
SSN	Text	Employee's SSN and foreign key field to link the Employees table to the Attendance table
CourseID	Text	Course ID Number and foreign key field to link the Courses table to the Attendance table
Attended	Date/Time	Date the course was taken
Passed	Yes/No	Did the employee pass the final test?

Comparing linked to imported tables

The data in a **linked table** is stored in a file that is separate from the open database. For example, you may want to create a linked table to connect an Excel workbook to an Access database. Even though the data is physically stored in the Excel workbook, you can still add, delete, and edit records from within Access. Because the data presented by a linked table is stored in an external file, you cannot change the structure (add, modify, or delete fields) of a linked table from within Access. An **imported table** is a copy of data from an external file. An imported table works exactly the same as a table originally created in Access. There are no restrictions on modifying the data or the structure of a table that was created through an import process.

Access 2002

Defining Text Fields

Field properties are the characteristics that apply to each field in a table, such as Field Size, Default Value, or Caption. These properties help ensure database accuracy and clarity because they can be used to restrict the way data is entered and displayed. Field properties are modified in Table Design View. See Table E-3 for more information on Text field properties. Fred decides to make field property changes to several Text fields in the Employees table.

Steps

1. **If not already selected, click Tables on the Objects bar, right-click the Employees table, then click Design View from the shortcut menu**
   The Employees table opens in Design View. The field properties appear in the lower half of the Table Design View window and display the properties of the selected field. Field properties change depending on the field's data type. For example, when a field with a Text data type is selected, the Field Size property is visible. However, when a field with a Date/Time data type is selected, Access controls the Field Size property, so that property is not displayed. Most field properties are optional, but if they require an entry, Access provides a default value.

2. **Click the SSN field name, look at the field properties, then click each of the field names while viewing the field properties**
   A small black triangle in the **field selector button** to the left of the field indicates which field is currently selected.

QuickTip

Press [F6] to move between field names and field properties in Table Design View.

3. **Click the Last field name, double-click 50 in the Field Size property text box, then type 30**
   Fifty is the default value for the Field Size property for a Text field, but you do not anticipate last name field values to be greater than 30.

4. **Change the Field Size property to 30 for the following field names: First, Title, Location, and Email**
   Changing the Field Size property to 30 for each of these text fields in this table will accommodate the longest entry for each field. The **Input Mask** property provides a visual guide for users as they enter data. It also helps determine what types of values can be entered into a field.

Trouble?

If the Input Mask Wizard is not installed on your computer, you can still complete this step by typing the 000-00-0000;;_ entry directly into the Input Mask property for the SSN field.

5. **Click the SSN field name, click the Input Mask property text box, click the Build button, click Yes if prompted to save the table, click Yes when alerted that some data may be lost (because you changed the field size of several fields from 50 to 30 in the previous step), click Social Security Number in the Input Mask list, click Next, click Next to accept the default input mask, click Next to accept the option to store the data without the symbols in the mask, then click Finish**
   The Design View of the Employees table should look like Figure E-5. Notice that the SSN field is selected, and the new Input Mask property is entered. The SSN field is also the primary key field for the Employees table as evidenced by the key symbol beside the field name.

6. **Click the Save button on the Table Design toolbar, click the Datasheet View button on the Table Design toolbar, maximize the datasheet, press [Tab] enough times to move to the SSN field for the first record, then type 115774444**
   The SSN Input Mask property creates an easy-to-use visual guide to facilitate accurate data entry.

7. **Close the Employees table**

FIGURE E-5: Changing Text field properties

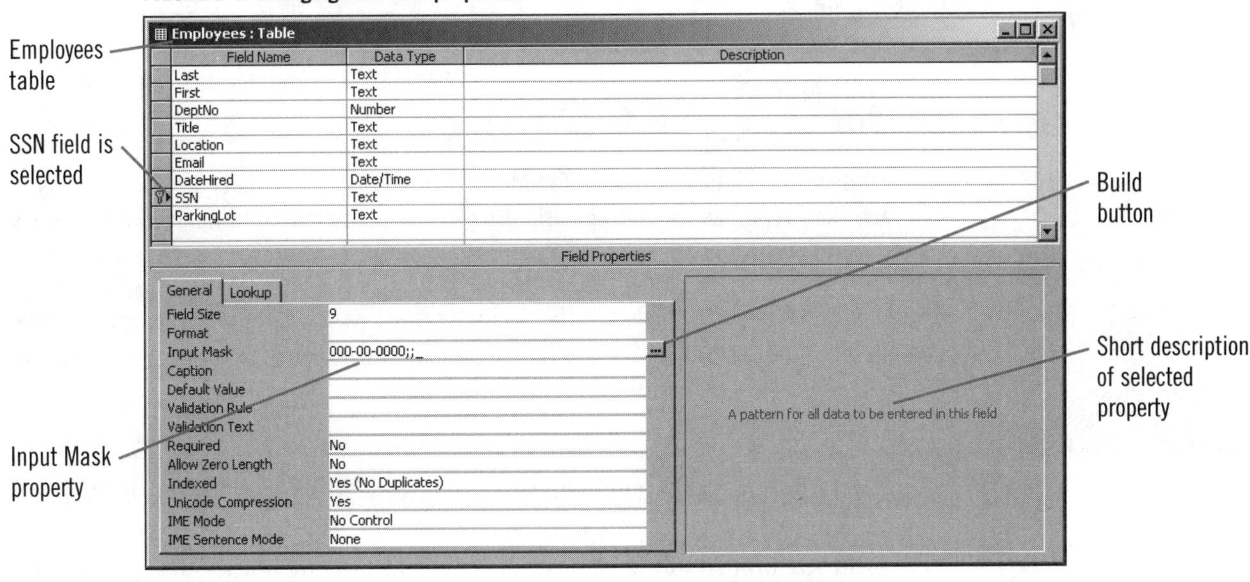

TABLE E-3: Common Text field properties

property	description	sample field name	sample property entry
Field Size	Controls how many characters can be entered into the field.	State	2
Format	Controls how information will be displayed and printed. < forces all characters to display lowercase even though the data is stored in the same way it was entered. > forces all characters to display uppercase even though the data is stored in the same way it was entered.	PartNo State	< >
Input Mask	Provides a pattern for data to be entered and contains three parts separated by semicolons. The first part controls what type of data can be entered and how it will be displayed: **9** represents an optional number; **0** represents a required number; **?** represents an optional letter; **L** represents a required letter. The second part determines whether all displayed characters (such as dashes in the SSN field) are stored in the field, or just the entry; the **0** (zero) entry stores all characters; the **1** (one) entry stores only the entered characters. The third part determines which character Access will display for the space where a character is typed in the input mask. Common entries are the asterisk (*), underscore (_), or pound sign (#).	Phone PartNo SSN ZIP Date	(999") "000-0000;1;_ LOL 0L0;0;* 000-00-0000;1;_ 00000-9999;1;# 99/99/0000;0;_
Caption	A label used to describe the field. When a Caption property isn't entered, the field name is used to label the field.	Emp#	Employee Number
Default Value	Value that is automatically entered in the given field for new records.	City	Kansas City
Required	Determines if an entry is required for this field.	LastName	Yes

Defining Number and Currency Fields

Even though some of the properties for Number and Currency fields are the same as for Text fields, each data type has its own specific list of valid properties. Numeric and Currency fields have very similar properties because they both contain numbers. One important difference, however, is that a Currency field limits the user's control over the field size. A Currency field is accurate to fifteen digits to the left of the decimal point and four digits to the right. The Courses table contains both a Number field (Hours), and a Currency field (Cost). Fred modifies the properties of these two fields.

Steps

1. Click the **Courses table**, click the **Design button** in the Training-E database window, then click the **Hours field name**
   The Field Size property for a Number field defaults to Long Integer. See Table E-4 for more information on common Number field properties.
2. Click the **Field Size property text box**, click the **Field Size list arrow**, then click **Byte**
   Choosing Byte and Integer Field Size property values for a Number field lowers possible values and the storage requirements for that field. The Byte Field Size property value allows entries only from 0 to 255.
3. Click the **Cost field name**, click the **Decimal Places property text box**, click the **Decimal Places list arrow**, then click **0**
   Your screen should look like Figure E-6. Because all of MediaLoft's courses are priced at a round dollar value, there is no need to display cents in each field entry.
4. Click the **Save button** on the Table Design toolbar, click **Yes** when prompted that some data may be lost (because you entered a more restrictive Field Size property for the Hours field in a previous step), then click the **Datasheet View button** on the Table Design toolbar
   Since none of the entries in the Hours field were greater than 255, the maximum value allowed by a Number field with a Byte Field Size, you won't lose any data. You want to test the new property changes.
5. Press **[Tab]** twice to move to the Hours field for the first record, type **1000**, then press **[Tab]**
   Because 1,000 is larger than the Byte Field Size property will allow, you are cautioned with an Access error message indicating that the value isn't valid for this field.
6. Click **OK**, press **[Esc]** to remove the inappropriate entry in the Hours field, then press **[Tab]** twice to move to the Cost field
   The Cost field displays zero digits after the decimal point.
7. Type **199.75** in the Cost field of the first record, press **[Enter]**, then click **200** in the Access1 record's Cost field
   Even though the Decimal Places property for the Cost field dictates that entries in the field are formatted to display zero digits after the decimal point, 199.75 is the actual value stored in the field. Formatting properties such as Decimal Places do not change the actual data, but only the way it is displayed.
8. Close the Courses table

QuickTip

Pressing [Esc] once removes edits from the current field. Pressing [Esc] twice removes edits from all fields of the current record.

FIGURE E-6: Changing Currency and Number field properties

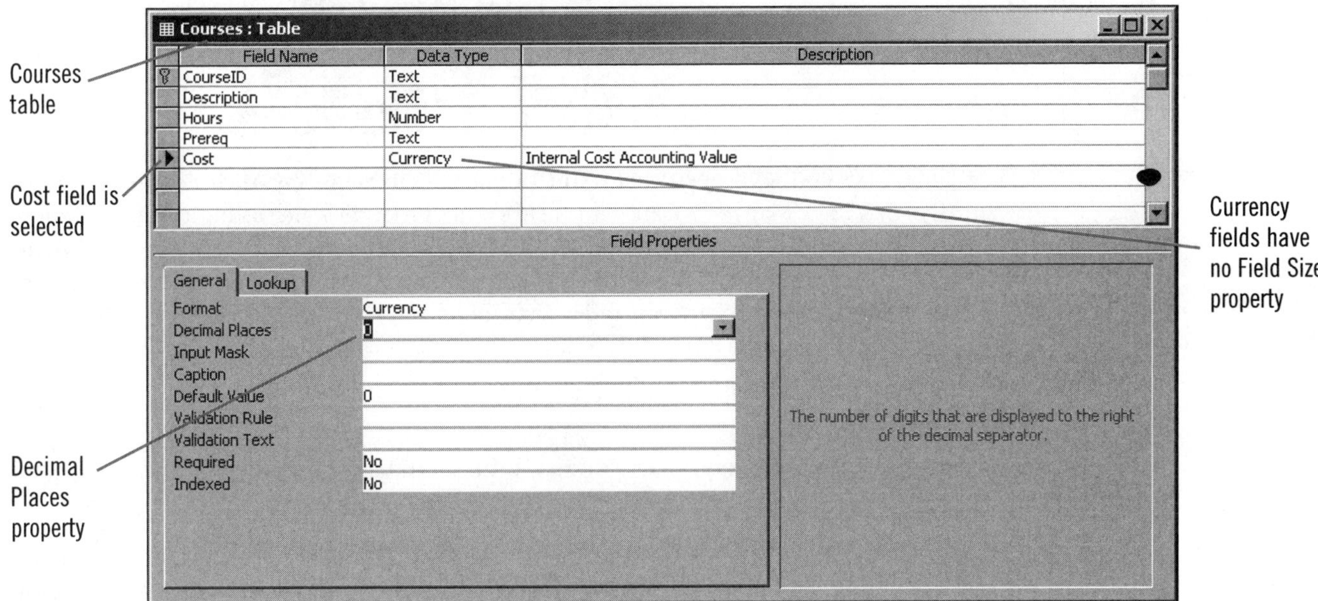

Access 2002

TABLE E-4: Common Number and Currency field properties

property	description
Field Size (for a Number field)	Determines the largest number that can be entered in the field, as well as the type of data (e.g., integer or fraction)
	Byte stores numbers from 0 to 255 (no fractions)
	Integer stores numbers from –32,768 to 32,767 (no fractions)
	Long Integer stores numbers from –2,147,483,648 to 2,147,483,647 (no fractions)
	Single stores numbers (including fractions with six digits to the right of the decimal point) times 10 to the –38th to +38th power
	Double stores numbers (including fractions with over 10 digits to the right of the decimal point) in the range of 10 to the –324th to +324th power
Decimal Places	The number of digits displayed to the right of the decimal point

Access 2002

Defining Date/Time and Yes/No Fields

A Date/Time field's **Format** property helps you format dates in many ways such as January 5, 2003; 05-Jan-03; or 1/5/2003. Many of a Date/Time field's other properties such as Input Mask, Caption, and Default Value are very similar to fields with a Text or Number data type. Fred wants to change the format of Date/Time fields in the database. He also wants to make sure that the Yes/No field is displayed as a check box rather than a text entry of "Yes" or "No."

Steps

1. Right-click the **Attendance table**, click **Design View** on the shortcut menu, then click the **Attended field name**
   You want the dates of attendance to display as 01/07/2002 instead of as 1/7/2002.
2. Click the **Format text box** in the Field Properties, then click the **Format list arrow**
   Although several predefined Date/Time formats are available, none matches the format you want. To define a custom format, enter symbols that represent how you want the date to appear.
3. Type **mm/dd/yyyy**
   The updated Format property for the Attended field shown in Figure E-7 forces the date to appear with two digits for the month, two digits for the day, and four digits for the year. The parts of the date will be separated by forward slashes. The **Display Control** property that determines how a Yes/No field appears is on the Lookup tab and you want to examine this property for the Passed field.

QuickTip

Click a property text box, then press F1 to open the Microsoft Access Help window to the specific page that describes that property.

4. Click the **Passed field name**, then click the **Lookup properties tab**
   A Yes/No field may appear as a check box in which checked equals "yes" and unchecked equals "no," as a text box that displays "yes" or "no," or as a combo box that displays "yes" and "no" in the drop-down list. By default, Yes/No fields appear as check boxes. The SSN field in this table would be improved if it contained the same Input Mask property as previously defined for the SSN field in the Employees table.
5. Click the **SSN field**, click the **General properties tab**, click the **Input Mask text box**, then type **000-00-0000;;_**
   While some properties provide helpful wizards such as the Input Mask Wizard, you can always directly enter a property if you know what it should be.
6. Click the **Save button** on the Table Design toolbar
   Access automatically added backslash (\) characters to the Input Mask property when you saved the table. A backslash in the Input Mask property causes the next character to be displayed as a literal character. Access provides default entries for many properties as well as syntax support throughout the program. **Syntax** refers to the technical rules that govern a language or program.

QuickTip

Click the check box or press the spacebar to check or uncheck it.

7. Click the **Datasheet View button** on the Table Design toolbar, press **[Tab]** to move to the SSN field, type **115774444**, press **[Tab]**, type **Comp1**, press **[Tab]**, type **1/25/02**, press **[Tab]**, then press **[Spacebar]**
   Your screen should look like Figure E-8. Double-check that the SSN and Attended fields are formatted correctly, too.
8. Press **[Enter]**, press **[Tab]** to move through the LogNo field, type **222334400**, press **[Tab]**, type **Comp1**, press **[Tab]**, type **1/25/02**, press **[Tab]**, then press **[Spacebar]**
   Two records are entered in the Attendance table.

FIGURE E-7: Changing Date/Time field properties

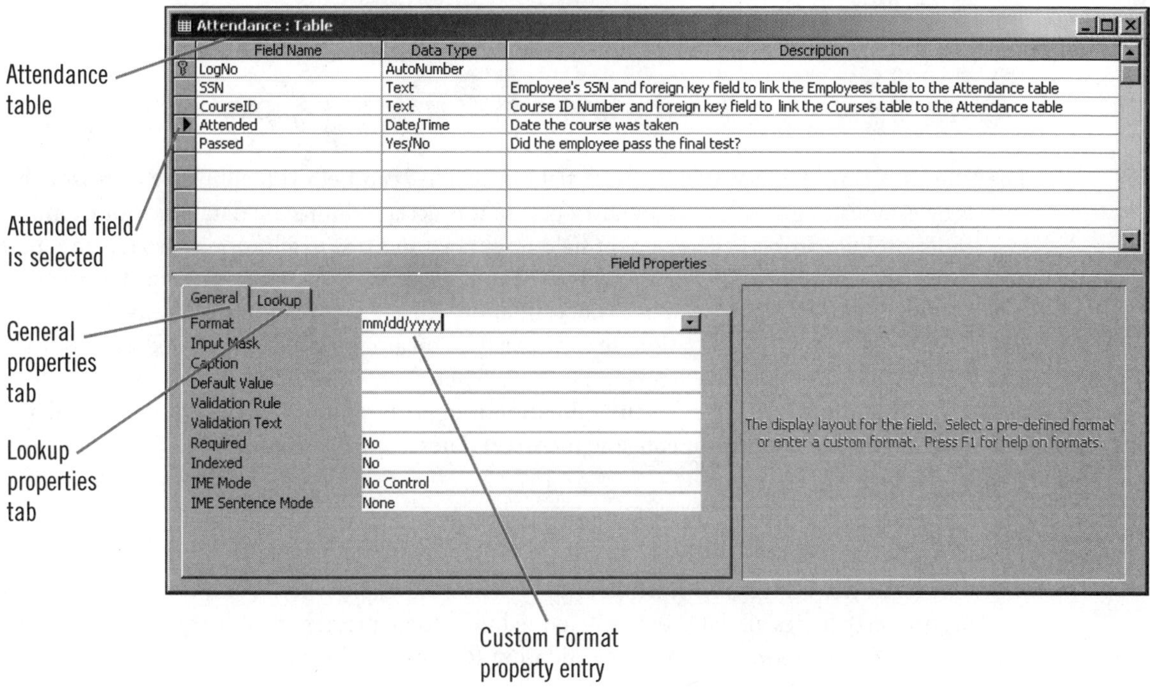

FIGURE E-8: Testing field property changes

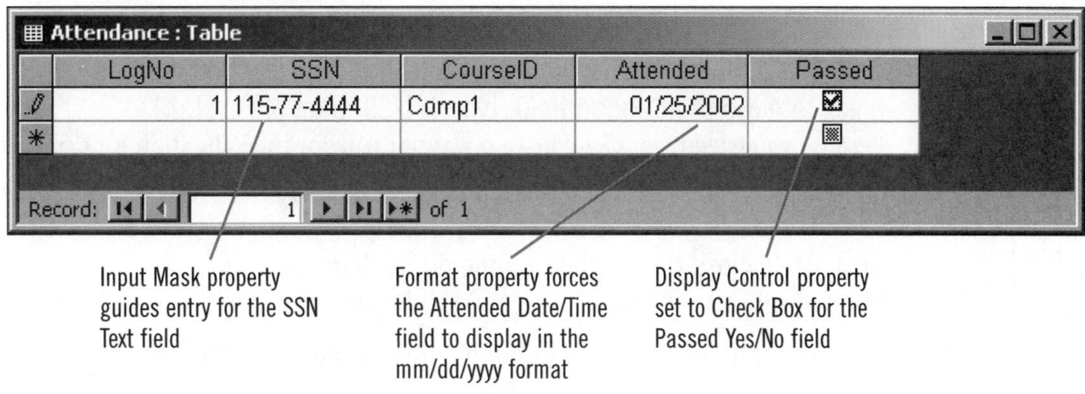

Access 2002

Defining Field Validation Properties

The **Validation Rule** and Validation Text field properties can help you eliminate unreasonable entries by establishing criteria for an entry before it is accepted into the database. For example, the Validation Rule property of a Gender field might be modified to allow only two entries: male or female. The **Validation Text** property is used to display an explanatory message when a user tries to enter data that doesn't pass the Validation Rule property for that field. Without a Validation Rule entry, the Validation Text property is meaningless. MediaLoft started providing in-house courses on January 17, 2002. Therefore, it wouldn't make sense to enter a date before that time. Fred modifies the validation properties of the Date field in the Attendance table to help prevent users from entering incorrect dates.

Steps

1. Click the **Design View button** on the Table Datasheet toolbar, click the **Attended field**, click the **Validation Rule property text box**, then type **>=1/17/2002**
   This property forces all dates in the Attended field to be greater than or equal to 1/17/2002. See Table E-5 for more examples of Validation Rule expressions.
2. Click the **Validation Text text box**, then type **Date must be on or after 1/17/2002**
   The Validation Text property provides a helpful message to the user in the event that he or she attempts to make an entry in that field that doesn't pass the criteria entered in the Validation Rule property. The Design View of the Attendance table should now look like Figure E-9. Once again, Access modified a property to include additional syntax by changing the entry in the Validation Rule property to >=#1/17/2002#. Pound signs (#) are used to surround date criteria.
3. Click the **Save button** on the Table Design toolbar, then click **Yes** when asked to test the existing data with new data integrity rules
   Because all dates in the Attended field are more recent than 1/17/2002, there are no date errors in the current data, and the table is saved. You should test the Validation Rule and Validation Text properties in the datasheet.
4. Click the **Datasheet View button** on the Table Design toolbar, press **[Tab]** three times to move to **Attended field**, type **1/1/99**, then press **[Tab]**
   Because you tried to enter a date that was not true for the Validation Rule property for the Attended field, a dialog box opens and displays the Validation Text entry as shown in Figure E-10.
5. Click **OK** to close the Validation Rule dialog box
   You know that the Validation Rule and Validation Text properties work properly.
6. Press **[Esc]** to reject the invalid date entry in the Attended field
7. Close the Attendance table

QuickTip

Access assumes that years entered with two digits in the range 30 to 99 refer to the years 1930 through 1999, whereas digits in the range 00 to 29 refer to the years 2000 through 2029. If you wish to indicate a year outside these ranges, you must enter all four digits of the year.

FIGURE E-9: Using the validation properties

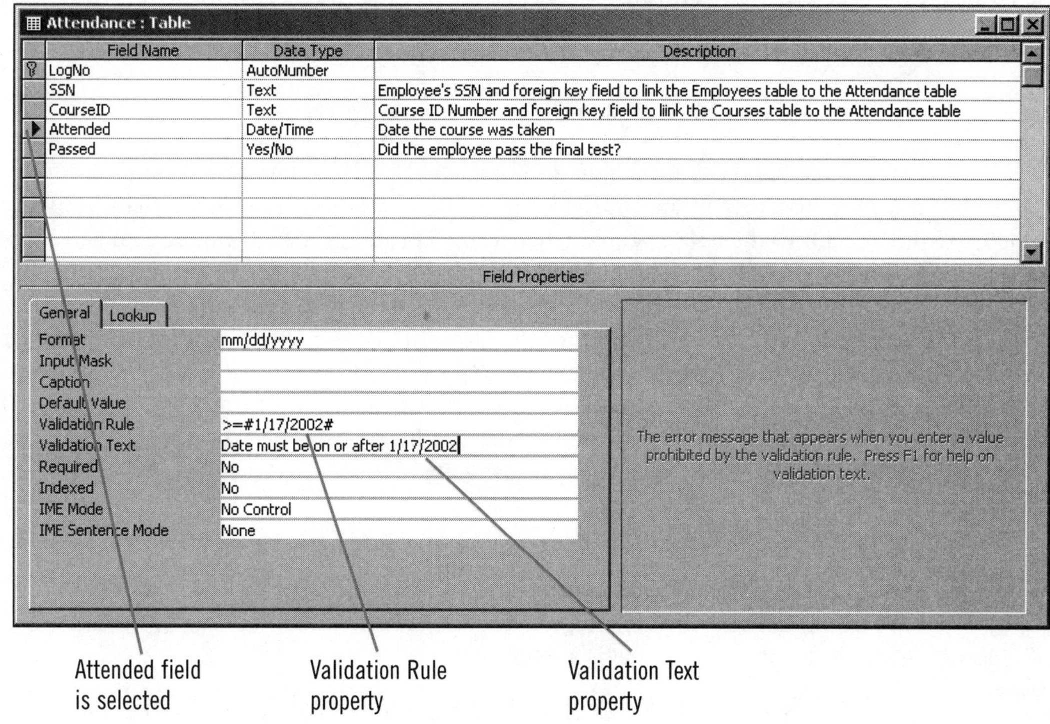

FIGURE E-10: Validation Text message

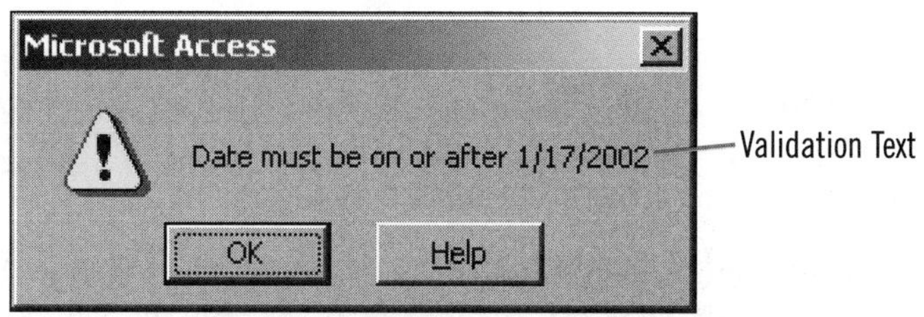

TABLE E-5: Validation Rule expressions

data type	validation rule expression	description
Number or Currency	>0	The number must be positive
Number or Currency	>10 And <100	The number must be between 10 and 100
Number or Currency	10 Or 20 Or 30	The number must be 10, 20, or 30
Text	"IA" Or "NE" Or "MO"	The entry must be IA, NE, or MO
Date/Time	>=#1/1/93#	The date must be on or after 1/1/1993
Date/Time	>#1/1/80# And <#1/1/90#	The date must be between 1/1/1980 and 1/1/1990

Access 2002

Creating One-to-Many Relationships

Once the initial database design and table design phase have been completed, you must link the tables together in appropriate one-to-many relationships. Some field properties that do not affect how the data is stored (such as the Format property) can be changed after the tables are linked, but other properties (such as the Field Size property) are more difficult to change once tables are linked. Therefore, it is best to complete all of the table and field design activities before linking the tables. Once the tables are linked, you can design queries, reports, and forms with fields from multiple tables. Fred's initial database sketch revealed that the SSN field will link the Employee table to the Attendance table, and that the CourseID field will link the Courses table to the Attendance table. Fred defines the one-to-many relationships between the tables of the Training-E database.

Trouble?

If the three tables do not appear in the Relationships window, click the Show Table button on the Relationships toolbar to add them.

QuickTip

To display all of a table's field names, drag the bottom border of the field list until all fields are visible. Drag the table's title bar to move the field list.

Trouble?

To delete a relationship from the Relationships window, click the relationship line then press [Delete].

1. Click the **Relationships button** on the Database toolbar
   The Employees, Attendance, and Courses table field lists appear in the Relationships window. The primary key fields are bold.
2. Click **SSN** in the Employees table field list, then drag it to the **SSN** field in the Attendance table field list
   Dragging a field from one table to another in the Relationships window links the two tables with the selected fields and opens the Edit Relationships dialog box as shown in Figure E-11. Referential integrity helps ensure data accuracy.
3. Click the **Enforce Referential Integrity check box** in the Edit Relationships dialog box, then click **Create**
   The **one-to-many line** shows the linkage between the SSN field of the Employees table and the Attendance table. The "one" side of the relationship is the unique SSN for each record in the Employees table. The "many" side of the relationship is identified by an infinity symbol pointing to the SSN field in the Attendance table. The CourseID field will link the Courses table to the Attendance table.
4. Click **CourseID** in the Courses table field list, drag it to **CourseID** in the Attendance table field list, click the **Enforce Referential Integrity check box**, then click **Create**
   The finished Relationships window should look like Figure E-12.
5. Click **File** on the menu bar, click **Print Relationships**, click the **Print button** on the Print Preview toolbar, close the Relationships report without saving it, then close the Relationships window
   A printout of the Relationships window, called the Relationships report, shows structural information including table names, field names, key fields, and relationships between tables.
6. Double-click the **Courses table** to open the datasheet, then click the **Comp1 expand button** [+]
   Your screen should look like Figure E-13. When a table is related to another, its datasheet will show an **expand button** [+] to the left of the record. Click the expand button to show related records in the "many" table as a **subdatasheet**. When the related records appear, the expand button becomes a **collapse button** [−]. Click the collapse button to close the subdatasheet.
7. Close the Courses table

FIGURE E-11: **Edit Relationships dialog box**

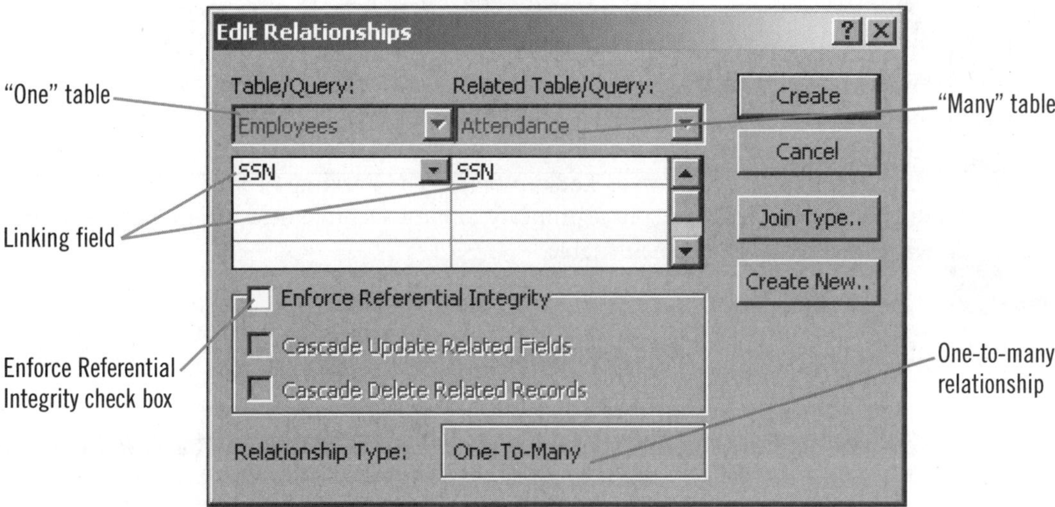

FIGURE E-12: **Final Relationships window**

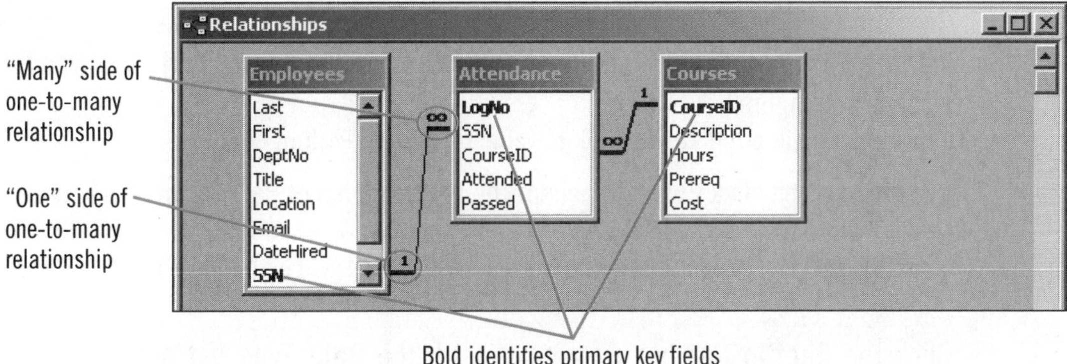

FIGURE E-13: **A subdatasheet allows you to view related records**

Courses : Table

CourseID	Description	Hours	Prereq	Cost
Access1	Introduction to Access	12	Comp1	$200
Access2	Intermediate Access	24	Access1	$400
AccessLab	Access Case Problems	12	Access2	$200
Comp1	Computer Fundamentals	12		$200
Excel1	Introduction to Excel	12	Comp1	$200
Excel2	Intermediate Excel	12	Excel1	$200
ExcelLab	Excel Case Problems	12	Excel2	$200

Subdatasheet (Comp1):

LogNo	SSN	Attended	Passed
1	115-77-4444	01/25/2002	☑
2	222-33-4400	01/25/2002	☑
*			

Expand button

Collapse button

One record in the Courses table is related to two records in the Attendance table

Subdatasheet

Enforcing referential integrity

Referential integrity is a set of rules that help ensure that no orphan records are entered or created in the database. An **orphan record** is a record in the "many" table that doesn't have a matching entry in the linking field of the "one" table. (In this case, an orphan record would be a record in the Attendance table that contains an SSN entry that is not present in the Employees table, or a CourseID entry that is not present in the Courses table.) Referential integrity also prevents the user from deleting a record from the "one" table if a matching entry exists in the linking field of the "many" table. You should enforce referential integrity on all one-to-many relationships if possible. Unfortunately, if you are working with a database that already contains orphan records, you will not be able to enforce this powerful set of rules.

Access 2002

Creating Lookups

A Lookup field may display values stored in a related table or you may enter a lookup list in the **Row Source** Lookup property of the field itself. The **Lookup Wizard** can also be used to set Lookup properties. Fred wants the ParkingLot and the DeptNo fields in the Employees table to behave as Lookup fields. The ParkingLot field will lookup a list of values stored in the field's Row Source property, and the DeptNo field will lookup the DeptName field values from the Departments table.

Steps

1. Right-click the **Employees table**, then click **Design View**
   The Lookup Wizard is the last entry in the Data Type list.
2. Click the **ParkingLot Text** data type, click the **Data Type list arrow**, then click **Lookup Wizard**
   The Lookup Wizard starts and prompts you for information about where the lookup column will get its values.
3. Click the **I will type in the values that I want option button**, click **Next**, click the first **cell** in the Col1 column, type **Red**, press **[Tab]**, type **Blue**, press **[Tab]**, then type **Green** as shown in Figure E-14
   These values will populate the lookup value list for the ParkingLot field.
4. Click **Next**, then click **Finish** to accept the default label of ParkingLot and to complete the wizard
   Note that the data type for the ParkingLot field is still Text. The Lookup Wizard is a process for setting Lookup property values for a field, and is not a data type itself.
5. Click the **DeptNo Number** data type, click the **Data Type list arrow**, then click **Lookup Wizard**
   In this case, you want the Lookup field to lookup department name values in another table. Department names are stored in the DeptName field in the Departments table.
6. Click **Next**, click **Table: Departments**, click **Next**, double-click **DeptName** to move it to the Selected Fields list, click **Next**, click **Next** to accept the column width, click **Finish**, then click **Yes** to save the table
   Now the DeptNo field in the Employees table will lookup and present department names from the Departments table.
7. Click the **Lookup properties tab** to observe the new Lookup properties for the DeptNo field, then click the **ParkingLot field name** to observe the new Lookup properties, as shown in Figure E-15
   The Lookup Wizard helped you enter the correct Lookup properties for these fields.
8. Click the **Datasheet button** on the Table Design toolbar, press **[Tab]** twice to move to the DeptNo field, click the **DeptNo list arrow**, click **Book**, press **[Tab]** six times to move to the ParkingLot field, click the **ParkingLot list arrow** as shown in Figure E-16, then click **Blue**
   Both the ParkingLot and DeptNo fields now present lookup values. The DeptNo field looks up actual department names from the DeptName field of the Departments table instead of showing the DeptNo number. The ParkingLot field looks up a list of values that you entered via the Lookup Wizard, which are stored in its Row Source Lookup property.
9. Close the Employees datasheet, close the Training-E database, then exit Access

FIGURE E-14: **Entering a Lookup list of values**

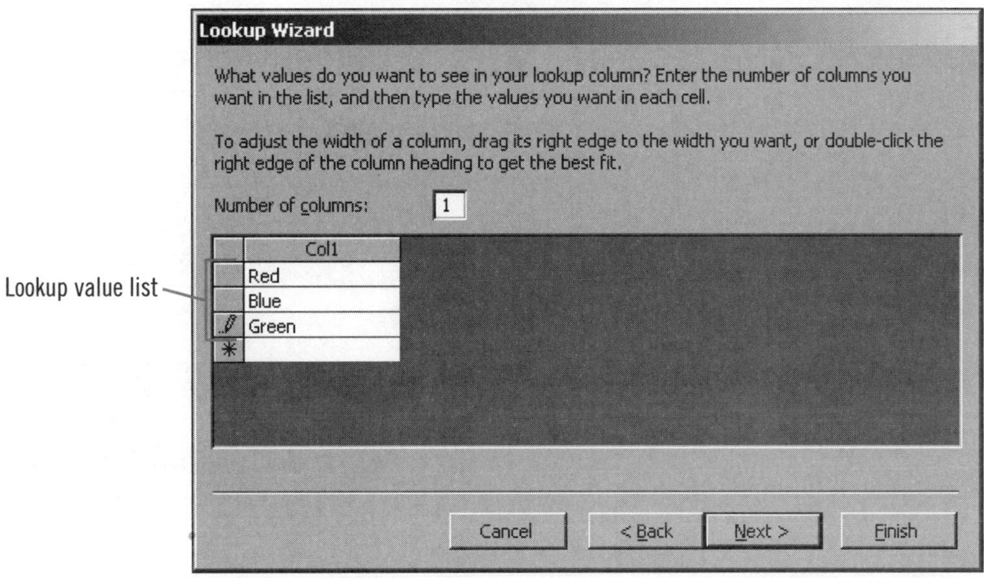

FIGURE E-15: **Viewing Lookup properties**

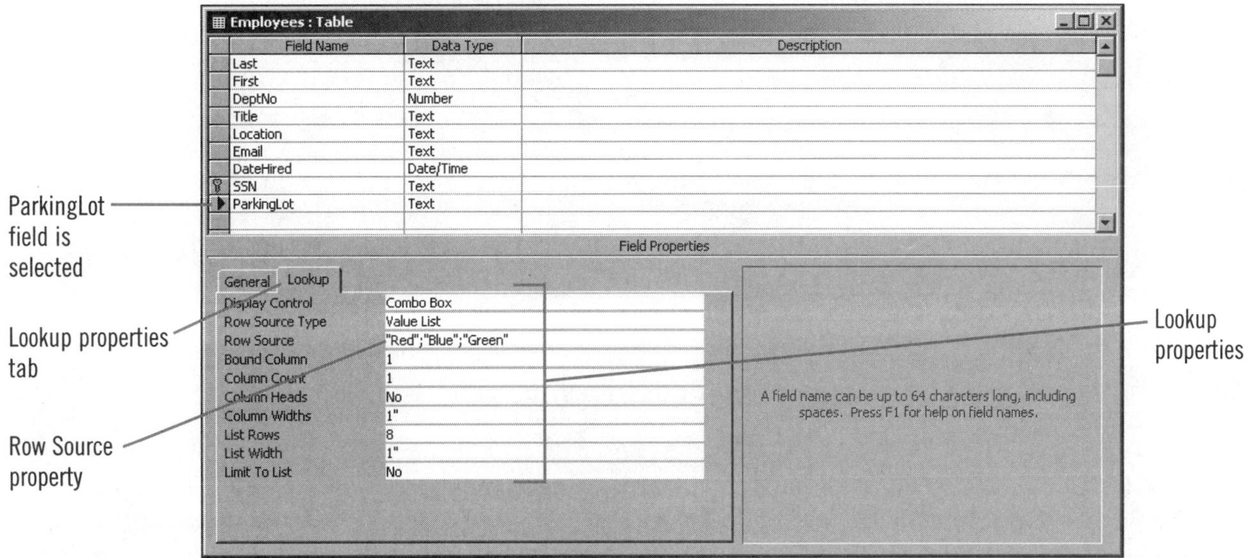

FIGURE E-16: **Using a Lookup field in a datasheet**

Employees : Table

Location	Email	DateHired	SSN	ParkingLot
New York	scolletti@medialoft.com	2/15/1998	115-77-4444	
San Francisco	nlee@medialoft.com	3/22/1998	134-70-3883	Red
Corporate	jshimada@medialoft.com	8/20/1998	173-48-5873	Blue
Corporate	lalber@medialoft.com	8/6/1998	222-33-4400	Green
Boston	mrath@medialoft.com	1/3/1997	234-56-7800	
Corporate	jfernandez@medialoft.com	7/1/1998	321-00-8888	
Corporate	ddumont@medialoft.com	1/1/1999	333-33-8887	
Seattle	jhayashi@medialoft.com	9/23/1998	333-44-0099	
Kansas City	mrollo@medialoft.com	4/6/1999	345-88-0098	

Record: 1 of 20

List of values for the ParkingLot Lookup field

Access 2002

Practice

► Concepts Review

Identify each element of the Table Design View shown in Figure E-17.

FIGURE E-17

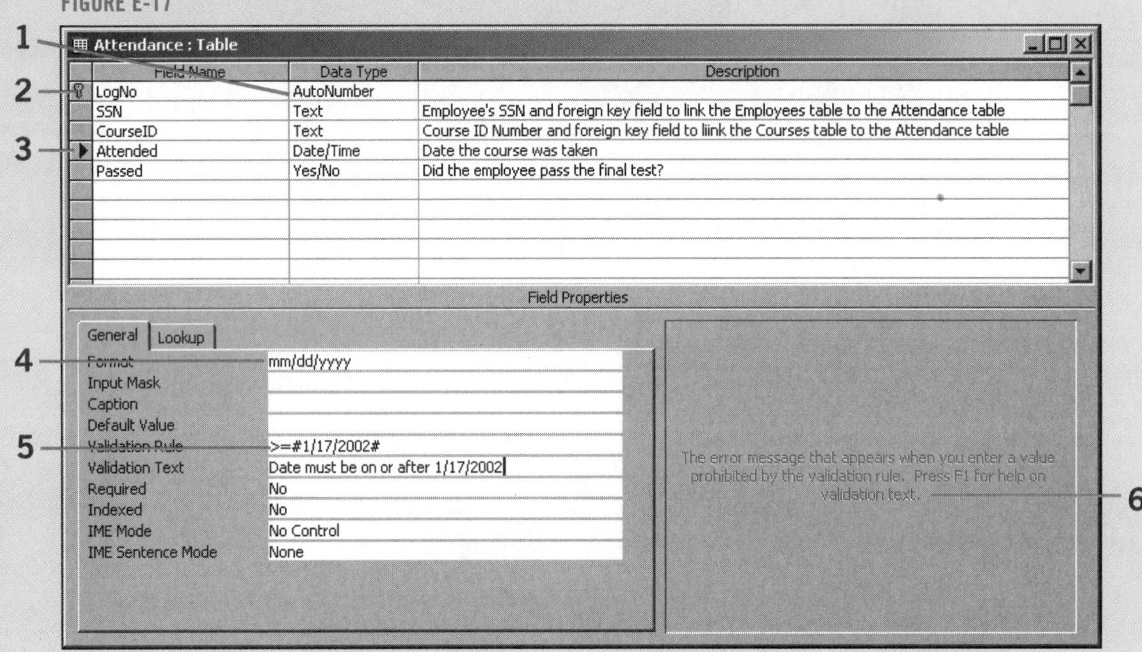

Match each term with the statement that describes its function.

7. Primary key
8. Properties
9. Table Design View
10. Validation Rule
11. Relational database

a. Several tables linked together in one-to-many relationships
b. A field that holds unique information for each record in the table
c. Where all characteristics of a table, including the field names, the primary key field, and all field properties are defined
d. Characteristics that apply to the fields of a table, such as Field Size, Default Value, or Format
e. Helps eliminate unreasonable entries by establishing criteria for the entry

Select the best answer from the list of choices.

12. Which of the following problems most clearly indicates that you need to redesign your database?
a. There is duplicated data in many fields and records of a table.
b. Referential integrity is enforced on table relationships.
c. Not all fields have Validation Rule properties.
d. The Input Mask Wizard has not been used.

13. Which of the following is NOT defined in Table Design View?
a. The primary key field
b. Duplicate data
c. Field Size properties
d. Field data types

► Skills Review

1. **Examine relational databases.**
   a. Examine your address book.
   b. Write down the fields you will need if you were to enter this information into an Access relational database.
   c. Identify those fields that contain duplicate values if all of the fields were to be stored in one table.
2. **Plan related tables and lookups.**
   a. Group the fields that you identified into subject matter tables, then identify the primary key field for each table.
   b. Your database will contain two tables: Names and Zips. If you did not identify these two tables earlier, regroup the fields within these two table names, then identify how the tables will be related.
   c. Identify potential lookups.
3. **Create related tables.**
   a. Start Access, then click the Blank Database link in the New section of the New File task pane.
   b. Type **Membership-E** as the filename, then save the database where your Project Files are located.
   c. Create a new table using Table Design View with the following field names and data types: **First**, Text; **Last**, Text; **Street**, Text; **Zip**, Text; **Birthday**, Date/Time; **Dues**, Currency; **MemberNo**, Text; **MemberType**, Text; **CharterMember**, Yes/No.
   d. Identify MemberNo as the primary key field, save the table as **Names**, then close it.
   e. Create a new table using Table Design View with the following field names and data types: **Zip**, Text; **City**, Text; **State**, Text.
   f. Identify Zip as the primary key field, save the table as **Zips**, then close it.
   g. Create a new table using Table Design View with the following field names and data types: **MemberNo**, Text; **ActivityDate**, Date/Time; **Hours**, Number.
   h. Save the table without a primary key field, name it **Activities**, then close it.
4. **Define Text fields.**
   a. Open the Zips table in Design View.
   b. Change the Field Size property of the State field to **2** and the Field Size property of the Zip field to **9**, then save the table.
   c. Use the Input Mask Wizard to create the Input Mask property for the Zip field. Choose the Zip Code Input Mask. Accept the other default options provided by the Input Mask Wizard, then click Finish.
   d. Save the changes, then close the Zips table. Open the Names table in Design View.
   e. Change the Field Size property of the First, Last, and Street fields to **30**, the MemberNo field to **5**, and the Zip field to **9**. Save the changes to the table.
   f. Use the Input Mask Wizard to create the Input Mask property for the Zip field. Choose the Zip Code input mask. Accept the other default options provided by the Input Mask Wizard. If the Input Mask Wizard is not installed on your computer, type **00000\-9999;;_** for the Input Mask property for the Zip field.
   g. Save the changes, then close Names table. Open the Activities table in Design View.
   h. Change the Field Size property of the MemberNo field to **5**, save the change, then close the Activities table.
5. **Define Number and Currency fields.**
   a. Open the Names table in Design View.
   b. Change the Decimal Places property of the Dues field to **0**. Save the change then close the Names table.
   c. Open the Activities table in Design View.
   d. Change the Field Size property of the Hours field to **Byte**. Save the change, then close the Activities table.
6. **Define Date/Time and Yes/No fields.**
   a. Open the Names table in Design View.
   b. Change the Format property of the Birthday field to **mm/dd/yyyy**.

   c. Check to ensure that the Display Control property (on the Lookup tab of the Field Properties) of the CharterMember field is set to **Check Box**.
   d. Save the changes, then close the Names table.
   e. Open the Activities table in Design View.
   f. Change the Format property of the ActivityDate field to **mm/dd/yyyy**.
   g. Save the change, then close the Activities table.

7. **Define field validation properties.**
   a. Open the Zips table in Design View.
   b. Click the State field name, click the Validation Rule text box, then type **=IA OR KS OR MO**
   c. Click the Validation Text text box, then type **State must be IA, KS, or MO**. Note the quotation marks, the additional syntax, that Access automatically added to the Validation Rule property.
   d. Save the changes then open the Zips table in Datasheet View.
   e. Test the Validation Text and Validation Rule properties by entering a new record with the Zip value of **661112222**, a City value of **Blue Valley**, and a State value of **MN**. Click OK when prompted with the Validation Text message, edit the State value to be **IA**, then close the Zips table.

8. **Create one-to-many relationships.**
   a. Open the Relationships window, double-click Activities, double-click Names, then double-click Zips to add all three tables to the Relationships window. Close the Show Table dialog box.
   b. Drag the Zip field from the Zips table to the Zip field in the Names table to create a one-to-many relationship between the Zips table and Names table using the common Zip field.
   c. Enforce referential integrity for this relationship.
   d. Drag the MemberNo field from the Names table to the MemberNo field in the Activities table to create a one-to-many relationship between the Names and the Activities table using the common MemberNo field.
   e. Enforce referential integrity for this relationship.
   f. Resize all of the field lists by dragging the borders of the lists so that all fields are visible.
   g. Click File on the menu bar, click Print Relationships to create a report of the Relationships window, add your name as a label to the Report Header section if desired, then print the report.
   h. Close the Relationships report without saving the report, then close the Relationships window. Save the changes to the Relationships window if prompted.

9. **Create lookups.**
   a. Open the Names table in Design View, then start the Lookup Wizard for the MemberType field.
   b. Select the option that allows you to enter your own values, use [Tab] to enter **Senior**, **Active**, and **Inactive** as the values for the lookup column, then accept the rest of the Lookup Wizard defaults.
   c. In Datasheet View, enter a new record using your name and the Zip value of **661112222** to test the Lookup properties for the MemberType field, then print, save, and close the Names datasheet.
   d. Close the Membership-E database then exit Access.

► Independent Challenge 1

As the manager of a music store's instrument rental program, you have decided to create a database to track instrument rentals to schoolchildren. The fields you need to track can be organized with four tables: Instruments, Rentals, Customers, and Schools.

   a. Start Access, then create a new blank database called **Music Store-E**, where your Project Files are located.
   b. Use Design View to create the four tables in the Music Store-E database using the following information. Note that the primary key fields are bold in the table.

c. Enter **>=#1/1/02#** as the Validation Rule property to the Date field of the Rentals table. This change will only allow dates of 1/1/02 or later to be entered into this field.

d. Enter **Dates must be on or later than 1/1/2002** as the Validation Text property to the Date field of the Rentals table.

e. Open the Relationships window, add all four tables to the window in the arrangement shown in Figure E-18, then create one-to-many relationships as shown.

f. Preview the Relationships report, then print the report making sure that all fields of each table are visible. (If you need your name on the printout, add your name as a label to the Report Header.)

g Close the Relationships report without saving it. Close the Relationships window, then save the layout if prompted.

h. Close the Music Store-E database, then exit Access.

FIGURE E-18

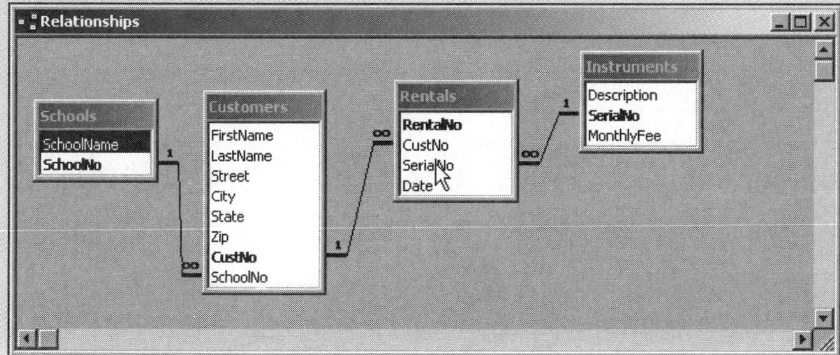

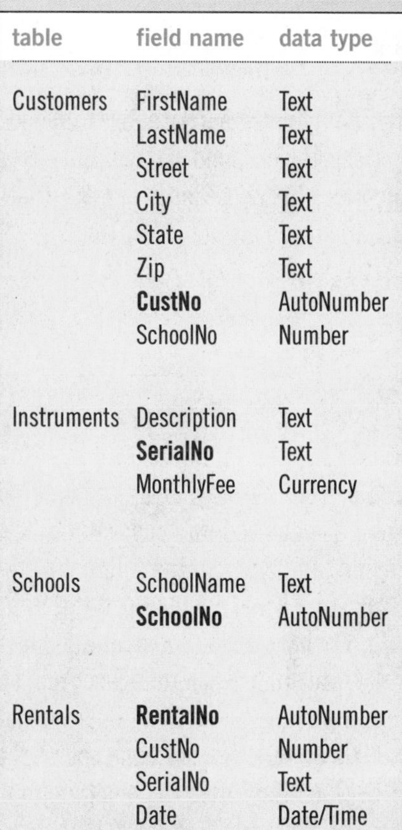

table	field name	data type
Customers	FirstName	Text
	LastName	Text
	Street	Text
	City	Text
	State	Text
	Zip	Text
	CustNo	AutoNumber
	SchoolNo	Number
Instruments	Description	Text
	SerialNo	Text
	MonthlyFee	Currency
Schools	SchoolName	Text
	SchoolNo	AutoNumber
Rentals	**RentalNo**	AutoNumber
	CustNo	Number
	SerialNo	Text
	Date	Date/Time

▶ Independent Challenge 2

You want to document the books you've read by creating and storing the information in a relational database. You will design the database on paper including the tables, field names, data types, and relationships.

a. On paper, create three balanced columns by drawing two vertical lines from the top to the bottom of the paper. At the top of the first column write **Table**. At the top of the second column write **Field Name**, and at the top of the third column write **Data Type**.

b. In the middle column, list all of the fields that need to be tracked to record information about the books you've read. You'll want to track such information as the book title, category (such as Biography, Mystery, or Science Fiction), rating (a numeric value from 1–10 that indicates how satisfied you were with the book), date you read the book, author's first name, and author's last name.

c. In the first column, identify the table where this field would be found. (Hint: You should identify two tables of information for this listing of fields.)

d. Identify the primary key fields found in the tables by circling the field name. If you do not find any fields that are good candidates for key fields, you may have to create additional fields. (*Hint:* Each book has an ISBN—International Standard Book Number—that is a unique number assigned to every book. To uniquely identify each author, you will have to create a new field. Don't use the author's last name as the primary key field as that precludes you from entering two authors with the same last name.)

e. In a third column, identify the appropriate data type for each field.

f. On a new piece of paper, sketch the fields as they would appear in the Relationships window of Access.

 Independent Challenge 3

You want to create a database that documents blood donations by employees. You will design the database on paper including the tables, field names, data types, and relationships. You'll want to track information such as employee name, employee Social Security number (SSN), employee department, employee blood type, date of donation, and hospital the donation was given to. Also, you'll want to track basic hospital information, such as the hospital name and address.

a. Complete Steps a. through f. as described in Independant Challenge 2 using the new case information. You should identify three tables for this case.

 Independent Challenge 4

You are on the staff of an economic development team whose goal is to encourage tourism in the Baltic Sea region. You have created an Access database called Baltic-E to track important fields of information for the countries in that region, and will use the Internet to find information about the area and enter it into existing forms.

a. Start Access, then open the **Baltic-E** database from the drive and folder where your Project Files are located.
b. Connect to the Internet, and then go to www.google.com, www.lycos.com, or any general search engine to conduct research for your database. Your goal is to find three upcoming events for Munich, Germany, and to print that Web page.
c. Open the Cities form, find the Munich record, and enter three more events for Munich into the Events fields. EventID is an AutoNumber field, so it will automatically increment as you enter the EventName and EventDate information.
d. Open the Cities table in Design View, then add a field called **MemberStatus** with a Text data type and a Field Size property of **11** to document the city's status with your economic development team.
e. Use the Lookup Wizard to provide the values **Charter**, **Active**, **Inactive**, and **No Interest** for the Lookup list.
f. Using the Report Wizard, create a report based on the Baltic Area Festivals query. Use all of the fields. View the data by Cities, do not add any more grouping levels, then sort the records by EventDate.
g. Use a Stepped layout, a Portrait orientation, and a Corporate style.
h. Title the report **Baltic Area Events**, then apply additional formatting embellishments as desired.
i. Add your name as a label to the Report Header section. Save, print, then close the report.
j. Close the Baltic-E database, then exit Access.

► Visual Workshop

Open the **Training-E** database, create a new table called **Vendors** using the Table Design View shown in Figure E-19 to determine field names and data types. Additional property changes include changing the Field Size property of the VState field to **2**, the VZip field to **9**, the VendorID and VPhone fields to **10**, and all other text fields to **30**. Be sure to specify that the VendorID field is the primary key field. Enter one record into the datasheet with your name in the VendorName field, then print the datasheet.

FIGURE E-19

Vendors : Table

Field Name	Data Type
VendorID	Text
VendorName	Text
VStreet	Text
VCity	Text
VState	Text
VZip	Text
VPhone	Text

General | Lookup

Field Size	10
Format	
Input Mask	
Caption	
Default Value	
Validation Rule	
Validation Text	
Required	No
Allow Zero Length	Yes
Indexed	Yes (No Duplicates)
Unicode Compression	Yes
IME Mode	No Control
IME Sentence Mode	None

Access 2002

Creating
Multiple Table Queries

Objectives

- MOUS ► **Create select queries**
- MOUS ► **Sort a query on multiple fields**
- MOUS ► **Develop AND queries**
- MOUS ► **Develop OR queries**
- MOUS ► **Create calculated fields**
- MOUS ► **Build summary queries**
- MOUS ► **Create crosstab queries**
- MOUS ► **Create PivotTables and PivotCharts**

Queries are database objects that answer questions about the data by pulling fields and records that match specific criteria into a single datasheet. A **select query**, the most common type of query, retrieves data from one or more linked tables and displays the results in a datasheet. In addition, queries can sort records, calculate new fields of data, or develop summary calculations such as the sum or average of the values in a field. **Crosstab queries** present information in a cross-tabular report, similar to PivotTables in Microsoft Excel. The MediaLoft Training database has been updated so that it contains information concerning which employees are taking which classes. Fred Ames, coordinator of training, creates select queries and crosstab queries to analyze the data in the database.

Access 2002

Creating Select Queries

You create queries by using the **Query Wizard** or by directly specifying requested fields and query criteria in **Query Design View**. The resulting query datasheet is not a duplication of the data that resides in the original table's datasheet; it is simply a logical *view* of the data. If you change or enter data in a query's datasheet, the data in the underlying table (and any other logical view) is automatically updated. Queries are often used to present and sort a subset of fields from multiple tables. Fred creates a query to answer the question, "Who is taking what courses?" He pulls fields from several tables into a query object to display a single datasheet that answers this question.

1. Start Access, then open the **Training-F** database from the drive and folder where your Project Files are stored
2. Click **Queries** on the Objects bar, then double-click **Create query in Design view**
   The Show Table dialog box opens and lists all the tables in the database. You use the Show Table dialog box to add the tables that contain the fields you want to view in the final query datasheet.
3. Click **Employees**, click **Add**, double-click **Attendance**, double-click **Courses**, then click **Close**
   The upper part of Query Design View displays **field lists** for the three tables. Each table's name is in the field list title bar. Drag the title bar of a field list to move it. Drag the edge of a field list to resize it. Key fields are bold, and serve as the "one" side of the one-to-many relationship between two tables. Relationships are displayed with **one-to-many join lines** between the linking fields, as shown in Figure F-1. The fields you want displayed in the datasheet must be added to the columns in the lower part of Query Design View. The lower pane of the Query Design View window is called the **query design grid**, or simply the **design grid**.
4. Click the **First field** in the Employees table field list, then drag the **First field** to the Field cell in the first column of the query design grid
   The order in which the fields are placed in the query design grid is the order they appear in the datasheet.
5. Double-click the **Last field** in the Employees field list, double-click the **Attended field** in the Attendance field list, double-click the **Description field** in the Courses field list, then double-click the **Hours field** in the Courses field list
   Your Query Design View should look like Figure F-2. You may delete a field from the query design grid by clicking the field selector above the field name and pressing [Delete]. Deleting a field from the query design grid removes it from the logical view of this query's datasheet, but does not delete the field from the database. A field is defined and the field's contents are stored in a table object only.
6. Click the **Hours field selector**, press **[Delete]** to remove the field from the query design grid, then click the **Datasheet View button** on the Query Design toolbar
   The resulting datasheet looks like Figure F-3. The datasheet shows the four fields selected in Query Design View and displays 153 records. The records represent the 153 different times a MediaLoft employee attended a class. Shayla Colletti appears in 11 records because she attended 11 classes.

Trouble?

If you add a table to Query Design View twice by mistake, click the title bar of the extra field list, then press [Delete].

QuickTip

When you drag a field to the query design grid, the existing fields move to the right to accommodate the new field.

Trouble?

If you add the wrong field, click the Field cell list arrow in the query design grid, then choose another field from the list. Choose a field from another table by clicking the Table cell list arrow in the query design grid, and choosing another table.

FIGURE F-1: Query Design View with multiple tables

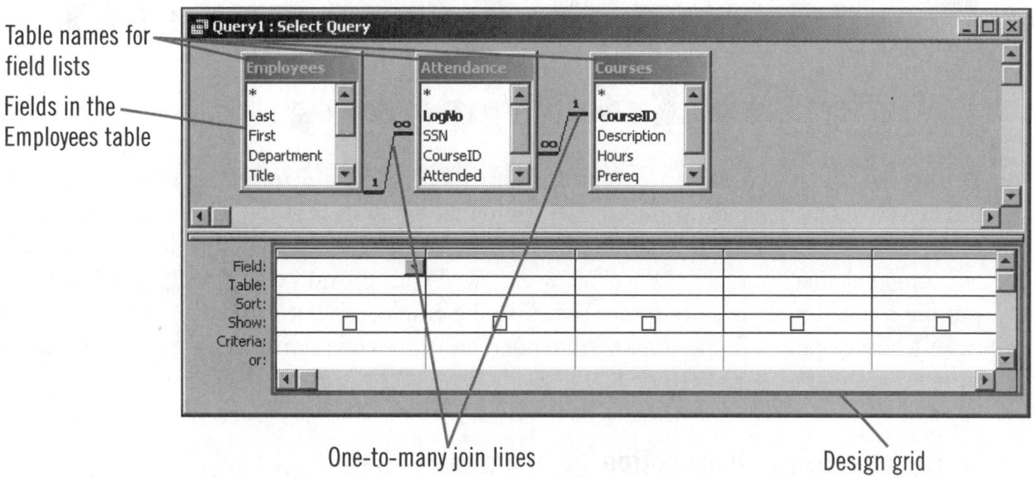

FIGURE F-2: Query Design View with five fields in the query design grid

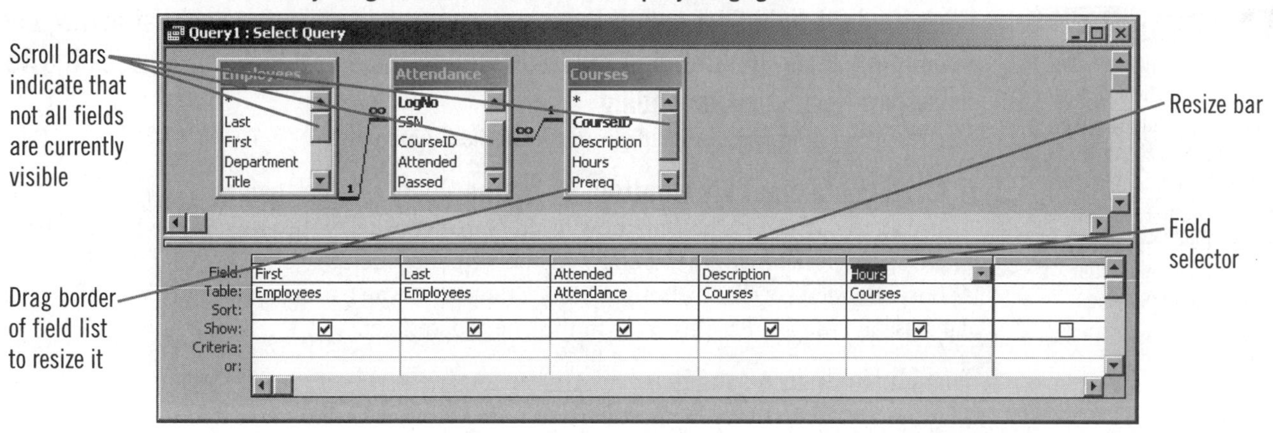

FIGURE F-3: Query datasheet showing related information from three tables

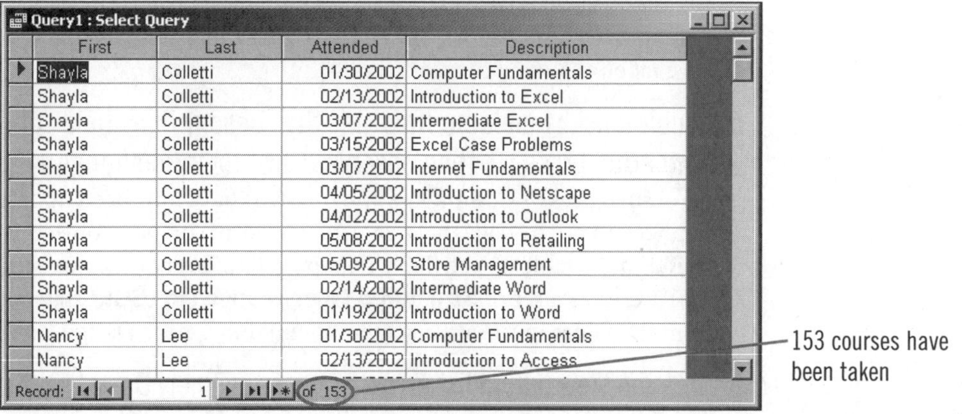

First	Last	Attended	Description
Shayla	Colletti	01/30/2002	Computer Fundamentals
Shayla	Colletti	02/13/2002	Introduction to Excel
Shayla	Colletti	03/07/2002	Intermediate Excel
Shayla	Colletti	03/15/2002	Excel Case Problems
Shayla	Colletti	03/07/2002	Internet Fundamentals
Shayla	Colletti	04/05/2002	Introduction to Netscape
Shayla	Colletti	04/02/2002	Introduction to Outlook
Shayla	Colletti	05/08/2002	Introduction to Retailing
Shayla	Colletti	05/09/2002	Store Management
Shayla	Colletti	02/14/2002	Intermediate Word
Shayla	Colletti	01/19/2002	Introduction to Word
Nancy	Lee	01/30/2002	Computer Fundamentals
Nancy	Lee	02/13/2002	Introduction to Access

Resizing Query Design View

Drag the **resize bar** up or down to provide more room for the upper (field lists) or lower (query design grid) panes of Query Design View. By dragging the resize bar down, you may have enough room to enlarge each field list so that you can see all of the field names for each table.

Sorting a Query on Multiple Fields

Sorting refers to reorganizing the records in either ascending or descending order based on the values in a field. Queries allow you to specify more than one sort field in Query Design View. Queries evaluate the sort fields from left to right. The sort field farthest to the left is the primary sort field. Sort orders defined in Query Design View are saved with the query object. Fred wants to put the records in alphabetical order based on the employee's last name. If more than one record exists for an employee (if the employee attended more than one class), Fred further sorts the records by the date the course was attended.

1. **Click the Design View button on the Query Datasheet toolbar**
   To sort the records according to Fred's plan, the Last field must be the primary sort field, and the Attended field the secondary sort field.

2. **Click the Last field Sort cell in the query design grid, click the Sort list arrow, click Ascending, click the Attended field Sort cell in the query design grid, click the Sort list arrow, then click Ascending**
   The resulting query design grid should look like Figure F-4.

QuickTip

You can resize the columns of a datasheet by pointing to the right column border that separates the field names, then dragging ↔ left or right to resize as needed. Double-click ↔ to automatically adjust the column width to fit the widest entry.

3. **Click the Datasheet View button on the Query Design toolbar**
   The records of the datasheet are now listed alphabetically by the entry in the Last field, then in chronological order by the entry in the Attended field, as shown in Figure F-5. Maria Abbott attended six classes, but you notice that her name has been incorrectly entered in the database as "Marie." Fix this error in the query datasheet.

4. **Type Maria, then press [↓]**
   This update shows that you are using a properly designed relational database because changing any occurrence of an employee's name should cause all other occurrences of that name to be automatically updated. The employee name is physically stored only once in the Employees table, although it is displayed in this datasheet once for every time the employee has attended a course. Similarly, the values in the Description field are physically stored only once in the Courses table, but appear many times in this datasheet because many employees have taken the same course.

5. **Double-click Fundamentals in the Description field of the third record, type Concepts, press [↓], then observe the automatic change to record 8**
   All occurrences of Computer Fundamentals have now been updated to Computer Concepts. Changes made to data through a query, form, or page object actually update data that is stored in the table object. Table data populates every other view of the information. A query object creates a set of **Structured Query Language (SQL)** statements that retrieves the data from the tables in the arrangement defined in Query Design View.

6. **Click the View button list arrow on the Query Datasheet toolbar, then click SQL View**
   The three SQL statements determine what fields are selected, how the tables are joined, and how the resulting records will be sorted. When you save a query, you are saving SQL statements. Fortunately, you do not have to be able to write or even understand SQL code to use Access. The easy-to-use Query Design View gives you a way to select and sort data from underlying tables without being an SQL programmer.

7. **Close the SQL window, click Yes when prompted to save the changes, type Employee Progress Query in the Query Name text box, then click OK**
   The query is now saved and listed as a query object in the Training-F database window.

FIGURE F-4: Specifying multiple sort orders in Query Design View

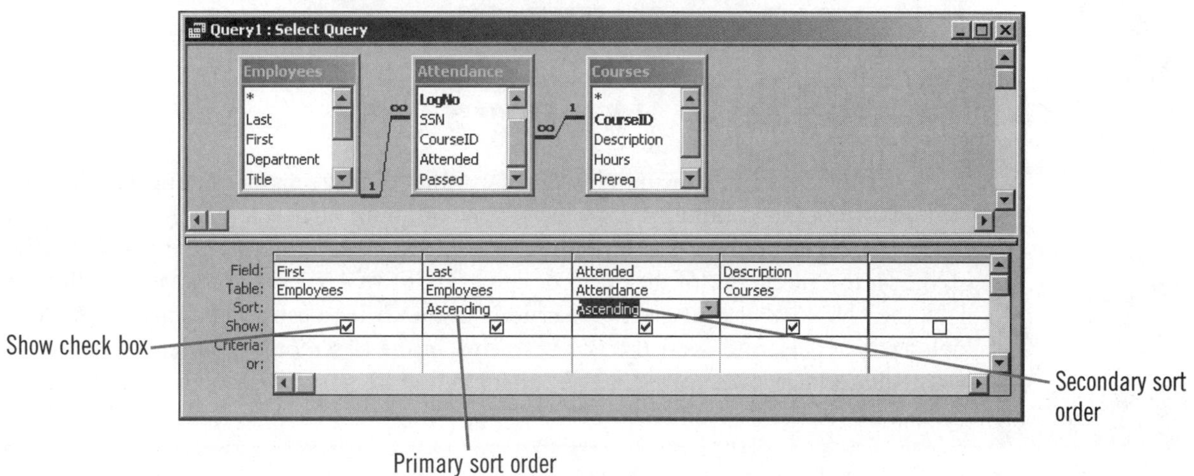

FIGURE F-5: Records sorted by Last, then Attended

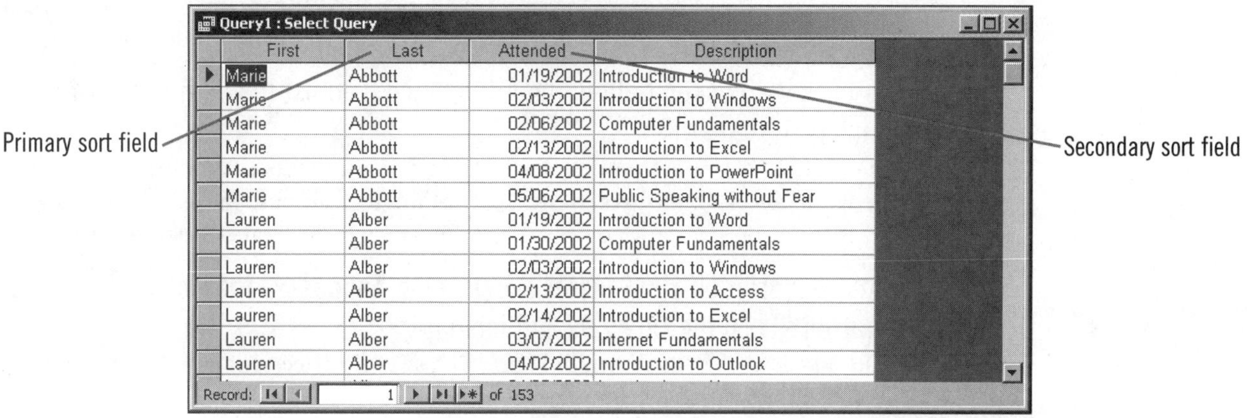

First	Last	Attended	Description
Marie	Abbott	01/19/2002	Introduction to Word
Marie	Abbott	02/03/2002	Introduction to Windows
Marie	Abbott	02/06/2002	Computer Fundamentals
Marie	Abbott	02/13/2002	Introduction to Excel
Marie	Abbott	04/08/2002	Introduction to PowerPoint
Marie	Abbott	05/06/2002	Public Speaking without Fear
Lauren	Alber	01/19/2002	Introduction to Word
Lauren	Alber	01/30/2002	Computer Fundamentals
Lauren	Alber	02/03/2002	Introduction to Windows
Lauren	Alber	02/13/2002	Introduction to Access
Lauren	Alber	02/14/2002	Introduction to Excel
Lauren	Alber	03/07/2002	Internet Fundamentals
Lauren	Alber	04/02/2002	Introduction to Outlook

CLUES TO USE

Specifying a sort order different from the field order in the datasheet

You cannot modify the left-to-right sort order hierarchy in Query Design View. However, if you wish to have the fields in the datasheet appear in an order different than the order by which they are sorted, there is a simple solution, as shown in Figure F-6. By adding a field to the query design grid twice and by unchecking the Show check box for the sort fields, the resulting datasheet can be sorted in one order (Department then Last) yet display data in another order (Last then Department).

FIGURE F-6: Query grid for sorting out of order

Field:	Department	Last	Last	Department
Table:	Employees	Employees	Employees	Employees
Sort:	Ascending	Ascending		
Show:	☐	☐	☑	☑
Criteria:				
or:				

Sort order is defined using fields that do not display on the datasheet

Show check boxes are unchecked

Access 2002

Access 2002

Developing AND Queries

Often, you'll want to limit the number of records that display on the resulting datasheet. **Criteria** are tests, or limiting conditions, for which the record must be true to be selected for a datasheet. To create an **AND query** in which two or more criteria are present, enter the criteria for the fields on the same Criteria row of the query design grid. If two AND criteria are entered for the *same* field, the AND operator separates the criteria in the Criteria cell for that field. Fred is looking for a person to assist the Access teacher in the classroom. In order to compile a list of potential candidates, he creates an AND query to find all employees who have taken MediaLoft's Access courses and passed the exams.

Steps

1. Right-click the **Employee Progress Query**, click **Design View** from the shortcut menu, click the **View button list arrow** on the Query Design toolbar, then click **Design View**
   Instead of creating a new query from scratch to find potential Access teachers, you decide to modify the Employee Progress Query as this query already contains most of the data you need. The only additional field you have to add to the query is the Passed field.
2. Double-click the **Passed field** in the Attendance field list to add it to the fifth column in the query design grid
   MediaLoft offers several Access courses, so the criteria must specify all the records that contain the word "Access" anywhere in the Description field. You use the asterisk (*), a **wildcard character** that represents any combination of characters, to create this criterion.
3. Click the **Description field Criteria cell**, type ***access***, then click the **Datasheet View button** on the Query Design toolbar
   The resulting datasheet, as shown in Figure F-7, shows thirteen records that match the criteria. The resulting records all contain the word "access" in some part of the Description field, but because of the placement of the asterisks, it didn't matter *where* (beginning, middle, or end) the word was found.
4. Click the **Design View button** on the Query Datasheet toolbar, click the **Passed field Criteria cell**, then type **yes**
   You added the criteria to display only those records where the Passed field equals Yes. The resulting query design grid is shown in Figure F-8. Access assists you with **criteria syntax**, rules by which criteria need to be entered. Access automatically adds quotation marks to surround text criteria in Text fields, and pound signs (#) to surround date criteria in Date/Time fields. The criteria in Number, Currency, and Yes/No fields are not surrounded by any characters. Notice that Access entered quotation marks around "*access*" in the Description field, and added the **Like operator**. See Table F-1 for more information on common Access comparison operators.
5. Click on the Query Design toolbar to view the resulting records
   Multiple criteria added to the same line of the query design grid (AND criteria) must *each* be true for the record to appear in the resulting datasheet, thereby causing the resulting datasheet to display *fewer* records. Only nine records contain "access" in the Description field and "yes" in the Passed field.
6. Click **File** on the menu bar, click **Save As**, type **Potential Access Assistants** in the Save Query 'Employee Progress Query' To: text box, then click **OK**
   The query is saved with the new name, Potential Access Assistants, as a new object in the MediaLoft-F database.
7. Close the Potential Access Assistants datasheet

FIGURE F-7: Datasheet for Access records

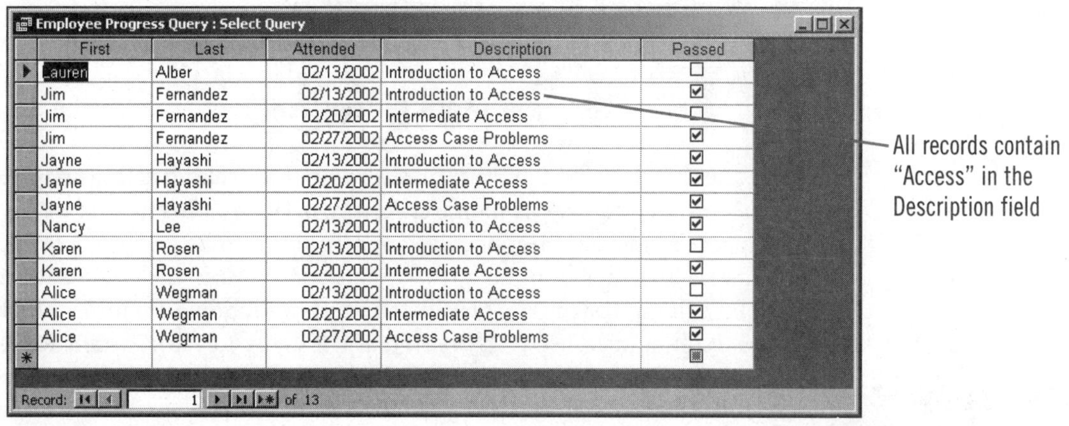

FIGURE F-8: AND criteria

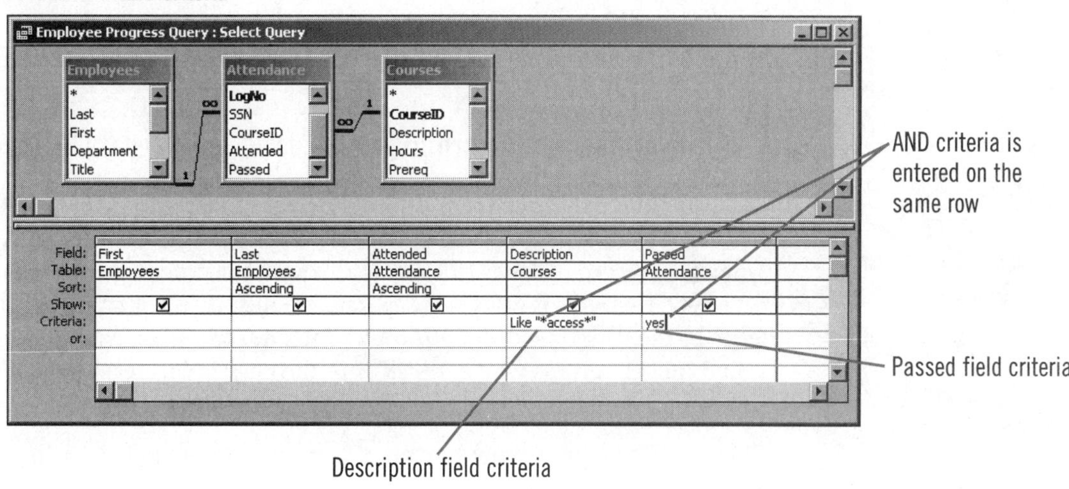

Access 2002

TABLE F-1: Common comparison operators

operator	description	example	result
>	greater than	>50	Value exceeds 50
>=	greater than or equal to	>=50	Value is 50 or greater
<	less than	<50	Value is less than 50
<=	less than or equal to	<=50	Value is 50 or less
<>	not equal to	<>50	Value is any number other than 50
Between...And	finds values between two numbers or dates	Between #2/2/01# And #2/2/03#	Dates between 2/2/2001 and 2/2/2003, inclusive
In	finds a value that is one of a list	In("IA","KS","NE")	Value equals IA or KS or NE
Null	finds records that have no entry in a particular field	Null	No value has been entered in a field
Is Not Null	finds records that have any entry in a particular field	Is Not Null	Any value has been entered in a field
Like	finds records that match the criteria	Like "A*"	Value starts with A
Not	finds records that do not match the criteria	Not 2	Numbers other than 2

Access 2002

Developing OR Queries

AND queries *narrow* the number of records in the resulting datasheet by requiring that a record be true for multiple criteria in one criteria row. **OR queries** *expand* the number of records that will appear in the datasheet because a record needs to be true *for only one* of the criteria rows. OR criteria are entered in the query design grid on different lines (criteria rows). Each criteria row of the query design grid is evaluated separately, adding the records that are true for that row to the resulting datasheet. Fred is looking for an assistant for the Excel courses. He modifies the Potential Access Assistants query to expand the number of records to include those who have passed Excel courses.

1. Click the **Potential Access Assistants** query, then click the **Design button** in the Training-F database window

   To add OR criteria, you have to enter criteria in the "or" row of the query design grid. You want to find all Excel courses.

2. Click the **or Description criteria cell** below Like "*access*", then type ***excel***

3. Click the **or Passed criteria cell** below Yes, then type **yes**, as shown in Figure F-9

   As soon as you clicked elsewhere in the design grid, Access added the appropriate criteria syntax. If a record matches *either criteria* row of the criteria grid, it is included in the query's datasheet. Each row is evaluated separately, which is why it was necessary to put the Yes criteria for the Passed field in both rows of the query design grid. Otherwise, the second row would pull all records where "excel" is in the description regardless of whether the test was passed or not.

4. Click the **Datasheet View button** on the Query Design toolbar

   The resulting datasheet displays 28 records, as shown in Figure F-10. All of the records contain course Descriptions that contain the word Access or Excel as well as Yes in the Passed field. Also, notice that the sort order (Last, then Attended) is still in effect.

5. Click **File** on the menu bar, click **Save As**, click between **Access and Assistants**, type **or Excel**, press **[Spacebar]**, then click **OK**

   The Potential Access or Excel Assistants query is saved as a separate database object.

6. Close the Potential Access or Excel Assistants query

   The Training-F database displays the three queries you created in addition to the two queries that were already in the database.

QuickTip

To rename an object from the Database window, right-click it, then choose Rename from the shortcut menu.

FIGURE F-9: OR criteria

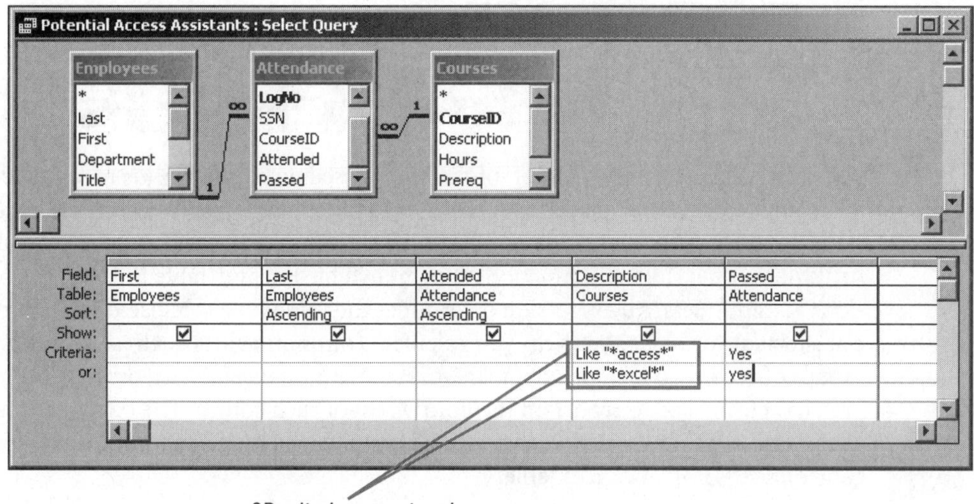

OR criteria are entered on different rows

FIGURE F-10: OR criteria adds more records to the datasheet

Potential Access or Excel Assistants : Select Query

First	Last	Attended	Description	Passed
Maria	Abbott	02/13/2002	Introduction to Excel	☑
Lauren	Alber	02/14/2002	Introduction to Excel	☑
Shayla	Colletti	02/13/2002	Introduction to Excel	☑
Shayla	Colletti	03/07/2002	Intermediate Excel	☑
David	Dumont	02/13/2002	Introduction to Excel	☑
Jim	Fernandez	02/13/2002	Introduction to Access	☑
Jim	Fernandez	02/14/2002	Introduction to Excel	☑
Jim	Fernandez	02/27/2002	Access Case Problems	☑
Jayne	Hayashi	02/13/2002	Introduction to Access	☑
Jayne	Hayashi	02/20/2002	Intermediate Access	☑
Jayne	Hayashi	02/27/2002	Access Case Problems	☑
Cynthia	Hayman	02/13/2002	Introduction to Excel	☑
Cynthia	Hayman	03/07/2002	Intermediate Excel	☑
John	Kim	02/13/2002	Introduction to Excel	☑
John	Kim	03/07/2002	Intermediate Excel	☑

Record: 1 of 28

Passed field is always "Yes"

Excel or Access records were found

28 records found

Access 2002

Using wildcard characters in query criteria

To search for a pattern, a wildcard character is used to represent any character in the criteria entry. Use a ? (question mark) to search for any single character and an * (asterisk) to search for any number of characters. Wildcard characters are often used with the Like operator. For example, the criterion **Like "10/*/03"** would find all dates in October of 2003, and the criterion **Like "F*"** would find all entries that start with the letter F.

Access 2002

Creating Calculated Fields

If you can calculate a new field of information based on existing fields in a database, never define it as a separate field in Table Design View. Rather, use a query object to create the new **calculated field** to guarantee that the new field always contains accurate, up-to-date information. **Arithmetic operators** and functions shown in Table F-2 and Table F-3 are used to create expressions within Access. An expression determines the value for a calculated field. **Functions** are special shortcut formulas that help you calculate common values such as counts and subtotals on groups of records, a loan payment (if working with financial data), or the current date. Fred has been asked to report on the hourly cost of each course. The data to calculate this answer already exists in the Cost (the cost of the course) and Hours (the number of contact hours per course) fields of the Courses table.

1. Click **Queries** on the Objects bar, double-click **Create query in Design View**, click **Courses** in the Show Table dialog box, click **Add**, then click **Close** in the Show Table dialog box
   The Courses field list is in the upper pane of the query design window.
2. Double-click the **Description field**, double-click the **Hours field**, then double-click the **Cost field**
   A **calculated field** is created by entering a new descriptive field name followed by a colon in the Field cell of the design grid followed by an expression. An **expression** is a combination of **operators** such as + (add), – (subtract), * (multiply), or / (divide); raw values (such as numbers or dates), functions; and fields that produce a result. Field names used in an expression are surrounded by square brackets.
3. Click the blank **Field cell** of the fourth column, type **HourlyRate:[Cost]/[Hours]**, then drag ✛ on the right edge of the fourth column selector to the right to display the entire entry, as shown in Figure F-11
4. Click the **Datasheet View button** on the Query Design toolbar
   It is not necessary to show the fields used in the calculated expression in the datasheet (in this case, Hours and Cost), but viewing these fields next to the new calculated field helps confirm that your new calculated field is working properly. The HourlyRate field appears to be accurate, but the data is not formatted in a useful way.
5. Click the **Design View button** on the Query Datasheet toolbar, right-click the **HourlyRate field** in the query design grid, then click **Properties** on the shortcut menu
   The Field Properties dialog box opens. The HourlyRate field represents dollars per hour.
6. Click the **Format text box**, click the **Format list arrow**, click **Currency**, close the property sheet, then click to display the records
   The data shown in the HourlyRate field displays as currency with dollar signs and is rounded to the nearest cent.
7. Press **[Tab]** twice, type **300** in the Introduction to Access Cost field, then press **[Enter]**
   The resulting datasheet is shown in Figure F-12. The HourlyRate field was recalculated as soon as the Cost field was updated. This is why it is extremely important to create calculated fields in queries rather than define them as fields in Table Design View. When created as calculated fields, they always display current data.
8. Click the **Save button** on the Query Datasheet toolbar, type **Hourly Rate** in the Save As dialog box, click **OK**, then close the datasheet
   The query is saved as an object in the database.

QuickTip

If an expression becomes too long to fit completely in a cell of the query design grid, you can right-click the cell, then click Zoom to use the Zoom dialog box for long entries.

FIGURE F-11: Entering a calculated field in Query Design View

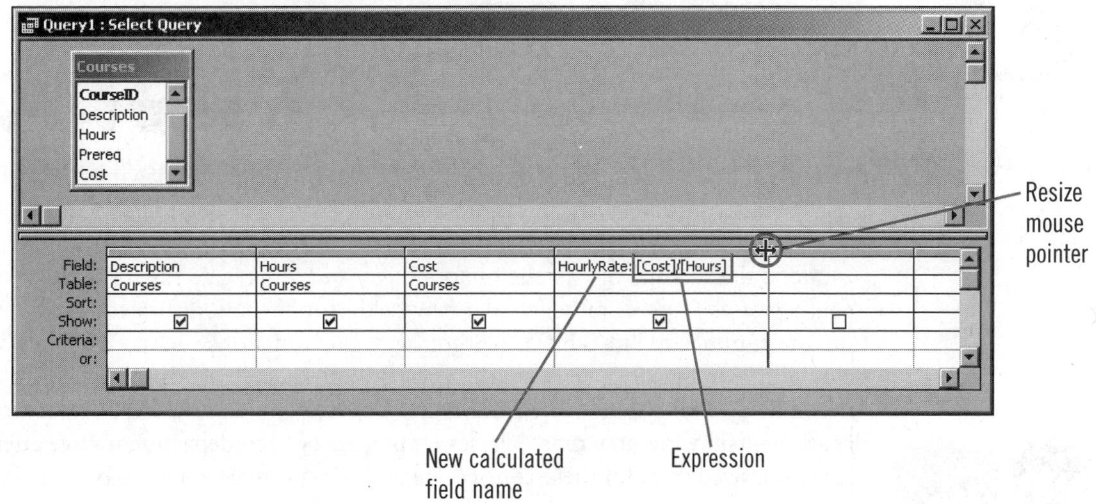

FIGURE F-12: Formatting and testing the calculated field

Query1 : Select Query

Description	Hours	Cost	HourlyRate
Introduction to Access	12	$300	$25.00
Intermediate Access	24	$400	$16.67
Access Case Problems	12	$200	$16.67
Computer Concepts	12	$200	$16.67
Introduction to Excel	12	$200	$16.67
Intermediate Excel	12	$200	$16.67
Excel Case Problems	12	$200	$16.67
Introduction to Internet Explorer	12	$200	$16.67
Intermediate Internet Explorer	12	$200	$16.67
Internet Fundamentals	12	$200	$16.67
Introduction to Netscape	12	$200	$16.67
Intermediate Netscape	12	$200	$16.67
Introduction to Networking	12	$200	$16.67

Record: 1 of 27

Calculated field with Currency format

Updated Cost field

TABLE F-2: Arithmetic operators

operator	description
+	Addition
–	Subtraction
*	Multiplication
/	Division
^	Exponentiation

TABLE F-3: Common functions

function	sample expression and description
DATE	DATE()-[BirthDate] Calculates the number of days between today and the date in the BirthDate field
PMT	PMT([Rate],[Term],[Loan]) Calculates the monthly payment on a loan where the Rate field contains the monthly interest rate, the Term field contains the number of monthly payments, and the Loan field contains the total amount financed
LEFT	LEFT([Lastname],2) Returns the first two characters of the entry in the Lastname field
RIGHT	RIGHT([Partno],3) Returns the last three characters of the entry in the Partno field
LEN	LEN([Description]) Returns the number of characters in the Description field

Access 2002

Building Summary Queries

As your database grows, you will probably be less interested in viewing individual records and more interested in analyzing information about groups of records. A **summary query** can be used to calculate information about a group of records by adding appropriate **aggregate functions** to the Total row of the query design grid. Aggregate functions calculate information about a *group of records* rather than a new field of information for *each record*. Aggregate functions are summarized in Table F-4. Some aggregate functions such as Sum can be used only on fields with Number or Currency data types, but others such as Min, Max, or Count can be used on Text fields, too. The Accounting Department has asked Fred for a report on costs by department showing how many classes employees of each department have attended as well as the summarized costs for these courses. He builds a summary query to provide this information.

Steps

1. Click **Queries** on the Objects bar, then double-click **Create query in Design View**
2. Double-click **Courses**, double-click **Attendance**, double-click **Employees**, then click **Close** in the Show Table dialog box
   Even though you won't explicitly use fields from the Attendance table, you need this table in your query to tie the fields from the Courses and Employees tables together.
3. Double-click the **Department field** in the Employees table, double-click the **Cost field** in the Courses table, then double-click the **Cost field** in the Courses table again
   You added the Cost field to the query grid twice because you wish to compute two different summary statistics (subtotal and count) on the data in this field.
4. Click the **Totals button** on the Query Design toolbar
   The **Total row** is added to the query grid below the Table row. Use the Total row to specify how you want the resulting datasheet grouped and summarized.
5. Click the **Cost field Total cell** in the second column, click the **Group By list arrow**, click **Sum**, click the **Cost field Total cell** in the third column, click the **Group By list arrow**, then click **Count**
   The query groups the records by the Department field, then sums (adds) and counts the data in the Cost field. Your Query Design View should look like Figure F-13.
6. Click the **Datasheet View button** on the Query Design toolbar
   The Accounting Department had $3,700 of internal charges for the 16 classes its employees attended, as shown in Figure F-14. By counting the Cost field in addition to summing it, you know how many records were combined to reach the total figure of $3,700. You can sort and filter summary queries, but you cannot enter or edit data in a summary query because each record represents the summarization of several records.
7. Click the **Save button** on the Query Datasheet toolbar, type **Internal Costs - Your Initials**, click **OK**, click the **Print button**, then close the datasheet

QuickTip

The query name is automatically placed in the header of the datasheet printout. So to uniquely identify your printout, include your name or initials in the query name.

FIGURE F-13: Summary Query Design View

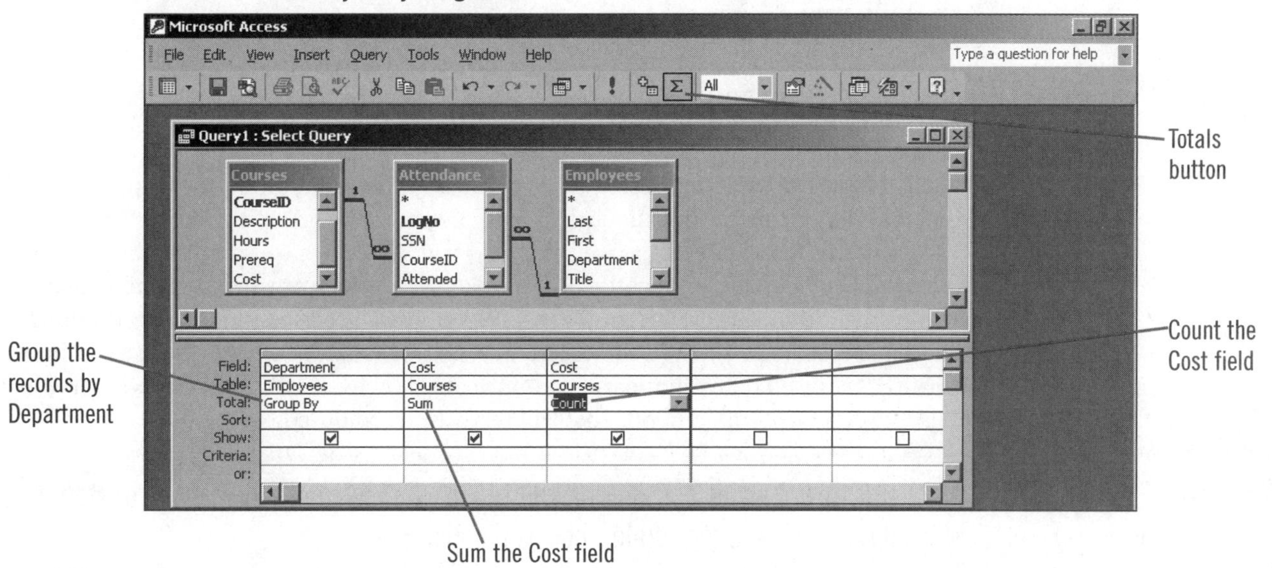

FIGURE F-14: Summarized records

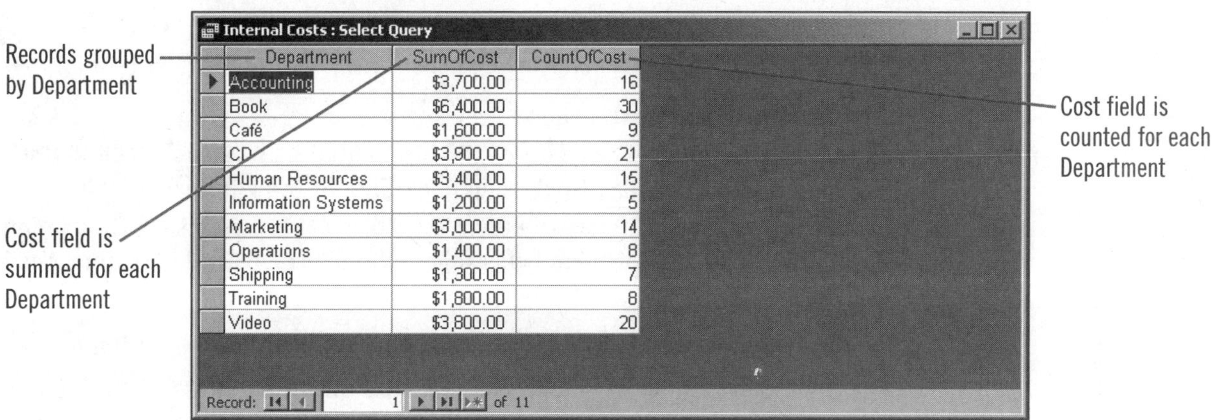

TABLE F-4: Aggregate functions

aggregate function	used to find the
Sum	Total of values in a field
Avg	Average of values in a field
Min	Minimum value in the field
Max	Maximum value in the field
Count	Number of values in a field (not counting null values)
StDev	Standard deviation of values in a field
Var	Variance of values in a field
First	Field value from the first record in a table or query
Last	Field value from the last record in a table or query

Creating Crosstab Queries

Crosstab queries provide another way to summarize information about groups of records. Crosstab queries calculate a statistic such as sum or average by grouping records according to a field that serves as a row heading as well as a field that serves as a column heading. You can use the **Crosstab Query Wizard** to identify how the datasheet will be organized or build the crosstab query directly within Query Design View. Fred needs to summarize the total cost within each department by the course description. A crosstab query can be used to find this information because Fred is summarizing information by two fields, one that will serve as the row heading (Description), and one that will serve as the column heading (Department).

Steps

Trouble?

The Create query by using wizard option in the database window creates a select query. You must click the New button to use the other query wizards.

1. **Click the New button on the database window toolbar, click Crosstab Query Wizard in the New Query dialog box, then click OK**
   The Crosstab Query Wizard dialog box opens. The first question asks you which table or query contains the fields for the crosstab query. The fields for this crosstab query were previously saved in the Crosstab Fields query.

2. **Click the Queries option button in the View section, click Crosstab Fields in the list of available queries, then click Next**
   The answers to the next questions in the Crosstab Query Wizard organize how the fields are displayed in the datasheet.

3. **Double-click Description to select it as the row heading, click Next, click Department for the column heading, click Next, then click Sum in the Functions list**
   The Sample portion of the Crosstab Query Wizard dialog box presents the Description field as the row heading, the Department field as the column heading, and the summarized Cost field within the body of the crosstab query, as shown in Figure F-15.

4. **Click Next, type Costs by Department and Course - Your Initials in the query name text box, then click Finish to display the crosstab query, as shown in Figure F-16**
   You can modify a crosstab query to change the row heading field, the column heading field, or the calculation statistic in Query Design View.

QuickTip

Click the Query Type button list arrow on the Query Design toolbar, then click Crosstab Query to change any select query into a crosstab query.

5. **Click the Design View button on the Query Datasheet toolbar**
   The Query Type button on the Query Design toolbar displays the crosstab icon indicating that the resulting datasheet will organize the records in a crosstab arrangement. The Total row shows that the datasheet is grouped by both the Description and the Department fields. The **Crosstab row** specifies that the Description field will be used as a Row Heading, and that the Department field will be used as a Column Heading.

6. **Click the Total Of Cost: Cost field Total cell, click the Sum list arrow, then click Count, as shown in Figure F-17**
   The Total Of Cost: Cost field creates the second column on the datasheet, and will now count the number of times each course was taken, rather than sum the costs for each row.

7. **Click the Datasheet View button on the Query Design toolbar, then click the Print button**

8. **Click the Save button, then close the crosstab query**
   Crosstab queries appear with a crosstab icon to the left of the query name in the Database window.

FIGURE F-15: Crosstab Query Wizard

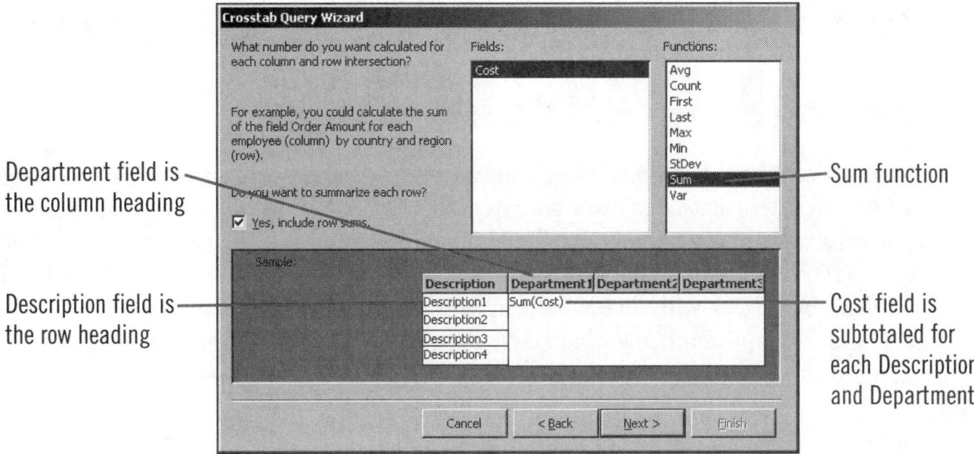

FIGURE F-16: Crosstab Query datasheet

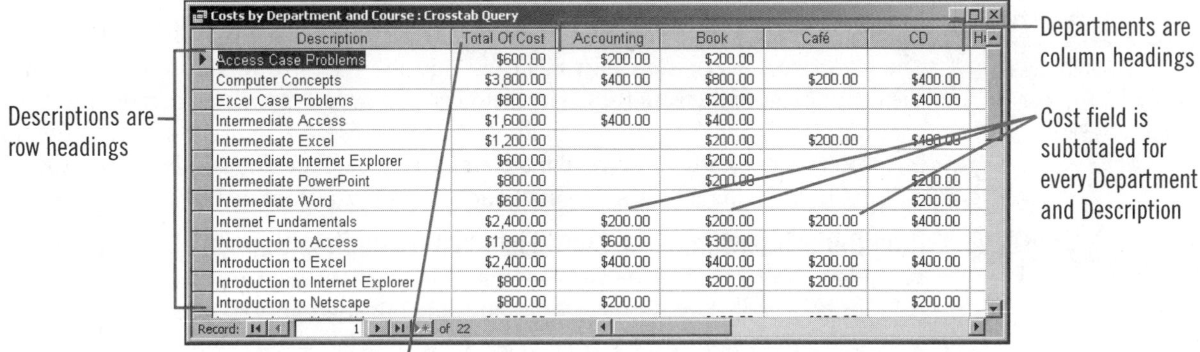

FIGURE F-17: Query Design View of a crosstab query

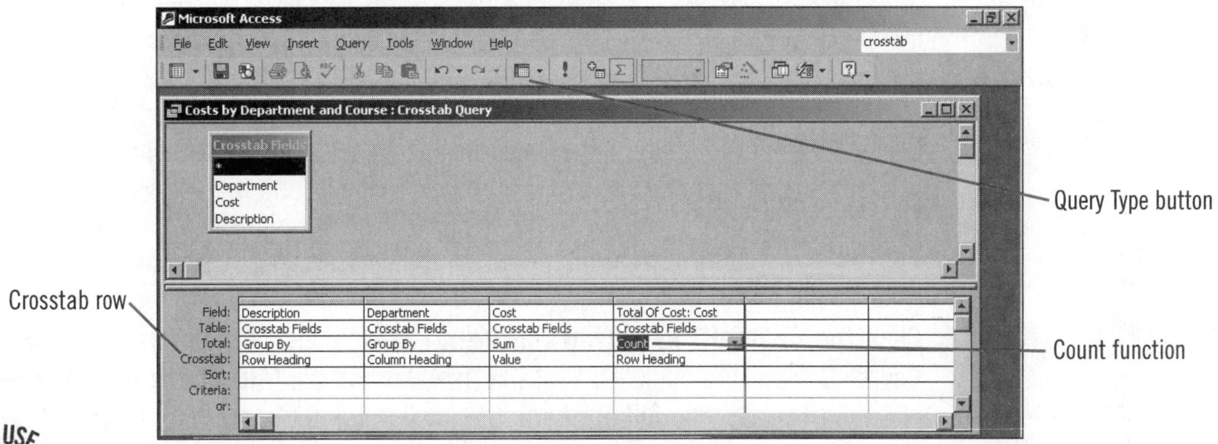

Query Wizards

The **Simple Query Wizard** is an alternative way to create a select query, rather than going directly into Query Design View. The **Find Duplicates Query Wizard** is used to determine whether a table contains duplicate values in one or more fields. The **Find Unmatched Query Wizard** is used to find records in one table that don't have related records in another table. To start the Find Duplicates, Find Unmatched, or Crosstab Query Wizards, you must click the New button when viewing the query objects within the Database window.

Access 2002

Creating PivotTables and PivotCharts

Summarized data can be presented using a PivotTable and PivotChart. Similar to a crosstab query, a **PivotTable** calculates a statistic such as sum or average, by grouping records according to a field that serves as a row heading as well as a field that serves as a column heading. A **PivotChart** is a graphical presentation of the data in the PivotTable. You build a PivotTable using **PivotTable View**. Similarly, you work with PivotCharts in **PivotChart View**. The PivotChart and PivotTable Views are bound to one another so that when a change is made in one view, the other is automatically updated as well. Fred uses PivotChart View to summarize data in the Training database.

1. **Double-click the PivotTable Fields query**
   The PivotTable Fields query datasheet opens. You can build a PivotTable and PivotChart based on the fields of an existing table, query, or form.

> **Trouble?**
> If the Chart Field List does not appear, click the Field List button to toggle it on.

2. **Click the Design View button list arrow, then click PivotChart View**
   The PivotChart View and Chart Field List appear, as shown in Figure F-18. In PivotChart View, you drag a field from the Chart Field List to a **drop area,** a position on the chart where you want the field to appear. The fields in the **Chart Field List** are the fields in the underlying object, in this case, the PivotTable Fields query. The relationship between drop areas on a PivotChart, PivotTable, and crosstab query are summarized in Table F-5.

> **Trouble?**
> If you drop a field to an incorrect area, drag it off the chart, then try again.

3. **Drag Department from the Chart Field List to the Drop Category Fields Here drop area**
   When you drag a field to a drop area, the drop area will display a blue border. Department field values now appear on the x-axis, also called the **category axis.**

> **Trouble?**
> Drag the title bar of the Chart Field List if you cannot see the Series drop area.

4. **Drag Cost from the Chart Field List to the Drop Data Fields Here drop area, drag Last to the Drop Filter Fields Here drop area, then drag CourseID to the Drop Series Fields Here drop area, as shown in Figure F-19**
   Cost field values are now displayed as bars on the chart, and are measured by the numbers displayed on the y-axis, also called the **value axis.** The CourseID field is in the legend, also called the **series,** position for the chart. The Last field is in the filter position for the chart. PivotChart and PivotTable Views are used to design a presentation of data as well as to analyze data. For example, PivotChart fields can be used to filter for only those records you wish to analyze.

5. **Click to toggle it off, click the CourseID list arrow, click the (All) check box to remove all checkmarks, click the Access1 check box, then click OK in the CourseID filter list**
   Now the PivotChart is filtered to display only the records for the Access1 CourseID. All PivotTable and PivotChart fields (except for the field summarized in the Data area) can be used to filter information.

> **QuickTip**
> If the data is filtered by that field, the field's list arrow will change from black to blue.

6. **Click the CourseID list arrow, click (All) to add all checkmarks, click OK in the CourseID filter list, click the Last list arrow, click the (All) check box to remove all checkmarks, click the Abbot check box, then click OK in the Last filter list**
   The resulting PivotChart shows you that Abbot is in the Marketing department, and has attended six classes. In order to see which classes Abbot attended, however, you need the CourseID values, which can be viewed in PivotTable View.

7. **Click on the Formatting (PivotTable/PivotChart) toolbar, then click PivotTable View**
   The PivotTable appears as shown in Figure F-20. The six CourseIDs are identified as column headings, and a grand total for each column and row is shown. You may also filter, reorganize, and analyze data in PivotTable View .

8. **Click the Save button, print and close the PivotTable, close the Training-F database, then exit Access**

FIGURE F-18: PivotChart drop areas

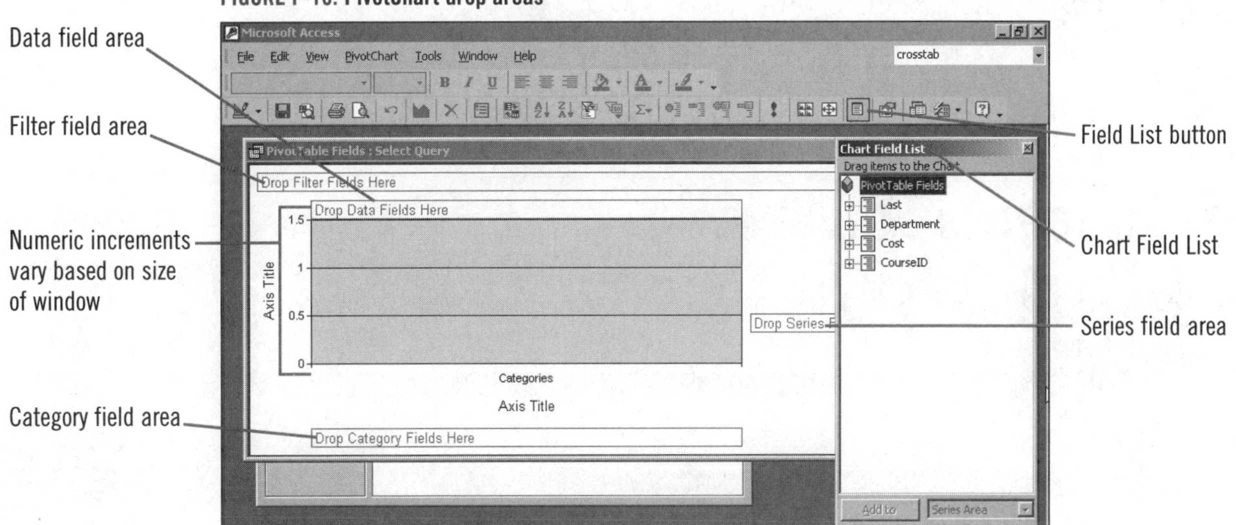

FIGURE F-19: PivotChart View

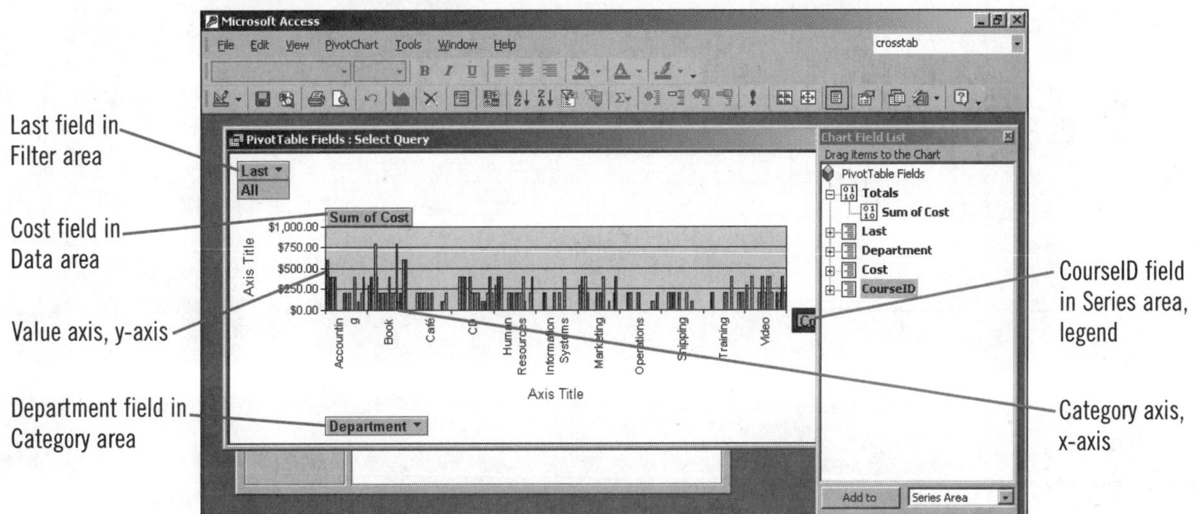

FIGURE F-20: PivotTable View

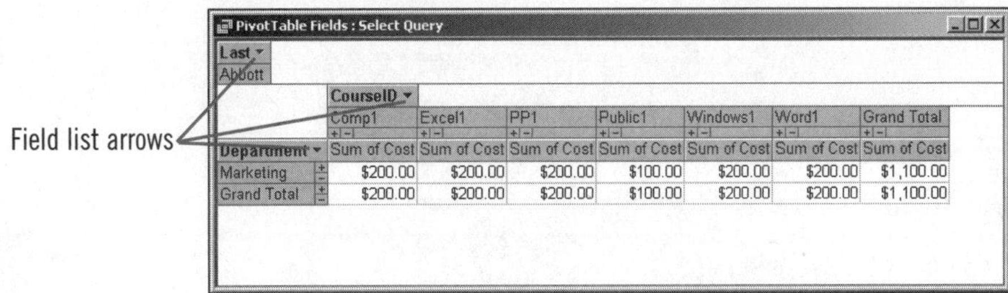

	CourseID						
	Comp1	Excel1	PP1	Public1	Windows1	Word1	Grand Total
Department	Sum of Cost	Sum of Cost	Sum of Cost	Sum of Cost	Sum of Cost	Sum of Cost	Sum of Cost
Marketing	$200.00	$200.00	$200.00	$100.00	$200.00	$200.00	$1,100.00
Grand Total	$200.00	$200.00	$200.00	$100.00	$200.00	$200.00	$1,100.00

TABLE F-5: PivotTable and PivotChart drop areas

drop area on PivotTable	drop area on PivotChart	crosstab query field position
Filter Field	Filter Field	(NA)
Row Field	Category Field	Row Heading
Column Field	Series Field	Column Heading
Totals or Detail Field	Data Field	Value

Practice

► Concepts Review

Identify each element of Query Design View shown in Figure F-21.

FIGURE F-21

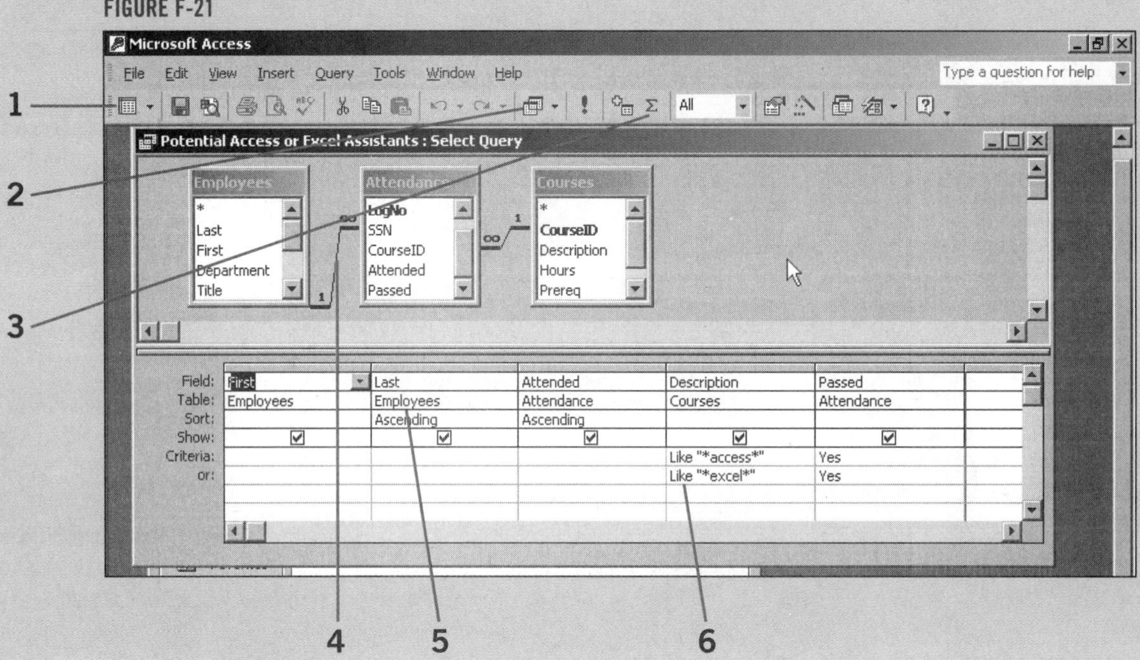

Match each term with the statement that describes its function.

7. Query	**a.** Placing the records of a datasheet in a certain order
8. Arithmetic operators	**b.** Used within mathematical calculations
9. AND criteria	**c.** A database object that answers questions about the data
10. Sorting	**d.** Entered on more than one row of the query design grid
11. OR Criteria	**e.** Entered on one row of the query design grid

Select the best answer from the list of choices.

12. The query datasheet can best be described as a:

- **a.** Duplication of the data in the underlying table's datasheet.
- **b.** Logical view of the selected data from an underlying table's datasheet.
- **c.** Separate file of data.
- **d.** Second copy of the data in the underlying tables.

13. Queries are often used to:

- **a.** Create copies of database files.
- **b.** Eliminate the need to build multiple tables.
- **c.** Create option boxes and list boxes from which to choose field values.
- **d.** Present a subset of fields from multiple tables.

14. **When you update data in a table that is displayed in a query:**
   a. You must also update the query.
   b. You must relink the query to the table.
   c. The data is automatically updated in the query.
   d. You have the choice whether or not you want to update the data in the query.

15. **To assemble several fields from different tables on one datasheet, use a(n):**
   a. Select query.
   b. Update query.
   c. Delete query.
   d. Append query.

16. **The order in which records are sorted is determined by:**
   a. The order in which the fields are defined in the underlying table.
   b. The alphabetic order of the field names.
   c. The left-to-right position of the fields in the query design grid that contain a sort order choice.
   d. The ascending fields are sorted first in the query design grid, then the descending fields are sorted second.

17. **Crosstab queries are used to:**
   a. Summarize information based on fields in the column and row headings areas.
   b. Update several records at the same time.
   c. Show a graphical representation of data.
   d. Calculate price increases on numeric fields.

18. **The PivotTable View is *not* available for which database object?**
   a. Tables
   b. Queries
   c. Forms
   d. Reports

19. **In Query Design View, which button identifies the type of query that is currently selected?**
   a. Query View
   b. Save
   c. Properties
   d. Query Type

20. **In a crosstab query, which field is the most likely candidate for the Value position?**
   a. FName
   b. Cost
   c. State
   d. Department

Skills Review

1. **Create select queries.**
   a. Start Access and open the **Membership-F** database from the drive and folder where your Project Files are stored.
   b. Create a new select query in Design View using the Names and Zips tables.
   c. Add the following fields to the query design grid in this order:
   First, Last, and Street from the Names table
   City, State, and Zip from the Zips table
   d. In Datasheet View, replace the current Last name with your last name in the Last field of the first record.
   e. Save the query as **Basic Address List**, print the datasheet, then close the query.
2. **Sort a query on multiple fields.**
   a. Open the Basic Address List query in Design View.
   b. Drag the First field from the Names field list to the right of the Last field in the query design grid to make the first three fields in the query design grid First, Last, and First.
   c. Add the ascending sort criteria to the second and third fields in the query design grid, and uncheck the Show check box in the third column. The query is sorted in ascending order by Last, then by First, but the order of the fields in the resulting datasheet is First, Last.
   d. Use Save As to save the query as **Sorted Address List**, view the datasheet, print the datasheet, then close the query.
3. **Develop AND queries.**
   a. Open the Basic Address List in Design View.
   b. Type **M*** (the asterisk is a wildcard) in the Last field criteria row to choose all people whose last name starts with M. Access assists you with the syntax for this type of criterion and enters Like "M*" in the cell when you click elsewhere in the query design grid.
   c. Enter **KS** as the criterion for the State field. Be sure to enter the criteria on the same line in the query design grid as the Like "M*" criteria.
   d. View the datasheet that selects only those people from Kansas with a last name that starts with the letter M.
   e. Enter a new value in the City field of the first record to uniquely identify the printout.
   f. Use Save As to save the query as **Kansas M Names**, print, then close the datasheet.
4. **Develop OR queries.**
   a. Open the Kansas M Names query in Design View.
   b. Enter **C*** in the second criteria row (the or row) of the Last field.
   c. Enter **KS** as the criterion in the second criteria row (the or row) of the State field so that only those people from KS with a last name that starts with either the letters M or C are selected.
   d. Use Save As to save the query as **Kansas C or M Names**, view and print the datasheet, then close the query.
5. **Create calculated fields.**
   a. Create a new select query using Design View using only the Names table.
   b. Add the following fields to the query design grid in this order: First, Last, Birthday.
   c. Create a calculated field called DaysOld in the fourth column of the query design grid by entering the expression: **DaysOld:Date()-[Birthday]** to determine the number of days old each person is based on the information in the Birthday field.
   d. Sort the query in descending order on the calculated DaysOld field, then view the datasheet.
   e. Return to Query Design View, open the Property sheet for the DaysOld field, then format the DaysOld field with a Standard format and **0** in the Decimal Places property text box.
   f. Save the query with the name **Age**, view the datasheet, print the datasheet, then close the query.

6. **Build summary queries.**
   a. Create a new select query in Design View using the Names and Activities tables.
   b. Add the following fields: First and Last from the Names table, Hours from the Activities table.
   c. Add the Total row to the query design grid, then change the function for the Hours field from Group By to Sum.
   d. Sort in descending order by Hours.
   e. Save the query as **Total Hours-Your Initials**, view the datasheet, print the datasheet, then close the query.
7. **Create crosstab queries.**
   a. Create a select query with the City and State fields from the Zips table, and the Dues field from the Names table. Save the query as **Crosstab Fields**, then close the query.
   b. Click the New button in the database window, click Crosstab Query Wizard in the New Query dialog box, click OK, then base the crosstab query on the Crosstab Fields query you just created.
   c. Select City as the row heading, State as the column heading, and sum the Dues field within the crosstab datasheet.
   d. Name the query **Crosstab of Dues by City and State-Your Initials**, then click Finish.
   e. View, print, then close the datasheet.
8. **Create PivotTables and PivotCharts.**
   a. Create a select query with the State field from the Zips table, and the CharterMember and Dues fields from the Names table. Save it as **Dues Analysis-Your Initials**.
   b. Switch to PivotChart View, open the Chart Field List if it is not already visible, then drag the State field to the Drop Category Fields Here drop area, the CharterMember field to the Drop Series Fields Here drop area, and the Dues field to the Drop Data Fields Here drop area.
   c. Use the CharterMember field to display only the data for the records where the CharterMember value is Yes, as shown in Figure F-22.
   d. Switch to PivotTable View, then print it.
   e. Save the changes to the Dues Analysis-Your Initials query, close it, close the Membership-F database, then exit Access.

FIGURE F-22

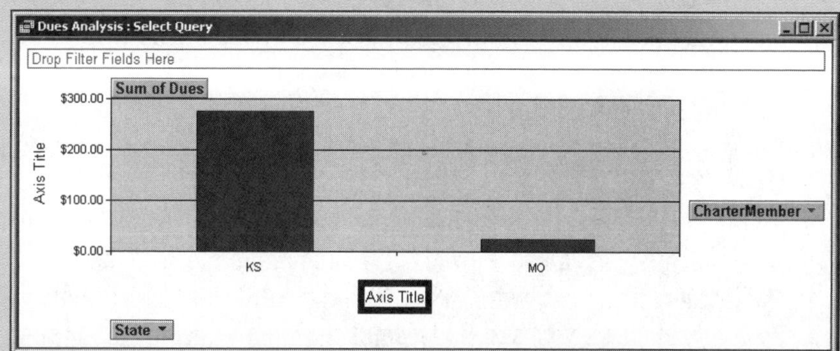

▶ Independent Challenge 1

As the manager of a music store's instrument rental program, you have created a database to track instrument rentals to schoolchildren. Now that several rentals have been made, you want to query the database for several different datasheet printouts to analyze school information.

a. Start Access and open the **Music Store-F** database from the drive and folder where your Project Files are stored.
b. In Query Design View create a select query with the SchoolName field from the Schools table, the Date field from the Rentals table, and the Description field from the Instruments table. (*Hint:* You will need to add the Customers table to this query to make the connection between the Schools table and the Rentals table even though you don't need any Customers fields in this query's datasheet.)
c. Sort ascending by SchoolName, then ascending by Date.
d. Save the query as **School Rentals**, replace the current entry in the first record with your elementary school name, then print the datasheet.

e. Modify the School Rentals query by deleting the Description field. Then, use the Totals button to group the records by SchoolName and to Count the Date field. Print the datasheet and save the query as **School Count**. Close the datasheet.
f. Use the Crosstab Query Wizard to create a crosstab query based on the School Rentals query. Use Description as the row heading and SchoolName as the column heading. Count the Date field.
g. Save the query as **School Crosstab**, then view, print, and close it.
h. Modify the School Rentals query so that only those schools with the word Elementary in the SchoolName field are displayed. (*Hint:* You will have to use wildcard characters in the criteria.)
i. Save the query as **Elementary Rentals**, then view, print, and close the datasheet.
j. Close the Music Store-F database, then exit Access.

► Independent Challenge 2

As the manager of a music store's instrument rental program, you have created a database to track instrument rentals to schoolchildren. The database has already been used to answer several basic questions, and now that you've shown how easy it is to get the answers using queries, more and more questions are being asked. You will use queries to analyze customer and rental information.

a. Start Access and open the **Music Store-F** database from the drive and folder where your Project Files are stored.
b. In Query Design View, create a select query with the Description and MonthlyFee fields from Instruments table, and the Zip and City fields from the Customers table. (*Hint:* You will need to add the Rentals table to this query to make the connection between the Customers table and the Instruments table even though you don't need any fields from the Rentals table in this query's datasheet.)
c. Add the Zip field to the first column of the query grid and specify an Ascending sort order for this field. Uncheck the Show check box for the first Zip field so that it will not display in the datasheet.
d. Specify an Ascending sort order for the Description field.
e. Save the query as **Zip Analysis**.
f. View the datasheet, replace Des Moines with a unique city entry in the first record's City field, then print and close the datasheet.
g. Modify the Zip Analysis query by adding criteria to find the records where the Description is equal to **viola**.
h. Save this query as **Violas**. How many records are in the datasheet?
i. Modify the Violas query with AND criteria that further specifies that the City must be **Des Moines**.
j. Save this query as **Violas in Des Moines**. How many records are in the datasheet?
k. Modify the Violas query with OR criteria that finds all violas or violins, regardless of where they are located.
l. Save this query as **Violas or Violins**. How many records are in the datasheet?
m. Using the Crosstab Query Wizard, create a crosstab query based on the School Analysis query that uses the Description field for the row headings, the SchoolName field for the column headings, and that Counts the RentalNo field.
n. Save the crosstab query as **Crosstab School and Instrument-Your Initials**, preview the datasheet, then print the datasheet in landscape orientation so that it fits on one page.
o. Close the **Music Store-F** database then exit Access.

► Independent Challenge 3

As the manager of a music store's instrument rental program, you have created a database to track instrument rentals to schoolchildren. Now that several rentals have been made, you wish to query the database to analyze customer and rental information.

a. Start Access and open the **Music Store-F** database from the drive and folder where your Project Files are stored.
b. In Query Design View, create a query that uses the following fields in the following order:
FirstName and LastName from the Customers Table
Description and MonthlyFee from the Instruments Table
(*Hint:* You will need to add the Rentals table to this query to make the connection between the Customers table and the Instruments table even though you don't need any fields from the Rentals table in this query's datasheet.)
c. Sort the records in ascending order by the LastName field.
d. Save the query as **Customer Rentals-Your Initials**, view the datasheet, enter your own last name in the first record's LastName field, then print the datasheet.
e. In Query Design View, modify the Customer Rentals query by deleting the FirstName and LastName fields. Then, click the Totals button to group the records by Description and to Sum the MonthlyFee field.
f. Add another MonthlyFee field as a third column to the query design grid, and use the Count function to find the total number of rentals within that group.
g. Sort the records in ascending order by the Description field.
h. Save the query as **Monthly Instrument Income-Your Initials**.
i. View, print, then close the datasheet.

FIGURE F-23

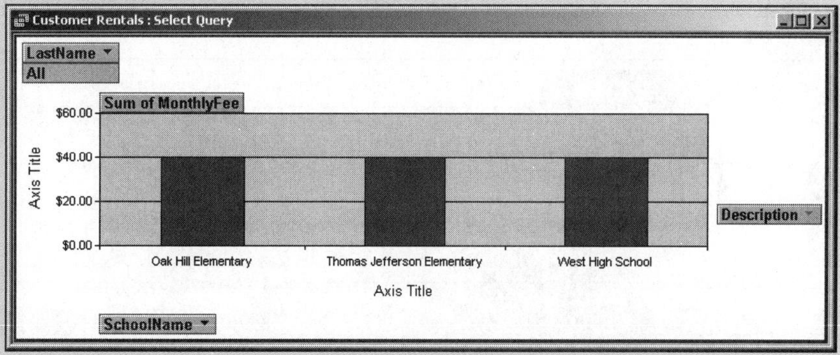

j. Open the Customer Rentals-Your Initials query in Design View, click the Show Table button on the Query Design toolbar to add the Schools table to the query, then add the SchoolName field as the fifth field in the query design grid.
k. Display PivotChart View, then create the PivotChart shown in Figure F-23. The Description field has been used as a filter to show only the cello records.
l. Print the PivotTable view, save and close the Customer Rentals-Your Initials query, close the **Music Store-F** database, then exit Access.

E-QUEST Independent Challenge 4

You are on the staff of an economic development team whose goal is to encourage tourism in the Baltic Sea region. You have created an Access database called Baltic-F to track important fields of information for the countries in that region, and are using the Internet to find information about the area that you then enter into existing forms.

a. Start Access and open the **Baltic-F** database from the drive and folder where your Project Files are stored.
b. Connect to the Internet, then go to www.hotbot.com, www.go.com or any general search engine to conduct some research for your database. Your goal is to find three upcoming events for Stockholm, Sweden, then print the Web page.
c. Open the Cities table datasheet, expand the Stockholm record, and enter three events for Stockholm into the subdatasheet. EventID is an AutoNumber field, so it will automatically increment as you enter the EventName and EventDate information.
d. Using Query Design View, create a select query with the following fields: Country and City from the Cities table and EventName and EventDate from the Events table.
e. Save the query with the name **Event Info**, then close it.
f. Use the Crosstab Query Wizard to create a query based on the Event Info query. City should be the row heading, Country the column heading, and the EventDate field should be Counted within the body of the crosstab query.
g. Title the query **Country Crosstab-Your Initials**, view, then print the datasheet.
h. Close the **Baltic-F** database, then exit Access.

Visual Workshop

Open the **Training-F** database from the drive and folder where your Project Files are located. In Query Design View create a new select query with the Department field from the Employees table, and the Cost and CourseID fields from the Courses table. Add the Attendance table to the query to connect the Employees table to the Courses table in the query. Display the query in PivotChart View, save it with the name **Accounting – Access - Your Initials**, then filter the records to show only the Access1, Access2, and AccessLab CourseIDs for the Accounting Department, as shown in Figure F-24. Print the PivotTable View of the Accounting – Access - Your Initials query.

FIGURE F-24

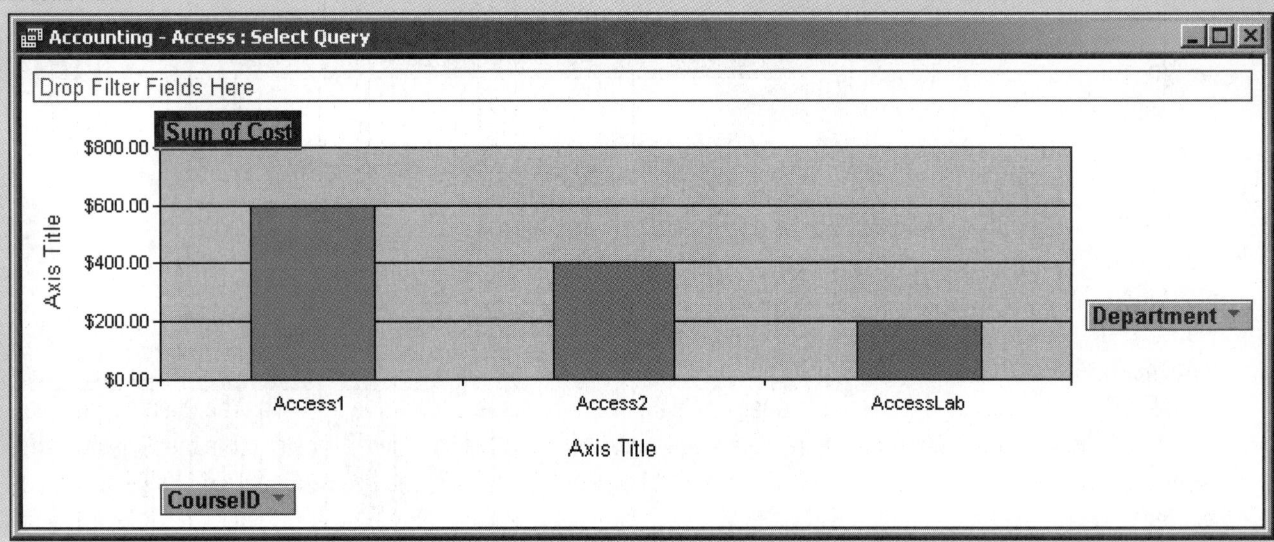

Developing

Forms and Subforms

Objectives

- MOUS ► **Understand the form/subform relationship**
- MOUS ► **Create subforms using the Form Wizard**
- MOUS ► **Create subforms using queries**
- MOUS ► **Modify subforms**
- MOUS ► **Add combo boxes**
- MOUS ► **Add option groups**
- MOUS ► **Add command buttons**
- MOUS ► **Add ActiveX controls**

Finding, entering, and editing data in a database must be easy and straightforward for all database users. A **form** can be designed to present data in any logical screen arrangement. It serves as the primary interface for most database users. Forms contain **controls** such as labels, text boxes, combo boxes, and command buttons to help identify and enter data. A form with a **subform** allows you to show a record and its related records from another object (table or query) at the same time. For example, you could display one customer and all of the orders placed by that customer at the same time. Fred Ames wants to improve the usability of several forms in the MediaLoft database by using subform controls. He also wants to improve several forms by adding various controls such as combo boxes, option groups, command buttons, and ActiveX controls.

Understanding the Form/Subform Relationship

A **subform** control is actually a form within a form. The primary form is called the **main form**, and it contains the subform control. The subform shows related records that are linked to the single record currently displayed in the main form. The relationship between the main form and subform is often called a **parent/child relationship**, because the "parent" record in the main form is linked to many "children" records displayed in the subform. The link between the main form and subform is established through a linking field common to both, the same way a one-to-many relationship is created between underlying tables in the database. Well-designed form/subforms encourage fast, accurate data entry, and shield the data entry person from the complexity of underlying tables, queries, and datasheets. Creating forms with subforms requires careful planning, so Fred studies form/subform planning guidelines before he attempts to create the forms in Access.

- **Sketch the layout of the form/subform on paper, identifying which fields belong in the main form and which belong in the subform**
  Fred sketched two forms with subforms that he wants to create. Figure G-1 displays employee information in the main form and attendance information in the subform. Figure G-2 displays course information in the main form and employee information in the subform.

- **Determine whether you are going to create separate queries upon which the main form and subform will be based, or if you are going to use the Form Wizard to collect fields from multiple tables to create the form and subform objects**
  This decision may have important consequences later because it determines the form's recordset. The **recordset** defines the fields and records that will appear on the form. To modify the recordset of forms created solely through the Form Wizard, you have to modify the form's **Record Source property**, where the recordset is defined. When the form is based on an intermediate query, changing the query object automatically updates the Record Source property for the form, because the query object name *is* the Record Source property entry for that form.

  If you use the Form Wizard to create a form with fields from multiple tables without an intermediary query object, the Record Source property of the form often displays an **SQL (Structured Query Language) statement.** This SQL statement can be modified to change the recordset, but requires some knowledge of SQL.

- **Create the form and subform objects based on the appropriate intermediary queries. If intermediary queries were not created, use the Form Wizard to gather the fields for both the form and subform**
  Fred uses the Form Wizard technique as well as the intermediary query technique so that he can compare the two.

FIGURE G-1: Employees Main Form with Attendance Subform

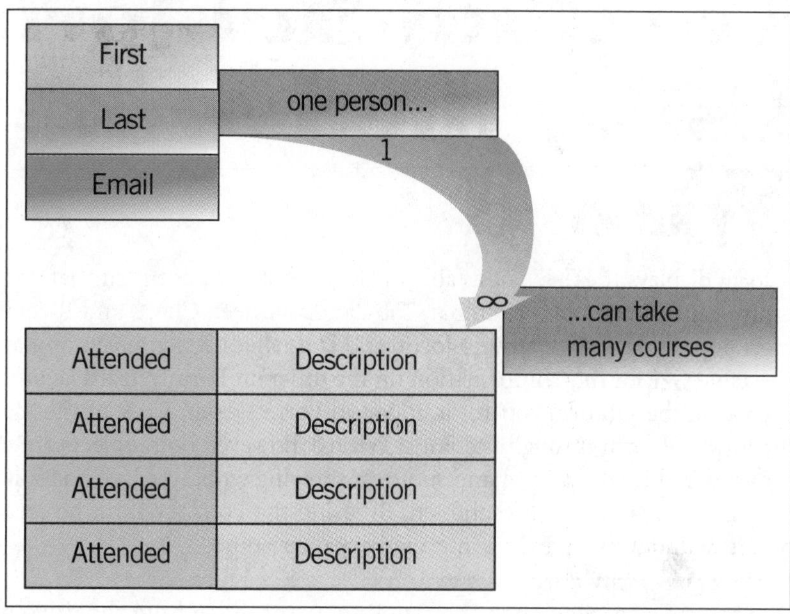

FIGURE G-2: Courses Main Form with Employee Subform

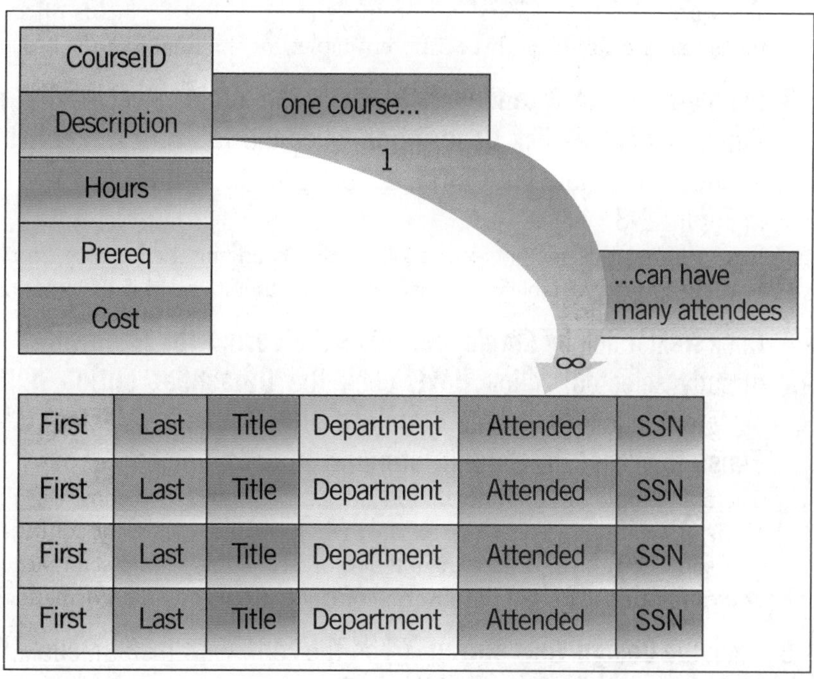

Access 2002

Creating Subforms Using the Form Wizard

A form displays the fields of a table or query in an arrangement that you design, based on one of five general **layouts**: Columnar, Tabular, Datasheet, Chart, and PivotTable. **Columnar** is the most popular layout for a main form, and **Datasheet** is the most popular layout for a subform. See Table G-1 for more information on the different Form Wizard layouts. Once the main form is created, the subform control is added in Form Design View of the main form. If you create the form/subform through the Form Wizard, however, both objects are created in one process. Fred creates a form and subform showing employee information in the main form and course information in the subform. By using the Form Wizard, he creates the form/subform objects without first creating intermediary query objects.

1. Start Access, then open the **Training-G** database from the drive and folder where your Project Files are stored
   The Training-G database opens. The database has three tables.
2. Click **Forms** on the Objects bar, then double-click **Create form by using wizard** in the Training-G Database window
   The **Form Wizard** appears and prompts you to select the fields of the form. You need five fields that are stored in three different tables for the final form/subform.
3. Double-click the **Attended field**, click the **Tables/Queries list arrow**, click **Table: Courses**, double-click **Description**, click the **Tables/Queries list arrow**, click **Table: Employees**, double-click **First**, double-click **Last**, then double-click **Email**, as shown in Figure G-3
   Next, you must decide how to view the data. Arranging the form by Employees places the fields from the Employees table in the main form, and the Attended and Description fields in a subform.
4. Click **Next**, click **by Employees**, click the **Form with subform(s) option button** (if not already selected), click **Next**, click the **Datasheet option button** (if not already selected), click **Next**, click **Standard** (if not already selected), click **Next**, then click **Finish** to accept the default form and subform names
   The final Employees main form and Attendance Subform is shown in Figure G-4. Two sets of Navigation buttons appear, one for the main form and one for the subform. The Navigation buttons show that 20 employees are in the recordset and that the first employee attended 11 courses. You can resize the form and subform control to display more information.
5. Click the **Design View button** on the Form View toolbar, click the **Employees Form Maximize button**, click the **subform control** so that sizing handles appear, then drag the bottom middle sizing handle of the subform control to the bottom of the screen using the ↕ pointer, as shown in Figure G-5
   The controls on the Attendance Subform appear within the subform control, and can be modified, just like controls in the main form. To select the subform control, click its edge.
6. Click the **Form View button** on the Form Design toolbar to view the resized subform, click the **Save button** on the Form View toolbar, then close the Employees form
   The Employees form and the Attendance Subform appear with other form objects in the Training-G Database window.

QuickTip

Use the Standard style when saving a database to a floppy disk. The other styles contain graphics that increase the storage requirements of the form.

Trouble?

If the subform control appears as a white box in Form Design View, click the Form View button, then click the Design View button to refresh the window.

FIGURE G-3: Form Wizard

Tables/Queries list arrow

Fields within the selected table or query

From Attendance table

From Courses table

From Employees table

Which fields do you want on your form?

You can choose from more than one table or query.

FIGURE G-4: Employees Main Form with Attendance Subform

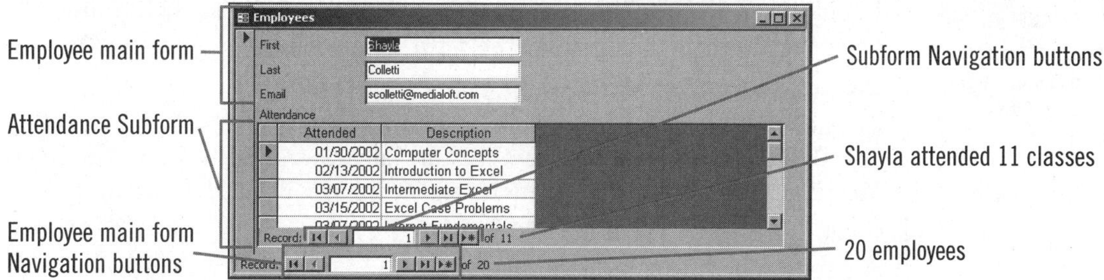

FIGURE G-5: Resizing the Attendance Subform

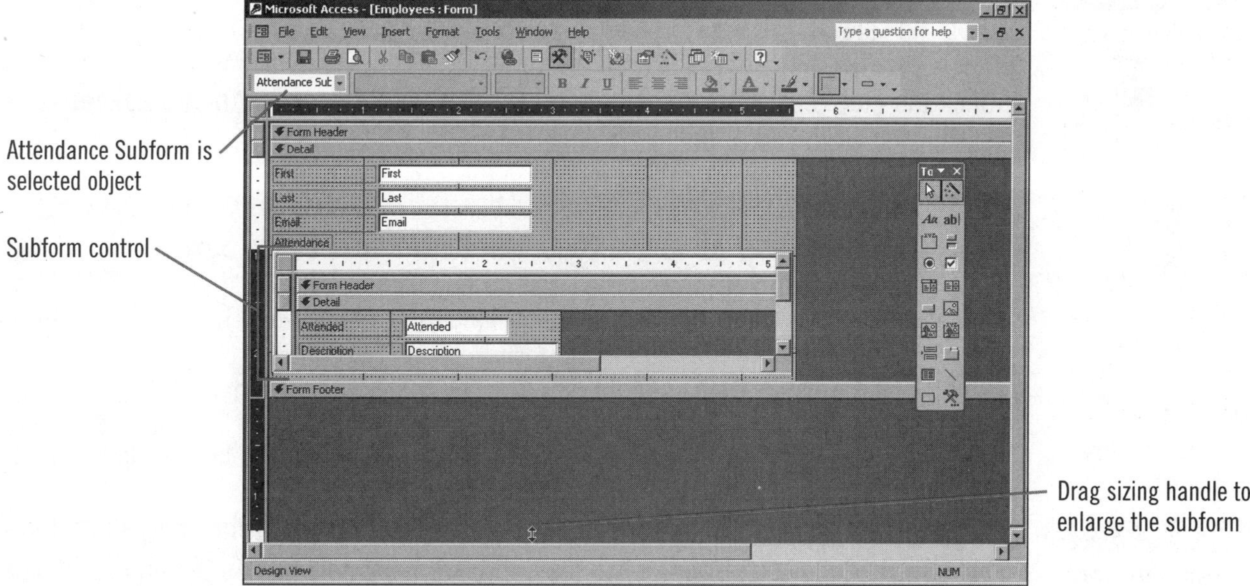

TABLE G-1: Form Wizard layouts

layout	description
Columnar	Each field appears on a separate line with a label to its left. The form displays one record at a time.
Tabular	Each field appears as a column heading and each record as a row. Multiple records appear just as they do in a Datasheet layout.
Datasheet	Each field appears as a column heading and each record as a row. The Datasheet layout shows multiple records at a time and emulates the datasheet of a table or query object. Formatting options are limited to the formats that you can apply to a datasheet. To display the data in the same general arrangement but preserve form design and formatting features, use the Tabular layout.
Justified	Each field name appears as a column heading with as much column width as needed to display field values. Unlike a Datasheet or Tabular layout, if all of the fields do not fit on one row, remaining fields will wrap to the second, third, etc., rows so that you can view all of the fields for the recordset on a form at the same time. The form displays one record at a time.

Access 2002

Creating Subforms Using Queries

Another way to create a form with a subform is to create both forms separately, basing them on either table or query objects, then linking the two forms together in a form/subform relationship. Although creating the forms by building them on separate query objects takes more work than building the form/subform using the Form Wizard, the advantage is your ability to quickly change the recordset of the form by modifying the underlying query. Fred creates a form and subform showing course information in the main form and employee information in the subform using query objects that he has already created.

Trouble?

If the property sheet doesn't show the word "Form" in the title bar, click the Form Selector button.

Trouble?

If you incorrectly drag and position the fields on the form, click Undo, then try again.

Trouble?

If the SubForm Wizard does not appear, delete the subform control, make sure that the Control Wizards button on the Toolbox toolbar is selected, then repeat Step 7.

1. Double-click **Create form in Design view**, click the **Properties button** on the Form Design toolbar to display the form's property sheet, click the **Data tab**, click the **Record Source list arrow**, then click **Employee Info**
   The field list for the Employee Info query opens to display the fields available to this form. The **Default View** property determines the initial layout of the form. The Datasheet Default View is a popular style for subforms because it arranges the fields horizontally.
2. Click the **Format tab**, click the **Default View list arrow**, click **Datasheet**, then click to toggle off the property sheet
   With the Record Source and Default View specified, you are ready to add the fields to the form.
3. Double-click the **Employee Info field list title bar** to select all fields in the list, then drag the **selected fields** to the form as shown in Figure G-6.
   You have added all of the fields from the Employee Info query to the form.
4. Click the **Field List button** to toggle off the field list, then click the **Datasheet View button** on the Form Design toolbar
   All forms can be viewed as datasheets, but in this case, the Datasheet View button appears on the Form Design toolbar because the Default View property was set to Datasheet.
5. Click the **Save button** on the Form View toolbar to open the Save As dialog box, type **Employee Info Subform** in the Form Name text box, click **OK**, then close the form
   The Employee Info Subform will be added later as a subform control to the Courses form, which will serve as the main form in this form/subform relationship.
6. Right-click **Courses**, then click **Design View** from the shortcut menu
   The Courses form displays fields from the Courses table in the upper portion of the form. It displays information on one course at a time. The Employee Info Subform will be related to the Courses form through the common CourseID field.
7. Click the **Toolbox button** on the Form Design toolbar to display the Toolbox toolbar (if not already displayed), click the **Subform/Subreport button** on the Toolbox toolbar, then drag + to create a rectangle, as shown in Figure G-7
   If you drag a control beyond the edges of an existing form, the form will automatically enlarge to accept the control. The SubForm Wizard appears.
8. Click **Employee Info Subform** in the Use an existing form list, click **Next**, click the **Show Employee Info for each record in Courses using CourseID** (if not already selected), click **Next**, click **Finish** to accept the default name for the new subform control, then click the **Form View button** on the Form Design toolbar
   The final form/subform is shown in Figure G-8. The first of 27 courses, Access1, is displayed in the main form. The six employees who completed that course are displayed in the subform. The number of fields displayed in the subform is dependent on the width of the subform control in Form Design View.

FIGURE G-6: Creating the Employee Info Subform

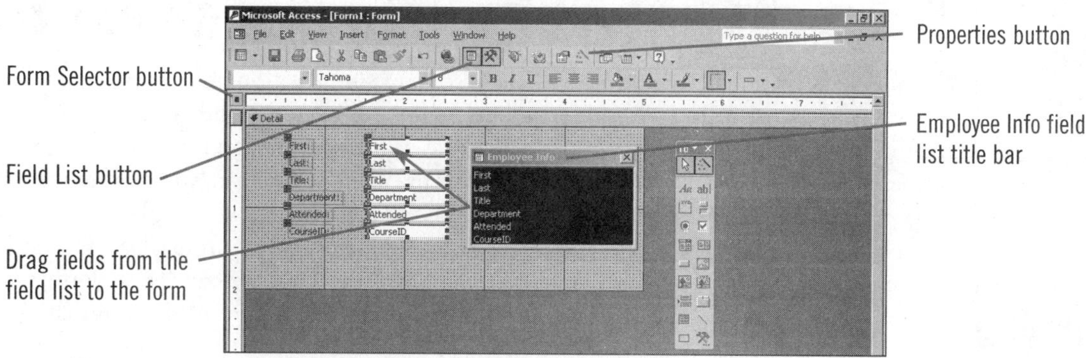

FIGURE G-7: Adding a subform control

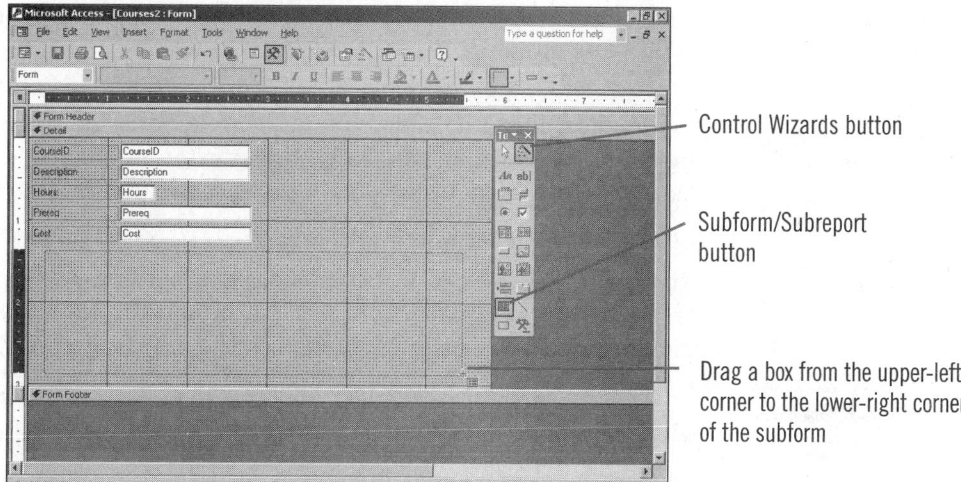

FIGURE G-8: Courses main form with Employee Info Subform

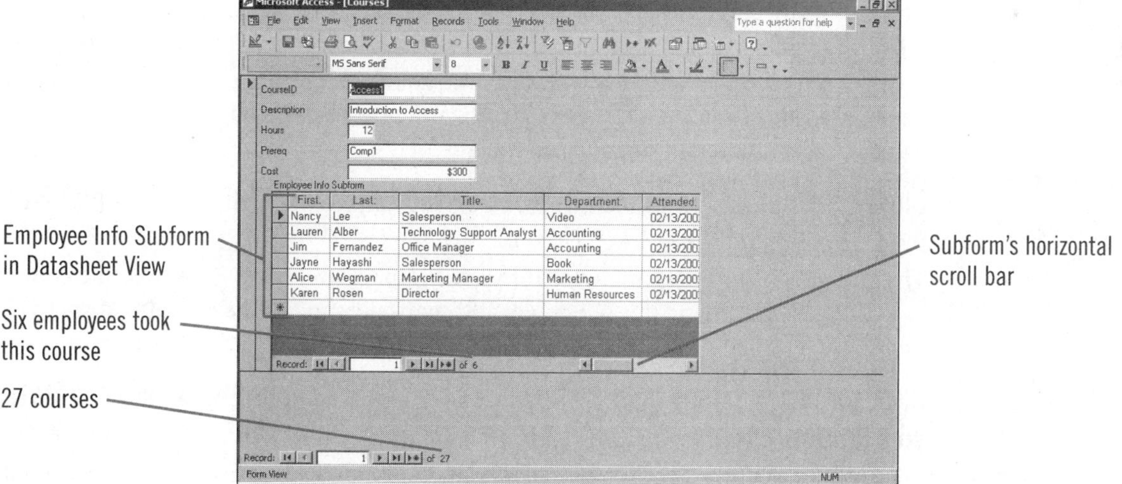

Access 2002

Linking the form and subform

If the form and subform do not appear to be correctly linked, examine the subform's property sheet, paying special attention to the **Link Child Fields** and **Link Master Fields** properties on the Data tab. These properties tell you which field serves as the link between the main form and subform. The field specified for this property should be present in the queries that underlie the main form and subform, and is the same field that creates a one-to-many relationship between tables.

Access 2002

Modifying Subforms

Because the form/subform arrangement packs so much information on one screen, it is important to modify and format the form/subform to present the data clearly. In Form View, you can resize, hide, or move the columns of the subform as well as change the font, grid color, or background color of the subform. To modify other aspects of either the form or subform, you need to work in Form Design View. You can modify the controls of both the main form and the subform when working in Design View of the main form. Fred likes the form/subform arrangement that displays each course in the main form and each employee who has taken that course in the subform, but he will improve upon the subform's design to display the employee subform information more clearly.

Steps

Trouble?

If sizing handles do not appear around the entire subform control or if the subform name is not in the Object box on the Formatting Form/Report toolbar, click outside the control, then click the subform control again to select it.

Trouble?

You do not see ✛ when pointing within the datasheet itself. It appears only when you point to the edge of the field selector (between field names at the top of the datasheet).

1. Click the **Design View button** on the Form View toolbar, click the edge of the **subform control** to select it (if it is not already selected), then drag the **middle right sizing handle** to the 7" mark on the horizontal ruler, as shown in Figure G-9

   Widening the subform control allows you to display more fields at the same time. Even though the fields of the subform appear to be in a vertical arrangement in the subform control, the Datasheet Default View property forces them to display horizontally, like a datasheet. Other options for a subform's Default View property are shown in Table G-2.

2. Click the **Form View button** on the Form Design toolbar to view the widened subform

   The appearance of a horizontal scroll bar on the subform tells you that not all of the fields are visible on the datasheet of the subform. You can resize the columns of the datasheet directly in Form View.

3. Point to the **column separator** between the First and Last fields, double-click with ✛ to automatically adjust the column to accommodate the widest entry, double-click each **column separator** in the subform, then click the **Save button** on the Form View toolbar

   Your screen should look like Figure G-10. Notice that the horizontal scroll bar disappears when all fields within the subform are visible. You can always sort, filter, and find records directly on a form or subform, but filters are not saved with the form object. By basing form objects on queries, you can easily modify the form's recordset by modifying the underlying query. MediaLoft's Accounting Department wants to use this form to display the subform data for the employees in their own department.

4. Close the Courses form, click **Queries** on the Objects bar, right-click **Employee Info**, then click **Design View**

   The Design View of the Employee Info query, upon which the Employee Info Subform is based, opens. Modifying this query will automatically modify the recordset displayed by the Employee Info Subform.

5. Click the **Department field Criteria cell**, type **Accounting**, then click the **Datasheet View button**

   The query now displays only the sixteen records that have a Department value equal to Accounting.

6. Click , then close the Employee Info query

7. Click **Forms** on the Objects bar, then double-click **Courses** to open it

   The Employee Info Subform that is based on the Employee Info query displays only those two employees from the Accounting department, as shown in Figure G-11.

8. Press **[Page Down]** several times to observe the data in the subform

FIGURE G-9: Widening a subform

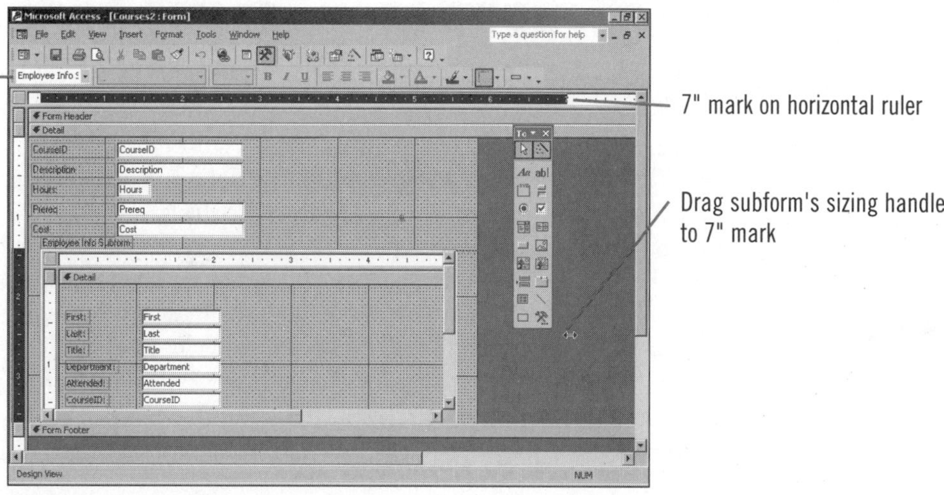

FIGURE G-10: Resizing columns of a subform

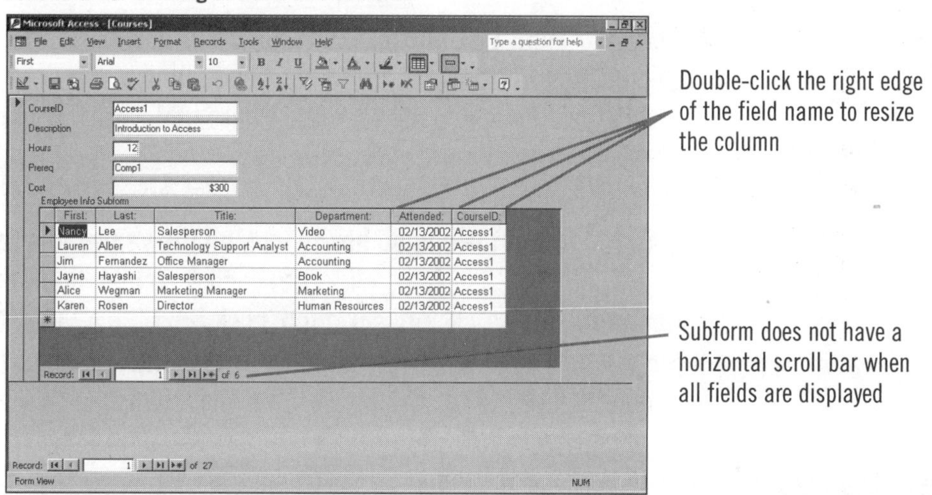

FIGURE G-11: The final form/subform

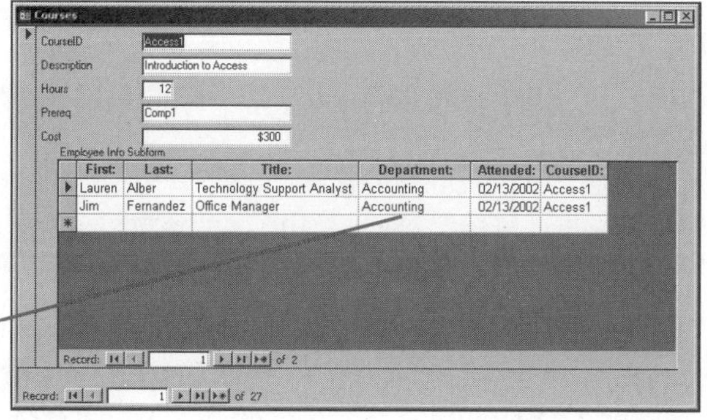

TABLE G-2: Default View property options for subforms

default view property	description
Single Form	Displays one record at a time. Gives the user full ability to format the controls.
Continuous Form	Displays multiple records at a time, and is often used as the Default View property for subforms. Gives the user the ability to format the controls in Design View.
Datasheet	Displays multiple records at the same time in a datasheet arrangement regardless of how they are formatted in Design View. This is the most common Default View property choice for subforms.

Access 2002

Adding Combo Boxes

By default, most fields are added to a form as text boxes, but sometimes other types of controls such as list boxes, combo boxes, or options buttons would work better for a particular field. Both the **list box** and **combo box** controls provide a list of values from which the user can choose an entry. A combo box also allows the user to make an entry from the keyboard; therefore, it is a "combination" of the list box and text box controls. You can create a combo box by using the Combo Box Wizard to guide your actions, or you can change an existing text box or list box into a combo box. Fred changes the Prereq text box (which specifies if a prerequisite course is required) from a text box into a combo box to give users a list of existing courses offered at MediaLoft when entering data into the Prereq field.

Steps

1. Click the **Design View button**, click the **Prereq text box** in the Detail section of the form, then press **[Delete]**
   Although you deleted the control, you can add the Prereq field back to the form as a combo box using the Combo Box Wizard.
2. Click the **Field List button** to toggle it on (if it is not already visible), click the **Combo Box button** on the Toolbox toolbar, then drag the **Prereq** field from the field list to the space between the Hours and Cost text boxes
   The Combo Box Wizard appears. You want the Prereq combo box to display the CourseID and Description field values from the Courses table.
3. Click the **I want the combo box to look up the values in a table or query option button** (if not already selected), click **Next**, click **Table: Courses**, click **Next**, double-click **CourseID**, double-click **Description**, click **Next** three times to move through the Combo Box Wizard and to accept column and value default options, type **Prereq** when prompted to enter a label for the combo box, then click **Finish**
   The new combo box control, bound to the Prereq field, is added to the form.
4. Move and resize the Prereq combo box so that the form looks similar to Figure G-12
   Your final step will be to change the Cost text box into a combo box as well. MediaLoft has only four internal charges for its classes, $100, $200, $300, and $400. You want to display these values in the combo box.
5. Right-click the **Cost text box**, point to **Change To** on the shortcut menu, then click **Combo Box**
   This action changed the control from a text box to a combo box. You need to use the combo box's property sheet to specify where this combo box will get its values since a wizard did not prompt you for this information.
6. Click the **Properties button**, click the **Data tab** (if not already selected), click the **Row Source Type text box,** click the **Row Source Type list arrow**, then click **Value List**
   This property choice indicates that the combo box will get its values from the list entered in the Row Source property.
7. Click the **Row Source property text box**, type **$100; $200; $300; $400**, press **[Enter]**, click the **Limit to List property list arrow**, click **Yes**, then click to close the property sheet
   The entries in the **Row Source** property list become the values for the combo box's list. By changing the **Limit to List** property to "Yes," the user cannot enter a new entry from the keyboard.
8. Click the **Save button**, click the **Form View button**, click the **Cost combo box list arrow**, click **$400**, then click the **Restore Window button** to restore the form window
   The updated form with two combo boxes should look like Figure G-13.

QuickTip

Press and hold [Ctrl], then press the arrow keys to move the control one pixel at a time.

Trouble?

Be sure to enter semicolons between the values in the Row Source property.

FIGURE G-12: Adding the Prereq combo box

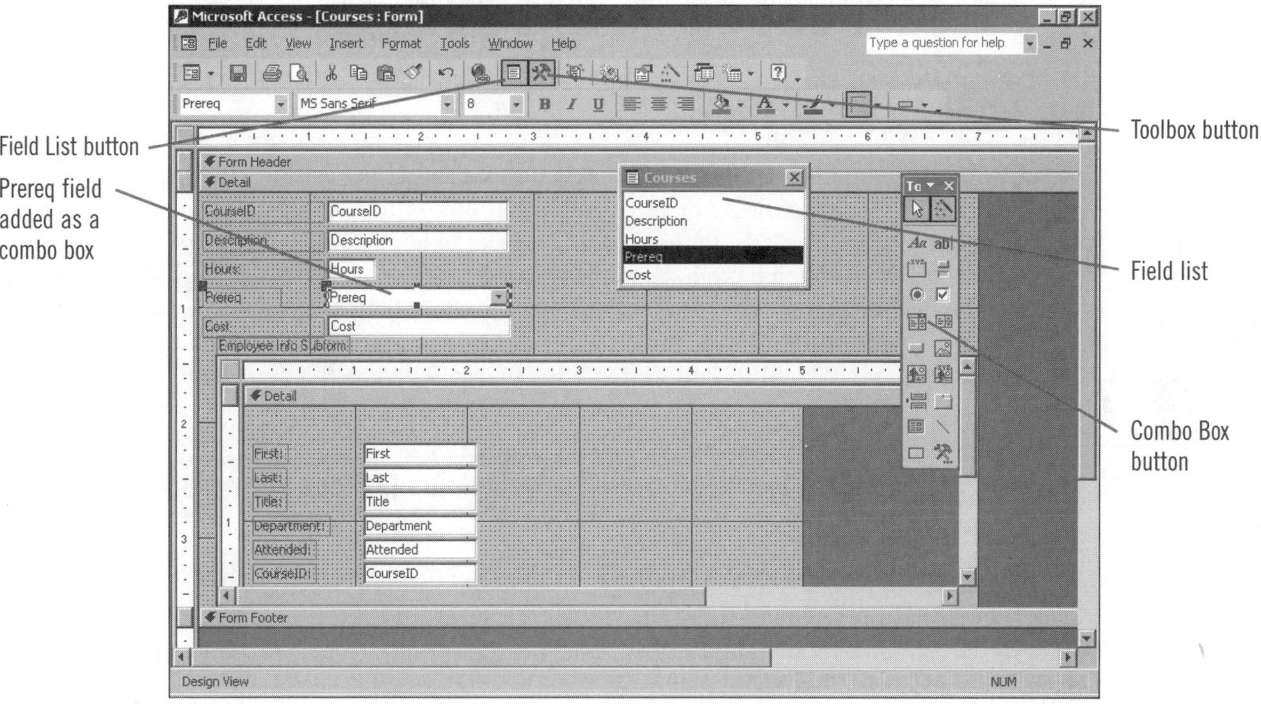

FIGURE G-13: Two new combo boxes

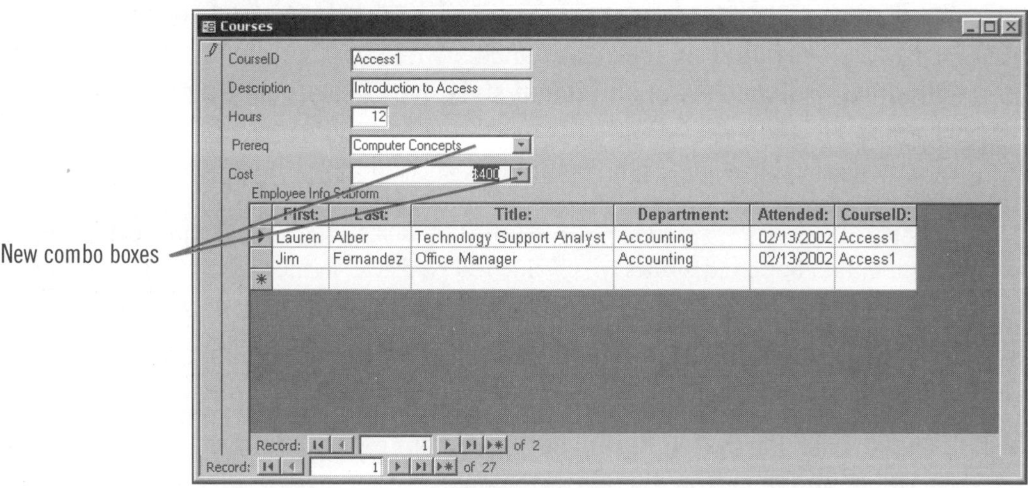

First:	Last:	Title:	Department:	Attended:	CourseID:
Lauren	Alber	Technology Support Analyst	Accounting	02/13/2002	Access1
Jim	Fernandez	Office Manager	Accounting	02/13/2002	Access1

Choosing between a combo box and a list box

The list box and combo box controls are very similar, but the combo box is more popular for at least two reasons. While both provide a list of values from which the user can choose to make an entry in a field, the combo box also allows the user to make a unique entry from the keyboard. More importantly, however, most users like the drop-down behavior of the combo box. A list box simply provides a list of values from which the user scrolls and selects a choice (the list box has no drop-down action). That's also why users often refer to the combo box as a drop-down list.

Access 2002

Adding Option Groups

An **option group** is a special type of bound control that is often used when a limited number of values are available for a field. You place **option button** controls within the option group to determine the value that is placed in the field. One option button exists for each possible entry. When the user clicks an option button, the numeric value associated with that option button is entered into the field bound to the option group. Option buttons within an option group are mutually exclusive, which means that only one can be chosen at a time. MediaLoft's classes are offered in 6-, 8-, 12-, and 16-hour formats. Because this represents a limited number of options, Fred uses an option group control for the Hours field to further simplify the Courses form.

Steps

1. Click the **Design View button**, click the **Hours text box**, then press **[Delete]**
   You can add the Hours field back to the form as an option group.
2. Click the **Option Group button** on the Toolbox, then drag the **Hours** field from the field list to the top of the right side of the form
   The **Option Group Wizard** helps guide the process of developing an option group. The first question asks about label names for the option buttons.
3. Type **6 hrs**, press **[Tab]**, type **8 hrs**, press **[Tab]**, type **12 hrs**, press **[Tab]**, type **16 hrs**, click **Next**, click the **No, I don't want a default option button**, then click **Next**
   The next question prompts you for the actual values associated with each option button.
4. Type **6**, press **[Tab]**, type **8**, press **[Tab]**, type **12**, press **[Tab]**, type **16**, click **Next**, click **Next** to accept **Hours** as the field that the value is stored in, click **Next** to accept **Option buttons controls** in an **Etched style**, type **Classroom Hours** as the caption, then click **Finish**
   An option group can contain option buttons, check boxes, or toggle button controls. The most common choice, however, are option buttons in an etched style. The **Control Source property** of the option group identifies the field it will update. The **Option Value property** of each option button identifies what value will be placed in the field when that option button is clicked. The new option group and option button controls are shown in Figure G-14.
5. Click the **Form View button**, then click the **16 hrs option button**
   Your screen should look like Figure G-15. You changed the Access1 course from 12 to 16 hrs.
6. Click, click the **Option Button button** on the Toolbox toolbar, then click below the **16 hrs option button** in the option group
   Your screen should look similar to Figure G-16. This option button in the group will represent the new 24-hour classes that were just announced.
7. Double-click the **label** of the new option button, then type **24 hrs**
   You changed the new option button's label. The Option Value property for the new option button must be changed to reflect the value that you want entered into the Hours field if this option button is clicked.
8. Double-click the new **option button** to open its property sheet, click the **Data tab**, double-click **5** in the Option Value property text box to select it, type **24**, close the property sheet, move the **24 hrs option button** as necessary to align it with the other option buttons, click the **Save button**, then click to observe the new option button in Form View

QuickTip

The option group control will darken while you are adding an option button to it.

FIGURE G-14: Adding an option group with option buttons

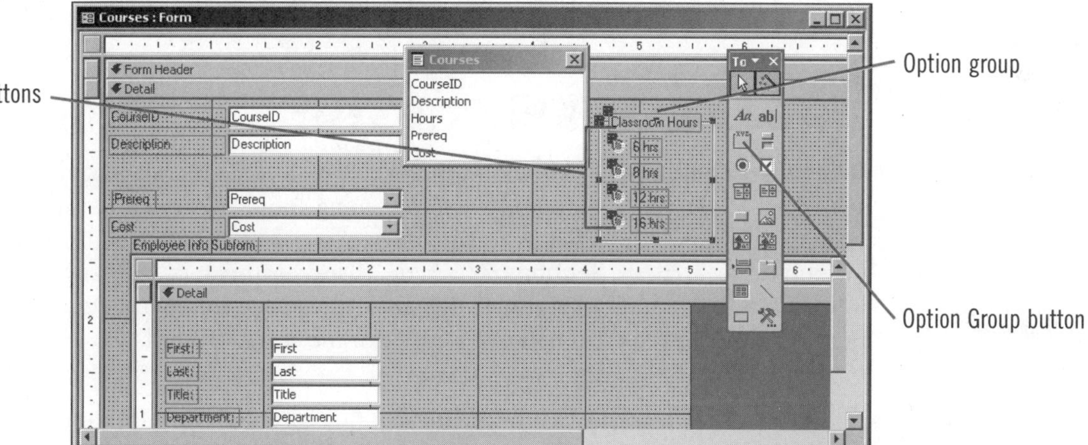

FIGURE G-15: Using an option group

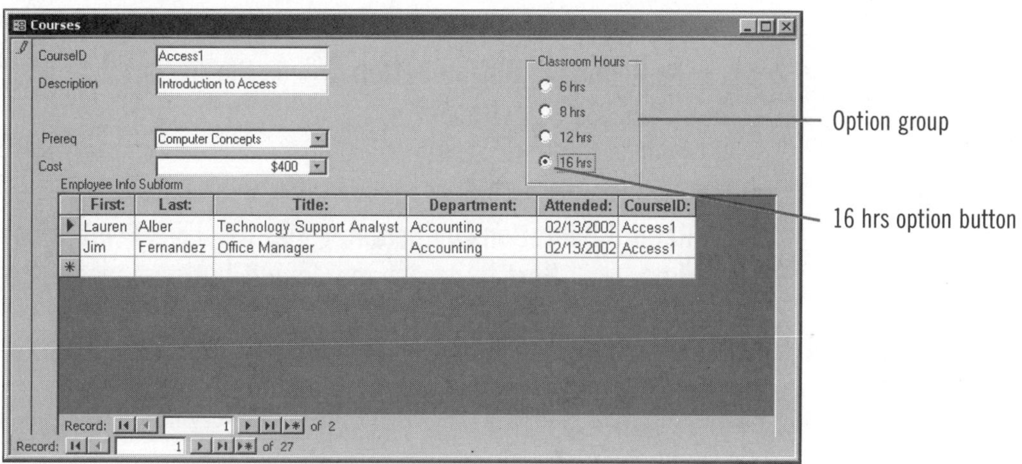

FIGURE G-16: Adding another option button

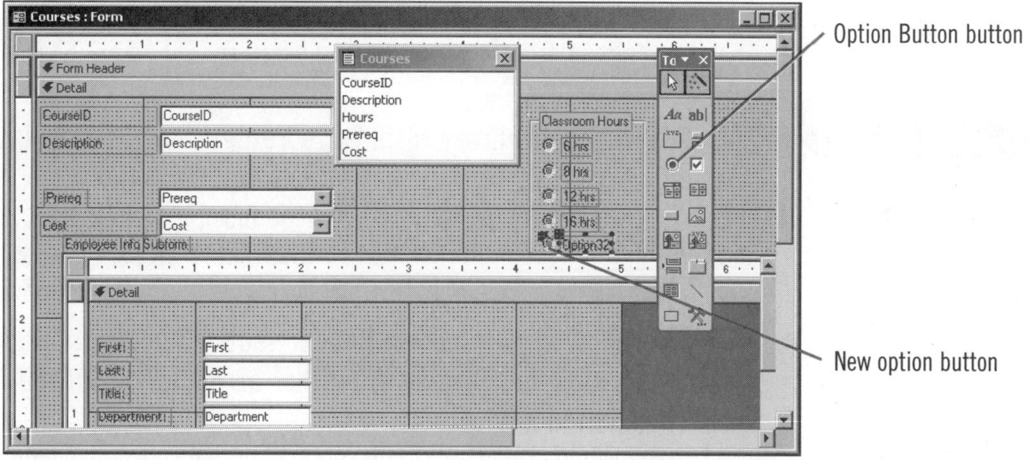

Protecting data

You may not want all the data that appears on a form to be able to be changed by all users who view that form. You can design forms to limit access to certain fields by changing the enabled and locked properties of a control. The **Enabled** property specifies whether a control can have the focus in Form View. The **Locked** property specifies whether you can edit data in a control in Form View.

Access 2002

Access 2002

Adding Command Buttons

A **command button** is a powerful unbound control used to initiate a common action in Form View such as printing the current record, opening another form, or closing the current form. Command buttons are added in Form Design View. They are often added to the **form header** or **form footer** sections. **Sections** determine where controls appear and print. See Table G-3 for more information on form sections. Fred adds a command button to the header section of the Courses form to help the users print the current record.

Steps

Trouble?

If the Form Header section is not visible, click View on the menu bar, then click Form Header/Footer.

1. Click the **Form Design View button**, point to the horizontal line that separates the Form Header and Detail section so that the pointer changes to ‡, then drag down to increase the size of the Form Header section about 0.5"

   Now that the Form Header is expanded, you can place controls in that section.

2. Click the **Command Button button** on the Toolbox toolbar, then click on the right side of the Form Header

   The Command Button Wizard opens, listing over 30 of the most popular actions for the command button, organized within six categories.

3. Click **Record Operations** in the Categories list, click **Print Record** in the Actions list, click **Next**, click **Next** to accept the default button appearance, type **Print Current Record** as the button name, then click **Finish**

   Your screen should look similar to Figure G-17. By default, the Print button on the Standard toolbar prints the entire recordset displayed by the form. Therefore, adding a command button to print only the current record is very useful.

4. Click the **Form View button** to view the new command button, double-click **Alber** in the first record of the subform, type your last name, click the **Print Record command button** in the Form Header section, save, then close the form

   The printout required two pages. You can adjust the left and right margins so that the printout fits neatly on one page.

QuickTip

Double-click the menu bar to immediately display all options for that menu.

5. Click **File** on the menu bar, click **Page Setup**, click the **Margins tab** (if not already selected), press **[Tab]** three times to select **1** in the Left text box, type **0.5**, press **[Tab]** once to select **1** in the Right text box, type **0.5**, then click **OK**

   You can also choose to not print controls in certain form sections. The **Display When** property of the Form Header determines when the controls in that section display and print.

6. Click , double-click the **Form Header section** to open its property sheet, click the **Format tab**, click the **Display When list arrow**, click **Screen Only**, then click the **Properties button**

   The **Display When** property determines whether that control will appear only on the screen, only when printed, or at all times.

Trouble?

If your printout is still too wide for one sheet of paper, drag the right edge of the form to the left in Form Design View to narrow it.

7. Click the **Save button**, click , then click the **Print Record command button**

   Your final Courses Main Form should look like Figure G-18, and your printout should fit on one page, without displaying the form header.

8. Close the Courses form

FIGURE G-17: Adding a command button

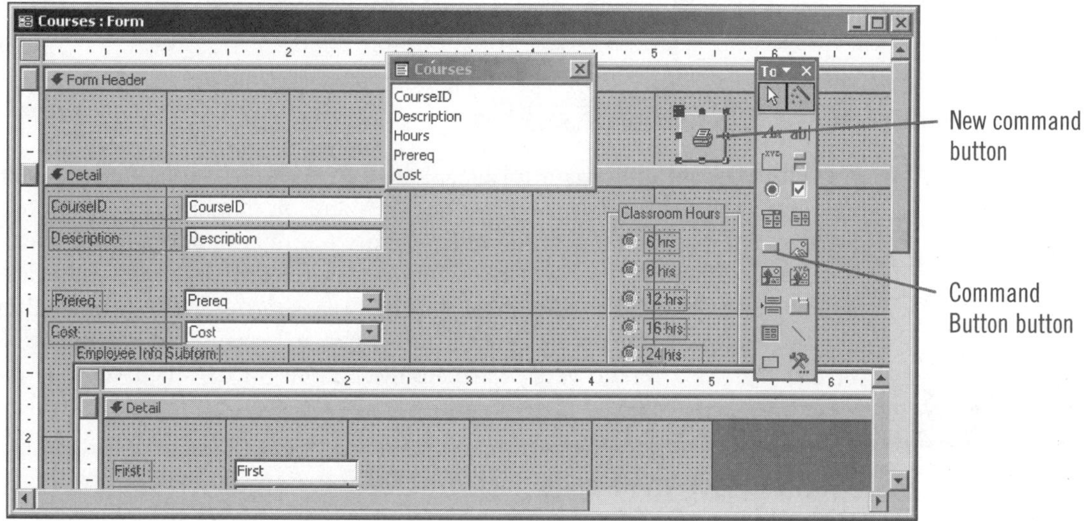

FIGURE G-18: The final Courses main form

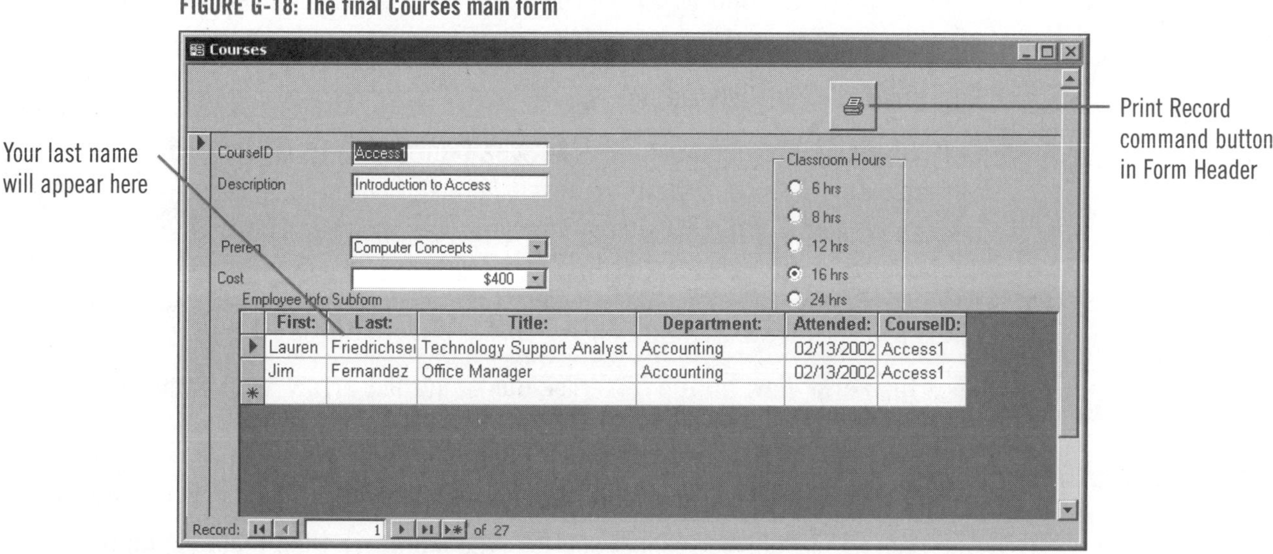

Access 2002

TABLE G-3: Form Sections

section	description
Detail	Appears once for every individual record
Form Header	Appears at the top of the form and often contains command buttons or a label with the title of the form
Form Footer	Appears at the bottom of the form and often contains command buttons or a label with instructions on how to use the form
Page Header	Appears at the top of a printed form with information such as page numbers or dates; the Page Header and Page Footer sections can be added to the form by clicking View on the menu bar, then clicking Page Header/Footer
Page Footer	Appears at the bottom of a printed form with information such as page numbers or dates

Access 2002

Adding ActiveX Controls

An **ActiveX Control** is a control that follows ActiveX standards. **ActiveX standards** are programming standards that were developed by Microsoft to allow developers to more easily share software components and functionality across multiple applications. For example, the same ActiveX control can be used in an Access form, in an Excel workbook, and on a Web page opened in Internet Explorer. The functionality of ActiveX controls range from multimedia players to charting programs to encryption software. Users of the Attendance form have asked Fred if there is a way to easily calculate the number of days between two dates. Fred uses a Calendar and Spreadsheet ActiveX control to give the users the functionality they have requested.

1. Right-click **Attendance**, then click **Design View** on the shortcut menu
   Right now, the form lists six fields in a horizontal arrangement. The ActiveX controls will be placed just below the text boxes in the Detail section.

QuickTip

ActiveX controls are also available by clicking the More Controls button on the Toolbox toolbar.

2. Click **Insert** on the menu bar, then click **ActiveX Control**
   The Insert ActiveX Control dialog box opens as shown in Figure G-19. All of the ActiveX controls available on your computer are listed alphabetically in the dialog box. The number and type of ActiveX controls will depend on the other programs loaded on your computer.
3. Press **C** to move to the ActiveX Controls that start with the letter "C", click **Calendar Control 10.0**, then click **OK**
4. Click **Insert** on the menu bar, click **ActiveX Control**, press **M,** click **Microsoft Office Spreadsheet 10.0**, click **OK** in the Insert ActiveX Control dialog box, then move and resize both new controls below the text boxes, as shown in Figure G-20
   The **Calendar control** appears with the current date chosen. You can use the Calendar control to find or display a date. The **Spreadsheet control** provides similar functionality to that of an Excel spreadsheet, such as calculating the number of days between two dates.
5. Click the **Form View button**, click the **Month list arrow**, click **January**, click the **Year list arrow**, then click **2002**
   Using the Calendar control, you can quickly find out what day of the week a particular class started on. In this case, you determine that the class for Shayla Colletti started on a Wednesday.
6. Click cell **A1** of the spreadsheet control, type **=today()**, then press **[Enter]**
   This formula returns today's date, which is stored in the battery of your computer.
7. Type **1/30/2002** in cell A2, click cell **A3**, type **=A1-A2**, then press **[Enter]**
   The formula in cell A3 determined the number of days between the two dates and presents it as the number of days since Shayla finished her Computer Concepts class. Right now, however, it is formatted as a date instead of as a whole number.
8. Right-click cell **A3**, click **Commands and Options** from the shortcut menu, click the **Number Format list arrow**, then click **General** as shown in Figure G-21
   Using ActiveX technology, programmers can build small programs such as the Calendar and Spreadsheet control, and reuse them in many different ways in different programs.
9. Close the Commands and Options dialog box, click cell **C1**, type **your name**, click the **Save button**, click **File** on the menu bar, click **Print**, click the **Selected Record Option** button, then click **OK**
10. Close the Attendance form, close the **Training-G** database, then exit Access

FIGURE G-19: Insert ActiveX Control dialog box

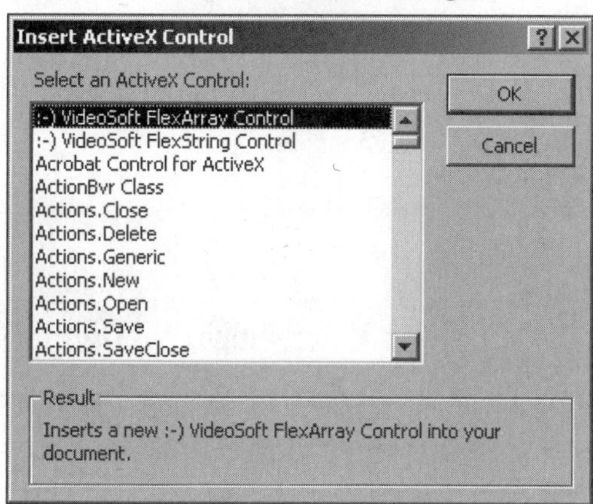

FIGURE G-20: ActiveX Controls in Form Design View

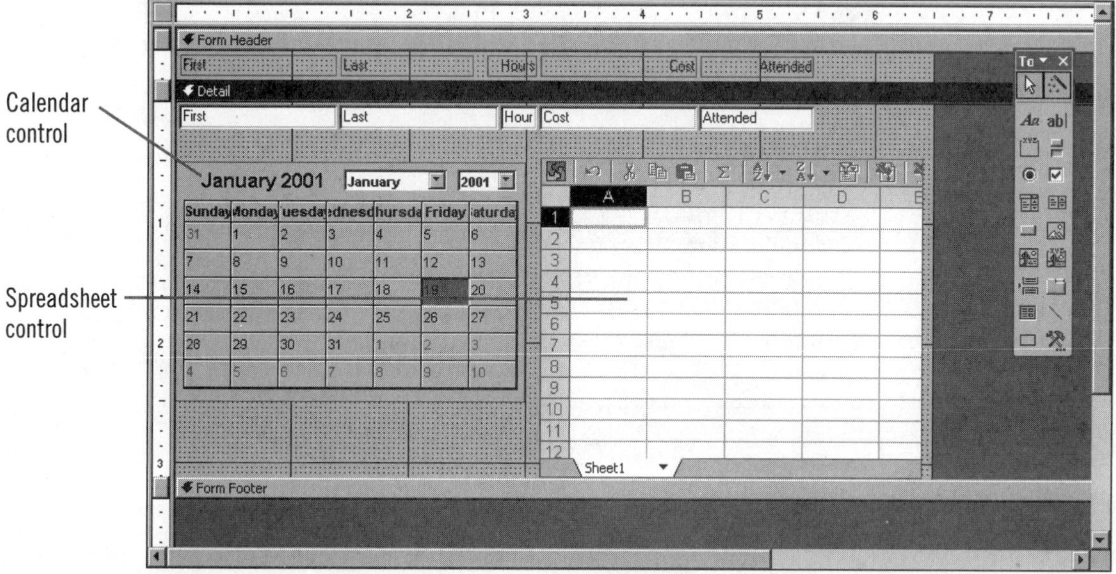

FIGURE G-21: Using ActiveX Controls

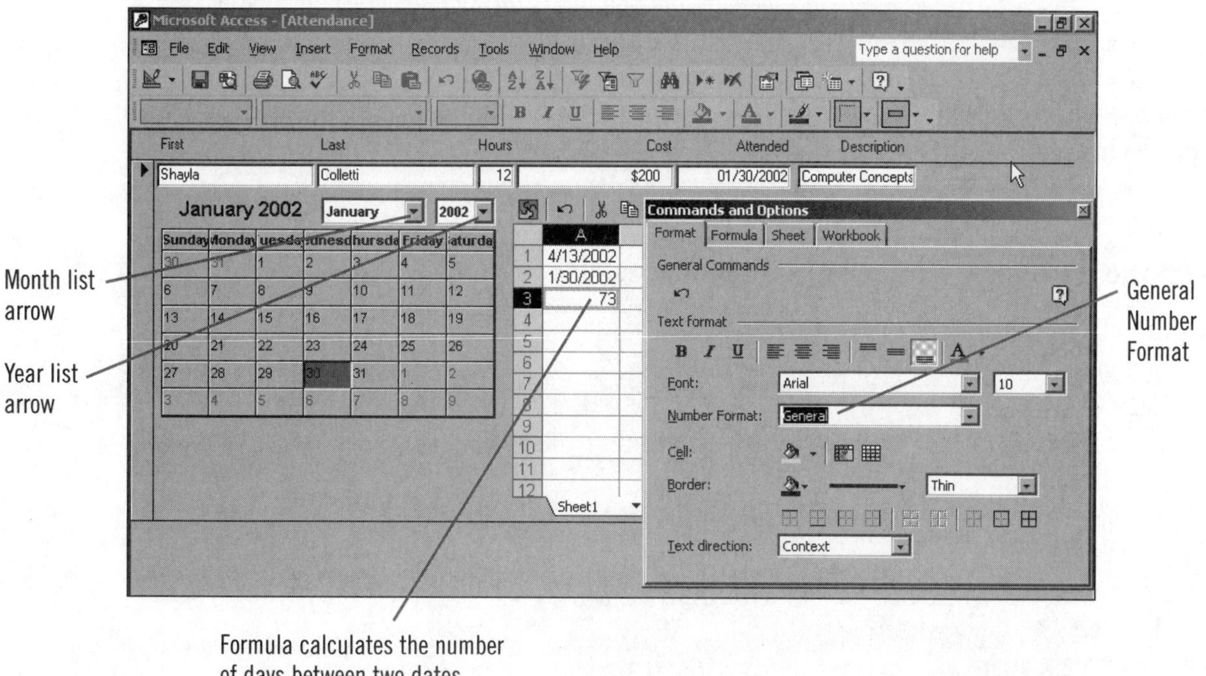

Access 2002

Practice

Concepts Review

Identify each element of the Form Design View shown in Figure G-22.

FIGURE G-22

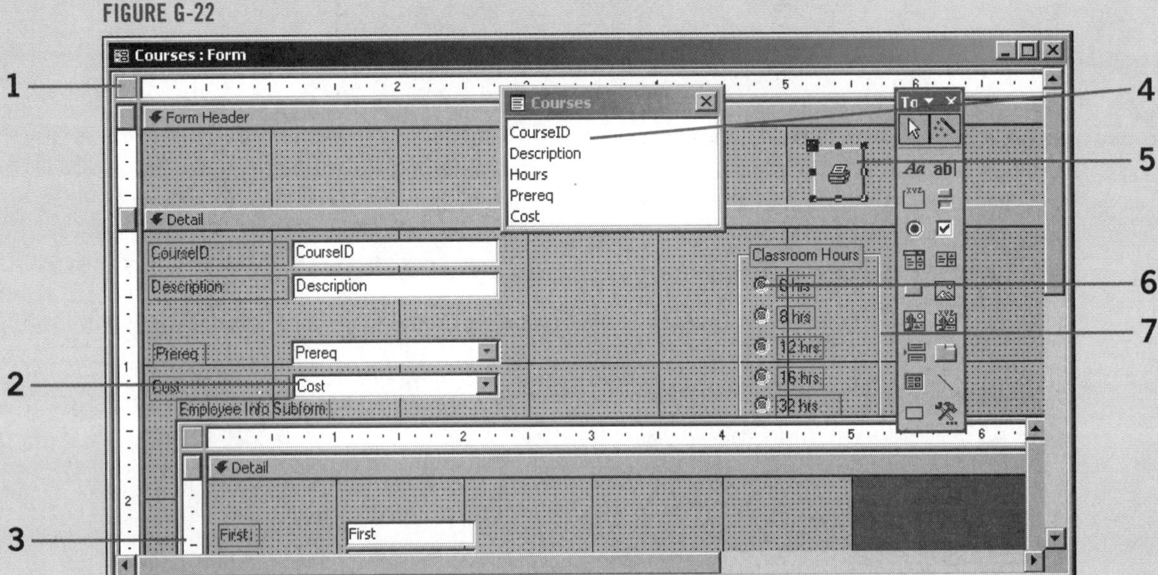

Match each term with the statement that describes its function.

8. **Option group**
9. **Controls**
10. **Command button**
11. **Subform**
12. **Combo box**

a. Elements you add to a form such as labels, text boxes, and list boxes
b. A control that shows records that are related to one record shown in the main form
c. An unbound control that executes an action when it is clicked
d. A bound control that is really both a list box and a text box
e. A bound control that displays a few mutually exclusive entries for a field

Select the best answer from the list of choices.

13. **Which control would work best to display two choices for a field?**
    a. Text box
    b. Label
    c. Option group
    d. Command button
14. **Which control would you use to initiate a print action?**
    a. Option group
    b. List box
    c. Text box
    d. Command button

15. **Which control would you use to display a drop-down list of 50 states?**
    a. Check box
    b. Field label
    c. List box
    d. Combo box
16. **To view linked records within a form use a:**
    a. Subform.
    b. List box.
    c. Design template.
    d. Link control.
17. **Which of the following defines what fields and records display on a form?**
    a. Recordset
    b. Toolbox
    c. Property sheet
    d. ActiveX control
18. **Which is a popular layout for a main form?**
    a. Datasheet
    b. PivotTable
    c. Columnar
    d. Global
19. **Which is a popular layout for a subform?**
    a. Datasheet
    b. PivotTable
    c. Columnar
    d. Global
20. **Which of the following is true of ActiveX controls?**
    a. They always display data from the recordset.
    b. They can be used in many applications.
    c. They are quite limited in scope and functionality.
    d. They are added to a form in Form View.

▶ Skills Review

1. **Understand the form/subform relationship.**
    a. Start Access and open the **Membership-G** database from the drive and folder where your Project Files are stored.
    b. Click the Relationships button on the Database toolbar.
    c. Double-click File on the menu bar, then click Print Relationships.
    d. The Relationships for Membership-G will appear as a previewed report. Click the Design View button, type your name as a label in the Report Header section, then print the report.
    e. Close the preview window without saving the report, and then close the Relationships window.
    f. Based on the one-to-many relationships defined in the Membership-G database, sketch two form/subform combinations that you could create.
2. **Create subforms using the Form Wizard.**
    a. Click Forms on the Objects bar in the Membership-G database window.
    b. Double-click Create form by using wizard.
    c. Select all of the fields from both the Activities and the Names tables.
    d. View the data by Names, then verify that the Form with subform(s) option button is selected.

e. Accept a Datasheet layout for the subform, a Standard style, and the default titles. Click Finish to view the Names form with the Activities subform.
f. Find the record for Lois Goode (record number 3) and change Lois's first and last name to your first and last name.
g. Resize the columns of the datasheet in the subform so that all of the data is clearly visible.
h. Click File on the menu bar, then click Print. Click the Selected records option button in the Print dialog box to print only the data for your name.
i. Save, then close the Names form.

3. **Create subforms using queries.**
   a. Open the Zips in IA or MO query in Design View, then add the criteria to find only those records from IA or MO in the State field. View the datasheet, then save and close the query.
   b. Using either the Form Wizard or Form Design View, build a columnar form based on the Zips in IA or MO query using all three fields in the query. Name the form **Zips in IA or MO.**
   c. Open the Zips in IA or MO form in Design View, and add a subform control about 5" wide by about 3" high below the three text boxes in the Detail section of the form.
   d. Use the Subform Wizard to specify that the subform will use an existing query, then select all of the fields in the Dues query for the subform.
   e. Allow the wizard to link the form and subform so that they show Dues for each record in Zips in IA or MO using Zip.
   f. Accept Dues Subform as the subform's name.
   g. Maximize the form, expand the size of the subform, move the subform as necessary, and display it in Form View.
   h. Resize the datasheet column widths so that all of the information in the subform is clearly visible. When all fields are visible, the horizontal scroll bar does not display in Form View and text from the subform doesn't overlap the main form.
   i. Find the record for Zip 64105, enter your last name in the Last field of the first record, and print only that record.
   j. Click File on the menu bar, click Save As, name the main form **Zips**, then save and close the form and subform.
4. **Modify subforms.**
   a. Click the Queries button in the Objects bar and open the Zips in IA or MO query in Design View.
   b. Delete the criteria that specifies that only the records with State values of IA or MO appear in the recordset.
   c. Use Save As to save the modified query as **All Zips**, then close the query.
   d. Click the Forms button on the Objects bar and open the Zips form in Design View.
   e. Open the property sheet for the form by double-clicking the Form Selector button in the upper-left corner at the intersection of the rulers. Click the Data tab, then change the Record Source property from Zips in IA or MO to **All Zips**.
   f. Close the property sheet, save the form, view the form in Form View, then navigate to record number 13, which displays Zip 64145 for Shawnee, Kansas.
   g. Change the city to the name of your hometown, print only this record, then close the Zips form.
5. **Add combo boxes.**
   a. Open the Names form in Design View, then delete the Zip text box.
   b. Use the Combo Box Wizard to add the Zip field back to the same location as a combo box.
   c. The Combo Box Wizard should look up values in a table or query.
   d. Choose the Zips table and the Zip field as the column values.
   e. Store the value in the Zip field, then label the Combo Box **ZipCode**.
   f. Reposition the new ZipCode label and combo box as necessary, save the form, then display it in Form View.
   g. Navigate to the third record, then change the Zip to **50266** using the new combo box.
6. **Add option groups.**
   a. Open the Names form in Design View, then delete the Dues text box.
   b. Add the Dues field back to the form below the CharterMember check box control using an Option Group control with the Option Group Wizard.

c. Enter **$25** and **$50** as the label names, then accept $25 as the default choice.
d. Change the values to **25** and **50** to correspond with the labels.
e. Store the value in the Dues field, choose Option buttons with an Etched style, type the caption **Annual Dues**, then click Finish.
f. Save the form, display it in Form View, find the record with your address, then change the Annual Dues to **$25**.
g. Save the form.

7. **Add command buttons.**
a. Open the Names form in Design View.
b. Open the Form Header to display about 0.5" of space, then add a command button to the upper-right corner using the Command Button Wizard.
c. Choose the Print Record action from the Record Operations category.
d. Display the text **Print Current Record** on the button, then name the button **Print**.
e. Save the form and display it in Form View. The final form should look similar to Figure G-23.
f. Navigate to the record with your own name, change the month and day of the Birthday entry to your own, then print the record using the new Print Current Record command button.
g. Save, then close the Names form.

FIGURE G-23

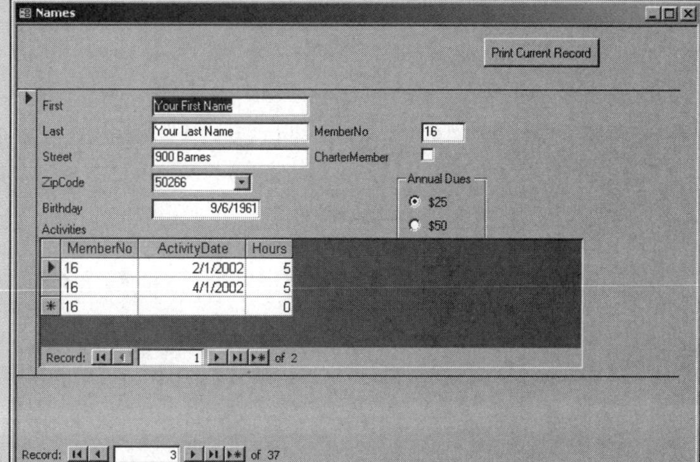

8. **Add ActiveX Controls.**
a. Open the Names form in Design View, then add a Microsoft Office Spreadsheet 10.0 ActiveX control to the Detail section of the main form.
b. Resize the spreadsheet control so that about three columns and four rows are visible, then move it to the upper right corner of the Detail section of the main form.
c. Save the form, then view it in Form View. The spreadsheet ActiveX control will be used to calculate the value of time donated to various activities.
d. Navigate to the record with your name. In cell A1 of the spreadsheet, type **10**, the total number of hours you have contributed based on the information in the subform.
e. In Cell A2 of the spreadsheet, type **12**, the value of one hour of work for the purposes of determining contribution to this club.
f. In Cell A3 of the spreadsheet, type **=A1*A2**, then press [Enter] to calculate the total value of the hours of time you have donated.
g. Click the Print Current Record button to print this record.
h. Save and close the Names form, close the Membership-G database, then exit Access.

► Independent Challenge 1

As the manager of a music store's instrument rental program, you have created a database to track instrument rentals to schoolchildren. Now that several rentals have been made, you wish to create a form/subform to facilitate the user's ability to enter a new rental record.

a. Start Access then open the database **Music Store-G** from the drive and folder where your Project Files are stored.
b. Using the Form Wizard, create a new form based on all of the fields in the Customers and Rentals tables.

c. View the data by Customers, choose a Datasheet layout for the subform and a Standard style, then accept the default form titles of Customers for the main form and Rentals Subform for the subform.
d. Add another record to the rental subform by pressing [Tab] through both the RentalNo and CustNo fields, then typing **888335** as the SerialNo entry and **5/1/03** as the Date entry.
e. Close the Customers form.
f. You want to add the Description field to the subform information. To do this, click the Queries button on the Objects bar, then double-click Create query in Design view. This query will include the Description field, and will serve as the record source for the subform.
g. Add the Rentals and Instruments tables, then close the Show Table dialog box.
h. Add all of the fields from the Rentals table and the Description field from the Instruments table to the query, save the query with the name **Rental Description**, view the query datasheet, then close it.
i. Open the Rentals Subform in Design View, then change the Record Source property of the form from Rentals to **Rental Description**.
j. Open the subform's field list (if it is not already open), then drag the Description field to just below the Date text box in the Detail section. The field may not line up perfectly with the others and the Description label may seem to be on top of other controls. Because the Default View of this form is set to Datasheet, this form will appear as a datasheet regardless of the organization of the controls in Design View.
k. Close the property sheet, save, then close the Rentals Subform.
l. Open the Customers form. It now contains a new Description field in the subform. Enter your first and last name in the first record of the main form, then print it.
m. Close the Customers form, close the Music Store-G database, then exit Access.

► Independent Challenge 2

As the manager of a music store's instrument rental program, you have created a database to track instrument rentals to schoolchildren. You add command buttons to a form to make it easier to use.

a. Start Access then open the database **Music Store-G** from the drive and folder where your Project Files are stored.
b. Using the Form Wizard, create a form/subform using all the fields of both the Customers and Schools tables.
c. View the data by Schools, use a Datasheet layout for the subform, then choose a Standard style.
d. Accept the default names of **Schools** for the main form and **Customers Subform** for the subform.
e. Maximize the main form then resize the columns of the subform so that as many fields as possible can be displayed. Save the form.
f. In Form Design View, widen the subform to the 6.5" mark on the horizontal ruler, then open the Form Header section by 0.5".
g. In Form Design View, add a command button in the Form Header using the Command Button Wizard. The action should print the current record and display the text **Print School Record**. Name the button **Print**.
h. Add a second command button to the Form Header section using the Command Button Wizard. The action should add a new record and display the text **Add New School**. Name the button **Add**.
i. Open the property sheet for the Form Header and give the Display When property the **Screen Only** value. Close the property sheet, then save the Schools form.
j. Display the form in Form View, resize the columns of the datasheet to display all fields, edit the first record in the subform datasheet to display your name and your address, then use the Print School Record button to print that record.
k. Click the Add New School button, then add the name of your elementary school to the SchoolName field, allow the SchoolNo to increment automatically, then add the name of a friend as the first record within the subform.
l. Use the Print School Record button to print this new school record.
m. Close the Schools form, save any changes, close the Music Store-G database, then exit Access.

► Independent Challenge 3

As the manager of a music store's instrument rental program, you have created a database to track instrument rentals to schoolchildren. Now that the users are becoming accustomed to forms, you add a combo box and option group to make the forms easier to use.

a. Start Access, then open the database **Music Store-G**.
b. Using the Form Wizard, create a form/subform using all the fields of both the Instruments and Rentals tables.
c. View the data by Instruments, use a Datasheet layout for the subform, and choose a Standard style.
d. Enter the name **Instruments Main Form** for the main form and **Rental Information** for the subform.
e. In Form Design View, delete the Condition text box and label in the main form.
f. Using the field list and the Toolbox toolbar, add the Condition field as a combo box under the MonthlyFee text box using the Combo Box Wizard. Choose the I will type in the values that I want option, then enter **Poor**, **Fair**, **Good**, and **Excellent** as the values for the first and only column.
g. Store the value in the Condition field, and label the new combo box as **Condition**.
h. Move, then resize the new combo box as necessary so that it is aligned with the three text boxes above it.
i. Delete the MonthlyFee textbox and associated label.
j. Using the field list and the Toolbox toolbar, add the MonthlyFee field as an option group to the right side of the main form using the Option Group Wizard.
k. Enter the Label Names as **$35**, **$40**, **$45**, and **$50**. Do not specify a default option. The corresponding values for the option buttons should be **35**, **40**, **45**, and **50**.
l. Store the value in the MonthlyFee field. Use Option buttons with an Etched style.
m. Caption the option group **Monthly Fee**, save the form, then view it in Form View.
n. Navigate to the second record for the cello, Serial Number 1234568, change the Monthly Fee to **$45**, choose **Excellent** for the Condition, then change the Description field to include your name.
o. Print only that record by clicking File on the menu bar, clicking Print, then choosing the Selected Records option button before clicking OK in the Print dialog box.
p. Save, then close the Instruments Main Form, close the Music Store-G database, and then exit Access.

Independent Challenge 4

You are in the process of organizing your family's photo library. After reviewing the general template sample databases, but not finding any good matches to use for your project, you decide to browse the template gallery featured at the Microsoft Web site to determine if there is a sample database that you can download and use or modify for this purpose.

a. Connect to the Internet, start Access, then click the Templates on Microsoft.com link in the New from template section of the New File task pane.
b. Click the category link for Personal Interests, Community, and Politics, then click the Personal Use link
c. Click the Photograph database link, click the Accept button at the bottom of the End-User License Agreement for Templates page, then click the Edit in Microsoft Access link.
d. A database is downloaded to your computer, which automatically opens a switchboard form that helps you navigate the sample Picture Library database. Click the Enter/View Rolls of Film link, scroll through the main form to view information about the five sample vacations that are presented in the main form, then view the sample photo information for each vacation in the subform.
e. Return to the first vacation record in the main form (the Paris Vacation), edit the Subject Name field entry in the first photo record of the subform to your name, then print the selected main form record.
f. Close the Rolls of Film form, then explore the rest of the sample Picture Library database.
g. Click the Exit This Database link on the Main Switchboard form to close the Photograph library database, then exit Access.

Visual Workshop

Open the **Training-G** database. Use the Form Wizard to create a new form, as shown in Figure G-24. The First, Last, and Department fields are from the Employees table, the Description field is from the Courses table, and the Attended and Passed fields are from the Attendance table. View the form by Employees, choose a Datasheet layout for the subform, and choose a Standard style. Name the form **Employee Basics**, then name the subform **Test Results**. The Department combo box contains the following entries: **Accounting**, **Book**, **Cafe**, **CD**, **Human Resources**, **Marketing**, **Operations**, **Shipping**, **Training**, and **Video**. Use the command buttons in the Form Header to print the current record then close the form. Add your name as a label to the Form Header section, then print the first record.

FIGURE G-24

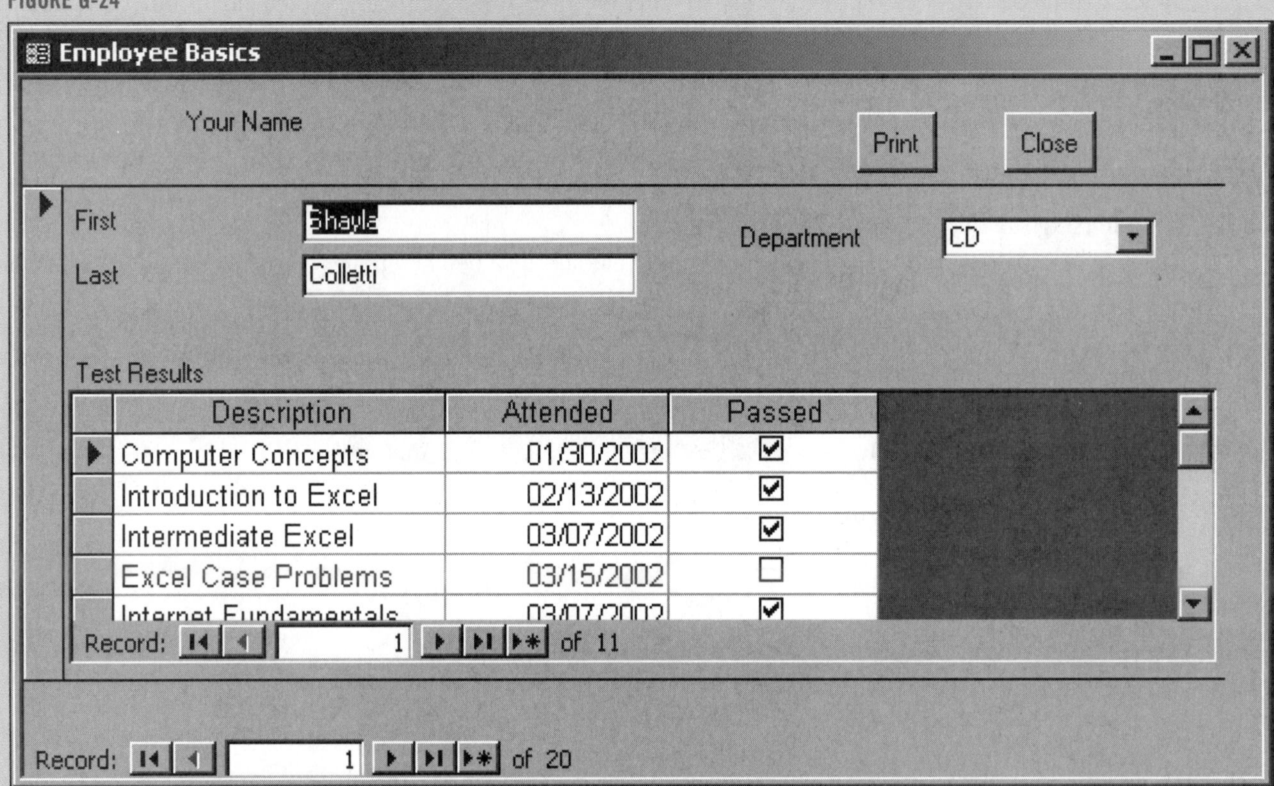

Sharing Information and Improving Reports

Objectives

- MOUS ► Use the Database Wizard
- MOUS ► Import data
- MOUS ► Apply advanced formatting
- MOUS ► Add lines
- MOUS ► Use the Format Painter and AutoFormats
- MOUS ► Create a Web page
- MOUS ► Export data
- MOUS ► Compact and repair a database

Although you can print data in forms and datasheets, **reports** give you more control over how data is printed and greater flexibility in presenting summary information. To create a report, you add bound controls such as text boxes that display values from underlying fields, and unbound controls such as lines, graphics, or labels to clarify or enhance the information. Using the export and Web page features of Access you can electronically share information with other people. Fred Ames, coordinator of training at Medialoft, will use the Access import and export features to share data between the Training-H database and other file formats such as Excel workbooks and Web pages. He will also use advanced reporting and formatting features such as conditional formatting, colors, and lines to improve his reports.

Access 2002

Using the Database Wizard

The **Database Wizard** is a powerful Access tool that creates a sample database file for a general purpose such as inventory control, event tracking, or expenses. These sample databases include several sample objects (tables, forms, reports, and others) that you can use or modify. The Accounting department tracks a training budget to determine how various departments are using MediaLoft's in-house classes, and has requested a quarterly update of this data, currently stored in the Training-H database. In addition, the Accounting department wants this information in an electronic format so that they can further analyze it on their own. Fred decides to create a separate Access database for the Accounting department into which he will regularly import quarterly information on course attendance and costs from the Training-H database.

Trouble?

If the task pane is not visible, click the New button on the Database toolbar.

1. Start Access, click the **General Templates...** link in the New from template section of the New File task pane, then click the **Databases tab** in the Templates dialog box
   The Databases tab of the Templates dialog box is shown in Figure H-1. **Templates** are sample databases that you can use and modify for your own purposes. Some templates invoke the Database Wizard, which prompt you with further questions about how to create the database and the type of information it will store.
2. Double-click **Expenses** in the Templates dialog box
   When you create a new database, you must first name the database file, regardless of whether it is created by a wizard or from scratch.
3. Type **Accounting** in the File name text box, click the **Save in list arrow**, navigate to the drive and folder where your Project Files are stored, then click **Create**
   The Database Wizard starts and provides information about what type of data the database will store.
4. Click **Next**
   The sample database will include the four tables, as shown in Figure H-2. The fields for the selected table appear in the second list. You can select or unselect suggested fields for the chosen table by clicking the check boxes to the left of the field names.
5. Click **Expense report information** in the Tables list to view the fields in this table, then click **Next** to accept the default field choices for all four tables
6. Click **Standard**, click **Next**, click **Corporate**, click **Next**, type **Accounting** as the database title, click **Next**, make sure that the **Yes, start the database check box** is checked, then click **Finish**
   It takes several seconds for Access to build all of the objects for the Accounting database and then open the Main Switchboard form, as shown in Figure H-3. When you use the Database Wizard, Access creates a **switchboard**, a special Access form with command buttons used to navigate through the database. You decide to directly explore the database rather than work with the Switchboard.

Trouble?

The Accounting database window is minimized in the Access window.

7. Click the **Main Switchboard Close button**, click the **Accounting database Maximize button**, review the available forms, click **Reports** on the Objects bar, click **Queries** on the Objects bar, then click **Tables** on the Objects bar
   The form, report, and table objects that were created by the wizard can be used, modified, or deleted just like any user-created object. The wizard did not create any query, page, or macro objects for this database. Not only did the Expenses Database Wizard create the four tables identified in the initial dialog box, a fifth table called Switchboard Items was also created to store information used in the Main Switchboard form.

FIGURE H-1: Database wizards

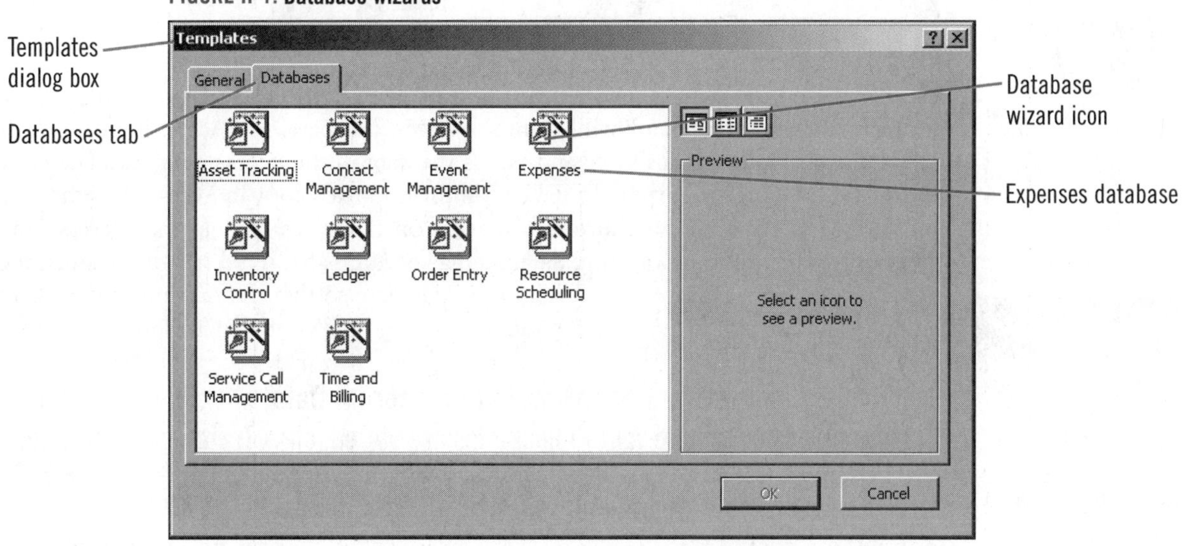

FIGURE H-2: Tables and fields within the Expenses Database Wizard

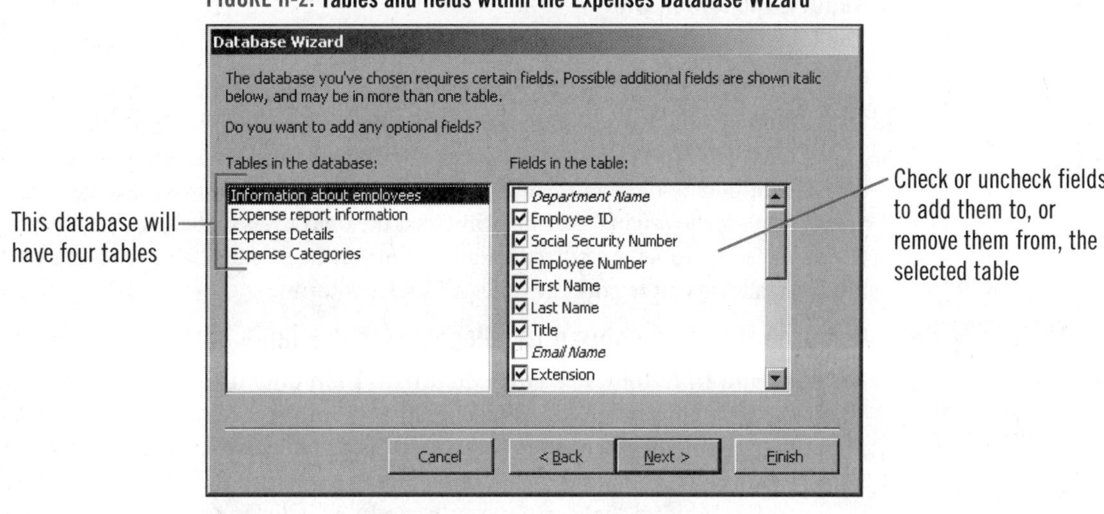

FIGURE H-3: Main Switchboard form for the Accounting database

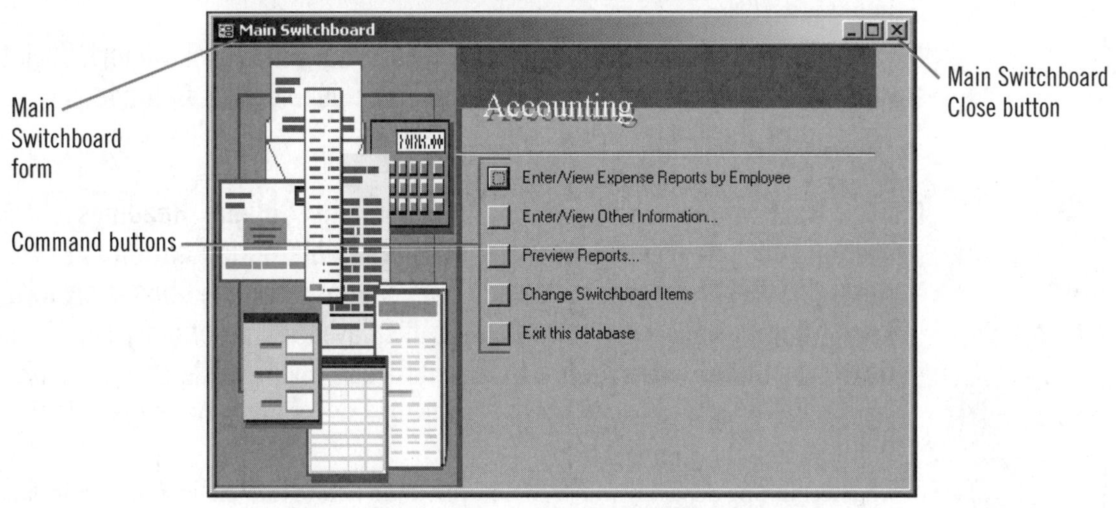

Access 2002

Access 2002

Importing Data

Importing is a process to quickly convert data from an external file, such as an Excel workbook or other database format, and bring it into an Access database. The Access import process copies the data from the original source and pastes the data in the Access database. Therefore, if you update data in either the original source or in the imported copy in Access, the other copy is not updated. See Table H-1 for more information on the types of data that Access can import. Now that the Accounting database has been created, Fred imports historical cost and attendance information from the Training-H database so that the Accounting department can analyze and manipulate this data without disturbing Fred's original Training-H database.

Steps

Trouble?

You can't import from the Training-H database if it is opened in another Access window.

1. Click **File** on the menu bar, point to **Get External Data**, click **Import**, navigate to the drive and folder where your Project Files are stored, click **Training-H**, then click **Import**
   The Import Objects dialog box opens, as shown in Figure H-4. Any object in the Training-H database can be imported into the Accounting database.
2. Click the **Tables tab** (if not already selected), click **1QTR-2002**, click **Courses**, click the **Queries tab**, click **Accounting Query**, click the **Reports tab**, click **Accounting Report**, then click **OK**
   The four selected objects are imported from the Training-H database into the Accounting database.
3. Click **Tables** on the Objects bar, then click the **Details button** in the Database window
   The Created and Modified dates of both the 1QTR-2002 and the Courses tables should be today's date. If you update these tables in the future, the Modified date will change. The Created date always displays the original date and time that the object was first created. By default, objects in the database window are sorted in ascending order by name, but clicking on the column headings allows you to sort the objects by that column.

QuickTip

You can resize the columns by dragging the ✣ pointer between column headings. Double-click ✣ to automatically widen the column to accommodate the widest item.

4. Click the **Modified column heading** to sort the Table objects in ascending order by the date and time they were last modified, then click the **Name column heading**
   The database window should look like Figure H-5. In this case, sorting by the Modified column doesn't provide much value because all of the tables were created on the same date, and none have been modified since that time. But you will find this technique very helpful when trying to find objects that were recently modified. Clicking the column heading a second time sorts the objects in descending order by that column. The MediaLoft Accounting department stores department codes in an Excel workbook that also needs to be imported into this database.
5. Click **File** on the menu bar, point to **Get External Data**, click **Import**, click the **Files of type list arrow**, click **Microsoft Excel**, then double-click **Deptcodes**
   The Import Spreadsheet Wizard presents the data that you are trying to import, and then guides you through the rest of the import process.
6. Click **Next**, make sure the **First Row Contains Column Headings** check box is checked, click **Next**, make sure the **In a New Table option button** is selected, click **Next**, click **Next** to accept the default field options, click the **Choose my own primary key option button**, make sure **Code** is displayed in the primary key list box, click **Next**, type **Codes** in the Import to Table text box, click **Finish**, then click **OK**
   The Deptcodes spreadsheet is now a table named Codes in the Accounting database.
7. Double-click the **Codes** table to open it
   The Accounting department has more work to do before they can use their new database, but using the Database Wizard and Access importing features helped them get off to a quick start.
8. Close the Codes datasheet, then close the Accounting database

FIGURE H-4: Import Objects dialog box

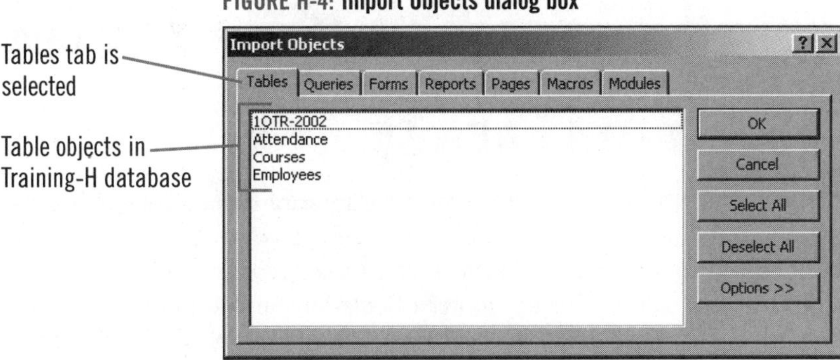

FIGURE H-5: Database window showing object details

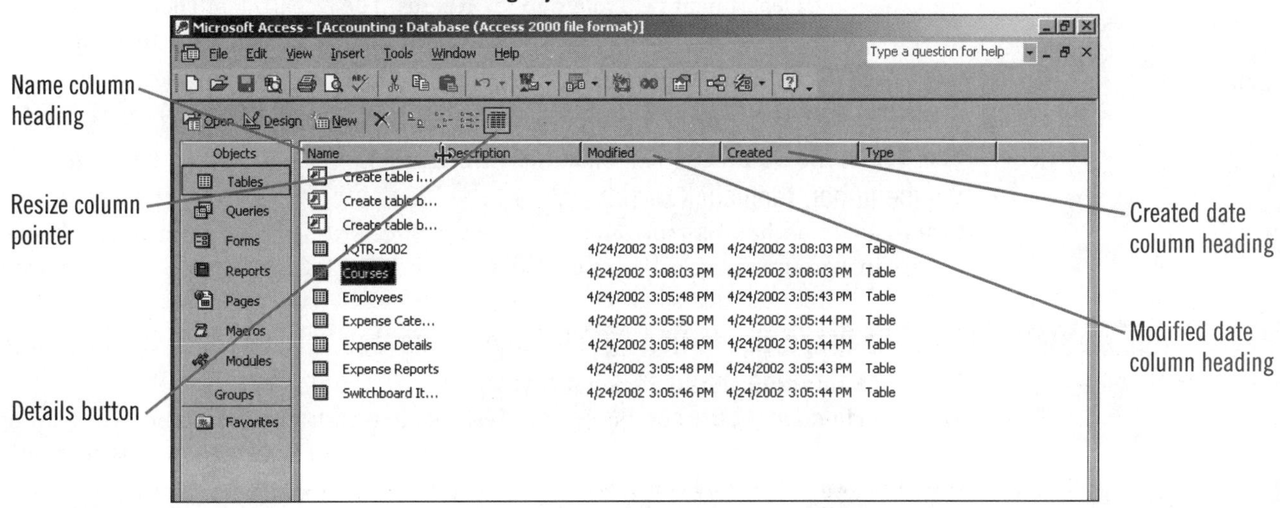

TABLE H-1: Data sources Microsoft Access can import

data source	version or format supported	data source	version or format supported
Microsoft Access database	2.0, 7.0/95, 8.0/97, 9.0/2000, and 10.0/2002	**Microsoft Exchange**	All versions
Microsoft Access project	9.0/2000, 10.0/2002	**Delimited text files**	All character sets
dBASE	III, IV, 5, 7	**Fixed-width text files**	All character sets
Paradox, Paradox for Windows	3.x, 4.x, 5.0, 8.0	**HTML**	1.0 (if a list) 2.0, 3.x (if a table or list)
Microsoft Excel	3.0, 4.0, 5.0, 7.0/95, 8.0/97, 9.0/2000, 10.0/2002	**XML Documents**	All versions
Lotus 1-2-3	.wks, .wk1, .wk3, .wk4	**SQL tables, Microsoft Visual FoxPro, and other data sources that support ODBC protocol**	**ODBC** (Open Database Connectivity) is a protocol for accessing data in **SQL** (Structured Query Language) database servers

Access 2002

Applying Advanced Formatting

Conditional formatting allows you to change the appearance of a control based on criteria you specify. **Grouping controls** allows you to identify several controls as a group in order to quickly apply the same formatting properties to them. Other report embellishments such as hiding duplicate values and adding Group Footer calculations also improve a report. Fred wants to improve the Attendance by Department report by applying conditional formatting. He explores other report techniques such as hiding duplicate values and grouping controls.

Steps

QuickTip

Click the Sorting and Grouping button on the Report Design toolbar to view the order of the grouping and sorting fields used for the report.

1. Open the **Training-H** database, click **Reports** on the Objects bar, right-click **Attendance by Department**, then click **Design View**

   The Attendance by Department report opens in Design View, as shown in Figure H-6. The report uses the Department field to group the records. The Department Footer section subtotals the Hours (of in-class training) for that department using a text box that contains the =Sum([Hours]) expression.

2. Click the **Last text box** in the Detail section, press and hold **[Shift]**, click the **First text box** in the Detail section, click the **Title text box**, release **[Shift]**, click **Format** on the menu bar, then click **Group**

   Group selection handles surround the group of three text boxes, so when you click on *any* control in a group, you select *every* control in the group. Clicking a control within a *selected group* still selects just that single control.

QuickTip

The title bar of the property sheet indicates that multiple controls have been selected.

3. Click the **Properties button**, click the **Format tab**, click the **Hide Duplicates text box**, click the **Hide Duplicates list arrow**, click **Yes**, then click

   With the **Hide Duplicates** property set to Yes, the First, Last, and Title values will print only once per employee rather than once for each record in the Detail section. It is common to copy and paste calculated controls from a Group Footer section to the Report Footer section in order to quickly create the same calculations for the entire report.

4. Right-click the **=Sum([Hours]) text box** in the Department Footer, click **Copy** on the shortcut menu, right-click the **Report Footer section**, then click **Paste**

   The text box containing the =Sum([Hours]) calculation has been pasted at the left edge of the Report Footer section.

5. Use the pointer to drag the **=Sum([Hours]) text box** in the Report Footer section to the right edge of that section

   You cannot group controls in different sections, but you can select multiple controls in different sections in order to apply the same formatting commands to all selected controls.

QuickTip

You can add up to three conditional formats for any combination of selected controls.

6. Press **[Shift]**, click the **=Sum([Hours]) text box** in the Department Footer section to add it to the current selection, click **Format** on the menu bar, click **Conditional Formatting**, click the **between list arrow**, click **greater than**, click the **text box**, type **200**, click the **Bold button** for Condition 1, then click the red **Font/Fore Color button** for Condition 1

   The Conditional Formatting dialog box should look like Figure H-7.

7. Click **OK** in the Conditional Formatting dialog box, click the **Save button** on the Report Design toolbar, click the **Print Preview button**, then zoom and position the report, as shown in Figure H-8

8. Click the **Design View button**, click the **Label button** on the Toolbox toolbar, click the right side of the Report Header section, then type your name

9. Save, print, then close the Attendance by Department report

FIGURE H-6: Attendance by Department report in Report Design View

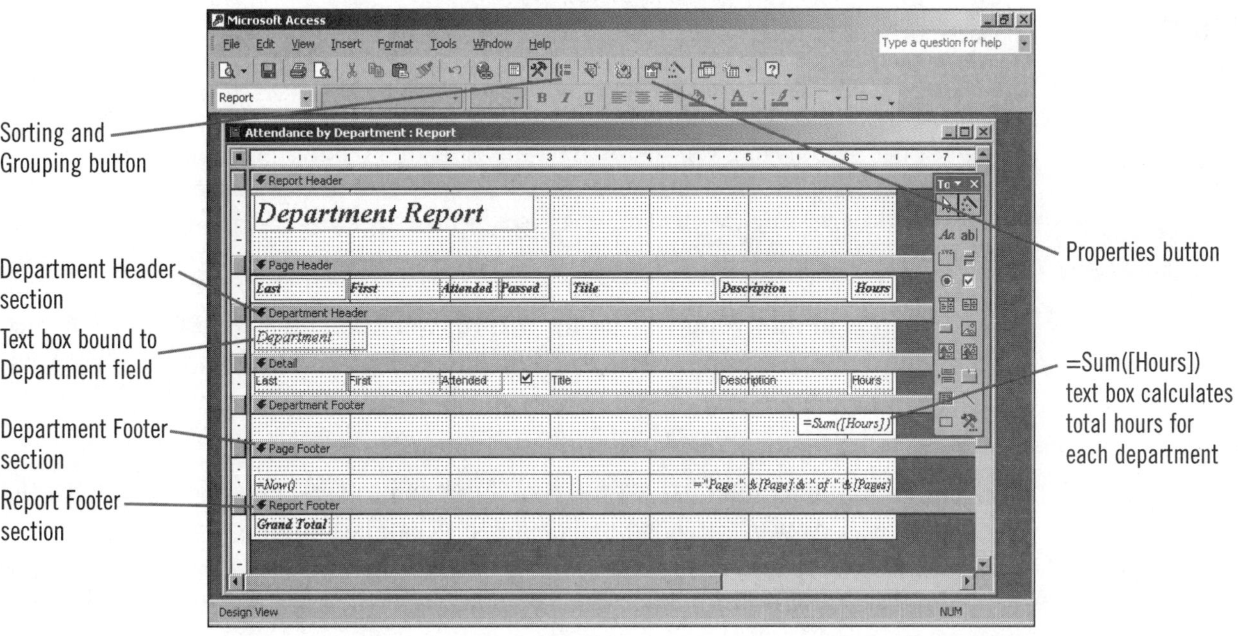

FIGURE H-7: Conditional Formatting dialog box

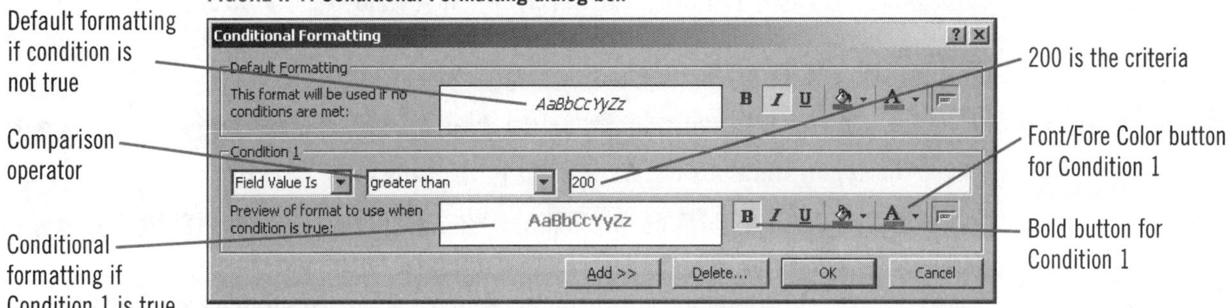

FIGURE H-8: Final Attendance by Department report for the Book department

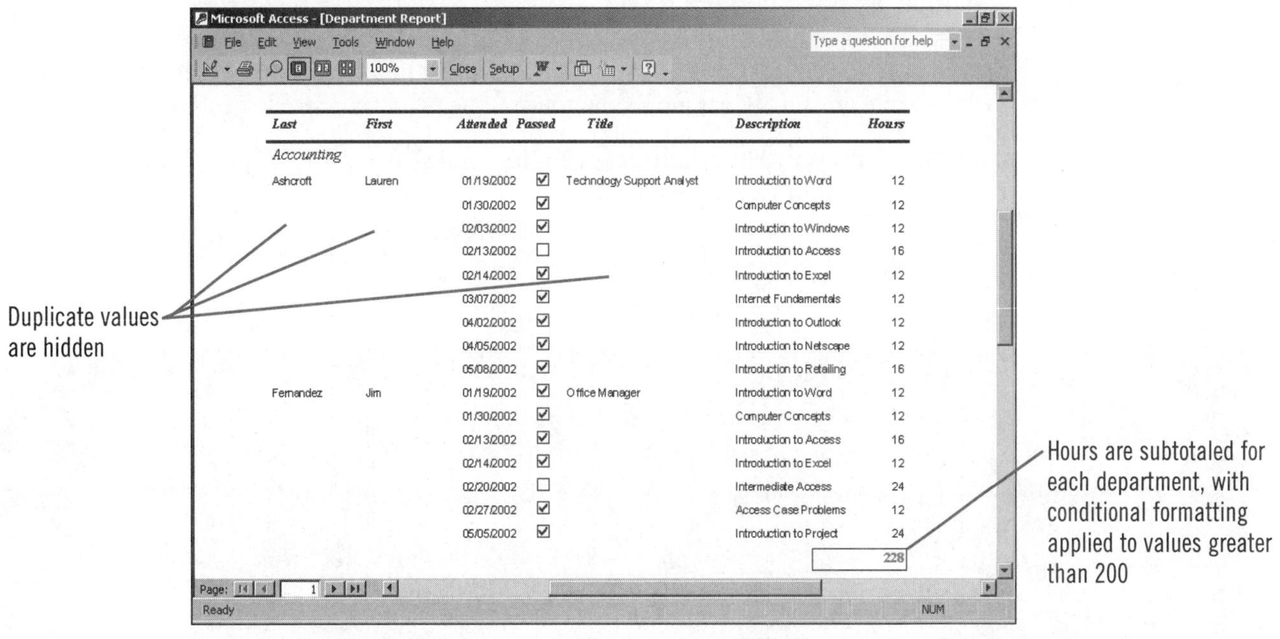

Access 2002

Access 2002

Adding Lines

Unbound controls such as labels, lines, and rectangles enhance the clarity of a report. The Report Wizard often creates line controls at the bottom of the Report Header, Page Header, or Group Header sections that visually separate the parts of a report. Lines can be formatted in many ways. The Personnel department has asked Fred to create a report that lists all of the Medialoft courses and to subtotal the courses by hours and costs. Fred uses line controls to enhance the appearance of this report.

1. Double-click **Create report by using wizard**, click the **Tables/Queries list arrow**, click **Query: Course Summary Query**, click the **Select All Fields button**, click **Next**, click **by Attendance**, click **Next**, double-click **Department**, then click **Next**
   After determining the grouping field(s), the wizard prompts for the sort field(s).
2. Click the **first sort field list arrow**, click **Attended** to sort the detail records by the date the classes were attended, then click the **Summary Options button**
   The Summary Options dialog box allows you to include the sum, average, minimum, or maximum value of fields to various sections of the report.
3. Click the **Hours Sum check box**, click the **Cost Sum check box**, click **OK**, click **Next**, click the **Outline 2 Layout option button**, click the **Landscape Orientation option button**, click **Next**, click the **Formal** Style, click **Next**, type **Course Summary Report** as the report title, click **Finish**, then click the **Zoom Out pointer** on the report
   The wizard created several line and rectangle controls identified in Figure H-9.
4. Click the **Design View button** on the Print Preview toolbar, click the **line control** near the top of the Detail section, then press **[Delete]**
5. Click the **Line button** on the Toolbox toolbar, press and hold **[Shift]**, drag a line from the bottom-left edge of the =Sum([Hours]) text box to the bottom-right edge of the =Sum([Cost]) text box in the Report Footer section, then release **[Shift]**
   Copying and pasting lines creates an exact duplicate of the line.
6. Click the **Copy button** on the Formatting (Form/Report) toolbar, click the **Paste button**, then press ↑
   Design View of the report should look like Figure H-10. Short double lines under the calculations in the Report Footer section indicate grand totals. Moving a control with the arrow keys while pressing [Ctrl] moves the control one **pixel** (picture element) at a time.
7. Click the **Print Preview button** on the Formatting (Form/Report) toolbar, then click the **Last Page Navigation button**
   The last page of the report should look like Figure H-11. The two lines under the final values indicate that they are grand totals.

Trouble?

If your report title doesn't display the entire title, widen the label that displays this text in Report Design View.

Trouble?

The easiest place to select the line control in the Detail section is between the Passed check box and Description text box.

Trouble?

Be sure to add the lines to the Report Footer section, and not the Department Footer section.

Line troubles

As you work with your report in Report Design View, it is easy to accidentally widen a line beyond the physical limits of the page, thus creating extra pages in your printout showing the portion of the line that extends off the right edge of the paper. The solution to this problem is to narrow the lines and the right edge of the report in Report Design View to within the margins set for a physical page. Remember, though, that lines are sometimes difficult to find in Report Design View because they are often hidden by the edge of a section. Also, remember to hold [Shift] down while resizing a line. This will keep the line perfectly horizontal as you resize it.

FIGURE H-9: First page of Course Summary Report

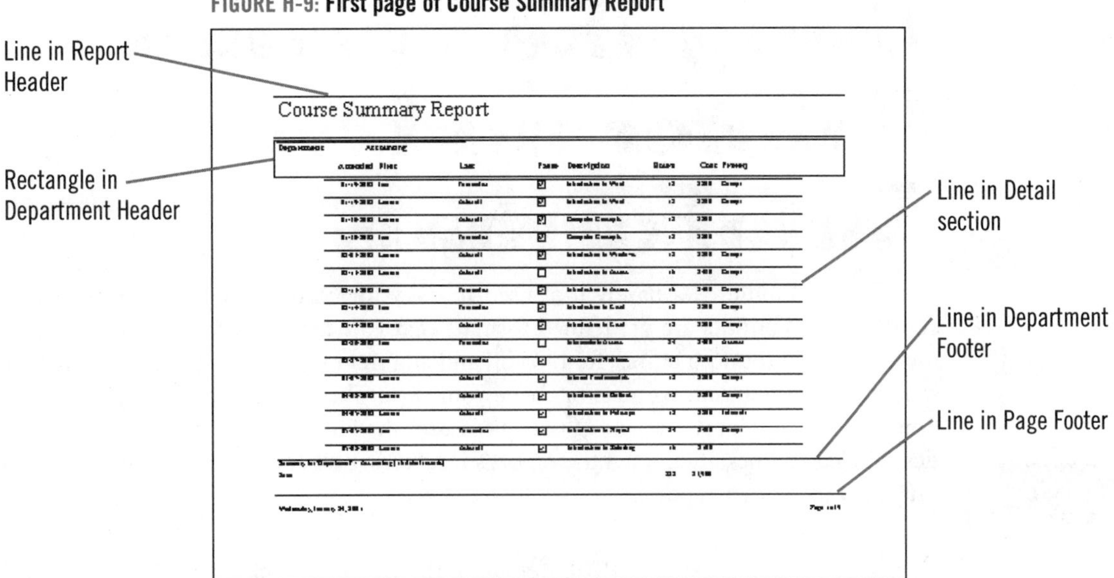

FIGURE H-10: Course Summary Report in Design View

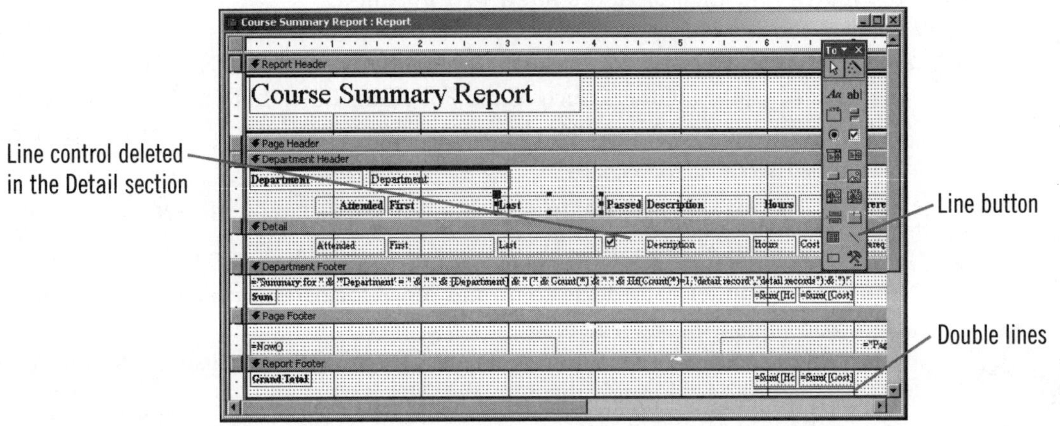

FIGURE H-11: Last page of modified Course Summary Report

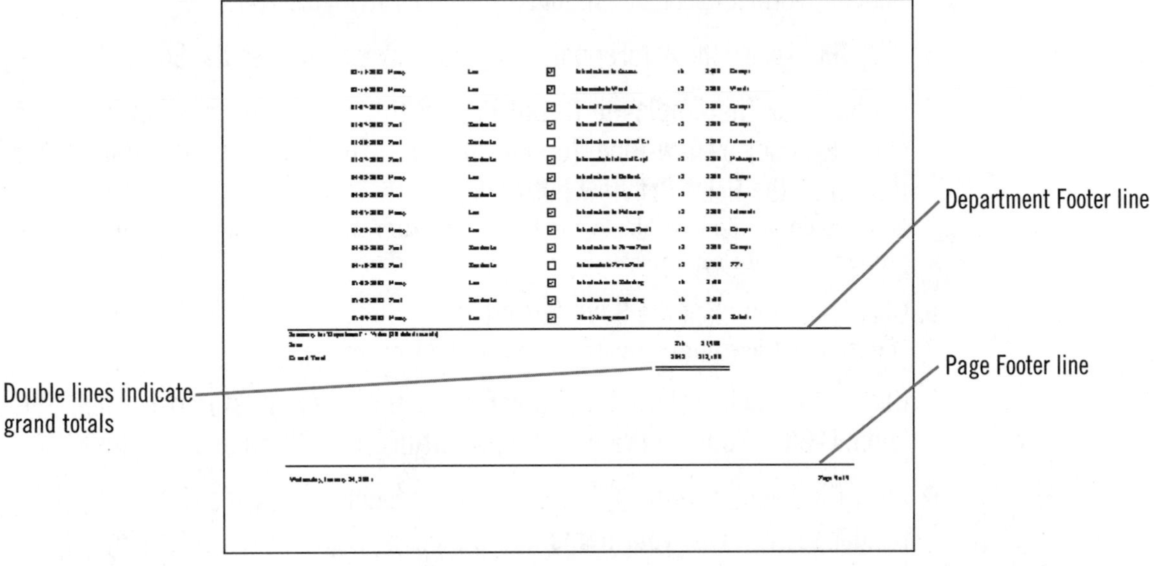

Access 2002

Access 2002

Using the Format Painter and AutoFormats

The **Format Painter** is a handy tool used to copy formatting properties from one control to another. **AutoFormats** are predefined formats that you can apply to a form or report to determine the background pictures, font, color, and alignment choices applied to the report. You can modify the existing AutoFormats or create your own. The report AutoFormats are available every time you use the Report Wizard. Fred uses the Format Painter to change the characteristics of selected lines, then saves the report's formatting scheme as a new AutoFormat so that he can apply it to other reports.

Steps 1 2 3 4

1. Click the **Design View button**, click the **Attended label** in the Department Header section, click the **Font/Fore Color button list arrow**, click the **blue** box in the second row, click the **Fill/Back Color button list arrow**, click the **yellow** box in the fourth row, then click the **Align Left button**
   Some of the buttons on the Formatting (Form/Report) toolbar such as the **Bold button** and the **Align Left button** display with a blue square to indicate that they are applied to the selected control. Others, such as the **Font/Fore Color button** and **Fill/Back Color button**, display the last color that was used for this report. The Format Painter can help you apply these formats to other controls very quickly.
2. Double-click the **Format Painter button** on the Formatting (Form/Report) toolbar, then click all of the **labels** in the Department Header section
   The Format Painter copied the color and other formatting properties from the Attended label, and pasted those formats to the other labels in the Department Header section, as shown in Figure H-12. You can save this set of formatting embellishments as an AutoFormat so that you can quickly apply them to another report.
3. Click to release it, click the **AutoFormat button** on the Report Design toolbar, click **Customize**, click the **Create a new AutoFormat based on the Report 'Course Summary Report' option button**, click **OK**, type **Yellow-Blue-YourFirstName**, then click **OK**
   The AutoFormat dialog box should look similar to Figure H-13.
4. Click **OK** to close the AutoFormat dialog box, save, then close the Course Summary Report
5. Double-click the **Employee Detail Report** to view the current formatting, click , click , click **Yellow-Blue-YourFirstName** in the Report AutoFormats list, click **OK**, then click the **Print Preview button**
   Your screen should look like Figure H-14. The AutoFormat you applied changed the formatting properties of labels in the Department Header section.
6. Click , then click the **Save button**
   You should delete AutoFormats that you will no longer use.
7. Click , click **Yellow-Blue-YourFirstName**, click **Customize**, click the **Delete 'Yellow-Blue-YourFirstName' option button**, click **OK**, then click **Close**
8. Click the **Label button** on the Toolbox toolbar, click the right side of the Report Header section, type **your name**, print, then save and close the Employee Detail Report

QuickTip

Press [Esc] to release the Format Painter.

FIGURE H-12: Using the Format Painter

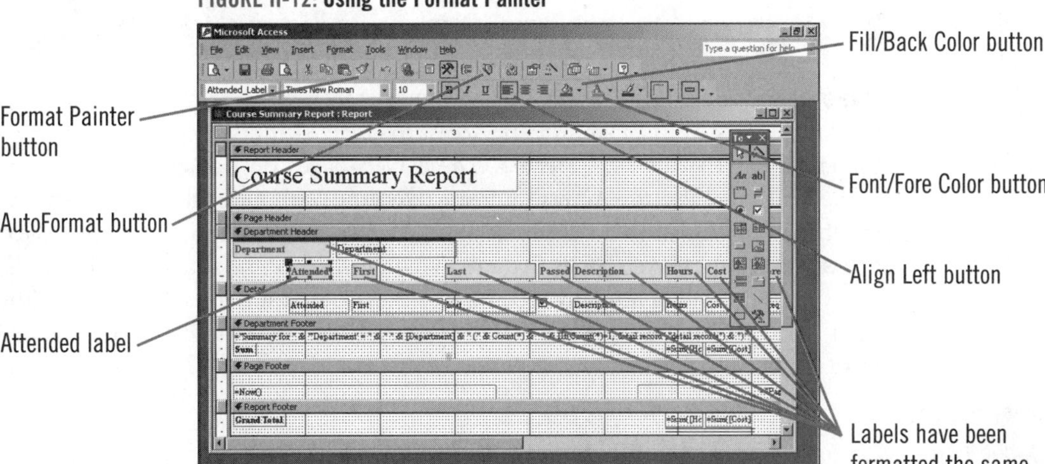

FIGURE H-13: The AutoFormat dialog box

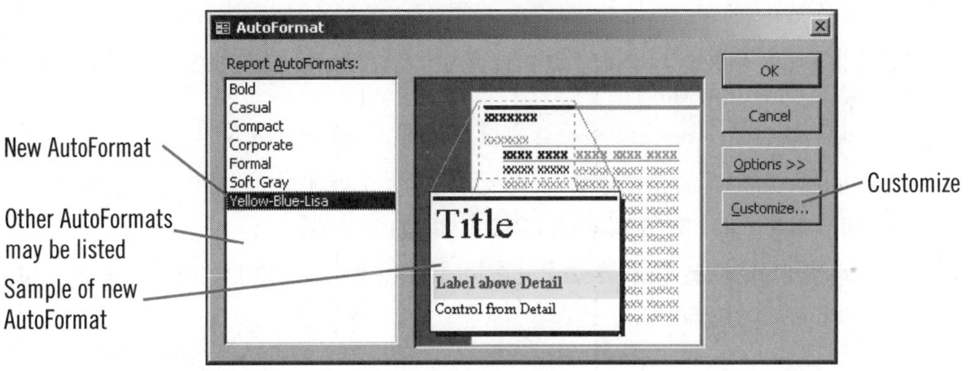

FIGURE H-14: Applying a custom AutoFormat to a different report

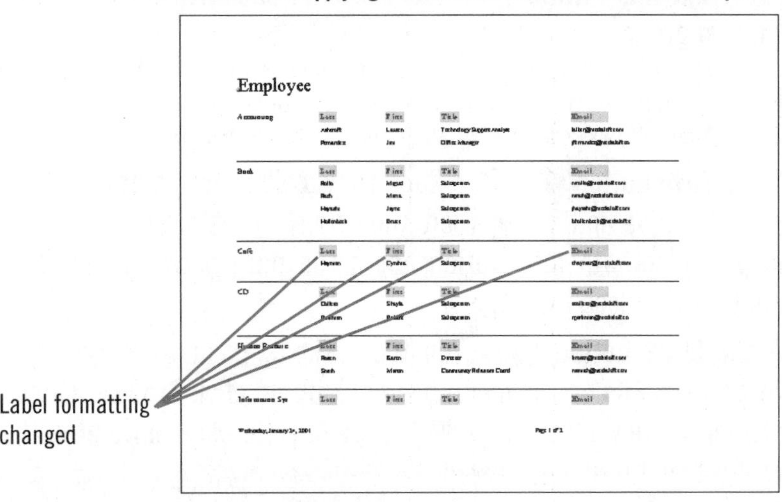

Creating summary reports

Sometimes you may not want to show all the details of a report, but rather only the summary information that is calculated in the Group Footer section. You can accomplish this by deleting all controls in the Detail section. Calculated controls in a Group Footer section will still calculate properly even if the individual records used within the calculation are not displayed on the report.

Access 2002

Creating a Web Page

A **Web page** is a file that is viewed using **browser** software such as Microsoft Internet Explorer. You can use the export capabilities of Access to create **static** Web pages that show data as of the moment the Web page was created. These Web pages do not change when the database is updated. You can also use Access to create **dynamic** Web pages that are automatically updated with the latest changes to the database and therefore show current data. The page object creates **data access pages**, Web pages that are dynamically connected to the database. The benefit of converting Access data into any type of Web page is that it makes the information more accessible to a larger audience. Fred uses the page object to create a dynamic Web page to report employee information.

Steps

1. Click **Pages** on the Objects bar, then double-click **Create data access page by using wizard**
   The Page Wizard opens with an interface similar to the Form and Report Wizards. First, you need to determine what fields you want the Web page to display.
2. Click the **Tables/Queries list arrow**, click **Table: Employees**, click the **Select All button** >>, then click **Next**
   Web pages, like reports, can be used to group and sort records.
3. Double-click **Department** to specify it as a grouping field, click **Next**, click the **first sort order list arrow**, click **Last**, then click **Next**
4. Type **Employees Info Web Page** for the title, click the **Open the page option button**, then click **Finish**
   The Web page opens in **Page View**, a special view within Access that allows you to see how your Web page will appear when opened in Internet Explorer. You modify the structure of a data access page in **Page Design View**.
5. Click the **Expand button** + to the left of the Department label to show the fields within that group
   Your page should look like Figure H-15. On a data access page, the **Navigation bars** not only allow you to move from record to record, they contain buttons to edit, sort, and filter the data. Page View shows you how the Web page will appear from within Internet Explorer (IE).
6. Click the **Save button** on the Page View toolbar, type **einfo** as the File name, navigate to the drive and folder where your Project Files are stored, click **Save**, click **OK** when prompted with information about the path between the Web page and the database, then close the page
7. Click the **Start button** Start on the taskbar, point to **Programs**, click **Internet Explorer**, click **File** on the menu bar, click **Open**, click **Browse**, navigate to the drive and folder where you saved the Web page, double-click **einfo.htm**, then click **OK**
   Internet Explorer loads and presents the Web page.
8. Click the **Next button** on the Employees-Department navigation toolbar, click + to the left of the Department label, then click the **Sort Descending button** on the Employees Navigation bar
   The Web page should look like Figure H-16. The address of the Web page displays the drive and folder where you saved the file.
9. Close Internet Explorer

Trouble?

If the Web page opens in Design View, click the Page View button to switch to Page View.

Trouble?

Web pages created through the page object in Access require Internet Explorer version 5.0 or later to support dynamic connectivity with the database.

FIGURE H-15: Web page in Page View

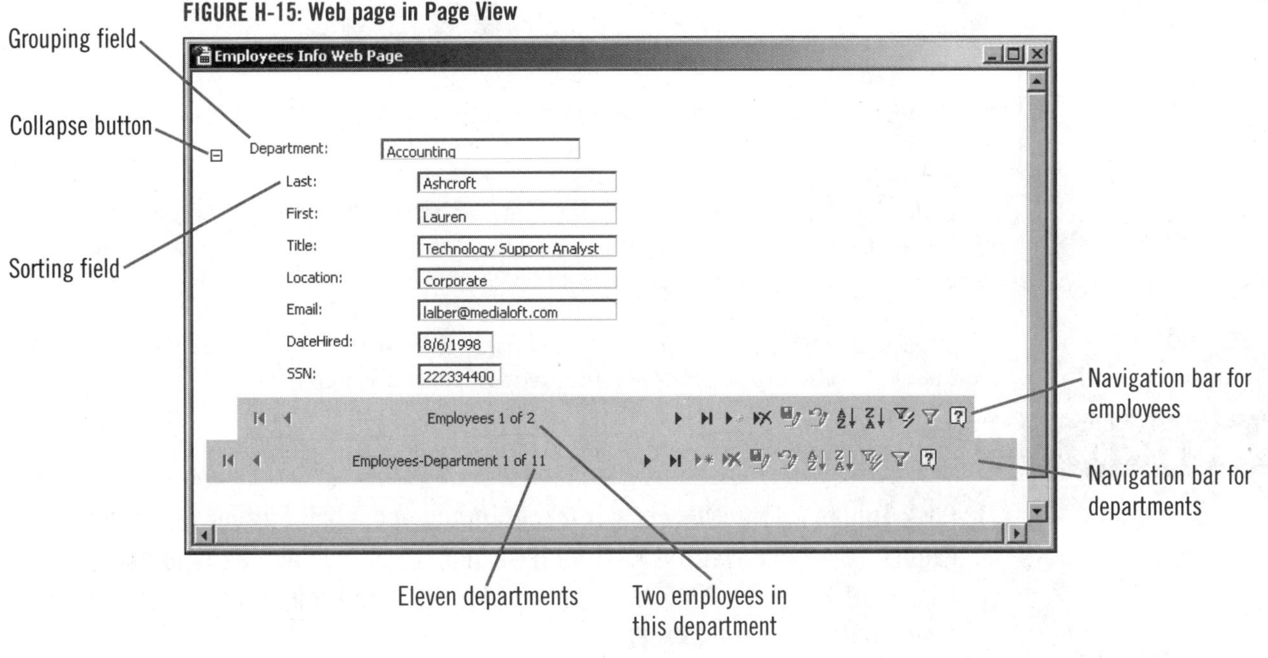

FIGURE H-16: einfo Web page in Internet Explorer

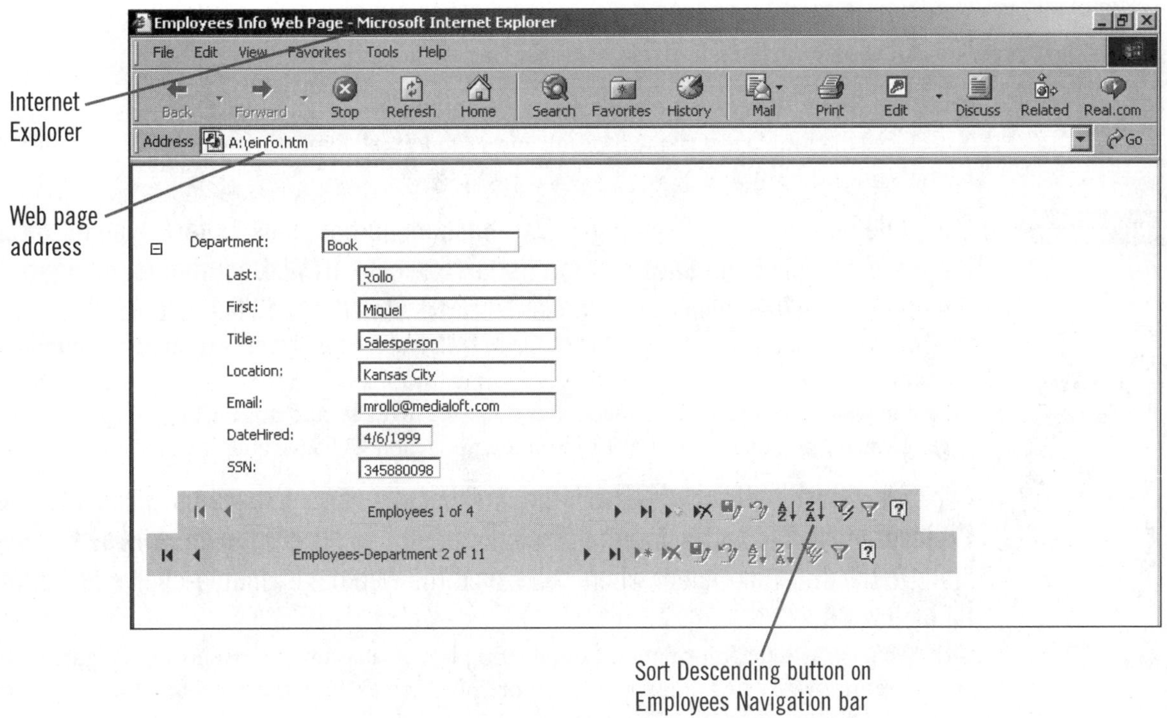

Access 2002

Exporting Data

Exporting is a process to quickly convert data from Access to another file format such as an Excel workbook, a Word document, or a static Web page. Importing is a process used to copy and paste data *into* an Access database, whereas exporting is a process used to copy and paste data *out of* the database. Since there is no dynamic link between the original Access database and an exported copy of the data, changes made to the information in the database will *not* affect the exported copy. See Table H-2 for more information on the types of data that Access can export.
Fred received a request from the Human Resources department to copy the data in the Employees table to an Excel workbook. Fred uses the export features to send this data to an Excel workbook. He also experiments with exporting data as a Web page.

Steps

1. Click **Tables** on the Objects bar, click **Employees**, click **File** on the menu bar, click **Export**, type **EmployeeData** as the file name, click the **Save as type list arrow**, click **Microsoft Excel 97-2002**, navigate to the drive and folder where your Project Files are stored, then click **Export**
   The export process creates the EmployeeData.xls Excel workbook that contains the Employees data.
2. Click the **Start button** on the taskbar, point to **Programs**, click **Microsoft Excel**, click the **Open button** on the Excel Standard toolbar, navigate to the drive and folder where you exported the Employees table, then double-click **EmployeeData**
   The Excel workbook appears, as shown in Figure H-17. All of the data has been successfully exported, but some of it is hidden because the columns are narrow.
3. Click the **Select All button**, point between column heading A and column heading B so that the pointer becomes ✚, then double-click
   With all columns selected, you can adjust the width of all of them at the same time so that you can clearly see that all Access data was successfully exported.
4. Click the **Save button**, click **File** on the menu bar, then click **Exit**
   You closed the EmployeeData workbook and exited Excel. Exporting Access data to other file formats, including Web pages, is a similar process.

QuickTip

If you want to create a *dynamic* Web page that automatically updates as the information is modified in the database, use the page object rather than the Export option.

5. Click **File** on the Access Training-H Database menu bar, click **Export**, type **edata** as the file name, click the **Save as type list arrow**, click **HTML Documents**, navigate to the drive and folder where your Project Files are stored, then click **Export**
   The Employees table is saved as an HTML file. **HTML** is short for **HyperText Markup Language**, a set of codes inserted into a text file that browser software such as Internet Explorer use to determine the way text, hyperlinks, images, and other elements should appear on a Web page. Web pages created using the export feature are *static*, and will not change after they are created.
6. Click the **Start button** on the taskbar, point to **Programs**, click **Internet Explorer**, click **File** on the Internet Explorer menu bar, click **Open**, click **Browse**, navigate to the drive and folder where you saved the Web page, double-click **edata.html**, then click **OK**
   The Web page with the information from the Employees table appears, as shown in Figure H-18. Static Web pages created through the export process can be viewed using either Microsoft Internet Explorer or Netscape Navigator.
7. Close **Internet Explorer**

FIGURE H-17: EmployeeData workbook

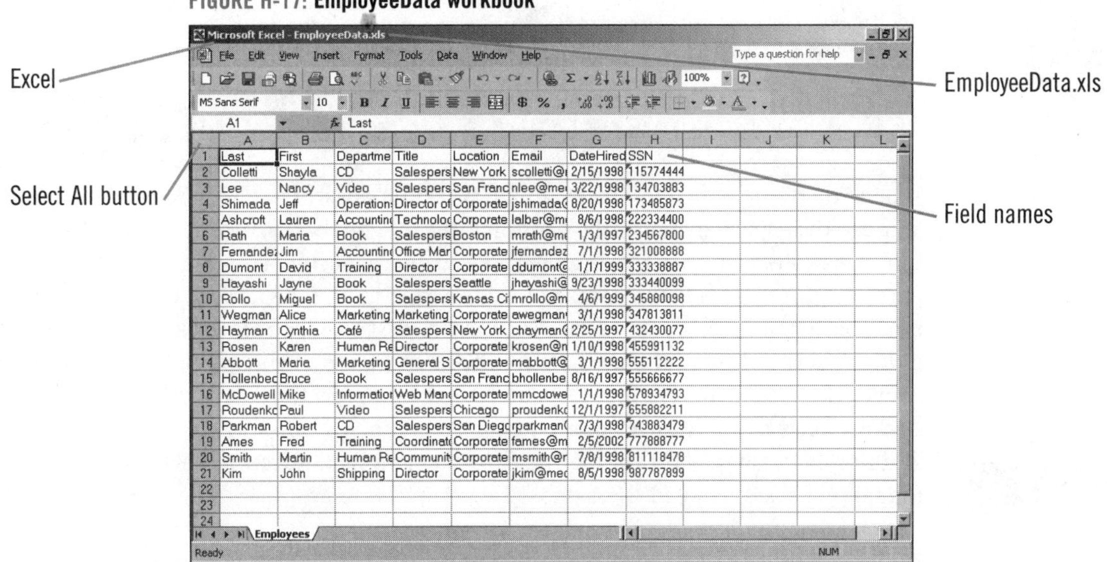

FIGURE H-18: edata Web page

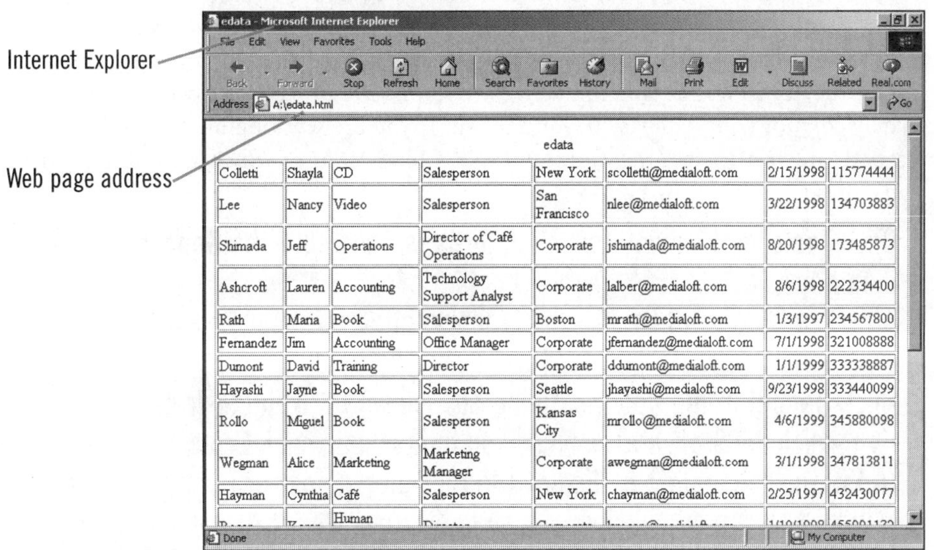

TABLE H-2: Data formats Microsoft Access can export

application	version or format supported	application	version or format supported
Microsoft Access database	2.0, 7.0/95, 8.0/97, 9.0/2000, 10.0/2002	**Lotus 1-2-3**	.wk2, .wk1, and .wk3
Microsoft Access project	9.0/2000, 10.0/2002	**Delimited text files**	All character sets
dBASE	III, IV, 5, and 7	**Fixed-width text files**	All character sets
Paradox, Paradox for Windows	3.x, 4.x, 5.0, and 8.0	**HTML**	1.0 (if a list), 2.0, 3.x, 4.x (if a table or list)
Microsoft Excel	3.0, 4.0, 5.0, 7.0/95, 8.0/97, 9.0/2000, 10.0/2002	**SQL tables, Microsoft Visual FoxPro, and other data sources that support ODBC protocol**	Visual FoxPro 3.0, 5.0, and 6.x
Microsoft Active Server Pages	All	**XML Documents**	All

Access 2002

Compacting and Repairing a Database

When you delete data and objects in an Access database, the database can become fragmented and use disk space inefficiently. **Compacting** the database rearranges the data and objects to improve performance by reusing the space formerly occupied by the deleted objects. The compacting process also repairs damaged databases. A good time to back up a database is right after it has been compacted. If hardware is stolen or destroyed, a recent **backup**, an up-to-date copy of the data files, can minimize the impact of that loss to the business. Use Windows Explorer to copy individual database files and floppy disks, or use back-up software such as Microsoft Backup to create back-up schedules to automate the process. Fred needs to secure the Training-H database. He explores the Compact and Repair feature, then uses Windows Explorer to make a backup copy of the database.

1. **Click Tools on the menu bar, click Options, then point to Database Utilities**
   The **Compact and Repair Database** option on the Database Utilities menu allows you to compact and repair an open database, but ***if you are working on a floppy disk, do not compact the database.*** The compaction process creates a temporary file that is just as large as the database itself. If the floppy disk does not have the needed space to build the temporary file, it will not be able to finish the compaction process or close your database, and you may corrupt your database beyond repair. If you are working on a hard drive, though, it's a good practice to use the **Compact on Close** feature, which compacts and repairs the database every time it is closed.
2. **Click Tools on the menu bar, click Options, then click the General tab of the Options dialog box**
   The Options dialog box with the Compact on Close option is shown in Figure H-19. By default, the Compact on Close option is not checked for new databases.

QuickTip

Make sure that you have a blank floppy disk ready to complete the following steps.

3. **Click Cancel in the Options dialog box, close the Training-H database, exit Access, right-click the Start button on the taskbar, click Explore, then click 3½ Floppy (A:) in the Folders list to display the files stored on your floppy disk**
   Windows Explorer should look similar to Figure H-20. You may see more files depending on how your Project Files are organized. You may see fewer details on each file depending on the current view of Windows Explorer. You will, of course, see different folders and drives that describe your own unique computer.
4. **Right-click 3½ Floppy (A:) in the Folders list, then click Copy Disk**
   The Copy Disk dialog box opens, as shown in Figure H-21. This command allows you to copy an entire floppy disk from one disk to another without first copying the contents to the computer's C: drive.
5. **Click Start**
   Windows Explorer will start copying your original Project Disk, the **source disk**, and will prompt you to insert a blank disk, the **destination disk**, where the files will be pasted.
6. **Insert the destination disk when prompted, then click OK**
   Explorer was able to copy all of the files from the Project Disk to the blank disk with one process. Sometimes you are prompted to reinsert the source disk and then the destination disk because all of the files cannot be copied in one process.
7. **Click Close in the Copy Disk dialog box, then close Windows Explorer**
8. **Remove the disk from the disk drive, then label the disk**

FIGURE H-19: Options dialog box

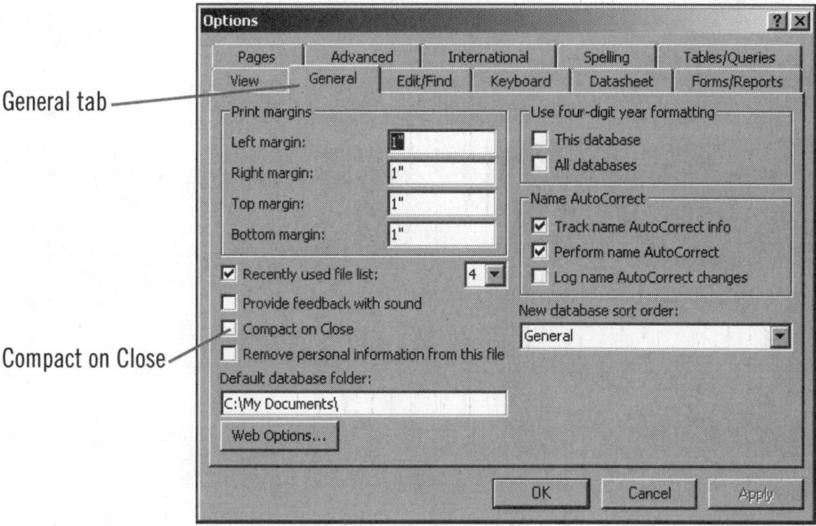

FIGURE H-20: Windows Explorer

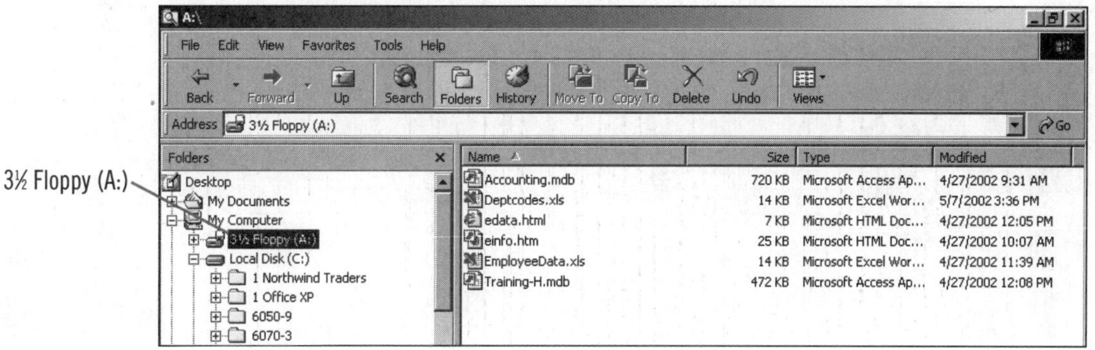

FIGURE H-21: Copy Disk dialog box

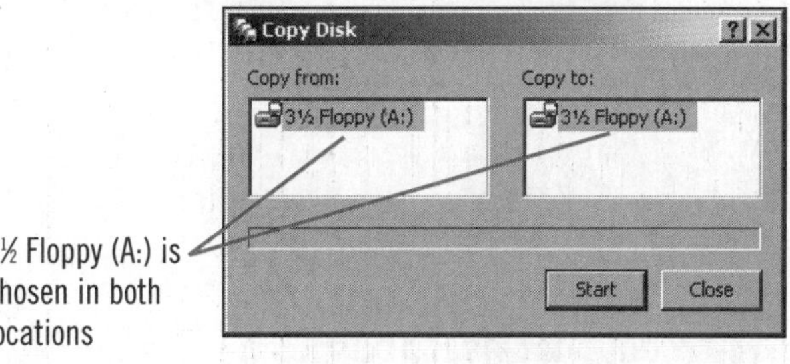

Backing up Project Files stored on your hard drive

If your Project Files are on the hard drive, the backup process is very similar. First, locate the folder that stores your Project Files in the Folders list within Windows Explorer. Right-click the folder, click Send To on the shortcut menu, then click 3½ Floppy (A:). Insert a blank floppy disk into the A: drive when prompted. If all of the copied files will not fit on one floppy disk, you will be prompted to insert another one. One file, however, cannot be larger than a single floppy disk for this backup method to work. If one file is larger than the storage space of a floppy disk, approximately 1.44 MB, you must use backup software such as Microsoft Backup or compression software such as WinZip to compress the files before copying them to a floppy. Or, you can copy them to a larger storage device such as a Zip, Jazz, or network drive or a Web site that allows you to upload and store files such as www.xdrive.com.

Practice

► Concepts Review

Identify each element of the Report Design View shown in Figure H-22.

FIGURE-H-22

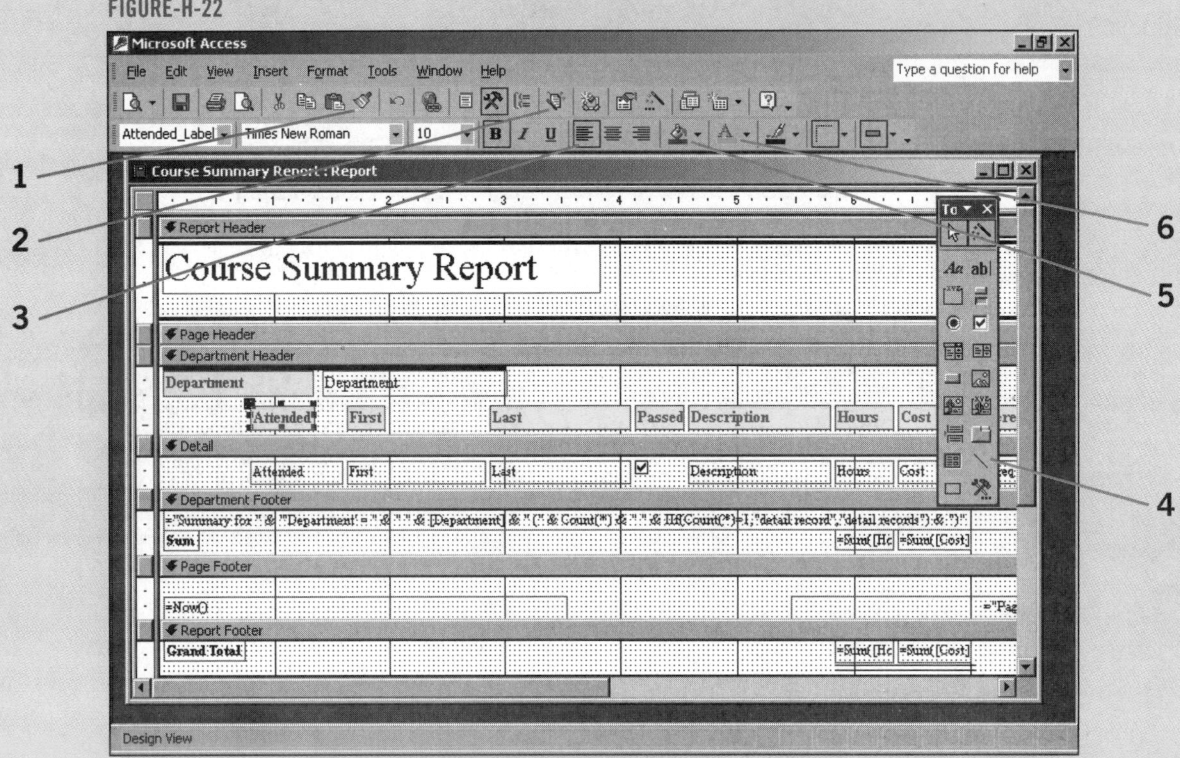

Match each term with the statement that describes its function.

7. **Exporting**
8. **Compacting**
9. **Backup**
10. **Format Painter**
11. **Importing**

a. A process to quickly copy data from an external source into an Access database
b. A process that rearranges the data and objects of a database to improve performance and to decrease storage requirements
c. An up-to-date copy of Project Files
d. Used to copy formatting properties from one control to another
e. A process to quickly copy data from an Access database to an external file

Select the best answer from the list of choices.

12. What Access tool creates a sample database file for a general purpose such as inventory control, event tracking, or expenses?
- **a.** Database Wizard
- **b.** Object Wizard
- **c.** Relationships Wizard
- **d.** AutoData Wizard

13. Which control would you use to visually separate groups of records on a report?
- **a.** Option group
- **b.** Image
- **c.** Bound Object Frame
- **d.** Line

14. Which wizard would you use to create a dynamic Web page?
- **a.** Page Wizard
- **b.** Table Wizard
- **c.** HTML Wizard
- **d.** Lookup Wizard

15. What feature allows you to apply the formatting characteristics of one report to another?
- **a.** AutoContent Wizard
- **b.** AutoFormat
- **c.** Report Layout Wizard
- **d.** PivotTables

16. Which of the following file types cannot be imported into Access?
- **a.** Excel
- **b.** Lotus 1-2-3
- **c.** Lotus Notes
- **d.** HTML

17. Sample databases that you can use and modify for your own purposes are called:
- **a.** MicroSamples.
- **b.** Templates.
- **c.** Controls.
- **d.** Datasets.

18. Which feature compacts and repairs the database every time it is closed?
- **a.** Compact on Close
- **b.** Conversion Wizard
- **c.** Backup Wizard
- **d.** Repair Wizard

19. Which Access feature would you use to create a static Web page?
- **a.** Web page Wizard
- **b.** Export
- **c.** Mailto: HTML
- **d.** Conversion Wizard

20. What feature allows you to change the appearance of a control on a form or report based on criteria you specify?
- **a.** Autoformat
- **b.** Behavioral formatting
- **c.** Event-driven formatting
- **d.** Conditional formatting

Skills Review

1. **Use the Database Wizard.**
   - a. Start Access, click the General Templates link in the New from template section of the task pane, then click the Databases tab.
   - b. Double-click the Contact Management Wizard, then create the new database with the name **Contacts**. If working on floppies, be sure to create the database on the floppy disk that contains the other Skills Review Project Files for this unit.
   - c. Respond to the prompts in the Database Wizard by accepting all of the default field suggestions. Use the Standard style for screen displays and the Soft Gray style for printed reports. Accept the name **Contact Management** as the title of the database.
   - d. After all of the objects are created, close the Main Switchboard form, then maximize the Contacts Database window.
2. **Import data.**
   - a. Click File on the menu bar, point to Get External Data, then click Import.
   - b. In the Import dialog box, click the Files of type list arrow, click Microsoft Excel, navigate to the drive and folder where your Project Files are stored, then double-click **Prospects**.
   - c. In the Import Spreadsheet Wizard, make sure that the Show Worksheets option button is selected, click Next, check the First Row Contains Column Headings check box, click Next, click the In a New Table option button, click Next, click Next to accept the default field options, click the Choose my own primary key option button, verify that ContactID is the primary key field, click Next, type **Prospects** in the Import to Table text box, then click Finish.
   - d. Click OK when prompted that the import was successful, then open the Prospects table.
   - e. Add your personal information as a new record using **10** as the entry for the ContactID field.
   - f. Print the datasheet in landscape orientation, close the datasheet, then close the Contacts database.
3. **Apply advanced formatting.**
   - a. Open the **Membership-H** database from the drive and folder where your Project Files are stored.
   - b. Using the Report Wizard, create a report based on the Member Activity Log using all of the fields in that query.
   - c. View the data by Names, do not add any additional grouping levels, sort ascending by ActivityDate, then Sum the Hours field.
   - d. Use the Outline 2 Layout, Portrait Orientation, Compact style, type **Member Activity Log** as the report title, then open the report in Design View.
   - e. Select the =Sum([Hours]) calculated field in the MemberNo Footer section.
   - f. Use Conditional Formatting to change the Font/Fore color to blue and text formatted with italics if the field value is greater than or equal to **10**.
   - g. Add a label to the Report Footer section with the text **Created by Your Name**.
   - h. Group all of the controls in the Report Footer section, then apply italics to the group.
   - i. Save, then print the last page of the report.
4. **Add lines.**
   - a. Open the Member Activity Log report in Design View, then delete the line at the top of the MemberNo Header section. Delete the line at the top of the Detail section. (*Hint*: Click between the ActivityDate and Hours text boxes.)
   - b. Delete the text box with the ="Summary for ..." calculation and the line at the top of the MemberNo Footer section.
   - c. Add a short horizontal line just above the =Sum([Hours]) calculation in the MemberNo Footer section. (*Hint*: Press and hold [Shift] while creating the line for it to be perfectly horizontal.)
   - d. Copy and paste the line into the Report Footer section, then move the line directly under the =Sum([Hours]) control in that section.

e. Copy and paste the line in the Report Footer section, then move the two lines under the =Sum([Hours]) control to indicate a grand total.
f. Save the report, then print the last page.

5. **Use the Format Painter and AutoFormats.**
   a. Open the Member Activity Log report in Design View.
   b. Format the MemberNo label in the MemberNo Header section with a bold Tahoma 12pt font.
   c. Use the Format Painter to copy that format to the five other labels in the MemberNo Header section (First, Last, Dues, ActivityDate, and Hours). Also, be careful to format the labels rather than the text boxes in the MemberNo Header section.
   d. Change the color of the two lines in the Report Header section to red.
   e. Create a new AutoFormat named **Red Lines-Your Name** based on the Member Activity Log report.
   f. Add a label with your name to the Report Header section, print the first page of the Member Activity Log report, then save it.
   g. In Design View, apply the Corporate AutoFormat. (*Hint*: Click the report selector button in the upper left corner of the report to select the entire report before applying an AutoFormat. If an individual section or control is selected when you apply an AutoFormat, it will be applied to only that section or control.)
   h. Use the Customize button in the AutoFormat dialog box to delete the Red Lines-Your Name style.
   i. Preview, then print the first page of the Member Activity Log report. Save, then close the report.

6. **Create a Web page.**
   a. Use the Page Wizard to create a Web page based on all of the fields in the Names table.
   b. Group the information by Zip, do not add any sorting orders, title the page **Zip Code Groups**, then open it in Page View.
   c. Navigate to the 50266 zip code, then navigate to the record for the name Kristen Larson. Enter your first and last name into the page, as shown in Figure H-23, then save and print that page.
   d. Save the data access page with the name **zip** to the drive and folder where your Project Files are stored, then click OK when prompted about the connection string.
   e. Close the zip Web page.

FIGURE-H-23

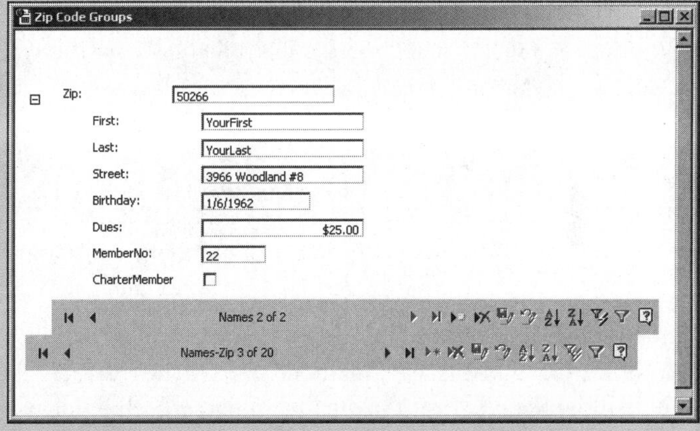

7. **Export data.**
   a. Export the Names table as an HTML Document with the name **list-yourinitials** (e.g., list-ab or list-kf) to the drive and folder where your Project Files are stored.
   b. Start Internet Explorer, click the File menu bar, click Open, then click Browse. Find and then double-click the **list-yourinitials** Web page, click OK to view it in Internet Explorer, then click Print on the Standard Buttons toolbar to print that page.
   c. Close Internet Explorer, then return to the Membership-H database window.

8. **Compact and repair a database.**
   a. If working on a hard drive, click Tools on the menu bar, point to Database Utilities, then click Compact and Repair Database. (*Note*: You can also complete this step on a floppy disk if your disk has enough space [in this case, about 400 KB of disk storage] to create the temporary file used during the compacting process.)
   b. Close the Membership-H database, then exit Access.

c. Start Explorer, right-click 3½ Floppy (A:) in the Folder's list, then click Copy Disk. Follow the prompts to make a back-up copy of your Project Files to a blank floppy disk, then exit Windows Explorer. If your Project Files are located on the hard drive or other storage device, locate and right-click the folder that contains your Project Files in the Folders list, then click Copy. Right-click 3½ Floppy (A:) in the Folders list, click Paste, then exit Windows Explorer.

► Independent Challenge 1

As the manager of a music store's instrument rental program, you created a database to track instrument rentals to schoolchildren. Now that several instruments have been purchased, you often need to print a report listing instruments in inventory. You create a single instrument inventory report based on a parameter query that prompts the user for the type of instrument to be displayed on the report. You conditionally format the report to highlight instruments in poor condition.

a. Start Access, then open the database **Music Store-H**.
b. Use the Report Wizard to create a report based on the Instruments by Type query. Select all of the fields, group by the Description field, sort in ascending order by the SerialNo field, do not specify any summary options, use a Stepped Layout, use a Portrait Orientation, apply a Corporate style, then title the report **Instruments in Inventory**.
c. Type **Cello** when prompted for the type of instrument.
d. Open the report in Design View, then add a label with your name to the Report Header.
e. Select the Condition text box in the Detail section, then use conditional formatting so that when the field value is equal to **Poor**, the Font/Fore Color is italic and red.
f. Save, then preview the report. Enter **Violin** when prompted for the type of instrument.
g. Print the report, then close the Instruments in Inventory report.
h. Close the Music Store-H database, then exit Access.

► Independent Challenge 2

As the manager of a music store's instrument rental program, you have created a database to track instrument rentals to schoolchildren. Now that several instruments have been rented, you need to create a conditionally formatted report that lists which schools have a large number of rentals.

a. Start Access, then open the database **Music Store-H**.
b. Use the Report Wizard to create a report with the following fields from the following tables:
   Schools: SchoolName
   Instruments: Description, MonthlyFee
   Rentals: Date
c. View the data by Schools, do not add any additional grouping levels, sort in ascending order by Date, then Sum the MonthlyFee field.
d. Use an Outline 1 Layout, Portrait Orientation, and Casual style.
e. Title the report **School Summary Report**.
f. Open the report in Design View, then click the =Sum([MonthlyFee]) control in the SchoolNo Footer section.
g. Use Conditional Formatting to specify that the field be Bold and have a bright yellow Fill/Back Color if the sum is greater than or equal to 200.
h. Add a label to the Report Header section with your name, then save the report.
i. Print the first page of the report.
j. Close the School Summary Report, close the Music Store-H database, then exit Access.

► Independent Challenge 3

As the manager of a music store's instrument rental program, you have created a database to track instrument rentals to schoolchildren. You need to build both static and dynamic Web pages for this database.

a. Start Access, then open the database **Music Store-H**.
b. Use the Page Wizard to create a data access page with the SchoolName field from the Schools table, the Date from the Rentals table, and all of the fields in the Instruments table.
c. Group the records by SchoolName, sort them in ascending order by Date, title the page **School Rentals**, then display it in Page View.
d. In Design View, click in the Click here and type title text prompt, then type your name.
e. Save the page as **school** in the folder where your Project Files are located, then open the school.htm file in Internet Explorer.
f. Find the record for the Thomas Jefferson Elementary school, then click the Expand button.
g. Double-click Excellent in the Condition field for the first record within this school, then click the Filter by Selection button in the upper Navigation bar to find all instruments rented to this school with that criteria.
h. Navigate to the third instrument with an Excellent condition for the Thomas Jefferson Elementary school, then print that page.
i. Close Internet Explorer, close the Music-H database, then exit Access.

Independent Challenge 4

As the manager of a Human Resources Department for a company that specializes in developing trade partners in Southeast Asia, you have developed an Access database to track personnel benefits. Eventually, you want to convert some of the existing Access reports and forms to Web pages, which would be accessible to employees across the world. You already have offices in both Singapore and Hong Kong, and are excited to use the World Wide Web to establish global communication. You decide to go to Microsoft's Web site to find some information about how Access can be used to create Web pages.

a. Connect to the Internet, then go to www.microsoft.com/access (which will redirect you to the homepage for Microsoft Access).
b. The Microsoft Web site is extremely large, and, depending on whether you are looking for tips, downloads, introductory articles, or specific technical support, there are many places where you could go to find good information. Explore the Web site at your own pace. Your goal is to find and read articles that discuss how Access 2002 can be used to create Web pages, then print the first page of one of the articles. (Note: Some articles are quite long. Click File on the menu bar, then click Print to open the Print dialog box to specify a print range.)
c. Web sites change often, but after searching on your own, try to find articles with these titles:
   - Upgrading to Access 2002 (includes a section on Web pages)
   - Choosing a Web browser for multilingual Web pages
   - Comparing the Three Types of Web Pages
   - Data Access Pages
   - Deploying Data Access Pages on the Internet or Your Intranet (from the Microsoft Developers Network, MSDN, Library)
d. Access 2002 offers many improvements to Web page development over Access 2000. Search the Microsoft site for What's New? or What's Improved? in Access 2002, then print that article. Highlight the sections on what is new in regard to Web pages and Web page development.
e. On the back of one of your printouts, write a paragraph about what you learned from the research you conducted. Write a second paragraph about what questions you still have about how to use Access to create Web pages.

Visual Workshop

Open the **Training-H** database and use the Report Wizard to create the report shown in Figure H-24. Select the First, Last, and Department fields from the Employees table, and the Description and Hours fields from the Courses table. View the data by Employees, do not add any more grouping levels, sort in ascending order by Description, and Sum the Hours. Use the Outline 1, Landscape, and Corporate style Report Wizard options. Title the report **Employee Education Report**. Enter your name as a label in the Report Header to uniquely identify your printout. In Report Design View, make the necessary changes so that your report matches the figure as shown. You'll need to move and resize some controls. You'll also have to delete the long, calculated control that counts the records, and work with line controls in the SSN Footer section. Print the first page of the report.

FIGURE H-24

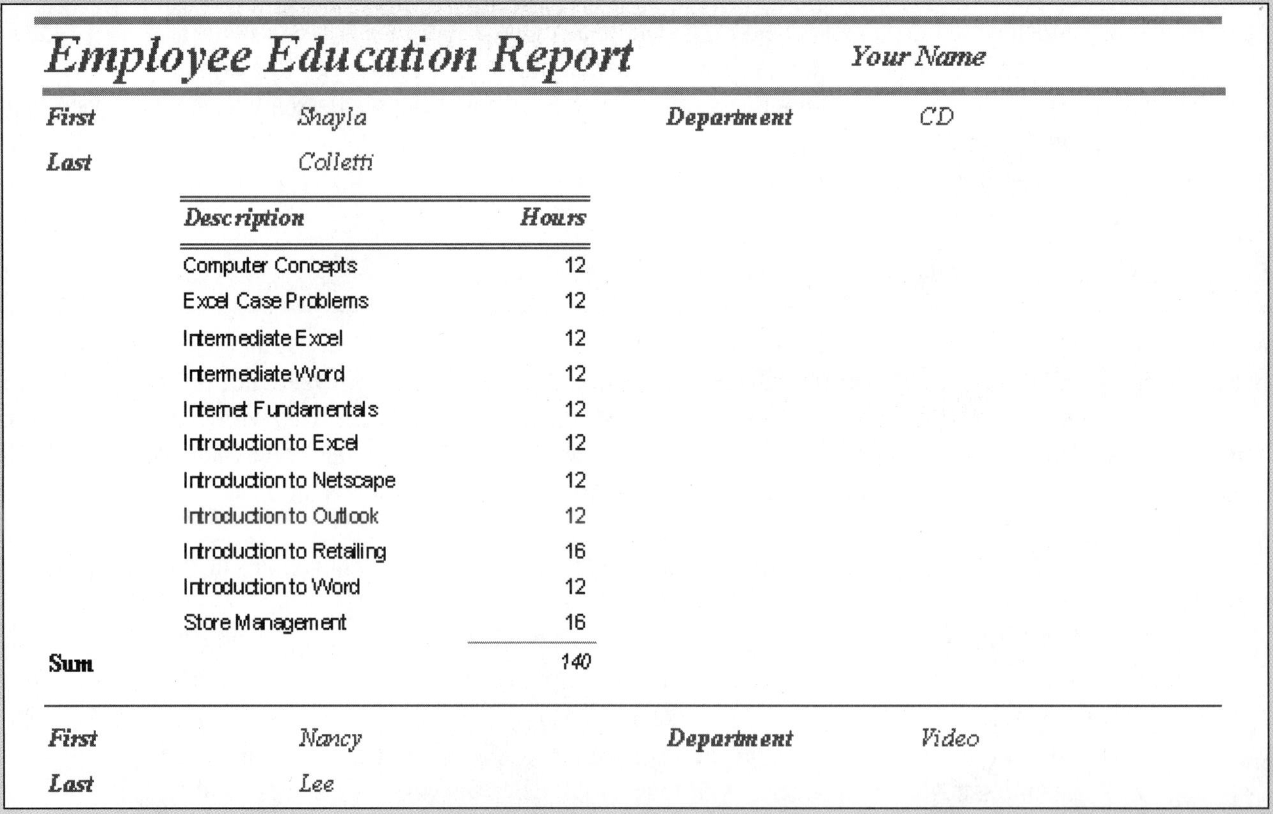

Employee Education Report *Your Name*

First *Shayla* ***Department*** *CD*

Last *Colletti*

Description	***Hours***
Computer Concepts	12
Excel Case Problems	12
Intermediate Excel	12
Intermediate Word	12
Internet Fundamentals	12
Introduction to Excel	12
Introduction to Netscape	12
Introduction to Outlook	12
Introduction to Retailing	16
Introduction to Word	12
Store Management	16

Sum *140*

First *Nancy* ***Department*** *Video*

Last *Lee*

Access 2002

Sharing Access Information with Other Office Programs

Objectives

- MOUS ▶ Examine Access objects
- MOUS ▶ Examine relationships
- MOUS ▶ Import XML data
- MOUS ▶ Link data
- MOUS ▶ Publish data to Word
- MOUS ▶ Analyze data with Excel
- MOUS ▶ Merge data with Word
- MOUS ▶ Export data to XML
- MOUS ▶ Use SQL Server

Access is a relational database program that can share data with many other Microsoft Office software products. Choosing the right tool for each task is important because you often need to use features from one program with data stored in another type of file. For example, you may want to analyze information in an Excel workbook using the powerful relational database capabilities of Access. Access provides tools to import or link to Excel data so that you will not need to rekey the data into the Access database. Or, you might want to send Access data to another file format. For example, you may want to merge records from an Access query into a Word document or export an Access report as a Web page. Fred Ames, coordinator of training at MediaLoft, has developed an Access database that tracks courses, employees, and course attendance for the staff training provided by MediaLoft. Fred will share Access data with other software programs so that each MediaLoft department can have the data they have requested in a format they can use.

Examining Access Objects

To become proficient with Access, you should understand the purpose of the seven Access objects. Fred reviews key Access terminology and the seven Access objects.

Details

- A **database** is a collection of data associated with a topic. The smallest piece of information in a database is called a **field**, or category of information, such as an employee's name, e-mail address, or department. A **primary key field** is a field that contains unique information for each record such as an employee's Social Security Number. A group of related fields, such as all descriptive information for one employee, is called a **record**. A collection of records for a single subject, such as all of the employee records, is called a **table**. When a table is opened, the fields and records are displayed as a **datasheet**, as shown in Figure I-1. Several related tables form a **relational database**. Click the **Expand button** [+] to the left of a record in a datasheet to see related records from another table.
- Tables are the most important **objects** in an Access database because they contain the data. An Access database can also contain six other object types: **queries**, **forms**, **reports**, **pages**, **macros**, and **modules**. They are summarized in Table I-1.
- Query objects are based on tables; form, page, and report objects can be based on either tables or queries. You can enter and edit data in four of the objects—tables, queries, pages, and forms—*but the data is physically stored in only one place: tables.* The relationships among database objects are shown in Figure I-2. The macro and module objects can provide additional database productivity and automation features such as **GUI** (**graphical user interface**) screens and buttons, which mask the complexity of the underlying objects. All of the objects (except for Web pages created by the page object) are stored in one database file.

FIGURE I-1: Table datasheet

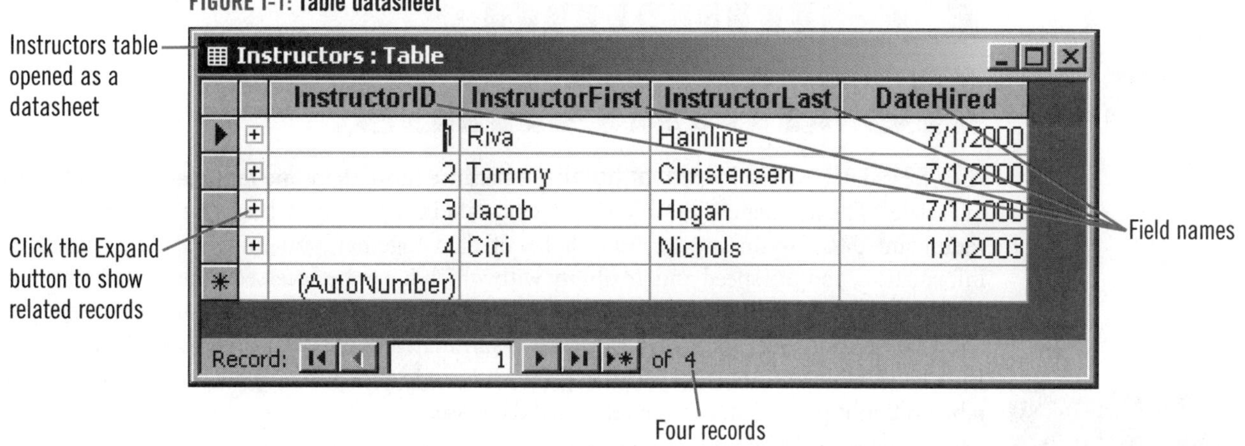

FIGURE I-2: Objects of an Access database

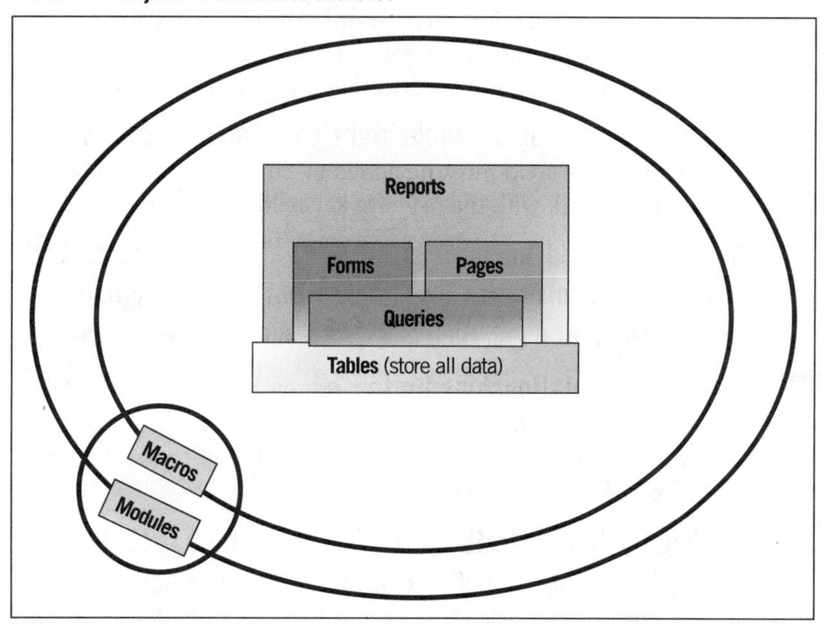

TABLE I-1: Access objects

object	purpose
Table	Contains all of the raw data within the database in a spreadsheet-like view called a datasheet
Query	Answers a "question" a user has about the data in the database, and presents the answer in a datasheet view
Form	Provides an easy-to-use data entry screen that generally shows only one record at a time
Report	Provides a professional printout of data that may contain enhancements such as headers, footers, and calculations on groups of records; mailing labels can also be created from report objects
Page	Creates Web pages from Access objects and provides Web page connectivity features to an Access database
Macro	Stores a collection of keystrokes or commands such as printing several reports or displaying a toolbar when a form opens
Module	Stores Visual Basic for Applications programming code that extends the functions and automated processes of Access

Access 2002

Examining Relationships

An Access database is a **relational database** because more than one table can share information, or "relate." The key benefit of organizing your data into a relational database is that it minimizes redundant data. By linking separate tables of data together, you improve the accuracy of the information, and the speed and flexibility with which it can be accessed. The process of designing a relational database is called **normalization**, and involves determining appropriate fields, tables, and table relationships. Relationship types are summarized in Table I-2. Fred develops an Instructors table to store one record for each teacher. He relates the Instructors table to the Courses table so that it participates in the relational database.

Steps

1. **Start Access, open the Training-I database from the drive and folder where your Project Files are stored, click Tables on the Objects bar, then double-click the Instructors table**
   The InstructorID field is the **primary key field** in the Instructors table and therefore contains unique data for each record. Because each instructor teaches many courses, the Instructors table should be related to the Courses table with a one-to-many relationship. The primary key field always acts as the "one" side of a one-to-many relationship.
2. **Close the Instructors table, right-click the Courses table, then click Design View**
   A **foreign key field** must be added to the table on the "many" side of a one-to-many relationship to link with the primary key field of the "one" table.
3. **Click the Field Name cell just below Cost, type InstructorID, press [Tab], press N to choose a Number data type, press [Tab], type Foreign Key, as shown in Figure I-3, click the Save button, then close the Courses table**
4. **Click the Relationships button on the Database toolbar**
   The Employees, Attendance, Courses, and Instructors tables appear in the Relationships window. Primary key fields appear in bold. Right now, the Instructors table is not related to the rest of the tables in the database.
5. **Drag the InstructorID field from the Instructors table to the InstructorID field in the Courses table, then click Create in the Edit Relationships dialog box**
   The link between the Courses and Instructors tables has been established, but the linking line doesn't display the "one" and "many" sides of the relationship.
6. **Double-click the linking line between the Instructors and Courses tables, then click the Enforce Referential Integrity check box, as shown in Figure I-4**
   Checking the **Enforce Referential Integrity** option means that you cannot enter values in the foreign key field unless you first enter them in the primary key field. It also means that you cannot delete records in the "one" table if the "many" table has corresponding related records. **Cascade Update Related Fields** automatically updates the data in the foreign key field when the matching primary key field is changed. **Cascade Delete Related Records** automatically deletes all records in the "many" table if the record with the matching key field in the "one" table is deleted.
7. **Click OK in the Edit Relationships dialog box**
   Printing the Relationships window shown in Figure I-5 creates a valuable report that helps you remember what fields are in which tables.
8. **Click File on the menu bar, click Print Relationships, click the Print button on the Print Preview toolbar, save and close the report with the default report name Relationships for Training-I, then close the Relationships window**

QuickTip
If a table's field list does not appear, click the Show Table button to add it.

QuickTip
To display all the fields in a table, resize the field list until the scroll bars are no longer visible.

QuickTip
Double-click the middle part of the linking line to edit the relationship.

FIGURE I-3: Adding the foreign key field to the Courses table in Design View

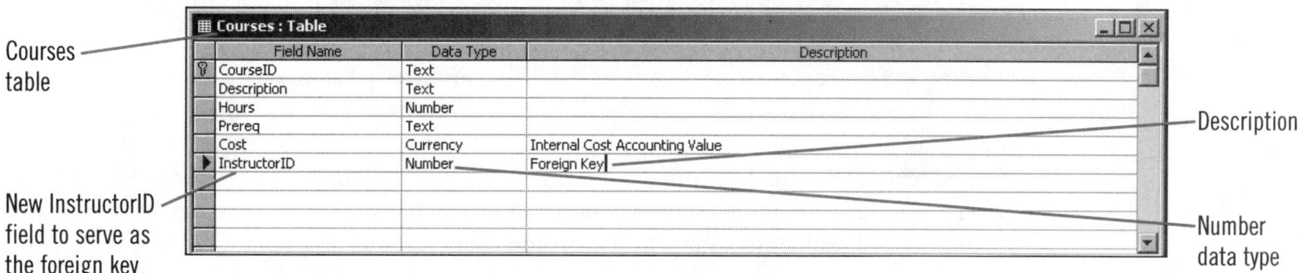

FIGURE I-4: Edit Relationships dialog box

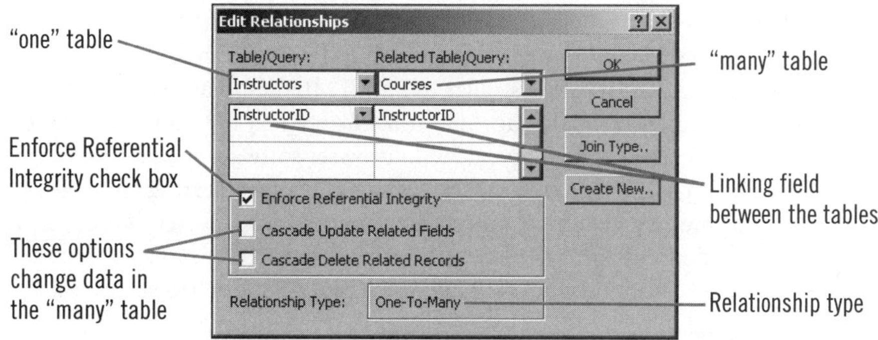

FIGURE I-5: Relationships window

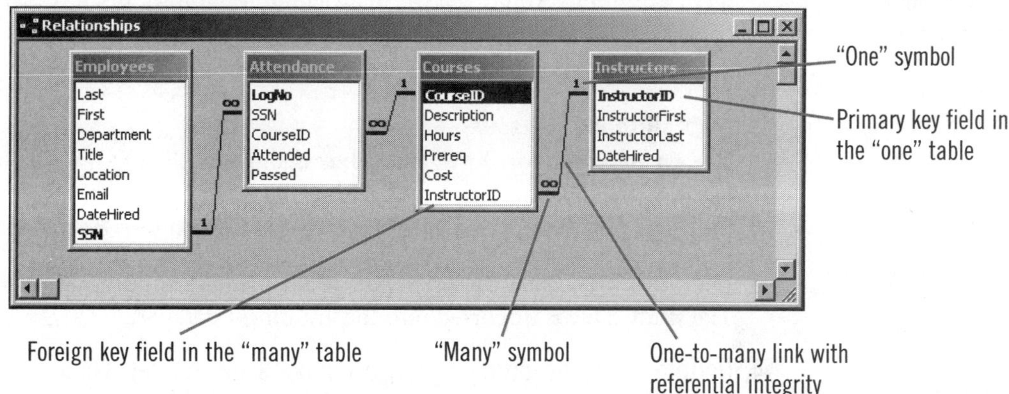

Access 2002

TABLE I-2: Relationship types

relationship	description	example	notes
One-to-One	A record in Table X has no more than one matching record in Table Y	A student table has no more than one matching record in a graduation table	This relationship is not common, because all fields related this way could be stored in one table.
One-to-Many	A single record in Table X has many records in Table Y	One product can be sold many times, one customer can make many purchases, or one student can enroll in many courses	The one-to-many relationship is by far the most common relationship type
Many-to-Many	A record in Table X has many records in Table Y, and a record in Table Y has many records	One employee can take several courses, and the same course can be attended by several employees. (In the MediaLoft database, the Attendance table serves as the in Table X	To create a many-to-many relationship in Access, you must first establish a third table, called a **junction table**, between two original tables. The junction table contains foreign key fields that link to the primary key fields of each of the original junction table between the Courses tables, and establishes separate one-to-many and Employees tables.) relationships with them.

Importing XML Data

Importing is a process to quickly convert data from an external source into an Access database. You can import data from one Access database to another, or from many other data sources such as data files created by Excel, dBase, Paradox, and FoxPro, or text files in an HTML, XML, or delimited text file format. In the past, you might have used a delimited text file to import information from one program to another. A **delimited text file** typically stores one record on each line, with the field values separated by a common character such as a comma, tab, or dash. Now, a more powerful way to share data is by using an XML file. An **XML file** is a text file that contains **Extensible Markup Language (XML)** tags that identify fields and contain data. XML has become a common method to deliver data from one application to another over the World Wide Web. You may be familiar with **Hypertext Markup Language (HTML)**, which adds tags to a text file to determine how content such as text and pictures should be formatted and positioned on a Web page. An XML file is similar to an HTML file because each uses **tags**, the programming codes defined by each language that transform a text file into a file that can be used to pass or present information when opened with browser software such as Internet Explorer. Think of an XML file not as a Web page itself, but as a container for storing and passing data from one computer to another via the World Wide Web. Karen Rosen, director of the Human Resources department, has asked the Training department to also track self-study materials for each course. This information is stored in an XML file called study.xml.

Trouble?

Import the study.xml file that contains the data rather than the study.xsd file that contains information about the structure of the data.

1. **Click File on the menu bar, point to Get External Data, click Import, navigate to the drive and folder where your Project Files are stored, click the Files of type list arrow, click XML Documents, then double-click study.xml**
   The Import XML dialog box opens.
2. **Click Options**
   The expanded Import XML dialog box is shown in Figure I-6. The upper portion shows the name of the table of data stored within the XML file that can be imported. The options in the lower portion of the dialog box help you determine how the data will be imported.
3. **Click OK, then click OK when you see a message indicating the report is finished**
   The study table is imported into the Training-I database.
4. **Double-click the study table to open its datasheet, then double-click the line that separates field names using the ↔ pointer to resize the columns to show all of the data in each field**
   The study datasheet, with the nine records, is displayed in Figure I-7. All of the data was successfully imported.
5. **Save, then close the study datasheet**

FIGURE I-6: Import XML dialog box

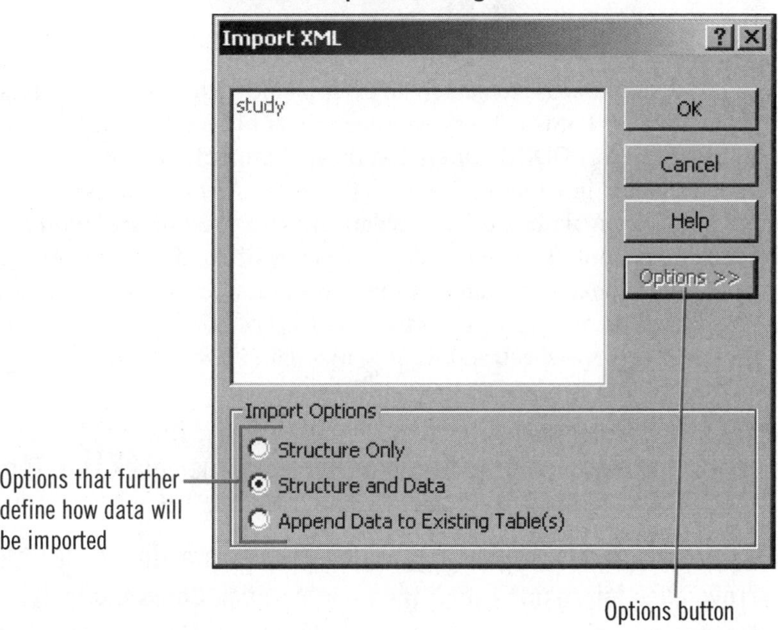

FIGURE I-7: Datasheet for study table

study : Table

CBTNo	CBTName	Format	Assessment
1	Intro to Access	CD	1
2	Intro to Word	CD	1
3	Intro to Excel	CD	1
4	Intro to PowerPoint	CD	1
5	Relational Database Design Issues	Videotape	0
6	How to Build an Attractive End Display	Videotape	0
7	Retail 101	Videotape	0
8	Customer Service Secrets	Book	0
9	Time Management Techniques	CD	0

Record: 1 of 9

Access 2002

Access 2002

Linking Data

Linking connects an Access database to data in an external file such as another Access, dBase, or Paradox database; an Excel or Lotus 1-2-3 spreadsheet; a text file; an HTML file; an XML file, or other data sources that support **ODBC** (**Open Database Connectivity**) standards. If you link, data can be entered or edited in either the original file or the Access database even though the data is only stored in the original file. Changes to data in either location are automatically made in the other. **Importing**, in contrast, makes a duplicate copy of the data in the Access database, so changes to either the original data source or the imported Access copy have no effect on the other. Fred asked the new instructors to make a list of all of their class materials. They created this list in an Excel spreadsheet, and want to maintain it there. Fred creates a link to this data from within the Training database.

Steps

1. Click **File** on the menu bar, point to **Get External Data**, then click **Link Tables**
   The Link dialog box opens, listing Access files in the current folder.
2. Navigate to the drive and folder where your Project Files are stored, click the **Files of Type list arrow**, click **Microsoft Excel**, then double-click **CourseMaterials**
   The Link Spreadsheet Wizard appears, as shown in Figure I-8. Data can be linked from different parts of the Excel spreadsheet. The data you want is on Sheet1.
3. Click **Next**, click the **First Row Contains Column Headings check box** to specify **CourseID**, **Materials**, and **Type** as field names, click **Next**, type **CourseSupplies** as the Linked Table Name, click **Finish**, then click **OK**
   The CourseSupplies table appears in the Database window with a linking Excel icon, as shown in Figure I-9. A linked table can and must participate in a one-to-many relationship with another table if it is to share data with the rest of the tables of the database.
4. Click the **Relationships button** on the Database toolbar, click the **Show Table button**, double-click **CourseSupplies**, then click **Close**
   Rearranging the tables in the Relationships window can improve the clarity of the relationships.
5. Drag the **CourseSupplies field list title bar** under the Attendance table, drag the **CourseID field** in the Courses table to the **CourseID field** in the CourseSupplies table, then click **Create** in the Edit Relationships dialog box
   Your screen should look like Figure I-10. A one-to-many relationship is established between the Courses and CourseSupplies tables. You cannot establish referential integrity when one of the tables is a linked table, but the linked table can now participate in queries, forms, pages, and reports that use fields from multiple tables.
6. Click the **Save** button, close the **Relationships window**, double-click the **CourseSupplies** table, click the **New Record button** on the Table Datasheet toolbar, type **Access1**, press **[Tab]**, type **MediaLoft.mdb**, press **[Tab]**, then type **File**
   You added a new record to a linked table, so the data was actually added to the original Excel workbook.
7. Close the **CourseSupplies table**, right-click the **Start button** on the taskbar, click **Explore**, navigate to the drive and folder where your Project Files are stored, double-click the **CourseMaterials Excel file** to open it in Excel, then press **[Page Down]**
   The new Access1 record was added as the last row of the Excel spreadsheet.
8. Close Excel, then close Explorer

FIGURE I-8: Link Spreadsheet Wizard dialog box

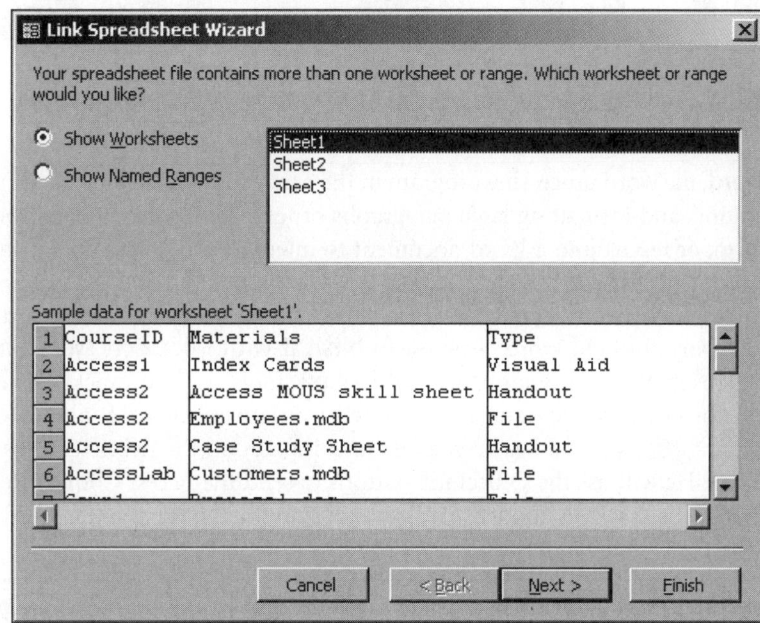

FIGURE I-9: CourseSupplies table is linked from Excel

FIGURE I-10: Relationships window with CourseSupplies table

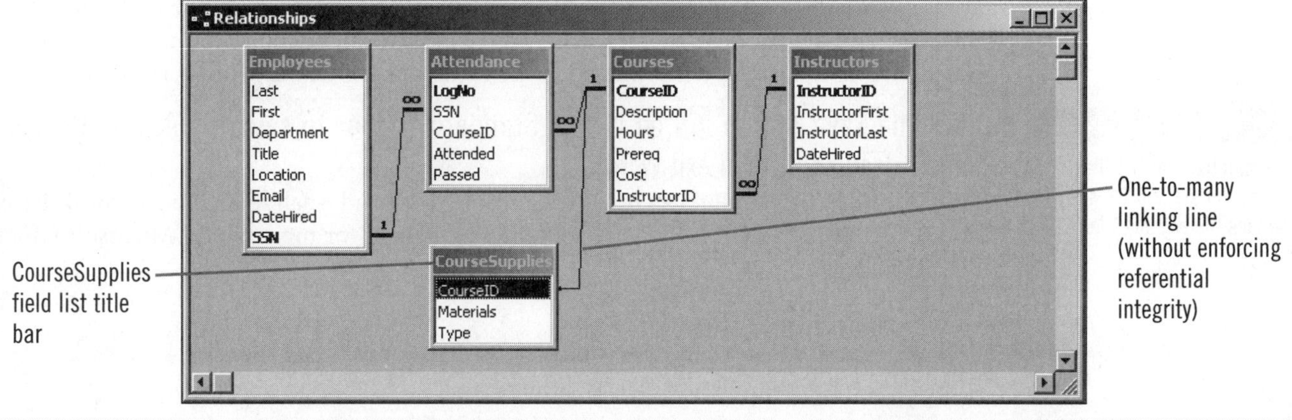

Access 2002

Publishing Data to Word

Word, the word processing program in the Microsoft Office Suite, is the premier tool for entering, editing, and formatting large paragraphs of text. You can copy data from an Access table, query, form, or report into a Word document to integrate the Access data with a larger word-processed document. You can use the **Publish It with Microsoft Word** feature to quickly copy Access data to Word which automatically copies the **recordset** (the fields and records) of a table, query, form, or report object to Word using the **Publish It with Microsoft Word button**. Publish It with Microsoft Word is one of three **OfficeLink** tools used to quickly send Access data to another Microsoft Office program. Table I-3 lists a variety of other techniques for copying Access data to Word. Fred has been asked to comment on the Access courses his department has provided. He will use the OfficeLink buttons to send the Access Courses Report to Word, then summarize his thoughts about the classes in a paragraph of text in the Word document.

Trouble?

If a dialog box opens indicating that the file already exists, click Yes to replace the existing file.

1. Click **Reports** on the Objects bar, click **Access Courses Report** (if not already selected), click the **OfficeLinks button list arrow** on the Database toolbar, click **Publish It with Microsoft Word**, then maximize the Word window

   The records from the Access Courses Report object appear in a Word document in an **RTF** (**rich text format**) file format, as shown in Figure I-11. The RTF format does not support all advanced Word features, but it does support basic formatting embellishments such as multiple fonts, colors, and font sizes. The RTF file format is commonly used when two different word processing programs need to use the same file.

2. Press **[Enter]** three times to increase the space between the top of the document and the Access information, press **[Ctrl][Home]** to position the insertion point at the top of the document, then type the following:

   To: **Management Committee**
   From: **your name**
   Re: **Analysis of Access Courses**
   Date: **today's date**

   The following information shows the recent demand for Access training. The information is sorted by department, and shows that the Accounting Department has had the greatest demand for Access courses.

3. Proofread your document, which should now look like Figure I-12, then click the **Print button** on the Standard toolbar

   Word's **word wrap** feature determines when a line of text extends into the right margin of the page, and automatically forces the text to the next line without you needing to press Enter. This allows you to enter and edit large paragraphs of text in Word very efficiently.

Trouble?

If prompted that the file already exists, click Yes to replace the existing file.

4. Click the **Save button** on Word's Standard toolbar to save the Access Courses Report document, then exit Word

   Files saved through the Publish It with Microsoft Word and Analyze It with Microsoft Excel feature are saved in the My Documents folder by default for most typical Microsoft Office installations.

FIGURE I-11: **Publishing an Access report to Word**

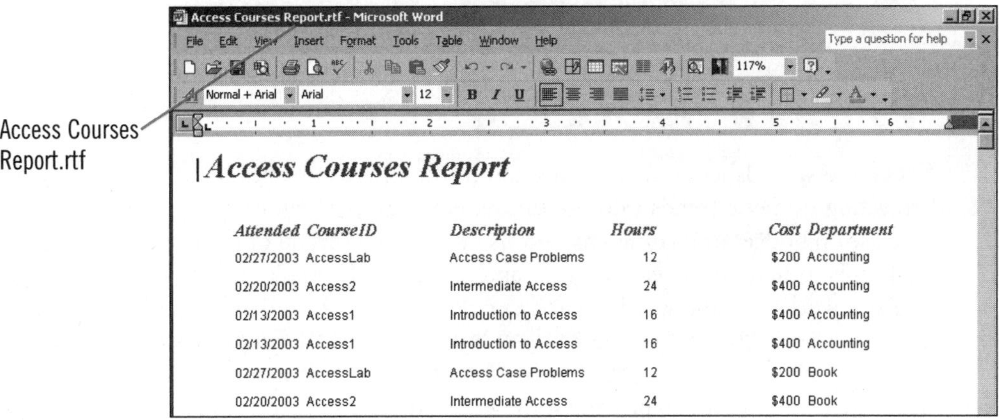

FIGURE I-12: **Using Word to enter text**

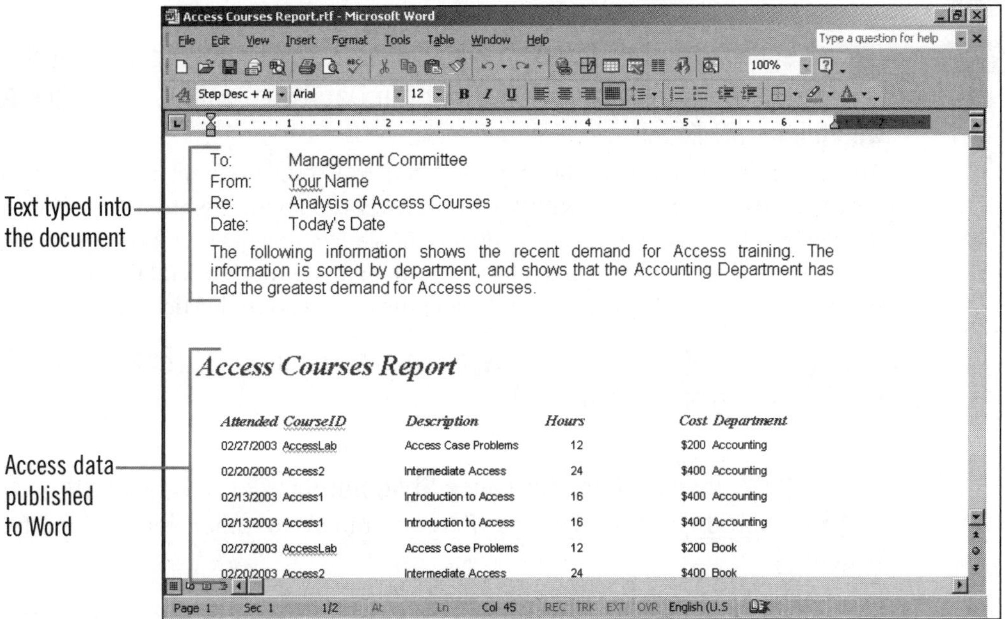

TABLE I-3: **Techniques to copy Access data to other applications**

technique	button or menu option	description
OfficeLinks	Analyze It with Microsoft Excel Publish It with Microsoft Word Merge It with Microsoft Word	Sends a selected table, query, form, or report object's records to Excel Sends a selected table, query, form, or report object's records to Word Helps merge the selected table or query recordset with a Word document
Office Clipboard	Copy and Paste	Click the Copy button to copy selected data to the Office Clipboard. The Office Clipboard can hold up to 24 different items. Open a Word document or Excel spreadsheet, click where you want to paste the data, then click the Paste button.
Exporting	File on the menu bar, then Export	Copies information from an Access object into a different file format
Drag and drop	Right-click an empty space on the taskbar, then click Tile Windows Horizontally or Tile Windows Vertically	With the windows tiled, drag the Access table, query, form, or report object icon from the Access window to the target (Excel or Word) window.

Analyzing Data with Excel

Excel, the spreadsheet software program in the Microsoft Office Suite, is an excellent tool for projecting numeric trends into the future. For example, you can analyze the impact of a price increase on budget or income projections by applying several different numbers. This reiterative analysis is sometimes called "what-if" analysis. **What-if analysis** allows you to change values in an Excel worksheet and watch related calculated formulas update instantly. This is a very popular use for Excel. You can use the **Analyze It with Microsoft Excel** feature to quickly copy Access data to Excel with the **Analyze It with Microsoft Excel button**. The Accounting department asked Fred to provide some Access data in an Excel spreadsheet so they can analyze how different increases in the cost of the Access classes would affect each of the departments. Fred has gathered the raw data into a report, called Access Courses Report, and uses Excel to analyze the effect of increased costs.

Trouble?

If a dialog box opens indicating that the file already exists, click Yes to replace the existing file.

1. Click **Reports** on the Objects bar, click the **Access Courses Report**, click the **OfficeLinks button list arrow** on the Database toolbar, then click **Analyze It with Microsoft Excel**

   The report data is automatically exported into an Excel workbook, as shown in Figure I-13. When you use the Analyze It with Microsoft Excel or Publish It with Microsoft Word buttons, the workbook or document you create has the same name as the Access object, and it is usually saved in the My Documents folder of your C: drive. You can send the recordset of a table, query, form, or report object to Excel using the Analyze It with Microsoft Excel button.

2. Click cell **G1** (column G, row 1), type **Cost Per Hour**, press **[Enter]**, type **=E2/D2** (in cell G2), and then press **[Enter]**

   Cell G2 contains a formula that divides the cost in cell E2 by the hours in cells D2, or 200/12.

3. Click cell **G2**, then click the **Currency Style button** on the Formatting toolbar

   You can quickly and easily copy Excel formulas to other cells using the **AutoFill** pointer +.

4. Point to the bottom right corner of cell G2 so that the pointer changes to +, then drag to cell G14

   The copied formulas are shown in Figure I-14. The workbook is now ready to perform what-if analysis by changing assumption values.

5. Click cell **E2**, type **400**, press **[Enter]**, type **500** (in cell E3), and then press **[Enter]**

   Your spreadsheet should look like Figure I-15. By changing any value in column E or D, Excel updates all formulas that depend on those values. In this case, Excel recalculated the formulas in cells G2 and G3.

6. Click the **Save button** on Excel's Standard toolbar to save the Access Courses Report workbook, then exit Excel

FIGURE I-13: Access Courses Report workbook

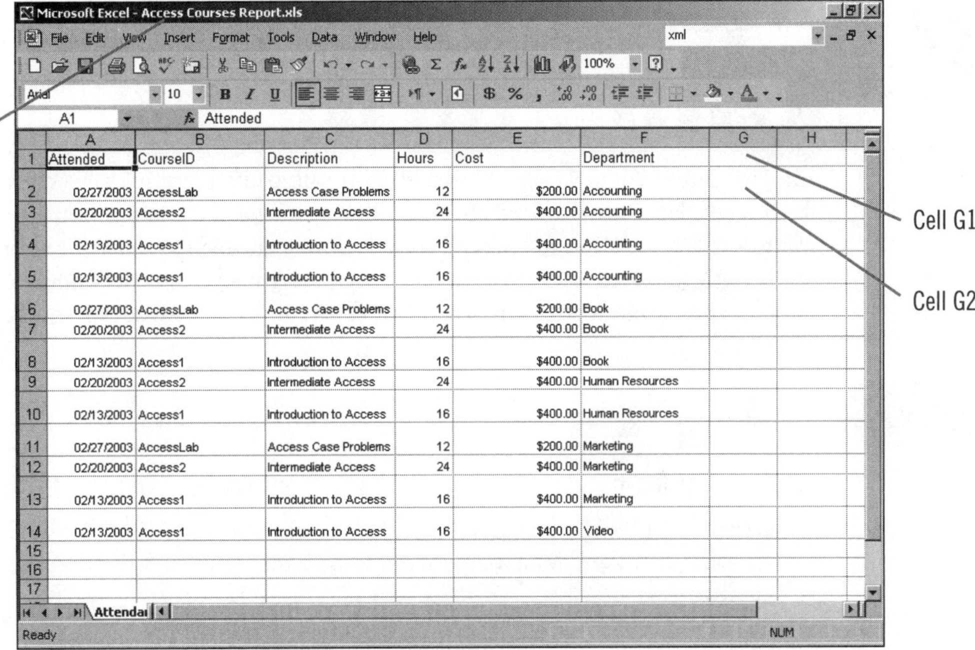

	Attended	CourseID	Description	Hours	Cost	Department
2	02/27/2003	AccessLab	Access Case Problems	12	$200.00	Accounting
3	02/20/2003	Access2	Intermediate Access	24	$400.00	Accounting
4	02/13/2003	Access1	Introduction to Access	16	$400.00	Accounting
5	02/13/2003	Access1	Introduction to Access	16	$400.00	Accounting
6	02/27/2003	AccessLab	Access Case Problems	12	$200.00	Book
7	02/20/2003	Access2	Intermediate Access	24	$400.00	Book
8	02/13/2003	Access1	Introduction to Access	16	$400.00	Book
9	02/20/2003	Access2	Intermediate Access	24	$400.00	Human Resources
10	02/13/2003	Access1	Introduction to Access	16	$400.00	Human Resources
11	02/27/2003	AccessLab	Access Case Problems	12	$200.00	Marketing
12	02/20/2003	Access2	Intermediate Access	24	$400.00	Marketing
13	02/13/2003	Access1	Introduction to Access	16	$400.00	Marketing
14	02/13/2003	Access1	Introduction to Access	16	$400.00	Video

FIGURE I-14: Copying a formula in the workbook

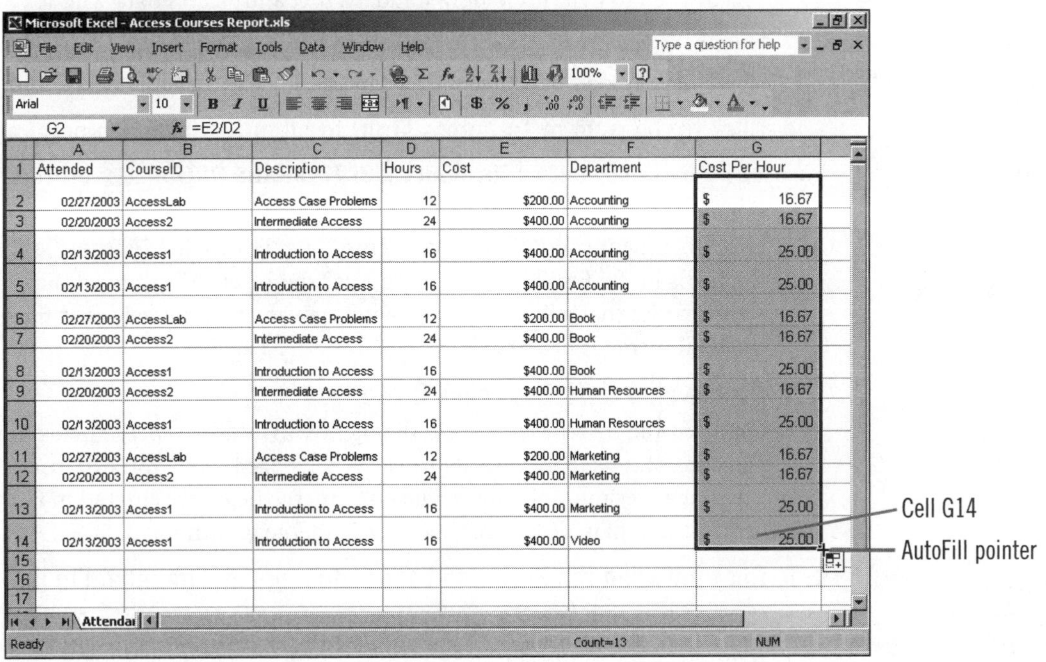

	Attended	CourseID	Description	Hours	Cost	Department	Cost Per Hour
2	02/27/2003	AccessLab	Access Case Problems	12	$200.00	Accounting	$ 16.67
3	02/20/2003	Access2	Intermediate Access	24	$400.00	Accounting	$ 16.67
4	02/13/2003	Access1	Introduction to Access	16	$400.00	Accounting	$ 25.00
5	02/13/2003	Access1	Introduction to Access	16	$400.00	Accounting	$ 25.00
6	02/27/2003	AccessLab	Access Case Problems	12	$200.00	Book	$ 16.67
7	02/20/2003	Access2	Intermediate Access	24	$400.00	Book	$ 16.67
8	02/13/2003	Access1	Introduction to Access	16	$400.00	Book	$ 25.00
9	02/20/2003	Access2	Intermediate Access	24	$400.00	Human Resources	$ 16.67
10	02/13/2003	Access1	Introduction to Access	16	$400.00	Human Resources	$ 25.00
11	02/27/2003	AccessLab	Access Case Problems	12	$200.00	Marketing	$ 16.67
12	02/20/2003	Access2	Intermediate Access	24	$400.00	Marketing	$ 16.67
13	02/13/2003	Access1	Introduction to Access	16	$400.00	Marketing	$ 25.00
14	02/13/2003	Access1	Introduction to Access	16	$400.00	Video	$ 25.00

FIGURE I-15: Performing "what-if" analysis

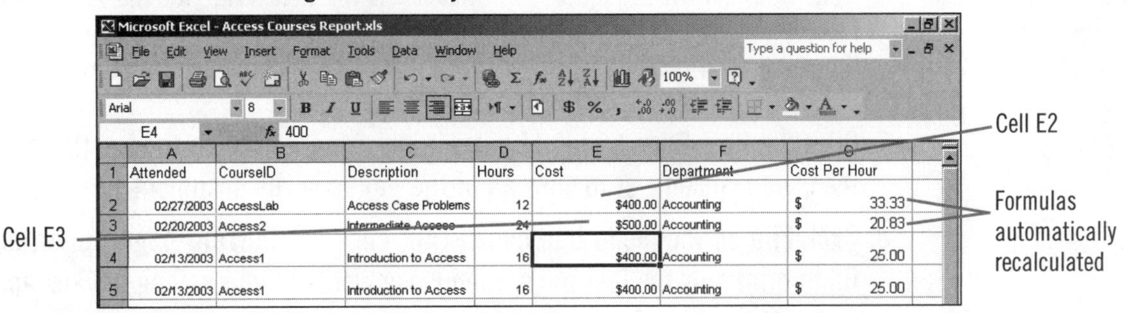

	Attended	CourseID	Description	Hours	Cost	Department	Cost Per Hour
2	02/27/2003	AccessLab	Access Case Problems	12	$400.00	Accounting	$ 33.33
3	02/20/2003	Access2	Intermediate Access	24	$500.00	Accounting	$ 20.83
4	02/13/2003	Access1	Introduction to Access	16	$400.00	Accounting	$ 25.00
5	02/13/2003	Access1	Introduction to Access	16	$400.00	Accounting	$ 25.00

Access 2002

Merging Data with Word

Another OfficeLink tool called **Merge It with Microsoft Word** merges Access records with a Word form letter, label, or envelope to create mass mailing documents. You use the **Merge It with Microsoft Word button** to send records from a table, query, form, or report to Word for a mail merge. Fred wants to send the MediaLoft employees a letter announcing two new courses. He uses the Merge It with Microsoft Word feature to customize a standard form letter to each employee.

Steps

1. Click **Tables** on the Objects bar, click **Employees**, click the **OfficeLinks button list arrow** on the Database toolbar, then click **Merge It with Microsoft Word**
   The Microsoft Word Mail Merge Wizard starts, requesting information about the merge process.
2. Click **Create a new document and then link the data to it**, then click **OK**
   Word starts and opens the **Mail Merge task pane** on the right side of the window and the **Mail Merge toolbar** at the top of the window. Both offer tools to help you with the mail merge process. The next important step, however, is to create the **main document**, the document used to determine how standard text and Access data will be combined.
3. Maximize the Word window, then type the text shown in Figure I-16
   This is the standard text that will be consistent for each letter created in the mail merge process.
4. Click to the right of **To:**, press **[Tab]** to align the insertion point at the same position as Your Name, click the **Insert Merge Fields button** on the Mail Merge toolbar, click **First**, then click **Insert**
   Your document should look like Figure I-17. The **Insert Merge Field** dialog box lists all of the fields in the Employees table. You use the Insert Merge Field dialog box to insert **merge fields**, codes that will be replaced with the values in the field that the code represents when the mail merge is processed.
5. Double-click **Last**, then click **Close**
   You used the Insert Merge Field dialog box to add two merge fields to a Word document—you cannot type them directly from the keyboard—but you can insert the same merge field into one letter multiple times. Once the merge fields are entered in the main document, you can edit the main document before you merge it with the data.
6. Click **between the First and Last codes**, press **[Spacebar]** to insert a space between the codes, click the **Merge to New Document button** on the Mail Merge toolbar, then click **OK** to merge all records
   The mail merge process combines field values from the Employees table with the Word form letter, and creates a letter for each record in the Employees table. The first letter is to Shayla Colletti, as shown in Figure I-18. "Shayla" is the field value for the First field in the first record, and "Colletti" is the field value for the Last field in the first record. The status bar of the Word document shows that this document contains 21 pages, one page for each of the 21 records in the Employees table.
7. Click the **Next Page button** below the vertical scroll bar to view the next page, and then keep clicking to view all of the pages in the document
8. Click **File** on the menu bar, click **Print**, click the **Current page option button**, click **OK** to print only the last page, then close Word without saving any documents

Trouble?

If your final merged document contains a mistake, close it without saving, edit the main document to correct the mistake, and click the Merge to New Document button again.

FIGURE I-16: Main document

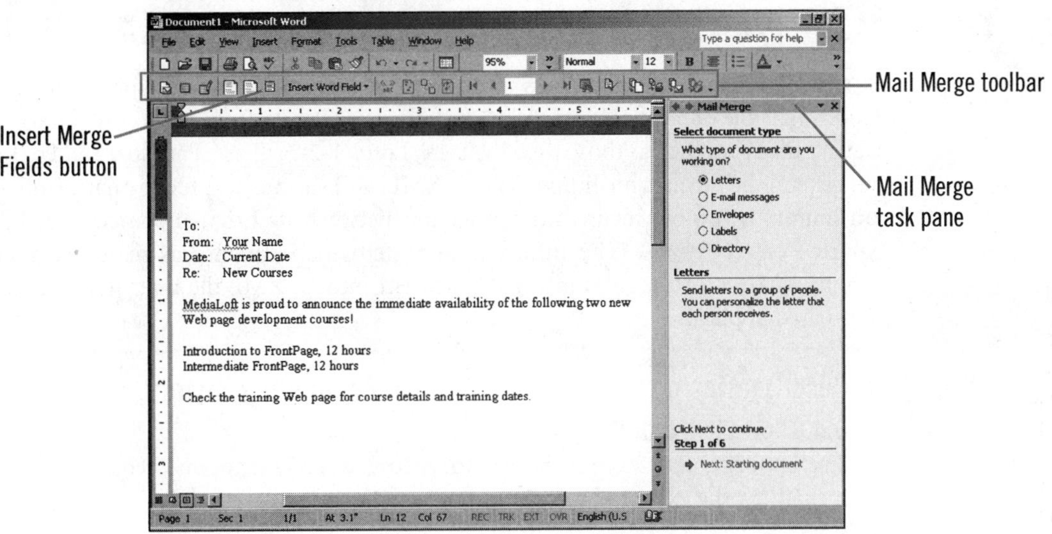

FIGURE I-17: Inserting merge fields

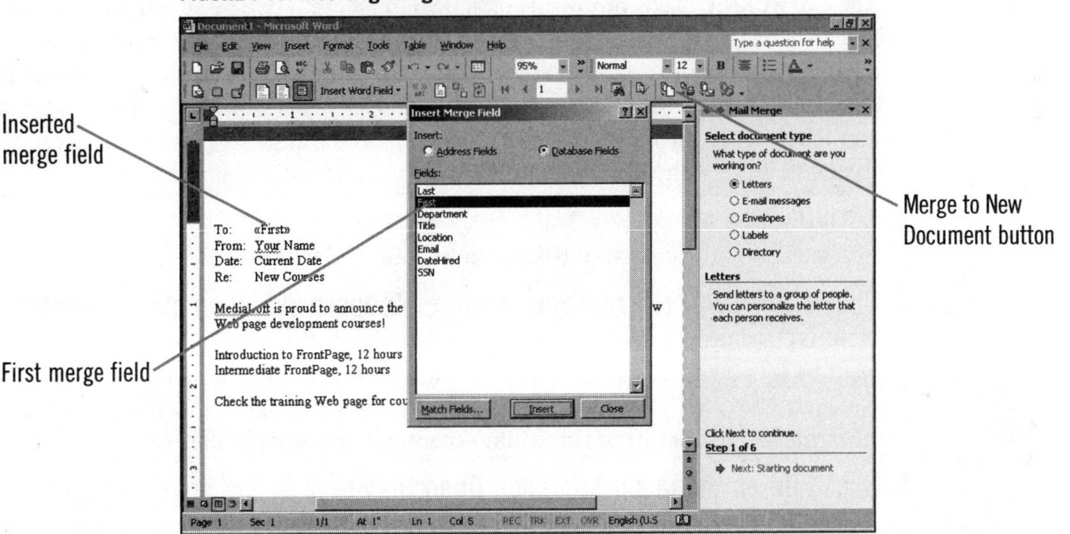

FIGURE I-18: Final merged document

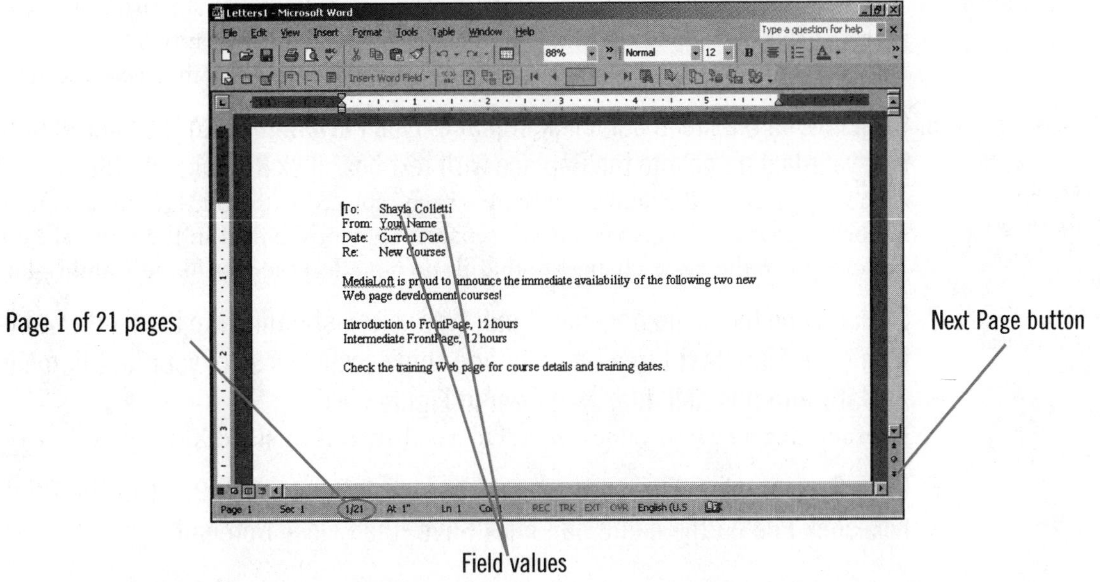

Access 2002

Exporting Data to XML

Exporting is a way to send Access information to another database, spreadsheet, or file format. Exporting is the opposite of importing. You can export data from an Access database to other proprietary file types such as those used by Excel, Lotus 1-2-3, dBase, Paradox, and FoxPro, and in several general file formats including HTML, XML, and various text file formats. Unlike linking, data you import or export retains no connection between its original source and the imported or exported copy. The Information Systems department has requested that Fred export training activity for the Accounting department into an XML file that they can use to develop a Web-based application.

Steps

QuickTip

You can also right-click an object in the Database window and click Export from the shortcut menu.

1. Click **Queries** on the Objects bar, click **Accounting History**, click **File** on the menu bar, then click **Export**

   The Export Query 'Accounting History' To... dialog box opens, requesting the location and format for the exported information.

2. Navigate to where your Project Files are located, type **acct** in the File name text box, click the **Save as type list arrow**, click **XML Documents**, then click **Export**

   The Export XML dialog box opens, as shown in Figure I-19. The **schema** of the data represents how the tables of the database are related. If you select this check box, Access creates and exports an accompanying **XSD (Extensible Schema Document)** file to store structural information about the database. The **presentation** of the data refers to formatting characteristics such as bold and font size. If you select this check box, Access creates and exports an accompanying **XSL (Extensible Stylesheet Language)** file to store presentation information.

3. Click **OK**

   Access exports the data and its schema to your Project Files folder.

4. Click **Start**, point to **Programs**, point to **Accessories**, then click **Notepad**

   Notepad is a text editing program that is provided with all versions of Windows. When you want to work with an HTML or XML file that is really just a text file with embedded tags, Notepad works well because it doesn't insert extra formatting features that the HTML or XML file cannot use, or which could potentially corrupt the file.

5. Click **File** on the menu bar, click **Open**, navigate to the drive and folder where your Project Files are located, click the **Files of type list arrow**, click **All Files**, double-click **acct.xml** in the file list, then maximize Notepad

   Your screen should look like Figure I-20. A less than symbol, <, and greater than symbol, >, surround each of the XML tags, and are a distinguishing characteristic of markup languages such as HTML and XML. XML data is positioned between two tags, also called the **start tag** and **end tag**. You can quickly find and change data using the Replace feature.

Trouble?

If you are using Windows 98 or Windows Me, Notepad doesn't include the Replace option on the Edit menu, so you will have to find Fernandez and replace it with your last name without using a Replace tool.

6. Click **Edit** on the menu bar, click **Replace**, type **Fernandez** into the Find what text box, type your last name into the Replace with text box, click **Replace All**, then click **Cancel**

   All occurrences of "Fernandez" have now been replaced with your last name. Since this file has been *exported* from Access, it is a separate copy of the data in the original Accounting History query; therefore, changes to this file do not affect the data in the Training-I database.

7. Click **Edit** on the menu bar, click **Find**, type your last name into the Find what text box, then click **Find Next** three times to find three occurrences of your last name inserted as data into this XML file, as shown in Figure I-21

   By examining how field values are stored, you better understand XML.

8. Click **Cancel**, click **File** on the menu bar, click **Print**, click **Print** in the Print dialog box, click **File** on the menu bar, click **Save**, then close Notepad

FIGURE I-19: Export XML dialog box

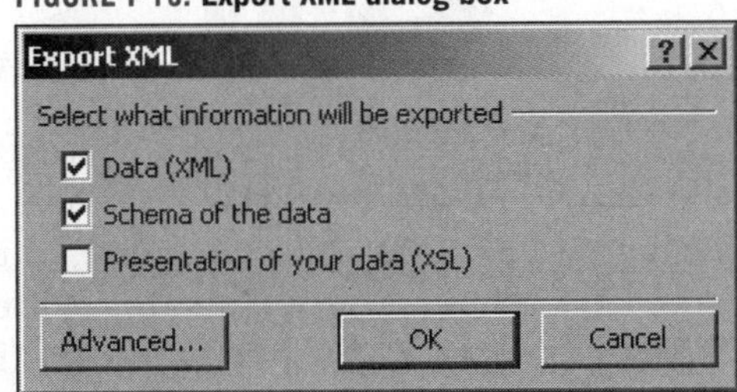

FIGURE I-20: Opening an XML file within Notepad

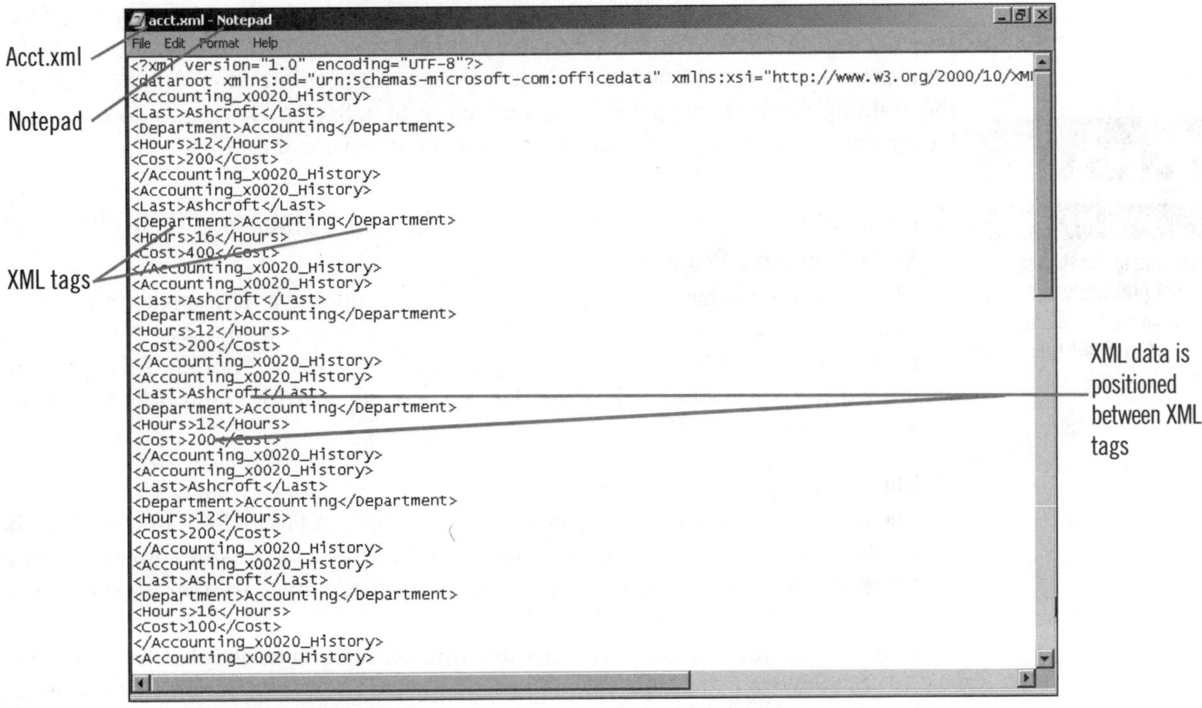

FIGURE I-21: Finding XML data

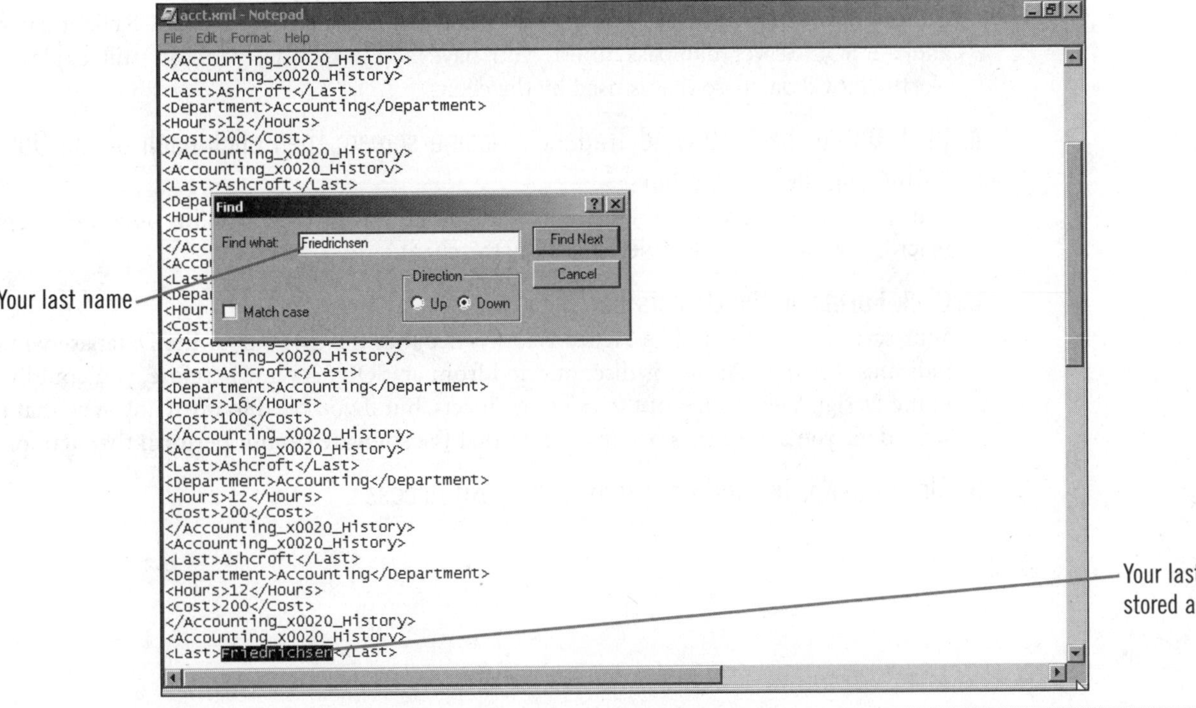

Access 2002

Using SQL Server

SQL Server is another database program provided by Microsoft. You use SQL Server for databases that are larger and more complex than those typically maintained in Access. If your Access database is growing rapidly, you can **upsize**, or convert, to SQL Server to handle more users or process large amounts of data more efficiently. Microsoft provides the sample **NorthwindCS** database as part of the full Access 2002 installation to illustrate how an Access database can connect to an SQL Server database. The NorthwindCS database is actually an Access **project**, a special Access file that contains no data. Rather, it contains form and report objects for the end user. All of the data used by those forms and reports is stored in an SQL Server database that is typically located on a shared file server. In this manner, you can use Access projects and an SQL server database to create efficient **client/server applications** which employ a server to manage shared data and clients to process the user interface. Fred anticipates the Training database may need to be upsized to SQL Server. He decides to open the sample NorthwindCS database to start learning about client/server computing.

Trouble?

If the sample databases were not previously installed on your computer, you are prompted to insert the Office CD.

1. Click **Help** on the menu bar, point to **Sample Databases**, then click **Northwind Sample Access Project**

   Although you can have multiple copies of Access running at any single time, you can only have one database open in an Access window. If the Training-I database was open when you clicked Northwind Sample Access Project, Access closed the Training-I database, and then opened the NorthwindCS database. You see a dialog box for connecting the project to an SQL Server database.

2. Click **OK**

   The Data Link Properties dialog box opens, as shown in Figure I-22. In this dialog box, you would enter all of the information required to make a successful connection to an SQL Server database such as the server name, database name, and any other information required by the firewall that protects the SQL Server. A **firewall** is a combination of hardware and software that adds a layer of security to corporate data. In its simplest form, a firewall consists of software that requires a valid user name and password before access to information is granted.

3. Click **Cancel**

   Although you can't make the physical connection between the NorthwindCS client database and an SQL Server database unless you have access to one, you can still explore the NorthwindCS database that is used by the client.

4. Click **OK** on the Northwind Traders welcome screen, then click each of the Objects buttons on the Objects bar

   You see that there are no tables in this file. Rather, this project contains only form, report, macro, page, and module objects used by the client.

5. Click **Forms** on the Objects bar

   Your screen should look like Figure I-23. Notice that the title bar of the Database window indicates that the database is disconnected from an SQL Server. Therefore, you could work in the Design View of any of the existing objects, but if you tried to open any view that presents data, you'd see a message indicating that the software cannot perform that action.

6. Close the NorthwindCS database, then exit Access

FIGURE I-22: Data Link Properties dialog box

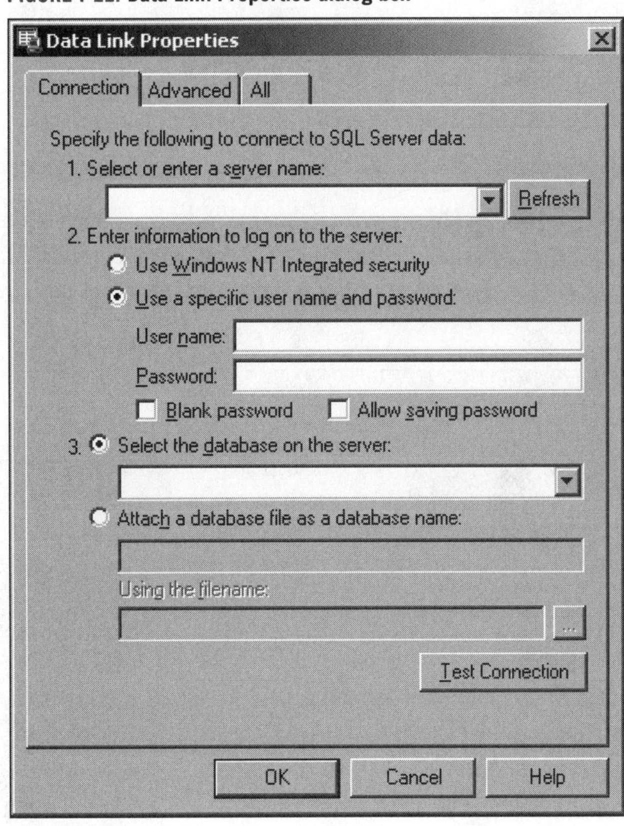

Access 2002

FIGURE I-23: NorthwindCS Project window

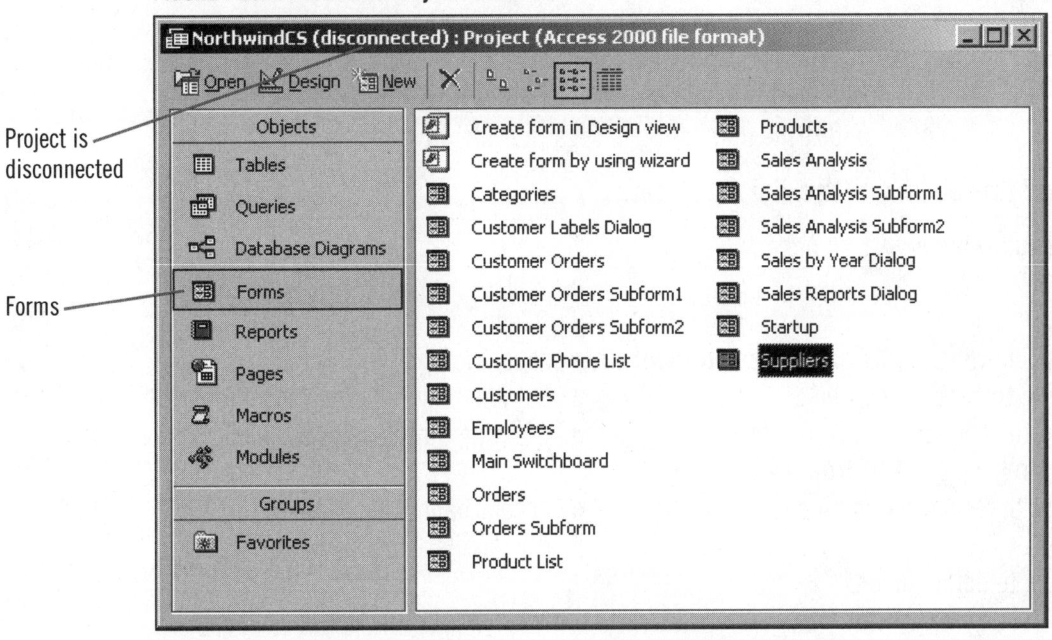

Practice

▶ Concepts Review

Identify each element of the Database window as shown in Figure I-24.

FIGURE I-24

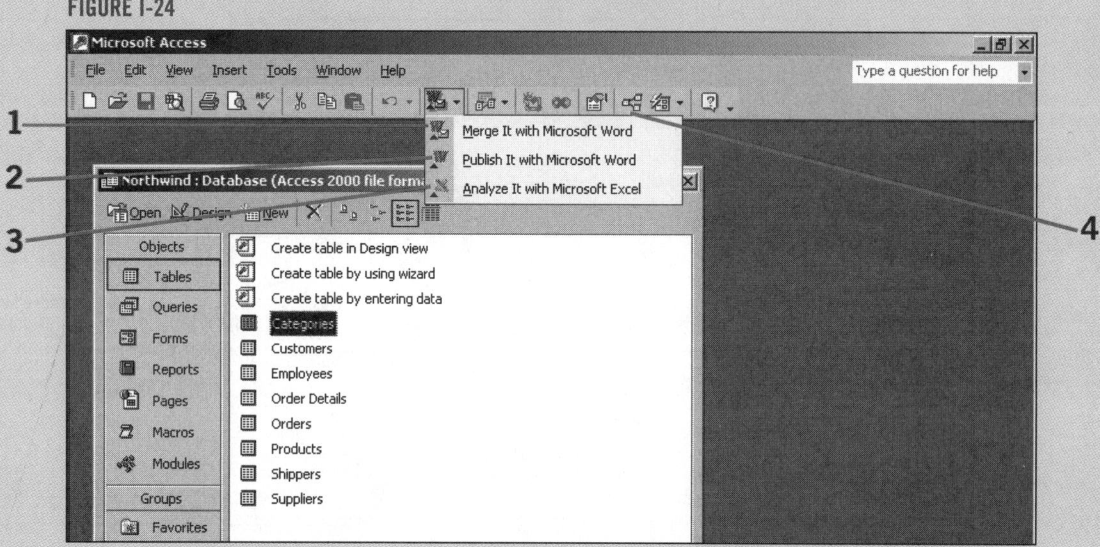

Match each term with the statement that describes its function.

5. XML
6. foreign key field
7. junction table
8. linking
9. what-if analysis
10. primary key field
11. normalization

a. A field that contains unique information for each record
b. Testing different assumptions in a spreadsheet
c. Contains foreign key fields that link to primary key fields
d. The process of determining the appropriate fields, records, and tables when designing a relational database
e. A way to connect to data in an external source without copying it
f. A field added to the table on the "many" side of a one-to-many relationship to link with the primary key field of the "one" table
g. A text file that contains tags that identify fields and contain data

Select the best answer from the list of choices.

12. Which of the following is NOT an Access object?
- **a.** Spreadsheet
- **b.** Report
- **c.** Table
- **d.** Query

13. Which of the following is NOT part of the normalization process?
- **a.** Determining the appropriate fields
- **b.** Identifying the correct number of tables
- **c.** Establishing table relationships
- **d.** Creating database hyperlinks

14. Which of the following is NOT true about XML?
- **a.** It is a popular format for sharing data over the Internet.
- **b.** It uses tags to define fields.
- **c.** Access cannot export data to an XML format.
- **d.** It is similar to HTML.

15. **Which of the following software products would most likely be used to analyze the effect on future sales and profits based on the change to several different assumptions?**
    a. Word
    b. Excel
    c. Access
    d. PowerPoint
16. **Which of the following is NOT an OfficeLinks button?**
    a. Analyze It with Microsoft Excel
    b. Publish It with Microsoft Word
    c. Present It with Microsoft PowerPoint
    d. Merge It with Microsoft Word

Skills Review

1. **Examine Access objects.**
   a. Start Access, then open the **Machinery-I** database from the drive and folder where your Project Files are located.
   b. On a separate piece of paper, list the seven Access objects and the number of each type that exist in the Machinery-I database.
   c. Use Table Datasheet View to determine the number of records in each table. Write down your answers.
   d. Use Table Design View to determine the number of fields in each table. Write down your answers.
2. **Examine relationships.**
   a. Click the Relationships button on the Database toolbar.
   b. Drag the ProductID field from the Products table to the ProductID field of the Inventory Transactions table to create a one-to-many relationship between those tables.
   c. Click Enforce Referential Integrity in the Edit Relationships dialog box, then click Create.
   d. Drag the PurchaseOrderID field from the Purchase Orders table to the PurchaseOrderID field of the Inventory Transactions table to create a one-to-many relationship between those tables.
   e. Click Enforce Referential Integrity in the Edit Relationships dialog box, then click Create.
   f. Click File on the menu bar, click Print Relationships, then view the relationships report in Design View.
   g. Add your name as a label to the Report Header section, print the report, then close report without saving it.
   h. Save the changes to the Relationships window, then close it.
3. **Import XML data.**
   a. Click File on the menu bar, point to the Get External Data option, then click Import.
   b. In the Import dialog box, change the Files of type list to XML Documents, then import the **employ** XML file stored on the drive and folder location where your Project Files are located.
   c. Open the datasheet for the new employ table, change the name in the first record to your own, then print it.
   d. Click the Design View button, then examine the data types for all of the fields. On the back of your paper, identify the data type that each field was automatically assigned, then close Table Design View.
4. **Link data.**
   a. Click File on the menu bar, point to the Get External Data option, then click Link Tables.
   b. In the Link dialog box, change the Files of type list to Microsoft Excel, then link to the **Vendors** Excel file stored on the drive and folder where your Project Files are located.
   c. In the Link Spreadsheet Wizard, be sure to specify that the first row contains column headings and that five data records are linked.
   d. Name the new table **Vendors**, then finish the wizard and close the Vendors table.
5. **Publish data to Word.**
   a. Click the Reports button on the Objects bar, click the Every Product We Lease report, click the Office Links list arrow, then click the Publish It with Microsoft Word button to send the information to Word.
   b. Press [Ctrl][Home] to go to the top of the document if the insertion point is not already positioned at the top of the page, press [Enter] twice, then press [Ctrl][Home] to return to the top of the document.

c. Type the following at the top of the document:
INTERNAL MEMO
From: [your name]
To: Sales Staff
Date: [today's date]
Do not forget to mention the long lead times on the Back Hoe and Thatcher to customers. We usually do not keep these expensive items in stock.

d. Proofread the document, save, then print it. Close the document, then exit Word.

6. **Analyze data with Excel.**
   a. Click the Tables button on the Objects bar, then click the Products table.
   b. Click the OfficeLinks button list arrow, then click Analyze It with Microsoft Excel.
   c. Click cell D12, type **=AVERAGE(D2:D11)**, then press [Enter]. This formula calculates the average Unit Price for all values in the range of cells from D2 through D11.
   d. Click cell A13, type your name, press [Enter], then click the Print button on the Standard toolbar.
   e. Click cell D7, type **499.75**, then press [Enter]. Changing the value of the most expensive product should make a big difference in the calculated average Unit Price.
   f. Save, print, and close the workbook, then exit Excel.

7. **Merge data with Word.**
   a. Click the Employees table. Click the OfficeLinks button list arrow, then click Merge It with Microsoft Word.
   b. Click the "Create a new document and then link the data to it" option button, then click OK.
   c. In the Word document, enter the following standard text to serve as the main document for the mail merge:
   Date: February 9, 2003
   To:
   From: your name
   Re: CPR Training
   The annual CPR Training session will be held on Monday, February 17, 2003. Please sign up for this important event in the lunch room. Friends and family over 18 years old are also welcome.
   d. Click to the right of To: and press [Tab] to position your cursor at the location for the first merge field.
   e. Click the Insert Merge Fields button on the Mail Merge toolbar, double-click FirstName and LastName, then click Close. Click between the FirstName and LastName codes, then press [Spacebar].
   f. Click the Merge to New Document button on the Mail Merge toolbar, then merge all records.
   g. Print the last page of the merged document, close both the merged document and the main document without saving them, then exit Word.

8. **Export data to XML.**
   a. Click the Products table. Click File on the menu bar, then click Export.
   b. Click the Save as type list arrow, click XML Documents, double-click Products in the File name and type **prod**, click Export, then export both the data and schema.
   c. Start Notepad, then open the **prod.xml** file in Notepad.
   d. Find the SerialNumber data for the Bird House (78999), then modify it so that your initials are added to the SerialNumber such as **78999LLF**.
   e. Save, then print the prod.xml document from within Notepad. Close Notepad, then close the Machinery-I database.

9. **Use SQL Server.**
   a. Click the Help menu, point to Sample Databases, then click Northwind Sample Access Project.
   b. When prompted to connect to an SQL Server, click OK.
   c. Write down four pieces of information from the Data Link Properties dialog box that you would probably have to supply if you were physically connecting to an SQL Server, then click Cancel.

d. Click OK on the Northwind welcome screen, click the Forms button, then double-click Orders. Click OK when prompted.
e. In a Word or Notepad document, explain why Access could not perform this operation, using the words client, server, data, Orders form, NorthwindCS, and SQL Server in your answer.
f. Close the NorthwindCS database, then exit Access.

▶ Independent Challenge 1

As the manager of a college women's basketball team, you have created a database called Basketball-I that tracks the players, games, and player statistics. You need to complete the table relationships.

a. Start Access and open the database **Basketball-I** from the drive and folder where your Project Files are located.
b. Click the Relationships button and create a one-to-many relationship using the GameNo field between the Games table and the Stats table. Enforce referential integrity.
c. Similarly, create a one-to-many relationship using the PlayerNo field between the Players and Stats table. Note that the Stats table should be the "many" side of both relationships.
d. Click File on the menu bar, click Print Relationships, and then view the relationships report in Design View.
e. Add a label to the Report Header section with your name as the caption, then close the report without saving it.
f. Save the changes to the Relationships window, and close it.
g. Click the Queries button on the Objects bar, then double-click the Players Query.
h. Change the first instance of Lindsey Swift to your name, press [Page Down], then print the first page of the datasheet. On the back of the printout, explain why every occurrence of Lindsey Swift changed to your name. Also explain why your name is listed 10 times on this datasheet.
i. Close the Basketball-I database, then exit Access.

▶ Independent Challenge 2

As the manager of a women's college basketball team, you have created a database called Basketball-I that tracks the players, games, and player statistics. You want to link to an Excel file that contains information on the player's course load. On a form, you also want to create a hyperlink to a Word document.

a. Start Access and open the database **Basketball-I** from the drive and folder where your Project Files are stored.
b. If relationships between the tables have not yet been established, complete Steps b. through f. of Independent Challenge 1.
c. Click the Reports button on the Objects bar, click the Player Statistics report, click the OfficeLinks button list arrow, then click the Publish It with Microsoft Word button.
d. Press [Enter] three times, then press [Ctrl][Home] to position the insertion point at the top of the document.
e. Type your name on the first line of the document, then save, print, and close the Player Statistics document. Exit Word. Close the Basketball-I database, then exit Access.

▶ Independent Challenge 3

As the manager of a women's college basketball team, you have created a database called Basketball-I that tracks the players, games, and player statistics. You want to export some information in the Basketball-I database to an Excel worksheet to analyze the data.

a. Start Access and open the database **Basketball-I** from the drive and folder where your Project Files are located.
b. Click the Games table, then choose the Analyze It with Microsoft Excel option from the OfficeLinks button on the Database toolbar. If prompted, click Yes to replace the existing file.

c. Click cell H1, type **Margin**, click cell H2, type **=E2-F2**, and then press [Enter].
d. Click cell H2 and then use the AutoFill handle to copy the formula down the entire column, through cell H23.
e. Click cell A25, type your name, change the print settings (use the Page Setup option on the File menu) to a landscape orientation, then print the spreadsheet.
f. Save and close the workbook, then exit Excel. Close the Basketball-I database, then exit Access.

Independent Challenge 4

You are the coordinator for the foreign studies program at your college. You have created a database that documents the primary and secondary languages used by foreign countries. The database also includes a table of common words and phrases, translated into various languages.

a. Start Access, open the **Languages-I** database from the drive and folder where your Project Files are located, then click Tables on the Objects bar.
b. Open the table datasheets to observe the entries. The Language1 and Language2 fields in the Countries table represent the primary and secondary languages for that country.
c. Click the Relationships button and create a one-to-many relationship using the LanguageID field in the Languages table and the Language1 field in the Countries table. Enforce referential integrity.
d. Similarly, create a one-to-many relationship using the LanguageID field in the Languages table and the Language2 field in the Countries table. Click No when prompted, and be sure to enforce referential integrity. The Languages table's field list will appear twice in the Relationships window with Languages_1 as the title for the second field list. The Words table is used for reference, and does not have a direct relationship to the other tables.
e. Click File on the menu bar, click Print Relationships, then view the relationships report in Design View.
f. Add a label to the Report Header section with your name as the caption, then close the report without saving it.
g. Connect to the Internet, and then go to www.ask.com, www.about.com, or any search engine. Your goal is to find a Web site that translates English to other languages, and to print one page of that Web site.
h. Add three new words or phrases to the Words table, making sure that the translation is made in all five of the represented languages: French, Spanish, German, Italian, and Portuguese.
i. Print the updated datasheet for the Words table, then close the Words table, close the Languages-I database, then exit Access.

Visual Workshop

Start Access and open the **Basketball-I** database from the drive and folder where your Project Files are stored. Use the Merge It with Microsoft Word feature to merge information from the Players table to a form letter. The final page of the merged document is shown in Figure I-25. Notice that the player's first and last names have been merged to the first line, and that the player's first name is merged a second time in the first sentence of the letter. Print the last page of the merged document, then close both documents without saving them.

FIGURE I-25

To: Jamie Johnson
From: Your Name
Date: Current Date
Re: Big 13 Champions!

Congratulations, Jamie, for an outstanding year at State University! Your hard work and team contributions have clinched the Big 13 Championship for State University for the third year in a row!

Thank you for your dedication!

Keep the faith,
Coach

Unit J

Access 2002

Creating Data Access Pages

Objectives

- Understand the World Wide Web
- Create Hyperlink fields
- MOUS Create pages for interactive reporting
- MOUS Create pages for data entry
- MOUS Create pages for data analysis
- MOUS Work in Page Design View
- Add hyperlinks
- Publish Web pages to Web servers

The Internet connects a vast amount of information, provides unlimited business opportunities, and supports fast, global communication. Most content provided via the Internet is accessed through a **Web page**, a hyperlinked document that makes the Internet easy to navigate. Web pages and their underlying infrastructure are referred to as the **World Wide Web**. Now, Web page technology has evolved to also include dynamic content. **Dynamic Web pages** are connected to a database, and are re-created with up-to-date data each time the Web page is opened. You can use dynamic Web pages to view, enter, or update data stored in an underlying database. Access 2002 provides the **page** object to create dynamic Web pages. Fred Ames, coordinator of training, wants to let MediaLoft employees access the Training-J database via the Internet. He will use the page object to create dynamic Web pages.

Access 2002

Understanding the World Wide Web

Creating Web pages that dynamically interact with an Access database is an exciting process that involves many underlying technologies. Understanding how the Internet, the World Wide Web, and Web pages interact helps you successfully connect a Web page to an underlying Access database. Fred reviews some of the history and key terminology of the Internet and World Wide Web to better prepare himself for the task of connecting a Web page to an Access database.

Details

- The **Internet** is a worldwide network of computer networks that sends and receives information through a common communications **protocol** (set of rules) called **TCP/IP** (Transmission Control Protocol/Internet Protocol).
- The Internet supports many services, including:
  - **E-Mail**: electronic mail
  - **File Transfer**: uploading and downloading files containing anything from text to pictures to music to software programs
  - **Newsgroups**: similar to e-mail, but messages are posted in a "public mailbox" that is available to any subscriber, rather than sent to one individual
  - **World Wide Web (WWW)**: a vast number of linked documents stored on thousands of Web servers that support a wide range of activities including research, education, advertising, entertainment, news, and e-commerce
- The Internet experienced tremendous growth in the past decade partly because of the following three major factors:
  - In the early 1990s, the U.S. government lifted restrictions on commercial Internet traffic, causing explosive growth in electronic commerce activities.
  - Technological breakthroughs resulted from innovations in hardware such as faster computer processors and storage devices, and in networking media such as fiber-optics and satellite transmission.
  - Less expensive and easier-to-use Internet systems and program software were developed for both **clients** (your computer) and **servers** (the computer that "serves" the information to you from the Internet).
- Behind all of these innovations are many amazing people. The World Wide Web was pioneered by a group of scientists who saw the need to easily share real-time information with colleagues, and started linking documents with similar content to one another. Table J-1 introduces more Internet and World Wide Web terminology. Figure J-1 shows how hyperlinks work on a Web page.

FIGURE J-1: **Hyperlinks on a Web page**

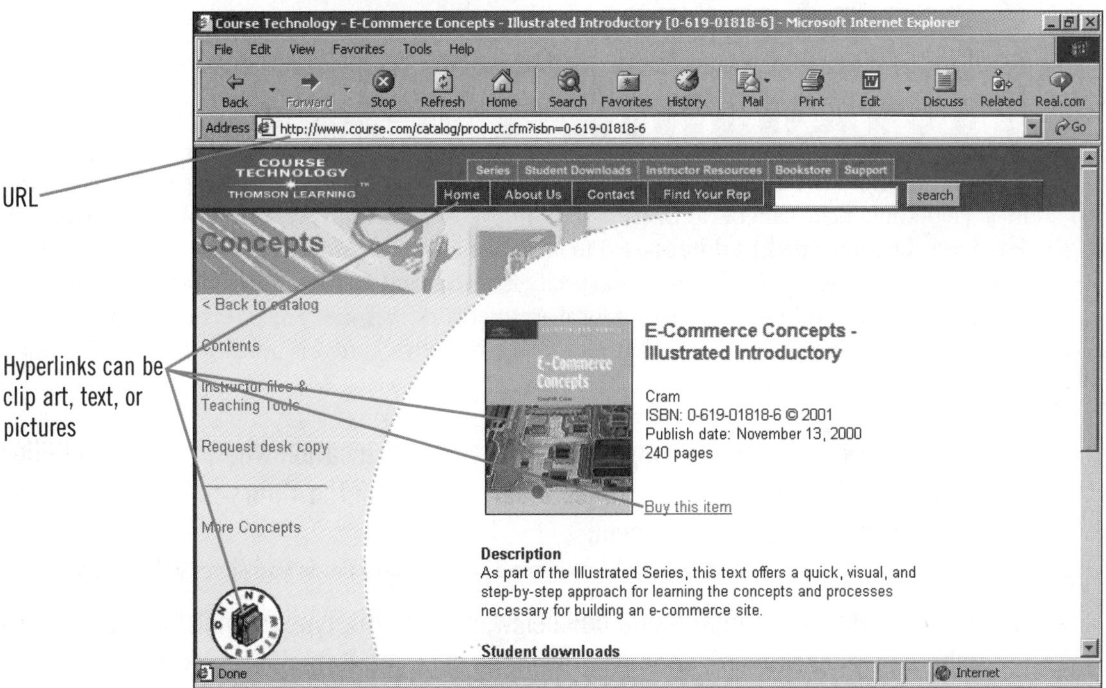

TABLE J-1: **Internet and World Wide Web terminology**

term	definition
Web page	A special type of file created with HTML code that contains hyperlinks to other files
Web server	A computer that stores Web pages
Hyperlink	Text (usually underlined), an image, or an icon on a Web page that when clicked, presents another Web page. Hyperlinks can jump to another part of the same Web page, a different page on the same Web server, or to a different Web server in another part of the world.
HTML (Hypertext Markup Language)	A special programming language used in Web pages. An HTML programmer writes HTML code to create a Web page. Nonprogrammers create HTML Web pages using FrontPage or by converting files such as Word, Excel, and PowerPoint into HTML Web pages using menu options within those programs.
Browser	Software such as Microsoft's Internet Explorer (IE) or Netscape Navigator used to find and display Web pages (HTML files created through the Access page object are best displayed with IE version 5 or later)
ISP (Internet Service Provider)	To access the Internet from a home computer, your computer first must connect to an ISP that then connects your computer with the Internet. National ISPs include America Online, the Microsoft Network, and Sprint's Earthlink. Hundreds of regional and local ISPs exist as well.
Modem	Short for *mod*ulate-*dem*odulate. A modem is hardware (usually located inside the computer) that converts digital computer signals to analog telephone signals to allow a computer to send and receive information across ordinary telephone lines. New and faster communication technologies such as DSL, satellite systems, and cable modems that can also connect your computer to the Internet without using the existing analog telephone systems are making traditional modems obsolete.
URL (Uniform Resource Locator)	Each resource on the Internet (including Web pages) has an address so that other computers can accurately and consistently locate and view it. For example, http://www.course.com/products/ is a URL for the Web page that displays information about Course Technology, Inc. (the publisher of this textbook). A URL never includes a space.
Domain name	The middle part of a URL, such as www.course.com. The middle part of the domain name is often either the company's name or words that describe the information you find at that site. The last part of the domain name indicates the type of site, such as commercial (com), educational (edu), military (mil), organizational (org), or governmental (gov).
Home page	The first page displayed on a Web server

Access 2002

Creating Hyperlink Fields

A **Hyperlink field** is a field defined with the Hyperlink data type in Table Design View. The entry in a Hyperlink field can be a **Universal Naming Convention (UNC) path** or a **Uniform Resource Locator (URL) address** used to locate a file on a network. Table J-2 gives more information about networks. URLs may also specify a newsgroup address, an FTP server location, an intranet Web page address, or a file on a local area network. Fred creates a Hyperlink field called OnlineResources to store the URL for a Web page that contains up-to-date information on the subject of each class.

Steps

1. Start **Access**, open the **Training-J** database from the location where your Project Files are stored, click **Tables** on the Objects bar, right-click the **Courses table**, then click **Design View** on the shortcut menu
   The Courses table opens in Design View, where you can add fields and specify their properties.
2. Click the first empty **Field Name cell** below InstructorID, type **OnlineResources**, press **[Tab]**, type **h**, click the **Save button**, then click the **Datasheet View button**
   The Courses table with the new OnlineResources field opens in Datasheet View.
3. Press [Tab] six times to move to the new OnlineResources field, type **www.microsoft.com/access**, press **[↓]**, point to the right edge of the **OnlineResources field name** so that the mouse pointer changes to ↔, then double-click to expand the column
   Your screen should look like Figure J-2. Hyperlink data in a datasheet appears underlined and in a bright blue color just like most text hyperlinks on Web pages.
4. Press **[Ctrl][']**, then press **[↓]**
5. Point to **www.microsoft.com/access** in either record so that the pointer changes to ☝, then click **www.microsoft.com/access**
   If you are currently connected to the Internet and have Microsoft Internet Explorer browser software, your screen should look similar to Figure J-3. Netscape Navigator is another popular browser program that will also open and display Web pages. Web pages are continually updated, so the content of the Web page itself may vary. If you are not already connected to the Internet, your **dialer** (software that helps you dial and connect to your Internet Service Provider, or ISP) may appear. Once connected to your ISP, the Microsoft Access Web page should appear.
6. Click the **Courses : Table button** in the taskbar, click the **OnlineResources field** for record **5** (Introduction to Excel), type **www.microsoft.com/excel**, click the **OnlineResources field** for record **11** (Introduction to Netscape), type **www.netscape.com**, then press **[Enter]**
7. Right-click the **Courses : Table button** on the taskbar, click **Close**, click **Yes** (if prompted) to save the changes to the layout of the table, then close any open browser windows

QuickTip

You can omit the first part of an Internet Web address (http://) when entering a URL into a Hyperlink field.

QuickTip

[Ctrl]['] copies the entry in the field of the previous record to the same field of the current record.

QuickTip

Visited links change to the color purple.

CLUES TO USE

Understanding the Universal Naming Convention (UNC)

The Universal Naming Convention (UNC) is another naming convention (in addition to URL) for locating a file on a network. The structure of a UNC is \\server\sharedfoldername\filename. UNCs are used for local resources, such as a file stored on a local area network. URL addresses are used for Web pages on the Internet or a company intranet.

FIGURE J-2: A hyperlink entry

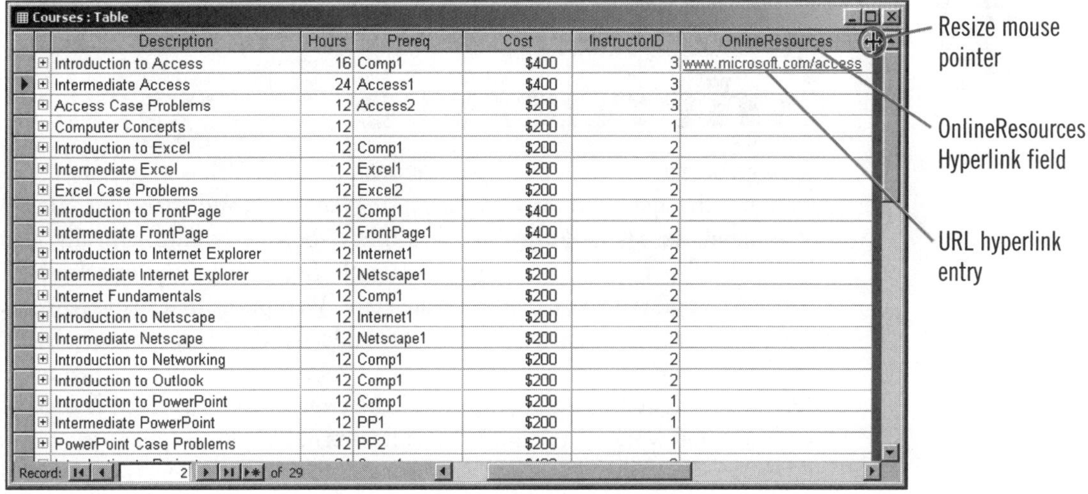

FIGURE J-3: Access home page

TABLE J-2: Types of networks

type of network	description
LAN (local area network)	Connects local resources such as file servers, user computers, and printers by a direct cable; LANs do not cross a public thoroughfare such as a street because of distance and legal restrictions on how far and where cables can be pulled
WAN (wide area network)	Created when a LAN is connected to an existing telecommunications network, such as the phone system, to reach resources across public thoroughfares such as streets and rivers
Internet	Largest WAN in the world, spanning the entire globe and connecting many diverse computer architectures
Intranet	WANs that support the same services as the Internet (i.e., e-mail, Web pages, and file transfer) and are built with the same technologies (e.g., TCP/IP communications protocol, HTML Web pages, and browser software), but are designed and secured for the internal purposes of a business

Creating Pages for Interactive Reporting

The **page** object, also called the **data access page (DAP)**, is a special Access object that creates dynamic Web pages used for viewing, editing, entering, and analyzing data stored in a Microsoft Access database. **Dynamic** means that the Web page is automatically reconnected with the database to display the most current data each time it is opened or refreshed by a browser such as Internet Explorer. You can also create static Web pages that display Access data by using the export to HTML feature after selecting any table, query, form, or report. **Static** Web pages retain no connection to the Access database and therefore do not change once they have been created. They can be viewed using any browser. The page object, however, is used to develop *dynamic* Web pages that work best using Microsoft Internet Explorer (IE) as the browser. Links to existing DAPs appear when you click the Pages button on the Objects bar. Table J-3 describes three major purposes for a DAP. Fred uses the page object to create an interactive report from the Training-J database as a Web page so it can be viewed using Internet Explorer.

1. Click **Pages** on the Objects bar, then double-click **Create data access page by using wizard**
2. Click the **Tables/Queries list arrow**, click **Query: Attendance Details**, click the **Select All Fields button** >>, click **Next**, double-click **Department** to select it as the grouping level field, then click **Next**

Trouble?
Click the Page View button if you are viewing Page Design View instead of Page View.

3. Click **Next** to bypass sorting options, type **Department Training Information** as the page title, click the **Open the page option button**, click **Finish**, then maximize the page
   Your screen should look like Figure J-4. **Page View** presents the Web page as it will appear within Internet Explorer. The **Expand button** indicates that detail records are grouped by that field. You can click the Expand button to view the detail records.
4. Click the **Expand button**, click **02/13/2003** in the Attended text box, then click the **Sort Ascending button** on the Attendance Details 1 of 16 navigation toolbar
   The upper navigation toolbar works with the detail records (the records within each department), and the lower navigation toolbar controls the grouping field itself, Department. Your screen should look like Figure J-5. The Expand button has become the **Collapse button**. When clicked, the Collapse button hides the detail records within that group.

Trouble?
You will not see the insertion point inside a text box that cannot be used for data entry.

5. Click the **Last button** on the lower Attendance Details-Department 1 of 11 navigation toolbar to display the Video group, click , click **Lee** in the Last field, then click the **Filter by Selection button** on the Attendance Details 1 of 20 navigation toolbar
   Your screen should look like Figure J-6.

QuickTip
Naming Web pages using one to eight lowercase letters helps ensure that the Web server operating system will be able to manage the file.

6. Click the **Filter Toggle button** on the Attendance Details 1 of 10 navigation toolbar to remove the filter, click the **Save button** on the Page View toolbar, navigate to the drive and folder where your Project Files are located, type **dept** in the File name text box, click **Save**, then click **OK** when prompted
   By saving the page, a Web page named dept.htm has been saved to the specified drive and folder.

QuickTip
Point to a DAP icon to display a ScreenTip that shows the path to the associated Web page.

7. Close the dept page
   The DAP icon contains a small linking symbol in the lower-left corner. When you double-click the DAP link, you open the external Web page in Access and use Page View as a browser to view this file. You could delete the DAP icon without disturbing the physical Web page file, but it's much easier to open the Web page in Access (for later modification) if the link to the Web page is available in the database window.

FIGURE J-4: **Department Training Information data access page**

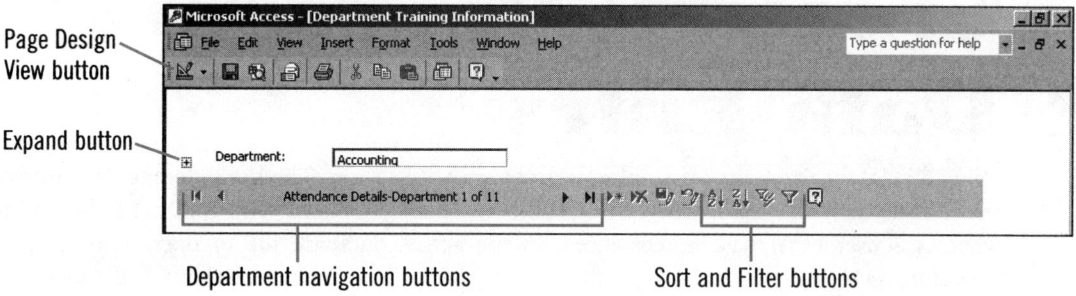

FIGURE J-5: **Expanded and sorted data access page**

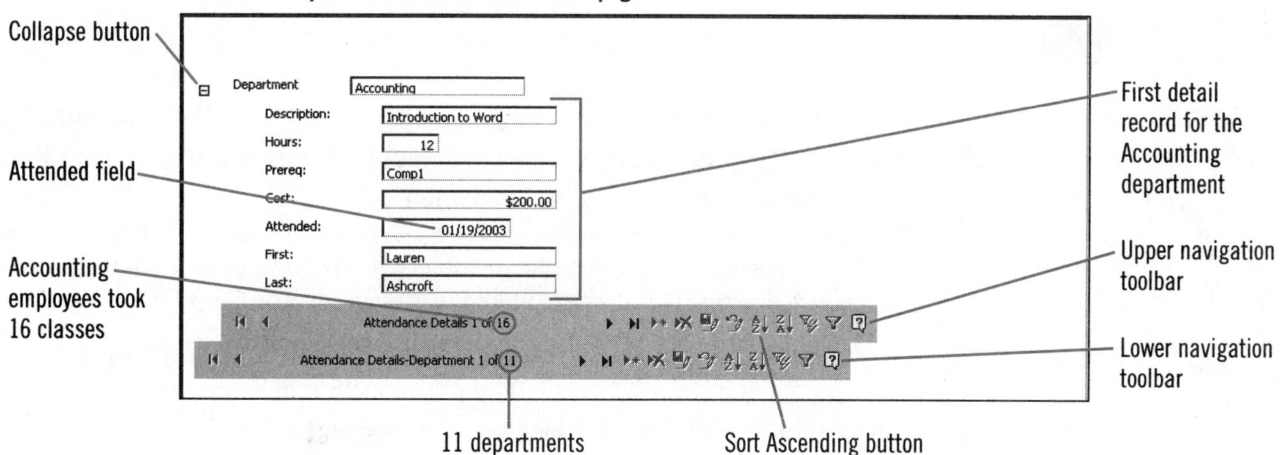

FIGURE J-6: **Filtered data access page**

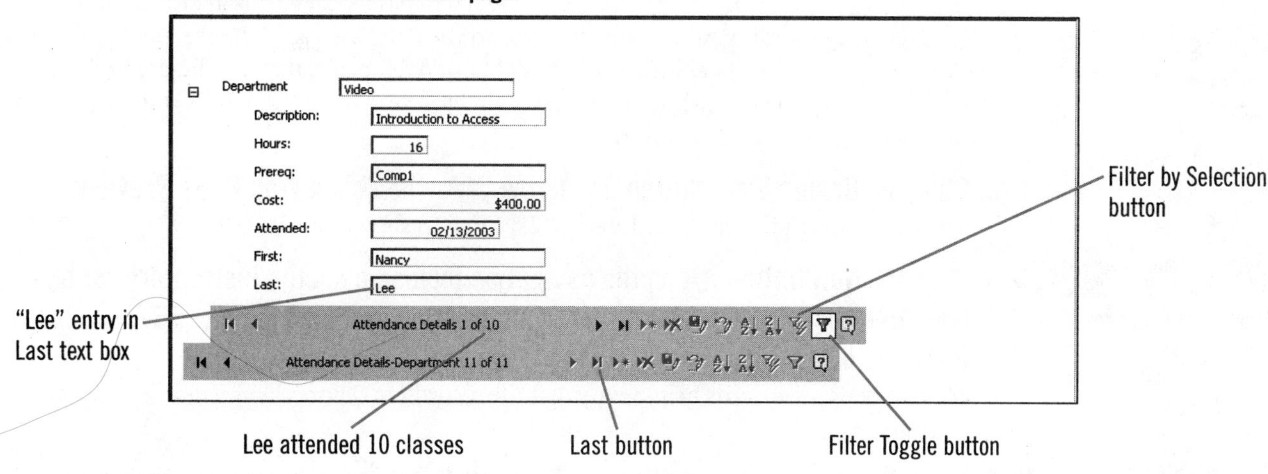

TABLE J-3: **Purposes for data access pages**

purpose	description
Data entry	Web pages that work as forms that can be used to view, add, or edit records
Interactive reporting	Web pages that work as reports that can be used to further sort, group, or filter data
Data analysis	Web pages that work as reports that can be used to analyze data using PivotTables and charts

Creating Pages for Data Entry

Using a DAP for data entry is similar to using an Access form. The big difference, of course, is that a dynamic Web page created by a page object can be opened with Internet Explorer (IE), whereas a user must have direct access to the actual database file to open a form object. Therefore, DAPs not only make a database more accessible, but can add a layer of database security because you can provide data entry and update features to other users without giving them direct access to the actual database file. The Human Resources department has offered to help Fred find, enter, and update information on instructors. Fred creates a data access page that works like a form to let the Human Resources department update data using the Internet Explorer browser.

1. Double-click the **Create data access page by using wizard**, click the **Tables/Queries list arrow**, click **Table: Instructors**, click the **Select All Fields button**, click **Next**, then click **Finish** to accept the rest of the default options
   The data access page opens in **Page Design View**, as shown in Figure J-7. The **Field List** window, which organizes database objects in a folder hierarchy, is open. Each item on the Page object is called a control just as it is in Report Design View or Form Design View.
2. Click the **Page View button** on the Page Design toolbar to view the data access page, click the **Save button** on the Page View toolbar, navigate to the drive and folder where your Project Files are located, type **instruct** in the File name text box, click **Save**, then click **OK** when prompted with a message about the connection string
   The instruct data access page shows the first of four records in the Instructors table. You *could* use this page object within Access to enter or edit data, but the purpose of a data access page isn't data entry if you can open the actual database file. (Forms are much more powerful data entry tools if you have direct access to the database file.) The real power of the data access page object is its ability to create dynamic Web pages that can be used to enter and update data by people who *do not* have direct access to the database, but who *do* have Internet Explorer browser software.
3. Click the **Design View Button list arrow**, then click **Web Page Preview**
   The instruct.htm file opens in Internet Explorer, as shown in Figure J-8.
4. Click the **New button** on the navigation toolbar, click the **InstructorFirst** text box, type **Delores**, press **[Tab]**, type **Hanneman**, press **[Tab]**, type **9/1/03**, click the **Previous button**, then click the **Next button**
   Moving between records helps verify that the record for Delores Hanneman was entered successfully.
5. Close **Internet Explorer**, click the **Training-J: Database button** on the taskbar, click **Tables** on the Objects bar, then double-click the **Instructors table** to open it in Datasheet View
   Your screen should look like Figure J-9. The new record appears in the table. You used a Web page opened in Internet Explorer to dynamically update an underlying Access database!
6. Close the **Instructors** datasheet, then close the **instruct** DAP

Trouble?

If you see #Name? errors on the Web page, click File on the IE menu bar, and then click Work Offline.

Trouble?

The [Page Up] and [Page Down] keys will not move the focus from record to record when viewing records through a Web page.

FIGURE J-7: Page Design View

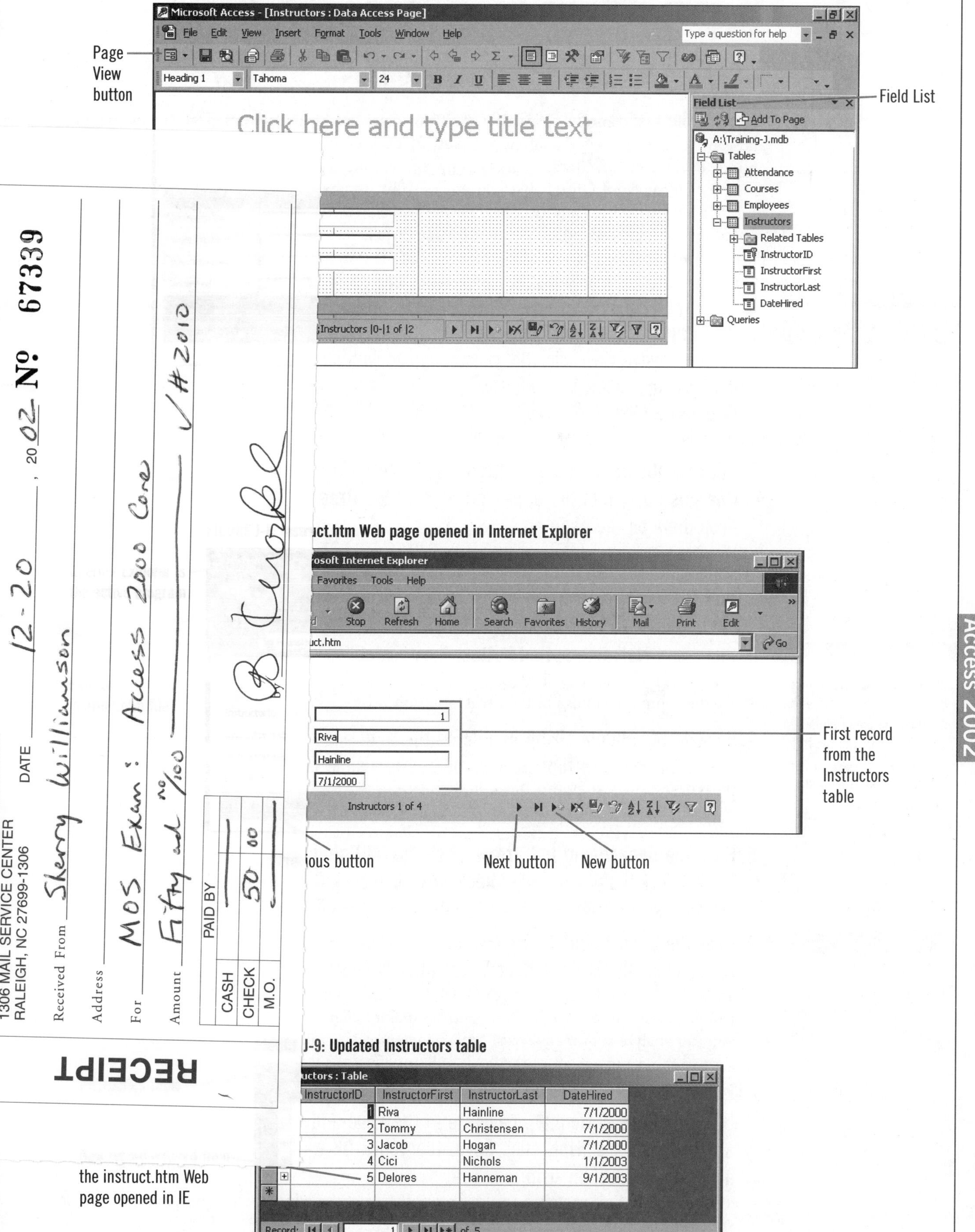

InstructorID	InstructorFirst	InstructorLast	DateHired
1	Riva	Hainline	7/1/2000
2	Tommy	Christensen	7/1/2000
3	Jacob	Hogan	7/1/2000
4	Cici	Nichols	1/1/2003
5	Delores	Hanneman	9/1/2003

Access 2002

Access 2002

Creating Pages for Data Analysis

A **PivotTable List** control displays data as a PivotTable—a table that summarizes data by columns and rows to make it easy to analyze. A typical **PivotTable** uses one field as the column heading, another field for the row heading, and summarizes a third field in the body of the PivotTable. For example, you could use a PivotTable to arrange data by summarizing sales (the field used within the body of the PivotTable) by product category (the field used as the row heading) and by state (the field used as the column heading). You cannot use the PivotTable List control to edit, delete, or add new data. Fred creates a data access page using the PivotTable List control so that he can view, summarize, and analyze information about course attendance in different ways.

Steps

QuickTip

Double-click the title bar of any window to maximize it.

1. Click **Pages** on the Objects bar (if not already selected), double-click **Create data access page in Design view**, click **OK** when prompted with a message about Access 2000, then maximize the Design View window

   Page Design View is very similar to that of Form Design View or Report Design View. Table J-4 summarizes some of the key terminology used in Page Design View.

2. Click the **Queries Expand button** in the Field List, then drag the **Department Charges** query into the upper-left area of the **Drag fields from the Field List and drop them on the page** area

   When you are dragging tables, queries, or fields from the Field List to Page Design View, a blue outline identifies the **drop zone**, the area on the page where you can successfully add that item. If the Control Wizards button is selected on the Toolbox toolbar, the **Layout Wizard** opens to guide you through the rest of the process of dynamically adding data to a DAP.

Trouble?

If the Layout Wizard dialog box doesn't open, delete the controls that were added to the page, click the Control Wizards button on the Toolbox toolbar, then redo Step 2.

3. Click the **PivotTable option button**, then click **OK**

   Your screen should look like Figure J-10. The fields within the Department Charges query are the column headings in the PivotTable control.

4. Point to the **middle sizing handle** on the right edge of the PivotTable control, drag ↔ to the right so that all four fields are visible as column headings within the PivotTable, then click the **Page View button** on the Page Design toolbar

   The data access page appears within Access, and the field names display list arrows.

5. Click the **Department list arrow**, click the **(All) check box** to clear all of the check marks, click the **Accounting check box**, then click **OK**

   Only the records with "Accounting" in the Department field appear.

QuickTip

To make a change to a PivotTable permanent, you must make the change in Page Design View, then save the page.

6. Click the **Department list arrow**, click the **(All) check box** to select all departments again, click **OK**, right-click the **Description field name**, then click **Move to Row Area**

   Your screen should look like Figure J-11. The Description field entries are now organized as row headings. The PivotTable List control's major benefit is that it quickly rearranges data so you can analyze it in many ways. Any change made to a PivotTable in Page View is temporary, so this arrangement of the fields will not affect the way the PivotTable is presented the next time it is opened in a browser.

7. Click the **Save button**, navigate to the drive and folder where your Project Files are located, type **pivot**, click **Save**, then click **OK** when prompted with a message about the connection string

   The new page link is stored in the Training-J database window and the pivot.htm file is stored in the location where your Project Files are stored.

FIGURE J-10: **PivotTable in Page Design View**

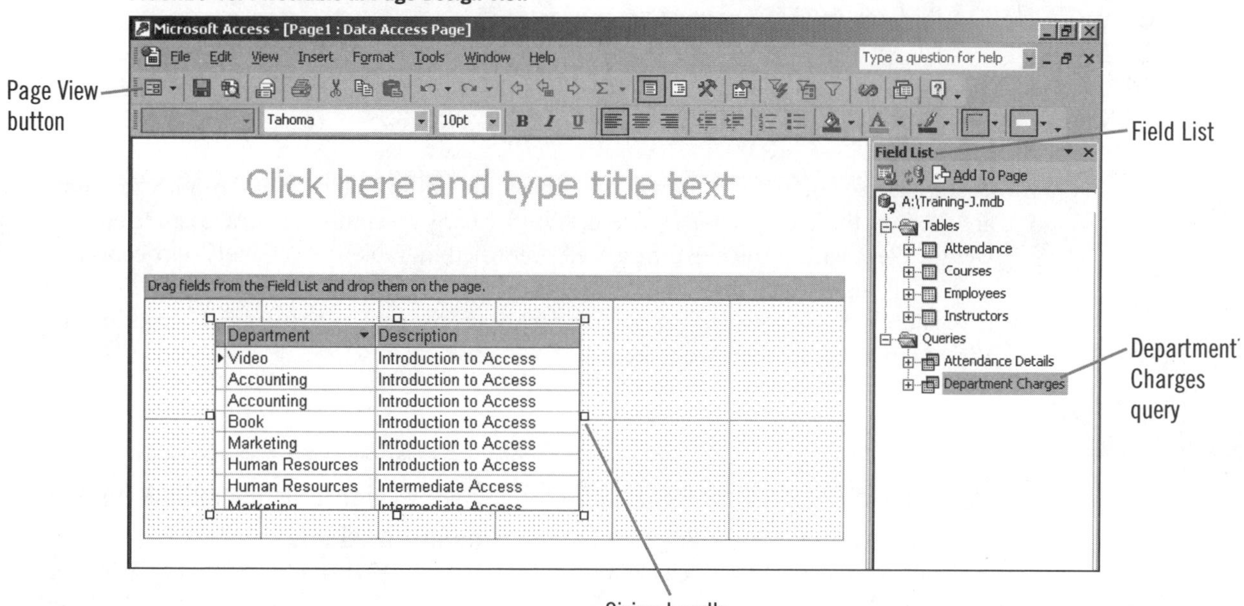

FIGURE J-11: **Modified PivotTable in Page View**

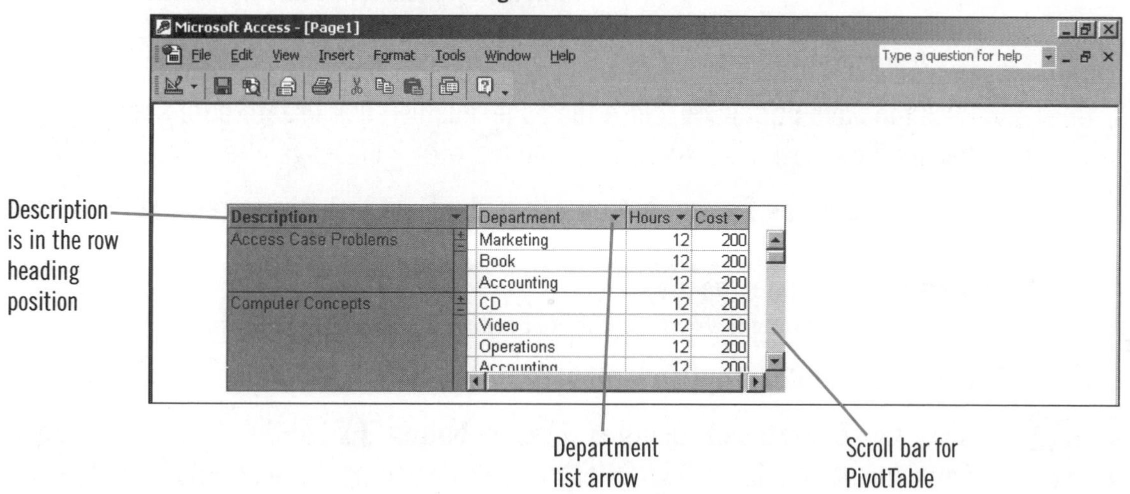

TABLE J-4: **Design View terminology**

term	definition
Field list	List that contains all of the field names that can be added in Design View
Toolbox toolbar	Toolbar that contains all of the bound and unbound controls that can be added in Design View
Control	Each individual element that can be added, deleted, or modified in Design View
Bound controls	Controls that display data from an underlying recordset; common bound controls are text boxes, list boxes, and PivotTable lists
Unbound controls	Controls that do not display data from an underlying recordset; common unbound controls for a page are labels, lines, and toolbars
Sections	Areas of the object that contain controls; sections determine where and how often a control will appear or print
Properties	Characteristics that further describe the selected object, section, or control

Access 2002

Working in Page Design View

You use Page Design View to modify the structure of the Web page and modify the controls that are used on the Web page. Page Design View closely resembles Form Design View and Report Design View, with some key differences, identified in Table J-5. A **PivotChart** control is used to graphically display data that is presented by a PivotTable control. You use Page Design View to add new controls or modify the existing characteristics of the page. Fred works in Page Design View to modify the pivot Web page.

Steps

1. Click the **Design View button** on the Page View toolbar, click **Click here and type title text**, then type **your name's Department PivotTable**
   Making an entry in the "Click here and type title text" area adds a title to a Web page.

2. Click the **PivotTable control** to select it, click the **PivotTable control** a second time to edit it, right-click the **Hours** field, click **Remove Field** on the shortcut menu
   Your screen should look like Figure J-12. The first click selects the control and the second click opens it for editing. You know that a PivotTable is open for editing when it displays a hashed border. Changes made and saved to the PivotTable in Page Design View permanently change how it appears when the Web page is opened in Page View or within Internet Explorer.

> **Trouble?**
> If you double-click the PivotTable control instead of single-clicking it twice, you open its property sheet. Close the property sheet and try again.

3. Click the **Save button**, close the page, double-click **Create data access page in Design View**, then click **OK** when prompted with a message about Access 2000

4. Click the **Queries Expand button** in the Field List, then drag the **Department Charges** query into the upper-left area of the **Drag fields from the Field List and drop them on the page** area
   The Layout Wizard allows you to choose between many presentations of the data.

5. Click the **PivotChart option button**, then click **OK**

6. Click the **Department Charges Expand button** in the Field List, drag the **Department field** to the Drop Category Fields Here, drag the **Cost field** to the Drop Data Fields Here area, drag the **Description field** to the Drop Filter Fields Here area, then click outside the PivotChart
   Your screen should look like Figure J-13. Depending on the amount of data, and how it is organized, you may have to spend some time resizing the control to display the data effectively.

> **Trouble?**
> If you drag the wrong field to the PivotChart, or drag a field to the wrong location, remove the field from the PivotChart by dragging it off the PivotChart, then try again.

7. Click the **PivotChart** to select it, drag the lower-right sizing handle using the ↘ mouse pointer to the lower-right corner of the screen to enlarge the chart, then click the **Page View button** to observe the final PivotChart
   The final PivotChart should look like Figure J-14. You can work with the fields on the PivotChart to filter and reorganize the data just as you could with a PivotTable.

> **QuickTip**
> Right-click the PivotChart and click Toolbar on the shortcut menu to toggle the PivotChart toolbar on or off.

8. Click , navigate to the drive and folder where your Project Files are located, type **chart** as the File name, click **Save**, click **OK** when prompted with a message about the connection string, then close the page

FIGURE J-12: **Modifying a PivotTable in Page Design View**

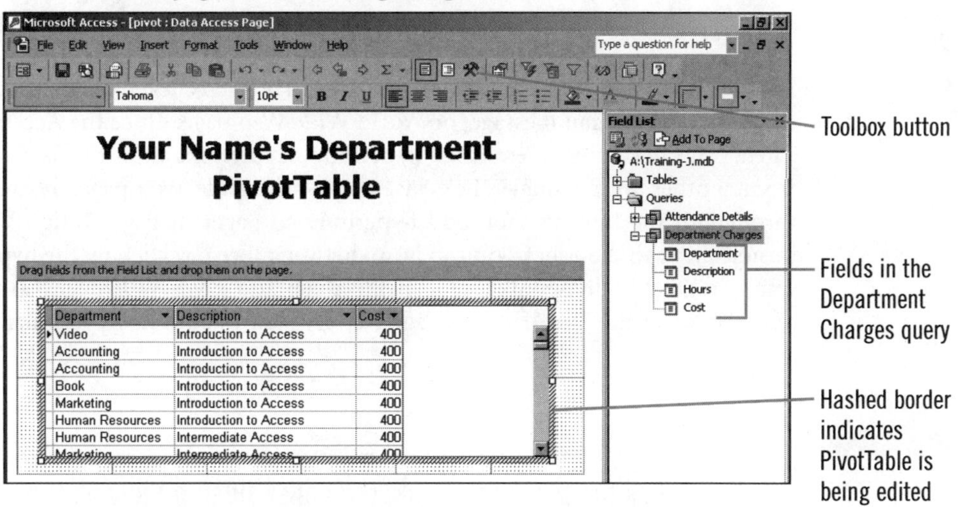

FIGURE J-13: **Building a PivotChart**

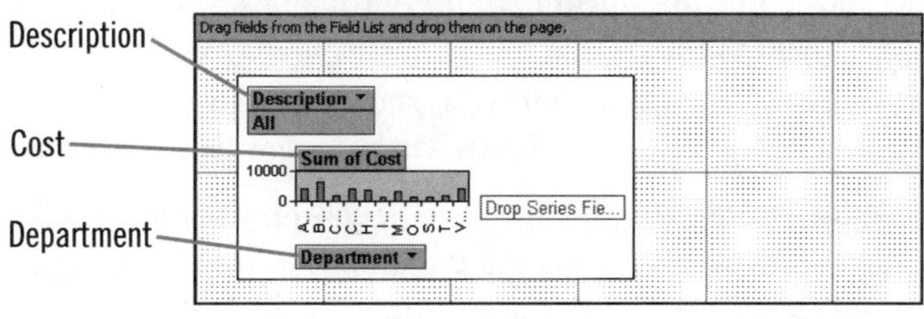

FIGURE J-14: **Viewing the updated Web page in Internet Explorer**

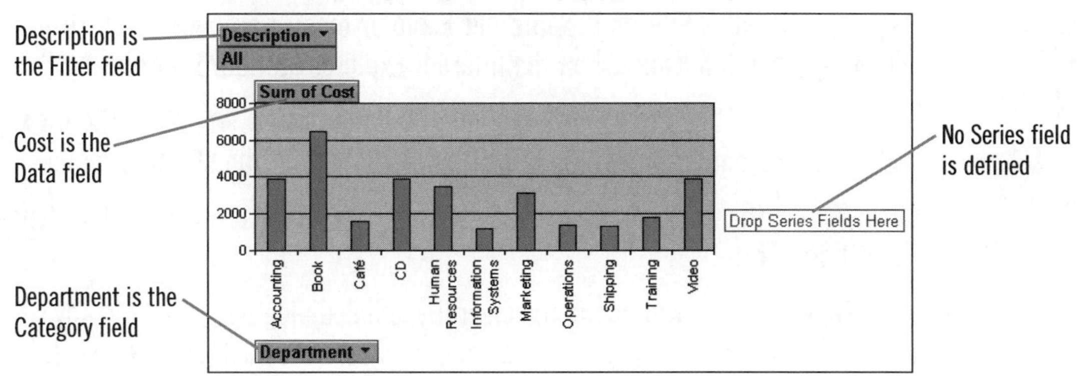

TABLE J-5: **New features in Page Design View**

item	description
Body	The area that displays text, controls, and sections
Sections	The record navigation section is used to display the navigation toolbar and the caption section is used to display text
Positioning	By default, the position of controls in the body of a page; by default, controls are positioned relative to one another
Toolbox	The Office PivotTable, Expand, and Record Navigation controls are new buttons on the Toolbox toolbar
Field List	The Field List window displays all tables, queries, and their fields

Access 2002

Adding Hyperlinks

A **hyperlink** is a single label, button, or image that when clicked opens another object, document or graphic file, e-mail message, or World Wide Web page. Once the Access page objects are finished, you can connect them using hyperlinks. Hyperlinks allow the user to access one Web page from another with a single click, just like World Wide Web pages reference other Web pages throughout the Internet. You add hyperlinks to pages in Page Design View. Then, when you browse through the pages, you can jump between them by clicking the hyperlinks. Fred wants to create a hyperlink between the chart and pivot Web pages so that one page can be accessed from the other. He uses Page Design View to add the hyperlinks to both pages.

Steps

1. Right-click the **pivot** page link, then click **Design View** on the shortcut menu
   Hyperlinks are added to page objects by using the **Hyperlink control**.
2. Click the **Toolbox button** to toggle on the Toolbox toolbar (if it is not already visible), click the **Hyperlink button** on the Toolbox, then click the **body** of the page about 0.5" below the PivotTable
   The Insert Hyperlink dialog box opens, as shown in Figure J-15. You can create hyperlinks to existing files, Web pages, pages in this database, new pages, or e-mail addresses.
3. Click the **Page in This Database** button, click **chart** from the Select a page in this database list, click **OK**, then click the **Page View button** on the Page Design toolbar
   The pivot Web page displays the new hyperlink.
4. Click the **chart hyperlink** to test the link
   The chart Web page opens within an Internet Explorer window.
5. If prompted with a message about making the page available offline, click **OK** in the message box, click **File** on the Internet Explorer menu bar, click **Work Offline**, then click the **Refresh button** on the Internet Explorer Standard buttons toolbar
6. Close the Internet Explorer window, click the **Save button**, close the **pivot** page, right-click the **chart** page, then click **Design View** from the shortcut menu
7. Click on the Toolbox, then click the **body** of the page about 0.5" below the PivotChart control
8. Click **Page in This Database** in the Insert Hyperlink dialog box (if not already selected), click the **pivot** page in the Select a page in this database list, click **OK**, click, then click
9. Click the **pivot hyperlink** in Page View, then click the **Print button** on the Internet Explorer Standard Buttons toolbar to print the final pivot Web page
   The pivot page should open in Internet Explorer, as shown in Figure J-16. Now you can move between the two related Web pages by clicking their hyperlinks.
10. Close Internet Explorer, save and close any open page objects, close the Training-J database, then exit Access

Trouble?

If Netscape opens the Web page, it means that the .htm file extension is associated with Netscape Navigator on your computer instead of Internet Explorer. To open the Web page in Internet Explorer, copy the Web page address from the Location bar within Netscape and paste it into the Address bar of an Internet Explorer window.

QuickTip

To make sure that Internet Explorer is displaying the latest version of a Web page, click the Refresh button on the Internet Explorer Standard Buttons toolbar.

FIGURE J-15: **Insert Hyperlink dialog box**

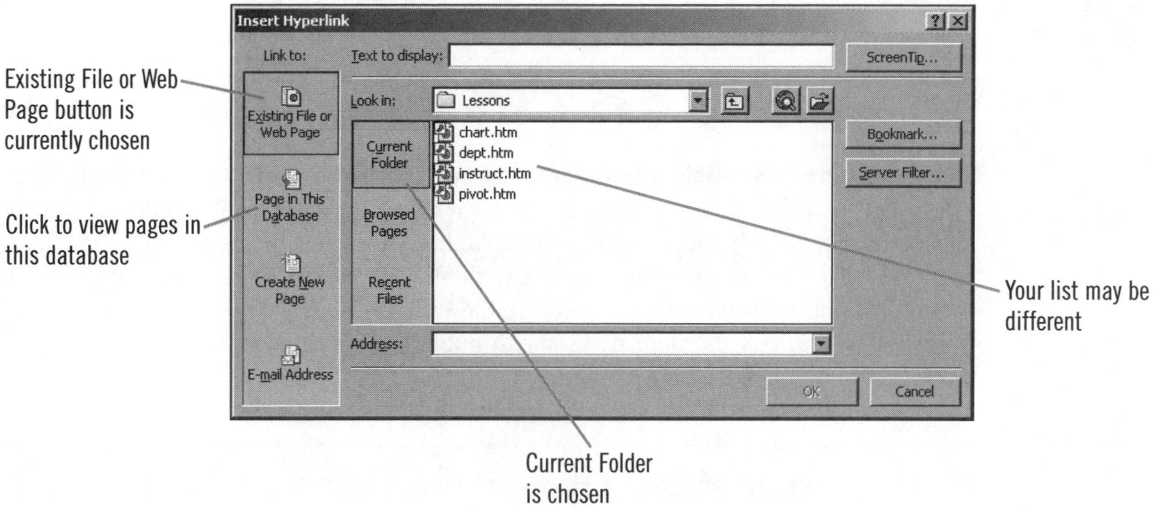

FIGURE J-16: **Pivot Web page open in IE with hyperlink**

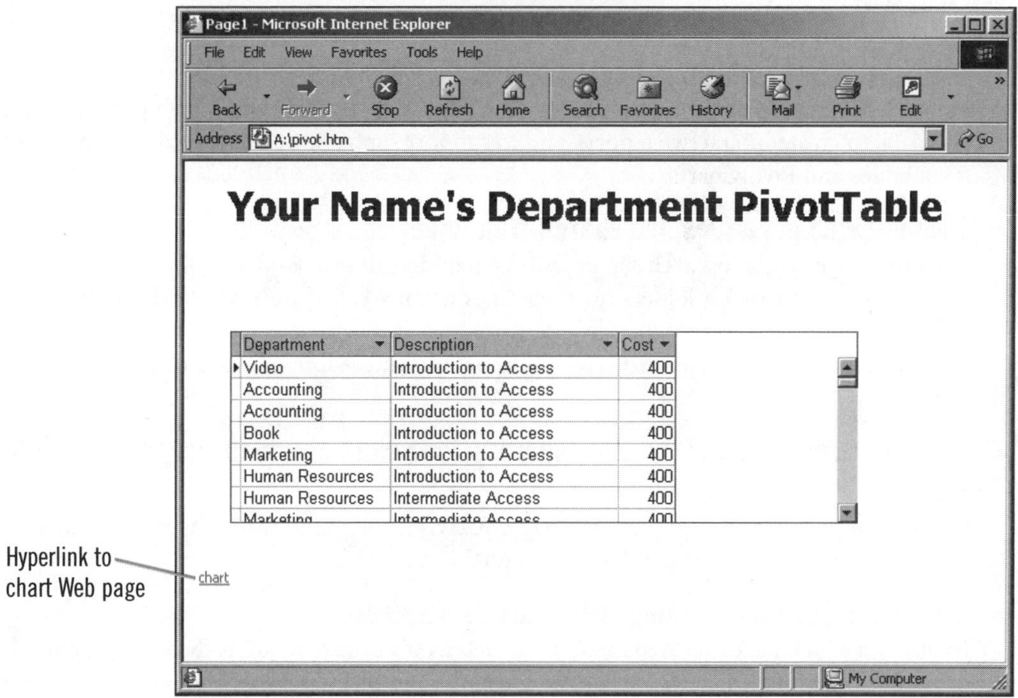

Creating a hyperlink from an image

Once an image is added to a form or a DAP, you can convert it to a hyperlink by using its property sheet to modify the image's **Hyperlink Address** property. Depending on what you enter for the Hyperlink Address property, clicking the hyperlinked image in Form View or Page View (or clicking the hyperlinked image as it appears on the Web page when opened in Internet Explorer) opens another file, Access object, or Web page. For example, C:\Colleges\JCCC.doc is the Hyperlink Address property to link to the JCCC.doc Word document on the C: drive in the Colleges folder. A Hyperlink Address property of http://www.jccc.net creates a link to that Web address.

Access 2002

Publishing Web Pages to Web Servers

Making Web pages available over the Internet or a company intranet requires publishing your Web pages to a **Web server**, a computer devoted to storing and downloading Web pages. Web servers contain **Web folders**, which are special folders dedicated to organizing Web pages. Once your Web page files are stored appropriately, **clients**, computers with appropriate browser and communication software that have access to the Web folder, may download and use those files. Fred reviews the steps necessary to publish the Web pages for use over MediaLoft's intranet.

Details

- **Store the Access database in a shared network folder on the Web server**
  On a network, most folders are not available to everyone, so be sure to put the Access database in a folder that the appropriate people have permission to use (**shared network folder**). Access databases are inherently **multi-user**, so that many people can enter and update information at the same time, provided they are given permission to use the files inside that folder. Two people cannot, however, update the same record at the same time (**record locking**).

- **Use the page object within Access to create dynamic Web pages**
  As you have experienced, you can use the page object to create dynamic Web pages to enter and edit data, to create interactive reports, and to support sophisticated data analysis tools including PivotTables and PivotCharts.

- **Save the Web page files in a shared Web folder**
  You must have access to a Web server with Web folders to save your Web files in these locations. Saving Web files to Web folders on a server is usually called **publishing**. Publishing is more complex than merely saving the file to your hard drive because any time you intend to share a Web page with others, you must have a compatible and secure network infrastructure already in place.

- **Give the users the URL or UNC address to access the Web pages using Internet Explorer**
  URLs are used to access Internet Web pages. UNCs can be used when the file is located on the same local area network as the client computer.

- **Use professional networking resources as necessary**
  Publishing a Web page to a Web folder on a Web server usually requires the knowledge and skills of professionals dedicated to the field of computer networking. People who build and maintain networks are often called **network administrators**. Those who work with Web servers, Web folders, and supporting Internet technologies are often called **Webmasters**. Table J-6 provides more tips and information about working with Web pages and Access. Figure J-17 illustrates the infrastructure involved with publishing a Web page to a Web server.

FIGURE J-17: Publishing to a Web server

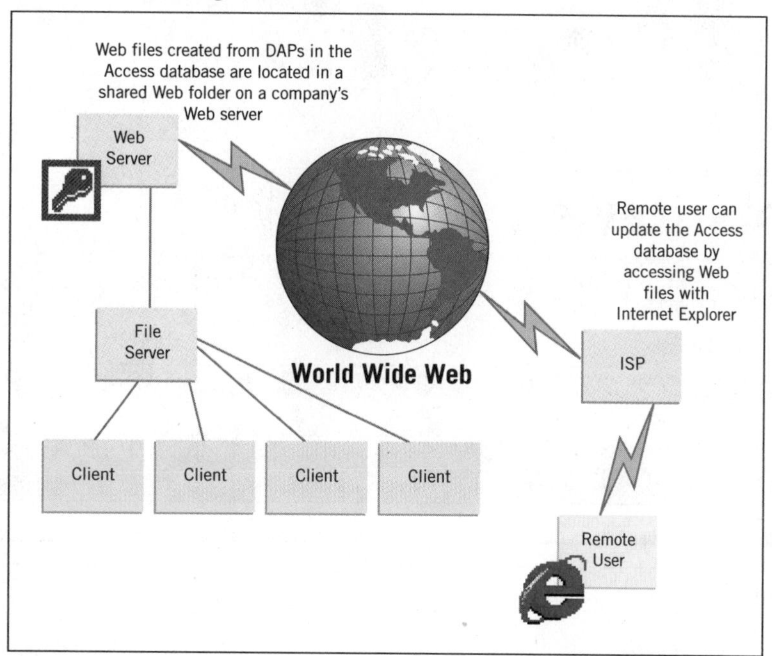

TABLE J-6: Tips for working with Web pages and Access

to...	do this...
Create DAPs from existing Access forms and reports	Select the form or report, click File on the menu bar, click Save As, then choose Data Access Page in the As list.
Open dynamic HTML files created by Access in a browser other than Internet Explorer	Use the Export option on the File menu to create server-generated Web pages from tables, queries, and forms. (Use the ASP file type for Microsoft Active Server Pages.) Server-generated HTML files pages are dynamic (and therefore change as your database changes).
Create static Web pages based on Access data	Use the Export option on the File menu to create static Web pages from tables, queries, forms, and reports. The files display a snapshot of the data at the time the static HTML file was created and can be viewed equally well in Internet Explorer and Netscape Navigator.
Open a Web page created by another program in Access	Right-click the file in the Open dialog box, then click Open in Microsoft Access on the shortcut menu.

The connection between the Web page and database file

The Web pages you create in this unit are linked to the database with path information that specifies the current drive, folder, and filenames for both the Web page and database files. Therefore, if you change the location or name of either the Web page or database file after the Web page is initially created, the link between the two may not work. However, it's not difficult to reestablish the connection. If you open a page in Page View and see the message "The HTML file associated with this link has been moved, renamed, or deleted," it means that the Web page file has been moved or renamed. To correct this, click the Update Link button in the error message dialog box, then locate the appropriate Web page associated with that page. If you open a page in Page View or view a Web page in Internet Explorer and see the message "Microsoft Office Web Components could not open the database drive:\path\databasename.mdb," #Name errors on the Web page, or any other errors indicating that the database cannot be found, it means that the database file has been moved or renamed. To correct this, open the page in Page Design View, open the Field List, right-click the name of the database at the top of the Field List, click Connection on the shortcut menu, click the Build button to the right of the database name on the Connection tab, then locate the appropriate database associated with that page.

Practice

► Concepts Review

Identify each element of the Web page shown in Figure J-18.

FIGURE J-18

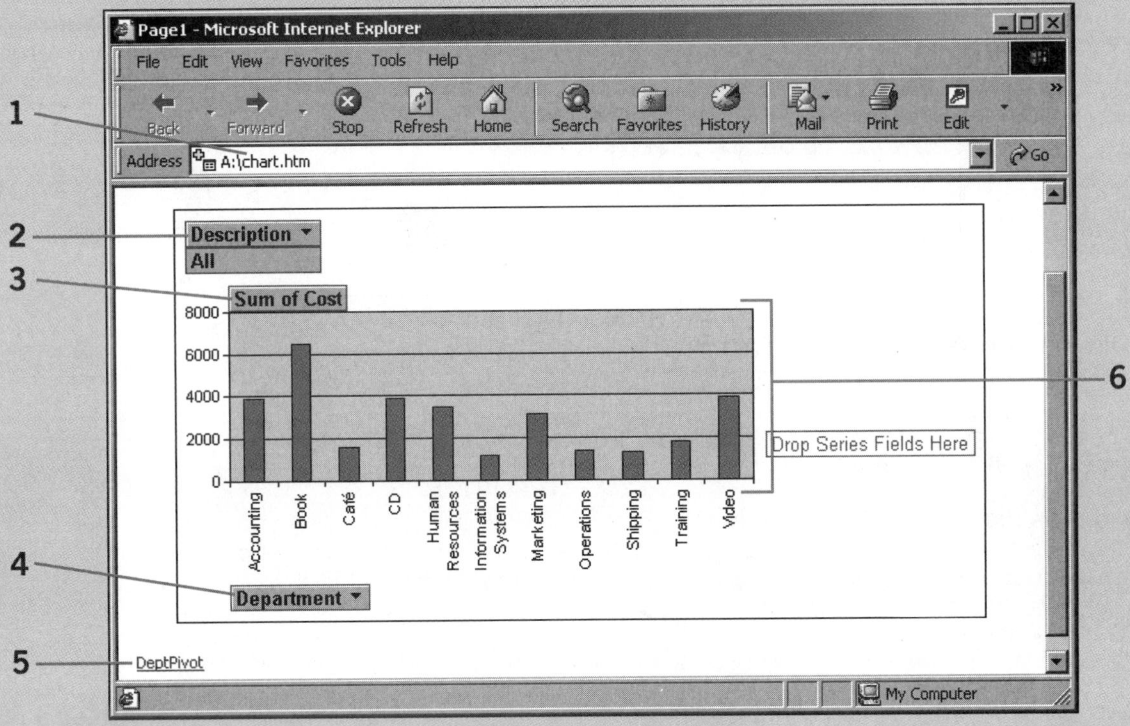

Match each term with the statement that describes its function.

7. **URL**
8. **HTML**
9. **World Wide Web pages**
10. **browser**
11. **data access page**
12. **Internet**

a. Programming language used in Web pages
b. Software loaded on a client used to find and display Web pages
c. Access 2002 object that creates dynamic Web pages
d. Worldwide network of computer networks
e. Hyperlinked documents that make the Internet easy to navigate
f. Web page address

13. The communications protocol for the Internet is:

a. TCP/IP.
b. HTML.
c. URL.
d. ISP.

14. To connect to the Internet through your home computer, you must first connect to a(n):

a. URL.
b. ISP.
c. Home page.
d. Webmaster.

15. Which of the following is NOT a service provided by the Internet?

a. E-mail
b. File transfer
c. World Wide Web
d. Electrical power

16. **Which of the following is browser software?**
    a. Windows NT
    b. Internet Explorer
    c. Microsoft Access
    d. Microsoft Excel
17. **Which of the following is a special type of Web page designed for viewing, editing, and entering data stored in a Microsoft Access database?**
    a. Browser
    b. Home page
    c. Data access page
    d. PivotTable
18. **Making Web pages created through Access available to other users is called:**
    a. Publishing.
    b. Uploading.
    c. Transferring.
    d. Rendering.
19. **DAPs create Web pages that are always:**
    a. Dynamic.
    b. Static.
    c. Used for data entry.
    d. Based on forms.
20. **Which of the following objects can NOT be converted to a DAP using the Save As option on the File menu?**
    a. Table
    b. Query
    c. Form
    d. Macro

Skills Review

1. **Understand the World Wide Web.**
   a. Interview five people and ask them to identify a Web site address where they have recently experienced the following activities:
      - To sell or purchase a product or service
      - For entertainment
      - To index or reference other Internet resources (search engines)
      - To gather information about a specific topic
      - To take a class
   b. Through interviews or research, identify five ISPs in your area, and write down their names. Identify which two ISPs appear to be the most popular. Research the costs and services for these two ISPs.
2. **Create Hyperlink fields.**
   a. Open the **Machinery-J** database from the drive and folder where your Project Files are located, then open the Products table in Design View.
   b. Add a new field named **HomePage** with a Hyperlink data type.
   c. Save the Products table, open it in Datasheet View, then enter the following home page URLs into the new field for the first six records:
      1) www.toro.com
      2) www.caseih.com
      3) www.snapper.com
      4) www.deere.com
      5) www.troybilt.com
      6) www.stihl.com
   d. Click the link for www.deere.com, then print the first page of the John Deere Web site. If you are not already connected to the Internet, your dialer may appear, prompting you to connect with your chosen ISP. Once connected to your ISP, the John Deere home page should appear.
   e. Close your browser, then close the Products datasheet.
3. **Create pages for interactive reporting.**
   a. Click Pages on the Objects bar, then double-click Create data access page by using wizard.
   b. Select the ProductName and the ReorderLevel fields from the Products table, then select the TransactionDate and UnitPrice fields from the Inventory Transactions table.
   c. Group the records by ProductName, then sort the records in ascending order by TransactionDate.

d. Type **ProductActivity** for the page title, then open the new page in Page View.
e. Open Page Design View, maximize the Design View window, click in the title area of the body of the page, then type the title **your name's Garden Shop Orders**.
f. Click the Page View button, click the ProductName text box, sort the ProductName in descending order, expand the ProductName group, navigate to the record with a 7/1/2003 TransactionDate entry within the Weed Wacker ProductName group, then print that page.
g. Save the HTML file with the name **garden** to the drive and folder where your Project Files are located, then close the page.

4. **Create pages for data entry.**
   a. Click Pages on the Objects bar, then double-click Create data access page by using the wizard.
   b. Select all of the fields in the Products table.
   c. Do not add any grouping levels, but sort the records in ascending order on ProductName.
   d. Title the page **Products**.
   e. In Design View, click in the title area of the body of the page, then type the title **your name's Products**.
   f. Save the Web page as **products** to the drive and folder where your Project Files are located, click OK when prompted about the connection string, then click the View button list arrow and choose Web Page Preview to view the new Web page in Internet Explorer. If you receive #Name? errors on the Web page, click File on the IE menu bar, then click Work Offline to toggle off that option.
   g. Find the Mulcher record, change the price of the mulcher from $69.50 to **$79.50**, then print the Web page within Internet Explorer in which you made this change.
   h. Navigate to the next record within Internet Explorer, then back to the Mulcher record to make sure that the price change was saved. Close Internet Explorer.
   i. Open the Products table in the Machinery-J database, then make sure the Mulcher record now displays $79.50 as the Unit Price. Add your initials to the end of the Serial Number entry for the Mulcher record, then print the Products datasheet in landscape mode.
   j. Close the Products table, then save and close the products Web page.
5. **Create pages for data analysis.**
   a. Click Pages on the Objects bar, double-click Create data access page in Design view, then click OK.
   b. Open the Field List window if not already visible, then click the Expand button to the left of the Queries folder.
   c. Drag the Products Query to the upper-left corner of the "Drag fields from the Field List and drop them on the page" area, click the PivotTable option button in the Layout Wizard dialog box, then click OK.
   d. Click the PivotTable control to edit it, right-click the ProductName field in the PivotTable control, then click Move to Row Area on the shortcut menu.
   e. Resize the control so that all three columns are clearly visible.
   f. Click in the title area of the body of the page, type the title **your name's Orders**, then display the page in Page View.
   g. Use the TransactionDate list arrow to select only the **7/1/03** dates, then print that page, as shown in Figure J-19.
   h. Save the page as **units** to the drive and folder where your Project Files are located, click OK when prompted about the connection string, then close the page.

FIGURE J-19

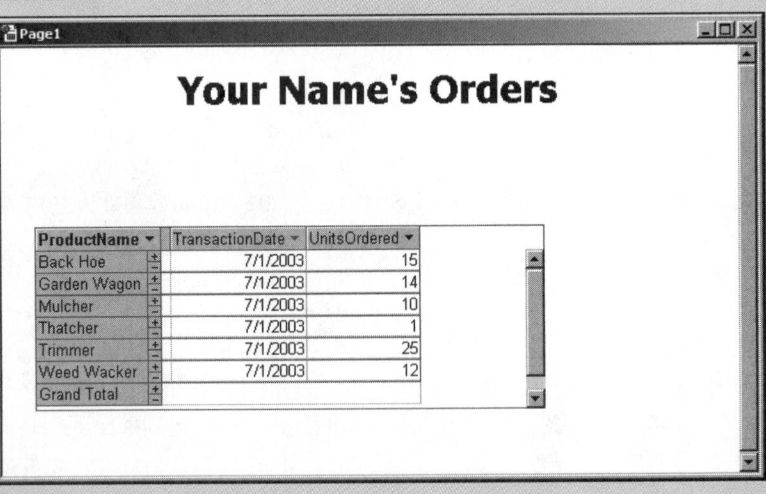

6. **Work in Page Design View.**
   a. Click the Pages button on the Objects bar, then double-click Create data access page in Design view.
   b. Expand the Queries folder in the Field List, and then drag the Products Query to the "Drag fields from the Field List and drop them on the page" area.
   c. Click PivotChart in the Layout Wizard dialog box, then click OK.
   d. Expand the Products Query in the Field List, then drag the ProductName field to the Drop Category Fields Here area of the PivotChart.
   e. Drag the TransactionDate field to the Drop Series Fields Here area of the PivotChart.
   f. Drag the UnitsOrdered field to the Drop Data Fields Here area of the PivotChart.
   g. Click in the title area of the body of the page, then type **your name's PivotChart of Orders**. Resize the PivotChart to clearly display the data.
   h. Save the page as **uchart** to the drive and folder where your Project Files are located, click OK when prompted about the connection string, open it in Page View, then print it.
   i. Close the uchart page.
7. **Add hyperlinks.**
   a. Open the products page in Design View, then use the Hyperlink button on the Toolbox toolbar to add a hyperlink to the units page. Place the hyperlink in the lower-left corner of the page.
   b. Save the products page, then close it.
   c. Open the units page in Design View, then use the Hyperlink button on the Toolbox toolbar to add a hyperlink to the products page. Place the hyperlink in the lower-left corner of the page.
   d. Save the units page, then open it in Page View.
   e. Click the products link, sort the products in descending order based on the UnitPrice field, then print that page.
   f. Close all Internet Explorer windows, close any open page objects within the Machinery-J database, then exit Access.
8. **Publish Web pages to Web servers.**
   a. Call your ISP and ask for information about the requirements to publish Web pages to their Web server. (If you are not currently connected to the Internet from home, research any ISP of your choice. You may also be able to find this information on the ISP's Web site.)
   b. If your ISP does not allow members to publish Web pages, continue researching ISPs until you find one that allows members to publish Web pages.
   c. Print or copy the documentation on how to publish Web pages to the ISP's Web server.
   d. Open Internet Explorer and type **www.geocities.com** in the Address list box.
   e. Follow the links on the Web page to determine how to create your own Web page at the geocities Web site, then print the documentation.

Independent Challenge 1

As the manager of a college women's basketball team, you want to enhance the Basketball-J database to include hyperlink field entries for opponents. You also want to develop a Web page to report information on player statistics.

a. Start Access, then open the **Basketball-J** database from the drive and folder where your Project Files are located.
b. Open the Games table in Design View, then add a field named **WebSite** with a Hyperlink data type.
c. Save the Games table, then open it in Datasheet View.
d. For the second record, enter **www.creighton.edu** in the WebSite field.
e. For the fifth record, enter **www.drake.edu** in the WebSite field.
f. Click the www.drake.edu link to display the Web page for Drake University, then print the first page.
g. Close the Drake Web page, close the Games table, click Pages on the Objects bar, then double-click Create data access page by using wizard.

h. Add all of the fields in the Players Query, group the information by the Last field, do not specify any sort fields, then title the page **pstats**.
i. In Design View, click in the title text area of the body of the page, then type the title **Iowa State Women's Basketball**. Include your initials in the title if you want them displayed on the printed solution.
j. Save the Web page as **pstats** to the drive and folder where your Project Files are stored, then open the Web Page Preview of the page (which opens the Web page in Internet Explorer).
k. Find and expand the details for the player with the last name of Hile, sort the detail records in descending order on the values in the TotalPts field, then print that record.
l. Close Internet Explorer, save and close the pstats DAP, close the Basketball-J database, then exit Access.

▶ Independent Challenge 2

As the manager of a college women's basketball team, you want to enhance the Basketball-J database by developing a Web page to enter new game information.

a. Start Access, then open the **Basketball-J** database from the drive and folder where your Project Files are located.
b. Click Pages on the Objects bar, then double-click Create data access page by using wizard.
c. Add all of the fields from the Games table, do not add any grouping levels, sort the records in ascending order by Date, then accept **Games** as the title for the page.
d. In Design View, click in the title area of the body of the page, then type the title **ISU Games**. Include your initials in the title to include them on the printed solution.
e. Save the Web page with the name **games** to the drive and folder location where your Project Files are stored, then display Web Page Preview to view the Games Web page in Internet Explorer.
f. Enter the following new record as record 23:

Date:	**3/1/03**
GameNo:	(The AutoNumber entry for the new record, 23, is automatically entered.)
Opponent:	**Kansas State**
Mascot:	**Wildcats**
Home-Away:	**H**
Home Score:	**100**
Opponent Score:	**52**
Web Site:	**www.ksu.edu**

g. Navigate to the first record, then back to the last.
h. Print this new record, which should look like Figure J-20, then close Internet Explorer.
i. Open the datasheet for the Games table to verify the entry in the Basketball-J database.
j. Close the Games datasheet, close the games Web page, close the Basketball-J database, then exit Access.

FIGURE J-20

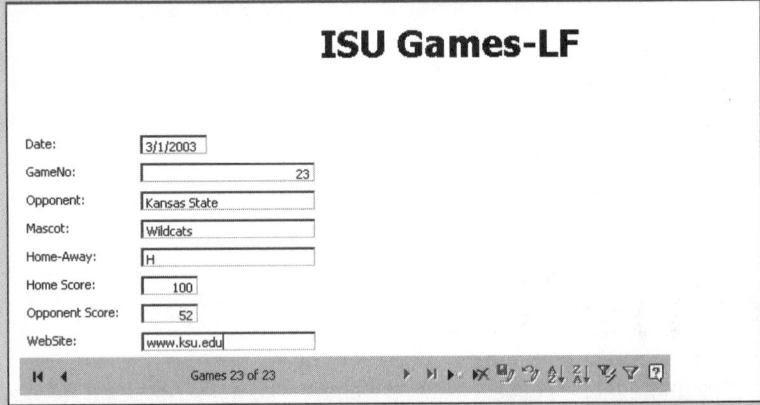

▶ Independent Challenge 3

As the manager of a college women's basketball team, you want to enhance the Basketball-J database by developing a Web page to display player statistical information as a PivotTable.

a. Start Access, then open the **Basketball-J** database from the drive and folder where your Project Files are located.
b. Click Pages on the Objects toolbar, double-click Create data access page in Design View, then click OK.

c. Expand the Queries folder in the Field List, then drag the Players Query to the upper-left corner of the "Drag fields from the Field List and drop them on the page" area.
d. Choose the PivotTable option, then click OK.
e. Widen the PivotTable control so that all of the seven fields are clearly displayed.
f. Click in the title area of the body of the Page, then type the title **Game Stats**. Include your initials in the title to include them on the printed solution.
g. Select the PivotTable to select it, click it again to edit it, right-click the Opponent field, then choose Move to Row Area on the shortcut menu.
h. Save the Web page as **gstats** to the drive and folder where your Project Files are located, then view the page in Web Page Preview so that it loads into Internet Explorer.
i. Click the Last list arrow in the PivotTable, click the All check box (to clear it), then click the Franco and Tyler check boxes to display only Denise Franco and Morgan Tyler's statistics.
j. Print this Web page, then close Internet Explorer.
k. Close the gstats Web page, close the Basketball-J database, then exit Access.

Independent Challenge 4

You are the coordinator of the foreign studies program at your college. You help place students in foreign college study programs which have curriculum and credits that are transferable back to your college. You have started to build a database that documents the primary and secondary language used by the foreign countries for which your college has developed transfer programs. The database also includes a table of common words and phrases, translated into various languages that you use in correspondence with the host colleges.

a. Start Access, then open the **Languages-J** database from the drive and folder where your Project Files are located.
b. Open the Words table, observe the field names that represent various languages, then click the Design View button to switch to Table Design View.
c. Add a field to the database that represents a language that doesn't currently exist in the database, then save the table and display its datasheet.
d. Connect to the Internet, then go to www.yahoo.com, www.msn.com, or any general search engine to conduct some research for your database. Your goal is to find a Web page that translates English to the new language that you added to the database, then to print one page of that Web page.
e. Using the features provided by the Web page, translate the existing six words in the English field of the Words table to the new language you added as a field, then print the Words datasheet in landscape mode.
f. Use the Page Wizard to create a Web page with all of the fields in the Words table. Do not add any grouping levels, but sort the records in ascending order based on the values in the English field.
g. Title the page **Translations**.
h. In Page Design View, type the title **Translations**. Include your initials in the title to include them on the printed solution.
i. Save the Web page with the name **trans** to the drive and folder where your Project Files are stored, then display Web Page Preview to view the Translations Web page in Internet Explorer.
j. Navigate to the record for the English word "hello," then print that page, as shown in Figure J-21.
k. Close Internet Explorer, close the trans Web page, close Languages-J, then exit Access.

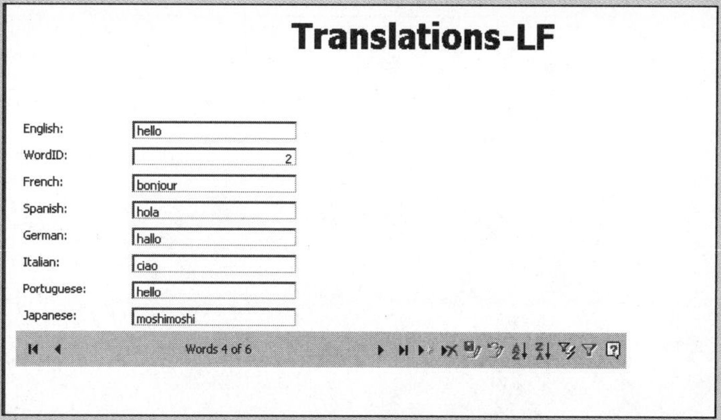

FIGURE J-21

Translations-LF

English: hello
WordID: 2
French: bonjour
Spanish: hola
German: hallo
Italian: ciao
Portuguese: hello
Japanese: moshimoshi
Words 4 of 6

 Visual Workshop

As the manager of a college women's basketball team, you need to enhance the **Basketball-J** database by developing a Web page to display player scoring information as a PivotTable. In Page Design View, use the Scoring query as the basis of the PivotTable. Move the Home-Away field and the Last field to the Row Area. Figure J-22 shows the final data access page, titled ISU Scoring. Include your initials in the title area if desired. Save the Web page with the name **scoring** to the drive and folder where your Project Files are located. Open, view, and print the page within Internet Explorer, then close all open applications.

FIGURE J-22

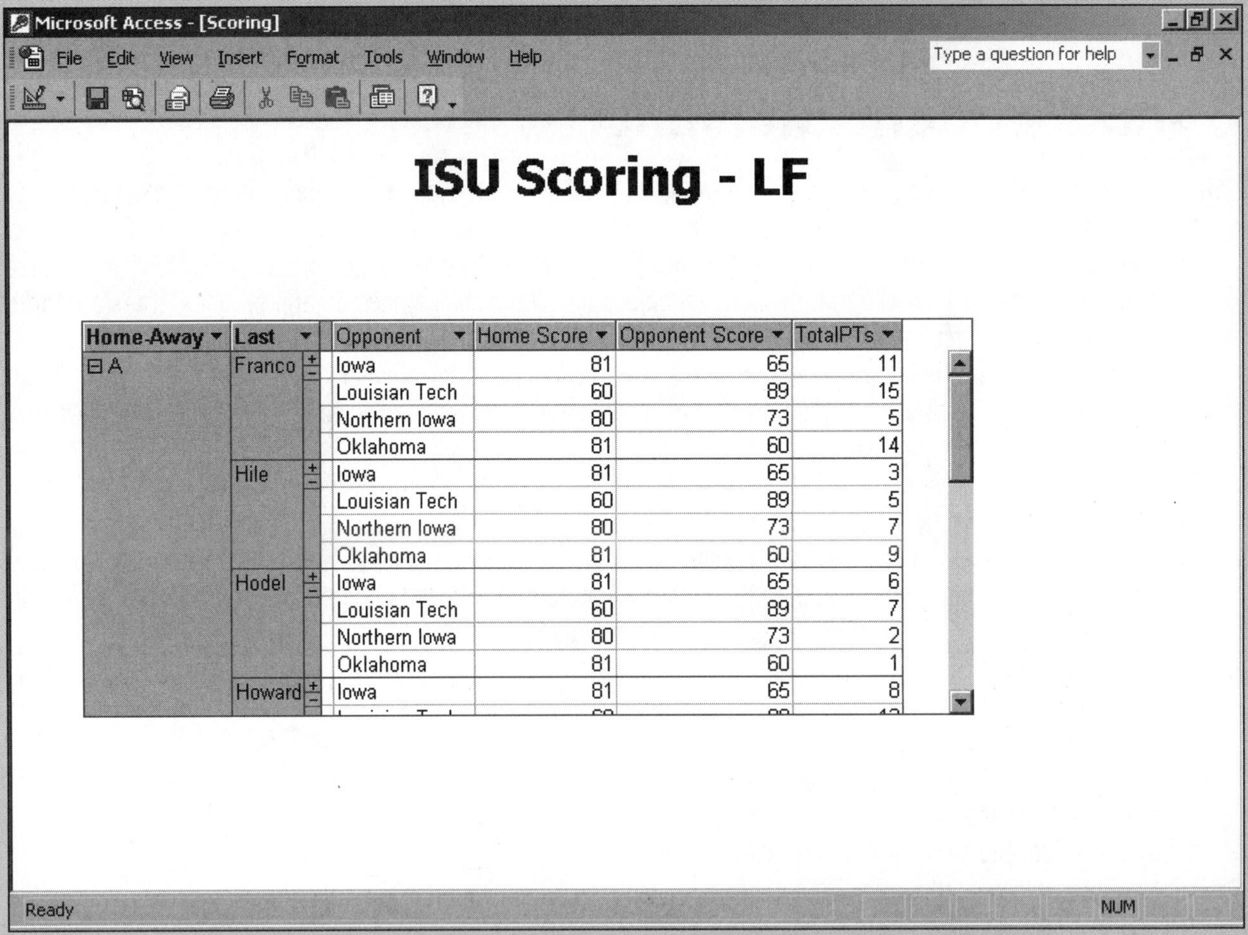

Microsoft Access - [Scoring]

File Edit View Insert Format Tools Window Help | Type a question for help

ISU Scoring - LF

Home-Away	Last	Opponent	Home Score	Opponent Score	TotalPTs
⊟ A	Franco	Iowa	81	65	11
		Louisian Tech	60	89	15
		Northern Iowa	80	73	5
		Oklahoma	81	60	14
	Hile	Iowa	81	65	3
		Louisian Tech	60	89	5
		Northern Iowa	80	73	7
		Oklahoma	81	60	9
	Hodel	Iowa	81	65	6
		Louisian Tech	60	89	7
		Northern Iowa	80	73	2
		Oklahoma	81	60	1
	Howard	Iowa	81	65	8

Ready | NUM

Access 2002

Creating
Advanced Queries

Objectives

- MOUS ► Query for top values
- MOUS ► Create a parameter query
- ► Modify query properties
- MOUS ► Create an update query
- MOUS ► Create a make-table query
- MOUS ► Create an append query
- MOUS ► Create a delete query
- ► Specify join properties

Queries are database objects that answer questions about the data. The most common query is the **select query**, which creates a single datasheet to display the fields and records that match specific criteria. Other types of queries, such as top value, parameter, and action queries, are powerful tools for displaying, analyzing, and updating data. An **action query** is one that makes changes to the data. There are four types of action queries: delete, update, append, and make-table. Fred Ames, coordinator of training at MediaLoft, has become very familiar with the capabilities of Access. Database users come to Fred with extensive data-analysis and data-update requests, confident that Fred can provide the information they need. Fred uses query features and new query types to handle these requests.

Access 2002

Querying for Top Values

Once a large number of records are entered into a table of a database, it is less common to query for all of the records, and more common to list only the most significant records by choosing a subset of the highest or lowest values from a sorted query. Use the **Top Values** feature in Query Design View to specify a number or percentage of records that you want to display in the query's datasheet. Employee attendance at MediaLoft classes has grown. To help plan future classes, Fred wants to print a datasheet listing the names of the top five classes, sorted by number of students per class. Fred creates a summarized Select Query to find the total number of attendees for each class, then uses the Top Values feature to find the five most attended classes.

Steps

1. Start Access, open the **Training-K** database, click **Queries** on the Objects bar, then double-click **Create query in Design view**
   You need fields from both the Attendance and Courses tables.
2. Double-click **Attendance**, double-click **Courses**, then click **Close** in the Show Table dialog box
   Query Design View displays the field lists of the two related tables in the upper portion of the screen.
3. Double-click **LogNo** in the Attendance field list, double-click **Description** in the Courses field list, then click the **Datasheet View button** on the Query Design toolbar
   The datasheet shows 153 total records with the LogNo and Description for each course taken at MediaLoft. You want to count the LogNo entries for the records grouped by values in the Description field so that you know how many people took each course.
4. Click the **Design View button**, click the **Totals button** on the Query Design toolbar, click **Group By** for the LogNo field, click the **Group By list arrow**, then click **Count**
   Your screen should look like Figure K-1. Sorting helps you further analyze the information and prepare for finding the top values.
5. Click the **LogNo field Sort cell**, click the **LogNo field Sort list arrow**, then click **Descending**
   Choosing a descending sort order will put the courses with the highest values in the LogNo field, those most attended by MediaLoft employees, at the top of the resulting datasheet.
6. Click the **Top Values list arrow** All on the Query Design toolbar
   The number or percentage specified in the Top Values list box determines which records will be displayed, starting with the first one on the datasheet. Therefore, the Top Values feature works best when the records are also sorted. See Table K-1 for more information on how to use the Top Values feature.
7. Click **5**, then click on the Query Design toolbar
   Your screen should look like Figure K-2. The datasheet shows the five most popular MediaLoft courses. For example, the Computer Fundamentals course had 19 attendees. If more than one course had 10 attendees (a summarized value of 10 in the CountOfLogNo field), then all courses that tied for fifth place would have been displayed, too.
8. Click the **Save button** on the Query Datasheet toolbar, type **Top 5 Courses**, click **OK**, then close the datasheet
   The Top 5 Courses query appears as a query object in the database window. The last Top Value entered (5) is saved with the query.

Trouble?

If you add a table's field list to Query Design View twice by mistake, click the title bar of the extra field list, then press [Delete].

QuickTip

Click the at any time during the query design development process to view the resulting datasheet.

FIGURE K-1: **Designing a summary query for top values**

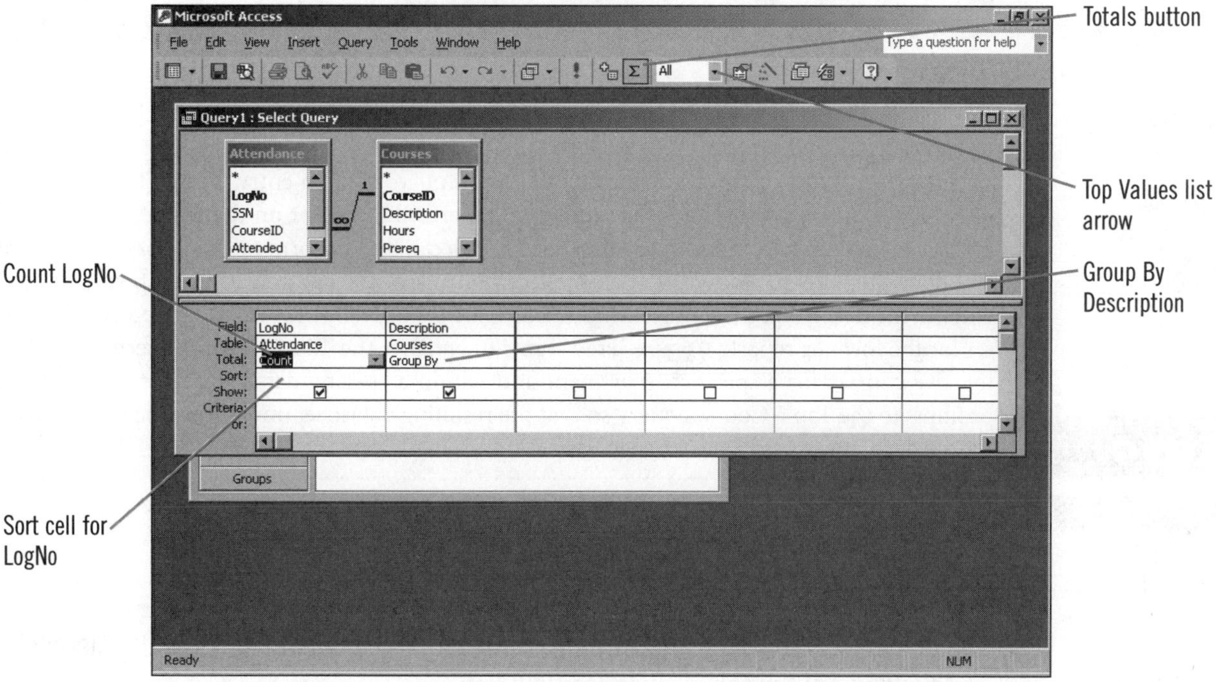
Totals button
Top Values list arrow
Group By Description
Count LogNo
Sort cell for LogNo
Microsoft Access
Query1 : Select Query
Attendance
Courses
Field: LogNo | Description
Table: Attendance | Courses
Total: Count | Group By
Sort:
Show:
Criteria:
or:
Ready

FIGURE K-2: **Top values datasheet**

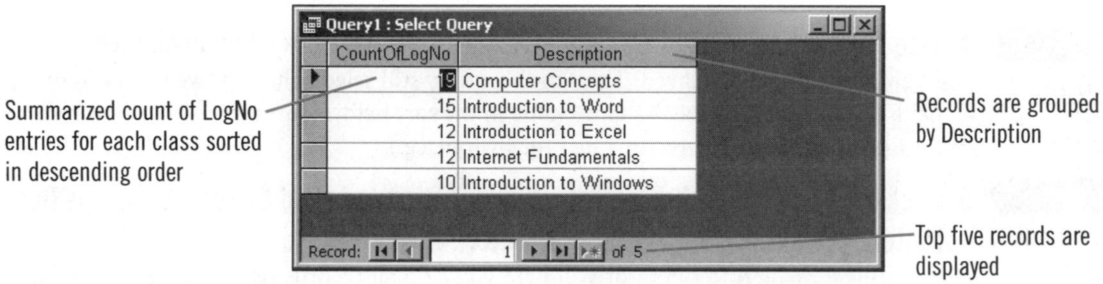
Summarized count of LogNo entries for each class sorted in descending order
Records are grouped by Description
Top five records are displayed
Query1 : Select Query
CountOfLogNo
Description
19 Computer Concepts
15 Introduction to Word
12 Introduction to Excel
12 Internet Fundamentals
10 Introduction to Windows
Record: 1 of 5

TABLE K-1: **Top Values options**

action	to display
Click 5, or 25, or 100 from the Top Values list	Top 5, 25, or 100 records
Enter a number such as 10 in the Top Values text box	Top 10, or whatever value is entered, records
Click 5% or 25% from the Top Values list	Top 5 percent or 25 percent of records
Enter a percentage, such as 10%, in the Top Values text box	Top 10%, or whatever percentage is entered, of records

Access 2002

Creating a Parameter Query

A **parameter query** displays a dialog box that prompts you for an entry. Your entry is used as criteria for the query, and narrows the number of records that appear on the final datasheet just like criteria entered directly in the query design grid. You can build a form or report based on a parameter query, too. Then, when you open the form or report, the parameter dialog box appears. The entry in the dialog box determines which records are collected by the query that become the recordset for the form or report. Fred wants to enhance the Top 5 Courses query to display the top five courses for a specific department and within a specific date range. He adds parameter prompts to the Top 5 Courses query so that the resulting datasheet only shows the top five courses for the department and dates he specifies.

Steps

QuickTip

You can drag the title bars of the field lists to rearrange them in a way that more clearly shows their relationships.

1. Right-click the **Top 5 Courses query**, click **Design View** on the shortcut menu, click the **Show Table button**, double-click **Employees**, then click **Close**
   The Employees table contains the Department field needed for this query.
2. Double-click the **Department field** in the Employees field list, then double-click the **Attended field** in the Attendance field list
   The Attended field contains the date that the course was taken. Both the Department and Attended fields will contain parameter prompts.
3. Click the **Department field Criteria cell**, type **[Enter department name:]**, and then click the **Datasheet View button**
   Your screen should look like Figure K-3. Parameter criteria must be entered within [square brackets]. The entry you make in the Enter Parameter Value dialog box is used as criteria for the field that contains the parameter criteria.

QuickTip

Query criteria are not case sensitive so "accounting" is the same as "Accounting."

4. Type **accounting** in the Enter department name: text box, then click **OK**
   Twelve records are displayed. Though this query still selects the top five values in the LogNo field, several records have the same value in the sort field, CountOfLogNo. (Four records tied for first place and eight records tied for fifth place.)

QuickTip

Right-click the Criteria cell, then click Zoom or press [Shift][F2] to open the Zoom dialog box, which clearly displays a long entry.

5. Click the **Design View button**, click the **Attended field Criteria cell**, type **Between [Enter start date:] And [Enter end date:]**, then click
   The **Between ... And** operator will help you find all records on or between two dates. The criteria >= [Enter start date:] and <= [Enter end date:] is equivalent to Between [Enter start date:] And [Enter end date:].
6. Type **book** in the Enter department name: text box, press **[Enter]**, type **1/1/03** in the Enter start date: text box, press **[Enter]**, type **3/31/03** in the Enter end date: text box, then press **[Enter]**
   Your screen should look like Figure K-4. Once again, a tie for the fifth place record caused the query to display more than five top records.
7. Click **File** on the menu bar, click **Save As**, type **Top 5-Department-Date-Your Name** then click **OK**
   Because the object name always appears in the header of a printed datasheet, descriptive query names can help identify the information or creator of the information.
8. Click the **Print button**, then close the query
   The new query also appears as an object in the database window.

FIGURE K-3: A parameter prompt

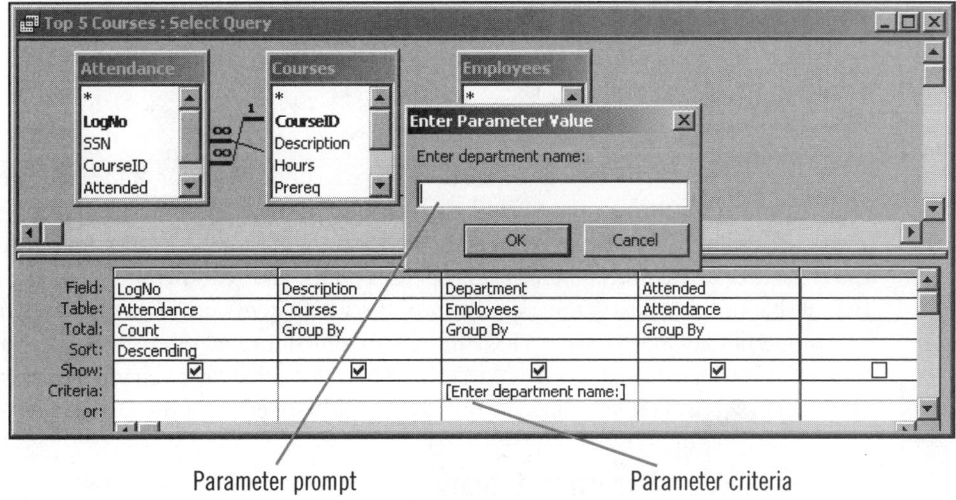

Parameter prompt

Parameter criteria

FIGURE K-4: Final datasheet for top 5 records between 1/1/03 and 3/31/03 in the Book department

Top 5 Courses : Select Query

CountOfLogNo	Description	Department	Attended
3	Introduction to Word	Book	01/19/2003
3	Introduction to Windows	Book	02/03/2003
3	Computer Concepts	Book	01/30/2003
2	Introduction to Excel	Book	02/13/2003
1	Introduction to Internet Explo	Book	03/20/2003
1	Introduction to Access	Book	02/13/2003
1	Internet Fundamentals	Book	03/07/2003
1	Intermediate Internet Explore	Book	03/27/2003
1	Intermediate Excel	Book	03/07/2003
1	Intermediate Access	Book	02/20/2003
1	Excel Case Problems	Book	03/15/2003
1	Computer Concepts	Book	02/06/2003
1	Access Case Problems	Book	02/27/2003

Record: 1 of 13

Tie for fifth place caused 13 records to appear in datasheet

Access 2002

Concatenating a parameter prompt to a wildcard character

You can concatenate (or combine) parameter prompts with a wildcard character such as the asterisk (*) to create more flexible queries. For example, the entry: LIKE [Enter the first character of the company name:] & "*" placed in the Criteria cell of the Company field searches for companies that begin with a specified letter. The entry: LIKE "*" & [Enter any character(s) to search by:] & "*" placed in the Criteria cell of the Company field searches for words that contain the specified characters anywhere in the field. The **ampersand (&)** is used to concatenate items in an expression and quotation marks (" ") are used to surround text criteria.

Access 2002

Modifying Query Properties

Properties are characteristics that define the appearance and behavior of the database objects, fields, sections, and controls. You can view the properties for an item by opening its property sheet. To open the property sheet for an item, click the item, then click the Properties button. You can also right-click an item, and then click Properties on the shortcut menu to open the property sheet. The title bar of the property sheet always indicates which item's properties are shown. If you change field properties in Query Design View, they are modified for that query only (as opposed to changing the field properties in Table Design View, which affects that field's characteristics throughout the database). Fred modifies the query and field properties of the Department Charges query.

Steps

QuickTip

Click the object column headings to sort the objects in ascending or descending order.

Trouble?

If the calculated field did not work correctly, return to Design View and make sure that you entered the expression PerHour:[Cost]/[Hours] accurately.

1. Right-click the **Department Charges** query, then click **Properties**

   The Department Charges Properties dialog box opens, providing information about the query and a text box where you can enter a description for the query.

2. Type **Lists the department, description, hours, and cost**, click **OK**, click the **Details button** in the Training-K database window, then maximize the database window

   Five columns of information about each query object appear, as shown in Figure K-5. The Description property you entered appears in the Description column.

3. Click the **Design button**, click the **Properties button** on the Query Design toolbar, click to the **right of the Employees field list**, click **Dynaset** in the Recordset Type property, click the **Recordset Type list arrow**, then click **Snapshot**

   Your screen should look like Figure K-6. Viewing the query property sheet from within Query Design View gives a complete list of the query's properties. The **Snapshot** entry in the Recordset Type property locks the recordset (prevents it from being updated). The **Recordset Type** property determines if and how records displayed by a query are locked.

4. Move the Query Properties dialog box by dragging its **title bar** (if it covers the first blank column in the query grid), click the **blank Field cell** for the next column in the query grid, type **PerHour:[Cost]/[Hours]**, click the **Datasheet View button**, double-click **12** in the Hours field for the first record, then try to type **15**

   The datasheet appears with the new calculated PerHour field in the last column. Because the query Recordset Type property was set to Snapshot, you can view the records but not update them.

5. Click the **Design View button**, click the **PerHour field** (if it's not already selected), click the **Format text box**, click the **Format list arrow**, click **Currency**, click the **Decimal Places text box**, click the **Decimal Places list arrow**, then click **2**

   When you click a property in a property sheet, a short description of the property appears in the status bar. You can press [F1] to open Microsoft Access Help for a longer description of the selected property.

6. Click to the **right of the Employees field list** to display the property sheet for the query, click **Snapshot**, click the **Recordset Type list arrow**, then click **Dynaset**

   Dynaset is the default property for the Recordset Type property, and allows updates to data.

7. Click to close the property sheet, click on the Query Design toolbar, double-click **12** in the Hours field for the first record, type **24**, then press **[Enter]** twice

   Your screen should look like Figure K-7. Not only are the values in the PerHour field now formatted with a currency symbol and two digits to the right of the decimal point, but you can update the recordset again.

8. Save, then close the Department Charges query

FIGURE K-5: Details view of objects

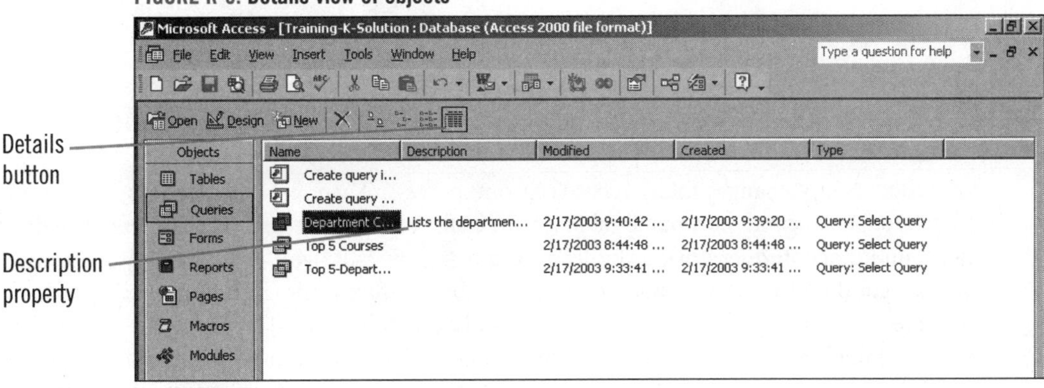

FIGURE K-6: Query property sheet

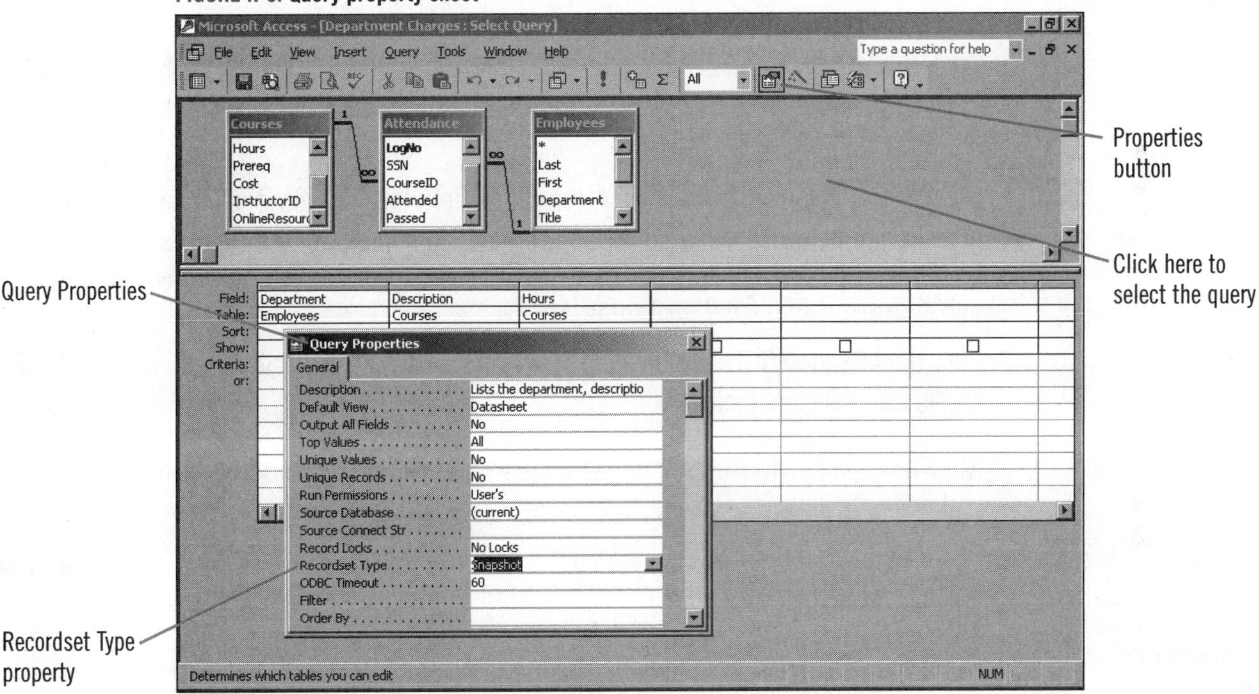

FIGURE K-7: Final datasheet

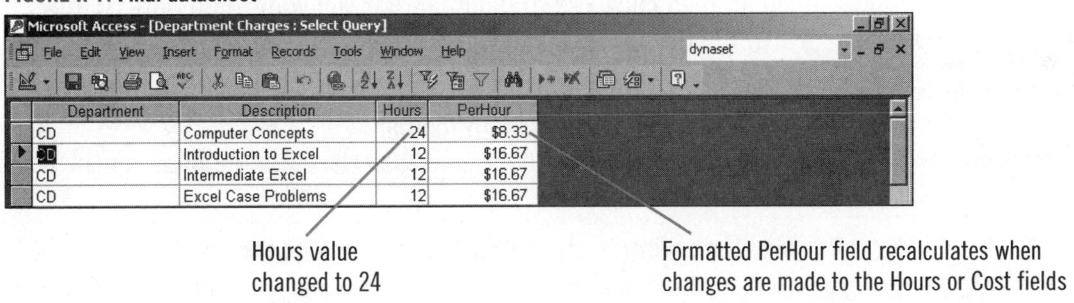

Access 2002

Access 2002

Creating an Update Query

An **action query** changes many records in one process. There are four types of action queries: delete, update, append, and make-table. In order for an action query to complete its action, you must run an action query using the Run button. Because you cannot undo this action, it is always a good idea to create a backup of the database before using an action query. See Table K-2 for more information on action queries. An **update query** is a type of action query that updates the values in a field. For example, you may want to increase the price of product in a particular category by 5%. Or you may want to update the value of an area code for a subset of customers. The Training Department upgraded their equipment on April 1, and Fred has received approval to increase by 5% the internal cost of all courses offered after that date. He creates an update query to quickly calculate and enter the new values.

Steps

1. Click the **List button** on the database window toolbar, double-click **Create query in Design view**, double-click **Attendance**, double-click **Courses**, then click **Close** in the Show Table dialog box

2. Double-click **CourseID** from the Attendance field list, double-click **Attended** from the Attendance field list, then double-click **Cost** from the Courses field list
   The three fields are added to the query design grid. You want to change the Cost value for only those courses offered on or after April 1.

3. Click the **Attended Criteria cell**, type **>=4/1/03**, then click the **Datasheet View button** on the Query Design toolbar
   Every action query starts as a select query, as reflected in the title bar of the query window. Always look at the datasheet of the select query before initiating any action that changes data to double-check which records will be affected. In this case, 51 records are selected.

Trouble?

Double-click the Query Type button list arrow to immediately display the entire list of menu options.

4. Click the **Design View button** on the Query Datasheet toolbar, click the **Query Type button list arrow** on the Query Design toolbar, then click **Update Query**
   The Query Type button displays the Update Query icon and the Update To: row appears in the query design grid, as shown in Figure K-8. All action query icons include an exclamation point to warn you that data will be changed when you click the Run button on the Query Design toolbar.

Trouble?

Be sure to enter the [Cost]*1.05 update criteria for the Cost field, *not* for the CourseID or Attended fields.

5. Click the **Cost field Update To cell**, type **[Cost]*1.05**, click on the Query Design toolbar, then click **Yes** to indicate that you want to update 51 rows
   When you run an action query, Access prompts you with an "Are you sure?" message before actually updating the data. The Undo button cannot undo changes made by action queries.

6. Click on the Query Design toolbar
   Your screen should look like Figure K-9. The datasheet of an update query shows only the updated field.

7. Close the update query without saving the changes
   You rarely need to save an update query, because once the data has been updated, you don't need the query object anymore. Also, if you double-click an action query from the database window, you run the query (as opposed to double-clicking a select query, which opens its datasheet). Therefore, don't save any queries that you won't need again, especially action queries that could inadvertently change data.

FIGURE K-8: Creating an update query

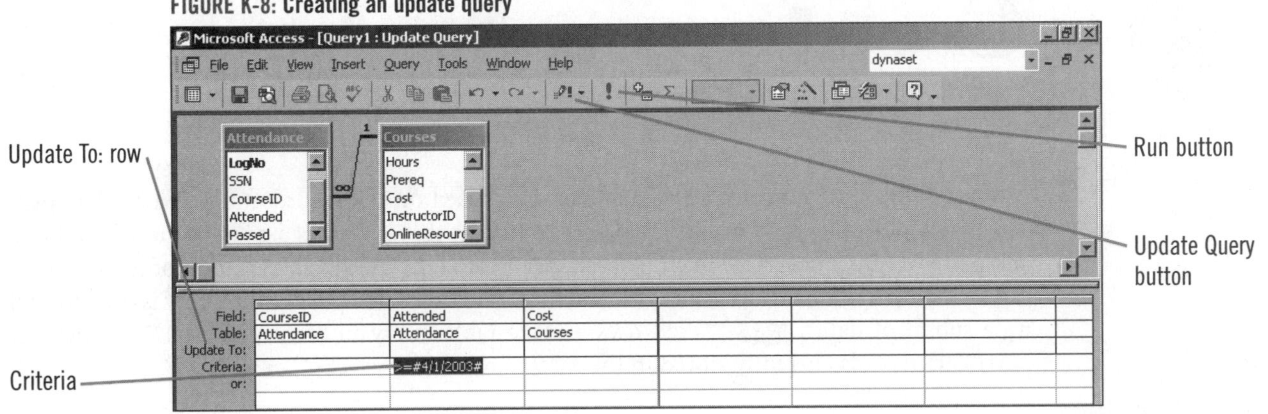

FIGURE K-9: Updated Cost values

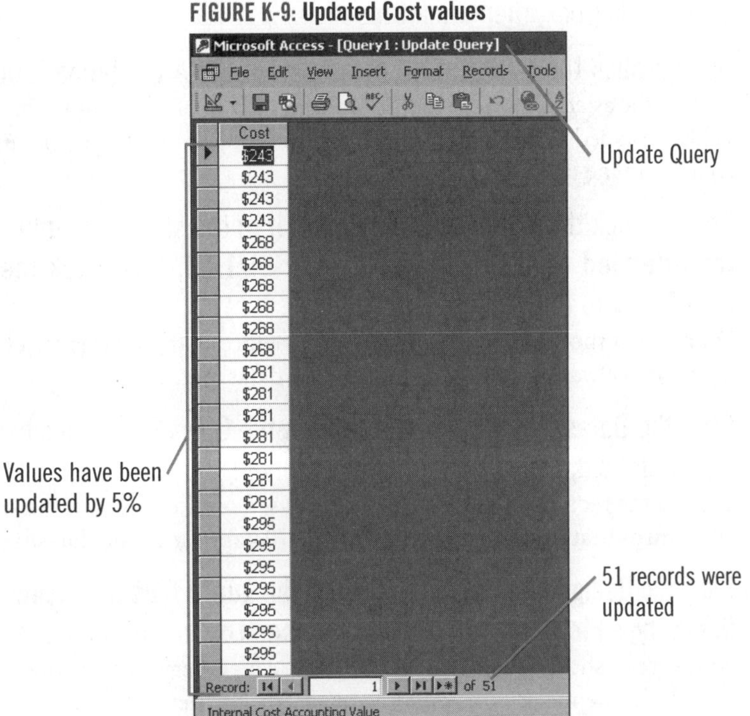

TABLE K-2: Action queries

type of action query	query icon	description	example
Delete		Deletes a group of records from one or more tables	Remove products that are discontinued or for which there are no orders
Update		Makes global changes to a group of records in one or more tables	Raise prices by 10 percent for all products
Append		Adds a group of records from one or more tables to the end of a table	Append the employee address table from one division to the address table from another
Make-Table		Creates a new table from data in one or more tables	Export records to another Access database or make a back-up copy of a table

Access 2002

Creating a Make-Table Query

A **make-table query** creates a new table of data based on the recordset defined by the query. The make-table query works like an export feature in that it creates a copy of the selected data and pastes it into a new table in a database specified by the query. The location of the new table can be the current or any other Access database. Sometimes the make-table query is used to back up a subset of data. Fred uses a make-table query to archive the 1/1/2003 through 3/31/2003 records currently stored in the Attendance table.

Steps

1. Double-click **Create query in Design view**, double-click **Attendance** in the Show Table dialog box, then click **Close**

2. Double-click the *** (asterisk)** at the top of the Attendance table's field list
   Adding the asterisk to the query design grid puts all of the fields in that table in the grid. Later, if fields are added to this table, they also will be added to this query because the asterisk represents all fields in the table.

3. Double-click the **Attended field** to add it to the second column of the query grid, click the **Attended field Criteria cell**, type **<4/1/03**, then click the **Attended field Show check box** to uncheck it
   Your screen should look like Figure K-10. Before changing this select query into a make-table query, it is always a good idea to view the datasheet.

4. Click the **Datasheet View button** on the Query Design toolbar, click any entry in the **Attended field**, then click the **Sort Descending button** on the Query Datasheet toolbar
   Sorting the records in descending order based on the values in the Attended field allows you to confirm that no records on or after 4/1/03 appear in the datasheet.

QuickTip

The sort and filter buttons work on a query datasheet in exactly the same way that they work in a table datasheet or form.

5. Click the **Design View button**, click the **Query Type list arrow**, click **Make-Table Query**, type **First Quarter 2003 Attendance Log** in the Table Name text box, then click **OK**
   Your screen should look like Figure K-11. The Query Type button displays the Make-Table icon. The make-table query is ready, but the new table has not yet been created. Action queries do not delete, update, append, or make data until you click the Run button.

6. Click on the Query Design toolbar, click **Yes** when prompted that you are about to paste 102 records, then close but do not save the query
   Once you've made a table of data, you do not need to save or run the make-table query again.

7. Click **Tables** on the Objects bar, then double-click **First Quarter 2003 Attendance Log** to view the new table's datasheet
   All 102 records were pasted into the new table, as shown in Figure K-12. Field properties such as the Input Mask for the SSN field and the Display Control for the Passed field were not duplicated, but you could modify the Design View of this table to change the appearance of the fields just like you could for any other table. (*Note*: –1 is used to designate "yes" and 0 is used to designate "no" when the Display Control property for a Yes/No field is set to Text Box.)

8. Close the First Quarter 2003 Attendance Log table

FIGURE K-10: Using the asterisk in a query grid

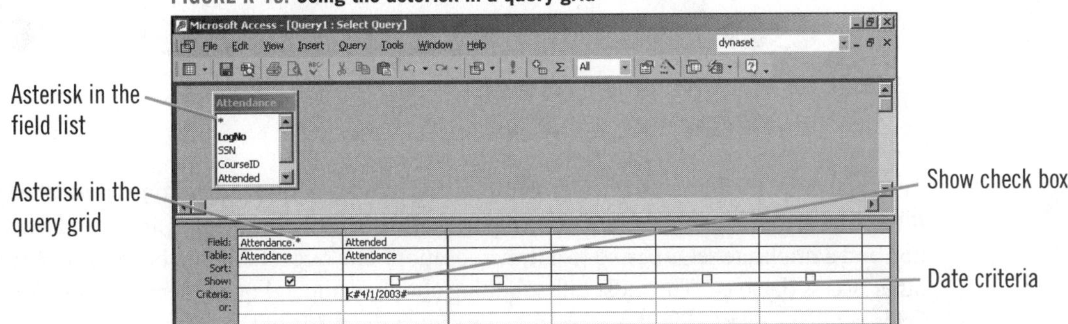

FIGURE K-11: Creating a make-table query

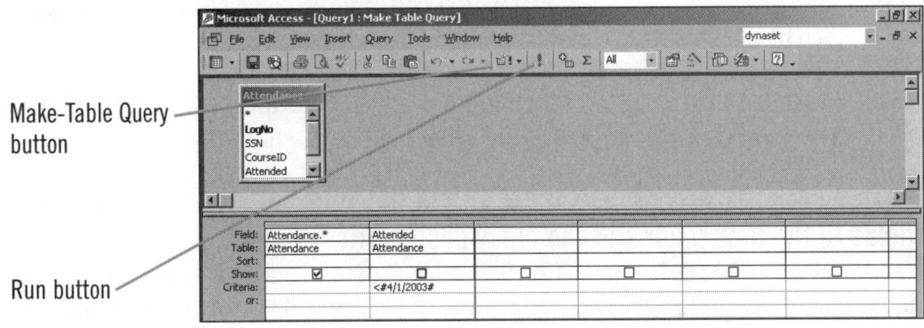

FIGURE K-12: First Quarter 2003 Attendance Log datasheet

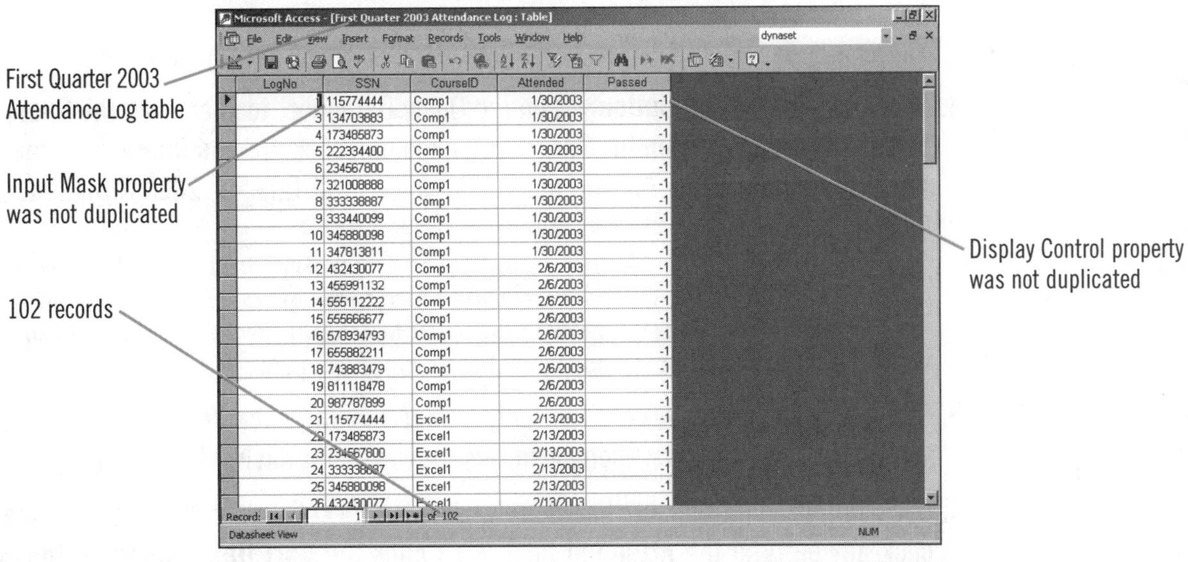

1900 versus 2000 dates

If you type only two digits of a date, Access assumes that the digits 00 through 29 are for the years 2000 through 2029. If you type 30 through 99, Access assumes the years refer to 1930 through 1999. If you want to specify years outside these ranges, you must type all four digits of the year.

Access 2002

Creating an Append Query

An **append query** adds a selected recordset defined by a query to an existing table called the **target table**. The append query works like an export feature because the records are copied from one location and a duplicate set is pasted to another location. The target table can be in the current or in any other Access database. The most difficult thing about an append query is making sure that all of the fields you have selected in the append query match the fields of the target table where you want to append (paste) them. If the target table has more fields than those you want to append, the append query will append the data in the matching fields and ignore the other fields. If the target table lacks a field that the recordset of the append query contains, an error message will appear indicating that the query has an unknown field name which will cancel the append action. Fred would like to append April's records to the First Quarter 2003 Attendance Log table. He uses an append query to do this, then he renames the table to accurately reflect its contents.

Steps

1. Click **Queries** on the Objects bar, double-click **Create query in Design view**, double-click **Attendance** in the Show Table dialog box, then click **Close**
2. Double-click the **Attendance table's field list title bar**, then drag the **highlighted fields** to the first column of the query design grid
   Double-clicking the title bar of the field list selects all of the fields, allowing you to add all the fields to the query grid quickly. To successfully complete the append process, the append query's Query Design View cannot have more fields than in the target table. Therefore, the technique of adding all of the fields to the query grid by using the asterisk in the field list and then adding the Attendance field again in order to enter the date criteria would not work for the append operation.
3. Click the **Attended field Criteria cell**, type **>=4/1/03 and <=4/30/03**, then click the **Datasheet View button** on the Query Design toolbar
   The datasheet should show 29 records with an April date in the Attended field.
4. Click the **Design View button** on the Query Datasheet toolbar, click the **Query Type button list arrow** on the Query Design toolbar, click **Append Query**, click the **Table Name list arrow** in the Append dialog box, click **First Quarter 2003 Attendance Log**, then click **OK**
   Your screen should look like Figure K-13. The Query Type button displays the Append Query icon and the Append To row was added to the query design grid. You would use the Append To row to choose fields in the target table if they were different from the query fields. The append action is ready to be initiated by clicking the Run button.
5. Click the **Run button** on the Query Design toolbar, click **Yes** to indicate that you want to append 29 rows, then close the query without saving the changes
6. Click **Tables** on the Objects bar, double-click the **First Quarter 2003 Attendance Log**, click any entry in the **Attended** field, then click the **Sort Descending button** on the Table Datasheet toolbar
   The April records were appended to the table for a total of 131 records, as shown in Figure K-14.
7. Close the First Quarter 2003 Attendance Log datasheet without saving changes, right-click **First Quarter 2003 Attendance Log** in the database window, click **Rename** on the shortcut menu, type **Jan-April 2003 Log**, then press **[Enter]**
   The backup table with attendance records from January through April 2003 has been renamed.

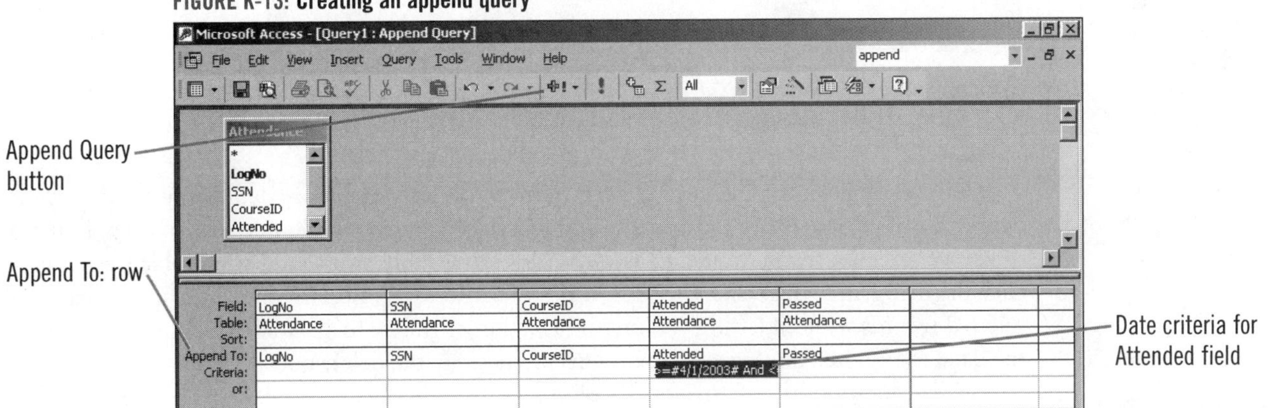

FIGURE K-13: Creating an append query

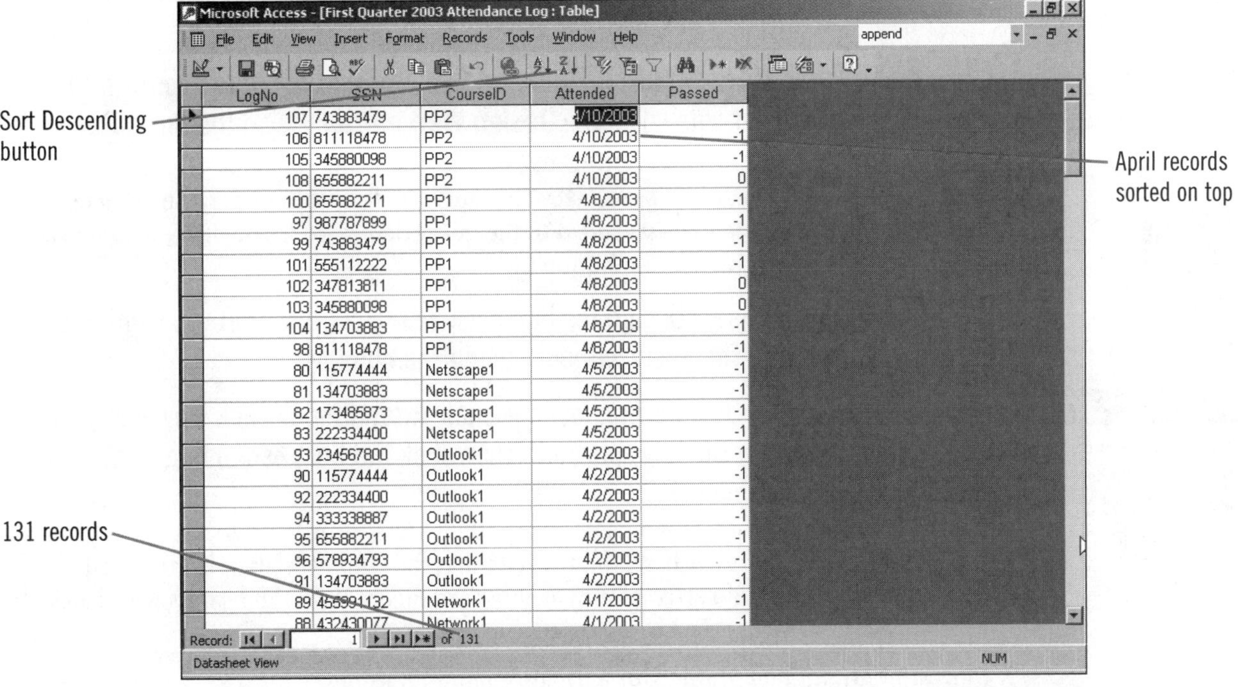

FIGURE K-14: Updated table with appended records

Access 2002

Access 2002

Creating a Delete Query

A **delete query** deletes a group of records from one or more tables as defined by a query. Delete queries always delete entire records, and not just selected fields within records, so they should be used very carefully. If you wanted to delete a field from a table, you would open Table Design View, click the field name, then click the **Delete Rows button**. Because the delete query deletes all selected records without letting you undo the action, it is wise to always have a current backup of the database before running any action query, especially the delete query. Now that Fred has the first four months of attendance records archived in the Jan-April 2003 Log table, he wants to delete them from the Attendance table. He uses a delete query to accomplish this task.

Steps 1 2 3 4

1. Click **Queries** on the Objects bar, double-click **Create query in Design view**, double-click **Attendance** in the Show Table dialog box, then click **Close**
2. Double-click the * **(asterisk)** at the top of the Attendance table's field list, then double-click the **Attended** field
   All the fields from the Attendance table are added to the first column of the query design grid by using the asterisk. The Attended field is added to the second column of the query design grid so you can enter limiting criteria for this field.
3. Click the **Attended field Criteria cell**, type **<=4/30/03**, then press **[Enter]**
   Before you initiate the delete action, check the datasheet to make sure that you have selected the same 131 records that were added to the Jan-April 2003 Log table.
4. Click the **Datasheet View button** on the Query Design toolbar to confirm that the datasheet has 131 records, click the **Design View button** on the Query Datasheet toolbar, click the **Query Type button list arrow**, then click **Delete Query**
   Your screen should look like Figure K-15. The Query Type button displays the Delete Query icon, and the Delete row was added to the query design grid. The delete action is ready to be initiated by clicking the Run button.
5. Click the on the Query Design toolbar, click **Yes** to confirm that you want to delete 131 rows, then close the query without saving the changes
6. Click **Tables** on the Objects bar, double-click **Attendance**, click **any entry in the LogNo field** (if it's not already selected), then click the **Sort Ascending button** on the Table Datasheet toolbar
   Sorting in ascending order by LogNo places the oldest records on top since LogNos are assigned in sequential order based on the date that the employee attends the actual course. The oldest records should start in May, as shown in Figure K-16. All records with dates earlier than 5/1/2003 were deleted by the delete query.
7. Close the Attendance datasheet without saving changes

QuickTip

The default sort order for the records in a datasheet is ascending order based on the values in the primary key field.

FIGURE K-15: Creating a delete query

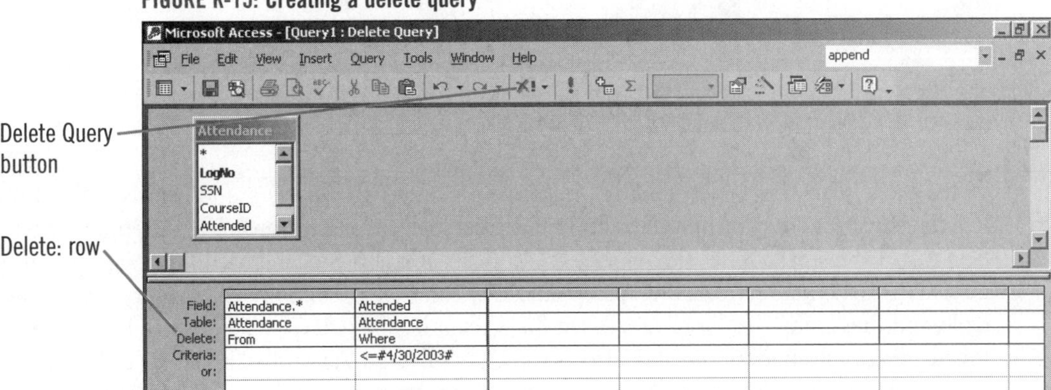

FIGURE K-16: Attendance table without January–April records

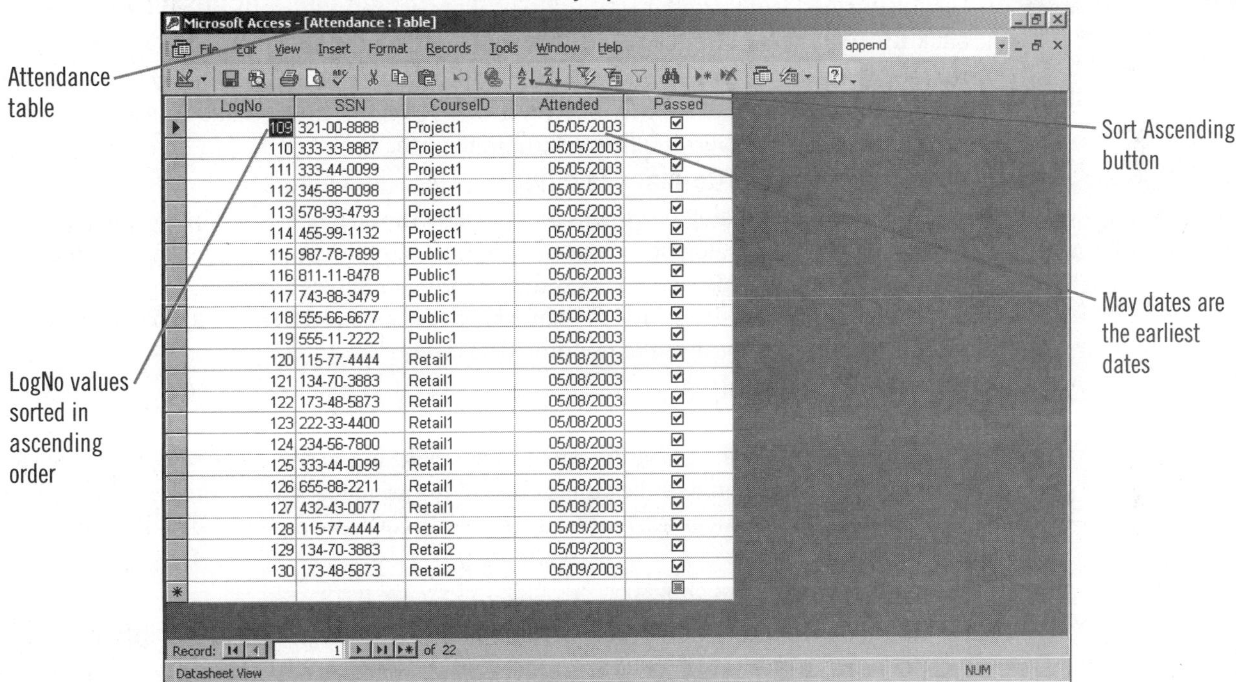

LogNo	SSN	CourseID	Attended	Passed
109	321-00-8888	Project1	05/05/2003	☑
110	333-33-8887	Project1	05/05/2003	☑
111	333-44-0099	Project1	05/05/2003	☑
112	345-88-0098	Project1	05/05/2003	☐
113	578-93-4793	Project1	05/05/2003	☑
114	455-99-1132	Project1	05/05/2003	☑
115	987-78-7899	Public1	05/06/2003	☑
116	811-11-8478	Public1	05/06/2003	☑
117	743-88-3479	Public1	05/06/2003	☑
118	555-66-6677	Public1	05/06/2003	☑
119	555-11-2222	Public1	05/06/2003	☑
120	115-77-4444	Retail1	05/08/2003	☑
121	134-70-3883	Retail1	05/08/2003	☑
122	173-48-5873	Retail1	05/08/2003	☑
123	222-33-4400	Retail1	05/08/2003	☑
124	234-56-7800	Retail1	05/08/2003	☑
125	333-44-0099	Retail1	05/08/2003	☑
126	655-88-2211	Retail1	05/08/2003	☑
127	432-43-0077	Retail1	05/08/2003	☑
128	115-77-4444	Retail2	05/09/2003	☑
129	134-70-3883	Retail2	05/09/2003	☑
130	173-48-5873	Retail2	05/09/2003	☑

Reviewing referential integrity

Referential integrity between two tables is established when tables are joined in the Relationships window. Referential integrity ensures that no orphaned records currently exist or are added to the database. Related tables have an **orphan record** when information in the foreign key field of the "many" table doesn't have a matching entry in the primary key field of the "one" table. An orphan record is sometimes called an **unmatched record**. The term "orphan" corresponds to general database terminology which often refers to the "one" table as containing **parent records**, and the "many" table as containing **child records**. Using this analogy, referential integrity means that a child record cannot be created without a corresponding parent record.

Access 2002

Specifying Join Properties

When more than one table's field list is used in a query, the tables are joined as defined in the Relationships window for the database. If referential integrity was enforced, a "1" appears next to the field that serves as the "one" side of the one-to-many relationship, and an infinity sign (∞) appears next to the field that serves as the "many" side. The "one" field is usually the primary key field for its table, and the "many" field is always called the foreign key field. If no relationships have been established, Access automatically creates join lines in Query Design View if the linking fields have the same name and data type in two tables. You can edit table relationships for an individual query in Query Design View by double-clicking the join line. Fred would like to create a query to find out which courses have never been attended. He modifies the join properties between the Attendance and Courses table to find this answer.

QuickTip

Right-click to the right of the field lists, then click Relationships to open the Relationships window.

Trouble?

Double-click the middle portion of the join line, not the "one" or "many" symbols, to open the Join Properties dialog box.

QuickTip

Filter criteria is not saved with query objects.

1. Click **Queries** on the Object bar, double-click **Create query in Design view**, double-click **Courses**, double-click **Attendance**, then click **Close**
   Because the Courses and Attendance tables already have a one-to-many relationship with referential integrity enforced in the Relationships window, the join line appears, linking the two tables using the CourseID field common to both.
2. Double-click the **one-to-many join line** between the field lists
   The Join Properties dialog box opens and displays the characteristics for the join, as shown in Figure K-17. The dialog box shows that option 1 is chosen, which means that the query will display only records where joined fields from *both* tables are equal. That means that if the Courses table has any records for which there are no matching Attendance records, those courses would not appear in the resulting datasheet.
3. Click the **2** option button
   By choosing option 2, you are specifying that you want to see ALL of the records in the Courses table, even if the Attendance table does not contain matching records. Because referential integrity is enforced, option 3 would be the same as option 1—referential integrity makes it impossible to enter records in the Attendance table that do not have a corresponding record in the Courses table.
4. Click **OK**
   The join line's appearance changes, as shown in Figure K-18.
5. Double-click **CourseID** from the Courses field list, double-click **Description** from the Courses field list, double-click **Attended** from the Attendance field list, then click the **Datasheet View button**
   All courses are now listed in the datasheet, regardless of whether anyone attended them. The courses without an entry in the Attended field are those that have never been taken. By using a filter, you can quickly isolate those courses.
6. Click the **Access1 Attended field** (it is null), then click the **Filter by Selection button** on the Query Datasheet toolbar
   The 25 filtered records represent the courses shown in Figure K-19. They contain a **null** (nothing) value in the Attended field, and represent the courses that have not been taken since May 1, 2003. (Recall that all records prior to this date were deleted from the Attendance table and added to the Jan-April 2003 Log table.)
7. Click the **Save button** on the Query Datasheet toolbar, type **No Attendance Since 5/1/03 – Your Initials** in the Query Name text box, click **OK**, click the **Access1 Attended field value**, click (to refilter for null values), then click the **Print button**
   If you wanted to permanently save the "is null" criteria for the Attended field, you would add it to Query Design View.
8. Close the datasheet without saving changes, then close the Training-K database

FIGURE K-17: Join Properties dialog box

Double-click join line to open the Join Properties dialog box

Default join property

FIGURE K-18: The join line's appearance changes when its properties are changed

Join line's appearance shows that *all* records from the Courses table will be included in the datasheet

FIGURE K-19: Filtering for courses with no attendance records

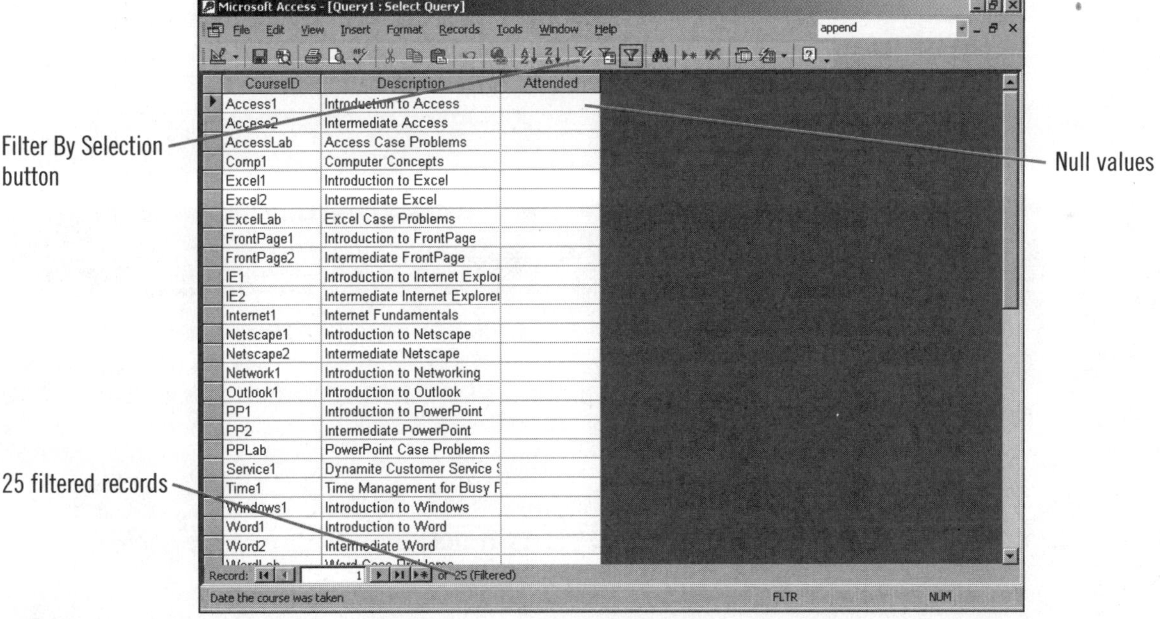

Filter By Selection button

Null values

25 filtered records

Finding duplicate and unmatched records

When referential integrity is enforced on a relationship before data is entered into a database, no one can enter a foreign key field value in the "many" table that doesn't already exist in a record on the "one" side of the relationship. Sometimes, though, you inherit a database in which referential integrity was not imposed from the beginning, and unmatched and duplicate records already exist in the database. Or, you may be asked to scrub, a database term for "find and correct," unmatched and duplicate records that are imported into your database from another source. The **Find Duplicates Query Wizard** and **Find Unmatched Query Wizard** can help you solve these database problems.

Access 2002

Practice

▶ Concepts Review

Identify each element of the Query Design View shown in Figure K-20.

FIGURE K-20

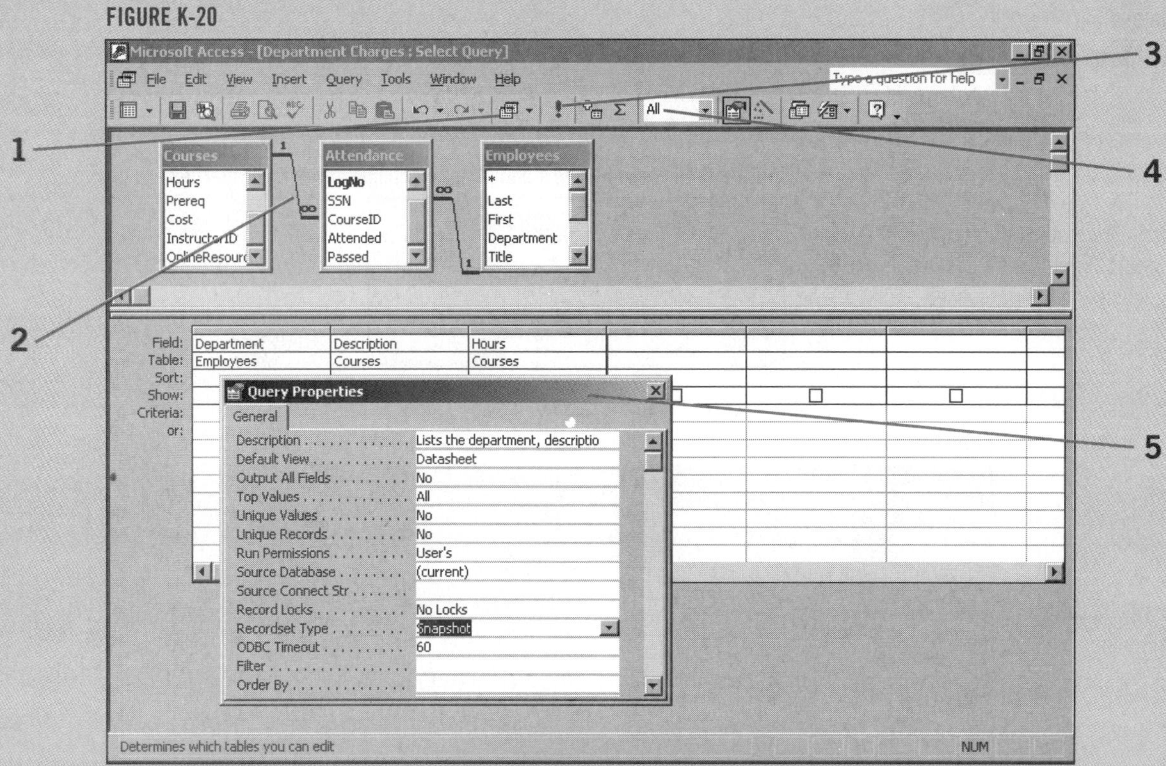

Match each term with the statement that describes its function.

6. Top values query	**a.** Displays a dialog box prompting you for criteria
7. Select query	**b.** Makes changes to data
8. Action query	**c.** Displays only a number or percentage of records from a sorted query
9. Properties	**d.** Displays fields and records that match specific criteria in a single datasheet
10. Snapshot	**e.** Makes the recordset not updateable
11. Parameter query	**f.** Characteristics that define the appearance and behavior of items within the database

Practice

Select the best answer from the list of choices.

12. Which entry for the Recordset Type query property will not allow you to modify the recordset?

- **a.** No Updates
- **b.** Snapshot
- **c.** Referential Integrity
- **d.** Dynaset (No Nulls)

13. Which of the following is a valid parameter criteria entry in the query design grid?

- **a.** >=(Type minimum value here:)
- **b.** >=Type minimum value here: }
- **c.** >=[Type minimum value here:]
- **d.** >=Type minimum value here:

14. You cannot use the Top Values feature to:

- **a.** Display a subset of records.
- **b.** Show the top 30 records.
- **c.** Update a field's value by 10 percent.
- **d.** Show the bottom 10 percent of records.

15. Which of the following is not an action query?

- **a.** Union query
- **b.** Delete query
- **c.** Make-table query
- **d.** Append query

16. Which of the following precautions should you take before running a delete query?

- **a.** Check the resulting datasheet to make sure the query selects the right records.
- **b.** Have a current backup of the database
- **c.** Understand the relationships between the records you are about to delete in the database.
- **d.** All of the above

17. When querying tables in a one-to-many relationship with referential integrity enforced, which records will appear (by default) on the resulting datasheet?

- **a.** Only those with matching values in both tables
- **b.** All records from the "one" table, and only those with matching values from the "many" side
- **c.** All records from the "many" table, and only those with nonmatching values from the "one" side
- **d.** All records from both tables will appear at all times

18. The process defined by an action query doesn't happen until you click which button?

- **a.** Properties
- **b.** Design View
- **c.** Save
- **d.** Run

Access 2002

19. **Which of the following queries is most often used to create a back-up copy of a table?**
    a. Update
    b. Delete
    c. Top Values
    d. Make-Table

20. **Where does an append query append the selected records?**
    a. To the first table in the current database
    b. To the last table in the current database
    c. To a new table in a new database
    d. To the target table which can be in the current or a different database

Skills Review

1. **Query for top values.**
   a. Start Access, then open the **Seminar-K** database from the drive and folder where your Project Files are located.
   b. Create a new select query with the EventName field from the Events table and the RegistrationFee field from the Registration table.
   c. Add the RegistrationFee field a second time, then click the Totals button on the Query Design toolbar. In the Total row of the query grid, Group By the EventName field, Sum the first RegistrationFee field, then Count the second Registration Fee field.
   d. Sort in descending order by the summed RegistrationFee field.
   e. Enter **2** in the Top Values list box to display the top two seminars in the datasheet.
   f. Save the query as **Top 2 Seminars – Your Initials**, view, print, then close the datasheet without saving it.

2. **Create a parameter query.**
   a. Create a new select query with the AttendeeLastName field from the Attendees table the RegistrationDate field from the Registration table, and the EventName field from the Events table.
   b. Add the parameter criteria **Between [Enter Start Date:] And [Enter End Date:]** in the Criteria cell for the RegistrationDate field.
   c. Specify an ascending sort order on the RegistrationDate field.
   d. Click the Datasheet View button, then enter **5/1/03** as the start date and **5/31/03** as the end date in order to find everyone who has attended a seminar in May of the year 2003. You should view 6 records.
   e. Save the query as **May Registration – Your Initials**, then print the datasheet.

3. **Modify query properties.**
   a. Open the May Attendance – Your Initials query in Query Design View, open the property sheet for the query, change the Recordset Type property to Snapshot, then close the Query Properties dialog box.
   b. Right-click the RegistrationDate field, then click Properties from the shortcut menu to open the Field Properties dialog box. Enter **Date of Registration** for the Caption property, change the Format property to Medium Date, then close the Field Properties dialog box.
   c. View the datasheet for records between **5/1/03** and **5/31/03**. Print, save, then close the datasheet.

4. **Create an update query.**
   a. Create a new select query, and select all the fields from the Registration table by double-clicking the Registration field list's title bar and dragging the selected fields to the query design grid.
   b. Enter **>=5/1/03** in the Criteria cell for the RegistrationDate field to find those records in which the

RegistrationDate is on or after 5/1/03. View the datasheet. Observe and note the values in the RegistrationFee field. There should be six records.

c. In Query Design View, change the query to an update query, then enter **[RegistrationFee]+5** in the RegistrationFee field Update To cell in order to increase each value in that field by $5.
d. Run the query to update the six records.
e. Using the Query Type button, change the query back to a select query, then view the datasheet to make sure that the RegistrationFee fields were updated properly.
f. Save the query as **Registration Fee Update – Your Initials**, print, then close the datasheet.

5. **Create a make-table query.**
   a. Create a new select query, and select all the fields from the Registration table by double-clicking the Registration field list's title bar and dragging the selected fields to the query design grid.
   b. Enter **<=3/31/03** in the Criteria cell for the RegistrationDate field to find those records in which the RegistrationDate is on or before 3/31/00.
   c. View the datasheet. There should be 15 records.
   d. In Query Design View, change the query into a make-table query that creates a new table in the current database. Give the new table the name **1Qtr2003 – Your Initials**.
   e. Run the query to paste 15 rows into the 1Qtr2003 – Your Initials table.
   f. Close the make-table query without saving it, click Tables on the Objects bar, open the 1Qtr2003 – Your Initials table, view the 15 records, print the datasheet, then close it.

6. **Create an append query.**
   a. Create a new select query, and select all the fields from the Registration table by double-clicking the Registration field list's title bar and dragging the selected fields to the query design grid.
   b. Enter **>=4/1/03 and <=4/30/03** in the Criteria cell for the RegistrationDate field to find those records in which the RegistrationDate is in April, 2003.
   c. View the datasheet. There should be one record.
   d. In Query Design View, change the query into an append query that appends to the 1Qtr2003 – Your Initials table.
   e. Run the query to append the row into the 1Qtr2003 – Your Initials table by clicking the Run button on the Query Design toolbar.
   f. Close the append query without saving it.
   g. Rename the 1Qtr2003 – Your Initials table to **Jan-Apr2003 –ß Your Initials**, open the datasheet (there should be 16 records), print it, then close it.

7. **Create a delete query.**
   a. Create a new select query, and select all the fields from the Registration table by double-clicking the Registration field list's title bar and dragging the selected fields to the query design grid.
   b. Enter <5/1/03 in the Criteria cell for the RegistrationDate field to find those records in which the RegistrationDate is before May 1, 2003.
   c. View the datasheet. There should be 16 records.
   d. In Query Design View, change the query into a delete query.
   e. Run the query to delete 16 records from the Registration table.
   f. Close the query without saving it.
   g. Open the Registration table in Datasheet View to confirm that there are only six records, then close it.

8. **Specify join properties.**
   a. Create a new select query with the following fields: AttendeeFirstName and AttendeeLastName from the Attendees table, and RegistrationFee from the Registration table.
   b. Double-click the link between the Attendees and Registration tables to open the Join Properties dialog box. Click the option button to include ALL records from Attendees and only those records from Registration where the joined fields are equal.
   c. View the datasheet, add your own first and last name as the last record, but do not enter anything in the RegistrationFee field for your record.
   d. Print the datasheet, save the query with the name **Registration Fee List**, then close the datasheet.
   e. Close the Seminar-K database, then exit Access.

Independent Challenge 1

As the manager of a college women's basketball team, you want to create several queries using the Basketball-K database.

a. Start Access, then open the **Basketball-K** database from the drive and folder where your Project Files are located.
b. Open the Player Stats query in Query Design View, then enter **Between [Enter start date:] and [Enter end date:]** in the Criteria cell for the Date field.
c. View the datasheet for all of the records between **1/1/2003** and **12/31/2003**. There should be 18 records.
d. Use the Save As option on the File menu to save the query with the name **2003 – Your Initials**, then print the datasheet.
e. In Query Design View of the 2003 – Your Initials query, sort the records in descending order on the TotalPts field, then use the **5%** Top Values option.
f. View the datasheet for all of the records between **1/1/2003** and **12/31/2003**. There should be two records.
g. Use the Save As option on the File menu to save the query with the name **2003 – Top 5% – Your Initials**. Print, then close the datasheet.
h. Open the Victories query in Query Design View, then add a new calculated field as the fifth field with the following field name and expression: **Win%:[Home Score]/[Opponent Score]**
i. View the datasheet to make sure that the Win% field calculates properly. Because the home score is generally greater than the opponent score, most values will be greater than 1.
j. In Query Design View, click the Win% field, click the Properties button, change the Format property of the Win% field to Percent and the Decimal Places property to **0**.
k. View the datasheet, use the Save As feature to save the query as **Victories – Your Initials**, print, then close it.
l. Close Basketball-K database, then exit Access.

Independent Challenge 2

As the manager of a college women's basketball team, you want to enhance the Basketball-K database and need to create several action queries using the Basketball-K database.

a. Start Access, then open the **Basketball-K** database from the drive and folder where your Project Files are located.
b. Create a new select query, and select all the fields from the Stats table by double-clicking the field list's title bar and dragging the selected fields to the query design grid.
c. Add criteria to find all of the records with the GameNo field equal to **1**, **2**, or **3**, then view the datasheet. There should be 18 records.
d. In Query Design View, change the query to a make-table query to paste the records into a table in the current database called **123 – Your Initials**.

e. Run the query to paste the 18 rows, then close the query without saving it.
f. Open the datasheet for the 123 – Your Initials table, then print it.
g. Create another new select query that includes all of the fields from the Stats table by double-clicking the field list's title bar and dragging the selected fields to the query design grid.
h. Add criteria to find all of the statistics for those records with the GameNo field equal to 4 or 5, then view the datasheet. There should be 12 records.
i. In Query Design View, change the query to an append query to append the records to the 123 – Your Initials table.
j. Run the query to append the 12 rows, then close the query without saving it.
k. Rename the 123 – Your Initials table to **12345 – Your Initials**, open the datasheet, then print it. There should be 30 records.
l. Close the 12345 – Your Initials table, close the Basketball-K database, then exit Access.

► Independent Challenge 3

As the manager of a college women's basketball team, you want to query the Basketball-K database to find specific information about each player.

a. Start Access, then open the **Basketball-K** database from the drive and folder where your Project Files are located.
b. Create a new select query in Query Design View using the Players and Stats tables.
c. Double-click the linking line to open the Join Properties dialog box, then change the join properties to include ALL records from Players and only those from Stats where the joined fields are equal.
d. Add the First and Last fields from the Players table, and the Assists fields from the Stats table.
e. Type **is null** in the Criteria cell for the Assists field, then view the datasheet to find those players who have never recorded an Assist value in the Stats table. There should be seven records.
f. Add your name as the last record, but do not enter an Assists value for this record.
g. Print the datasheet, save the query as **Redshirts**, then close the datasheet.
h. Close Basketball-K, then exit Access.

Independent Challenge 4

Your culinary club is collecting information on international chocolate factories and museums, and has asked you to help build a database to organize the information.

a. Start Access, then open the **Chocolate-K** database from the drive and folder where your Project Files are located.
b. Open the Places of Interest report, then print it.
c. Connect to the Internet, then go to a search engine such as www.google.com or www.about.com to search for information about international chocolate factories and museums. Or, you might look for information by going directly to a chocolate company's home page and searching for places to visit from there. Your goal is to find a Web page with information about an international chocolate factory or museum to add to the existing database, and to print that Web page.
d. Using the Countries form, add the record you found on the World Wide Web to the database, then close the Countries form.
e. Open the Places of Interest query in Query Design View, double-click the link line between the Countries and ChocolatePlaces tables, then choose option 2, which includes ALL records from the Countries table.
f. Open the Places of Interest report in Report Design View, add your name as a label to the header, preview, then print the report. On the printout, circle the record you added to the database. On the printout, circle any countries that do NOT have any related records in the ChocolatePlaces table.
g. Close the Places of Interest report, close Chocolate-K, then exit Access.

 Visual Workshop

As the manager of a college women's basketball team, you want to create a query from the **Basketball-K** database with the fields from the Players and Stats tables as shown. The query is a parameter query that prompts the user for a start and end date. Figure K-21 shows the datasheet where the start date of 1/1/03 and end date of 1/31/03 are used. Save and name the query **Offense – Your Initials**, then print the datasheet.

FIGURE K-21

Query1 : Select Query

First	Last	FG	3P	FT	Date
Lindsey	Swift	3	2	1	1/2/2003
Ellyse	Howard	3	0	1	1/2/2003
Amy	Hodel	0	0	1	1/2/2003
Denise	Franco	4	1	3	1/2/2003
Megan	Hile	1	2	1	1/2/2003
Morgan	Tyler	3	0	3	1/2/2003
Lindsey	Swift	4	2	3	1/5/2003
Ellyse	Howard	4	0	4	1/5/2003
Amy	Hodel	2	0	5	1/5/2003
Denise	Franco	1	2	1	1/5/2003
Megan	Hile	1	0	1	1/5/2003
Morgan	Tyler	1	0	5	1/5/2003
Lindsey	Swift	4	2	3	1/9/2003
Ellyse	Howard	4	1	3	1/9/2003
Amy	Hodel	2	1	5	1/9/2003
Denise	Franco	5	1	1	1/9/2003

Record: 1 of 18

Access 2002

Unit L

Creating
Advanced Forms and Reports

Objectives

- MOUS ▶ Add check boxes and toggle buttons
- MOUS ▶ Use conditional formatting in a form
- MOUS ▶ Create custom Help
- MOUS ▶ Add tab controls
- MOUS ▶ Add charts
- MOUS ▶ Modify charts
- MOUS ▶ Add subreport controls
- MOUS ▶ Modify section properties

Advanced controls such as tab controls, charts, and subreports are powerful communication tools. Conditional formatting allows you to highlight exceptional information within a form or report to more clearly present key information. Using these advanced features to enhance forms and reports improves the value of your database. Fred Ames, coordinator of training at MediaLoft, wants to enhance existing forms and reports to more professionally and clearly present the information. Fred will use form and report controls such as check boxes, conditional formatting, tab controls, charts, and subreports to improve the forms and reports in the Training-L database.

Access 2002

Adding Check Boxes and Toggle Buttons

A **check box** control is often used to display the value of a Yes/No field on a form or report. A check box can appear in only one of two ways: checked or unchecked. A check means "Yes," and the absence of a check means "No." It is much easier to answer Yes/No questions on a form by clicking a check box rather than typing the word "Yes" in a text box. A **toggle button** control can also display the value of a Yes/No field. You click a toggle button to change the value from "No" to "Yes" just like a check box. When a toggle button appears indented or pushed in, it means "Yes," and when appears raised or not pushed in, it means "No." By default, Access represents any field with a Yes/No data type as a check box control on a form, regardless of whether the field was added to the form through the Form Wizard, AutoForm options, or in Form Design View. Fred would like to improve the visual appeal of the Employee Course Attendance form and Attendance Subform.

1. Open the **Training-L** database, click **Forms** on the Objects bar, then double-click the **Employee Course Attendance form**
   The form opens in Form View. The Attendance Subform is presented as a datasheet.
2. Click the **Design View button** on the Form View toolbar, then maximize the Employee Course Attendance form
   Your screen should look like Figure L-1. To change the appearance of the controls on the subform, you must change the **Default View** property for the form from Datasheet (which allows no special formatting) to Continuous Forms.
3. Click the **subform** to select it, double-click the subform's **Form Selector button**, click the **Format tab** (if not already selected) on the Form property sheet, click **Datasheet** in the Default View property, click the **Default View list arrow**, then click **Continuous Forms**
4. Click the **Properties button** on the Form Design toolbar, then click the **Form View button** on the Form Design toolbar
   Because of the change to the subform's Default View property, the subform displays the records as continuous forms, the way they also appear in Form Design View, rather than as a datasheet.
5. Click on the Form View toolbar, right-click the **Passed check box** in the subform, point to **Change To**, then click **Toggle Button**
   Table L-1 provides more information on which controls are interchangeable.
6. Point to the **middle-right resize handle** on the toggle button, drag ⟷ to the right edge of the form, click the **toggle button**, type **Passed the test?**, then click
   Your screen should look similar to Figure L-2. You also can change the text displayed on the button using the Caption property on the Format tab in the toggle button's property sheet.
7. Click the **Save button** on the Form View toolbar
   The changes are saved to the Employee Course Attendance form and the Attendance Subform.
8. Close the Employee Course Attendance form

Trouble?

If the subform appears as a white rectangle, click the Form View button, then click the Design View button to refresh the screen.

FIGURE L-1: Form and subform in Form Design View

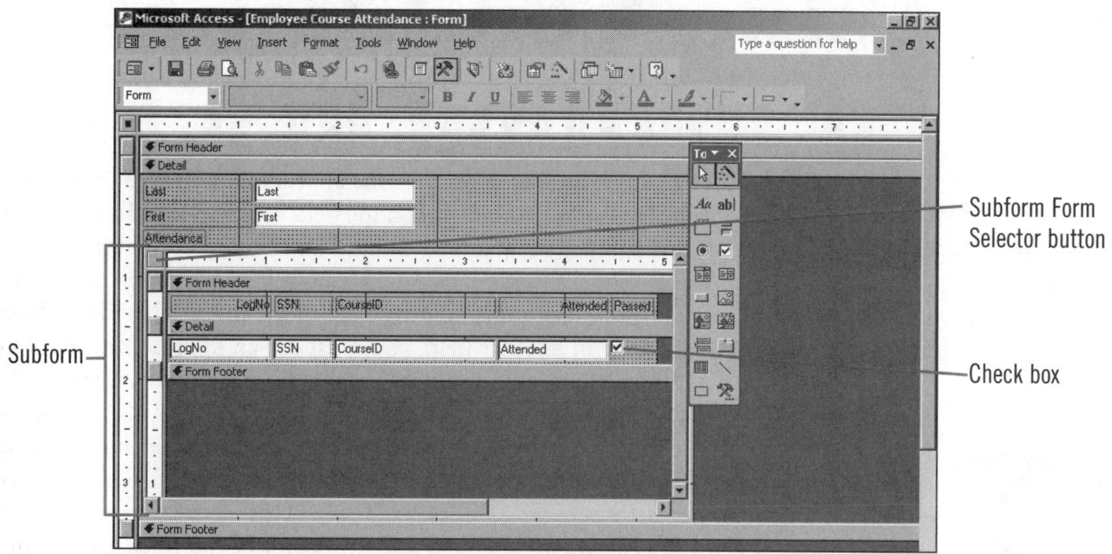

FIGURE L-2: Toggle buttons displaying "Yes" and "No" values

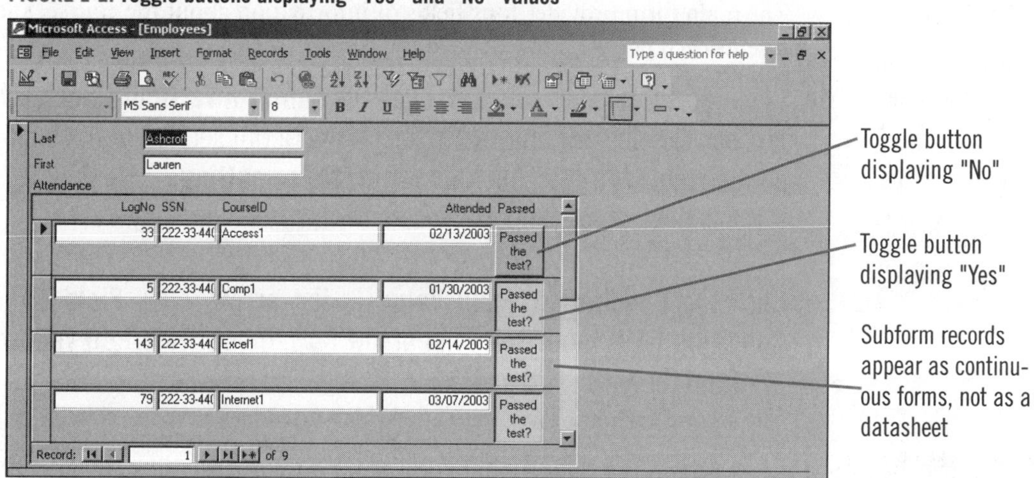

TABLE L-1: Interchangeable bound controls

control	Toolbox toolbar button	can be interchanged with	used most commonly when the field has
Text box	abl	List box, combo box	An unlimited number of choices such as a Price, LastName, or Street field
List box		Text box, combo box	A limited number of predefined values such as a Manager, Department, or State field
Combo box		Text box, list box	A limited number of common values, yet you still need the ability to enter a new value from the keyboard, such as a City field
Check box		Toggle button, option button	Only two values, "Yes" or "No," such as a Veteran field
Option button		Check box, toggle button	A limited number of values, such as "female" or "male" for a Gender field; most commonly used with an option group that can contain several option buttons, each representing a possible value for the field
Toggle button		Check box, option button	Only two values, "Yes" or "No," and you want the appearance of the field to look like a button

Access 2002

Using Conditional Formatting in a Form

Conditional Formatting can be used to determine the appearance of a field on a form or report based on its value, a value in another field, or when the field has the focus. **Focus** is when a field can receive user input through the keyboard or mouse. Conditional formatting also provides a way to alert the user to exceptional situations as data is being entered or reported. Format changes include changing the text color, background color, or style of the control. If you conditionally format a control based on a value in another field, you must use an **expression**, which contains a combination of field names, operators, and values that calculate an answer. The users of the Courses form (which includes the Course-Employee Subform) would like Fred to modify the form so that they can quickly identify those course attendees with the title of "Salesperson." Additionally, Fred uses conditional formatting to more clearly show which text box has the focus.

Steps

Trouble?

If the subform appears as a white rectangle, click the Form View button, then click the Design View button to refresh the screen.

QuickTip

You can include up to three conditions in the Conditional Formatting dialog box.

1. Double-click the **Courses form**, view the overall layout of the form and subform, then click the **Design View button** on the Form View toolbar

   The main form provides four fields of information about the course, and the subform represents each person who attended the course.

2. Click the **subform** to select it, click the **subform vertical ruler** to the left of the Last text box to select all four text boxes in the Detail section of the subform, click **Format** on the menu bar, then click **Conditional Formatting**

   The Conditional Formatting dialog box opens. The first condition will highlight the field with the focus.

3. Click the **Condition 1 Field Value Is list arrow**, click **Field Has Focus**, click the **Condition 1 Fill/Back Color list arrow**, then click **bright yellow** (fourth row, third box from the left)

   The second condition will highlight which attendees have the title of "Salesperson."

4. Click **Add** in the Conditional Formatting dialog box, click the **Condition 2 Field Value Is list arrow**, click **Expression Is**, press **[Tab]**, type **[Title]="Salesperson"**, click the **Condition 2 Bold button**, click the **Condition 2 Font/Fore Color list arrow**, then click **bright red** (third row, first box from the left)

   Your screen should look like Figure L-3. When an expression is used in the Conditional Formatting dialog box, the expression must evaluate to be either "true," which turns the formatting on, or "false," which turns the formatting off.

5. Click **OK**, click the **Form View button** on the Form Design toolbar, then click **Lee** (the value in the Last field for the first record) in the subform

   Your screen should look like Figure L-4.

6. Press **[Tab]** three times to move the focus to the Salesperson entry for the first record, type **Sales Manager**, then press **[Tab]**

   Your screen should look like Figure L-5, in which the values in the first record in the subform are no longer red and boldface. Conditional formatting reverts to default formatting if the condition is no longer true.

7. Save, then close the Courses form

FIGURE L-3: Conditional Formatting dialog box

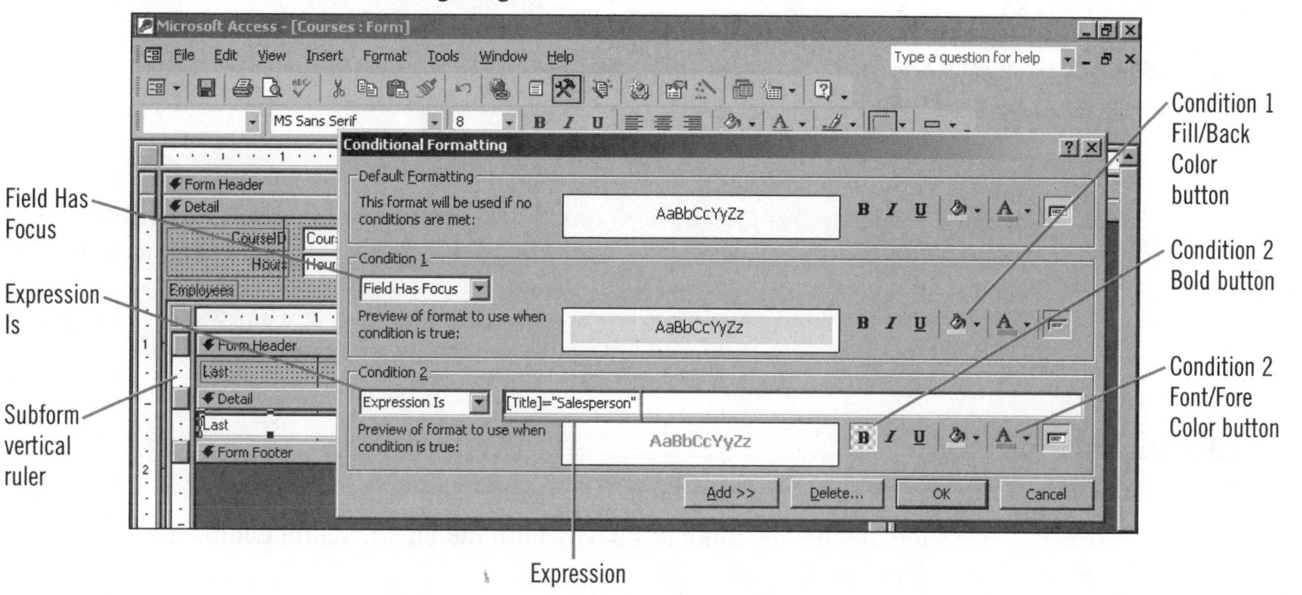

FIGURE L-4: The control with the focus has a bright yellow back color

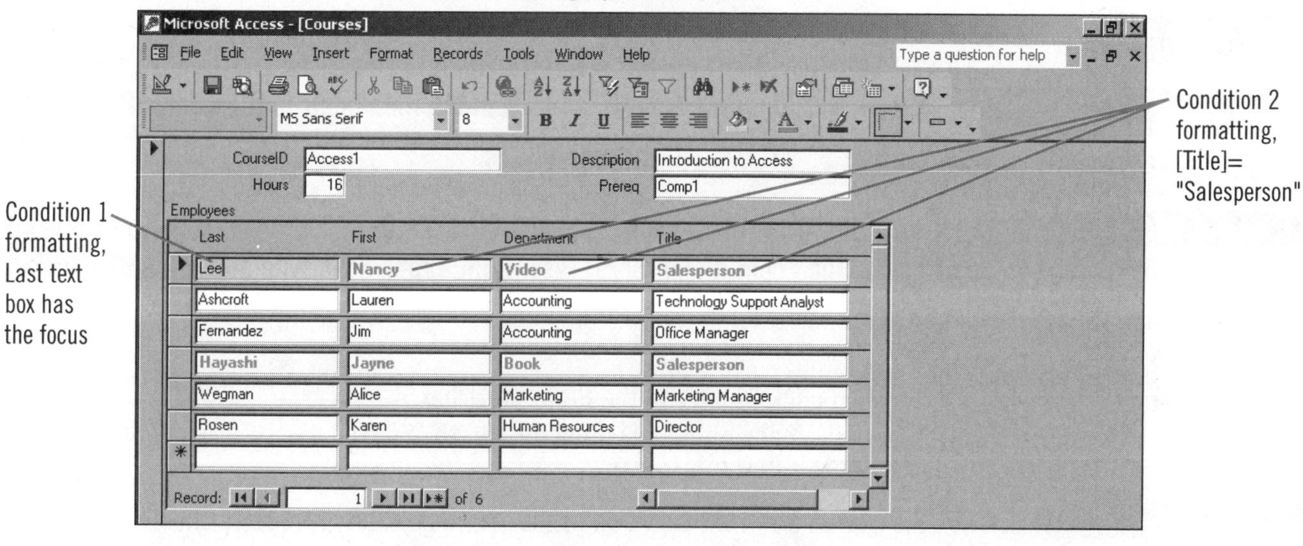

FIGURE L-5: Conditional formats change as data is edited

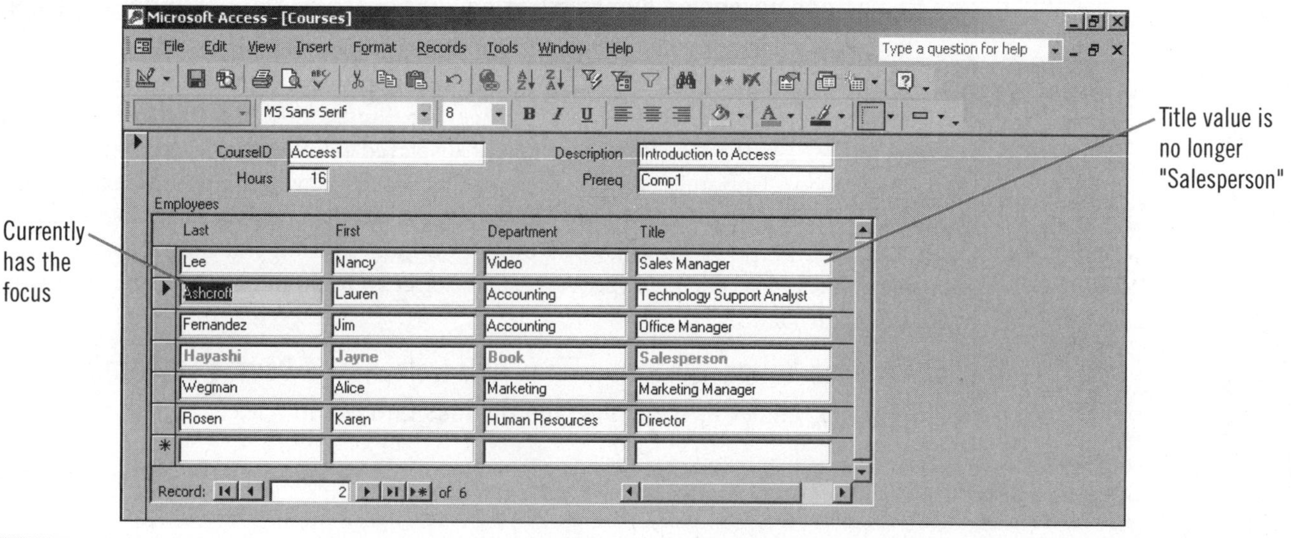

Access 2002

Creating Custom Help

You can create several types of custom Help for a form or a control on a form. If you want to display a textual tip that pops up over a control when you point to it, use the **ControlTip Text** property for that control. Or use the **Status Bar Text** property to display helpful information about a form or control in the status bar. Fred wants to allow other users to enter new course records as those courses become available. He quickly creates a new form based on the Courses table, then adds custom Help to guide the new users as they enter the data.

Steps

Trouble?

The AutoForm tool uses the same AutoFormat that was chosen during the Form Wizard process. Therefore, your form may not have a standard AutoFormat as shown in the figures.

1. Click the **New button** in the Database window toolbar, click **AutoForm: Columnar**, click the **Choose the table or query where the object's data comes from list arrow**, click **Courses**, then click **OK**
   The Courses form is created. You can modify the ControlTip Text and Status Bar Text properties for text boxes and other bound controls in Form View.
2. Click **View** on the menu bar, click **Properties**, click the **Other tab** in the Text Box: CourseID property sheet, click the **ControlTip Text property text box**, type **Use a 1 suffix for an introductory course**, press **[Enter]**, then point to the **CourseID text box**
   A control tip pops up, as shown in Figure L-6. You can view and enter long entries using the Zoom dialog box.

QuickTip

Click a property, then press [Shift][F2] to open the Zoom dialog box for that property.

3. Right-click the **ControlTip Text property**, click **Zoom**, click to the right of the word **"course"** in the Zoom dialog box, press **[Spacebar]**, then type **and a 2 suffix for an intermediate course**
   The Zoom dialog box should look like Figure L-7.
4. Click **OK**, then click **Comp1** in the Prereq text box
   The property sheet now shows the properties for the Prereq text box (even though the title bar still shows Text Box: CourseID).

QuickTip

Click a property, then press [F1] to open the Microsoft Access Help window for the specific explanation of that property.

5. Click the **Status Bar Text text box** in the Text Box: Prereq property sheet
   When the property sheet is open, a short description of the selected property appears in the status bar.
6. Type **Comp1 can be waived by achieving an 80% score on the Computers 101 test**, close the property sheet, then point to the **CourseID text box**
   Your screen should look like Figure L-8. The status bar displays the entry in the Status Bar Text property for the Prereq text box because the Prereq text box has the focus. The ControlTip Text for the CourseID text box is displayed because you are pointing to the CourseID text box. Unbound controls such as labels do not have a Status Bar Text property because they cannot have the focus, but a label can display ControlTip Text. To modify the ControlTip Text property for a label or other unbound control, you must be able to first select the control to access its property sheet. To select an unbound control, you must work in Form Design View.
7. Click the **Save button** on the Form View toolbar, type **Course Entry** in the Form Name text box, click **OK**, then close the Courses Entry form

FIGURE L-6: Using the ControlTip Text property

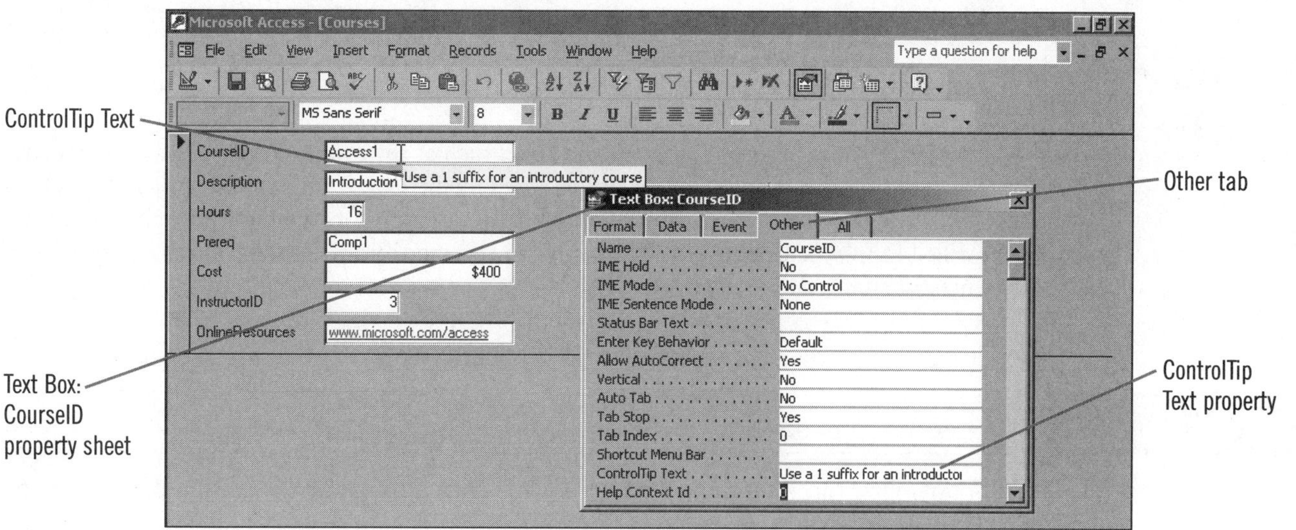

FIGURE L-7: Zoom dialog box

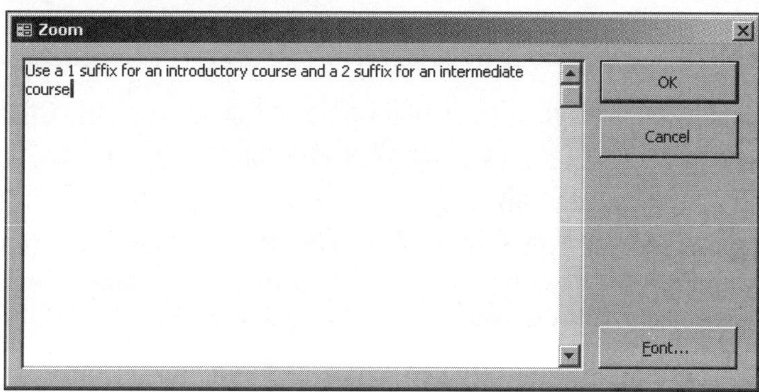

FIGURE L-8: Using the Status Bar Text property

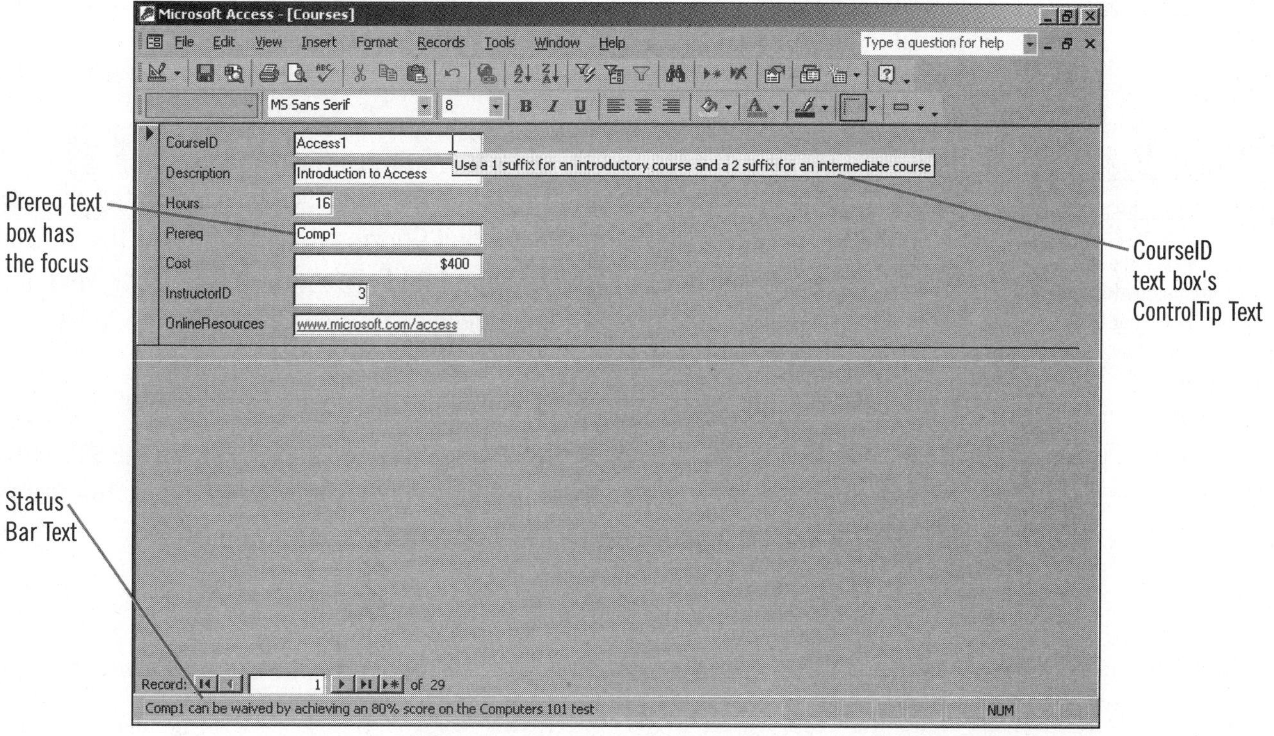

Access 2002

Adding Tab Controls

The **tab control** is a powerful unbound control used to organize the controls on a form and to give the form a three-dimensional look. You are already familiar with using tab controls because you have used them in many Access dialog boxes such as the property sheet. The property sheet uses tab controls to organize properties identified by their category name such as Format, Data, Event, Other, and All. Fred created a form to be used for many employee update activities called Employee Update Form. He wants to add tab controls to the form to better organize and present some of the information.

Steps

1. Right-click the **Employee Update Form**, click **Design View** on the shortcut menu, click the **Toolbox button** to toggle the Toolbox on (if it is not already visible), click the **Tab Control button** on the Toolbox toolbar, then click immediately below the **First text box** in the Detail section of the form
   Your screen should look like Figure L-9. By default, the tab control is added with two "pages," with the default names of Page17 and Page18, on the respective tabs.

QuickTip

To add more pages, right-click the tab control in Form Design View, then click Insert Page on the shortcut menu.

2. Double-click **Page17** to open its property sheet, click the **Other tab** (if it is not already selected), double-click **Page17** in the Name property text box, type **Personnel Info**, click the **Page18 tab** on the form, double-click **Page18** in the Name text box of the property sheet, type **Course Attendance**, then close the property sheet
   The tabs now describe the information they will organize, but you still need to add the appropriate controls to each page of the tab control.

QuickTip

The page will become dark gray when you are successfully adding control(s) to that page.

3. Click the **Personnel Info tab**, click the **Field List button** on the Form Design toolbar to toggle it on (if it is not already visible), click **Department** in the field list, press and hold **[Shift]**, click **SSN** in the field list (you may have to scroll) to select all fields between the Department and SSN, release **[Shift]**, then drag the **highlighted fields** to the top middle area of the Personnel Info page
   Your screen should look similar to Figure L-10. The six fields are added to the Personnel Info page on the tab control.

Trouble?

The Control Wizards button must be selected before you click the Subform/Subreport button on the Toolbox toolbar in order to use the SubForm Wizard.

4. Click the **Course Attendance tab**, click the **Subform/Subreport button** on the Toolbox toolbar, click the **Course Attendance page**, click **Yes** if prompted to install the wizard, click the **Use existing Tables and Queries** option button in the SubForm Wizard dialog box, click **Next**, click the **Select All Fields button** >>, click **Next**, click **Show Attendance for each record in Employees using SSN** (if not already selected), click **Next**, type **Attendance Info**, then click **Finish**
   You can add any type of control, even a subform control, to a tab control page.
5. Use ↔ to drag the left-middle and right-middle sizing handles of the subform to the edges of the main form, click the **Form View button**, click the **Course Attendance tab**, then maximize the Employee Update Form window
   Your screen should look similar to Figure L-11.
6. Save, then close the Employee Update Form

FIGURE L-9: Adding a tab control

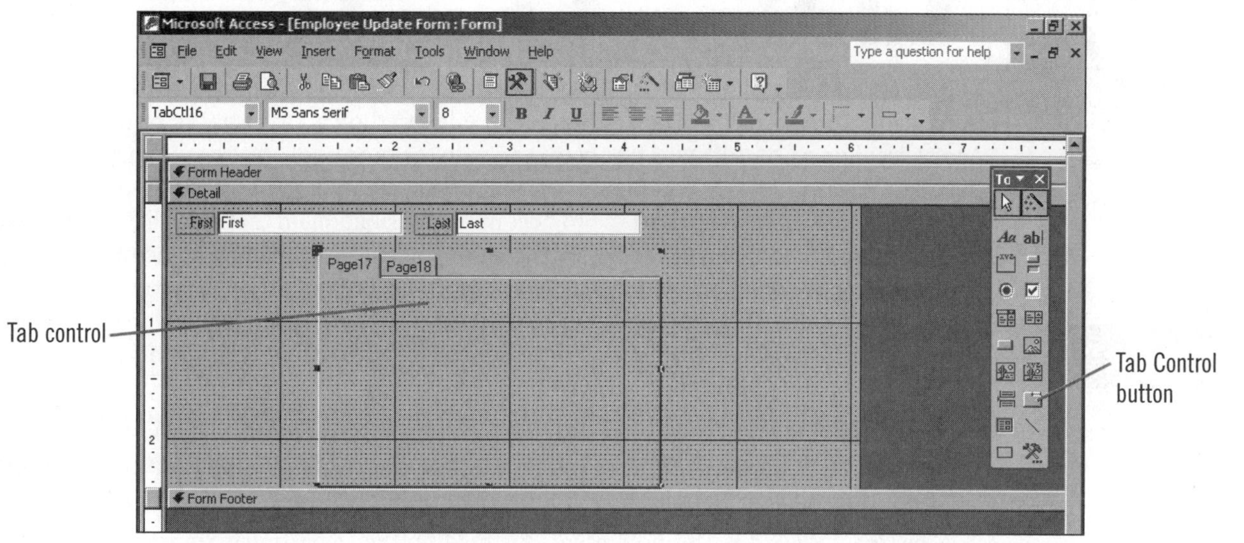

FIGURE L-10: Adding fields to a page on a tab control

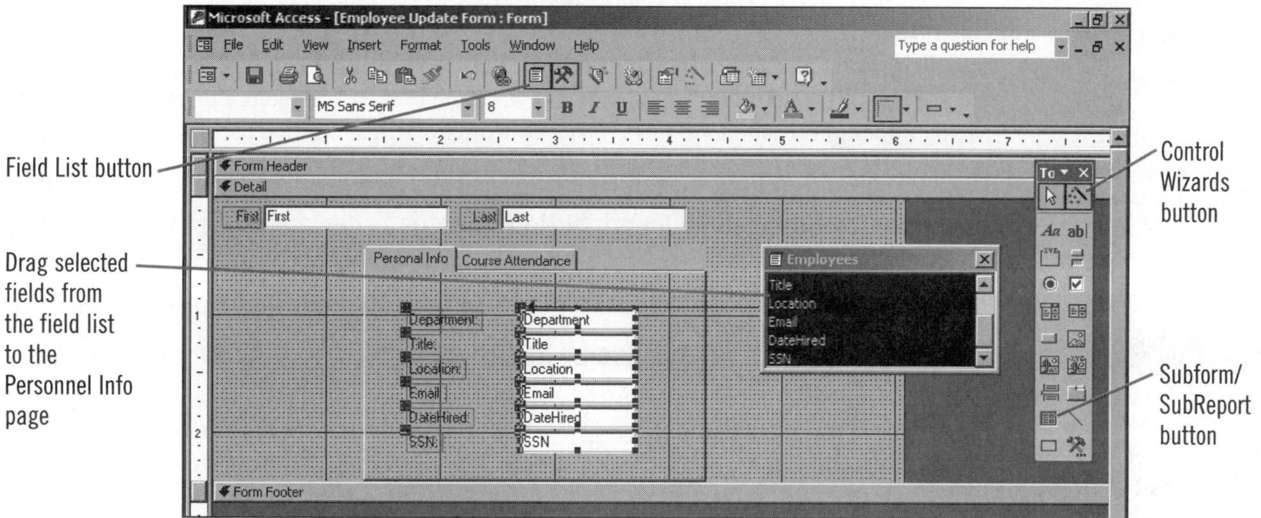

FIGURE L-11: The tab control in Form View

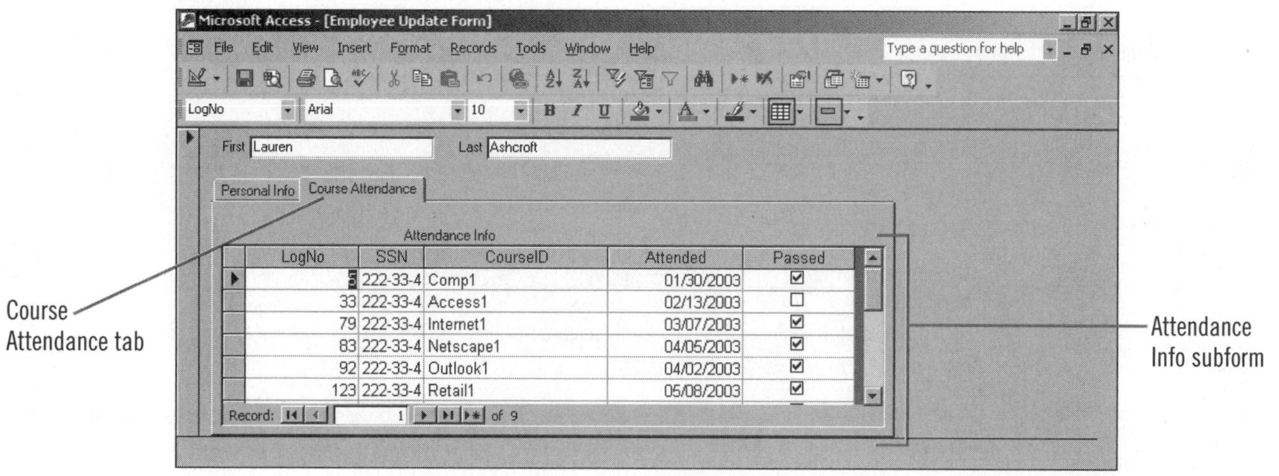

Access 2002

Adding Charts

Charts, also called graphs, are visual representations of numeric data that help users see comparisons, patterns, and trends in data. Charts can be inserted on a form, report, or data access page. Access provides a **Chart Wizard** that helps you with the process of creating the chart. Before using the Chart Wizard, however, you should determine what data you want the graph to show and what chart type you want to use. Table L-2 provides more information on common chart types. Fred created a Department Summary query with two fields: Attended from the Attendance table, and Department from the Employees table. Instead of reporting this information as a datasheet of values, he uses the Chart Wizard to graphically display both a total count of employees who attended internal MediaLoft courses, and a count of employees subtotaled by department.

1. Click **Reports** on the Objects bar, click the **New button** in the database window toolbar, click **Chart Wizard**, click the **Choose the table or query where the object's data comes from list arrow**, click **Department Summary**, then click **OK**
   The Chart Wizard starts and presents the fields in the Department Summary query.

QuickTip

Click any chart button to read a description of that chart in the lower-right corner of the Chart Wizard dialog box.

2. Click the **Select All Fields button** >>, then click **Next**
   The Chart Wizard lists the chart types that you can create, as shown in Figure L-12. The Column Chart is the default chart type.
3. Click **Next**
   The next dialog box determines which fields will be used for the x-axis, bar, and series (legend) areas of the chart. For this chart, you want the bars to represent a total count of number of values in the Attended field. The Department field should be used as x-axis labels.

QuickTip

Double-click a button in the Data area to change the way it is summarized.

4. Drag the **Attended field button** from the field buttons on the right to the **Data** area, then drag the **Attended by month button** from the Series area out of the chart area, as shown in Figure L-13
   Because the Attended field holds date data, bars should count the number of entries.

Trouble?

Depending on the size of your chart, the scale on the y-axis, the labels on the x-axis, or the chart title may appear slightly different.

5. Click **Next**, type **Total Attendance by Department** as the title for your chart text box, then click **Finish**
   Your chart should look similar to Figure L-14. The chart is difficult to read as it currently appears, but you can modify a chart in Design View to improve its appearance.

TABLE L-2: Common chart types

chart type	chart icon	most commonly used to show	example
Column		Comparisons of values	Each bar represents the annual sales for a different product for the year 2003
Line		Trends over time	Each point on the line represents monthly sales for one product for the year 2003
Pie 2003		Parts of a whole	Each slice represents total quarterly sales for a company for the year
Area		Cumulative totals	Each section represents monthly sales by representative, stacked to show the cumulative total sales effort for the year 2003

FIGURE L-12: Chart types

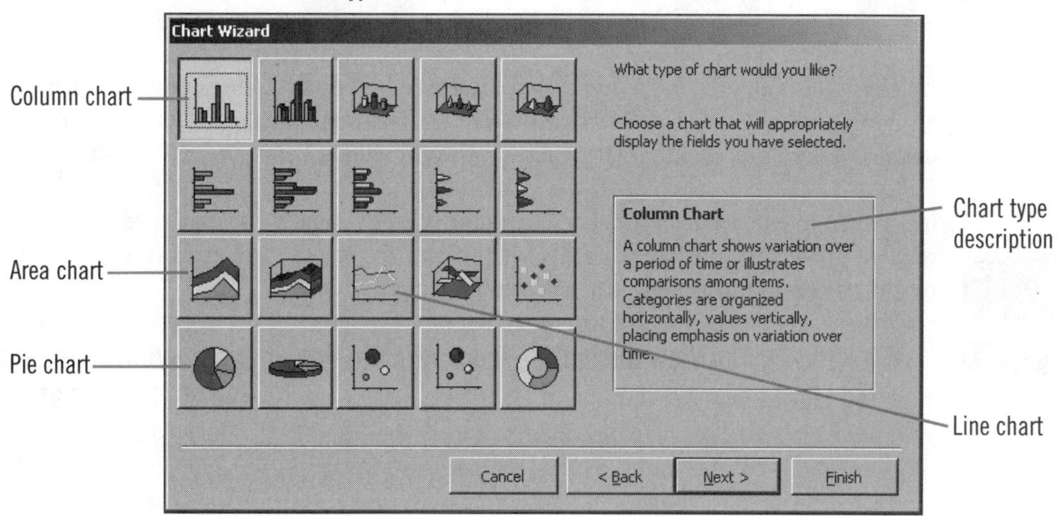

FIGURE L-13: Determining chart layout

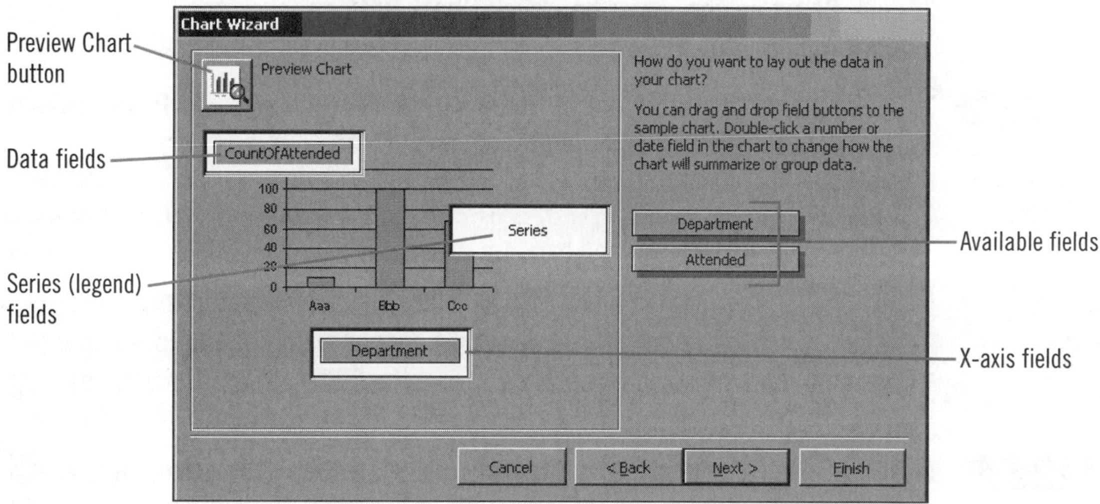

FIGURE L-14: Total Attendance by Department chart

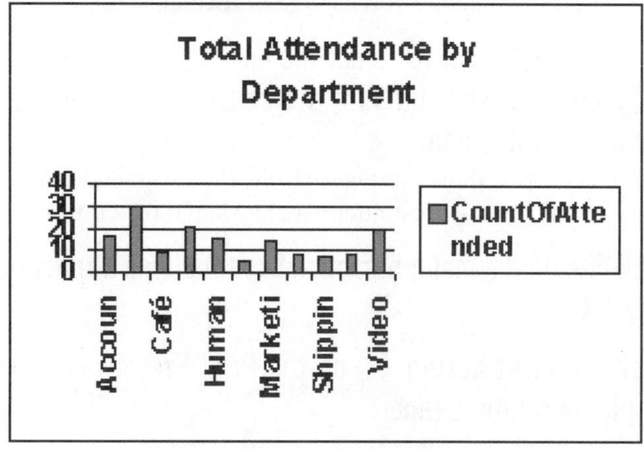

Access 2002

Access 2002

Modifying Charts

All charts are modified in Design View of the form or report that contains the chart. Modifying a chart is challenging because Design View doesn't show you the actual chart values, but instead, displays a chart placeholder that represents the embedded chart object. To modify the chart, you modify the chart placeholder. To view the changes as they apply to the real data you are charting, return to either Form View for a form, or Print Preview for a report. Fred wants to remove the legend and resize the chart to better display the values on the axes. He makes all modifications to the existing chart in Report Design View.

QuickTip

Drag the title bar of the Chart datasheet to move it.

Trouble?

Depending on the size of your chart, the scale on the y-axis, the labels on the x-axis, or the chart title may appear slightly different.

Trouble?

You must expand *both* the size of the chart placeholder *and* the Chart Area in order to successfully resize the chart to display all elements clearly.

1. Click the **Design View button**, maximize the Report Design View window, click the **Field List button** to close it (if it's visible), then double-click the **chart** to edit it

   The chart is now ready to be edited, as shown in Figure L-15. The hashed border of the chart placeholder control indicates that the chart is in **edit mode**, and the Chart menu bar and Chart Standard toolbar appear. You can delete, move, or resize the chart object without being in edit mode, but if you want to modify any of the individual chart elements such as the title, legend, or axes, you must double-click the chart placeholder to open edit mode. In edit mode, you can select and then modify individual items within the chart. If you double-click the *edge* of the chart placeholder, you will open its property sheet instead of opening it in edit mode.

2. Click **Chart** on the menu bar, click **Chart Options**, click the **Legend tab**, click the **Show legend check box** to toggle it off, then click **OK**

3. Click **outside the chart** to exit Chart edit mode, then click the **Print Preview button** on the Report Design toolbar

   Your chart should look similar to Figure L-16. Because the chart has only one series of bars, a clear title (rather than a legend) is used to describe the series. But most of the elements, including the x-axis labels and bars, are still too small to clearly display the information.

4. Click on the Print Preview toolbar, click the **chart placeholder** to select the control, then use to drag the **lower-right corner sizing handle** down and to the right to the **5"** mark on the horizontal ruler and the **3.5"** mark on the vertical ruler

   With the chart placeholder resized, you can expand the size of the chart within it.

5. Double-click the **chart placeholder**, click the **View Datasheet button** on the Chart Standard toolbar to toggle it off, then use to drag the **lower-right corner sizing handle** of the Chart Area (identified by the hashed border) to just within the border of the chart placeholder

   Your chart should look similar to Figure L-17. You can modify any element such as the labels on the x-axis, also called the Category Axis, or the y-axis, also called the Value Axis, but you must select them before you change or format them.

6. Click the **East label** to select the entire Category Axis, click the **Font Size list arrow** 8.5, click **10**, click **outside the chart** to exit chart edit mode, then click on the Report Design toolbar

   The final chart is shown in Figure L-18. It clearly shows that of all the departments, the Book Department has the most attendees at MediaLoft's internal training courses.

7. Click **File** on the menu bar, click **Save As**, type **Department Graph-Your Initials**, then click **OK**

8. Click the **Print button** on the Print Preview toolbar, then close the Department Graph-Your Initials report

FIGURE L-15: **Editing a chart in Design View**

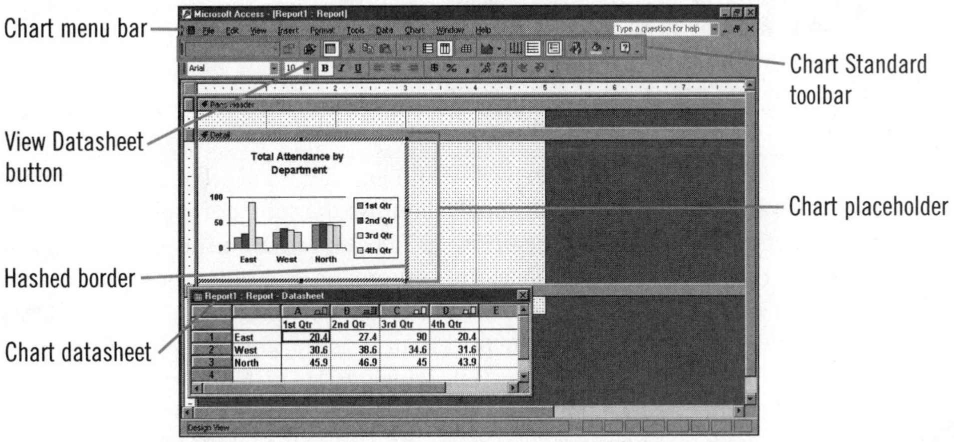

Chart menu bar

Chart Standard toolbar

View Datasheet button

Chart placeholder

Hashed border

Chart datasheet

FIGURE L-16: **Chart still needs improvement**

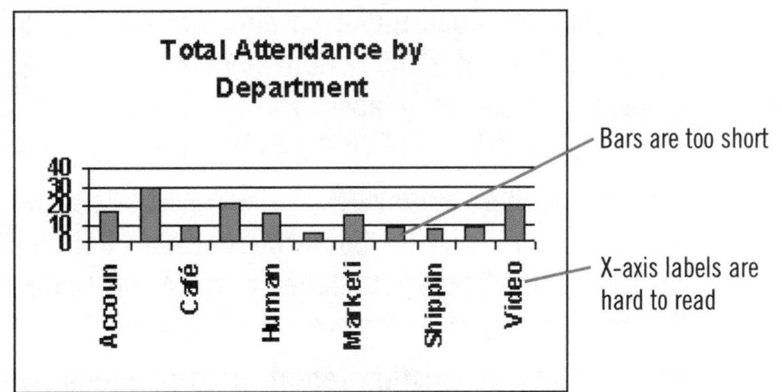

FIGURE L-17: **Increasing the chart size**

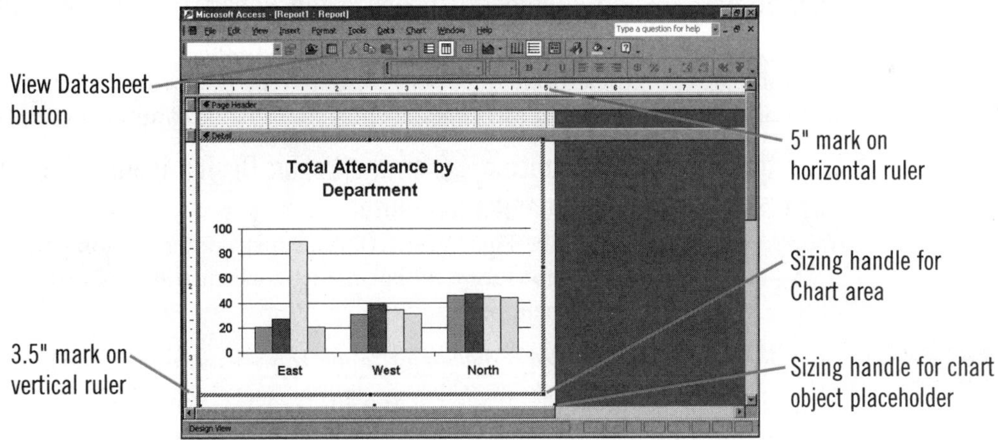

FIGURE L-18: **Final chart**

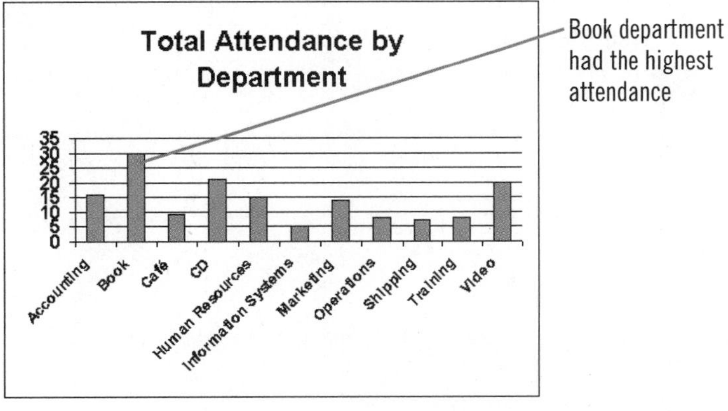

Access 2002

Adding Subreport Controls

A **subreport** control displays a report within another report. The report that contains the subreport control is called the **main report**. You use the subreport control when you want to link two reports together to automate printing. You also can use a subreport control when you want to change the order in which information automatically prints. For example, if you want report totals (generally found in the Report Footer section, which prints on the last page) to print on the first page, you could use a subreport to present the grand total information, and place it in the main report's Report Header section, which prints first. Now that Fred has created the Department Graph report, he will add it as a subreport to the Department Enrollment report so that both reports are viewed and printed at the same time.

Steps

1. Right-click the **Department Enrollment** report, click **Design View** on the shortcut menu, scroll, point to the **bottom edge** of the report, then use ‡ to drag the bottom edge of the report down about **1"**
   You've expanded the size of the Report Footer section to make room for the subreport control.
2. Click the **Toolbox button** on the Report Design toolbar to toggle it on (if it's not already visible), click the **Subform/Subreport button** on the Toolbox toolbar, then click below the **Grand Total label** in the Report Footer section
   The SubReport Wizard opens, as shown in Figure L-19.
3. Click the **Use an existing report or form option button**, click **Department Graph Report-Your Initials**, click **Next**, click **Finish** to accept the name **Department Graph-Your Initials** for the subreport, maximize the Report Design View window (if not already maximized), then scroll down to view the Report Footer section
   The subreport control appears in Report Design View, as shown in Figure L-20, and automatically expands the size of the Report Footer section to accommodate the large control.
4. Click the **Print Preview button** on the Report Design toolbar, then click the **Last page button** on the navigation buttons
   Your screen should look like Figure L-21. The Report Footer section contains the subreport—the Department Graph–Your Initials report—which will now print on the last page of the Department Enrollment report.
5. Click **File** on the menu bar, click **Print**, click the **Pages** option button, type **8** in the From: text box, press **[Tab]**, type **8** in the To: text box, then click **OK** to print the last page of the Enrollment Report
6. Close the Department Enrollment report, then click **Yes** to save the changes when prompted

Trouble?

If your report has a different total number of pages, to print the graph, replace 8 with the last page number for your report.

FIGURE L-19: SubReport Wizard

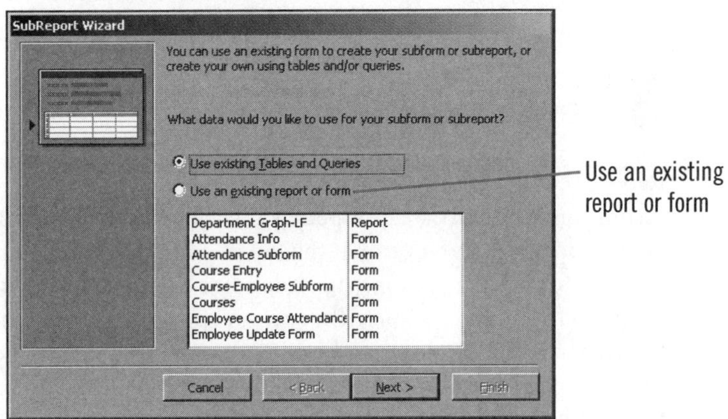

FIGURE L-20: Subreport in Report Design View

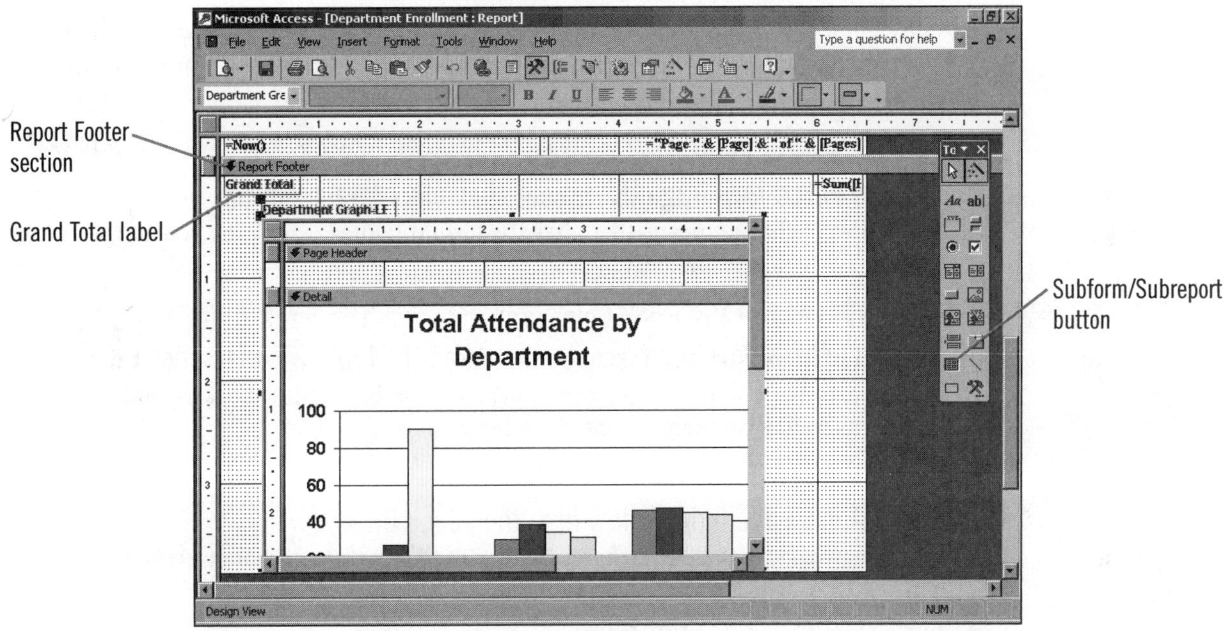

FIGURE L-21: Department graph displayed as a subreport

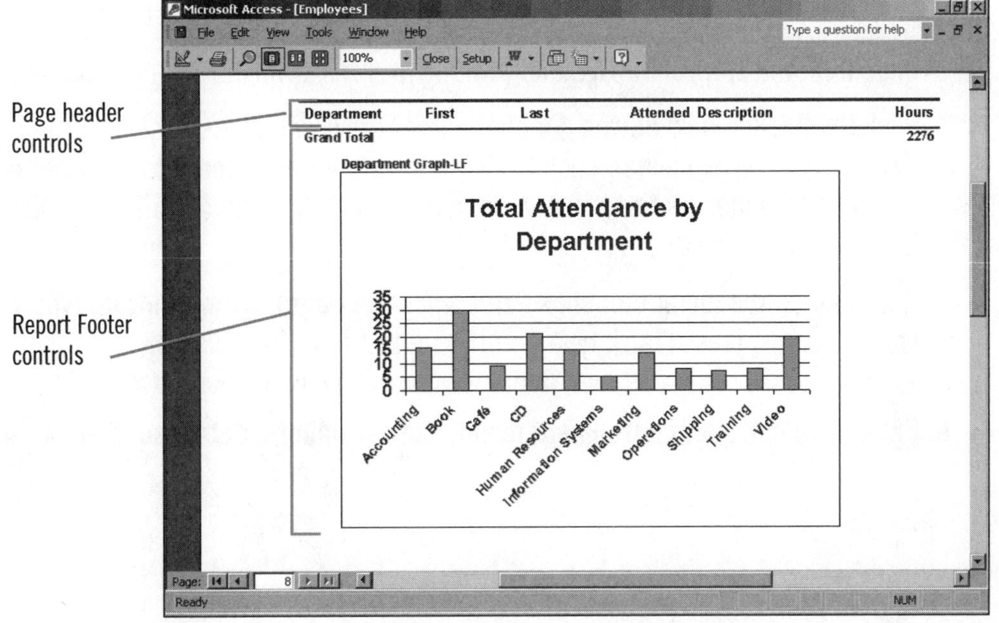

Access 2002

Access 2002

Modifying Section Properties

Report **section properties** can be modified to improve report printouts. For example, if the records on the report are grouped by the values in the Department field, you may want each new Department Header to print at the top of a new page. Or, you may want to modify section properties to format the section with color. For example, you could change the section's Back Color property to emphasize where the section appears on the printout. Fred wants to change the Department Enrollment report so that the records for each new department start at the top of a new page. He also wants to highlight Department Header and Department Footer sections by changing their Back Color property. He makes these section property changes in Report Design View.

Steps

1. Right-click the **Department Enrollment report**, click **Design View** on the shortcut menu, double-click the **Department Footer section** to open its property sheet, then click the **Format tab** in the property sheet
   The property sheet for the Department Footer section opens, as shown in Figure L-22.
2. Click the **Force New Page list arrow**, then click **After Section**
   This property change means that after the Group Footer prints, the rest of the report will continue at the top of the next page.
3. Click **16777215** in the Back Color property, click the **Back Color Build button**, click the **light yellow box** (second column on the top row), then click **OK**
   The Department Footer section will appear with a light yellow background color in Print Preview, as well as on the printout if a color printer is used.
4. Click the **Department Header section**, click **16777215** in the Back Color property, click , click the **light yellow box**, then click **OK**
   You formatted both the Department Header and Department Footer sections with the same light yellow background color.
5. Click the **Properties button** on the Report Design toolbar to close the property sheet, click the **Print Preview button**, then click to zoom out
   Your screen should look like Figure L-23. By modifying section color properties, you have clarified where each new department starts and stops. You have also forced the report to continue at the top of the next page after printing each Department Footer section.
6. Click the **Design View button** on the Print Preview toolbar, click the **Label button** on the Toolbox toolbar, click to the right of the **Department Enrollment label** in the Report Header section, type **your name**, then click the **Save button** on the Report Design toolbar
7. Click **File** on the menu bar, click **Print**, click the **Pages option button**, type **1** in the From: text box, press **[Tab]**, type **1** in the To: text box, then click **OK**
   The first page of the Department Enrollment report is sent to the printer.
8. Close the **Department Enrollment** report, close **Training-L database**, then exit **Access**

Trouble?

Colors print as shades of gray on a black and white printer, and some bright colors will appear solid black. Test all colors on the printer you are use before relying too heavily on them, especially when the colors are used as background color.

FIGURE L-22: Using section properties

Section: GroupFooter1 property sheet
Force New Page list arrow
Back Color property
Department Footer section
Microsoft Access - [Department Enrollment : Report]
Section: GroupFooter1
Force New Page .... None
New Row Or Col .... None
Keep Together .... Yes
Visible .... Yes
Can Grow .... No
Can Shrink .... No
Height .... 0.3542"
Back Color 16777215
Special Effect .... Flat
Where do you want the section to start printing?

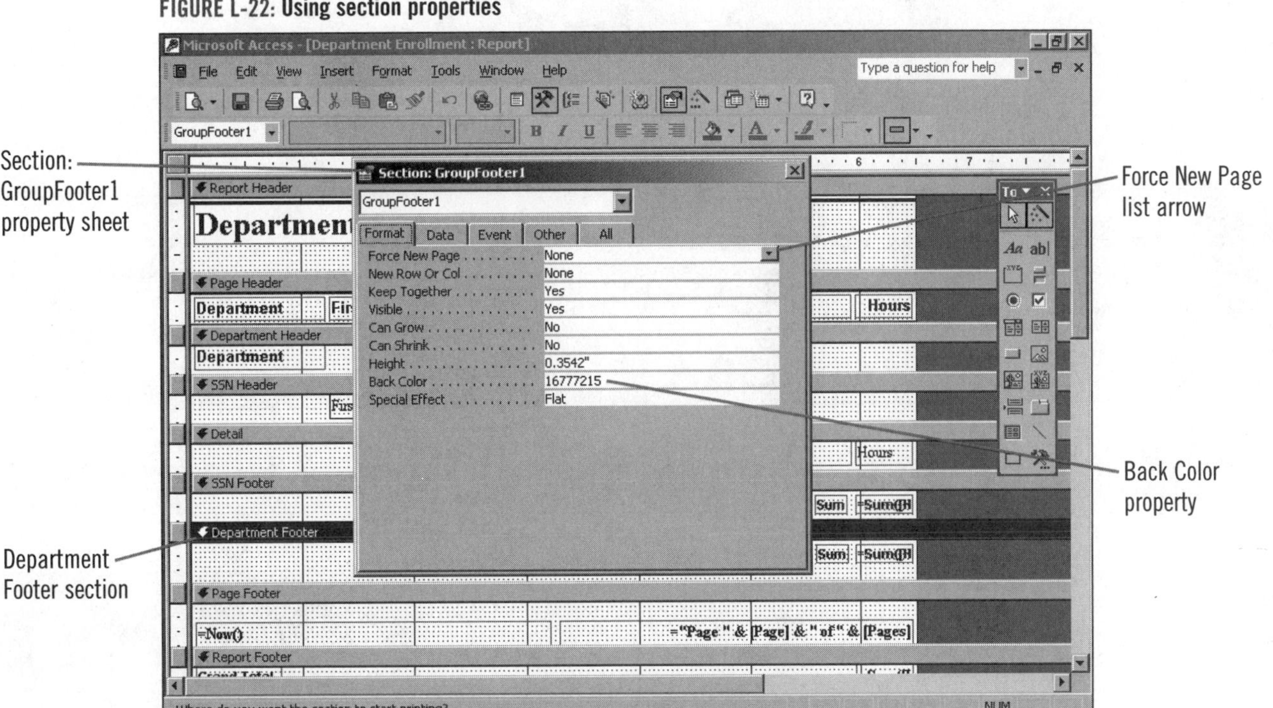

FIGURE L-23: Using section colors

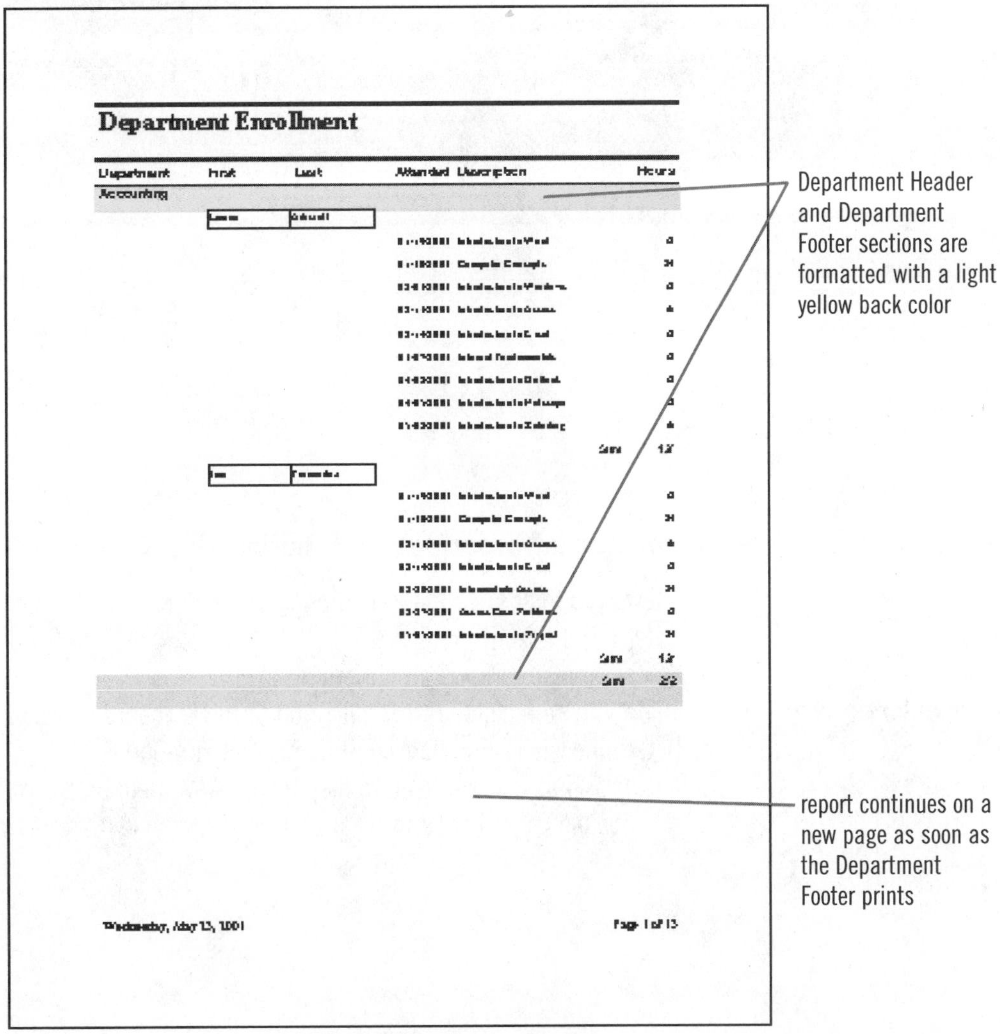

Department Enrollment
Department Header and Department Footer sections are formatted with a light yellow back color
report continues on a new page as soon as the Department Footer prints

Practice

▶ Concepts Review

Identify each element of the Report Design View shown in Figure L-24.

FIGURE L-24

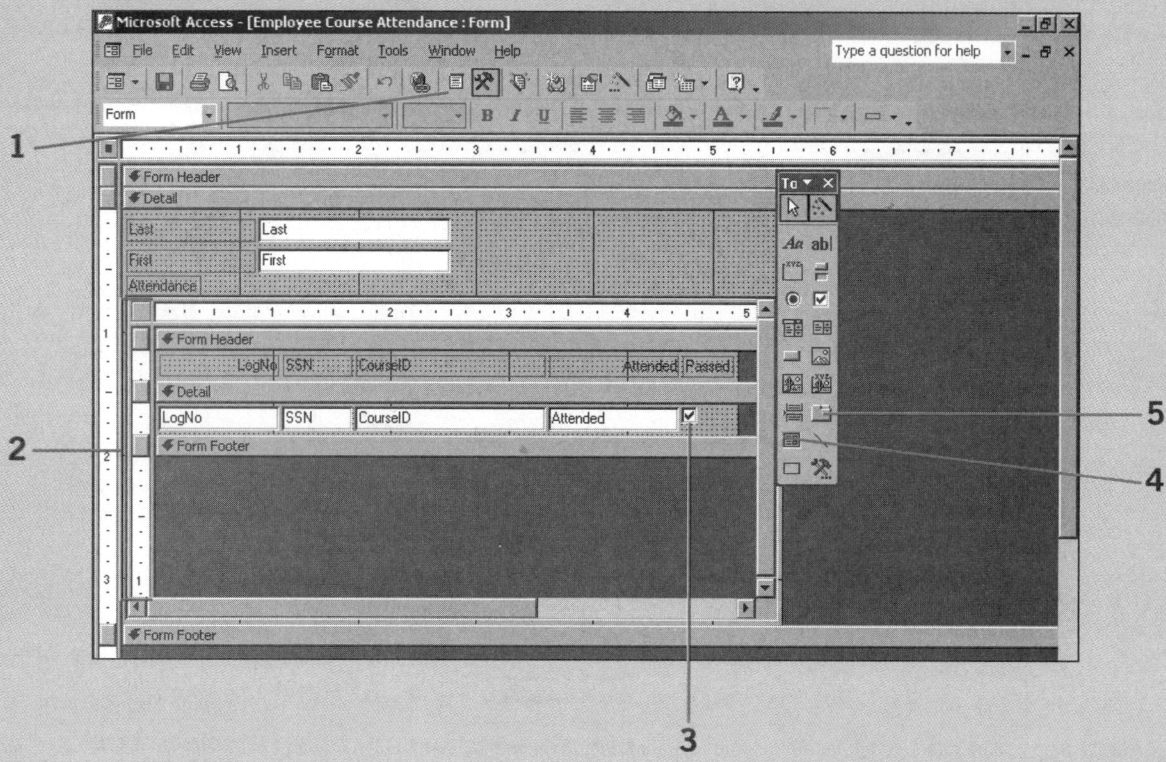

Match each term with the statement that describes its function.

6. **Focus**
7. **Tab control**
8. **Sections**
9. **Conditional formatting**
10. **Charts**
11. **Check box**

a. Allows you to change the appearance of a control on a form or report based on criteria you specify

b. Visual representations of numeric data

c. The ability to receive user input through the keyboard or mouse

d. Determine where and how controls print on a report

e. A control that is often used to display a Yes/No field on a form

f. An unbound control used to organize a form and give it a three-dimensional look

Select the best answer from the list of choices.

12. Which controls are NOT interchangeable?
- **a.** Text box and combo box
- **b.** Combo box and list box
- **c.** Check box and toggle button
- **d.** Check box and option group

13. When would you most likely use a toggle button control?
- **a.** For a field with a limited set of choices
- **b.** For a field with only two choices: Yes or No
- **c.** In place of a command button
- **d.** In place of an unbound label

14. Which control would be the best candidate for a City field?
- **a.** Toggle button
- **b.** Combo box
- **c.** Check box
- **d.** Command button

15. Which control property would you use to automatically display text when you point to a control?
- **a.** ControlTip Text
- **b.** Status Bar Text
- **c.** Popup Text
- **d.** Help Text

16. Which type of chart would be the best candidate to show an upward sales trend over several months?
- **a.** Pie
- **b.** Column
- **c.** Scatter
- **d.** Line

17. Which type of control would you use to combine two reports into one?
- **a.** Report Footer
- **b.** Subreport
- **c.** Calculated properties
- **d.** Main report

18. Which property would you use to force a new group of records to start printing at the top of the next page?
- **a.** Force New Page
- **b.** Subreport
- **c.** Visible
- **d.** Section Break

19. To modify a chart legend, you must open the chart in:
- **a.** Edit mode.
- **b.** Chart mode.
- **c.** Property mode.
- **d.** Design mode.

20. Which view do you use to add more pages to the tab control?
- **a.** Form Design View
- **b.** Form View
- **c.** Report Print Preview
- **d.** Page View

► Skills Review

1. Add check boxes and toggle buttons.
- **a.** Start Access, then open the **Seminar-L** database from the drive and folder where your Project Files are located.
- **b.** Open the Attendees form in Form View, then check the EarlyBirdDiscount check box for the first record in the subform of the first person, Phuong Pham.
- **c.** Open Design View of the Attendees form. If the subform appears as a white box, click the Form View button, then click the Design View button a second time to refresh the screen, which will display the controls within the subform.
- **d.** Maximize the form, then use the subform's Form Selector button to open its property sheet and change the Default View property of the subform to Continuous Forms. Close the property sheet.
- **e.** Change the EarlyBirdDiscount check box in the subform into a toggle button.
- **f.** Expand the height of the subform by dragging the lower-middle sizing handle for the subform down about two inches, then use the middle-right sizing handle for the EarlyBirdDiscount toggle button to widen it to the right edge of the subform.

g. Click the toggle button, then type the text **Early Bird Discount?**

h. View the form in Form View. The subform should be large enough to clearly display three or four records, as shown in Figure L-25. Use Form Design View to make modifications as needed.

i. Open the form in Form View, then click the toggle button to enter Yes in the EarlyBirdDiscount field for the second record in the subform for Phuong Pham.

j. Enter your own last name in place of Pham, then print only this record.

k. Save, then close the form.

FIGURE L-25

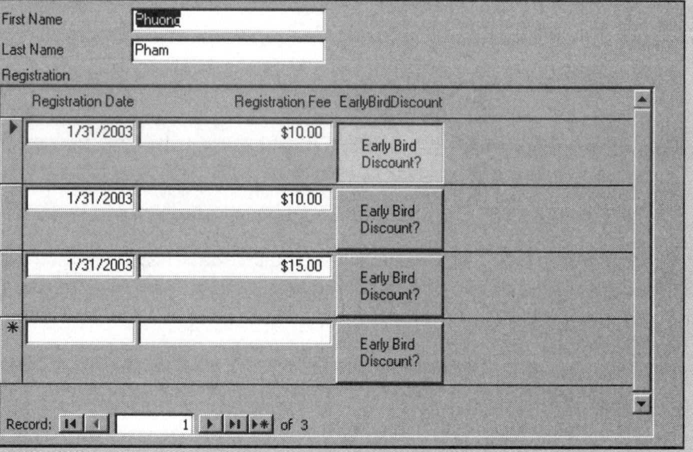

2. **Use conditional formatting in a form.**
   a. Open the Attendees form in Design View. If the subform appears as a white box, click the Form View button, then click the Design View button again to refresh the screen and display the controls within the subform.
   b. Click the RegistrationDate text box, then press and hold [Shift] while clicking the RegistrationFee text box to select both controls in the Detail section of the subform.
   c. Click Format on the menu bar, click Conditional Formatting, set Condition 1 to Expression Is, then enter **[RegistrationFee]>10** as the criteria.
   d. Apply a bold and blue Font/Fore Color for the Condition 1 format, then save the form.
   e. Click the AttendeeFirstName text box, then press and hold [Shift] while clicking the AttendeeLastName text box control to select both controls in the Detail section of the main form.
   f. Click Format on the menu bar, click Conditional Formatting, then set Condition 1 to Field Has Focus.
   g. Apply a light blue Fill/Back color for the Condition 1 format, then save the form.
   h. Display the form in Form View, then enter your own first name in place of Phuong in the first record.
   i. Change the Registration Fee to **$11** for the first record in the subform, then tab through the record to make sure that both the RegistrationDate and RegistrationFee text boxes change format based on the new RegistrationFee.
   j. Save the form, print the first record, then close the form.
3. **Create custom Help.**
   a. Open the Attendees form in Design View.
   b. Open the property sheet for the EarlyBirdDiscount toggle button, then select the Other tab.
   c. Type **To qualify, registration must be one month before the event** for the ControlTip Text property. Use the Zoom dialog box to make this long entry, if desired.
   d. Type **Discounts can also be given for group registrations** for the Status Bar Text property. Use the Zoom dialog box to make this long entry, if desired.
   e. Close the property sheet, save the form, then open the form in Form View.
   f. Point to the toggle button for the third record in the subform to make sure that the ControlTip Text property works.
   g. Click the toggle button for the third record in the subform, then observe the status bar to make sure that the Status Bar Text property works.
   h. Save, then close the Attendees form.

4. **Add tab controls.**
   a. Open the Events form in Design View.
   b. Add a tab control under the Event Name label.
   c. Modify the Page5 Name property of the first tab to be **Event Info**.
   d. Modify the Page6 Name property of the second tab to be **Participants**.
   e. Open the field list, then add the Location, Date, and AvailableSpaces fields from the field list to the middle of the Event Info page.
   f. Add a subform to the Participants page, using the SubForm Wizard to guide your actions. Click the Existing tables or queries option button in the SubForm Wizard, then select the RegistrationDate field from the Registration table, and the AttendeeFirstName and AttendeeLastName fields from the Attendees table.
   g. Link the main form to the subform by using the Show Registration for each record in Events using EventID option.
   h. Type **Registration** as the name of the subform.
   i. Expand the height and width of the subform control to use the existing room on the form, then view the form in Form View.
   j. Click the Participants tab to make sure both tabs work correctly, select Estate Planning and type **Your Name Seminar** (to uniquely identify your printout), then print the first record twice, once with the Event Info tab displayed and once with the Participants tab displayed.
   k. Save, then close the Events form.
5. **Add charts.**
   a. Click Reports on the Objects bar, then click the New button on the database window toolbar.
   b. Click the Chart Wizard option, and choose the Registration table for the object's data.
   c. Select the EventID and RegistrationFee as the fields from the Registration table for the chart.
   d. Choose a Column Chart type.
   e. Sum the RegistrationFee field in the Data area, and use the EventID field as the x-axis. (*Hint*: These should be the defaults, but click the Preview Chart button to verify these choices.)
   f. Type **Registration Fee Totals-Your Initials** for the chart title, then save it with the name **Registration Fee Totals**.
6. **Modify charts.**
   a. Open the Registration Fee Totals report in Design View.
   b. Double-click the chart to edit it.
   c. Remove the legend, then increase the size of both the control and the chart within it to as large as reasonably fits on your screen.
   d. Click any value in the y-axis to select it, click Format on the menu bar, then click the Number option.
   e. Click the Number tab in the Format Axis dialog box, click the Currency category, change the Decimal places text box to **0**, then click OK in the Format Axis dialog box.
   f. Click outside the chart object to return to Report Design View, preview the report, print it, save the changes, then close the Registration Fee Totals report.
7. **Add subreport controls.**
   a. Use the Report Wizard to create a report on all of the fields in the Events table.
   b. Do not add any grouping levels, but sort the records in ascending order by EventID.
   c. Use a Tabular layout, a Portrait orientation, and a Casual style.
   d. Type **Event Information** as the title for the report.
   e. Open Event Information in Report Design View, then open the Report Footer section by dragging the bottom edge of the report down about one inch.
   f. Add a subreport control to the upper-left part of the Report Footer section.
   g. Use the SubReport Wizard to guide your actions in creating the subreport. Use the existing Registration Fee Totals report for the subreport, and accept the name **Registration Fee Totals** for the subreport name.
   h. Preview the report, print it, save, then close the Event Information report.

8. **Modify section properties.**
   a. Use the Report Wizard to create a report on all of the fields in the Registration table, as well as the EventName field in the Events table.
   b. View the data by Events, but do not add any more grouping or sorting fields.
   c. Use an Outline 2 layout, a Landscape orientation, and a Compact style.
   d. Type **Event Details** for the report title.
   e. Open Event Details in Design View, then open the property sheet for the Events_EventID Header section.
   f. Change the Force New Page property on the Format tab to Before Section. Change the Back Color property to light blue. (*Hint*: Use the Build button to locate the color on the palette.)
   g. Close the property sheet, use a label control to add your name to the Page Header section, preview the report, then print the first two pages.
   h. Save, then close the Event Details report. Close Seminar-L, then exit Access.

► Independent Challenge 1

As the manager of a college women's basketball team, you want to enhance the forms within the Basketball-L database.

a. Start Access, then open the database **Basketball-L** from the drive and folder where your Project Files are located.
b. Click the Forms button on the Objects bar, then double-click the Create form by using wizard option.
c. Select all of the fields in the Players table.
d. Use a Columnar layout and a Standard style, then type **Player Information** as the title for the form.
e. Maximize the Player Information form, open it in Design View, then change the Lettered? check box to a toggle button with the text **Varsity Letter?**
f. Resize the toggle button so that it clearly displays the text and is as wide as the form.
g. Open the toggle button's property sheet, then type **Must have 200 minutes of playing time to letter** for the ControlTip Text property.
h. In the toggle button's property sheet, type **For the year 2003** for the Status Bar Text property.
i. Close the property sheet, display the form in Form View, enter your own last name in the first record, then click the toggle button to indicate you've earned a varsity letter.
j. Print the first record, save the form, close the Player Information form and the Basketball-L database, then exit Access.

► Independent Challenge 2

As the manager of a college women's basketball team, you want to enhance the forms within the Basketball-L database.

a. Start Access, then open the database **Basketball-L** from the drive and folder where your Project Files are located.
b. Open the Player Statistics form in Design View, then add a tab control just below the Last label.
c. Modify the Page5 Name property of the first tab to be **Player Background**.
d. Modify the Page6 Name property of the second tab to be **Statistics**.
e. Add the Height, PlayerNo, Year, Position, HomeTown, and HomeState fields from the field list to the middle of the Player Background page.
f. Add a subform to the Statistics page based on all the fields from the Stats table. Link the main form to the subform by using the "Show Stats for each record in Players using PlayerNo" option.
g. Type **Stats** as the name of the subform.
h. Expand the height and width of the subform control to the existing margins of the form, then view the form in Form View.

i. Click the Statistics tab to make sure both tabs work correctly, move to the second record and enter your name in the First text box, then print the second record twice to show both pages of the tab control.
j. Save, then close the Player Statistics form. Close the Basketball-L database, then exit Access.

▶ Independent Challenge 3

As the manager of a college women's basketball team, you want to create a chart from the Basketball-L database to summarize three-point goals.

a. Start Access, then open the database **Basketball-L** from the drive and folder where your Project Files are located.
b. Click the Reports button on the Objects bar, click the New button on the database window toolbar, click Chart Wizard, then base the object on the Stats table.
c. Select the PlayerNo, 3P (three pointers), and 3PA (three pointers attempted) fields for the chart.
d. Select Column Chart for the chart type.
e. Drag the 3PA field to the Data area of the chart so that both the SumOf3P and SumOf3PA fields are in the Data area, and the PlayerNo field is in the Axis area of the chart.
f. Type **3 Pointers–Your Initials** for the title of the chart.
g. Print the chart, then save the report with the name **3 Pointers**.
h. Close the 3 Pointers report, close the Basketball-L database, then exit Access.

Independent Challenge 4

Tab controls appear in many styles and are used on many Web pages to help users navigate a Web site. In this independent challenge, surf the Internet to find Web pages that present information organized similarly to how tab controls are used on Access forms.

a. Connect to the Internet, go to www.course.com, the home page for Course Technology, the publisher of this textbook, then explore the navigation aids on the page to determine if any controls work the way tab controls work on a form. Go back to the home page and print only the first page. On the printout, identify the area of the Web page that worked like tab controls. If you didn't think that the Web page used tab controls, explain why.
b. Go to www.bta.org.uk or www.travelbritain.org, a travel guide to Britain (substitute your own favorite international travel site if desired), and explore the site to identify tab controls. Print a page that uses tab controls (they may not look exactly like tabs). On that printout, identify the area of the Web page that worked like tab controls. If you didn't think that the Web page used tab controls, explain why.
c. Go to www.soccerage.com, a Web site with international soccer information (substitute your own favorite international sports site if desired), and explore the site to identify tab controls. Print a page that uses tab controls (they may not look exactly like tabs). On the printout, identify the area of the Web page that worked like tab controls. If you didn't think that the Web page used tab controls, explain why.
d. Not all Web pages organize their content by using hyperlinks that look like tab controls. On a piece of paper, write a paragraph about the other types of hyperlinks you found that help organize and navigate a site, and identify and explain the characteristics of the controls you liked best.

Visual Workshop

As the manager of a college women's basketball team, you want to create a form that highlights outstanding statistics if either scoring or rebounding totals are equal to or greater than **10** for an individual game effort. Start Access, then open the **Basketball-L** database from the drive and folder where your Project Files are located. Open the Players form in Design View, then use the conditional formatting feature to format the FG (field goals), 3P (three-point shots), and FT (free throws) text boxes in the Stats Subform1 to have bold text and a yellow background if the following expression that totals their scoring for that game is true: **2*[FG]+3*[3P]+[FT]>=10**. Conditionally format the Reb-O (offensive rebounds) and Reb-D (defensive rebounds) text boxes to have a bold text and green background if the following expression that totals rebounds is true: **[Reb-O]+[Reb-D]>=10**. Display the record for Ellyse Howard, which should look like Figure L-26. Enter your own name in the First and Last text boxes, then print that record.

FIGURE L-26

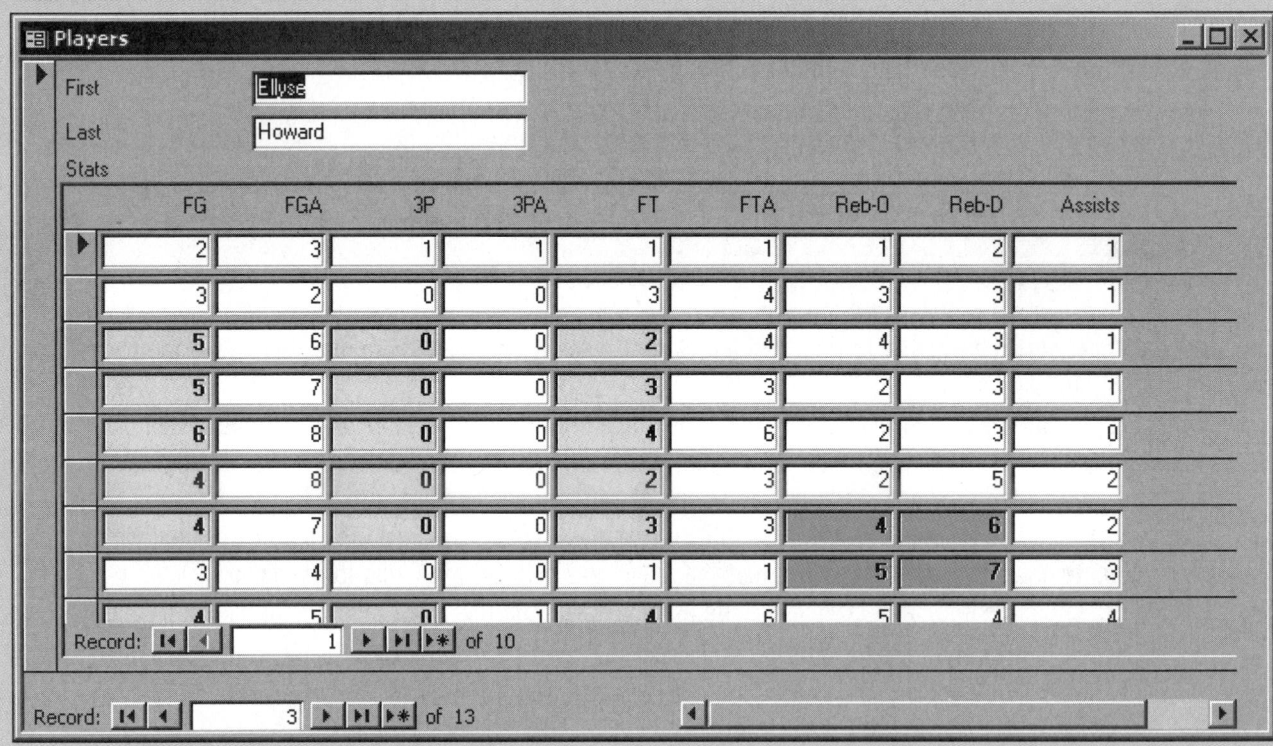

Access 2002

Unit M

Managing Database Objects

Objectives

- Work with objects
- Use the Documenter
- Group objects
- Modify shortcuts and groups
- MOUS Create a dialog box
- MOUS Create a pop-up form
- MOUS Create a switchboard
- MOUS Modify a switchboard

As your database grows in size and functionality, the number of objects (especially queries and reports) grows as well. Your ability to find, rename, delete, and document objects, and your proficiency to present objects in an organized way to other database users will become important skills. Kristen Fontanelle is the network administrator at MediaLoft headquarters. She has developed a working database to document MediaLoft computer equipment. The number of objects in the database makes it increasingly difficult to find and organize information. Kristen will use powerful Access documentation, object grouping, and switchboard features to manage the growing database.

Access 2002

Working with Objects

Working with Access objects is similar to working with files in Windows Explorer. For example, you can use the **View buttons** (Large Icons, Small Icons, List, and Details) on the database window toolbar to arrange the objects in four different ways just as you arrange files within Windows Explorer. Similarly, you can right-click an object within Access to open, copy, delete, or rename it just as you would right-click a file within Windows Explorer. Kristen deletes, renames, sorts, and adds descriptions to several objects to make the Database window easier to use.

Steps

1. **Start Access, open the Technology-M database from the drive and folder where your Project Files are located, maximize the database window, click Queries on the Objects bar (if it is not already selected), then click the Details button on the Database window toolbar**

   Your screen should look like Figure M-1, with five columns of information for each object: Name, Description, Modified (date the object was last changed), Created (date the object was originally created), and Type. By default, objects are sorted in ascending order by name, and the Description column is blank.

> **QuickTip**
> Point to the line between column headings, then drag ↔ left or right to resize that column.

2. **Click the Created column heading to sort the objects in ascending order on the date they were originally created, click the Created column heading again to sort the objects in descending order on the date they were originally created, then click the Name column heading**

   The query objects are now sorted in ascending order by name. You use the Description column to further describe the object.

3. **Right-click the Equipment Specs query, then click Properties on the shortcut menu**

   The Equipment Specs Properties dialog box opens, as shown in Figure M-2.

4. **Enter Includes memory, hard drive, and processor information in the Description text box, then click OK**

   Part of the description appears in the Database window and helps identify the selected object. If an object is no longer needed, you should delete it to free up disk space and keep the database window organized.

5. **Right-click the Employees Query, click Delete on the shortcut menu, then click Yes when prompted**

   Although object names can be 64 characters long and can include any combination of letters, numbers, spaces, and special characters except a period (.), exclamation point (!), accent (`), or brackets ([ ]), keep them as short, yet descriptive, as possible. Short names make objects easier to reference in other places in the database, such as in the Record Source property for a form or report.

6. **Right-click the Human Resources query, click Rename on the shortcut menu, type HR, press [Enter], right-click the Information Systems query, click Rename on the shortcut menu, type IS, then press [Enter]**

   Your final screen should look like Figure M-3. With shorter query names, you can see all of the object names in the Database window without resizing the columns.

FIGURE M-1: Viewing object details

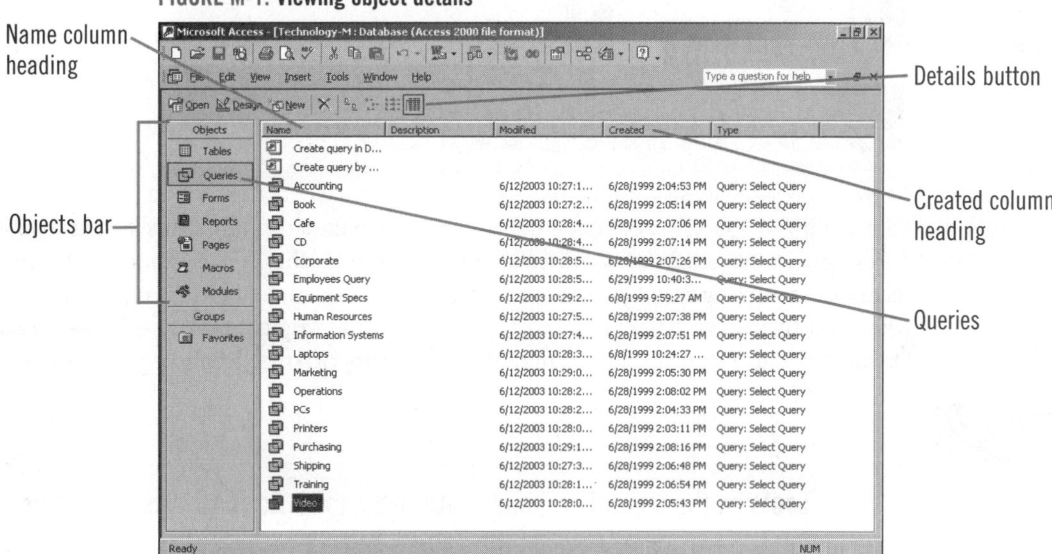

FIGURE M-2: Equipment Specs Properties dialog box

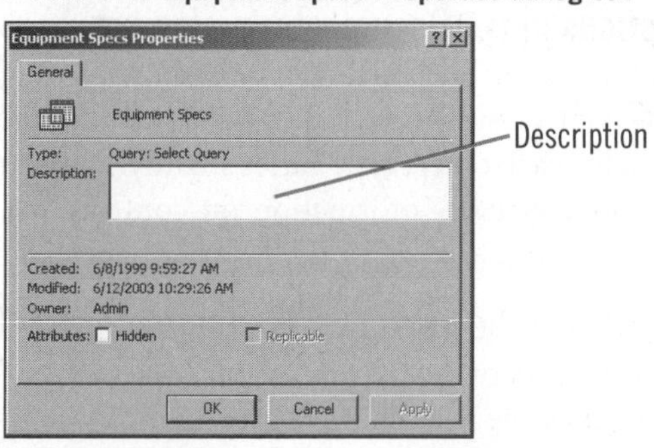

FIGURE M-3: Final Database window

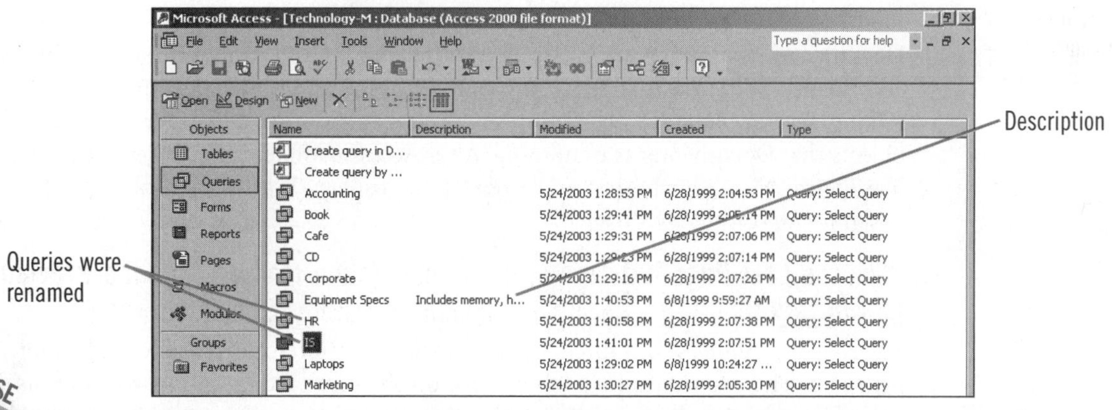

CLUES TO USE

Updating names with Name AutoCorrect

Name AutoCorrect fixes discrepancies between references to field names, controls on forms and reports, and object names when you change them. For example, if a query includes the field "LastName," but you change that field name to "LName" in Table Design View, the Name AutoCorrect feature will update the field name to "LName" within the query as well. Similarly, if a report is based on a query named "Department Income," and you change the query name to "Dept Inc," the Name AutoCorrect feature will automatically update the Record Source property for the report to "Dept Inc" to match the new query name. However, Name AutoCorrect will not repair references in Visual Basic for Applications code, replicated databases, linked tables, or a number of other database situations. Click Tools on the menu bar in the database window, click Options, and then click the General tab to view the Name AutoCorrect options.

Using the Documenter

As your Access database becomes more successful, users will naturally find new ways to use the data. Your ability to modify a database depends on your understanding of existing database objects. Access provides an analysis feature called the **Documenter** that creates reports on the properties and relationships among the objects in your database. This documentation is especially helpful to those who need to use the database, but did not design the original tables. Kristen uses the Documenter to create paper documentation to support the Technology-M database for other MediaLoft employees.

1. Click **Tools** on the menu bar, point to **Analyze**, click **Documenter**, click **Yes** if prompted to install the feature, then click the **Tables tab**
   The Documenter dialog box opens, displaying tabs for the object types.
2. Click **Options** in the Documenter dialog box
   The Print Table Definition dialog box, shown in Figure M-4, opens. This dialog box gives you some control over what type of documentation you will print for the table. The documentation for each object type varies slightly. For example, the documentation on forms and reports would include information on controls and sections, which are not part of table objects.
3. Click **Cancel** in the Print Table Definition dialog box
   You can also select or deselect individual objects by clicking the check box beside their name, or you can click the Select All button to quickly select all objects of that type.
4. Click **Select All**, click the **Forms tab**, click **Select All**, click **OK**, then click on the report preview to zoom in
   Documenter is now creating a report about all of the table and form objects in the Technology-M database, and will display it as an Access report. This can be a lengthy process (taking several seconds) depending on the speed of your computer and the number of objects that Documenter is examining. After Access completes the report, your screen looks like Figure M-5, which shows a report that displays information about the first table, Assignments, on the first page.
5. Click the **Last Page button** in the navigation toolbar, click the **Previous Page button**, then scroll down so that your screen looks like Figure M-6
   The report contains about three pages of documentation for each table, and about six pages per form. The properties for each control on the form are listed in two columns. Because most form controls have approximately 50 properties, you can quickly see why the documentation that lists each control and section property can become so long. You can print the report, or send it to a Word document using the OfficeLinks buttons, but you cannot modify the report in the Report Design View or save the report as an object within the database window.
6. Click **Close** on the Print Preview toolbar

QuickTip

Information about the progress of Documenter appears in the status bar.

FIGURE M-4: Print Table Definition dialog box

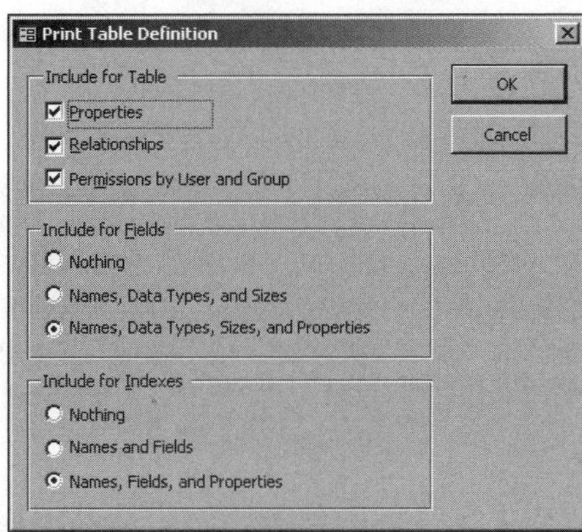

FIGURE M-5: First page of documentation

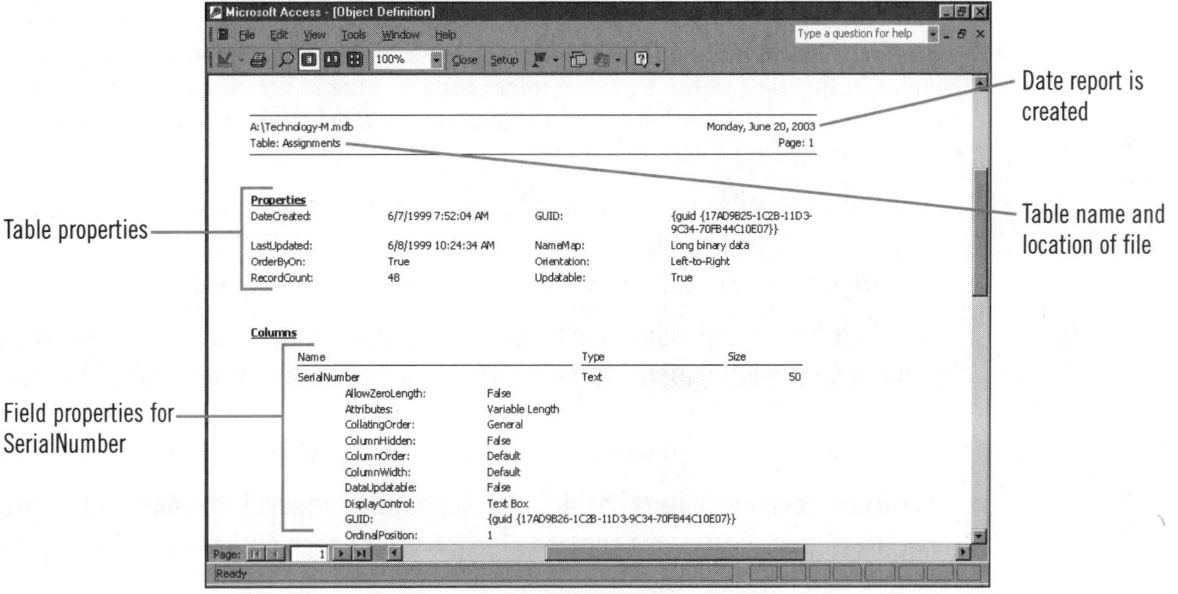

FIGURE M-6: Second to last page of documentation

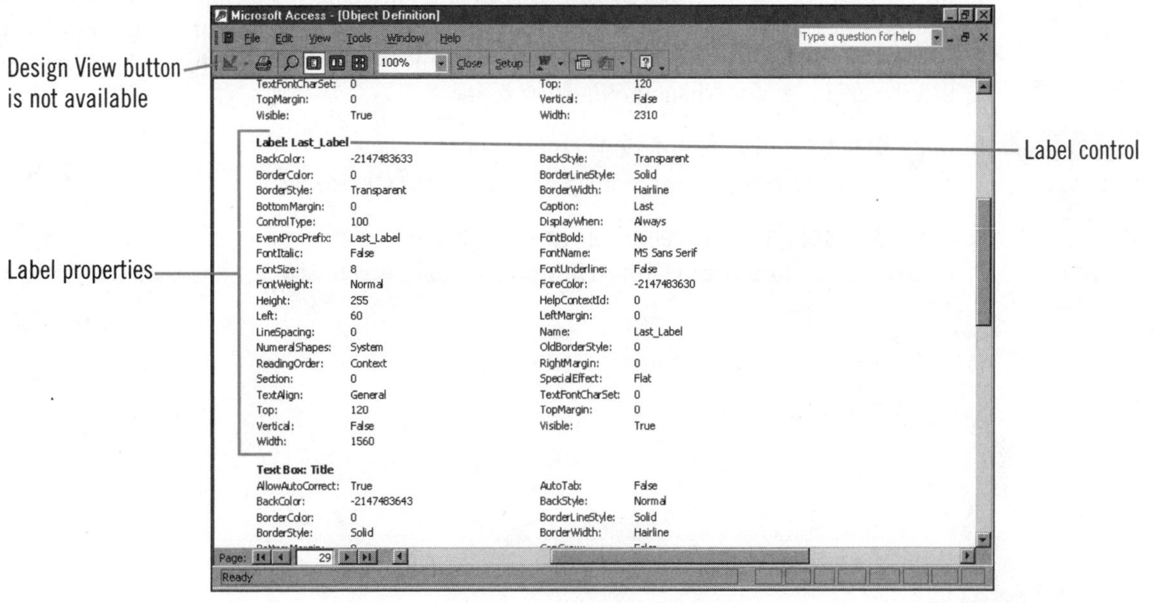

Access 2002

Grouping Objects

Viewing every object in the database window can be cumbersome when your database contains many objects. You can place objects in **groups** to easily organize or classify objects. For example, you might create a group for each department that uses the database so that the forms and reports used by each department are presented as a set. A group consists of **shortcuts** (pointers) to each database object that belongs to the group and does not affect the original location of the object. To work with groups, click the **Groups bar** below the Objects bar in the Database window. Kristen organizes the objects in the Technology-M database by creating groups for the objects used by two different departments: Human Resources (HR) and Accounting.

Steps

1. Right-click **Favorites** on the Groups bar, click **New Group** on the shortcut menu, type **HR**, click **OK**, then click **HR** on the Groups bar

   Your screen should look like Figure M-7. Because you just created the HR group, it doesn't contain any objects. The **Favorites group** is provided for every new Access database and is similar in function to the Favorites folder used in other Microsoft programs. Within an Access database, the Favorites group organizes *objects* rather than files because it is an Access group (rather than a folder).

2. Right-click **Favorites** on the Groups bar, click **New Group** on the shortcut menu, type **Accounting**, then click **OK**

   After creating the new groups, you are ready to use them to organize other database objects.

3. Click **Queries** on the Objects bar, drag the **Accounting query** to the **Accounting group**, drag the **Equipment Specs query** to the **Accounting group**, then drag the **HR query** to the **HR group**

   Dragging an object to a group icon places a shortcut to that object within that group.

4. Click **Reports** on the Objects bar, drag the **Accounting report** to the **Accounting group**, drag the **Human Resources report** to the **HR group**, then click the **Accounting group**

   Your screen should look like Figure M-8, with three shortcut icons representing two queries and one report in the Accounting group. Because both a query and a report object were named "Accounting," Access added a "1" to the "Accounting" shortcut icon that represents the Accounting report. These shortcuts are just pointers to the original objects, and therefore do not change the name of the original object. You can open or design an object by accessing it through a shortcut icon. You also can drag an object to more than one group, thereby creating more than one shortcut to it.

5. Click **Groups** on the Groups bar three times

   You can expand, collapse, or restore this section of the Objects bar.

6. Click **Objects** on the Objects bar three times

   Displaying all Objects and Groups buttons is a good way to arrange the database window for a new user.

QuickTip

You can resize the Groups or Objects sections by pointing to the top edge of the Objects or Groups button and dragging ↕ to resize that section of the Objects bar.

FIGURE M-7: Creating groups

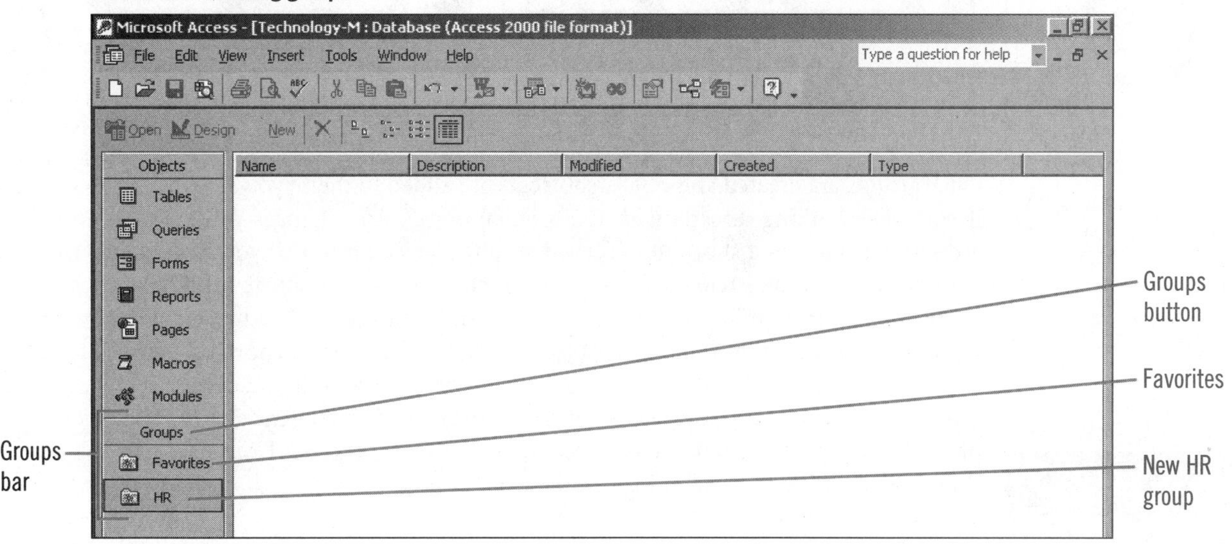

FIGURE M-8: Dragging objects to groups

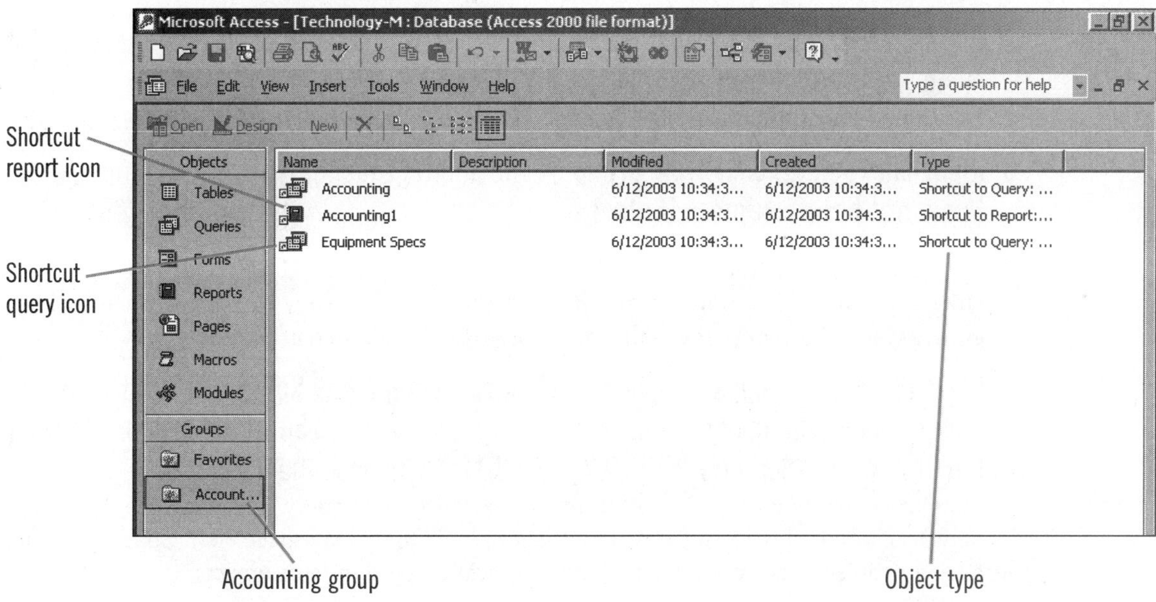

Speech recognition–interface of the future?

Speech recognition means being able to talk to your computer, and having it respond appropriately to the instruction you gave it. For example, to display the query objects in the database window, it would be faster and easier for most people to say "Queries," than to click the Queries button on the Objects bar, especially if your hand wasn't already resting on the mouse. Office XP products including Access 2002 support speech recognition, but you must have a microphone, install the speech recognition software, and train the software to recognize the sound of your unique voice. For more information on speech recognition, open Microsoft Access Help to the "About speech recognition" page.

Modifying Shortcuts and Groups

Once groups are created and object shortcuts are added to them, you work with the shortcut as if you were working directly with the original object. Any changes you make to an object by accessing it through a shortcut are saved with the object, just as if you had opened that object without using the shortcut. You can delete, rename, or copy a shortcut by right-clicking it and choosing the appropriate command from the shortcut menu. The biggest difference between working with shortcuts and actual objects is that if you delete a shortcut, you delete only that pointer, which does not affect the original object it references. If you delete an object, however, it is, of course, permanently deleted, and any shortcuts that reference it will no longer function properly. You can also rename or delete entire groups. Kristen modifies groups and shortcuts to clarify the Technology-M database.

1. Right-click the **Accounting1 shortcut** in the Accounting group, click **Rename** on the shortcut menu, type **Accounting Report**, then press **[Enter]**

   A shortcut name does not have to use the same name as the object that it points to, but the shortcuts should be clearly named. The shortcut icon to the left of the shortcut indicates the type of object it represents.

2. Right-click **Accounting** on the Groups bar, click **Rename Group** on the shortcut menu, type **Acctg**, then press **[Enter]**

   The Groups bar should look like Figure M-9.

3. Right-click **Acctg**, click **New Group** on the shortcut menu, type **IS** in the New Group Name text box, then press **[Enter]**

4. Drag the **Equipment Specs shortcut** from the Acctg group to the IS group

   Dragging a shortcut from one group to another creates a copy of that shortcut in both groups. Shortcuts that point to the same object can have different names.

5. Click **IS** on the Groups bar, double-click the **Equipment Specs shortcut** in the IS group to open the query in Datasheet View, double-click **256** in the Memory field for the first record (SerialNo JK123FL3), type **512**, then close the datasheet

   Edits and entries made to Query Datasheet View through a query shortcut work exactly the same as if you had made the change in the original Query Datasheet View. Changes to data from any object view modify data that is physically stored in table objects.

6. Click **Tables** on the Objects bar, double-click the **PCSpecs table** to open its datasheet, click the **Find button** on the Table Datasheet toolbar, type **JK123FL3** in the Find what text box, press **[Enter]**, then click **Cancel**

   The Memory field for the JK123FL3 record contains the value 512, as shown in Figure M-10.

7. Close the PCSpecs datasheet

FIGURE M-9: Modifying groups

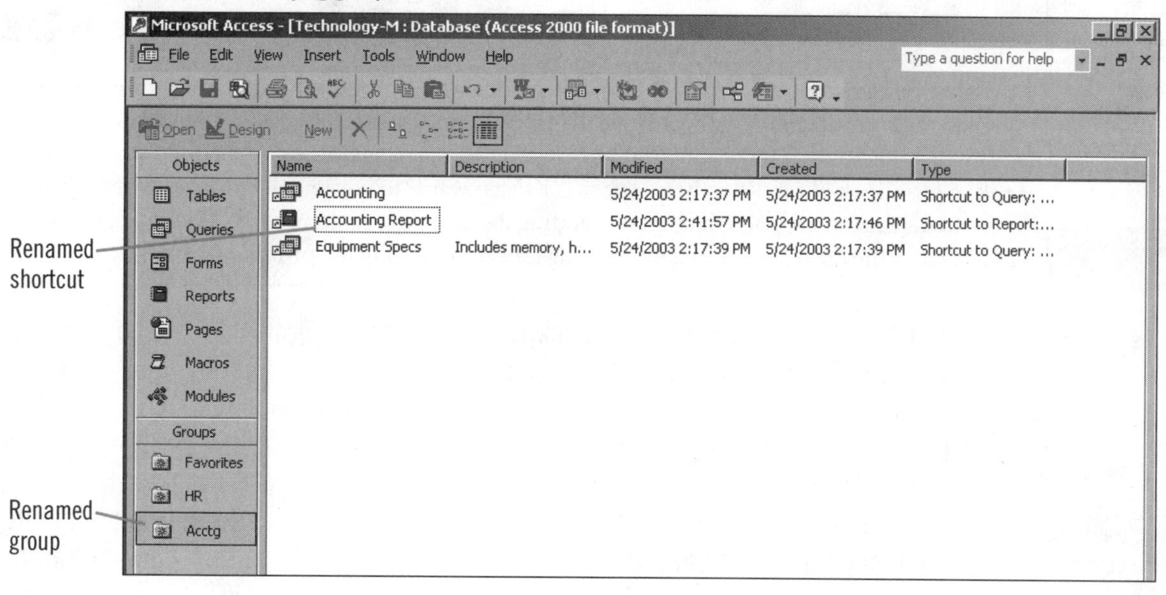

FIGURE M-10: A change made through a shortcut

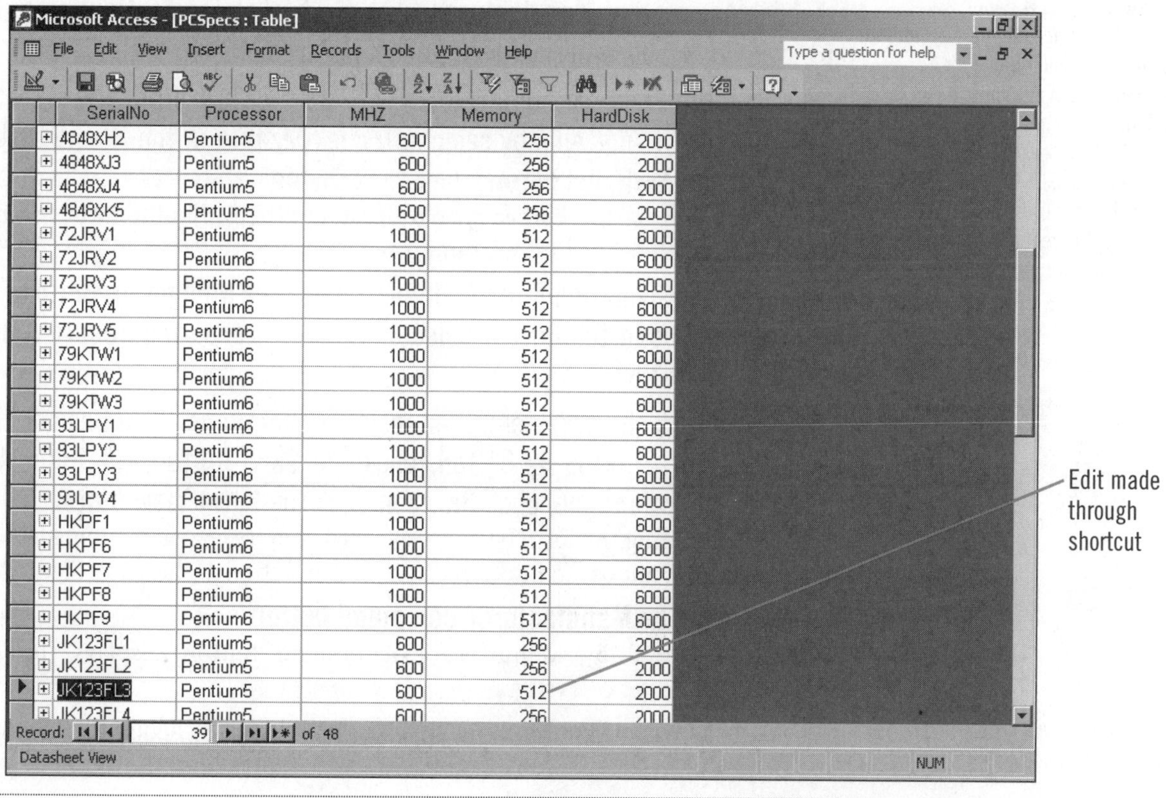

SerialNo	Processor	MHZ	Memory	HardDisk
4848XH2	Pentium5	600	256	2000
4848XJ3	Pentium5	600	256	2000
4848XJ4	Pentium5	600	256	2000
4848XK5	Pentium5	600	256	2000
72JRV1	Pentium6	1000	512	6000
72JRV2	Pentium6	1000	512	6000
72JRV3	Pentium6	1000	512	6000
72JRV4	Pentium6	1000	512	6000
72JRV5	Pentium6	1000	512	6000
79KTW1	Pentium6	1000	512	6000
79KTW2	Pentium6	1000	512	6000
79KTW3	Pentium6	1000	512	6000
93LPY1	Pentium6	1000	512	6000
93LPY2	Pentium6	1000	512	6000
93LPY3	Pentium6	1000	512	6000
93LPY4	Pentium6	1000	512	6000
HKPF1	Pentium6	1000	512	6000
HKPF6	Pentium6	1000	512	6000
HKPF7	Pentium6	1000	512	6000
HKPF8	Pentium6	1000	512	6000
HKPF9	Pentium6	1000	512	6000
JK123FL1	Pentium5	600	256	2000
JK123FL2	Pentium5	600	256	2000
JK123FL3	Pentium5	600	512	2000
JK123FL4	Pentium5	600	256	2000

Access 2002

Creating a Dialog Box

A **dialog box** is a special form that displays information or prompts a user for a choice. For example, you might create a dialog box to give the user a list of reports to view or print. Use dialog boxes to simplify the Access interface. You use form properties such as **Border Style** and **Auto Center** to make a form look like a dialog box. Kristen wants to create a dialog box that lets database users access the three reports that the Accounting department regularly prints. She also wants to add a shortcut to the dialog box in the Accounting group to simplify the printing process.

Steps

1. Click **Forms** on the Objects bar, click the **List button** on the Database window toolbar, then double-click **Create form in Design view**
   You create a dialog box in Form Design View. A dialog box is not bound to an underlying table or query, and therefore doesn't use the Record Source property. A dialog box often contains command buttons to automate tasks.

Trouble?

Make sure that the Control Wizards button is selected on the Toolbox before you click to start the Command Button Wizard.

2. Click the **Toolbox button** on the Form Design toolbar (if the Toolbox is not already visible), click the **Command Button button** on the Toolbox, then click in the upper-left corner of the form
   The **Command Button Wizard** shown in Figure M-11 assists you in creating new command buttons. The Command Button Wizard organizes over 30 of the most common command button actions within six categories.
3. Click **Report Operations** in the Categories list, click **Preview Report** in the Actions list, click **Next**, click **Accounting** as the report choice (if it is not already selected), click **Next**, click the **Text option button**, press **[Tab]**, type **Sorted by Name**, click **Next**, type **Name** in the button name text box, then click **Finish**
   The command button appears in Form Design View, as shown in Figure M-12. The name of the command button appears in the Object box on the Formatting (Form/Report toolbar).

Trouble?

Every command button must be given a unique name that is referenced in underlying Visual Basic for Applications (VBA) code. Deleting a command button from Design View does not delete the underlying code, so each new button name must be different, even if the button has been deleted.

4. Click the **Command Button button**, click below the first command button, click **Report Operations** in the Categories list, click **Preview Report** in the Actions list, click **Next**, click **Accounting Manufacturer**, click **Next**, click the **Text option button**, press **[Tab]**, type **Sorted by Manufacturer**, click **Next**, type **Mfg**, then click **Finish**
5. Double-click the **Form Selector button** to open the form's property sheet, click the **Format tab** (if it is not already selected), click **Sizable** in the Border Style property, click the **Border Style list arrow**, then click **Dialog**
   The **Dialog** option for the Border Style property indicates that the form will have a thick border and may not be maximized, minimized, or resized.
6. Click **Yes** in the Navigation Buttons property, click the **Navigation Buttons list arrow**, click **No**, click **Yes** in the Record Selectors property, click the **Record Selectors list arrow**, then click **No**
7. Close the property sheet, restore, then resize the form and Form Design window so it is approximately 3" wide by 3" tall, click the **Save button**, enter **Accounting Reports** as the form name, click **OK**, then click the **Form View button**
   Restoring and resizing the form best displays the property changes you made to the Border Style, Navigation Buttons, and Record Selectors properties, as shown in Figure M-13.
8. Click the **Sorted by Manufacturer command button**
   Clicking the Sorted by Manufacturer command button displays the Accounting Manufacturer report.
9. Close the Accounting Manufacturer report, then close the Accounting Reports form

FIGURE M-11: Command Button Wizard

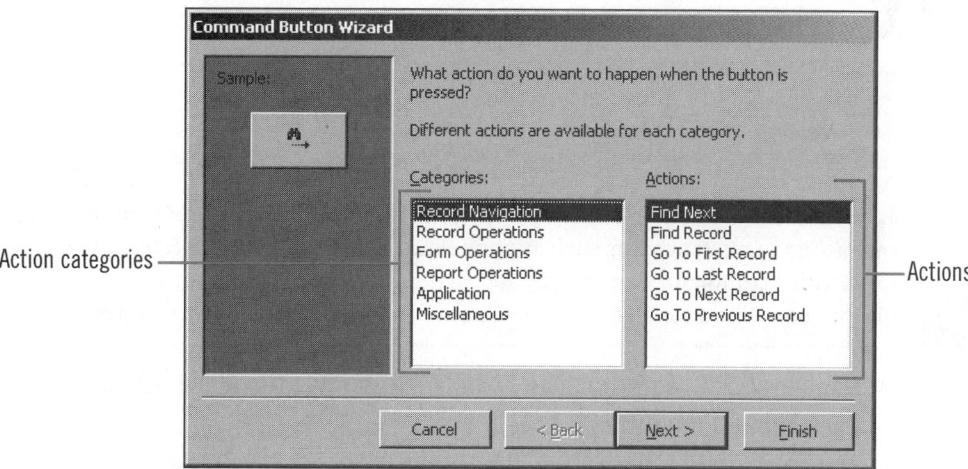

FIGURE M-12: Adding a command button

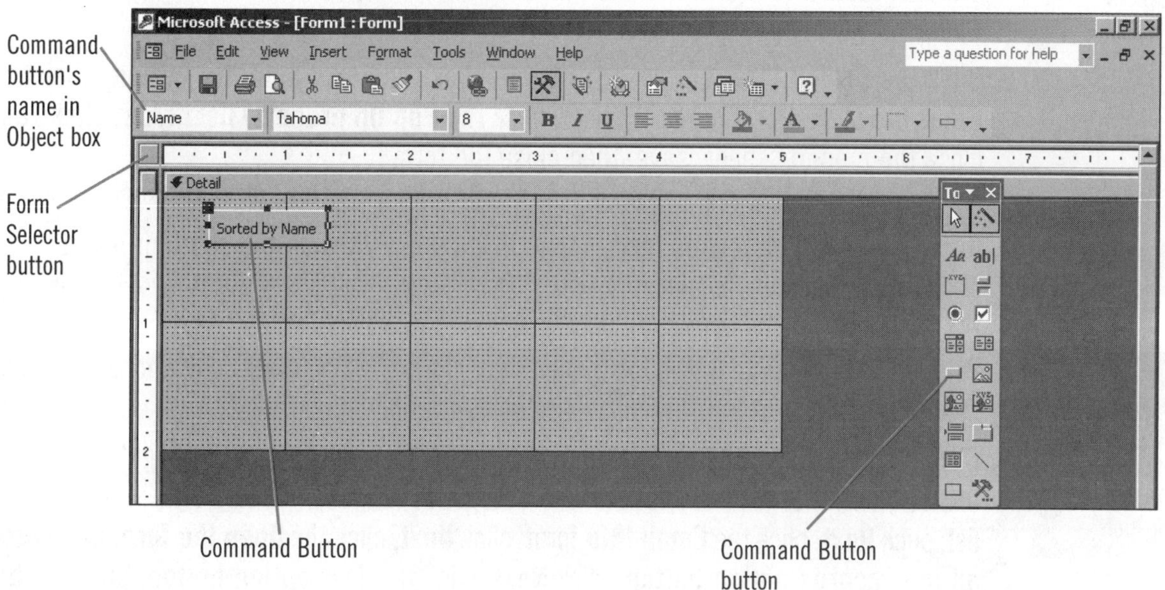

FIGURE M-13: The final dialog box in Form View

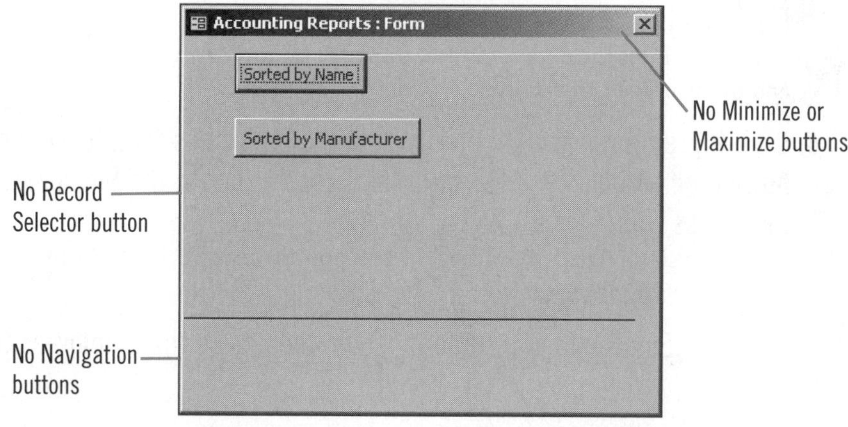

Access 2002

Access 2002

Creating a Pop-up Form

A **pop-up form** is another special type of form that stays on top of other open forms, even when another form is active. For example, you might want to create a pop-up form to give the user easy access to reference lists such as phone numbers or e-mail addresses. You can open a pop-up form with a command button. Kristen creates a pop-up form to access employee e-mail information. She adds a command button on the Employees form to open the pop-up form.

Steps

1. Double-click **Create form by using wizard**, click the **Tables/Queries list arrow**, then click **Table: Employees**
   You want to add three fields to the pop-up form.
2. Double-click **First**, double-click **Last**, double-click **Email**, click **Next**, click the **Tabular option button**, click **Next**, click **Standard** for the style (if it is not already selected), click **Next**, type **Email Info** for the title of the form, then click **Finish**
   The Email Info form opens in Form View, as shown in Figure M-14. You change a form into a pop-up form by changing form properties in Form Design View.
3. Click the **Design View button**, double-click the **Form Selector button**, click the **Other tab** in the Form property sheet, click the **Pop Up property list arrow**, click **Yes**, close the property sheet, save, then close the form
   You want to open the Email Info pop-up form with a command button on the Employees form.
4. Right-click the **Employees form**, then click **Design View** on the shortcut menu
   The Employees form contains four bound fields: Last, First, Department, and Title, as well as a subform that displays the equipment assigned to that employee.
5. Point to the **right edge of the form**, then drag ✛ to the **6.5"** mark on the horizontal ruler
   You want to put the command button in the upper-right corner of the form.
6. Click the **Command Button button** on the Toolbox, click ⁺▭ to the right of the Title text box, click **Form Operations** in the Categories list, click **Open Form** in the Actions list, click **Next**, click the **Email Info** form, click **Next**, click the **Open the form and show all the records option button**, click **Next**, click the **Text option button**, press **[Tab]**, type **Email**, click **Next**, type **Email** as the name of the button, then click **Finish**
   Your screen should look similar to Figure M-15.
7. Click the **Form View button**, click the **Email command button**, resize the **Email Info window**, then drag the **Email Info title bar** down so that your screen looks like Figure M-16
   The power of pop-up forms is that they stay on top of all other forms and can be turned on and off as needed by the user.
8. Click **Ingraham** in the Last text box in the Employees form, click the **Sort Ascending button**, double-click **Maria** in the First text box of the Employees form, type **Mary**, then press **[Tab]**
   "Maria" also changed to "Mary" in the pop-up form because both forms are tied to the underlying Employee table.
9. Close the Email Info pop-up form, save, then close the Employees form

QuickTip

If the field list is in the way, drag its title bar to move it or click the Field List button on the Form Design toolbar to toggle it off.

FIGURE M-14: Creating the Email Info pop-up form

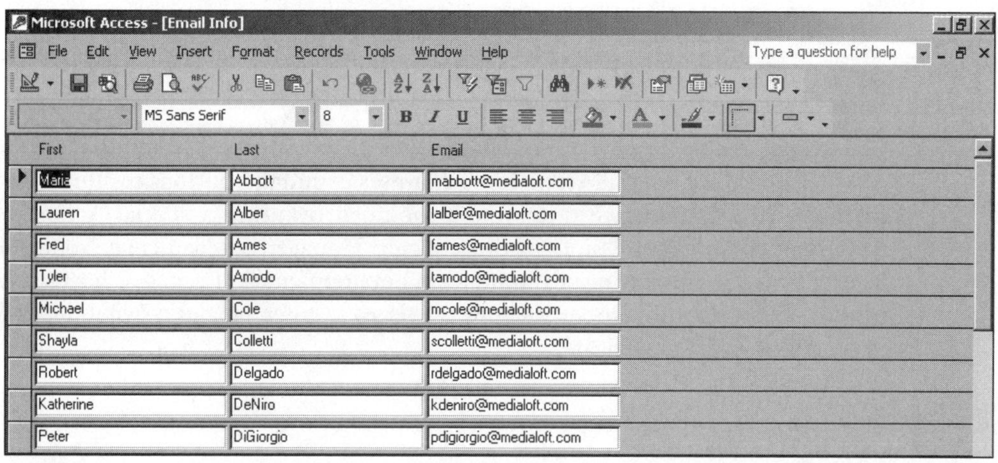

FIGURE M-15: Adding a command button to the Employees form

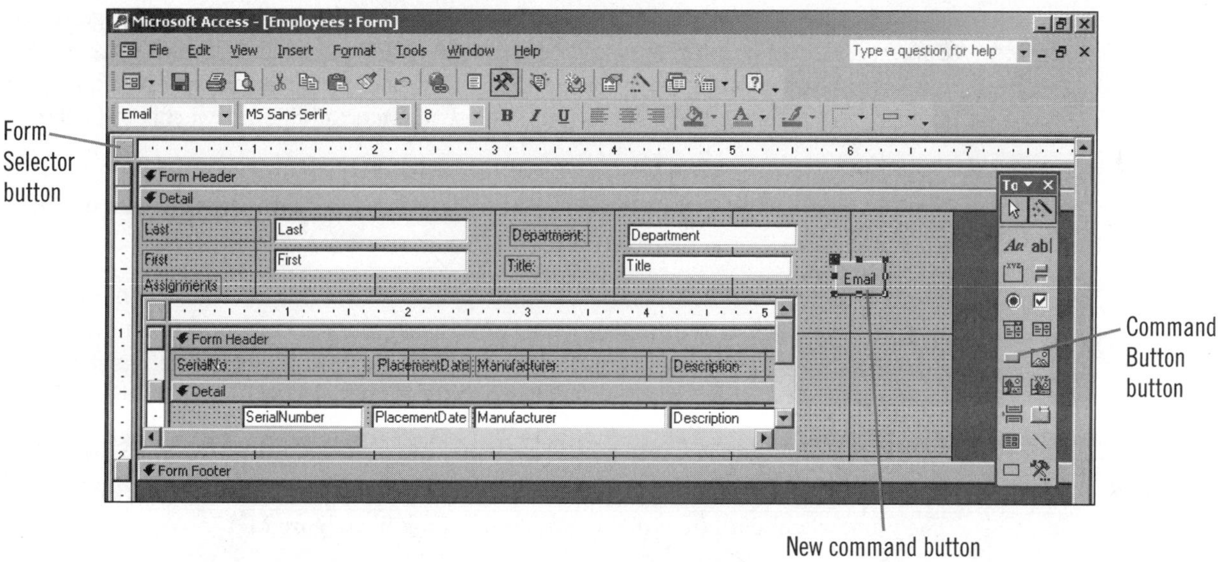

FIGURE M-16: The final form and pop-up form

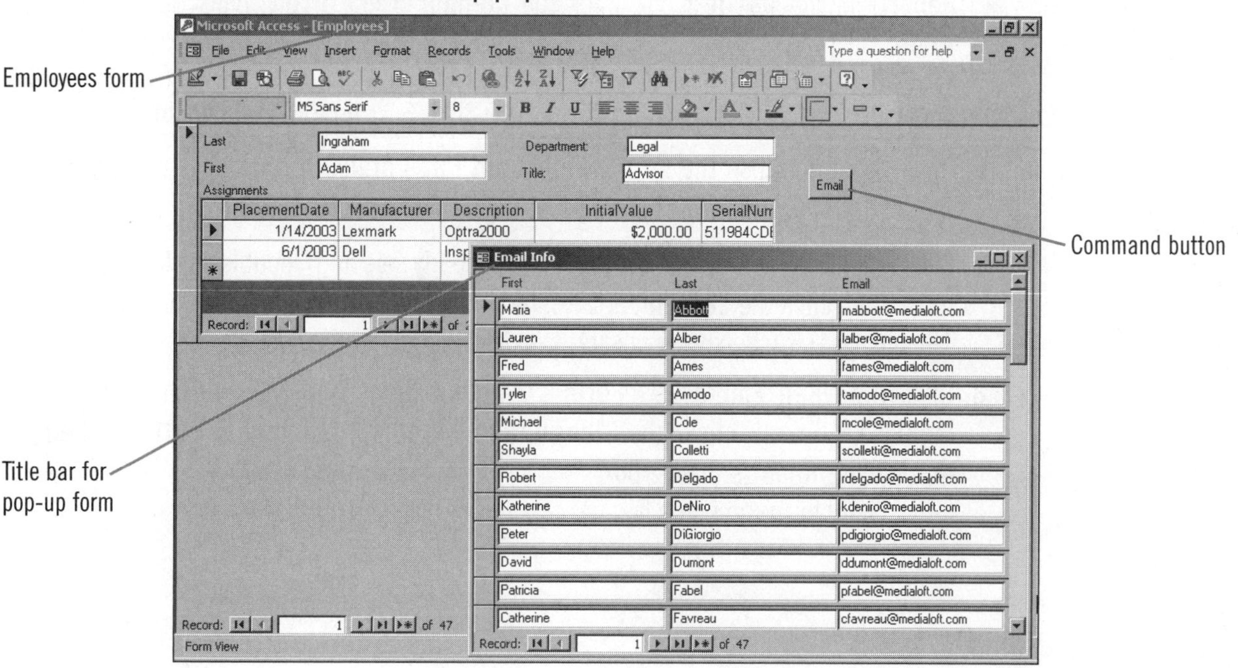

Access 2002

Creating a Switchboard

A **switchboard** is a special Access form that uses command buttons to simplify and secure the database. Switchboards are created and modified by using a special Access tool called the **Switchboard Manager**. Using the Switchboard Manager, you can create sophisticated switchboard forms without having advanced form development skills, such as how to work with controls or how to modify property settings. Kristen creates a switchboard form to make the database easier to navigate.

Steps

1. **Click Tools on the menu bar, point to Database Utilities, click Switchboard Manager, then click Yes when prompted to create a switchboard**
   The Switchboard Manager dialog box opens and presents the first switchboard page, which you can edit or delete. Each new switchboard form you create is listed in the Switchboard Pages list of this dialog box. One switchboard page must be designated as the **default switchboard**, the first switchboard in the database, and the one you use to link to additional switchboard pages.

2. **Click Edit**
   The Edit Switchboard Page dialog box opens. The switchboard form does not contain any items.

3. **Click New**
   The Edit Switchboard Item dialog box opens, prompting you for three important items: Text (a label on the switchboard form that identifies the corresponding command button), Command (which corresponds to a database action), and Switchboard (which further defines the command button action). Switchboard options depend on the action selected in the Command list.

4. **Type Open Employees Form in the Text text box, click the Command list arrow, click Open Form in Edit Mode, click the Form list arrow, then click Employees**
   The Edit Switchboard Item dialog box should look like Figure M-17.

5. **Click OK to add the first command button to the switchboard, click New, type Accounting Reports in the Text text box, click the Command list arrow, click Open Form in Edit Mode, click the Form list arrow, click Accounting Reports, then click OK**
   The Edit Switchboard Page dialog box should look like Figure M-18. Each entry in this dialog box represents a command button that will appear on the final switchboard.

6. **Click Close to close the Edit Switchboard Page dialog box, then click Close to close the Switchboard Manager dialog box**

7. **Click Forms on the Objects bar (if it is not already selected), double-click the Switchboard form, then click the Switchboard Restore Window button (if it is maximized)**
   The finished switchboard opens in Form View, as shown in Figure M-19.

8. **Click the Open Employees Form command button on the Switchboard, close the Employees form, click the Accounting Reports command button, then close Accounting Reports dialog box**
   Switchboard forms provide a fast and easy way to help users navigate a large database.

FIGURE M-17: Edit Switchboard Item dialog box

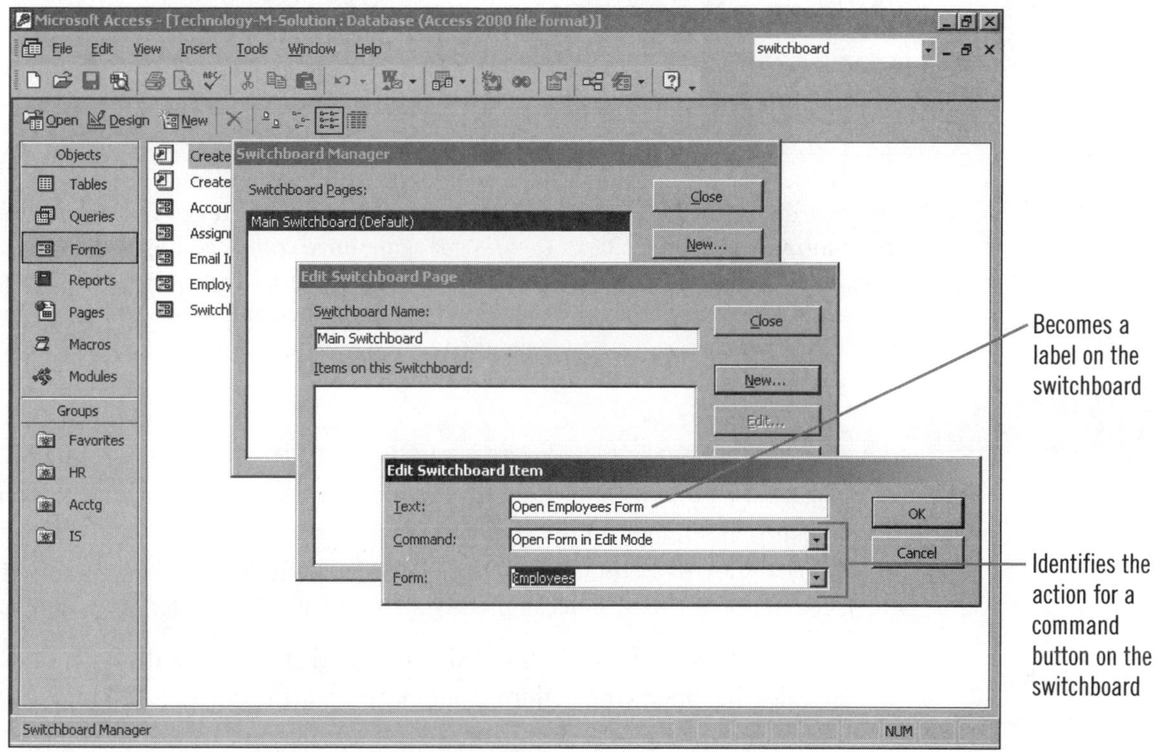

FIGURE M-18: Edit Switchboard Page dialog box

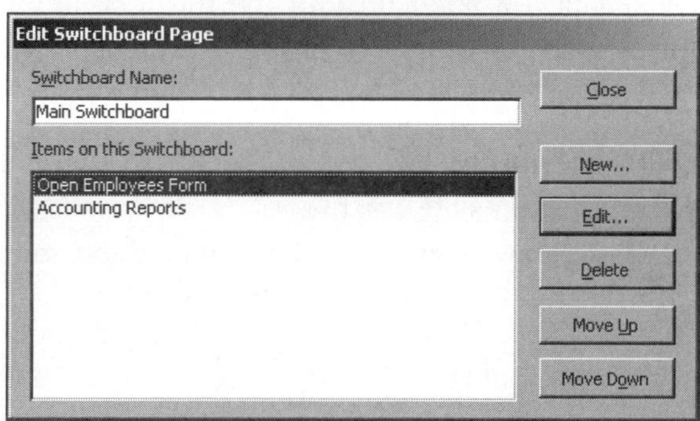

FIGURE M-19: Switchboard

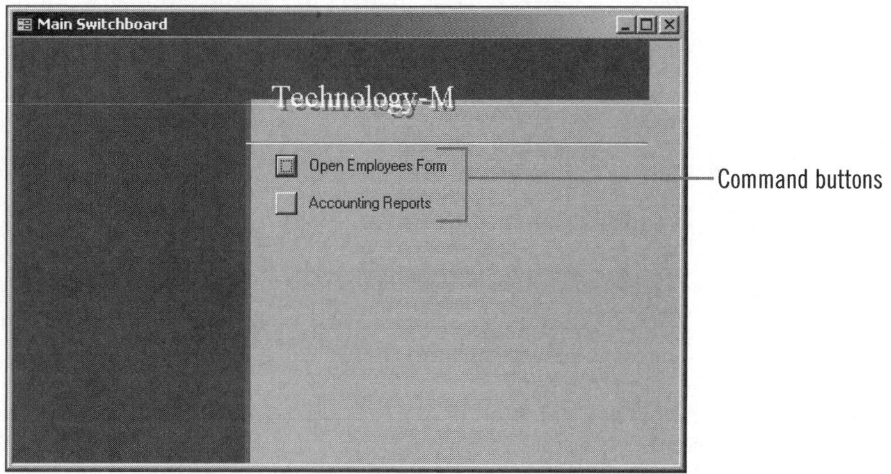

Access 2002

Access 2002

Modifying a Switchboard

Always use the Switchboard Manager to add, delete, move, and edit the command buttons and text that describes the command buttons on a switchboard form. Use Form Design View to make formatting modifications such as changing form colors, adding clip art, or changing the switchboard title. Kristen is happy with the initial switchboard form she created, but she would like to improve it by changing the title, colors, and order of the command buttons. She uses Form Design View to make the formatting changes and the Switchboard Manager to change the order of the buttons.

Steps

1. Click the **Design View button** on the Form View toolbar, then click the **dark green rectangle** on the left of the Detail section
   The dark green blocks on the left and top portion of the Switchboard are actually rectangles, added to provide color. You can modify them just as you would modify any clip art object.
2. Click the **Fill/Back Color button list arrow** on the Formatting (Form/Report) toolbar, click the **yellow box** (third column and fourth row from the top), click the **dark green rectangle** on the top of the Detail section, click , then click the **red box** (first column and third row from the top)
3. Click the **white Technology-M label** to select it, point to the edge, use to drag the white Technology-M label up into the red rectangle, click the **gray Technology-M** label to select it, then press **[Delete]**
   The modified switchboard should look like Figure M-20.
4. Click the **Label button** on the Toolbox toolbar, click the **yellow rectangle**, type **your name**, then press **[Enter]**
   You use Form Design View to modify colors, titles, and make other formatting changes. Notice that the text describing each command button does not appear in Form Design View. This text and other information about the command buttons on the Switchboard form are stored in a table called Switchboard Items.
5. Click the **Save button** on the Form Design toolbar, close the switchboard, click **Tools** on the menu, point to **Database Utilities**, click **Switchboard Manager**, then click **Edit**
   You use the Switchboard Manager to edit the text that accompanies command buttons.
6. Click **Accounting Reports**, click **Edit**, click to the left of the **A** in the Text text box, type **Preview**, press **[Spacebar]**, then click **OK**
   You can add, delete, move, or edit command buttons from the Edit Switchboard Page dialog box.
7. Click **Move Up** to make Preview Accounting Reports the first item in the switchboard, click **Close**, then click **Close**
8. Double-click the **Switchboard** form to open it in Form View, click on the Form View toolbar to print the Switchboard, close the switchboard, then exit Access
   The modified switchboard should look like Figure M-21.

Trouble?

If you need to delete your Switchboard form and start over, you must first delete the Switchboard Items table before you can re-create the form.

FIGURE M-20: Switchboard in Form Design View

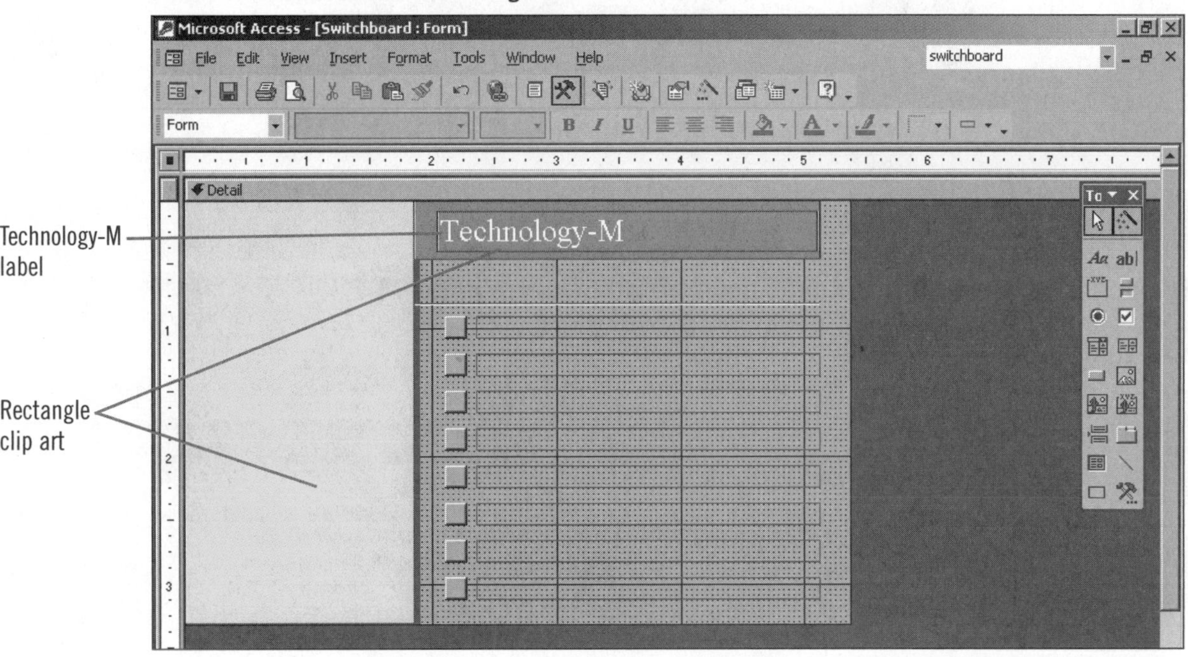

FIGURE M-21: Modified switchboard

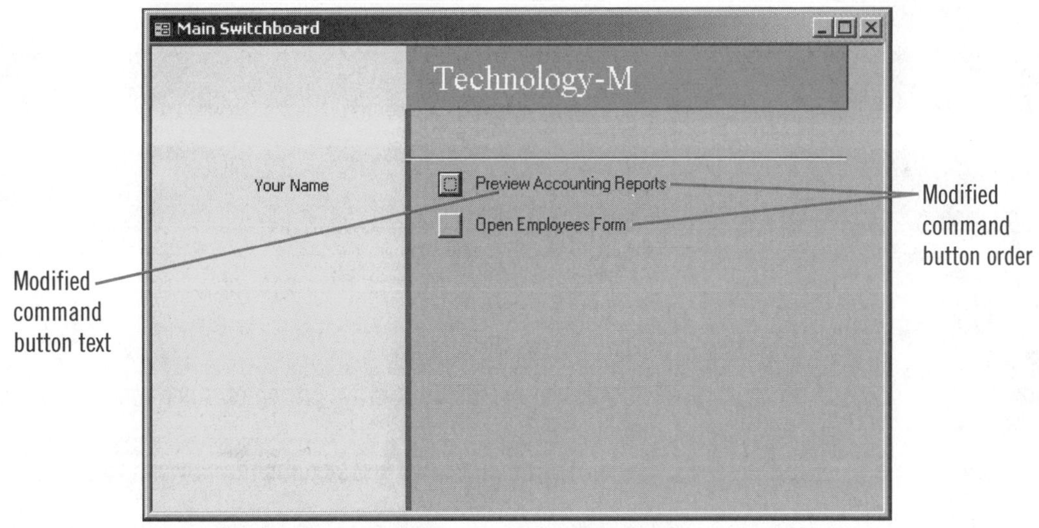

The Northwind database

Microsoft provides a sample database with Access 2002 called **Northwind** that illustrates how to use Access switchboards and dialog boxes. To open the Northwind database, click Help on the menu bar, point to Sample Databases, then click Northwind Sample Database. If this is the first time the database has been opened, you will be prompted to install it. Northwind not only contains sample switchboard forms, but it is a robust relational database that provides many useful sample objects of all types.

Practice

► Concepts Review

Identify each element of the Database window shown in Figure M-22.

FIGURE M-22

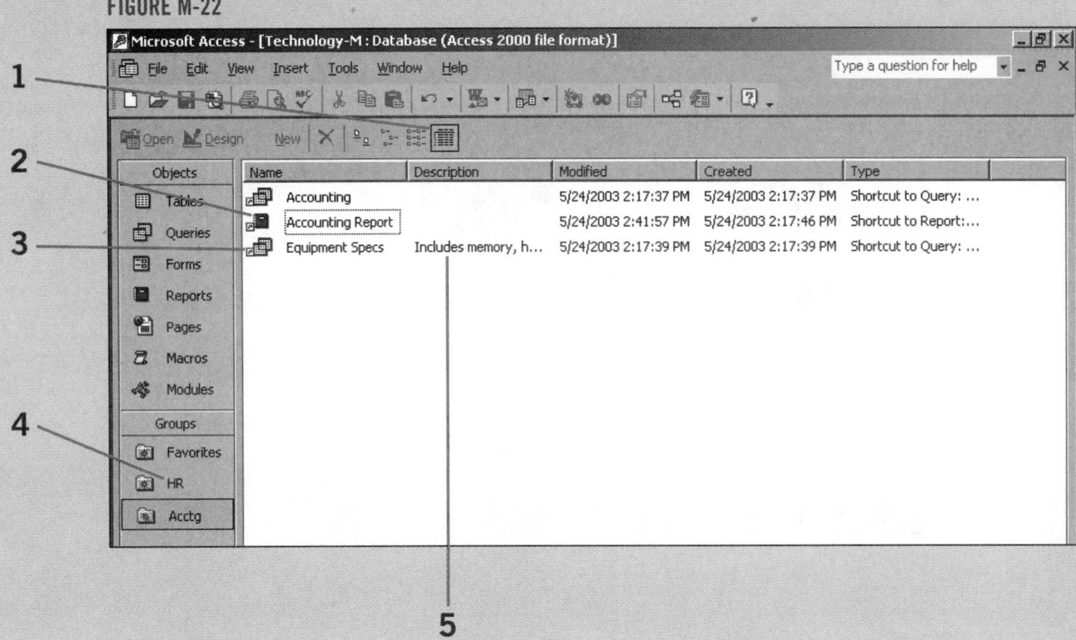

Match each term with the statement that describes its function.

6. Group
7. Pop-up form
8. Shortcut
9. Northwind
10. Documenter
11. Switchboard

a. Creates reports on the properties and relationships among the objects in your database
b. Pointer to database objects
c. Special type of form that stays on top of other open forms, even when another form is active
d. Special type of form that uses command buttons to simplify and secure access to database objects
e. Sample database used to illustrate many Access features, including switchboards
f. Helps you easily organize and classify objects

Select the best answer from the list of choices.

12. Which View button do you use to see the date that the object was created?
- **a.** List
- **b.** Small Icons
- **c.** Date
- **d.** Details

13. Which feature fixes discrepancies between references to field names, controls, and objects when you rename them?
- **a.** Documenter
- **b.** Renamer
- **c.** Name AutoCorrect
- **d.** Switchboard Manager

14. If you wanted to add a command button to a switchboard, which view or tool would you use?
- **a.** Form Design View
- **b.** Report Design View
- **c.** Switchboard Manager
- **d.** Switchboard Analyzer

15. Which item would NOT help you organize the Access objects that the Human Resources (HR) Department most often uses?
- **a.** A report that lists all HR employees
- **b.** A switchboard that provides command buttons to the appropriate HR objects
- **c.** A dialog box with command buttons that reference the most commonly used HR forms and reports
- **d.** An HR group with shortcuts to the HR objects

16. Northwind is the name of a sample:
- **a.** Switchboard form.
- **b.** Database.
- **c.** Pop-up form.
- **d.** Dialog box.

17. A dialog box is which type of object?
- **a.** Table
- **b.** Form
- **c.** Macro
- **d.** Report

18. A switchboard is which type of object?
- **a.** Table
- **b.** Form
- **c.** Macro
- **d.** Report

19. If you wanted to modify the text that identifies each command button on the switchboard, which view or tool would you use?
- **a.** Table Design View
- **b.** Form Design View
- **c.** Switchboard Manager
- **d.** Documenter

20. If you wanted to change the clip art on a switchboard, which view or tool would you use?
- **a.** Form View
- **b.** Form Design View
- **c.** Switchboard Manager
- **d.** Switchboard Documenter

Skills Review

1. Work with objects.
- **a.** Open the **Basketball–M** database, then maximize the Database window.
- **b.** Click the Details button to view the details, then click Reports on the Objects bar.
- **c.** Open the property sheet for the Player Field Goal Stats report (resize the columns to view the entire report name if needed), then type **Forwards and Guards** for the Description property.
- **d.** Click Queries on the Objects bar, then rename the Games query with the name **Score Delta**.
- **e.** Open the Games Summary Report in Design View, open the report property sheet, then check the Record Source property on the Data tab. Because the Games Summary Report was based on the former Games Query object, the new query name should appear in the Record Source property.
- **f.** Close the property sheet, save, then close the Games Summary Report.

2. Use the Documenter.
- **a.** Click Tools on the menu bar, point to Analyze, then click Documenter.
- **b.** Click the Tables tab, click Select All, click the Reports tab, click the Games Summary Report check box, then click OK.
- **c.** Watch the status bar to track the progress of the Documenter.
- **d.** The final report is several pages long. Click File on the menu bar, click Print, click the Pages option button, enter **1** in the From text box, enter **1** in the To text box, then click OK to print the first page. Write your name on the printout.
- **e.** Close the report created by Documenter.

3. **Group objects.**
   a. Create a new group named **Forwards**.
   b. Create shortcuts for the Forward Field Goals query and the Forward Field Goal Stats report in the Forwards group.
   c. Create a new group named **Guards**.
   d. Create shortcuts for the Guard Field Goals query and Guard Field Goal Stats report in the Guards group.
4. **Modify shortcuts and groups.**
   a. Rename the Forward Field Goals query shortcut in the Forwards group to **Forward FG Query**.
   b. Rename the Forward Field Goal Stats report shortcut in the Forwards group to **Forward FG Report**.
   c. Rename the Guard Field Goals query shortcut in the Guards group to **Guard FG Query**.
   d. Rename the Guard Field Goal Stats report shortcut in the Guards group to **Guard FG Report**.
   e. Double-click the Forward FG Query shortcut in the Forwards group, then enter your name to replace Amy Hodel on any record where her name appears.
   f. Print the datasheet, save, then close the Forward Field Goals query.
5. **Create a dialog box.**
   a. Start a new form in Form Design View.
   b. Add a command button to the upper-left corner of the form using the Command Button Wizard. Select Report Operations from the Categories list, select Preview Report from the Actions list, then select the Games Summary Report.
   c. Type **Preview Games Summary Report** as the text for the button, then type **GamesReport** for the button name.
   d. Add a second command button below the first to preview the Player Field Goal Stats report.
   e. Type **Preview Player FG Stats** as the text for the button, then type **PlayersReport** for the button name.
   f. Below the two buttons, add a label to the form with your name.
   g. In the property sheet for the form, change the Border Style property of the form to Dialog, the Record Selectors property to No, and the Navigation Buttons property to No.
   h. Close the property sheet, restore the form (if it is maximized), resize the form and Form Design View window until it is approximately 3" wide by 3" tall, then save the form as **Team Reports**.
   i. Open the Team Reports form in Form View, test the buttons, then print the form. Your Team Reports form should be similar to Figure M-23.

FIGURE M-23

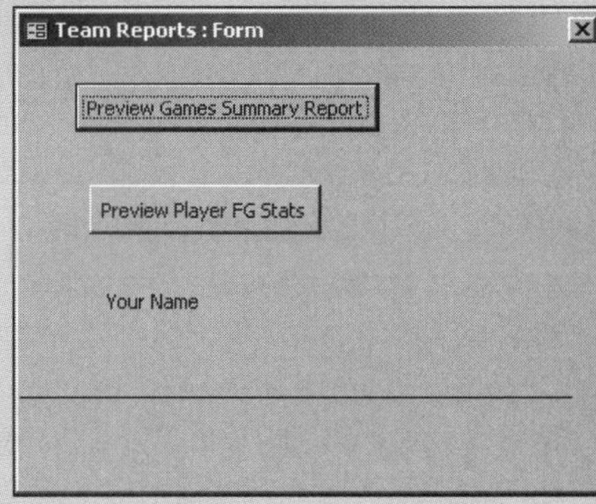

6. **Create a pop-up form.**
   a. Using the Form Wizard, create a form with the following fields from the Players table: First, Last, and PlayerNo.
   b. Use a Tabular layout, a Standard style, and title the form **Player Pop-up**.
   c. In Design View of the Player Pop-up form, resize the First and Last labels and text boxes to about half of their current width.
   d. Move the Last and PlayerNo labels and text boxes next to the First label and text box so that the entire form can be narrowed to no larger than 3" wide. Resize the form to 3" wide.
   e. Open the property sheet for the Player Pop-up form, change the Pop Up property to Yes, then close the property sheet.
   f. Save, then close the Player Pop-up form.
   g. Open the Team Reports form in Form Design View, then add a command button to the bottom of the form using the Command Button Wizard.
   h. In the Command Button Wizard, select the Form Operations category, the Open Form action, and the Player Pop-up form to open. The form should be opened to show all of the records.
   i. Type **Open Player Pop-up** as the text for the button, then name the button **PlayerPopup**.

j. Save the Team Reports form, then open it in Form View. Click the Open Player Pop-up command button to test it. Test the other buttons as well. The Player Pop-up form should stay on top of all other forms and reports until you close it.
k. Save, then close all open forms and reports.

7. **Create a switchboard.**
   a. Click Tools on the menu bar, point to Database Utilities, click Switchboard Manager, then click Yes to create a new switchboard.
   b. Click Edit to edit the Main Switchboard, then click New to add the first item to it.
   c. Type **Select a Team Report** as the Text entry for the first command button, select Open Form in Add Mode for the Command, select Team Reports for the Form, then click OK to add the first command button to the switchboard.
   d. Click New to add a second item to the switchboard. Type **Open Player Entry Form** as the Text entry, select Open Form in Add Mode for the Command, select Player Entry Form for the Form, then click OK to add the second command button to the switchboard.
   e. Close the Edit Switchboard manager dialog box, then close the Switchboard Manager dialog box. Open the Switchboard form and click both command buttons to make sure they work. Notice that when you open a form in Add Mode (rather than using the Open Form in Edit Mode action within the Switchboard Manager), the navigation buttons indicate that you can only add a new record, and not edit an existing one.
   f. Close all open forms including the Switchboard form.

8. **Modify a switchboard.**
   a. Click Tools on the menu bar, point to Database Utilities, click Switchboard Manager, then click Edit to edit the Main Switchboard.
   b. Click the Open Player Entry Form item, then click Edit.
   c. Select Open Form in Edit Mode for the Command, select Player Entry Form for the Form, then click OK.
   d. Move the Open Player Entry Form item above the Select a Team Report item, then close the Switchboard Manager.
   e. In Form Design View of the Switchboard form, delete both the white and gray Basketball–M labels, add a label with the name of your favorite team's name to the top of the form, then add a label with your own name to the left side of the form. Format the labels with a color and size that makes them easy to read in Form View.
   f. View the modified switchboard in Form View, as shown in Figure M-24, then test the buttons. Notice the difference in the Open Player Entry Form button (the form opens in Edit Mode versus Add Mode).
   g. Save, print, then close the Switchboard form.
   h. Close the Basketball–M database, then exit Access.

FIGURE M-24

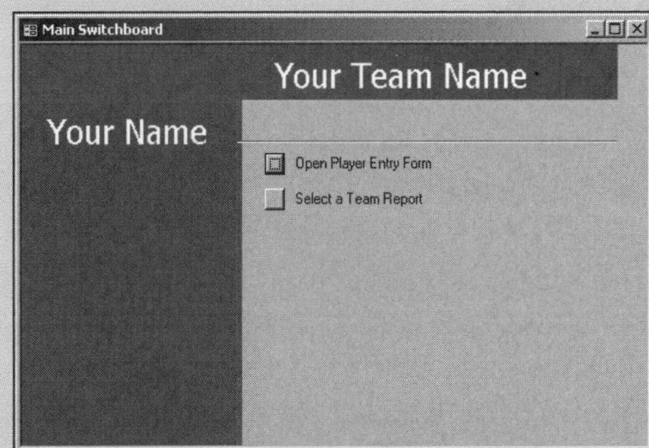

Independent Challenge 1

As the manager of a doctor's clinic, you have created an Access database called Patients-M to track insurance claim reimbursements that are fixed (paid at a predetermined fixed rate), or denied (not paid by the insurance company). You want to create two groups to organize database objects. You also want to document the database's relationships.

a. Start Access, then open the database **Patients–M** from the drive and folder where your Project Files are located.
b. Create two new groups, **Fixed** and **Denied**.
c. Add shortcuts for the Monthly Query–Fixed query, the Date of Service Report–Fixed report, and the Monthly Claims Report–Fixed report to the Fixed group.

d. Add shortcuts for the Monthly Query–Denied query, the Date of Service Report–Denied report, and the Monthly Claims Report–Denied report to the Denied group.
e. Click Tools on the menu bar, point to Analyze, then click Documenter. On the Current Database tab, click Relationships, then click OK.
f. Print the Documenter's report, then close it. Write your name on the printout.
g. Close the Patients–M database, then exit Access.

▶ Independent Challenge 2

As the manager of a doctor's clinic, you have created an Access database called Patients–M to track insurance claim reimbursements that are fixed (paid at a predetermined fixed rate) or denied (not paid by the insurance company). You want to create a new dialog box to make it easier to preview the reports within your database.

a. Start Access, then open the database **Patients–M** from the drive and folder where your Project Files are located.
b. Start a new form in Form Design View.
c. Using the Command Button Wizard, add a command button to the form. Select Report Operations from the Categories list, select Preview Report from the Actions list, then select the Date of Service Report–Denied report.
d. Type **Preview Date of Service–Denied** as the text for the button, then type **PDOSD** for the button name.
e. Using the Command Button Wizard, add a second command button under the first. Select Report Operations from the Categories list, select Preview Report from the Actions list, then select the Date of Service Report–Fixed report.
f. Type **Preview Date of Service–Fixed** as the text for the button, then type **PDOSF** for the button name.
g. Using the Command Button Wizard, add a third command button under the second. Select Report Operations from the Categories list, select Preview Report from the Actions list, then select the Monthly Claims Report–Denied report.
h. Type **Preview Monthly Claims–Denied** as the text for the button, then type **PMCD** for the button name.
i. Using the Command Button Wizard, add a fourth command button under the third. Select Report Operations from the Categories list, select Preview Report from the Actions list, then select the Monthly Claims Report–Fixed report.
j. Type **Preview Monthly Claims–Fixed** as the text for the button, then type **PMCF** for the button name.
k. Below the buttons, add a label to the form with your name.
l. Open the property sheet for the form, change Border Style property to Dialog, the Record Selectors property to No, and the Navigation Buttons property to No.
m. Close the property sheet, restore the form (if it is maximized), resize the form and Form Design View window so they are approximately 3" wide by 3" tall, then save the form as **Report Dialog Box**.
n. Open the Report Dialog Box form in Form View, test the buttons, then print the form. It should look like Figure M-25.
o. Close the Report Dialog Box form, close the Patients–M database, then exit Access.

FIGURE M-25

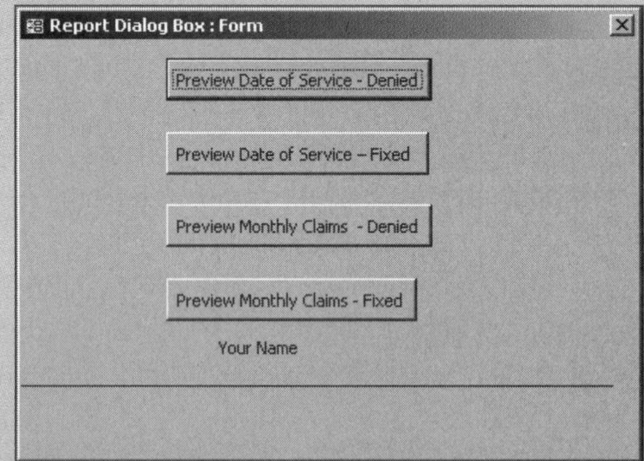

Independent Challenge 3

As the manager of a doctor's clinic, you have created an Access database called Patients–M to track insurance claim reimbursements that are fixed (paid at a predetermined fixed rate), or denied (not paid by the insurance company). You want to create a pop-up form to provide physician information. You want to add a command button to the Claim Entry Form to open the pop-up form.

a. Start Access, then open the database **Patients–M** from the drive and folder where your Project Files are located.
b. Use the Form Wizard to create a form with all three of the fields in the Doctors table.
c. Use a Tabular layout, a Standard style, and type **Doctor Pop-up** for the form title.
d. In Form Design View of the Doctor Pop-up form, resize all three labels and text boxes to about half their current width.
e. Move the PodLastName and PodCode labels and text boxes next to the PodFirstName label and text box, then resize the form to no wider than 3".
f. Open the property sheet for the form, then change the Pop-Up property to Yes.
g. Save, then close the Doctor Pop-up form.
h. In Form Design View of the Claim Entry Form, use the Command Button Wizard to create a command button placed in the right of the Form Header section.
i. Select Form Operations from the Categories list, select Open Form from the Actions list, select the Doctor Pop-up form, then choose the option button to open the form and show all of the records.
j. Type **Open Doctor Pop-up** as the text for the button, then type **Docs** for the button name.
k. Add a label to the Form Header with your name.
l. Save the Claim Entry Form, open it in Form View, then click the Open Doctor Pop-up command button.
m. Move through the records of the Claim Entry form. The Doctor Pop-up form should stay on top of all other forms.
n. Print the first record in the Claim Entry form. Close all open forms, close the Patients–M database, then exit Access.

Independent Challenge 4

Switchboard forms appear in many styles and are used on many Web pages to help you navigate that Web site. In this independent challenge, surf the Internet to find Web pages that present information organized similarly to how switchboards are used on Access forms.

a. Connect to the Internet, go to www.unisa.ac.za, the home page for the University of South Africa (substitute your own school or company home page, if desired), then explore the navigation aids on the page to determine if they have any controls that work similarly to how a switchboard works. Go back to the home page and print only the first page. On the printout, identify the area of the Web page that worked like a switchboard. If you didn't think that the Web page used a switchboard, explain why.
b. Go to www.google.com, a search engine (substitute your own favorite search engine, if desired), then explore the home page to determine if the page works like a switchboard. Return to the home page, then print only the first page. On the printout, identify the area of the Web page that worked like a switchboard. If you didn't think that the Web page worked like a switchboard, explain why.
c. Go to www.web100.com, a Web page that logs popular Web sites (substitute your own favorite reference or portal Web site, if desired), then explore the navigation aids on the page to determine if they have any controls that work similarly to how a switchboard works. Go back to the home page, then print only the first page. On the printout, identify the area of the Web page that worked like a switchboard. If you didn't think that the Web page used a switchboard, explain why.

d. Not all Web pages organize their content by using hyperlinks that work like switchboards. On a piece of paper, write a paragraph about the other types of hyperlinks you found that help organize and navigate a site, then identify and explain the characteristics of the controls you liked best.

Visual Workshop

As the manager of a doctor's clinic, you have created an Access database called **Patients–M** to track insurance claim reimbursements that are fixed (paid at a predetermined fixed rate), or denied (not paid by the insurance company). Create a switchboard form to give the users an easy interface, as shown in Figure M-26. Both command buttons on the switchboard open forms in Edit Mode. Add and modify the labels shown at the top of the switchboard in Form Design View, and be sure to add your own name as the manager. Print the switchboard.

FIGURE M-26

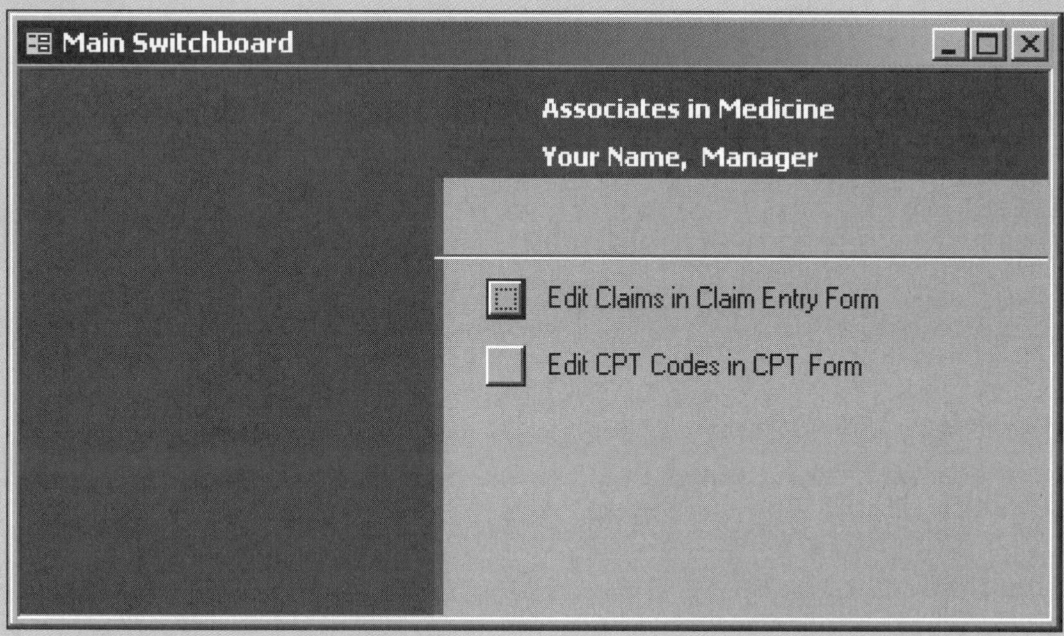

Access 2002

Creating

Macros

Objectives

- Understand macros
- Create a macro
- Modify actions and arguments
- Create a macro group
- Set conditional expressions
- Work with events
- Customize toolbars
- Troubleshoot macros

A **macro** is a database object that stores Access actions. When you **run** a macro, you execute the stored set of actions. **Actions** are the tasks that you want the macro to perform. Access provides about 50 actions from which to choose when creating a macro. Almost any repetitive Access task such as printing a report, opening a form, or exporting data is a good candidate for a macro. Automating routine and complex tasks by using a macro builds efficiency, accuracy, and flexibility into your database. Kristen Fontanelle, a network administrator at MediaLoft, has noticed that several tasks are repeated on a regular basis and can be automated with macros.

Understanding Macros

A macro object may contain one or more actions, or tasks that you want Access to perform. When you run a macro, the actions are executed in the order in which they are listed in **Macro Design View**. Each action has a specified set of **arguments** that provide additional information on how to carry out the action. For example, the OpenForm action contains six arguments including Form Name (identifies which form to open) and View (determines whether the form should be opened in Form View or Design View). Creating macros is easy because after choosing the appropriate macro action, the associated arguments for that action automatically appear in the lower pane of Macro Design View. Kristen studies the major benefits of using macros, macro terminology, and the components of Macro Design View before building her first macro.

The major benefits of using macros include:

- saving time by automating routine tasks.
- increasing accuracy by ensuring that tasks are executed consistently.
- improving the functionality and ease of use of forms by adding command buttons that execute macros.
- ensuring data accuracy in forms by using macros to respond to data entry errors.
- automating data transfers such as exporting data to an Excel workbook.
- creating your own customized environment by using macros to customize toolbars and menus.

Macro terminology:

- A **macro** is an Access object that stores a series of actions to perform one or more tasks.
- Each task that you want the macro to perform is called an **action**. Each macro action occupies a single row in Macro Design View.
- **Macro Design View** is the window in which you create a macro, as shown in Figure N-1. See Table N-1 for a description of Macro Design View components.
- **Arguments** are properties of an action that provide additional information on how the action should execute.
- A **macro group** is an Access macro object that stores more than one macro. The macros in a macro group run independently of one another, but are grouped together to organize multiple macros that have similar characteristics. For example, you may want to put all of the macros that print reports in one macro group.
- An **expression** is a combination of values, fields, and operators that result in a value.
- A **conditional expression** is an expression that results in either a true or false answer that determines if a macro action will execute or not. For example, if the Country field contains a null value (nothing), you may want the macro to execute an action that sends the user a message.
- An **event** is something that happens on a form, window, toolbar, or datasheet—such as the click of a command button or an entry in a field—that can be used to initiate the execution of a macro.

FIGURE N-1: Macro Design View of a macro group

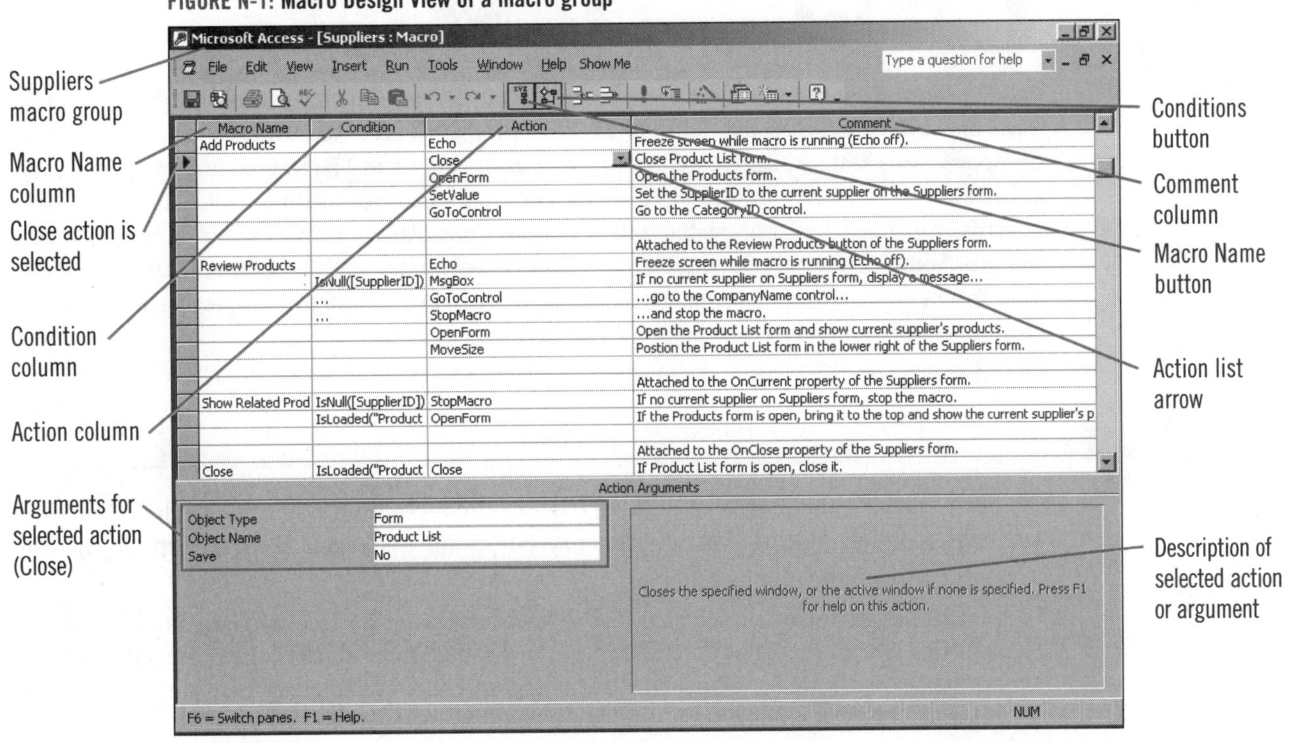

TABLE N-1: Macro Design View components

Component	Description
Macro Name column	Contains the names of individual macros within a macro group. If the macro object contains only one macro, it isn't necessary to use this column because you can run the macro by referring to the macro by the macro object's name. View this column by clicking the Macro Names button. The Macro Names button works as a toggle to open and close the Macro Name column.
Condition column	Contains conditional expressions that are evaluated either true or false. If true, the macro action on that row is executed. If false, the macro action on that row is skipped. View this column by clicking the Conditions button. The Conditions button works as a toggle to open and close the Condition column.
Action column	Contains the actions, or the tasks, that the macro executes when it runs
Comment column	Contains optional explanatory text for each row
Action Arguments pane	Displays the arguments for the selected action
	Indicates which row is currently selected

Creating a Macro

In some software programs, you can create a macro by using a "macro recorder" to record, or save, the keystrokes and mouse clicks you use to perform a task. Access doesn't use that method. In Access, you create a macro by choosing a series of actions in Macro Design View that accomplish the job you want to automate. Therefore, if you are to become proficient with Access macros, you must be comfortable with macro actions. Access provides more than 50 macro actions. Some of the most common actions are listed in Table N-2. Kristen observes that time can be saved opening the All Equipment report from the Employees form, so she decides to create a macro to automate this task.

Steps

1. Start Access, open the **Technology-N** database from where your Project Files are located, click **Macros** on the Objects bar, then click the **New button** on the Database window toolbar

   Macro Design View opens, ready for your first action. The Macro Name and Condition columns are not visible by default, but can be toggled on by clicking their respective buttons on the Macro Design toolbar. They are only needed, of course, if you are creating multiple macros in the same macro object or using conditional expressions.

2. Click the **Action list arrow**, press **o** to quickly scroll to the actions that start with the letter "o", then click **OpenReport**

   The OpenReport action is added as the first line, and the arguments that further define the OpenReport action appear in the Action Arguments pane in the lower half of Macro Design View. The OpenReport action has two required arguments: Report Name and View. The Filter Name and Where Condition arguments are optional.

QuickTip

Press [F6] to jump between the actions and Action Arguments panes in Macro Design View.

3. Click the **Report Name argument text box** in the Action Arguments pane, click the **Report Name List arrow**, then click **All Equipment**

   All of the report objects in the Technology-N database display in the Report Name argument list.

4. Click the **View argument text box** in the Action Arguments pane, click the **View list arrow**, then click **Print Preview**

   Your screen should look like Figure N-2. Macros can be one or many actions long. In this case, the macro is only one action long and has no conditional expressions.

5. Click the **Save button** on the Macro Design toolbar, type **Preview All Equipment Report** in the Macro Name text box, click **OK**, then close Macro Design View

   The Technology-N database window shows the Print All Equipment Report object as a macro object.

6. Click the **Run button** in the Database window toolbar

   The All Equipment report opens in Print Preview.

7. Close the All Equipment preview window

FIGURE N-2: Macro Design View with OpenReport action

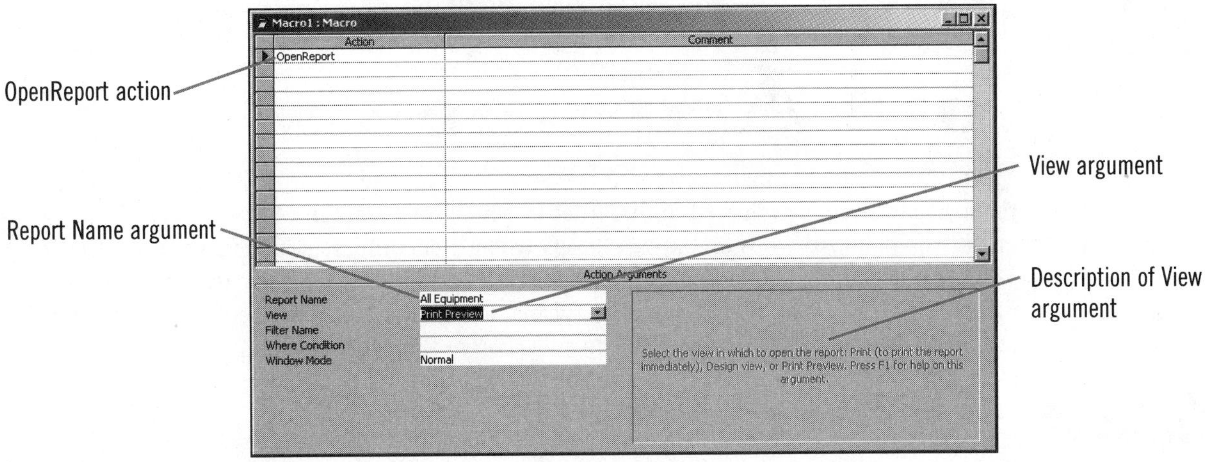

TABLE N-2: Common macro actions

subject area	macro action	description
Handling data in forms	ApplyFilter	Restricts the number of records that appear in the resulting form or report by applying limiting criteria
	FindRecord	Finds the first record that meets the criteria
	GoToControl	Moves the focus (where you are currently typing or clicking) to a specific field or control
	GoToRecord	Makes a specified record the current record
Executing menu options	RunCode	Runs a Visual Basic function (a series of programming statements that do a calculation or comparison and return a value)
	RunCommand	Carries out a specified menu command
	RunMacro	Runs a macro or attaches a macro to a custom menu command
	StopMacro	Stops the currently running macro
Importing/Exporting data	TransferDatabase TransferSpreadsheet TransferText	Imports, links, or exports data between the current Microsoft Access database and another database, spreadsheet, or text file
Manipulating objects	Close	Closes a window
	Maximize	Enlarges the active window to fill the Access window
	OpenForm	Opens a form in Form View, Design View, Print Preview, or Datasheet View
	OpenQuery	Opens a select or crosstab query in Datasheet View, Design View, or Print Preview; runs an action query
	OpenReport	Opens a report in Design View or Print Preview, or prints the report
	OpenTable	Opens a table in Datasheet View, Design View, or Print Preview
	PrintOut	Prints the active object, such as a datasheet, report, form, or module
	SetValue	Sets the value of a field, control, or property
Miscellaneous	Beep	Sounds a beep tone through the computer's speaker
	MsgBox	Displays a message box containing a warning or an informational message
	SendKeys	Sends keystrokes directly to Microsoft Access or to an active Windows-based application

Modifying Actions and Arguments

Macros can contain as many actions as necessary to complete the process that you want to automate. Each action is evaluated in the order in which it appears in Macro Design View, starting at the top. A macro stops executing actions when it encounters a blank row in Macro Design View. While some macro actions manipulate data or objects, others are used only to make the database easier to use. **MsgBox** is a useful macro action because it displays an informational message. Kristen decides to add an action to the Print All Equipment Report macro to clarify what is happening when the macro runs. She adds a MsgBox action to the macro to display a descriptive message for the user.

1. Click the **Design button** on the Database window toolbar
   The Print All Equipment Report macro opens in Macro Design View.
2. Click the **Action cell** for the second row, click the **Action list arrow**, press **m** to quickly scroll to the actions that start with the letter "m", then click **MsgBox**
   Each action has its own arguments that further clarify what the action will do.
3. Click the **Message argument text box** in the Action Arguments pane, then type **Click the Print button to print the All Equipment report**
   The Message argument determines what text appears in the message box. By default, the Beep argument is set to "Yes" and the Type argument is set to "None."
4. Click the **Type argument text box** in the Action Arguments pane, read the description in the lower-right corner of Macro Design View, click the **Type list arrow**, then click **Information**
   The Type argument determines which icon will appear in the dialog box that is created by the MsgBox action.
5. Click the **Title argument text box** in the Action Arguments pane, then type **To print this report...**
   Your screen should look like Figure N-3. The Title argument specifies what text will display in the title bar of the resulting dialog box. If you leave the Title argument empty, the title bar of the resulting dialog box will display "Microsoft Access."
6. Click the **Save button** on the Macro Design toolbar, then click the **Run button** on the Macro Design toolbar
   If your speakers are turned on, you should hear a beep, then the message box should appear, as shown in Figure N-4.
7. Click **OK** in the dialog box, close the All Equipment report, then close Macro Design View

QuickTip

Press [F1] to display Help text for the action and argument currently selected.

FIGURE N-3: **New MsgBox action**

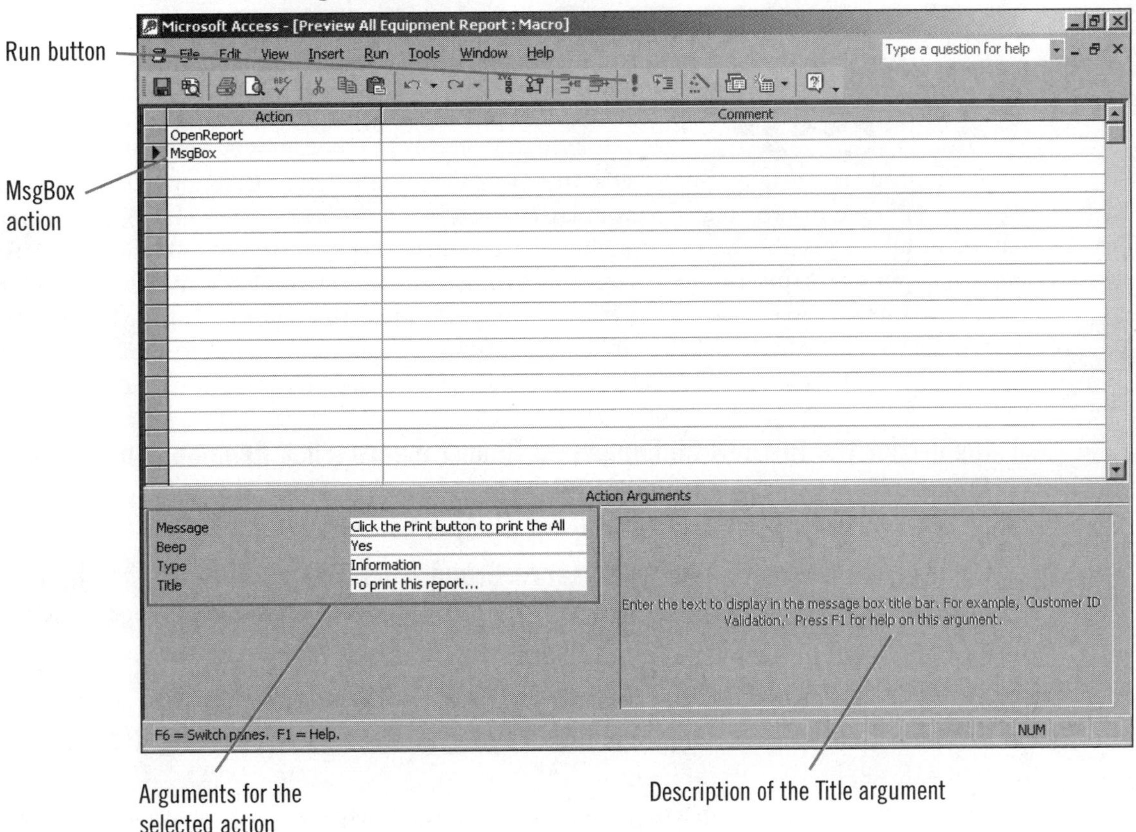

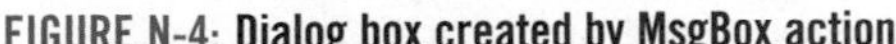

FIGURE N-4: **Dialog box created by MsgBox action**

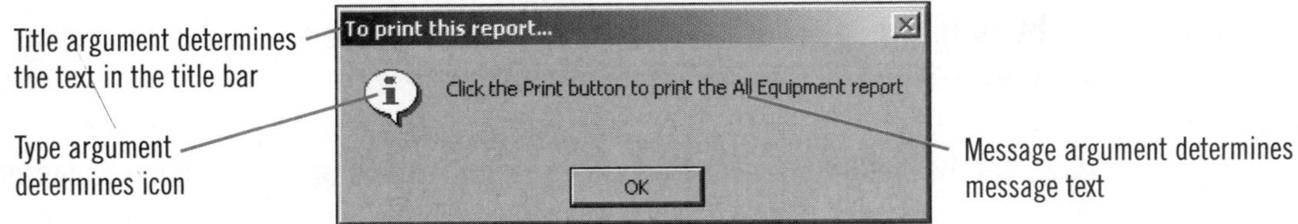

Access 2002

Creating a Macro Group

A **macro group** is a macro object that stores more than one macro. Macro groups are used to organize multiple macros that have similar characteristics, such as all the macros that print reports or all the macros that are used by the same form through various command buttons. When you put several macros in the same macro object to create a macro group, you must enter a unique name for each macro in the Macro Name column (in the same row as the first macro action) to identify where each macro starts. Kristen adds a macro that prints the Accounting Report in an existing macro object thereby creating a macro group.

Steps

1. Right-click the **Preview All Equipment Report macro**, click **Rename**, type **Preview Reports Macro Group**, then press **[Enter]**
   Object names should identify the object as clearly as possible.
2. Right-click the **Preview Reports Macro Group**, click **Design View** on the shortcut menu, click the **Macro Names button** on the Macro Design toolbar, type **Preview All Equipment** in the Macro Name column, then press **[Enter]**
   An individual macro in a macro group is named in the Macro Name column.
3. Click the **Macro Name cell** in the fourth row, type **Preview Accounting Report**, then press **[Enter]**
   An individual macro in a macro group stops when it hits a blank row, or when a new macro name is entered in the Macro Name column. Therefore, a blank row between macros is not required, but it does help to clarify where macros start and stop even when the Macro Name column is not visible.
4. Click the **Action list arrow**, scroll and click **OpenReport**, click in the **Report Name argument text box** in the Action Arguments pane, click the **Report Name list arrow**, click **Accounting Report**, click the **View argument text box**, click the **View list arrow**, then click **Print Preview**
   Your screen should look like Figure N-5. One benefit of creating several macros in one macro group is that you can copy and paste actions from one macro to another.
5. Click the **row selector of the MsgBox action of the Preview All Equipment macro**, click the **Copy button** on the Macro Design toolbar, click the **record selector for the fifth row**, then click the **Paste button** on the Macro Design toolbar
   Action argument values are copied with the action, but need to be edited as necessary to work with the new macro.
6. Select **All Equipment** in the Message property text box in the Action Arguments pane, type **Accounting,** then click the **Save button** on the Macro Design toolbar
   Your screen should look like Figure N-6. To run a macro (other than the first macro) from within a macro group, you use the Tools menu.
7. Click **Tools** on the menu bar, point to **Macro**, click **Run Macro**, click the **Macro Name list arrow** in the Run Macro dialog box, click **Preview Reports Macro Group.Preview Accounting Report**, then click **OK**
   Referring to a specific macro within a macro group by separating them with a period is called **dot notation**. Dot notation is also used when developing modules with Visual Basic programming code.
8. Click **OK**, then close the Accounting report and Macro Design View
   The Preview Reports Macro Group contains two macros.

QuickTip

To resize the columns of Macro Design View, point between the column headings then drag ↔.

FIGURE N-5: Creating a macro group

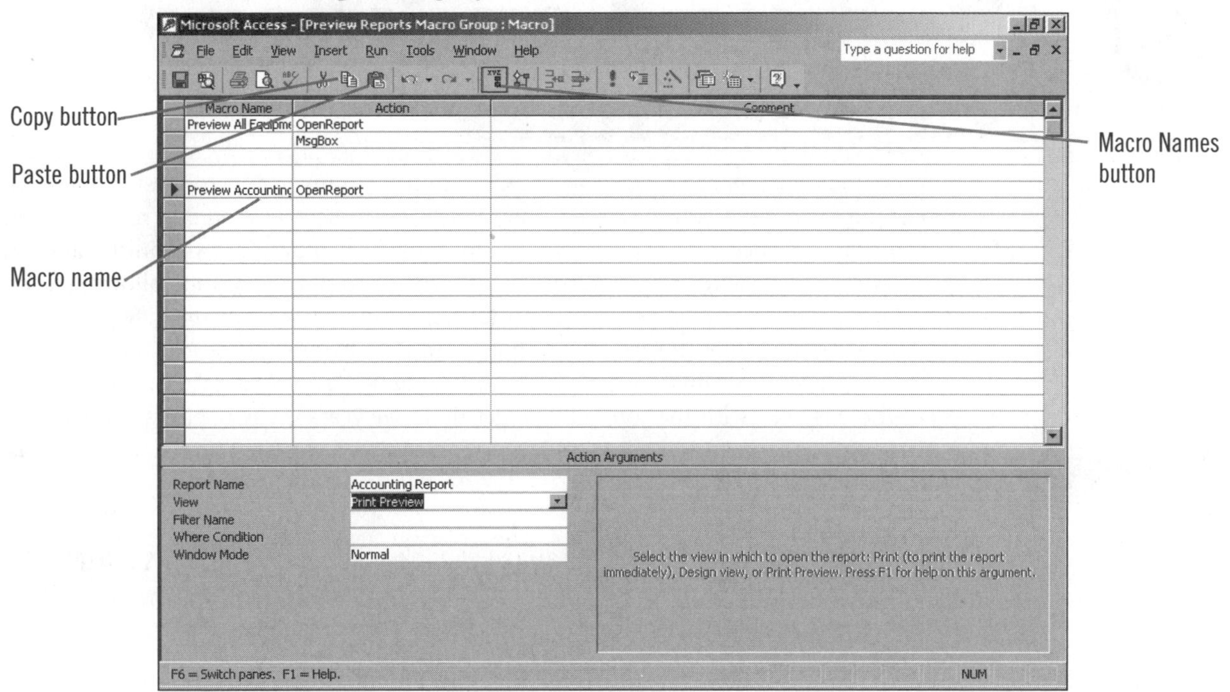

FIGURE N-6: Creating the Print Accounting Report macro

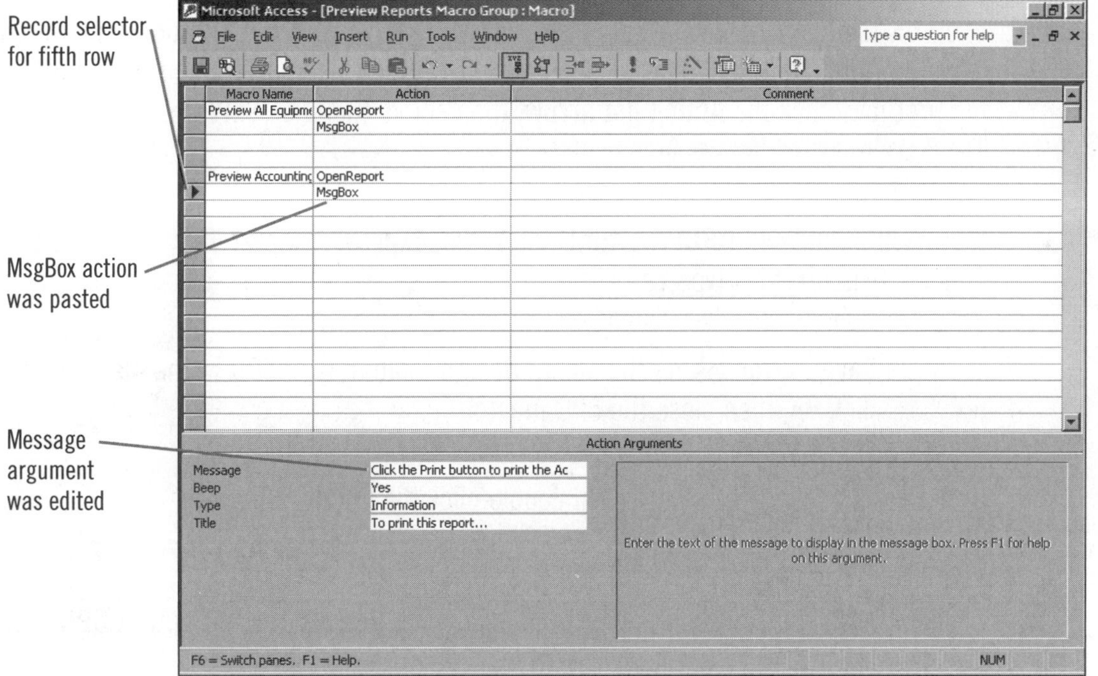

Assigning a macro to a key combination

You can assign a key combination (such as [Ctrl][L]) to a macro by creating a macro group with the name **AutoKeys**. Enter the key combination in the Macro Names column for the first action of the associated macro. Any key combination assignments you make in the AutoKeys macro override those that Access has already specified. Therefore, be sure to check the Keyboard Shortcuts information in the Microsoft Access Help system to make sure that the AutoKey assignment that you are creating doesn't override an Access quick keystroke that a user may already be using for another purpose.

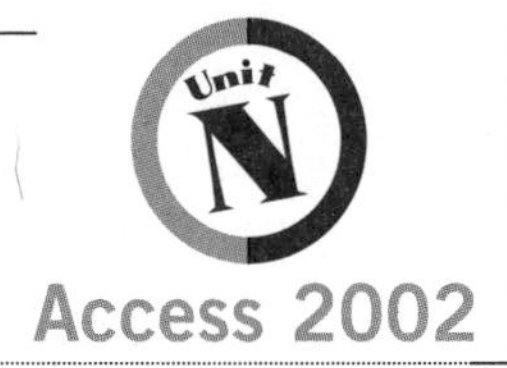

Access 2002

Setting Conditional Expressions

Conditional expressions are entered in the Condition column of Macro Design View. They result in a true or false value. If the condition evaluates true, the action on that row is executed. If the condition evaluates false, the macro skips that row. When building a conditional expression that refers to a value in a control on a form or report, use the following syntax: [Forms]![*formname*]![*controlname*] or [Reports]![*reportname*]![*controlname*]. Separating the object type (Forms or Reports) from the object name and from the control name by using [square brackets] and exclamation points ! is called **bang notation.** At MediaLoft, everyone who has been with the company longer than five years is eligible to take their old PC equipment home as soon as it has been replaced. Kristen uses a conditional macro to emphasize this information in a form.

1. Click the **New button** in the database window, click the **Conditions button** on the Macro Design toolbar, right-click the **Condition cell** in the first row, click **Zoom**, then type **[Forms]![Employees]![DateHired]<Date()-(5*365)** in the Zoom dialog box
   The Zoom dialog box should look like Figure N-7. This conditional expression says "Check the value in the DateHired control on the Employees form and evaluate true if that value is earlier than five years from today. Evaluate false if that value is not earlier than five years ago."
2. Click **OK** to close the Zoom dialog box, drag ✛ between the Condition and Action columns to expand the Condition column to its widest value, click the **Action cell** for the first row, click the **Action list arrow**, then scroll and click **SetValue**
   The SetValue action has two arguments.
3. Click the **Item argument text box** in the Action Arguments pane, type **[Forms]![Employees]![PCProgram]**, click the **Expression text box** in the Action Arguments panel, then type **Yes**
   Your screen should look like Figure N-8.
4. Click the **Save button** on the Macro Design toolbar, type **5PC** in the Macro Name text box, click **OK**, then close the 5PC macro
   Test the macro using the Employees form.
5. Click **Forms** on the Objects bar, then double-click the **Employees form**
   The record for Evelyn Storey, hired 1/1/92, appears. You use the 5PC macro to determine whether the PC Program check box should be checked.
6. Click **Tools** on the menu bar, point to **Macro**, click **Run Macro**, verify that **5PC** is in the Macro Name text box, then click **OK**
   After evaluating the date of this record and determining that this employee has been working at MediaLoft longer than five years, the PC Program check box was automatically checked (set to "Yes"), as shown in Figure N-9.
7. Click the **Last Record button** on the main form Navigation buttons, click **Tools** on the menu bar, point to **Macro**, click **Run Macro**, verify that **5PC** is in the **Macro Name text box**, then click **OK**
   Because Kristen Fontanelle was not hired more than five years ago, the PC Program check box was not checked (set to "yes") when you ran the macro.
8. Close the Employees form

FIGURE N-7: Zoom dialog box

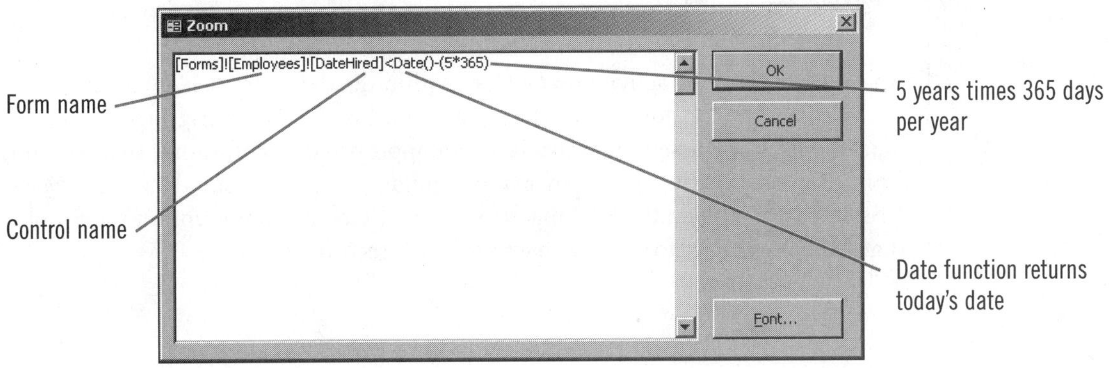

Zoom

[Forms]![Employees]![DateHired]<Date()-(5*365)

OK

Cancel

Font...

Form name

Control name

5 years times 365 days per year

Date function returns today's date

FIGURE N-8: Creating a conditional expression

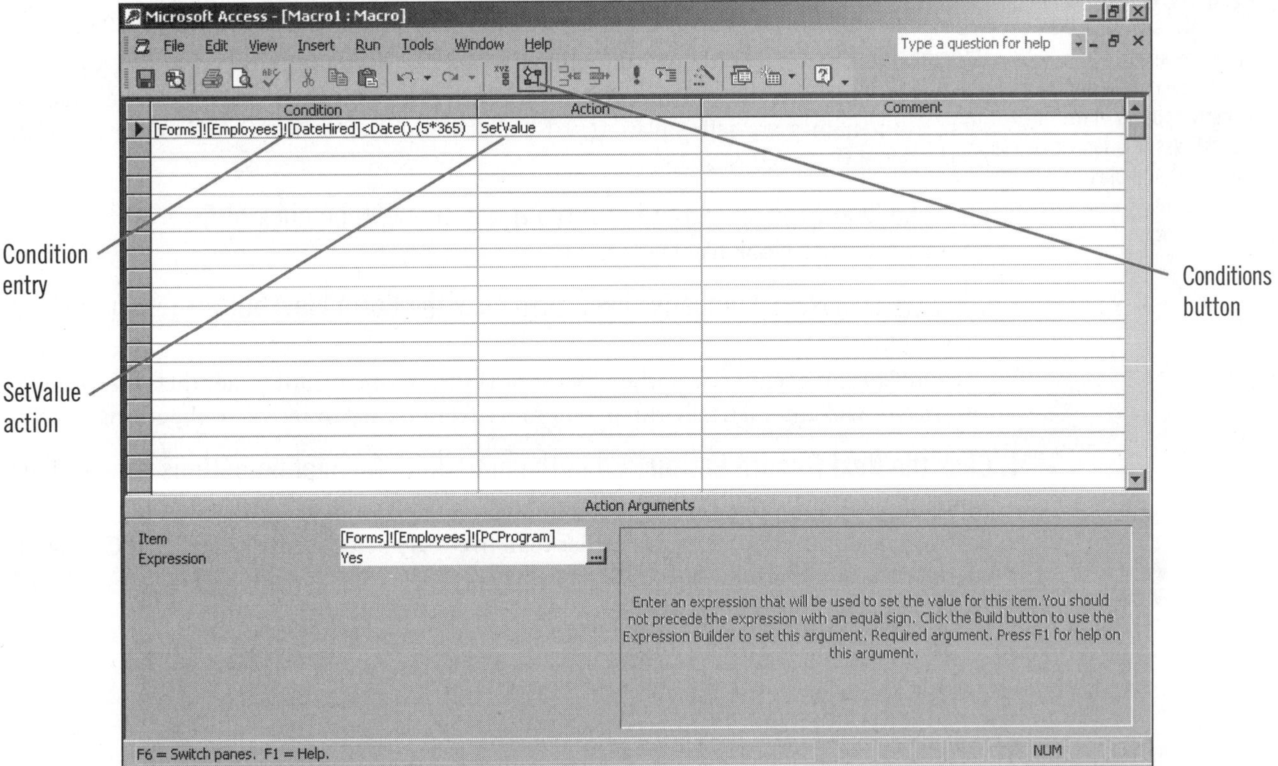

FIGURE N-9: Running the 5PC macro

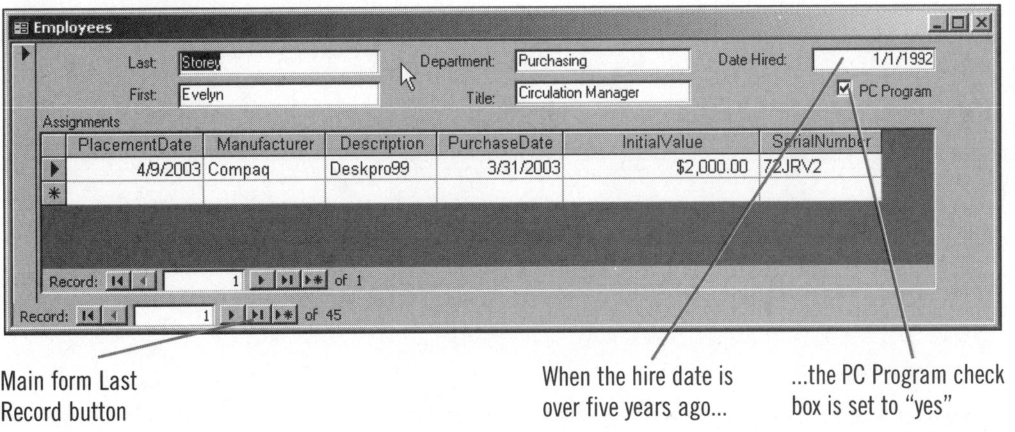

Access 2002

Access 2002

Working with Events

An **event** is a specific activity that occurs within the database such as clicking a command button, editing data, or opening or closing a form. Events can be triggered by the user, or by the database itself. By assigning a macro to an appropriate event, rather than running the macro from the Tools menu, you further automate and improve your database. Now that Kristen has developed the 5PC macro, she will attach it to an event on the Employees form so that she doesn't have to run the macro for each record.

QuickTip

In the property sheet, a short description of the current property appears in the status bar. Press [F1] for more help on that property.

1. Right-click the **Employees form**, click **Design View** on the shortcut menu, then click the **Properties button** to open the property sheet for the form
   All objects, sections, and controls have a variety of events to which macros can be attached. Most event names are self-explanatory for that item, such as the On Click event (which occurs when that item is clicked).
2. Click the **Event tab**, click the **On Current list arrow**, then click **5PC**
   Your screen should look like Figure N-10.
3. Click to close the property sheet, then click the **Form View button** on the Form View toolbar
   The On Current event occurs when focus moves from one record to another, therefore the 5PC macro will automatically run as you move from record to record in the form.
4. Click the **Next Record button** in the main form Navigation buttons fifteen times while observing the PC Program check box
   For every Date Hired value that is earlier than five years before today's date, the PC Program check box is automatically checked (set to "yes").
5. Save, then close the Employees form

FIGURE N-10: Assigning a macro to an event

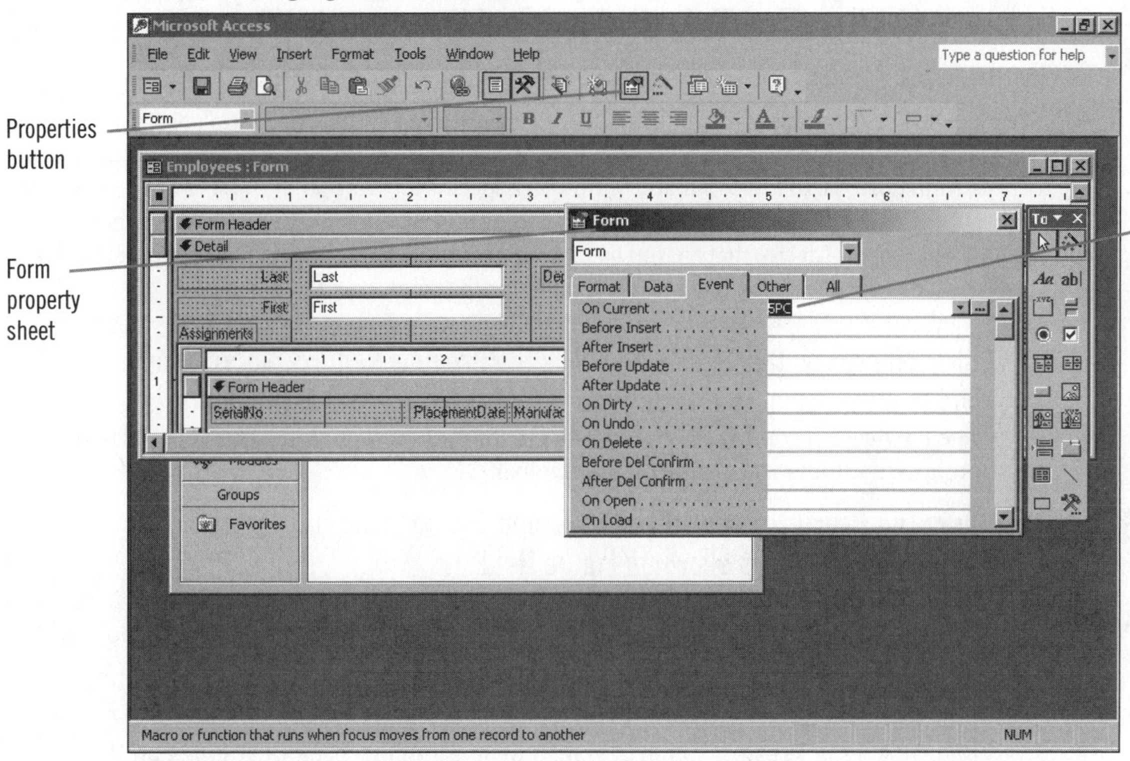

Access 2002

Assigning a macro to a command button

CLUES TO USE

A common way to run a macro from a form is to first add a command button to the form, and then run the macro from the command button. To do this, add a command button to the form using the Command Button Wizard. Select the Run Macro action from the Miscellaneous category. The selected macro is assigned to the **On Click** event for the command button, and runs when you click the command button in Form View.

Access 2002

Customizing Toolbars

There are many ways to run a macro: by clicking the Run button in Macro Design View, by using commands on the Tools menu, by assigning the macro to an event on a control, or by assigning it to a toolbar, menu, or shortcut menu. The benefit of assigning a macro to a toolbar button as compared to assigning the macro to a command button on a specific form is that the toolbar can be made available to the user at all times, whereas a command button on a form is available only when that specific form is open. Macros that are run from multiple forms are great candidates for custom toolbars. Kristen decides to create a new toolbar for the print macros.

1. Click **Macros** on the Objects bar, click the **Preview Reports Macro Group**, click **Tools** on the menu, point to **Macro**, then click **Create Toolbar from Macro**
   The Preview Reports Macro Group toolbar appears on your screen. All of the macros in that group are automatically added to the toolbar.
2. Drag the **Preview Reports Macro Group toolbar title bar** to dock it just below the Database toolbar, as shown in Figure N-11
   Because this toolbar contains buttons for only two macros (the two found in the Print Reports Macro Group), the entire name of the macro fits comfortably on the toolbar. If you wanted the toolbar to support many macros, you'd either have to shorten the text, or use icons in order to fit all of the macros on the toolbar.
3. Right-click the **Preview Reports Macro Group toolbar**, click **Customize** on the shortcut menu, right-click the **Preview All Equipment macro button** on the Preview Reports Macro Group toolbar, then point to **Change Button Image** on the shortcut menu
   Your screen should look like Figure N-12. The shortcut menu that allows you to modify toolbar button images and text is available only when the Customize dialog box is open.
4. Click the **Shoes icon** on the icon palette, right-click the **Preview All Equipment macro button** again, then click **Default Style** on the shortcut menu
   The Default Style for a button displays only the button image, not the text.
5. Right-click the **Preview Accounting Report macro button** on the Preview Reports Macro Group toolbar, point to **Change Button Image** on the shortcut menu, click the **Scales icon** on the icon palette, right-click the **Preview Accounting Report macro button**, then click **Default Style** on the shortcut menu
   Any image on any button on any toolbar button can be edited.
6. Right-click on the Preview Reports Macro Group toolbar, then click **Edit Button Image**
   The Button Editor dialog box opens, which allows you to change the appearance of the picture pixel by pixel.
7. Click the **green box** on the Colors palette, then click all 11 squares in the **left scale**, as shown in Figure N-13
   With enough time and patience, you could create any number of unique button images.
8. Click **OK**, then click **Close** to close the Customize dialog box
   The new Preview Reports Macro Group toolbar can be turned on or off from anywhere within the database, just like any other toolbar. New buttons can be added or modified at any time.
9. Point to , then point to on the Preview Reports Macro Group toolbar
   Each button on the Preview Reports Macro Group toolbar has a ScreenTip like buttons on other toolbars.

QuickTip

If the new toolbar docks in the wrong location, point to the left edge of the toolbar so that your mouse pointer changes to ✥, then drag it to the desired location.

QuickTip

With the Customize dialog box open, right-click any button, click Copy Button Image on the shortcut menu, right-click any other button, then click Paste Button Image on the shortcut menu to copy an image from one button to another.

FIGURE N-11: Preview Reports Macro Group toolbar

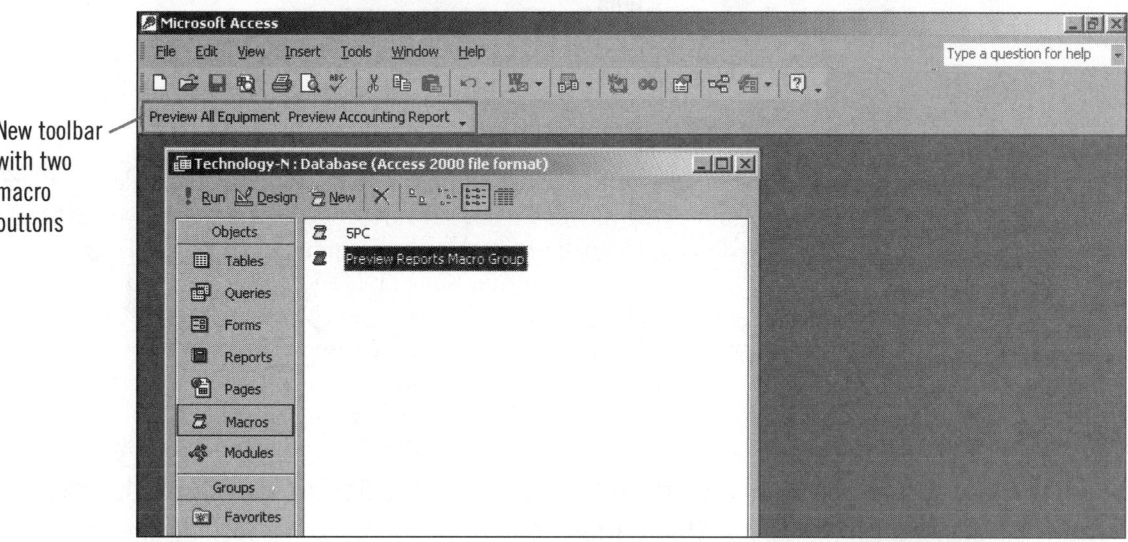

FIGURE N-12: Customizing a button image

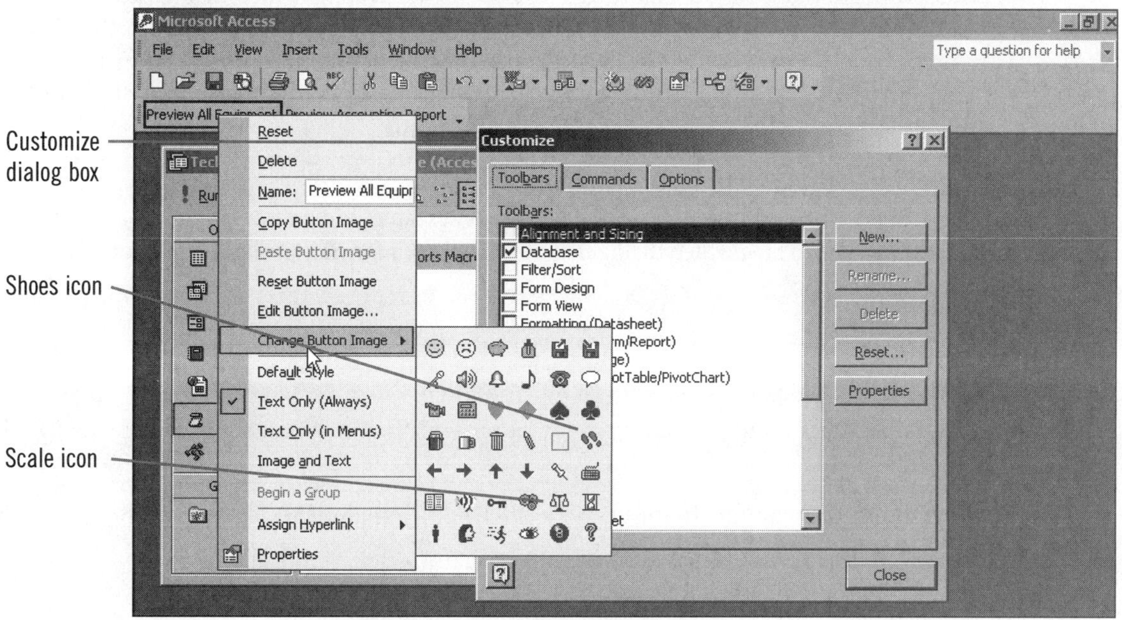

FIGURE N-13: Button Editor dialog box

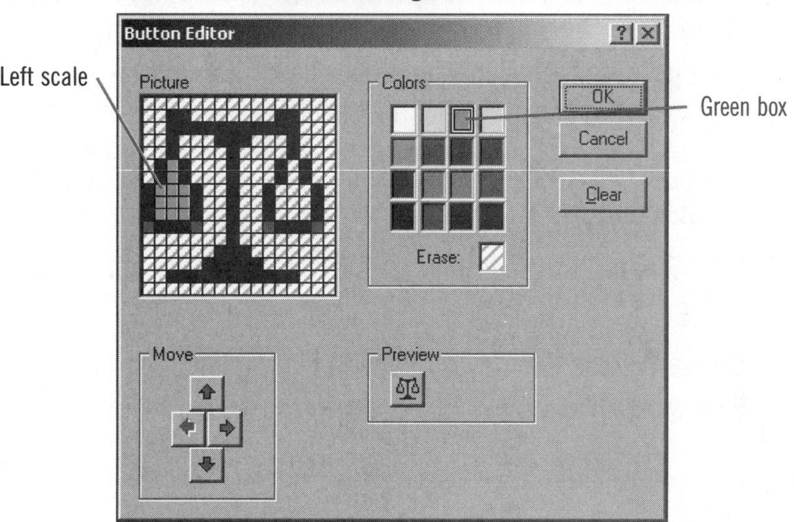

Access 2002

Troubleshooting Macros

When macros don't execute properly, Access supplies several techniques to debug them. **Debugging** means to determine why the macro doesn't run properly. It usually involves breaking a dysfunctional macro down into small pieces that can be individually tested. For example, you can **single step** a macro, which means to run it one line (one action) at a time to observe the effect of each specific action in the Macro Single Step dialog box. Another debugging technique is to disable a particular macro action(s) by entering false in the Condition cell for the action(s) that you wish to temporarily skip. Before building more sophisticated macros, Kristen uses the Preview Reports Macro Group to learn debugging techniques.

1. **Right-click Preview Reports Macro Group, click Design View from the shortcut menu, click the Single Step button on the Macro Design toolbar, then click the Run button on the Macro Design toolbar**
   The screen should look like Figure N-14, with the Macro Single Step dialog box open. This dialog box displays information including the name of the macro, whether the current action's condition is true, the action's name, and the action arguments. From the Macro Single Step dialog box you can step into the next macro action, halt execution of the macro, or continue running the macro without single stepping.

2. **Click Step in the Macro Single Step dialog box**
   Stepping into the second action lets the first action execute, and pauses the macro at the second action. The Macro Single Step dialog box now displays information about the second action.

3. **Click Step**
   The second action, the MsgBox action, executes, displaying the message box.

4. **Click OK, then close the All Equipment report**
   You can use the Condition column to temporarily ignore an action while you are debugging a macro.

5. **Click to stop single stepping, click the Conditions button on the Macro Design toolbar, click the Condition cell for the first row, then type False**
   Your screen should look like Figure N-15.

6. **Click the Save button on the Macro Design toolbar, then click the Run button**
   Because the Condition value is False for the OpenReport action, it did not execute, and the macro jumped to the second action, the MsgBox action.

7. **Click OK, double-click False in the Condition cell, then press [Delete]**
   Closing the Condition column does not delete or change the values stored in that column. To change the Preview All Equipment macro so that the All Equipment report opens in Print Preview the next time you run this macro, you must delete the False entry for the OpenReport action.

8. **Click File on the menu bar, click Print, then click OK in the Print Macro Definition dialog box**

9. **Save and close the Preview Reports Macro Group, close the Technology-N database, then exit Access**

QuickTip

If you add your name to the Comment cell for any macro action, it will appear on the printout.

FIGURE N-14: Single stepping through a macro

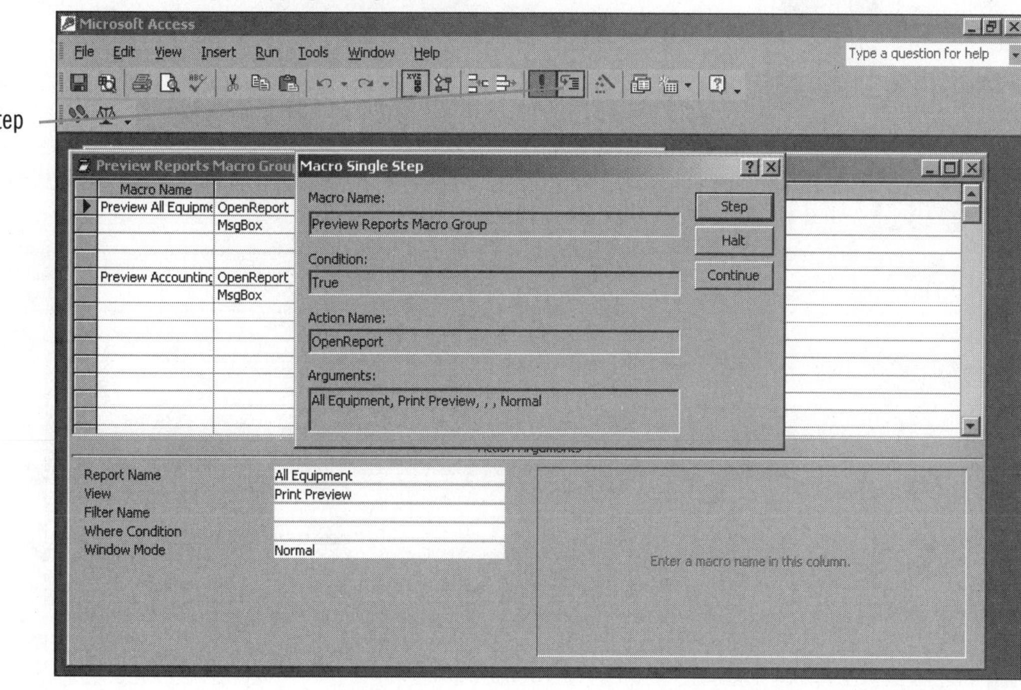

FIGURE N-15: Using a False condition

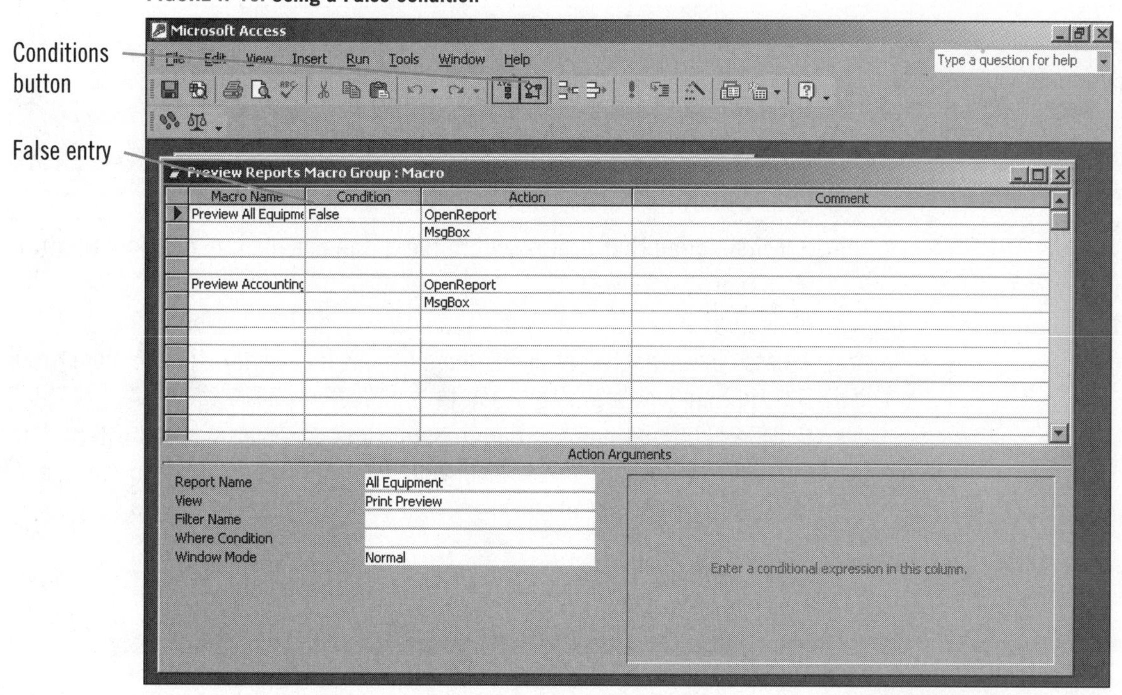

Access 2002

Access 2002

Practice

▶ Concepts Review

Identify each element of Macro Design View shown in Figure N-16.

FIGURE N-16

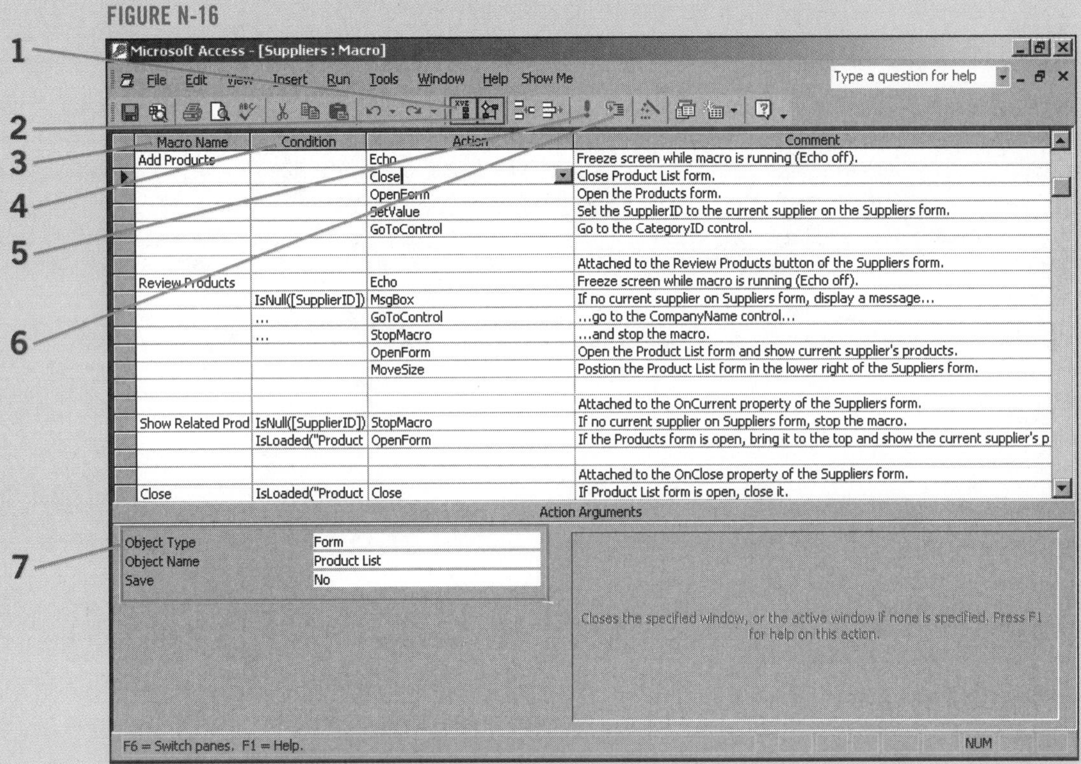

Match each term with the statement that describes its function.

8. Macro	**a.** Specific action that occurs within the database such as clicking a button or opening a form
9. Conditional expression	**b.** Individual steps that you want the Access macro to perform
10. Arguments	**c.** Access object that stores one or more actions that perform one or more tasks
11. Debugging	**d.** Determining why a macro doesn't run properly
12. Actions	**e.** Provide additional information to define how an Access action will perform
13. Event	**f.** Evaluates as either true or false, which determines whether Access executes that action or not

Select the best answer from the list of choices.

14. Which of the following is *not* a major benefit of using a macro?
- **a.** To save time by automating routine tasks
- **b.** To ensure consistency in executing routine or complex tasks
- **c.** To make the database more flexible or easy to use
- **d.** To redesign the relationships among the tables of the database

15. Which of the following *best* describes the process of creating an Access macro?
- **a.** Use the macro recorder to record clicks and keystrokes as you complete a task.
- **b.** Use the single-step recorder to record clicks and keystrokes as you complete a task.
- **c.** Use the Macro Wizard to determine which tasks are done most frequently.
- **d.** Open Macro Design View and add actions, arguments, and conditions to accomplish the desired task.

16. Which of the following would *not* be a way to run a macro?
- **a.** Click the Run button on the Database window toolbar.
- **b.** Assign the macro to an event of a control on a form.
- **c.** Add the macro as a button on a toolbar, then click the button.
- **d.** Add the macro as an entry on the title bar, then click the title bar.

17. Which is *not* a reason to run a macro in single-step mode?
- **a.** You want to change the arguments of a macro while it runs.
- **b.** You want to observe the effect of each macro action individually.
- **c.** You want to debug a macro that isn't working properly.
- **d.** You want to run only a few of the actions of a macro.

18. Which is *not* a reason to use conditional expressions in a macro?
- **a.** More macro actions are available when you are also using conditional expressions.
- **b.** Conditional expressions allow you to skip over actions when the expression evaluates as false.
- **c.** You can enter false in the Conditions column for an action to skip it.
- **d.** Conditional expressions give the macro more power and flexibility.

19. Which example illustrates the proper syntax to refer to a specific control on a form?
- **a.** {Forms}!{*formname*}!(*controlname*)
- **b.** (Forms)!(*formname*)!(*controlname*)
- **c.** Forms!*formname.controlname*
- **d.** [Forms]![*formname*]![*controlname*]

20. Which event executes every time you move from record to record in a form?
- **a.** New Record
- **b.** On Current
- **c.** On Move
- **d.** Next Record

Skills Review

1. Understand macros.
- **a.** Start Access, then open the **Basketball-N** database from where your Project Files are stored.
- **b.** Open the Print Macro Group in Macro Design View, then record your answers to the following questions on a sheet of paper:
  - How many macros are in this macro group?
  - What are the names of the macros in this macro group?

Access 2002

- What actions does the first macro in this macro group contain?
- What arguments does the first action contain? What values were chosen for those arguments?

c. Close Macro Design View for the Print Macro Group object.

2. Create a macro.

a. Start a new macro in Macro Design View.
b. Add the OpenQuery action to the first row of Macro Design View.
c. Select Score Delta as the value for the Query Name argument of the OpenQuery action.
d. Select Datasheet for the View argument of the OpenQuery action.
e. Select Edit for the Data Mode argument for the OpenQuery action.
f. Save the macro object with the name **View Score Delta**.
g. Run the macro to make sure it works, then close the Score Delta query and the View Score Delta Macro Design View.

3. Modify actions and arguments.

a. Open the View Score Delta macro in Macro Design View.
b. Add a MsgBox action in the second row of Macro Design View.
c. Type **We had a great season!** for the Message argument in the Action Arguments pane of the MsgBox action.
d. Select Yes for the Beep argument of the MsgBox action.
e. Select Warning! for the Type argument of the MsgBox action.
f. Type **Iowa State Cyclones** for the Title argument of the MsgBox action.
g. Save the macro, then run it to make sure the MsgBox action works as intended.
h. Click OK in the dialog box created by the MsgBox action, then close the Score Delta query and the View Score Delta macro.

4. Create a macro group.

a. Rename the View Score Delta macro, changing it to **Query Macro Group**.
b. Open Query Macro Group in Macro Design View.
c. Open the Macro Name column, then type the name **View Score Delta** on the first line for the first macro.
d. Start another macro by typing **View Forward FG** in the Macro Name cell of the fourth row.
e. Add an OpenQuery action for the first action of the Forward FG Macro.
f. Select Forward Field Goals for the Query Name argument of the OpenQuery action, and use the default entries for the other two arguments.
g. Add a MsgBox action for the second action of the View Forward FG macro.
h. Type **Forward Field Goals** as the Message argument for the MsgBox action.
i. Select Yes for the Beep argument of the MsgBox action.
j. Select Critical for the Type argument of the MsgBox action.
k. Type **2002-2003 Season** for the Title argument of the MsgBox action, then save the macro.
l. Click Tools on the menu bar, point to Macro, click Run macro, then run the View Forward FG macro.
m. Click OK, close the query datasheet, then close the Query Macro Group.

5. Set conditional expressions.

a. Start a new macro in Macro Design View.
b. Click the Conditions button on the Macro Design toolbar to open the Condition column.
c. Enter the following condition in the Condition cell of the first row: **[Forms]![Game Summary Form]![Home Score]>[Opponent Score]** (*Hint:* Use the Zoom dialog box or widen the column to more clearly view the entry.)
d. Add the SetValue action to the first row.
e. Type the following entry in the Item argument value for the SetValue action: **[Forms]![Game Summary Form]![Victory]**
f. Type **Yes** for the Expression argument for the SetValue action.
g. Save the macro with the name **Victory Calculator**, then close Macro Design View.

6. **Work with events.**
   a. Open the Game Summary Form in Form Design View.
   b. Open the property sheet for the form.
   c. Assign the Victory Calculator macro to the On Current event of the form.
   d. Close the property sheet, save the form, then open the Game Summary Form in Form View.
   e. Navigate through the first four records. The Victory check box should be marked for the first three records, but not the fourth.
   f. Print the third and fourth records, then close the Game Summary Form.
7. **Customize toolbars.**
   a. Click Macros on the Objects bar, click the Print Macro Group, click Tools on the menu bar, point to Macro, then click Create Toolbar from Macro.
   b. Dock the toolbar with the three text buttons just below the Database toolbar in the database window.
   c. Right-click the new toolbar, then click Customize on the shortcut menu to open the Customize dialog box.
   d. Change the button image for each of the three macros to the question mark icon and a default style (image only).
   e. Edit the button images so that the second macro question mark button is red (instead of yellow) and the third is blue (instead of yellow).
   f. Close the Customize dialog box, then point to each icon to make sure that the ScreenTip relates to the three macro names in the Print Macro Group.
8. **Troubleshoot macros.**
   a. Open the Print Macro Group in Macro Design View.
   b. Click the Single Step button on the Macro Design toolbar, then click the Run button on the Macro Design toolbar.
   c. Click Step twice to step through the two actions of this macro, then click OK in the resulting message box.
   d. Open the Condition column by clicking the Conditions button on the Macro Design toolbar (if it's not already opened).
   e. Enter the value **False** as a condition to the first row, the OpenReport action of the Games Summary macro.
   f. Save the macro, then click the Run button.
   g. Click the Step button twice to move through the actions of the macro. This time the Games Summary report should *not* be printed. Click OK when prompted.
   h. Delete the False condition in the first row, save the macro, then click the Single Step button to toggle it off.
   i. Click File on the menu bar, click Print, click OK in the Print Macro Definition dialog box, then close Macro Design View.
   j. Close the Basketball-N database, then exit Access.

► Independent Challenge 1

As the manager of a doctor's clinic, you have created an Access database called Patients-N to track insurance claim reimbursements. You will use macros to help automate the database.

a. Start Access, then open the database **Patients-N** from the drive and folder where your Project Files are located.
b. Open Macro Design View of the CPT Form Open macro. (CPT stands for Current Procedural Terminology, which is a code that describes a medical procedure.) If the Single Step button is toggled on, click it to toggle it off.
c. On a separate sheet of paper, identify the macro actions, arguments for each action, and values for each argument.
d. In two or three sentences, explain in your own words what tasks this macro automates.
e. Close the CPT Form Open macro.
f. Open the Claim Entry Form in Form Design View. Maximize the window.
g. In the footer of the Claim Entry Form are several command buttons. (*Hint:* Scroll the main form to see these buttons.) Open the property sheet of the Add CPT Code button, then click the Event tab.
h. On your paper, write the event to which the CPT Form Open macro is assigned.

i. Open the Claim Entry Form in Form View, then click the Add CPT Code button in the form footer.
j. On your paper, write the current record number that is displayed for you.
k. Scroll up the CPT form, then find the record for CPT Code 99243. Write the RBRVS value for this record, then close the CPT form and Claim Entry form. (RBRVS stands for Resource Based Relative Value System, a measurement of relative value between medical procedures.)
l. Close the Patients-N database, then exit Access.

Independent Challenge 2

As the manager of a doctor's clinic, you have created an Access database called Patients-N to track insurance claim reimbursements. You will use macros to help automate the database.

a. Start Access, then open the database **Patients-N** from the drive and folder where your Project Files are located.
b. Start a new macro in Macro Design View, then click the Macro Names button on the Macro Design toolbar to open the Macro Name column. If the Single Step button is toggled on, click it to toggle it off.
c. Type **Preview DOS-Denied** as the first macro name, then add the OpenReport macro action in the first row.
d. Select Date of Service Report–Denied for the Report Name argument, then select Print Preview for the View argument of the OpenReport action. Leave the other two arguments blank.
e. In the third row, type **Preview DOS-Fixed** as a new macro name, then add the OpenReport macro action in the third row.
f. Select Date of Service Report–Fixed for the ReportName argument, then select Print Preview for the View argument of the second OpenReport action. Leave the other two arguments blank.
g. Save the object with the name **Preview Group**, close Macro Design View, then click the Preview Group macro object to select it.
h. Click File on the menu bar, click Print, then click OK in the Print Macro Definition dialog box.
i. Run the Preview DOS-Denied macro to test it, then close Print Preview.
j. Run the Preview DOS-Fixed macro to test it, then close Print Preview.
k. Close the Patients-N database, then exit Access.

Independent Challenge 3

As the manager of a doctor's clinic, you have created an Access database called Patients-N to track insurance claim reimbursements. You will use macros to help automate the database.

a. Start Access, then open the **Patients-N** database from the drive and folder where your Project Files are located.
b. Start a new macro in Macro Design View, then click the Conditions button on the Macro Design toolbar to open the Condition column. If the Single Step button is toggled on, click it to toggle it off.
c. Enter the following in the Condition cell of the first row: **[Forms]![CPT Form]![RBRVS]=0**
d. Select the SetValue action for the first row.
e. Enter the following as the Item argument value for the SetValue action: **[Forms]![CPT Form]![Research]**
f. Type **Yes** as the Expression argument value for the SetValue action.
g. Save the macro with the name **Value Research**, close Macro Design View, then click the Value Research macro object to select it.
h. Click File on the menu bar, click Print, then click OK in the Print Macro Definition dialog box.
i. Open the CPT Form in Form Design View, and open the property sheet for the form.
j. Assign the Value Research macro to the On Current event of the form.
k. Close the property sheet, save the form, then open the CPT Form in Form View.

l. Use the Next Record button to move quickly through all 64 records in the form. Notice that the macro places a check mark in the Research check box only when the RBRVS value is equal to zero.
m. Save and close the CPT Form, then close the Patients-N database.

Independent Challenge 4

Your culinary club is collecting information on international chocolate factories, museums, and stores, and has asked you to help build a database to organize the information. You collect some information on the World Wide Web to enter into the database, then tie the forms together with macros attached to command buttons.

a. Go to www.godiva.com. Your goal is to determine if there is a Godiva Boutique store in Toronto, Canada, where some members of your group will be visiting. Because Web sites change often, the links to find the Godiva Boutique stores in Toronto from the Godiva home page may vary from those provided. Therefore, if you cannot find the following links, or if the links don't work, use the Search text box to find the stores.
b. Click the links from the Godiva home page to locate the Godiva Boutique stores in Toronto, Canada.
c. Once you find the page that lists the Godiva store locations in Toronto, Canada, select that information on the Web page, then print the selection.
d. Open the **Chocolate-N** database from the drive and folder where your Project Files are stored, then open the Countries form in Form View.
e. Click the New Record button for the main form, then type **Canada** in the Country text box.
f. In the subform for the Canada record, enter **Godiva Boutique** in the Name field, **S** in the Type field (S for store), the address information that you found on the Web site in the Street field, **Toronto** in the City field, and **Ontario** in the StateProvince field.
g. Open Macro Design View for a new macro, then add the PrintOut action to the first row. If the Single Step button is toggled on, click it to toggle it off. Modify the Print Range argument to Selection, save the macro with the name PrintRecord, then close it.
h. In Form Design View of the Countries form, add a label with your name to the left section of the Form Header section, then add a command button to the right section. If the Command Button Wizard starts, click Cancel.
i. In the property sheet for the Command button, click the On Click property on the Event tab. Click the list arrow for the On Click property, then click PrintRecord. You attached the PrintRecord macro to the On Click property for this command button. Therefore, when the command button is clicked in Form View, the PrintRecord macro should run.
j. Double-click the text on the command button, then type **Print Current Record**.
k. Save the form, then view it in Form View.
l. Find the Canada record, then click the Print Current Record command button. Only that record should print.
m. Close the Countries form, then exit Access.

▶ Visual Workshop

As the manager of a doctor's clinic, you have created an Access database called **Patients-N** to track insurance claim reimbursements. Develop a new macro called **Query Group** with the actions and argument values shown in Figure N-17 and Table N-3. Run both macros to test them, and debug them if necessary. Print the macro by clicking File on the menu bar. Click Print, and then click OK in the Print Macro Definition dialog box.

TABLE N-3: Macro actions and arguments for the Query Group

macro name	action	argument	argument value
Denied	OpenQuery	Query Name	Monthly Query – Denied
		View	Datasheet
		Data Mode	Edit
	Maximize		
	MsgBox	Message	These claims were denied
		Beep	Yes
		Type	Information
		Title	Denied
Fixed	OpenQuery	Query Name	Monthly Query – Fixed
		View	Datasheet
		Data Mode	Edit
	Maximize		
	MsgBox	Message	These claims were fixed
		Beep	Yes
		Type	Information
		Title	Fixed

FIGURE N-17

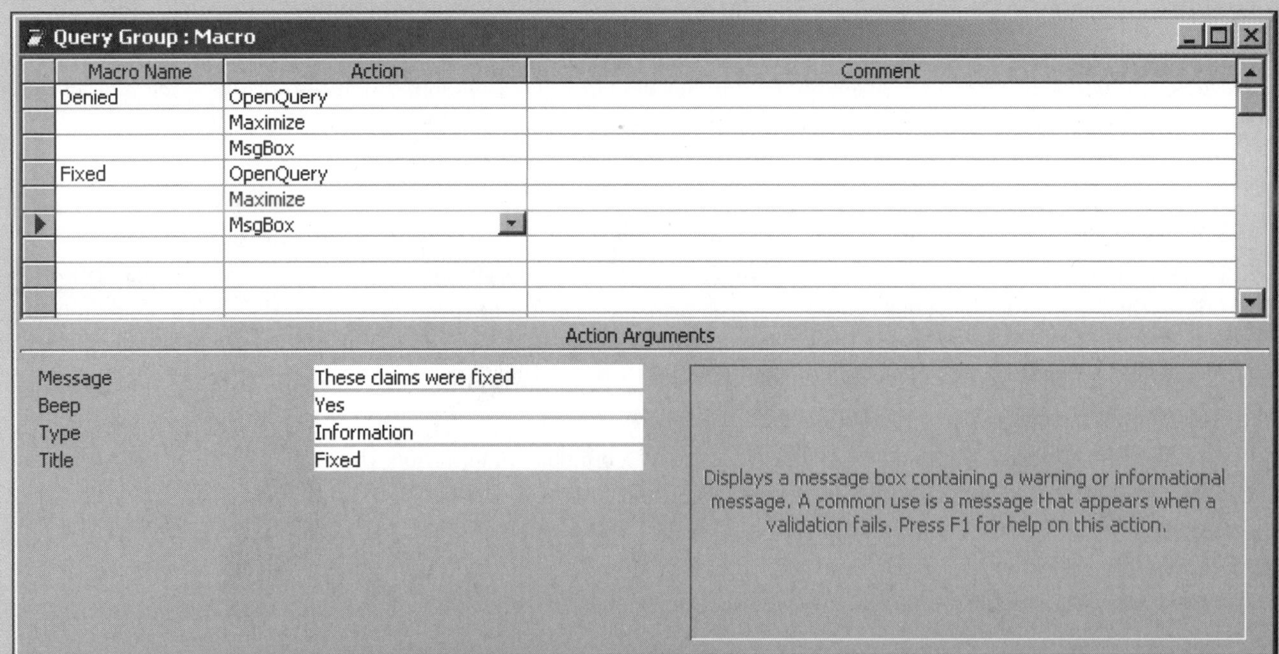

Access 2002

Unit O

Creating

Modules

Objectives

- Understand modules
- Compare macros and modules
- MOUS Create functions
- MOUS Use If statements
- MOUS Document procedures
- MOUS Examine class modules
- MOUS Create sub procedures
- Troubleshoot modules

Access is a robust and easy-to-use relational database program. End users can quickly create reports and forms that previously took programmers hours to build. Because Access provides so many user-friendly tools such as wizards and graphical Design Views to accomplish complex tasks, many Access database administrators don't need to work with the Microsoft Office programming language, **Visual Basic for Applications (VBA)**, to meet most user needs. When programming *is* required, however, Access provides the VBA development environment to write the programming code. The Access **module** object stores VBA code. Kristen Fontanelle, network administrator for MediaLoft, uses VBA to enhance the capabilities of the database.

Access 2002

Understanding Modules

A **module** is an Access object that stores Visual Basic for Applications (VBA) programming code. VBA is written in the **Visual Basic Editor Code window** (**Code window**), shown in Figure O-1. The components and text colors of the Code window are described in Table O-1. An Access database has two kinds of modules: **class modules**, which contain VBA code used only within a form or report, and store the code within the form or report object itself; and **standard modules**, which contain global code that can be executed from anywhere in the database. Standard modules are displayed as module objects in the database window when you click the Modules button on the Objects bar. Kristen asks some questions about VBA.

- **What does a module contain?**
  A module contains VBA programming code organized in **procedures**. A procedure is several lines of VBA code, each of which is called a **statement**. Modules may also contain **comments** that help explain the code.
- **What is a procedure?**
  A **procedure** is a series of VBA statements that perform an operation or calculate an answer. There are two types of procedures: Functions and Subs. **Declaration statements** precede procedure statements and help set rules for how the statements in the module are processed.
- **What is a function?**
  A **function** is a procedure that returns a value. Access supplies many built-in statistical, financial, and date functions, such as Sum, Pmt, and Now, that can be used in an expression in a query, form, or report to calculate a value. You might need to create a new function, however, to help perform calculations unique to your database. For example, you could create a new function called StockOptions, to calculate the date an employee is eligible for stock options.
- **What is a sub?**
  A **sub** (also called **sub procedure**) performs a series of VBA statements, but does not return a value and cannot be used in an expression like a function procedure. You use subs to manipulate controls and objects. They are generally executed based on an event, such as clicking a command button or check box.
- **What are arguments?**
  Arguments are constants, variables, or expressions passed to a procedure (usually a function procedure) that are required for it to execute. For example, the full syntax for the Sum function is Sum(*expr*), where *expr* represents the argument for the Sum function, the item that is being summed. Arguments are specified immediately after a procedure's name and are enclosed in parentheses. Multiple arguments are separated by commas.
- **What is an object?**
  In VBA, an **object** is any item that can be identified or manipulated, including the traditional Access objects (table, query, form, report, page, macro, module), and smaller pieces of the traditional objects including controls, sections, and existing procedures.
- **What is a method?**
  A **method** is an action that *an object can perform*. Procedures are often written to invoke methods in response to user actions. For example, you could invoke the GoToPage method when the user clicks a command button to move the focus to a specific control.
- **What is an event?**
  An **event** is a specific action that occurs *on or to an object*, and is usually the result of a user action. Clicking a command button, editing data, or closing a form, are examples of events.

FIGURE O-1: Visual Basic Editor Code window for a standard module

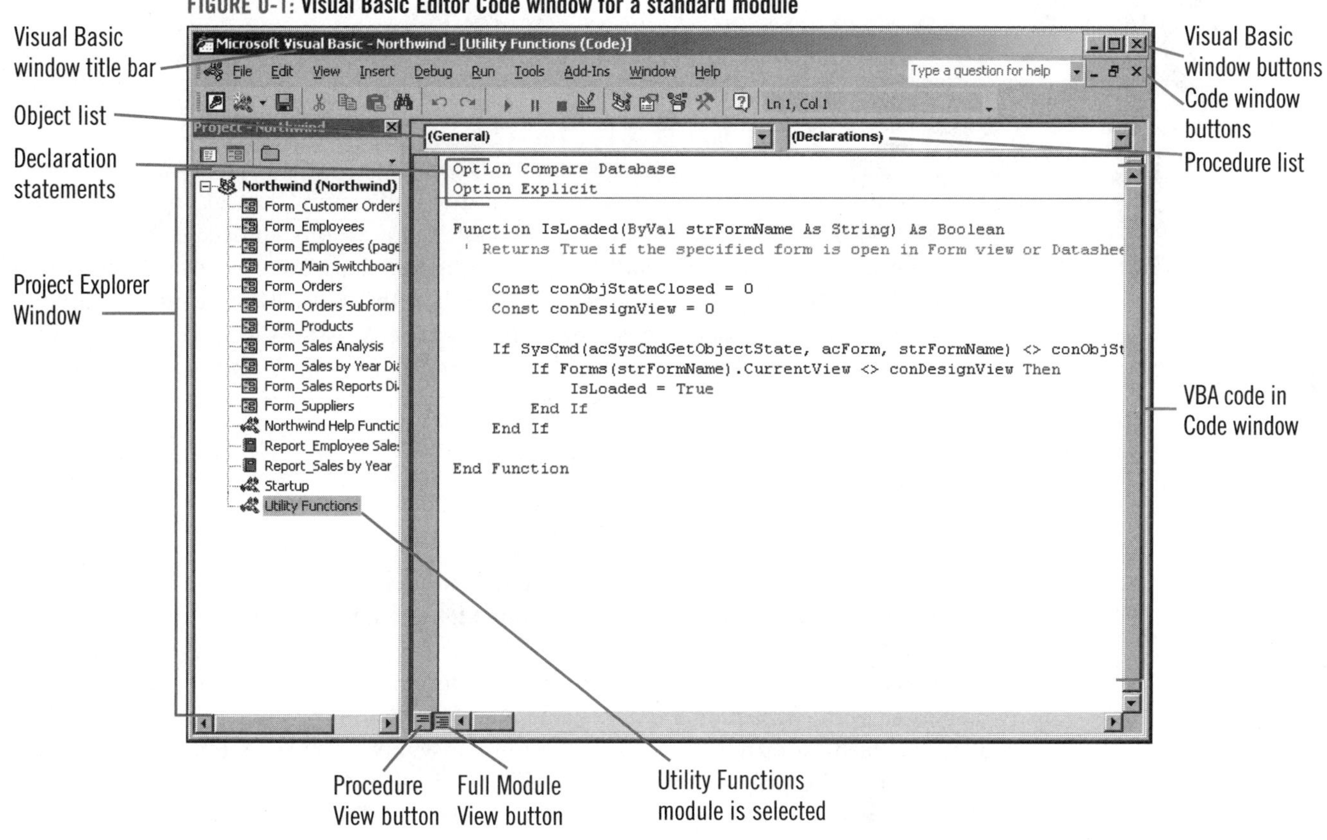

TABLE O-1: Components and text colors for the Visual Basic window

component or color	description
Visual Basic window	The entire Microsoft Visual Basic program window that contains smaller windows including the Code window and Project Explorer window
Code window	Contains the VBA for the project selected in the Project Explorer window
Project Explorer window	Displays a hierarchical list of the projects in the database; a **project** can be a module itself, or an object that contains class modules such as a form or report
Procedure View button	Shows the statements that belong only to the current procedure
Full Module View button	Shows all the lines of VBA (all of the procedures) in the current module
Declaration statements	Statements that apply to every procedure in the module such as declarations for variables, constants, user-defined data types, and external procedures in a dynamic link library
Object list	In a class module, lists the objects associated with the current form or report
Procedure list	In a standard module, lists the procedures in that module; in a class module, lists the events (such as Click or Dblclick) that the item selected in the Object box can use
Blue	Keyword text—blue words are reserved by VBA and are already assigned specific meanings
Black	Normal text—black words are the unique VBA code developed by the user
Red	Syntax error text—a line of code in red indicates that it will not execute correctly because there is a syntax error (perhaps a missing parenthesis or a spelling error)
Green	Comment text—any text after an apostrophe is considered documentation, and is therefore ignored in the execution of the procedure

Access 2002

Comparing Macros and Modules

Both macros and modules help run your database more efficiently (faster) and effectively (with fewer errors). To create either a macro or a module requires some understanding of programming concepts, an ability to follow a process through its steps, and patience. Some tasks can be accomplished by using either an Access macro or with VBA, and there are guidelines to help guide your choice of which object is best for the task. Also, note that creating macros in the other Microsoft Office products (Excel, Word, and PowerPoint) actually creates VBA code. Kristen learns how macros and modules compare by asking more questions.

For what types of tasks are macros best suited?

Macros are an easy way to handle repetitive, simple tasks such as opening and closing forms, showing and hiding toolbars, and printing reports.

Which is easier to create, a macro or a module, and why?

Macros are generally easier to create because you don't have to know any programming syntax. The hardest part of creating a macro is choosing the correct action (Access presents a limited list of about 50 actions from which you must choose). But once the action is chosen, the arguments associated with that action are displayed automatically in the Action Arguments pane, eliminating the need to learn any special programming syntax. To create a module, however, you must know a robust programming language, VBA, as well as the correct **syntax** (rules) for each VBA statement. The additional flexibility and power of VBA means that it is inherently more complex as well.

When must I use a macro?

You must use macros to make global, shortcut key assignments. You can also use an automatic macro that executes when the database first opens.

When should I use a module?

- Class modules, like the one shown in Figure O-2, are stored as part of the form or report object in which they are created. If you develop forms and reports in one database and copy them to another, class module VBA automatically travels with the object that stores it.
- You must use modules to create unique functions. Macros cannot create functions. For instance, you might want to create a function called COMMISSION that calculates the appropriate commission on a sale using your company's unique commission formula.
- Access error messages can be confusing to the user. But using VBA procedures, you can detect the error when it occurs and display your own message.
- You can't use a macro to accomplish many tasks outside of Access, but VBA code stored in modules works with other products in the Microsoft Office suite.
- VBA code can contain nested If statements, Case statements, and other programming logic which makes them much more powerful and flexible than macros. Some of the most common VBA keywords are shown in Table O-2. VBA keywords appear blue in the Code window.

Converting macros to Visual Basic

You can convert existing macros to Visual Basic. Click the Macros button on the Objects bar, then click the name of the macro you want to convert. Click the File menu, click Save As, click the As list arrow, click Module, then click OK. If the macro is stored in a form or report, open the form or report in Design View, click the Tools menu, point to Macro, then click Convert Form's (or Report's) Macros to Visual Basic.

FIGURE O-2: Code window for a class module

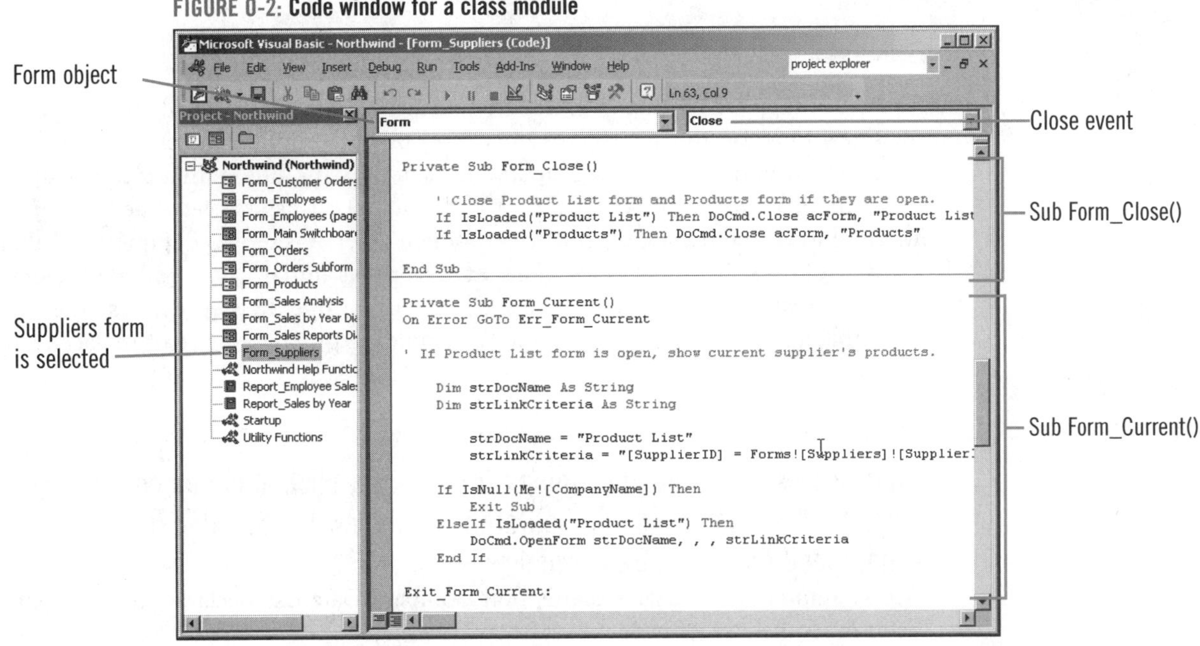

TABLE O-2: Common VBA keywords

statement	explanation
Function	Declares the name and arguments that create a new function procedure
End Function	When defining a new function, the End Function statement is required as the last statement to mark the end of the VBA code that defines the function
Sub	Declares the name for a new sub procedure; **Private Sub** indicates that the sub is accessible only to other procedures in the module where it is declared
End Sub	When defining a new sub, the End Sub statement is required as the last statement to mark the end of the VBA code that defines the sub
If...Then	Executes code (the code follows the Then statement) when the value of an expression is true (the expression follows the If statement)
End If	When creating an If...Then statement, the End If statement is required as the last statement
Const	Declares the name and value of a **constant**, an item that retains a constant value throughout the execution of the code
Option Compare Database	A declaration statement that determines the way string values (text) will be sorted
Option Explicit	A declaration statement that specifies that you must explicitly declare all variables used in all procedures; if you attempt to use an undeclared variable name, an error occurs at **compile time**, the period during which source code is translated to executable code
Dim	Declares a **variable**, a named storage location that contains data that can be modified during program execution
On Error GoTo	Upon error in the execution of a procedure, the On Error GoTo statement specifies the location (the statement) where the procedure should continue
Select Case	Executes one of several groups of statements called a **Case** depending on the value of an expression; use the Select Case statement as an alternative to using **ElseIf** in **If...Then...Else** statements when comparing one expression to several different values
End Select	When defining a new Select Case group of statements, the End Select statement is required as the last statement to mark the end of the VBA code

Access 2002

Creating Functions

While Access supplies hundreds of functions such as Sum and Count, you might need to create a new function to calculate a value based on the unique business rules used by your company. You would create a new function in a standard module so that it can be used in any query, form, or report in the database. MediaLoft has implemented a program that allows employees to purchase computer equipment when it is replaced. Equipment that is less than a year old will be sold to employees at 75% of its initial value, and equipment that is more than a year old will be sold at 50% of its initial value. Kristen defines a new function called EmployeePrice that will determine the employee purchase price of replaced computer equipment.

Steps

1. Start Access, open the **Technology-O** database, click **Modules** on the Objects bar, click the **New button** on the Database window toolbar, then maximize the Code window and the Visual Basic window

   Access automatically inserts the Option Compare Database declaration statement, which determines the way string values (text) will be sorted.

2. Type **Function EmployeePrice(startingvalue)**, then press **[Enter]**

   The Function statement declares a new function name, EmployeePrice, which contains one argument, startingvalue. VBA automatically adds the End Function statement, a required statement to mark the end of the code that defines the new function. Because both Function and End Function are VBA keywords, they are blue. The insertion point is positioned between the statements so that you can further define how the new EmployeePrice function will calculate.

3. Press **[Tab]**, type **EmployeePrice = startingvalue * 0.5**, then press **[Enter]**

   Your screen should look like Figure O-3. The second statement explains how the EmployeePrice function will calculate. The function will return a value that is calculated by multiplying the startingvalue by 0.5. It is not necessary to indent statements, but indenting code between matching Function/End Function, Sub/End Sub, or If/End If statements enhances the program's readability. Also, it is not necessary to enter spaces around the equal sign and an asterisk used as a multiplication sign, but when you press [Enter], Access will add spaces as appropriate to enhance the readability of the statement.

4. Click the **Save button** on the Standard toolbar, type **Functions** in the Save As dialog box, then click **OK**

   Now that the function is created, it can be used in a query, form, or report.

5. Close the Visual Basic window, click **Queries** on the Objects bar, right-click the **Employee Pricing query**, then click **Design View** on the shortcut menu

   The Employee Pricing query opens in Query Design View. You can create calculated expressions in a query using either Access functions or the ones you define in standard modules.

6. Click the **blank Field cell** to the right of the InitialValue field, type **Price:EmployeePrice ([InitialValue])**, click the **Datasheet View button** on the Query Design toolbar, then maximize the datasheet

   Your screen should look like Figure O-4. In this query, you created a new field called Price that used the EmployeePrice function you created in a standard module. The value in the InitialValue field was used as the startingvalue argument. The InitialValue field was multiplied by 0.5 to create the new Price field.

7. Save the Employee Pricing query, then close the datasheet

QuickTip

Field names used in expressions are not case sensitive, but they must exactly match the spelling of the field name as originally defined in Table Design View.

FIGURE O-3: Creating the EmployeePrice function

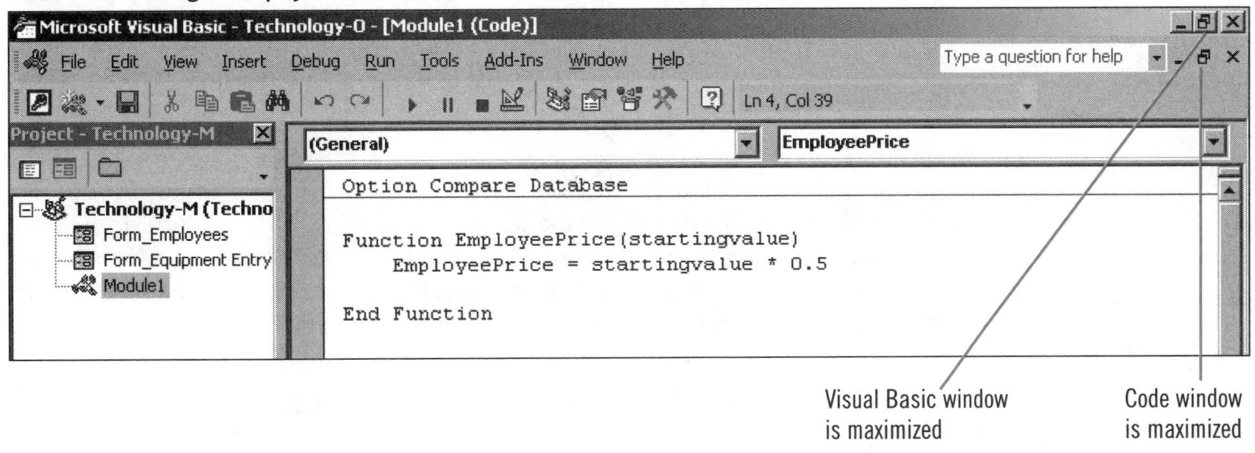

FIGURE O-4: Creating the Price field using the EmployeePrice function

Microsoft Access - [Employee Pricing : Select Query]

SerialNo	Manufacturer	Description	PurchaseDate	InitialValue	Price
242XG1	Micron	Transtrek3000	6/30/2003	$2,000.00	1000
242XG2	Micron	Transtrek3000	6/30/2003	$2,000.00	1000
295XT4	Micron	Prosignet303	7/14/2003	$1,800.00	900
295XT5	Micron	Prosignet303	7/14/2003	$1,800.00	900
295XT6	Micron	Prosignet303	7/14/2003	$1,800.00	900
295XT7	Micron	Prosignet303	7/14/2003	$1,800.00	900
300RZ1	Micron	Prosignet303	7/31/2003	$1,700.00	850
300RZ2	Micron	Prosignet303	7/31/2003	$1,700.00	850
300RZ3	Micron	Prosignet303	7/31/2003	$1,700.00	850
330RZ4	Micron	Prosignet303	7/31/2003	$1,700.00	850
388MQS1	Compaq	Centuria8088	5/31/2003	$1,500.00	750
388MQS2	Compaq	Centuria8088	5/31/2003	$1,500.00	750
388MQS3	Compaq	Centuria8088	5/31/2003	$1,500.00	750
388MQS4	Compaq	Centuria8088	5/31/2003	$1,500.00	750
4848XH1	Micron	Transtrek3000	7/14/2003	$1,900.00	950
4848XH2	Micron	Transtrek3000	7/14/2003	$1,900.00	950
4848XJ3	Micron	Transtrek3000	7/31/2003	$1,800.00	900
4848XJ4	Micron	Transtrek3000	7/31/2003	$1,800.00	900
4848XK5	Micron	Transtrek3000	8/14/2003	$1,750.00	875
511984CDE1	Lexmark	Optra2000	1/4/2003	$2,000.00	1000
511984CDE2	Lexmark	Optra2000	1/4/2003	$2,000.00	1000
72JRV1	Compaq	Deskpro99	3/31/2003	$2,000.00	1000
72JRV2	Compaq	Deskpro99	3/31/2003	$2,000.00	1000
72JRV3	Compaq	Deskpro99	3/31/2003	$2,000.00	1000

Record: 1 of 53

Datasheet View NUM

Calculated field price

Access 2002

Using If Statements

If...Then...Else logic allows you to test logical conditions and execute statements only if the conditions are true. If...Then...Else code can be composed of one or several statements, depending on how many conditions you want to test, how many possible answers you want to provide, and what you want the code to do based on the results of the tests. Kristen needs to add an If statement to the EmployeePrice function to test the age of the equipment, and then calculate the answer based on that age. As originally designed, the calculation *always* multiplies the startingvalue argument by 50%. But if the equipment is less than one year old, the function should return a value that multiplies the startingvalue argument by 75%.

Steps

1. Click **Modules** on the Objects bar, right-click the **Functions module**, then click **Design View**
   The Functions Code window with the EmployeePrice function opens. To determine the age of the equipment, the EmployeePrice function needs another argument, the purchase date of the equipment.
2. Click just before the **right parenthesis** in the Function statement, type **,** (a comma), press **[Spacebar]**, then type **purchasedate**
   The new function now contains two arguments. The statement is
   `Function EmployeePrice (startingvalue, purchasedate)`
   Now that another argument has been established, the argument can be used in the function.
3. Click to the right of the **right parenthesis** in the Function statement, press **[Enter]**, press **[Tab]**, type **If (Now() – purchasedate) >365 Then**, then press **[Enter]**
   This expression evaluates whether today's date, represented by the Access function Now(), minus the value represented by the purchasedate argument is greater than 365 days. If true, this would indicate that the equipment is older than one year.
4. Indent, then enter the rest of the statements exactly as shown in Figure O-5
   The Else statement will be executed only if the expression is false (if the equipment is less than 365 days old). The End If statement is needed to mark the end of the If block of code.
5. Click the **Save button** on the Standard toolbar, close the Visual Basic window, click **Queries** on the Objects bar, right-click the **Employee Pricing query**, then click **Design View** on the shortcut menu
   Now that the EmployeePrice function has two arguments, you need to modify the expression in the query to consider two arguments in order for it to calculate the correct answer.
6. Right-click the **Price field** in the query design grid, click **Zoom** on the shortcut menu, click between the **right square bracket** and **right parenthesis**, then type **,[PurchaseDate]**
   Your Zoom dialog box should look like Figure O-6. Both of the arguments used to calculate the EmployeePrice function are field names, so they must be typed exactly as shown, and surrounded by square brackets. Commas separate multiple arguments in the function.
7. Click **OK** in the Zoom dialog box, then click the **Datasheet View button** on the Query Design toolbar
8. Click any entry in the **PurchaseDate field**, then click the **Sort Ascending button** on the Query Datasheet toolbar
   The EmployeePrice function now calculates two ways, depending on the age of the equipment determined by the date in the PurchaseDate field, as shown in Figure O-7. The new calculated Price field is based on the current date on your computer, so your results may vary.
9. Save, then close the Employee Pricing query

QuickTip

Indentation doesn't affect the way the function works, but does make the code easier to read.

Trouble?

If you get a compile or syntax error, open the Visual Basic window, check your function against Figure O-5, then correct any errors.

FIGURE O-5: If…Then…Else statements

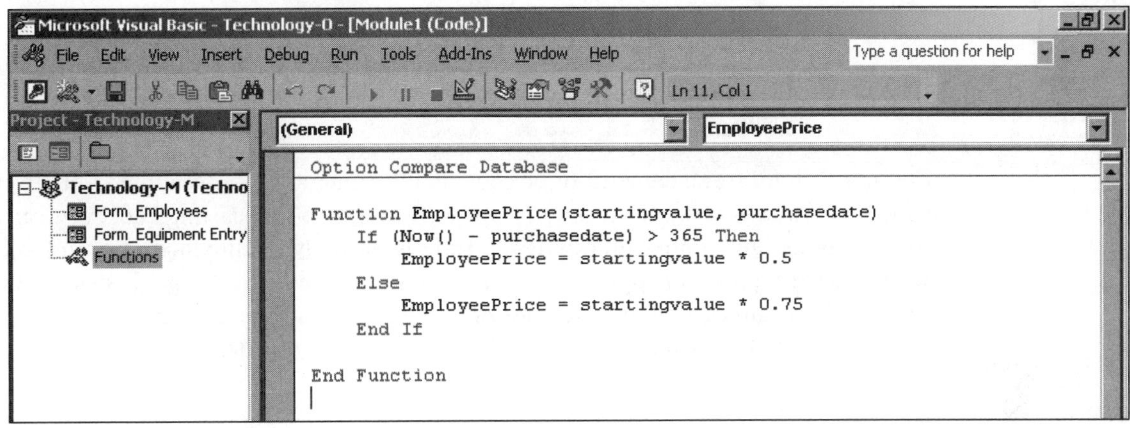

FIGURE O-6: Modifying the expression

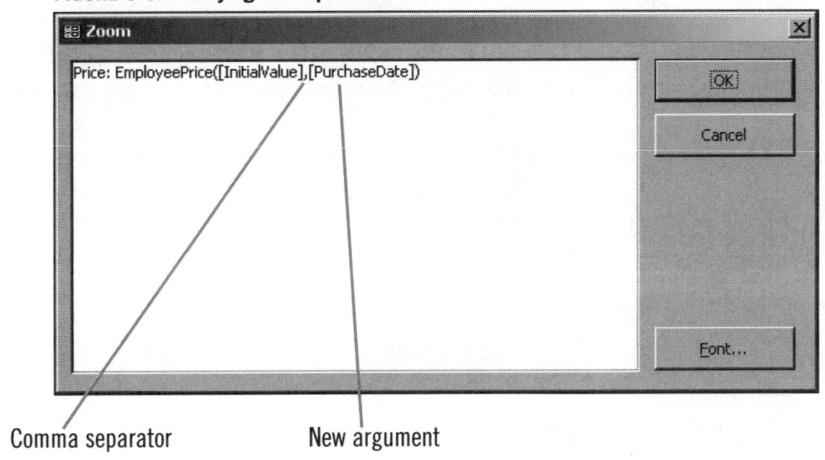

FIGURE O-7: Price field is calculated two ways

Microsoft Access - [Employee Pricing : Select Query]

SerialNo	Manufacturer	Description	PurchaseDate	InitialValue	Price
XPX5QRST2	HP	Deskjet 900XJ2	1/10/2000	$500.00	250
XPX5QRST1	HP	Deskjet 900XJ2	1/10/2000	$500.00	250
HKPF9	Dell	XPS480	1/4/2002	$2,000.00	1500
HKPF7	Dell	XPS480	1/4/2002	$2,000.00	1500
HKPF6	Dell	XPS480	1/4/2002	$2,000.00	1500
HKPF1	Dell	XPS480	1/4/2002	$2,000.00	1500
HKPF8	Dell	XPS480	1/4/2002	$2,000.00	1500
XPX5QRST3	HP	Deskjet 900XJ2	1/4/2002	$500.00	375

InitialValue *0.75 InitialValue *0.5

Access 2002

Access 2002

Documenting Procedures

Comment lines are statements in the code that document the code, and do not affect how the code runs. At any future time, if you want to read or modify existing code, you can write the modifications much more quickly if the code is properly documented. Comment lines start with an apostrophe, and appear in green in the Code window. Kristen documents the EmployeePrice function in the Functions module with descriptive comments. This will make it easier for her to follow the purpose and logic of the function later.

Steps

1. Click **Modules** on the Objects bar, right-click the **Functions** module, then click **Design View**
   The Code window for the Functions module opens.

2. Click to the left of the **Function statement**, press **[Enter]**, press **[Up arrow]**, type **'This function is called EmployeePrice and has two arguments**, then press **[Enter]**
   As soon as you move to another statement, the comment statement will become green in the Code window.

> **QuickTip**
> You also can create comments by starting the statement with Rem (for remark).

> **Trouble?**
> Be sure to use an ' (apostrophe) and not a " (quotation mark) to begin the comment line.

3. Type **'Created by Your Name on Today's Date**, then press [Enter]
   Your screen should look like Figure O-8. You also can place comments at the end of a line by entering an apostrophe to mark that the next part of the statement is a comment. The utility project contains VBA code that helps Access with certain activities such as presenting the Zoom dialog box. It automatically appears in the Project Explorer window when you use the Access features that utilize this code.

4. Click to the right of **Then** at the end of the If statement, press **[Spacebar]**, then type **'Now() is today's date**
   This comment explains that the Now() function is today's date. All comments are green, regardless of whether they are on their own line or at the end of an existing line.

5. Click to the right of **0.5**, press **[Spacebar]**, then type **'If > 1 yr, value is 50%**

6. Click to the right of **0.75**, press **[Spacebar]**, then type **'If < 1 yr, value is 75%**, then press [↓]
   Your screen should look like Figure O-9. Table O-3 provides more information about the Standard toolbar buttons in the Visual Basic window.

7. Click the **Save button** on the Standard toolbar, click **File** on the menu bar, click **Print**, then click **OK**

8. Click **File** on the menu bar, then click **Close and Return to Microsoft Access**

FIGURE O-8: Adding comments to the Code window

Comment lines

utility project

```
Option Compare Database

'This function is called EmployeePrice and has two arguments
'Created by Your Name on Today's Date

Function EmployeePrice(startingvalue, purchasedate)
    If (Now() - purchasedate) > 365 Then
        EmployeePrice = startingvalue * 0.5
    Else
        EmployeePrice = startingvalue * 0.75
    End If

End Function
```

FIGURE O-9: Adding comments at the end of a statement

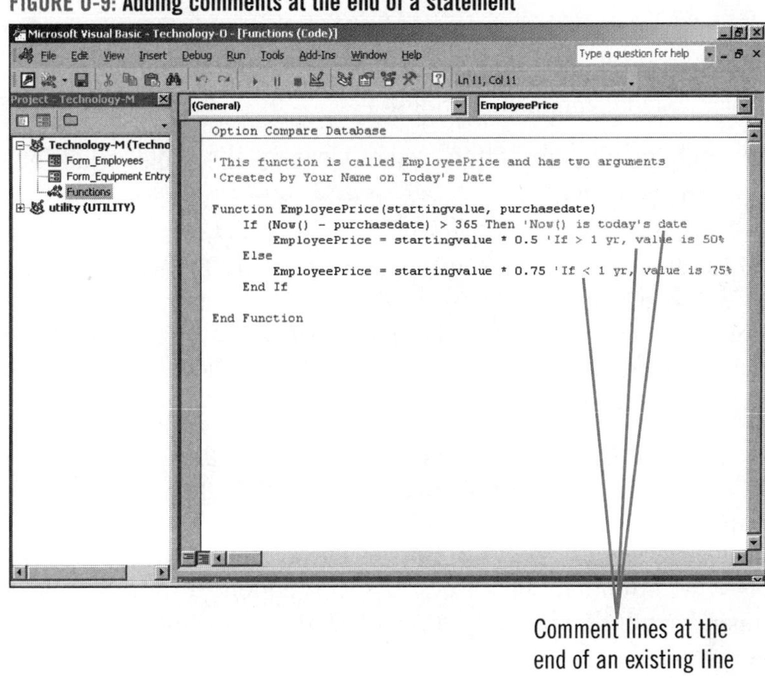

TABLE O-3: Standard toolbar buttons in the Visual Basic window

button name	button	description
View Microsoft Access		Toggles between the Access and the active Visual Basic window
Insert Module		Opens a new module or class module Code window, or inserts a new procedure in the current Code window
Run Sub/UserForm		Runs the current procedure if the insertion point is in a procedure, or runs the UserForm if it is active
Break		Stops execution of a program while it's running, and switches to **break mode**, the temporary suspension of program execution in which you can examine, debug, reset, step through, or continue program execution
Reset		Resets the procedure
Project Explorer		Displays the Project Explorer, which displays a hierarchical list of the currently open projects (set of modules) and their contents
Object Browser		Displays the **Object Browser**, which lists the defined modules and procedures as well as available methods, properties, events, constants, and other items that you can use in the code

Examining Class Modules

Class modules are contained and executed within specific forms and reports. Class modules most commonly contain sub procedures and execute in response to an event such as the click of a command button. You do not always have to know VBA code to create class modules. The Command Button Wizard, for example, creates sub procedures. You can examine them to see how sub procedures work and how they are executed through specific events. Kristen used the Command Button Wizard to create four command buttons on the Equipment Entry Form. She examines the sub procedures in this form in order to understand class modules.

1. **Click Forms on the Objects bar, right-click the Equipment Entry Form, click Design View on the shortcut menu, then maximize the form**
   The form has four command buttons.
2. **Click each command button while viewing the Object list on the Formatting (Form/Report) toolbar**
   Your screen should look like Figure O-10. The Object list identifies the name of the selected control as determined by the control's Name property. In this case, the word "object" is used as a VBA programmer would use it. Within VBA, an object is any item that can be identified or manipulated, including the traditional Access objects (table, query, form, report, page, macro, module), and smaller pieces of the traditional objects including controls, sections, and existing procedures.
3. **Click the Code button on the Form Design toolbar**
   The Code window for the VBA code stored in the Equipment Entry Form class module appears, as shown in Figure O-11. All of the code for each of the four command buttons was created by using the Command Button Wizard. The names of the subs, AddNewRecordButton and DeleteThisRecordButton, correspond with the names of the command buttons on the form. The _Click() suffix identifies the event that will cause the sub to execute.
4. **Close the Visual Basic window, double-click the Print This Record command button to open its property sheet, click the Event tab, click [Event Procedure] in the On Click property, then click the Build button**
   The class module is opened in the specific location where the PrintThisRecordButton_Click() sub is stored. To create a sub that executes based on a specific event associated with that command button (for example, to display a message box when the command button is double-clicked) you could use the property sheet to help you correctly name the new sub.
5. **Close the Visual Basic window, click the On Got Focus property, click , click Code Builder in the Choose Builder dialog box, then click OK**
   The class module Code window opens, as shown in Figure O-12. Because you entered the Code window through a specific event (On Got Focus) of a specific control (PrintThisRecordButton), VBA knew what to name the sub, PrintThisRecordButton_GotFocus(). It also automatically supplied the last line of the procedure, the End Sub statement. The rest of the sub's statements, however, would require individual programming, because you are not using a wizard to create the code.
6. **Select the Private Sub PrintThisRecordButton_GotFocus() statement and the End Sub statement, press [Delete], close the Visual Basic window, then save and close the Equipment Entry Form**

FIGURE O-10: Four command buttons in Form Design View

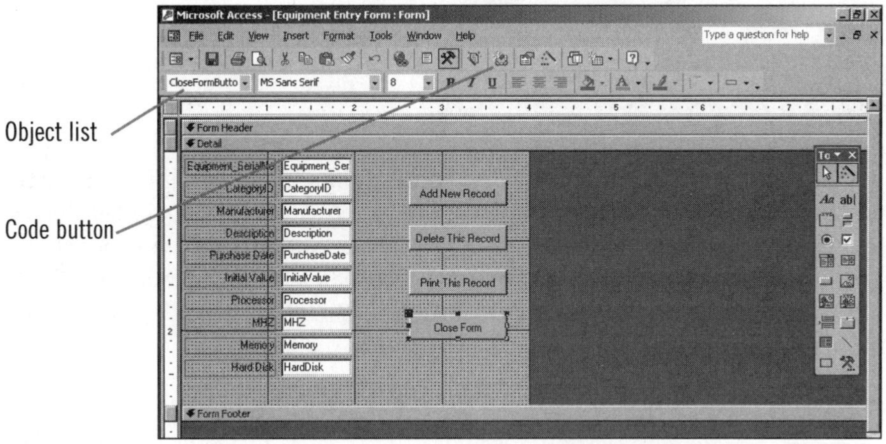

Object list

Code button

FIGURE O-11: Class module containing four sub procedures

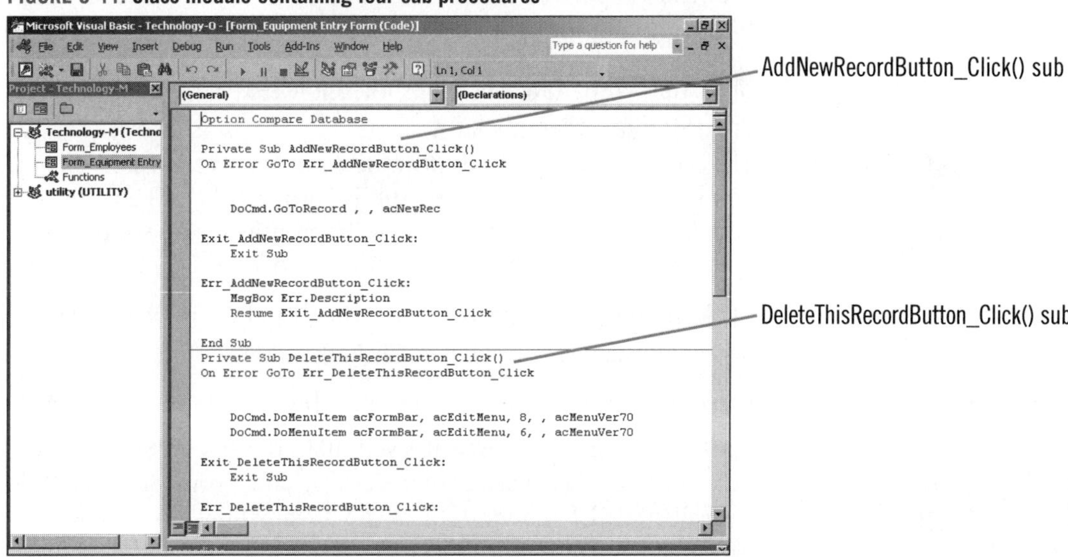

FIGURE O-12: Examining a new sub name

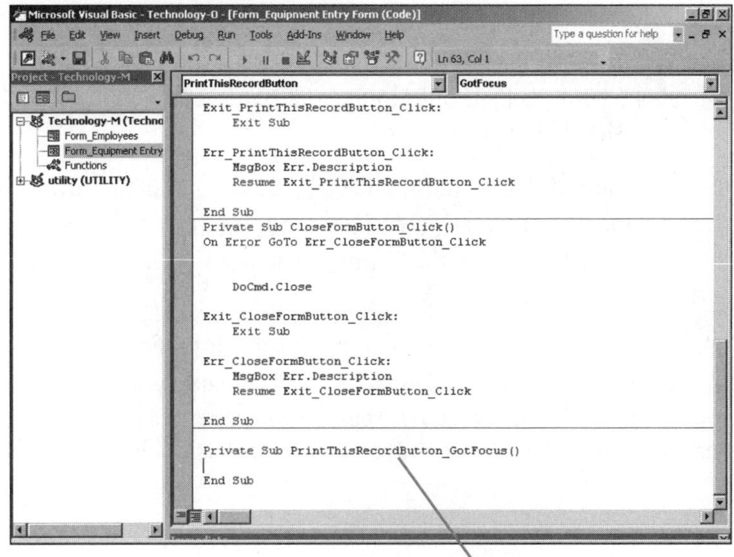

Access 2002

Access 2002

Creating Sub Procedures

While it is easiest to create class module sub procedures using wizards, not all subs can be created this way. The Command Button Wizard, for example, always attaches its code to the **On Click** event of a command button. You might want to create a sub that executes based on another action, such as double-click, or one that is assigned to a control other than a command button. Kristen would like to add built-in documentation to a form that the user can access by clicking the form. To accomplish this, she writes a sub procedure in a form class module.

Steps

1. Right-click the **Equipment Entry Form**, click **Design View** on the shortcut menu, then click the **Properties button** on the Form Design toolbar to open the property sheet (if it's not already visible)
2. Click the **Event tab**, click the **On Click text box**, click the **Build button**, click **Code Builder**, then click **OK**
   The class module opens with two new statements to identify the first and last lines of the new sub. The name of the new sub is Form_Click(). The name of the new sub references both the specific object and the specific event you chose in the property sheet. You can use the Object and Procedure lists within the Code window to change these choices, however.
3. Click the **Object list arrow** below the Standard toolbar, then click **FormFooter**
   A new sub, named FormFooter_Click(), is created.
4. Click the **Procedure list arrow** below the Standard toolbar, click **DblClick**, then scroll up to view the three new subs you just created, as shown in Figure O-13
   The Form_Click(), FormFooter_Click(), and FormFooter_DblClick(Cancel As Integer) were all created, but none of them contain anything more than the first and last statements. Now that you know how to use the Object and Procedure lists to create new subs, you can return to the original task of creating documentation for the form that appears when the user clicks the form.
5. Click the **Undo button** on the Standard toolbar twice to remove both FormFooter subs, type **MsgBox ("Created by Your Name on Today's Date")** as the single statement for the Form_Click() sub, then click the **Save button** on the Standard toolbar
   Your screen should look like Figure O-14.
6. Close the Visual Basic window, click , click the **Form View button** on the Form Design toolbar, then click the **record selector** to the left of the record
   The MsgBox statement in the Form_Click() sub creates the dialog box, as shown in Figure O-15.
7. Click **OK** in the message box, then click the **Close Form** command button
   VBA is as robust and powerful as Access itself. It takes years of experience to appreciate the vast number of objects, events, methods, and properties that are available. With only modest programming skills, however, you can create basic sub procedures.

FIGURE O-13: Using the Object and Procedure lists

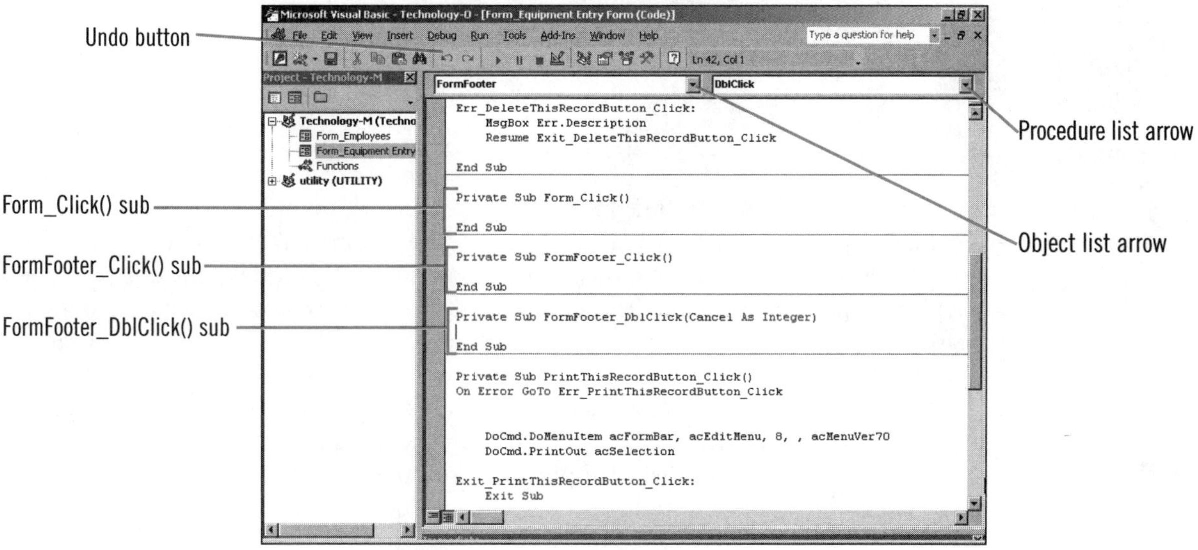

Undo button

Form_Click() sub

FormFooter_Click() sub

FormFooter_DblClick() sub

Procedure list arrow

Object list arrow

FIGURE O-14: Creating a sub procedure

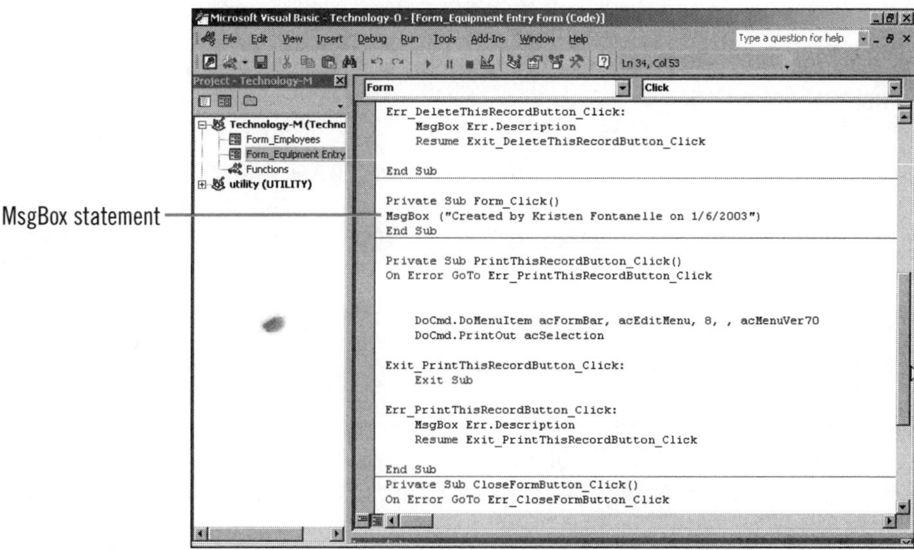

FIGURE O-15: Form_Click() sub executes the MsgBox statement

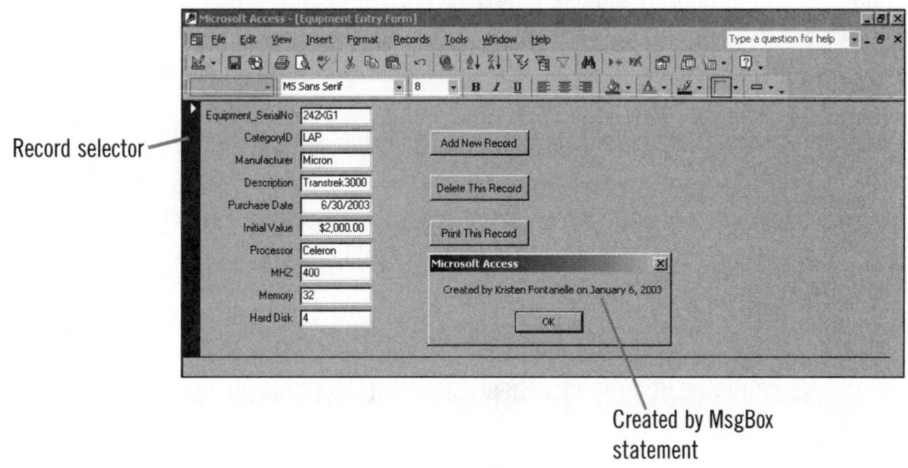

Access 2002

Access 2002

Troubleshooting Modules

You might encounter three types of errors as your code runs, and Access provides several techniques to help you **debug** (find and resolve) these errors. **Compile-time errors** occur as a result of incorrectly constructed code. For example, you may have forgotten to write an End If statement following an If clause, or you may have a **syntax error**, such as a missing parenthesis. This type of error is easiest to find because your code will turn red as soon as it detects a syntax error. **Run-time errors** occur after the code starts to run, and include attempting an illegal operation such as dividing by zero or moving focus to a control that doesn't exist. When you encounter a run-time error, VBA will stop executing your procedure at the line in which the error occurred so you can examine it. **Logic errors** are the most difficult to troubleshoot because they occur when the code runs without problems, but the procedure still doesn't produce the desired result. Kristen studies debugging techniques using the Functions module.

Steps

1. **Click Modules on the Objects bar, right-click Functions, click Design View, click to the right of the End If statement, type your name, then press [↓]**
   Because entering your name is not a valid way to start a VBA statement, when you move out of that statement, VBA displays it in bright red.

2. **Click OK in the Compile error message box, delete your name, then click anywhere in another statement**
   The Option Compare Database statement changes to blue (reserved VBA keywords are blue) as soon as you successfully delete your name and click elsewhere in the Code window. Another VBA debugging tool is to set a **breakpoint**, a bookmark that suspends execution of the procedure at that statement to allow the user to examine what is happening.

> **QuickTip**
> Click the gray bar to the left of the VBA statement to toggle breakpoints on and off.

3. **Click anywhere in the If statement, click Debug on the menu bar, then click Toggle Breakpoint**
   Your screen should look like Figure O-16.

> **QuickTip**
> If you suspend the execution of a procedure by using a breakpoint, pointing to an argument in the Code window will display a ScreenTip with the argument's current value.

4. **Click the View Microsoft Access button on the Standard toolbar, click Queries on the Objects bar, then double-click Employee Pricing**
   When the Employee Pricing query opens, it immediately runs the EmployeePrice function. Because you set a breakpoint at the If statement, that statement is highlighted, as shown in Figure O-17, indicating that the code has been suspended at that point.

5. **Click View on the menu bar, click Immediate Window, type ? purchasedate, then press [Enter]**
   Your screen should look like Figure O-18. The Immediate window is an area where you can determine the value of any argument at the breakpoint. If the date appears as a two-digit year and you would like it to appear as a four-digit year, you can specify that change for the existing database or for all databases using the Options dialog box. Click Tools on the menu bar, click Options, and the click then General tab to find the four-digit year formatting options.

6. **Click Debug on the menu bar, click Clear All Breakpoints, click the Continue button on the Standard toolbar to execute the remainder of the function, then save, print, and close the Functions module**
   The Employee Pricing query's datasheet should be visible.

7. **Close the Employee Pricing datasheet, close the Technology-O database, then exit Access**

FIGURE O-16: Setting a breakpoint

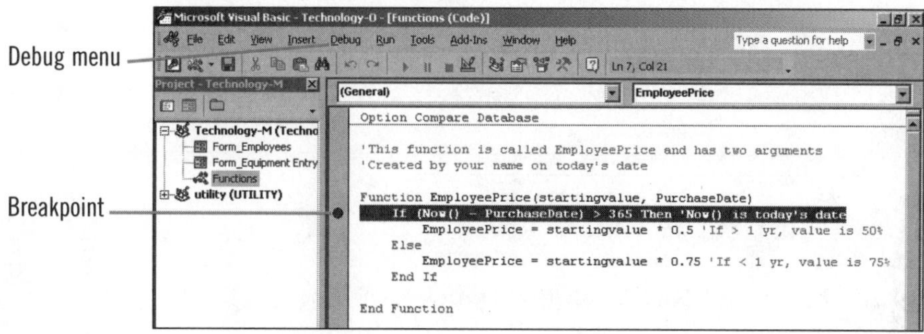

FIGURE O-17: Stopping execution at a breakpoint

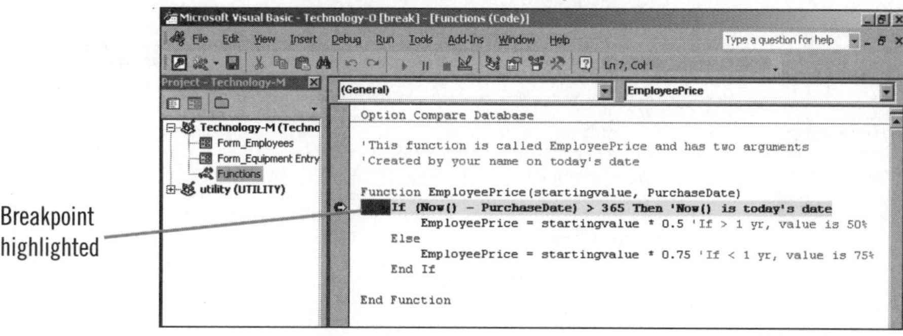

FIGURE O-18: Using the Immediate window

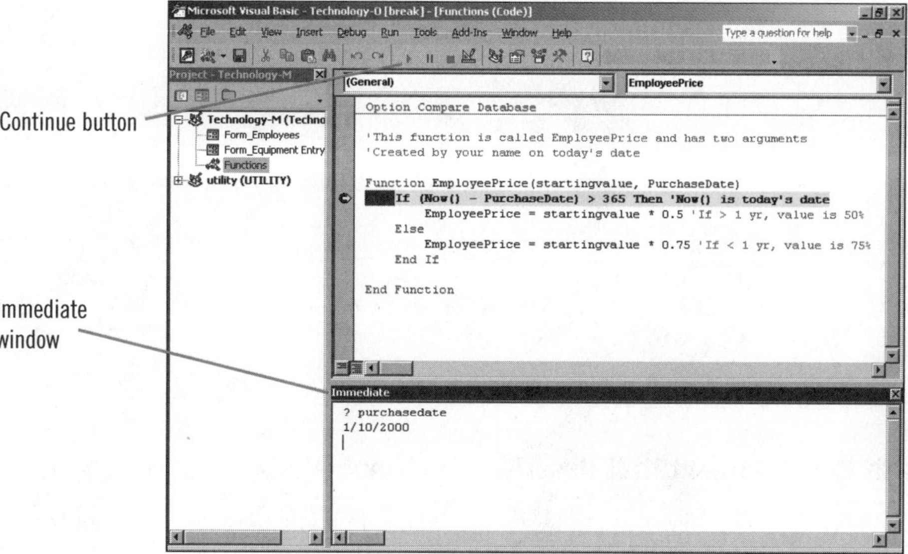

Interpreting Visual Basic syntax

When you enter a Visual Basic keyword such as MsgBox, shown in Figure O-19, Visual Basic prompts appear to help you complete the statement. In the MsgBox function syntax, the bold italic words are the **named arguments** of the function. Arguments enclosed in brackets are optional. (Do not type the brackets in your Visual Basic code.) For the MsgBox function, the only argument you must provide is the text for the prompt.

FIGURE O-19: MsgBox function

```
MsgBox |
MsgBox(Prompt, [Buttons As VbMsgBoxStyle = vbOKOnly], [Title], [HelpFile], [Context])
As VbMsgBoxResult
```

Practice

► Concepts Review

Identify each element of the Visual Basic window shown in Figure O-20.

FIGURE O-20

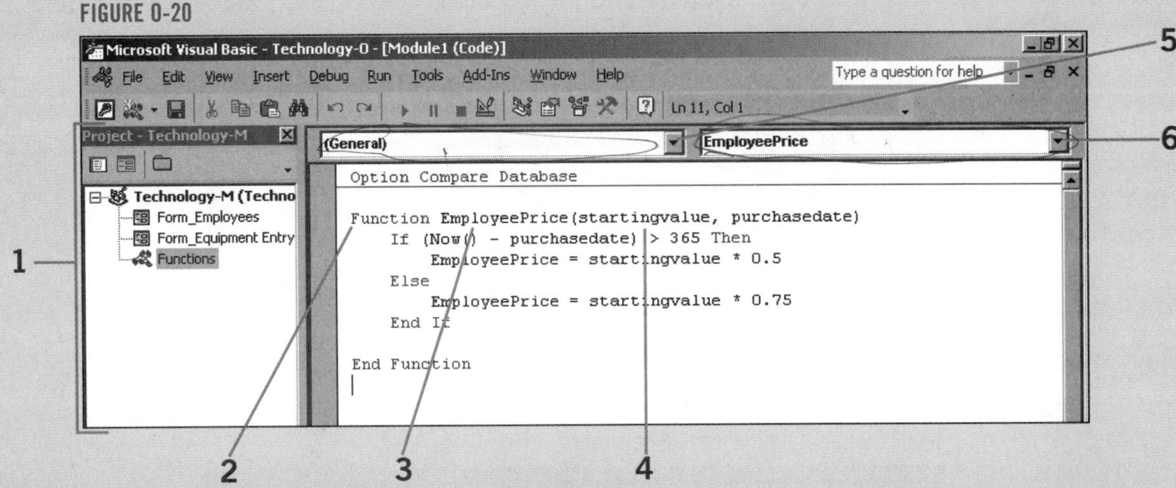

Match each term with the statement that describes its function.

7. Procedure
8. If…Then…Else statement
9. Debugging
10. Class modules
11. Visual Basic for Applications
12. Function
13. Arguments
14. Breakpoint
15. Module

a. Allows you to test a logical condition and execute commands only if the condition is true
b. The programming language used in Access modules
c. A line of code that automatically suspends execution of the procedure
d. A procedure that returns a value
e. Constants, variables, or expressions passed to a procedure to further define how it should execute
f. Stored as part of the form or report object in which they are created
g. The Access object where VBA code is stored
h. A series of VBA statements that perform an operation or calculate a value
i. A process to find and resolve programming errors

Practice

Select the best answer from the list of choices.

16. A module contains VBA programming code organized in units called:

a. Macros.
b. Arguments.
c. Breakpoints.
d. Procedures.

17. Which type of procedure returns a value?

a. Sub
b. Function
c. Sub procedure
d. Class module

18. Which of the following is NOT a reason to use modules rather than macros?

a. Modules are used to create unique functions.
b. Modules contain code that can work with other Microsoft Office software programs.
c. Modules can contain procedures that mask error messages.
d. Modules are usually easier to write than macros.

19. Which of the following is NOT a type of VBA error?

a. Compile time
b. Run time
c. Logic
d. Class action

20. Which of the following is a specific action that occurs on or to an object, and is usually the result of a user action?

a. Argument
b. Sub
c. Function
d. Event

▶ Skills Review

1. Understand modules.

a. Start Access, then open the **Basketball-O** database from the drive and folder where your Project Files are located.
b. Open the Code window for the Shot Statistics module.
c. Record your answers to the following questions on a sheet of paper.
- What is the name of the function defined in this module?
- What are the names of the arguments defined in this module?
- In your own words, what is the purpose of the If statement?
- What is the purpose of the End Function statement?
- Why is the End Function statement in blue?
- Why are some of the lines indented?

2. Compare macros and modules.

a. If not already opened, open the Code window for the Shot Statistics module.
b. Record your answers to the following questions on a sheet of paper.
- Why was a module rather than a macro used to create this function?
- Why is code written in the Shot Statistics Code window generally more difficult to create than a macro?
- Identify each of the keywords or keyword phrases, and explain the purpose for each.

3. Create functions.

a. If not already opened, open the Code window for the Shot Statistics module.
b. Create a function called Contribution below the End Function statement of the TotalShotPercentage function by typing the following VBA statements: (*Hint:* Type the function exactly as written below.)

```
Function Contribution(fg, threept, ft, offreb, defreb, assists)
        Contribution = (fg * 2 + threept * 3 + ft + offreb * 2 + defreb + assists * 2)
End Function
```

c. Save the Shot Statistics module, then close the Visual Basic window.

Access 2002

d. Use Query Design View to create a new query using the First and Last fields from the Players table and all of the fields from the Stats table.

e. Create a calculated field named **Rank** in the first available column by carefully typing the Contribution function as follows:
Rank: Int(Contribution([FG], [3P], [FT], [Reb-O], [Reb-D], [Assists]))
(*Note:* The Int function converted the result to an integer rather than text for later sorting purposes.)

f. Sort the query in ascending order on the GameNo field, then in descending order on the Rank field. This will put the records in order from most valuable player to least for each game.

g. View the datasheet, as shown in Figure O-21, change PlayerNo 21 to your first and last name, then print the first page of the datasheet in landscape orientation.

h. Save the query with the name **Rankings**, then close the Rankings datasheet.

4. Use If statements.

FIGURE O-21

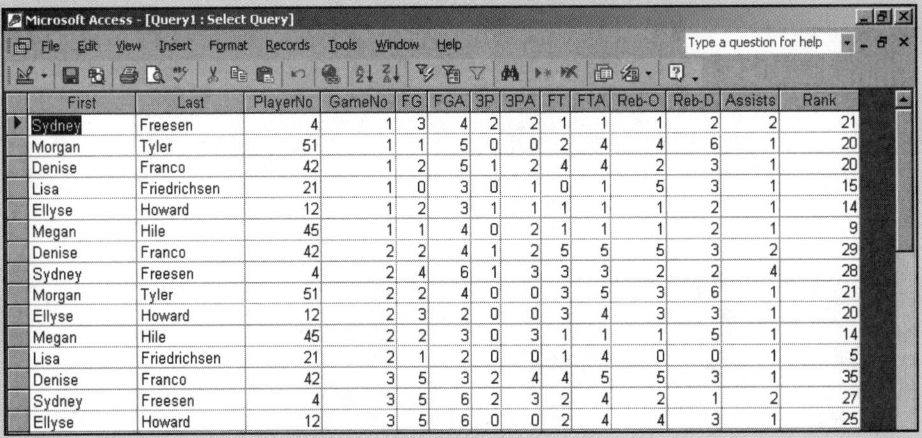

Microsoft Access - [Query1 : Select Query]

File Edit View Insert Format Records Tools Window Help — Type a question for help

First	Last	PlayerNo	GameNo	FG	FGA	3P	3PA	FT	FTA	Reb-O	Reb-D	Assists	Rank
Sydney	Freesen	4	1	3	4	2	2	1	1	1	2	2	21
Morgan	Tyler	51	1	1	5	0	0	2	4	4	6	1	20
Denise	Franco	42	1	2	5	1	2	4	4	2	3	1	20
Lisa	Friedrichsen	21	1	0	3	0	1	0	1	5	3	1	15
Ellyse	Howard	12	1	2	3	1	1	1	1	1	2	1	14
Megan	Hile	45	1	1	4	0	2	1	1	1	2	1	9
Denise	Franco	42	2	2	4	1	2	5	5	5	3	2	29
Sydney	Freesen	4	2	4	6	1	3	3	3	2	2	4	28
Morgan	Tyler	51	2	2	4	0	0	3	5	3	6	1	21
Ellyse	Howard	12	2	3	2	0	0	3	4	3	3	1	20
Megan	Hile	45	2	2	3	0	3	1	1	1	5	1	14
Lisa	Friedrichsen	21	2	1	2	0	0	1	4	0	0	1	5
Denise	Franco	42	3	5	3	2	4	4	5	5	3	1	35
Sydney	Freesen	4	3	5	6	2	3	2	4	2	1	2	27
Ellyse	Howard	12	3	5	6	0	0	2	4	4	3	1	25

a. Click Modules on the Objects bar, open the Shot Statistics Code window, click to the right of the Function Contribution statement, press [Enter], then modify the function with the statements shown below:
(*Hint:* You can use copy and paste to copy repeating statements, then edit for the differences.)

```
Function Contribution(fg, threept, ft, offreb, defreb, assists)
   If fg+threept+ft = 0 Then
        Contribution = (fg * 2 + threept * 3 + ft + offreb * 2 + defreb + assists * 2)/2
   ElseIf offreb+defreb = 0 Then
        Contribution = (fg * 2 + threept * 3 + ft + offreb * 2 + defreb + assists * 2)/3
   Else
       Contribution = (fg * 2 + threept * 3 + ft + offreb * 2 + defreb + assists * 2)
   End If
End Function
```

b. Save the Shot Statistics module, then close the Visual Basic window.

c. Rename the Rankings query to **Rankings-your initials**, then open and print the first pages of the datasheet in landscape orientation. You should see the calculated Ranking field change for PlayerNo 21 for Games 1, 2, and 3 in which the player had either zero offense or zero rebounds.

d. Close the datasheet.

5. Document procedures.

a. Click Modules on the Objects bar, open the Shot Statistics Code window, and edit the Contribution function to include the following five comment statements:

```
Function Contribution(fg, threept, ft, offreb, defreb, assists)
'If no field goals, 3 pointers, or free throws were made
   If fg + threept + ft = 0 Then
'Then the Contribution statistic should be divided by 2
      Contribution = (fg * 2 + threept * 3 + ft + offreb * 2 + defreb + assists * 2) / 2
'If no offensive or defensive rebounds were grabbed
   ElseIf offreb + defreb = 0 Then
```

```
'Then the Contribution statistic should be divided by 3
      Contribution = (fg * 2 + threept * 3 + ft + offreb * 2 + defreb + assists * 2) / 3
   Else
      Contribution = (fg * 2 + threept * 3 + ft + offreb * 2 + defreb + assists * 2)
   End If
End Function
'This function was created by Your Name on today's date
```

b. Save the changes to the Shot Statistics module, print the module, then close the Visual Basic window.

6. Examine class modules.

a. Open the Player Entry Form in Form Design View.

b. On the right side of the form, select the Command Button that is named PrintCurrentRecord and displays a printer icon.

c. Open the property sheet for the button, click the Event tab, click the On Click property, then click the Build button to open the class module.

d. Edit the comment on the last line to show your name and the current date; save and print the module, then close the Visual Basic window.

7. Create sub procedures.

a. Open the Player Entry Form in Form Design View, if it's not already opened.

b. Open the property sheet for the form, click the Event tab, click the On Mouse Move property text box, click the Build button, click Code Builder, then click OK.

c. Enter the following statement between the Private Sub and End Sub statements:
`[First].ForeColor = 255`

d. Enter a comment below this statement as follows:
`'When the mouse moves, the First control will become red.`

e. Save, then close the Visual Basic window.

f. Close the property sheet, save, then open the Player Entry Form in Form View.

g. Move the mouse beyond the edge of the Detail section of the form. The color of the First text box should turn red.

h. Save, then close the Player Entry Form.

8. Troubleshoot modules.

a. Open the Code window for the Shot Statistics module.

b. Click anywhere in the If fg + threept + ft = 0 statement.

c. Click Debug on the menu bar, then click the Toggle Breakpoint option to set a breakpoint at this statement.

d. Save and close the Visual Basic window, then return to Microsoft Access.

e. Click Queries on the Objects bar, then double-click the Rankings-your initials query. This action will use the Contribution function, which will stop and highlight the statement where you set a breakpoint.

f. Click View on the menu bar, click Immediate Window (if not already visible), type **?fg**, then press [Enter]. On a piece of paper, write down the current value of the fg variable.

g. Type **?offreb**, then press [Enter]. On a piece of paper, write down the current value of the offreb variable.

h. Click Debug on the menu bar, click Clear All Breakpoints, click the Continue button on the Standard toolbar.

i. Return to the Rankings-your initials query in Datasheet View. Using both Query Design View and Query Datasheet View, answer the following questions:

- When calculating the Rank field, what field was used for the fg argument?
- When calculating the Rank field, what field is used for the offreb argument?
- What is the value of the fg argument for the first record?
- What is the value of the offreb argument?

j. Close the Rankings-your initials query, close the Basketball-O database, then exit Access.

Independent Challenge 1

As the manager of a doctor's clinic, you have created an Access database called Patients-O to track insurance claim reimbursements and general patient health. You want to modify an existing function within this database.

a. Start Access, then open the **Patients-O** database from the drive and folder where your Project Files are located.

b. Open the Body Mass Index module in Design View, then record your answers to the following questions on another sheet of paper:
   - What is the name of the function in the module?
   - What are the function arguments?
   - How many comments are in the function?

c. Edit the BMI function by adding a comment at the end of the code with your name and today's date.

d. Edit the BMI function by adding a comment above the Function statement with the following information:
```
'A healthy BMI is in the range of 21-24.
```

e. Edit the BMI function by adding the following If statement between the Function and BMI statements:
```
If height = 0 Then BMI = 0 Else
```

f. Edit the BMI function by adding an End If statement between the BMI and End Function statements, then indent the code to clarify the If clause. The final BMI function code should look as follows:
```
'This function calculates BMI, body mass index.
'A high BMI indicates an unhealthy weight to height ratio.
'A healthy BMI is in the range of 21-24.
    Function BMI(weight, height)
        If height = 0 Then
            BMI = 0
        Else
            BMI = (weight * 0.4536) / (height * 0.0254) ^ 2
        End If
    End Function
'Your Name and today's date.
```

g. Save and print the module, then close the Visual Basic window.

h. Double-click the BMI Query to open its datasheet, then test the If statement by entering **0** in the Height field for the first record for Sara Johnson. When you press [Tab] to move to the Weight field, the bmicalc field should recalculate to 0.

i. Edit the first record to contain your first and last name, print, save, then close the BMI Query datasheet.

j. Close the Patients-O database, then exit Access.

Independent Challenge 2

As the manager of a doctor's clinic, you have created an Access database called Patients-O to track insurance claim reimbursements. You want to study the existing sub procedures stored as class modules in the Claim Entry Form.

a. Start Access, then open the **Patients-O** database from the drive and folder where your Project Files are located.

b. Open the Claim Entry Form in Form Design View.

c. Click the Code button on the Form Design toolbar, then record your answers to the following questions on another sheet of paper:
   - What are the names of the sub procedures in this class module?
   - What Access functions are used in the PtFirstName_AfterUpdate() sub?
   - How many arguments do the functions in the PtFirstName_AfterUpdate() sub have?
   - What do the functions in the PtFirstName_AfterUpdate() sub do? (*Hint:* You may have to use the Visual Basic Help system if you are not familiar with the functions.)
   - What is the purpose of the On Error command? (*Hint:* Use the Visual Basic Help system if you are not familiar with this command.)

d. Close the Visual Basic window, close the Claim Entry Form, then close the Patients-O database.
e. Exit Access.

Independent Challenge 3

As the manager of a doctor's clinic, you have created an Access database called Patients-O to track insurance claim reimbursements that are fixed (paid at a predetermined fixed rate) or denied (not paid by the insurance company). You want to enhance the database with a class module.

a. Start Access, then open the **Patients-O** database from the drive and folder where your Project Files are located.
b. Open the CPT Form in Form Design View.
c. Expand the width of the CPT Form to about the 5" mark on the horizontal ruler.
d. Use the Command Button Wizard to add a command button in the Form Header section. Choose the Add New Record action from the Record Operations category.
e. Enter **Add Record** as the text on the button, then name the button **AddRecordButton.**
f. Use the Command Button Wizard to add a command button in the Form Header section to the right of the existing Add Record button. (*Hint:* Move and resize controls as necessary to put two command buttons in the Form Header section.)
g. Choose the Delete Record action from the Record Operations category.
h. Enter **Delete Record** as the text on the button, and name the button **DeleteRecordButton**.
i. Save and view the CPT Form in Form View, then click the Add Record command button.
j. Add a new record (it will be record number 65) with a CPTCode value of **999** and an RBRVS value of **1.5.**
k. To make sure that the Delete Record button works, click the new record you just entered, click the Delete Record command button, then click Yes to confirm the deletion.
l. In Form Design View, click the Delete Record command button, then press the [Delete] key.
m. Click the Code button on the Standard toolbar to examine the class module associated with this form, then record your answers to the following questions on another sheet of paper:
   - How many subs exist in this class module and what are their names?
   - What was the effect of deleting the command button in Form Design view on the associated Visual Basic code?
n. Add a comment as the last line of code in the Code window with your name and the current date, save, print, then close the Visual Basic window.
o. Save and close the CPT Form, close the Patients-O database, then exit Access.

Independent Challenge 4

Learning a programming language is sometimes compared to learning a foreign language. But have you ever wondered how it would feel to learn a new software program or programming language if English wasn't your primary language, or if you had some other type of accessibility challenge? Advances in technology are helping to break down many barriers to those with vision, hearing, mobility, cognitive, and language impairments. In this exercise, you explore the Microsoft Web site for resources to address these issues.

a. Go to www.microsoft.com/enable, then print that page. Explore the Web site.
b. Go back to www.microsoft.com/enable, click the Guides by Disability link, then click the Cognitive and Language Impairments link.
c. After exploring the Web site (you may want to print some pages as well, but be careful as some articles are quite long), write a one-page, double-spaced paper describing some of the things that you learned about how Microsoft products accommodate people with Cognitive and Language impairments.
d. Go back to www.microsoft.com/enable, scroll to the bottom, click the International Sites list arrow, click Spanish, then click Go. Print that page, then exit Access.

Visual Workshop

As the manager of a college basketball team, you are helping the coach build meaningful statistics to compare the relative value of the players in each game. The coach has stated that one offensive rebound is worth as much to the team as two defensive rebounds, and would like you to use this rule to develop a "rebounding impact statistic" for each game. Open the **Basketball-O** database and use Figure O-22 to develop a function called **ReboundImpact** in a new module called **Rebound Statistic** to calculate this statistic. Include your name and the current date as a comment in the last row of the function. Print the function.

FIGURE O-22

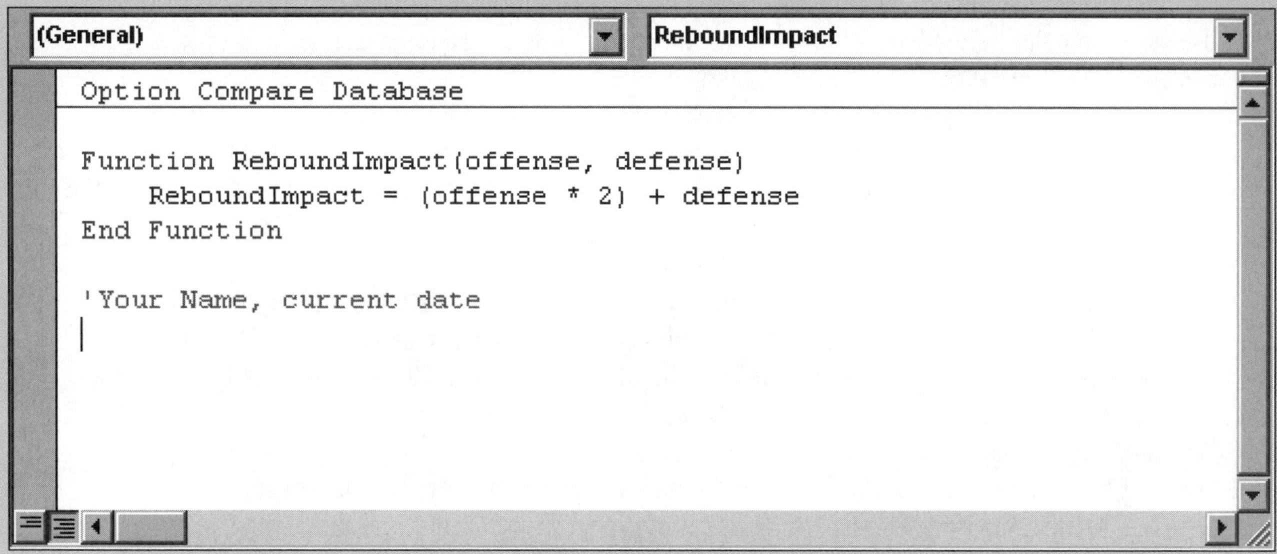

Managing the Database

Objectives

- Convert databases
- MOUS Set passwords
- MOUS Change startup options
- MOUS Encrypt a database
- Analyze performance
- MOUS Split a database
- MOUS Replicate using the Briefcase
- MOUS Synchronize using the Briefcase

Access databases are unlike the other Microsoft Office files in that they are typically used by more people and for much longer than Word documents or Excel spreadsheets. Therefore, spending a few hours to secure a database and improve its performance is a practical and wise investment. As more and more users become dependent on the database, any effort you take to make the database faster, easier, and more reliable will provide tremendous benefits. Database administration is an important responsibility. Kristen Fontanelle, network administrator at MediaLoft, will examine several administrative issues such as setting passwords, changing startup options, and analyzing database performance to protect, improve, and enhance her database.

Access 2002

Converting Databases

When you **convert** a database you change the file into one that can be opened in another version of Access. In Access 2002, however, the default file format for new databases is Access 2000, as evidenced by the information in the Database window title bar. This means that you can open an Access 2000 database in Access 2002 or Access 2000 without converting the database. While Microsoft Word and Microsoft Excel have enjoyed this type of backward and forward compatibility in previous versions, Access 2002 is the first version of Access that can share files with an older version of Access without first going through a conversion tool. If you want to open an Access 2000 database in Access 97, however, you need to convert it to an Access 97 database first. Kristen has been asked by the Training department to convert the Technology-P database to a version that they can open and use in Access 97 for a training class.

Steps

1. **Start Access, then open the Technology-P database from the drive and folder where your Project Files are located**
   To convert a database, you must make sure that no other users have it open. Because you are the sole user of this database, you can start the conversion process.

2. **Click Tools on the menu bar, point to Database Utilities, point to Convert Database, then click To Access 97 File Format**
   The Convert Database Into dialog box opens, prompting you for the name of the database.

3. **Make sure the Save In list references the drive and folder where your Project Files are located, then type Technology97 in the File name text box**
   Your screen should look like Figure P-1. Because both Access 2000 and Access 97 databases have the same **.mdb** file extension, it is helpful to identify the version of Access in the filename if you are going to be working with both file types on the same computer.

4. **Click Save in the Convert Database Into dialog box, then click OK when prompted about the Access 97 File Format**
   Access starts the conversion process; you can follow the progress on the status bar. Access creates a database file Technology97 in an Access 97 format. When the conversion is finished, you are returned to your original Access 2000 file, Technology-P.

5. **Right-click the Start button on the taskbar, click Explore on the shortcut menu, then scroll and locate your Project Files in the Folder list**
   You may need to click expand buttons [+] or collapse buttons [−] in the Folders list.

6. **Click View on the menu bar, then click Details**
   Your screen should look similar to Figure P-2. By viewing file details, the Name, Size, Type, and Modified columns display the name, size in KB, file type, and date the file was last modified. Notice that the list includes Technology97, the database that was just created by converting the Technology-P Access 2000 database to an Access 97 version database. The filename Technology-P appears twice, though, both with an .mdb and an .ldb extension. The **.ldb** file is a temporary file that keeps track of record-locking information when the database is open. It helps coordinate the multiuser capabilities of an Access database so that several people can read and update the same database at the same time. The .ldb file may already be closed if your Project Files are stored on the hard drive.

7. **Close Windows Explorer**

Trouble?

If you do not see the extensions on the file names, click Tools on the menu bar, click Folder Options, click the View tab, then uncheck the Hide file extensions for known file types check box.

FIGURE P-1: Convert Database Into dialog box

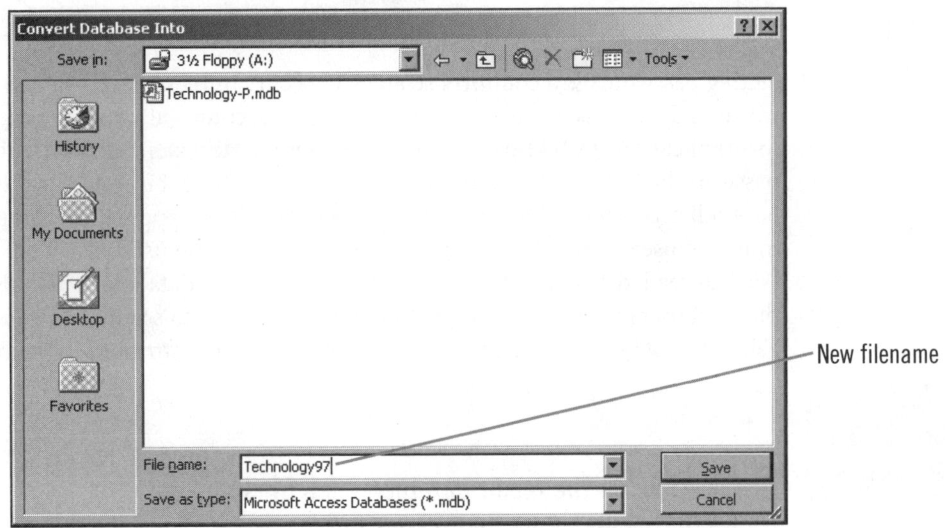

FIGURE P-2: Using Windows Explorer to view files

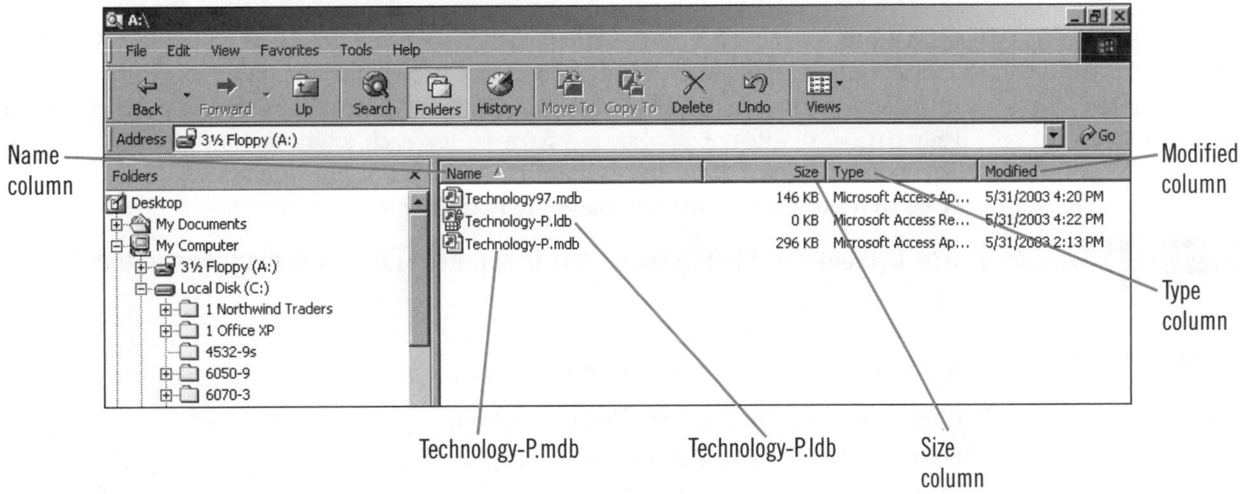

CLUES TO USE

Converting from Access 2000 to Access 2002

The *Access 2002 software application* provides some powerful new features not available in Access 2000 such as PivotTable View, PivotChart View, speech recognition, improved dynamic Web page connectivity, XML support, improved SQL Server connectivity, and more. *Access database files* themselves, however, have not dramatically changed between the Access 2000 and Access 2002 versions. Therefore, use the default Access 2000 version for new databases created in Access 2002 as shown in the Database window title bar unless your database is extremely large (a 2002 database will perform better if the database is very large), or are planning extensive future programming projects (a 2002 database will incorporate new properties and events for future releases of Access). By using the 2000 file format default option for new databases, you preserve seamless forward and backward compatibility with Access 2000 software users.

Setting Passwords

Setting passwords is a common strategy to secure information. You can set three types of passwords on an Access database: database, security account (also called user-level), and Visual Basic for Applications (VBA) passwords. If you set a **database password**, all users must enter that password before they are allowed to open the database, but once they open the database, they have full access to it. **Security account passwords** are applied to **workgroups**, files that determine the user(s), objects, and permissions to which the user(s) of that workgroup are granted (such as read, delete, or edit) for specific objects in the database. **VBA passwords** prevent unauthorized users from modifying VBA code. Other ways to secure an Access database are listed in Table P-1. Kristen uses a database password to further secure the information.

QuickTip

It's always a good idea to back up a database before creating a database password.

1. Click **File** on the menu bar, then click **Close**

   The Technology-P database closes, but the Access application window remains open.

2. Click the **Open button** on the Database toolbar, navigate to the drive and folder where your Project Files are stored, click **Technology-P**, click the **Open list arrow** in the Open dialog box, then click **Open Exclusive**

   To set a database password, you must open it in exclusive mode. **Exclusive mode** means that you are the only person who has the database open, and others will not be able to open the file during this time.

3. Click **Tools** on the menu bar, point to **Security**, then click **Set Database Password**

   The Set Database Password dialog box opens, as shown in Figure P-3. Passwords are case sensitive, and if you lose or forget your password, it can't be recovered. For security reasons, your password will not appear as you type; for each keystroke, an asterisk will appear. Therefore, you must enter the exact same password in both the Password and Verify text boxes to make sure you haven't made a typing error.

QuickTip

Check to make sure the Caps Lock light is not on before entering a password.

4. Type **cyclones** in the Password text box, press **[Tab]**, type **cyclones** in the Verify text box, then click **OK**

   Passwords should be easy to remember, but not as obvious as your name, the word "password," the name of the database, or the name of the company.

5. Click **File** on the menu bar, then click **Close**

   Of course, it's important to test the new password.

6. Click on the Database toolbar, navigate to the drive and folder where your Project Files are located, then double-click **Technology-P**

   The Password Required dialog box opens, as shown in Figure P-4.

7. Type **cyclones**, then click **OK**

   The Technology-P database opens, giving you full access to all of the objects. To remove a password, you must exclusively open a database, just as you did when you set a database password.

8. Click **File** on the menu bar, click **Close**, click on the Database toolbar, click **Technology-P**, click the **Open list arrow** in the Open dialog box, click **Open Exclusive**, type **cyclones** in the Password Required dialog box, then click **OK**

9. Click **Tools** on the menu bar, point to **Security**, click **Unset Database Password**, type **cyclones**, then click **OK**

FIGURE P-3: Set Database Password dialog box

FIGURE P-4: Password Required dialog box

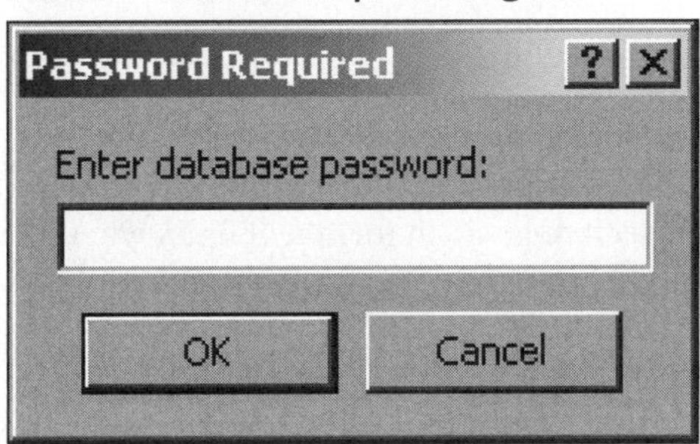

Access 2002

TABLE P-1: Methods to secure an Access database

method	description
passwords	Passwords can be set at the database, workgroup, or VBA level
encryption	Compacts the database and makes the data indecipherable to other programs
startup options	Hides or disables certain functions when the database is opened
show/hide objects	Shows or hides objects in the Database window; a simple way to prevent users from unintentionally deleting objects is to hide them in the Database window by checking the Hidden property in the object's property sheet
split a database	Separates the back-end data from the front-end objects (such as forms and reports) into two databases that work together; splitting a database allows you to give each user access to only those front-end objects they need as well as add additional security measures to the back-end database that contains the data

Creating workgroups

The most extensive way to secure an Access database is to use the Workgroup Administrator to create workgroups that define the specific users and object permissions to which the users have access. To start the Workgroup Administrator, click Tools on the menu bar, point to Security, then click Workgroup Administrator. Using Workgroup Administrator, you can grant or deny permissions to any object in the database to any group or individual that is defined within the workgroup information file. Microsoft refers to a database that is protected with workgroup-level security as a secure database.

Access 2002

Changing Startup Options

Startup options are a series of commands that execute when the database is opened. Many common startup options can be defined through the Startup dialog box, such as what form and menu bar to display when the database opens. Other startup options require that a **command-line option**, a special series of characters added to the end of the path to the file (for example, C:\My Documents\MediaLoft.mdb /excl), execute a command when the file is opened. See Table P-2 for information on several startup command-line options. Because she knows that most users immediately open the Employees form as soon as they open the Technology-P database, Kristen uses the Startup dialog box to specify that the Employees form opens as soon as the Technology-P database opens.

Steps

1. Click **Tools** on the menu bar, then click **Startup**
   The Startup dialog box opens, as shown in Figure P-5.
2. Click the **Display Form/Page list arrow**, then click **Employees**
   In addition to specifying which form will open when the Technology-P database opens, the Startup dialog box provides several other options to customize and secure the database.
3. Click in the **Application Title text box**, type **MediaLoft Computer Assets**, click the **Allow Toolbar/Menu Changes check box** to clear the check box, then click **OK**
   Clearing the Allow Toolbar/Menu Changes check box will not allow users to customize or change the view of toolbars or menus in any way. Provided the correct toolbars appear on each screen, not allowing the users to change them can simplify, secure, and improve the usability of the database. The text entered in the Application Title text box appears in the Access title bar.
4. Close the Technology-P database, click the **Open button** on the Database toolbar, navigate to the drive and folder where your Project Files are located, then double-click **Technology-P**
   The Technology-P database opens, followed by the Employees form, as shown in Figure P-6. If the database were password protected, you would have to remove the password before you could bypass the startup options.
5. Close the Employees form, then click **View** on the menu bar
   The Toolbars option is no longer available because you disabled toolbar changes in the Startup dialog box.
6. Right-click the **Database toolbar**
   No shortcut menus are available from any toolbars because you disabled toolbar changes in the Startup dialog box.

QuickTip

Press and hold [Shift] while opening a database to bypass the startup options.

FIGURE P-5: **Startup dialog box**

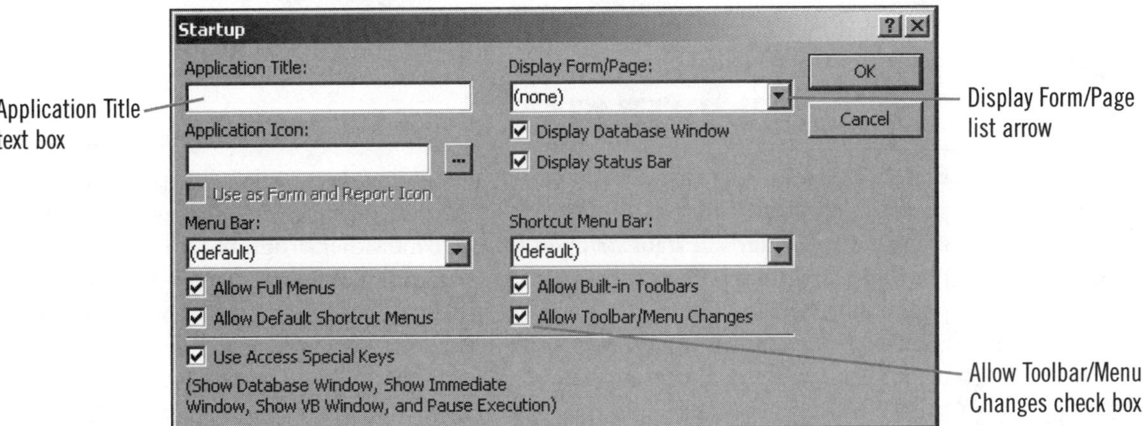

FIGURE P-6: **Employees form automatically opens**

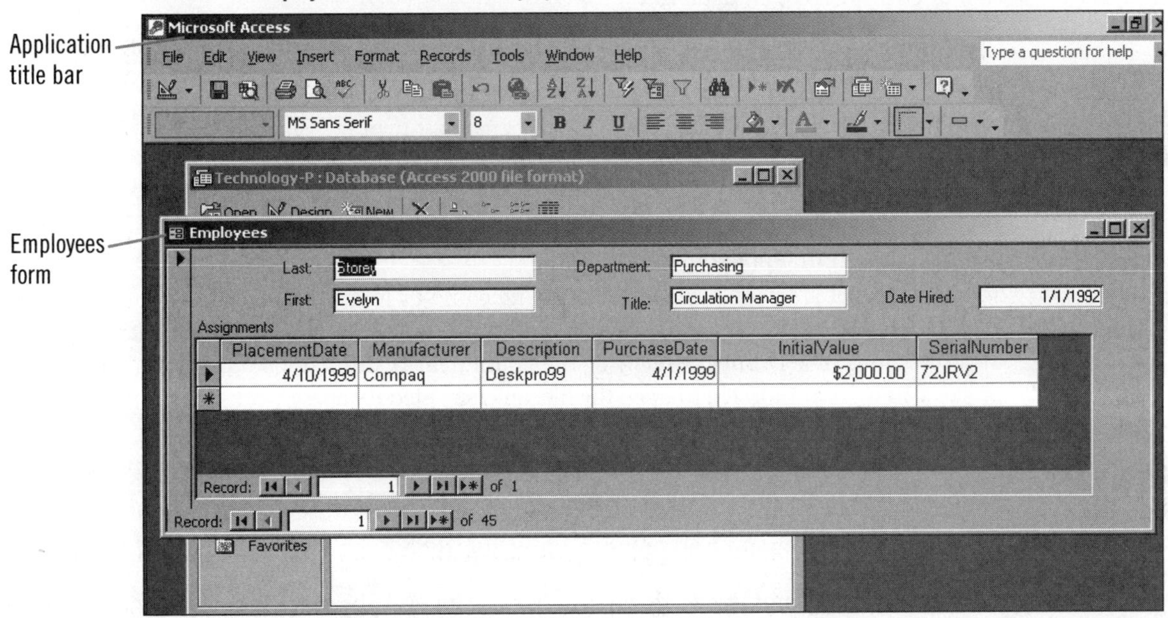

TABLE P-2: **Startup command-line options**

option	effect
/excl	Opens the database for exclusive access
/ro	Opens the database for read-only access
/pwd *password*	Opens the database using the specified *password*
/repair	Repairs the database (In Access 2000 and 2002, compacting the database also repairs it. If you choose the Compact on Close command, you don't need the /repair option.)
/convert *target database*	Converts a previous version of a database to an Access 2000 database with the *target database* name
/x *macro*	Starts Access and runs specified *macro*
/nostartup	Starts Access without displaying the task pane
/wrkgrp *workgroup information file*	Starts Access using the specified *workgroup information file*

Access 2002

Encrypting a Database

Encrypting means to make the Database objects and data itself indecipherable to other programs. **Decrypting** reverses encryption. If you are concerned that your Access database file might be stolen and the data stripped from it by another program (such as another database program, a word processor, or a utility program), encryption may be warranted. Other potential threats to your database are described in Table P-3. MediaLoft has recently connected their corporate file servers to the Internet, so Kristen is more concerned than ever before about keeping corporate data secure. She explores the encryption and decryption features of Access.

QuickTip

It's always a good idea to back up a database before encrypting it.

1. **Click File on the menu bar, then click Close**
   The Technology-P Database window closes, but the Access application is still running. You cannot encrypt an open database.
2. **Click Tools on the menu bar, point to Security, click Encrypt/Decrypt Database, then navigate to the drive and folder where your Project Files are located**
   The Encrypt/Decrypt Database dialog box opens, as shown in Figure P-7.
3. **Double-click Technology-P to choose it as the database to encrypt, double-click Technology-P again to choose it as the name for the encrypted database, then click Yes when prompted to replace the existing file**
   You can encrypt a database file to the same filename or to a new filename. In either case, a back-up copy of the database on a separate disk protects your file should the encryption be unsuccessful (unlikely but possible) or the equipment malfunctions during the encryption process. To users authorized to open the file, an encrypted database works in exactly the same way as the original file; it is not restricted until you create workgroup security accounts. Whether or not you are using workgroup accounts, though, encryption still helps protect data when it is sent over network connections. You decrypt a database using the same steps.
4. **Click Tools on the menu bar, point to Security, then click Encrypt/Decrypt Database**
5. **Double-click Technology-P to choose it as the database to decrypt, double-click Technology-P again as the name for the decrypted database, then click Yes when prompted to replace the existing file**
   The status bar presents information about the progress of the encryption or decryption process.

Creating an MDE File

An Access MDE file is a special copy of the database that prevents others from opening or editing form, report, or module objects in Design View. You can still enter data and use the MDE file just like the original database, but an MDE file gives you a way to distribute the database without revealing the development work you put into the forms, reports, and modules. An MDE file is also much smaller and runs faster than a regular database MDB file. To create an MDE file, close all open databases, but leave Access running. Click Tools on the menu bar, point to Database Utilities, and then click the Make MDE File option. Then enter the names of the original database and the MDE file.

Also, if you are using an Access 2000 version database, you must first convert the database to an Access 2002 version database before you can convert it to an MDE file. To convert an Access 2000 version database to an Access 2002 version, click Tools on the menu bar, point to Database Utilities, point to Convert Database, and then click To Access 2002 File Format. You will be prompted for both the original database (if it is not currently open), as well as the name for the Access 2002 version database.

FIGURE P-7: Encrypt/Decrypt Database dialog box

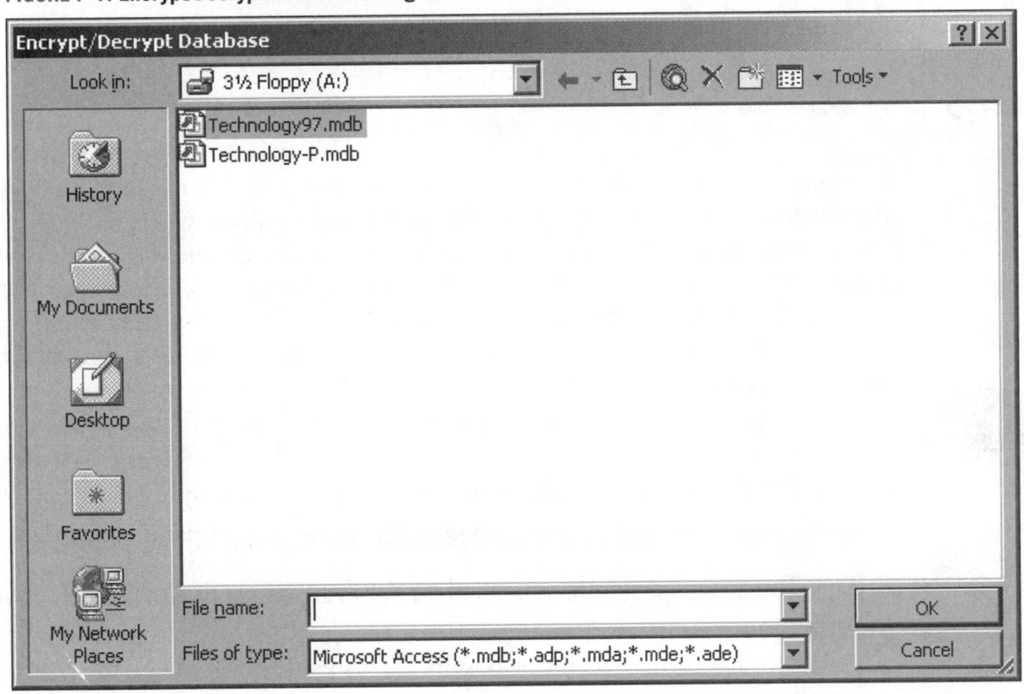

Access 2002

TABLE P-3: Database threats

incident	what can happen	appropriate actions
Virus	Viruses can cause a vast number of damaging actions, ranging from profane messages to destruction of files.	Purchase the leading virus-checking software for each machine, and keep it updated.
Power outage	Power problems such as **brown-outs** (dips in power often causing lights to dim) and **spikes** (surges in power) can cause damage to the hardware, which may render the computer useless.	Purchase a **UPS** (Uninterruptible Power Supply) to maintain constant power to the file server (if networked). Purchase a **surge protector** (power strip with surge protection) for each end user.
Theft or intentional damage	Computer thieves or other scoundrels steal or vandalize computer equipment.	Place the file server in a room that can be locked after hours. Use network drives for end user data files, and back them up on a daily basis. Use off-site storage for backups. Set database passwords and encryption so that files that are stolen cannot be used. Use computer locks for equipment that is at risk, especially laptops.

Access 2002

Analyzing Performance

Access provides a tool called the **Performance Analyzer** that studies the structure and size of your database and makes a variety of recommendations on how you could improve its performance. With adequate time and Access skills, you can alleviate many performance bottlenecks by using software tools and additional programming techniques to improve database performance. With extra money, however, you can often purchase faster processors and more memory to accomplish the same thing. See Table P-4 for tips on optimizing the performance of your computer. Kristen uses the Performance Analyzer to see whether Access provides any recommendations on how to easily maintain peak performance of the Technology-P database.

Steps

1. Open the **Technology-P database** from the drive and folder where your Project Files are located, then close the **Employees form** that automatically opens
2. Click **Tools** on the menu bar, point to **Analyze**, click **Performance**, then click the **Forms tab**

   The Performance Analyzer dialog box opens, as shown in Figure P-8. You can choose to analyze selected tables, forms, other objects, or the entire database.
3. Click the **All Object Types tab**, click **Select All**, then click **OK**

   The Performance Analyzer examines each object and presents the results in a dialog box, as shown in Figure P-9. The key shows that the analyzer gives four levels of advice regarding performance: recommendations, suggestions, ideas, and items that were fixed.
4. Click **Table 'Assignments': Change data type of field 'SSN' from 'Text' to 'Long Integer'** in the Analysis Results list

   The icon tells you that this is an idea. The Analysis Notes section of the Performance Analyzer dialog box gives you additional information regarding that specific item. In this case, the idea is to change the data type of the field SSN from Text to Number (with a Long Integer field size). While this might not be an appropriate action for an SSN field, the three fields in the PCSpecs table—Memory, HardDisk, and MHz—all represent numeric values that could be changed from Text to Number with the suggested field size. All of the Performance Analyzer's ideas should be considered, but they are not as important as recommendations and suggestions.
5. Click **Close** to close the Performance Analyzer dialog box

FIGURE P-8: Performance Analyzer dialog box

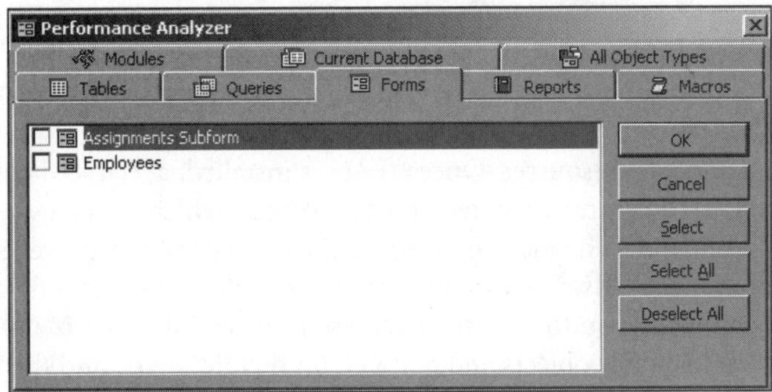

FIGURE P-9: Performance Analyzer results

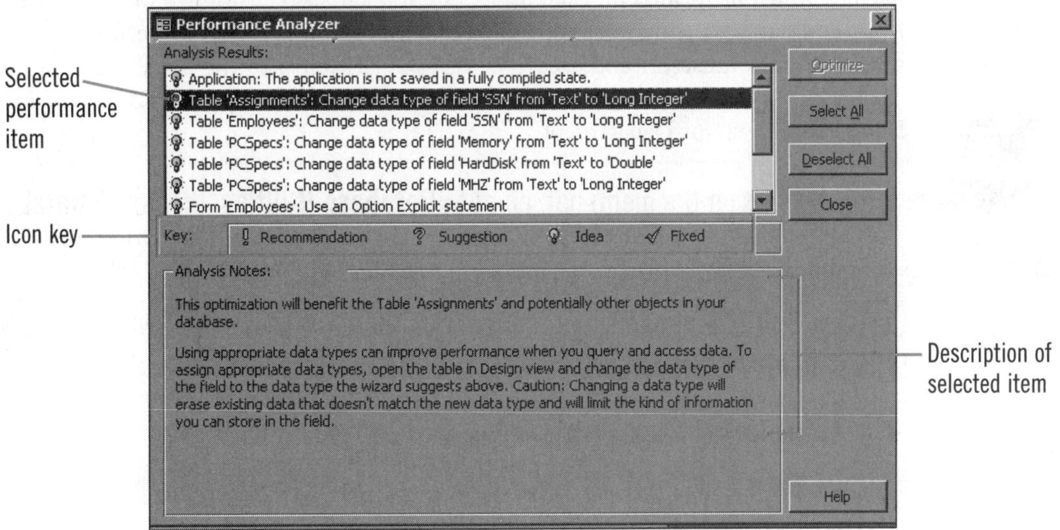

Access 2002

TABLE P-4: Tips for optimizing performance

degree of difficulty	tip
Easy	To free up memory and other computer resources, close all applications that you don't currently need
Easy	If they can be run safely on an "as-needed" basis, eliminate memory-resident programs such as complex screen savers, e-mail alert programs, and virus checkers
Easy	If you are the only person using a database, open it in exclusive mode
Easy	Use the Compact on Close feature to regularly compact and repair your database
Easy	Convert the database to an Access 2002 database
Moderate	Add more memory to your computer; once the database is open, memory is the single most important determinant of overall performance
Moderate	If others don't need to share the database, load it on your local hard drive instead of the network's file server (but be sure to back up local drives regularly, too)
Moderate	**Split** the database so that the data is stored on the file server, but other database objects are stored on your local, faster hard drive
Moderate to difficult	If using disk compression software, stop doing so or move the database to an uncompressed drive
Moderate to difficult	Run Performance Analyzer on a regular basis, examining and appropriately acting on each recommendation, suggestion, and idea
Moderate to difficult	Make sure that all PCs are running the latest versions of Windows and Access; this may involve purchasing more software or upgrading hardware to properly support these robust software products

Splitting a Database

A successful database grows and creates the need for higher levels of database connectivity. **Local area networks (LANs)** are installed to link multiple PCs together so they can share hardware and software resources. Once a LAN is installed, a shared database will often be moved to a **file server**, a centrally located computer from which every user can access the database by using the network. The more users share the same database, however, the slower it will respond. The **Database Splitter** feature improves the performance of a database shared among several users by allowing you to split the database into two files: the **back-end database**, which contains the actual table objects and is stored on the file server, and the **front-end database**, which contains the other database objects (forms, reports, so forth), and links to the back-end database tables. You copy the front-end database for as many users as needed because the front-end database must be located on each user's PC. You can also customize the objects and links each front-end database contains. Front-end databases not only improve performance, but also add a level of customization and security. Kristen uses the Database Splitter to split the Technology-P database into two databases in preparation for the new LAN being installed in the Information Systems Department.

QuickTip

It's always a good idea to back up a database before splitting it.

1. **Click Tools on the menu bar, point to Database Utilities, then click Database Splitter**
   The Database Splitter dialog box opens, and provides additional information on the process and benefits of splitting a database, as shown in Figure P-10.
2. **Click Split Database, then navigate to the drive and folder where your Project Files are located**
   The Create Back-end Database dialog box suggests the name Technology-P_be.mdb ("be" stands for "back-end") for your back-end database.
3. **Click Split**
   The status bar provides information about the split process.
4. **Click OK when prompted that the split was successful**
   The Technology-P database has become the front-end database, with all database objects intact except for the table objects. Technology-P no longer contains any table objects, but rather, contains links to the Technology-P_be database that stores the actual data, as shown in Figure P-11.
5. **Click Forms on the Objects bar, then double-click the Employees form**
   Even though the data is physically stored in the Technology-P_be.mdb database, the other objects in the Technology-P database can access this data through the linked tables.
6. **Close the Employees form, click Tables on the Objects bar, right-click Equipment, click Design View, then click Yes when warned that some properties cannot be modified**
7. **Press [F6] to move the focus to the Field Size property for the SerialNo field, then press [↓] to move through the properties while viewing the right side of the Field Properties pane**
   Most field properties cannot be modified in a linked table, including those that affect the actual size or structure of the data being stored. Properties that do not affect the physical data, but only how it appears to the user, such as Format and Input Mask, may be modified in a linked table.
8. **Close the Equipment table, close the Technology-P database, then exit Access**

FIGURE P-10: Database Splitter dialog box

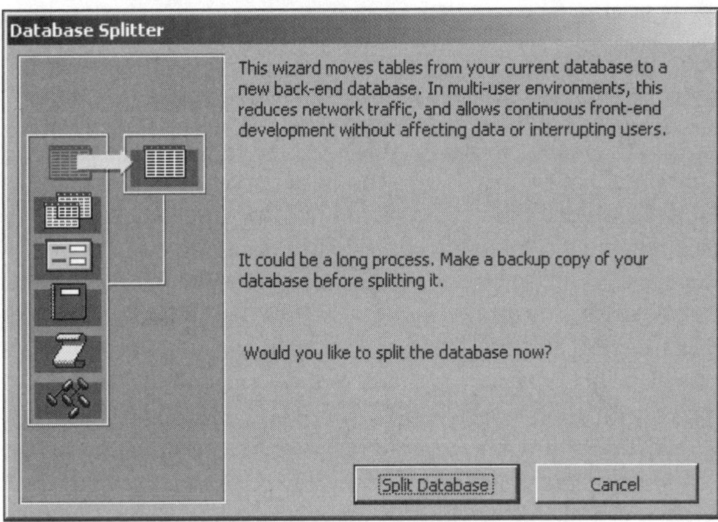

FIGURE P-11: Tables are linked in the front-end database

Access 2002

Client/Server computing

Splitting a database into a front-end and back-end database that work together is an excellent example of client/server computing. **Client/Server computing** can be defined as two or more information systems cooperatively processing to solve a problem. In most implementations, the **client** is defined as the user's PC and the server is defined as the shared file server, mini-, or mainframe computer. The **server** usually handles corporate-wide computing activities such as data storage and management, security, and connectivity to other networks. Within Access, client computers generally handle those tasks specific to each user, such as storing all of the objects (other than table objects) used by that particular user. Effectively managing a vast client/server network in which many front-end databases link to a single back-end database is a tremendous task, but the performance and security benefits are worth the effort.

Access 2002

Replicating Using the Briefcase

If you want to copy a database to another computer, such as a home PC or a laptop computer that you use when traveling, the Windows Briefcase can help you keep the copied database synchronized with the original database. The **Briefcase** makes a special copy of the original database (called a **replica**) and keeps track of changes made in both the original database (called the **master**) and the replica so that they can be resynchronized at a later date. The master database and all replica database files created from the master are called the **replica set**. The process of making the copy is called **replication**, and the process of reconciling and updating changes between the replica and the master is called **synchronization**. Kristen works with the Briefcase program to learn how to replicate and synchronize a database.

Steps

QuickTip

It's always a good idea to back up a database before replicating it.

1. Right-click the **Start button** on the taskbar, click **Explore** on the shortcut menu, locate your Project Files in the Folder list, right-click **Technology-P_be**, click **Copy** on the shortcut menu, then close Explorer
   You placed the Technology-P_be.mdb file on the Windows Clipboard.
2. Minimize all open windows, right-click the **desktop**, then click **Paste**
   You copied the master database to the desktop because you can't create a replica set with a master and replica both stored on floppy disks. Continue the exercise using the copy of the database on the desktop as the master database, and creating the replica on a new floppy disk.

Trouble?

If the My Briefcase window contains other files, move or delete them.

3. Right-click the **Technology-P_be** file on the desktop, click **Copy**, double-click **My Briefcase**, click **Edit** on the menu bar, click **Paste**, click **Yes** to continue, click **No** when prompted about a backup, then click **OK** to accept the Original copy as the database that will allow design changes
   Your screen should look like Figure P-12.
4. Close the My Briefcase window, remove any disks from **drive A**, insert a blank formatted disk into **drive A**, right-click on the desktop, point to **Send To**, then click **3½ Floppy (A)**
   The floppy disk with the replica database can now be removed and used on another computer. Any changes made to the replica can be synchronized later with the master because you used the Briefcase to create the replica.
5. Double-click the **My Computer icon**, double-click **3½ Floppy (A)**, double-click **My Briefcase**, double-click **Technology-P_be**, click **OK** if prompted about synchronization, then double-click the **Employees table**
   The Replicated Employees table opens. You can enter, delete, or edit data in this table just as you could in the master database.
6. Press **[Tab]**, type **Mike** in the First field for the first record, then close the Employees table
   Your screen should look like Figure P-13. Both the title bar of the database and the table icons indicate that you are working with a replica. The replica contains the record you just added, but the master does not.
7. Click **File** on the menu bar, then click **Exit**

FIGURE P-12: My Briefcase

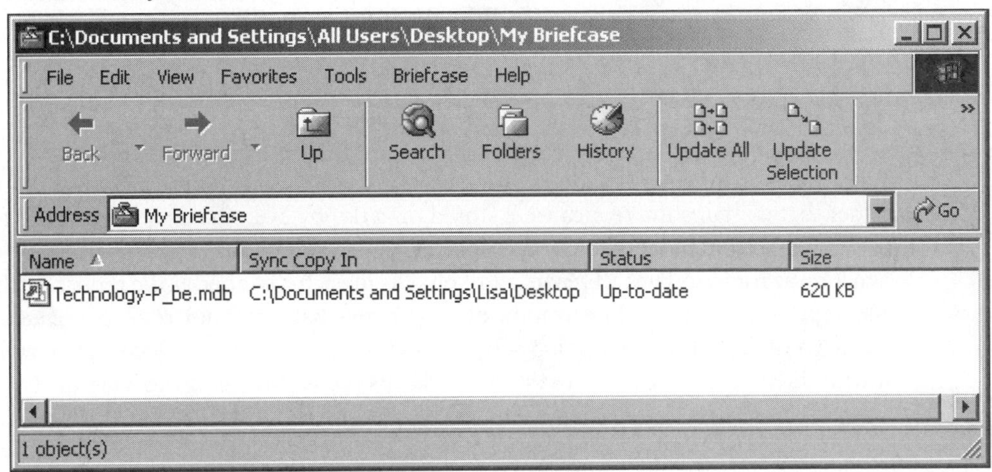

FIGURE P-13: Replica database

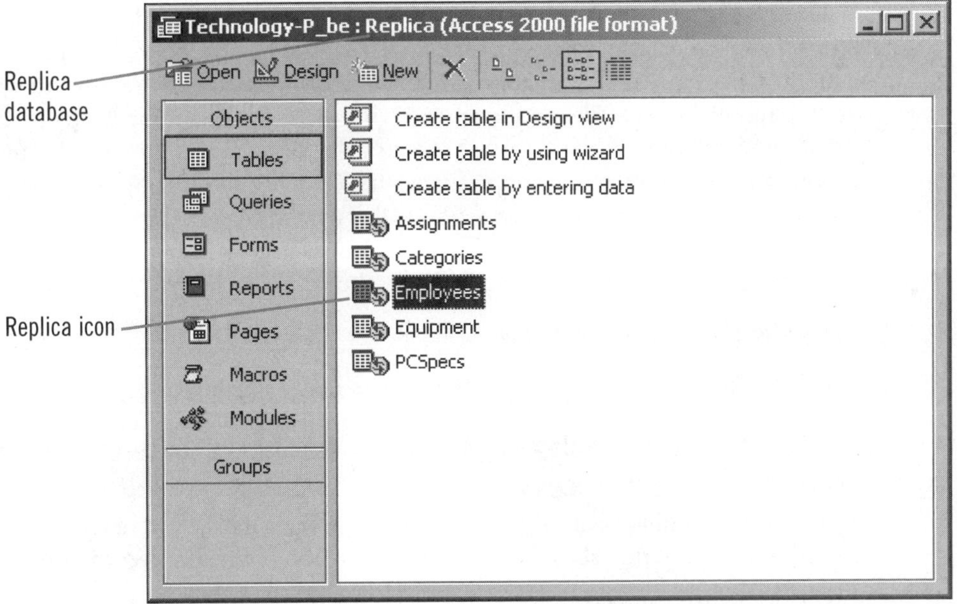

Access 2002

CLUES TO USE

Creating a Briefcase folder

By default, the desktop displays a single Briefcase icon called "My Briefcase." A **Briefcase** is actually a special type of folder designed to help users with two computers to keep the files that are used on both computers updated. If there is no Briefcase folder on the desktop, you can easily create as many new Briefcase folders as you need. You create, delete, copy, move, and rename a Briefcase folder in exactly the same manner as with a regular folder. For example, if you want to create a new Briefcase folder on the desktop, you can right-click the desktop, point to New, then click Briefcase.

Access 2002

Synchronizing Using the Briefcase

The Briefcase controls synchronization of the master and replica databases. If the Briefcase folder that contains the replica were stored on a floppy disk, the disk would have to be inserted into the computer on which the master is stored before synchronization could occur. Synchronization updates all records and objects in each member of the replica set. The Briefcase also reports on any synchronization discrepancies that it cannot resolve. Kristen has created a replica of the Technology-P_be database and has edited a record. She will synchronize it with the master to see how the Briefcase keeps the replica set up-to-date.

Steps

1. Click the **My Briefcase button** on the taskbar (if not already selected), then click the **Update All button** on the My Briefcase Standard Buttons toolbar
   Your screen should look like Figure P-14. The Briefcase program reads both the master and the replica and determines that the replica has been updated but the master has not. Therefore, it recommends the replace action. If the Briefcase contained many files, each one would be listed with a suggested action (replace, skip, merge).
2. Click **Update**
   The Briefcase replaces the master file on your desktop with the replica file on your floppy and displays the My Briefcase window with an "Up-to-date" Status message for the Technology-P_be.mdb file, as shown in Figure P-15. Had you made changes to both the master and the replica, the Briefcase window would have recommended a more complex action: merge. The **merge** action evaluates the changes in each object and applies them to the other. For example, the merge action will resynchronize the two databases if you edit or add records in both the master and replica. You also can add new objects to both. You can make design changes only to existing objects, however, in the master database.
3. Close the My Briefcase window
4. Close the 3½ Floppy (A:) window, then close the My Computer window
5. Double-click the **Technology-P_be Design Master** database on the desktop, then double-click the **Employees** table
   Your screen should look like Figure P-16. Because the databases were synchronized, the first record of the master database contains the edit made to the first record in the replica.
6. Close the Employees table, close the Technology-P_be Design Master database, then exit Access
7. Right-click the **Technology-P_be Design Master** on the desktop, then click **Delete** on the shortcut menu

FIGURE P-14: Update My Briefcase window–Replace action

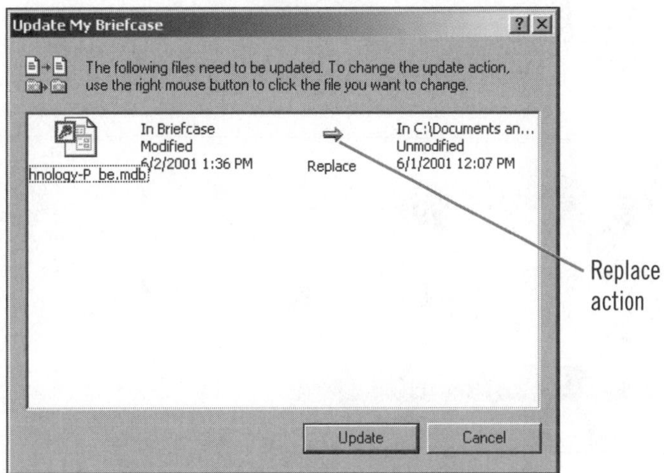

FIGURE P-15: My Briefcase window showing an up-to-date file

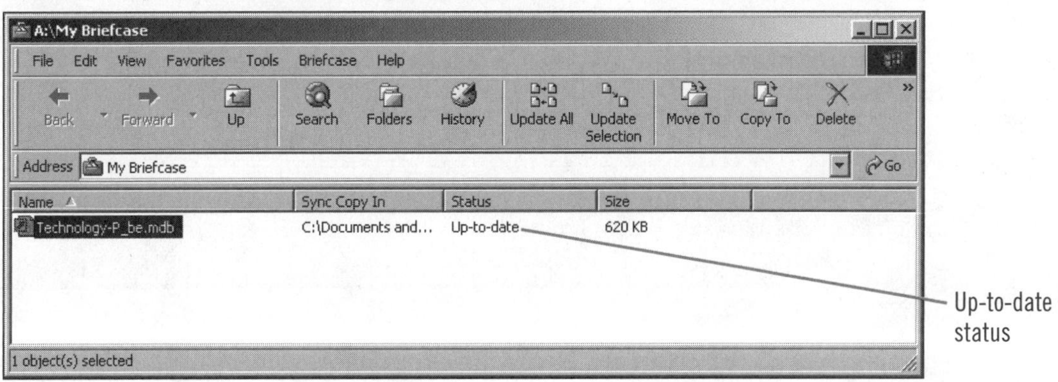

FIGURE P-16: Master database is synchronized

Employees : Table (Replicated)

Last	First	Department	Title	Location	Email
Ray	Mike	Accounting	Assistant	Corporate	mray@medialoft.com
Redwing	Helen	Information Systems	Manager	Corporate	hredwing@medialoft.com
Reed	Elizabeth	Corporate	Vice President	Corporate	ereed@medialoft.com
Colletti	Shayla	CD	Salesperson	New York	scolletti@medialoft.com
Lee	Nancy	Video	Salesperson	San Francisco	nlee@medialoft.com
Shimada	Jeff	Operations	Director of Café Operations	Corporate	jshimada@medialoft.com
Murphy	Eileen	Advertising	Copywriter	Corporate	emurphy@medialoft.com
Alber	Lauren	Accounting	Technology Support Analyst	Corporate	lalber@medialoft.com
Rath	Maria	Book	Salesperson	Boston	mrath@medialoft.com

Edit was made when databases were synchronized

CLUES TO USE

Using the Briefcase with a laptop computer

You might use the Briefcase when a master database is stored on a file server and the replica is stored on the hard drive of a laptop computer. When you are in the office, your laptop computer is connected to the network through a **docking station**, so you would use the master database just like all of the other users. When you are in the field, however, you would work on the replica stored in a Briefcase folder on the laptop's hard drive. When you return to the office, you would use the Briefcase update features to resynchronize the master on the hard drive and replica database on your laptop.

Access 2002

Practice

► Concepts Review

Identify each element of the Startup dialog box in Figure P-17.

FIGURE P-17

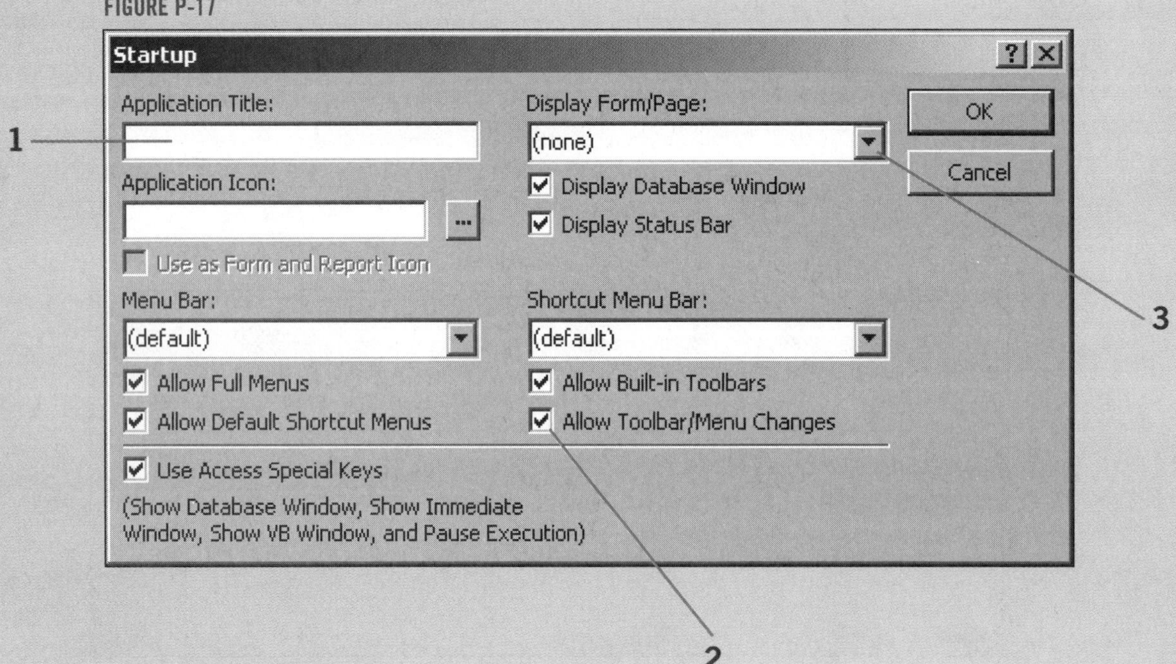

Match each term with the statement that describes its function.

4. **Exclusive Mode**
5. **Database Splitter**
6. **Encrypting**
7. **Performance Analyzer**
8. **Synchronization**

a. Studies the structure and size of your database, and makes a variety of recommendations on how you can improve its speed.

b. Breaks the database into two files to improve performance. One database contains the tables and the other contains the rest of the objects with links to the tables.

c. Updates the files in a replica set so that they all have the same information.

d. Scrambles data so that it is indecipherable when opened by another program.

e. Means that no other users will have access to the database file while it's open.

Select the best answer from the list of choices.

9. Changing a database file into one that can be opened in Access 97 is called:
- a. Splitting.
- b. Analyzing.
- c. Converting.
- d. Encrypting.

10. Which is NOT a type of password that can be set on an Access database?
- a. Database
- b. Security account
- c. Object
- d. Visual Basic for Applications

11. Which of the following determines the users, objects, and permissions to which the users are granted?
- a. Passwords
- b. Workgroups
- c. Permission logs
- d. Briefcase names

12. Which character precedes a command-line option?
- a. !
- b. @
- c. /
- d. ^

13. Which of the following is NOT an advantage of splitting the database using the Database Splitter?
- a. It keeps the data centralized in the back-end database for all users to access.
- b. It gives the users local control over form and report objects.
- c. It helps increase the overall performance of a database used on a LAN.
- d. It creates replica sets that can be used to synchronize files on laptops.

14. Startup command-line options are:
- a. A special series of characters added to the end of the file path that start with a forward slash.
- b. Entered in the Startup dialog box.
- c. Used to automate the synchronization of a replica set.
- d. Special objects that execute first when the database is opened.

15. Client/server computing can be defined as:
- a. Two or more information systems cooperatively processing to solve a problem.
- b. A process to resynchronize a replica set.
- c. A LAN, WAN, or the Internet.
- d. A way to study the structure and size of your database to make a variety of recommendations on how you could improve its performance.

16. If you want to copy a database to another computer, such as a home or laptop computer, which of the following features would keep the databases up-to-date?
- a. Database Splitter
- b. Performance Analyzer
- c. Startup options
- d. Briefcase

17. After you split a database, the original is referred to as the:
- a. Replica set.
- b. Replica.
- c. Synchronization set.
- d. Master.

18. The Briefcase is a special type of:
- a. Folder.
- b. File.
- c. Drive.
- d. Object.

19. Which of the following is NOT a way to improve performance?
- a. Convert the database to an Access 2002 database.
- b. Encrypt the database.
- c. Compact and repair the database.
- d. Open the database in exclusive mode.

20. Which of the following is NOT a startup command-line option?
- a. /ro
- b. /compact
- c. /excl
- d. /nostartup

Skills Review

1. **Convert a database.**
   a. Start Access, then open the **Basketball-P** database from the drive and folder where your Project Files are stored.
   b. Click Tools on the menu bar, point to Database Utilities, point to Convert Database, then click To Access 97 File Format.
   c. Navigate to the drive and folder where your Project Files are stored, enter **Basketball97** as the File Name, click Save in the Convert Database Into dialog box, then click OK when prompted.
   d. Start Windows Explorer, navigate to the drive and folder where your Project Files are stored, then check to make sure that both the Basketball-P and Basketball97 databases are present. You also will see a Basketball-P.ldb file, because Basketball-P.mdb is currently open.
   e. Close Explorer.
2. **Set passwords.**
   a. Close the Basketball-P database, but leave Access open.
   b. Click the Open button on the Database toolbar, navigate to the drive and folder where your Project Files are located, then click **Basketball-P**.
   c. Click the Open list arrow, then click Open Exclusive.
   d. Click Tools on the menu bar, point to Security, then click Set Database Password.
   e. Check to make sure the Caps Lock light is not on, type **big12** in the Password text box, press [Tab], type **big12** in the Verify text box, then click OK. (Remember that passwords are case sensitive.)
   f. Close the Basketball-P database, but leave Access open.
   g. Reopen the **Basketball-P** database in exclusive mode. Type **big12** as the password.
   h. Click Tools on the menu bar, point to Security, click Unset Database Password, type **big12**, then click OK.
   i. On a piece of paper, explain why it was necessary for you to open the database in Exclusive Mode in steps c. and g.
3. **Change startup options.**
   a. Click Tools on the menu bar, then click Startup to open the Startup dialog box.
   b. Type **Iowa State Cyclones** in the Application Title text box, click the Display Form/Page list arrow, click the Player Entry Form, clear the Allow Toolbar/Menu Changes check box, then click OK. Notice the change in the Access title bar.
   c. Close the Basketball-P database, but leave Access open.
   d. Open the **Basketball-P** database.
   e. Close the Player Entry Form that automatically opened when the database was opened.
   f. Right-click the Database toolbar to make sure that you are unable to change or modify any of the toolbars.
   g. On a piece of paper, identify one reason for changing each of the three startup options modified in step b.
   h. Close the Basketball-P database, but leave Access open.
4. **Encrypt a database.**
   a. To encrypt the database, click Tools on the menu bar, point to Security, then click Encrypt/Decrypt Database.
   b. Navigate to the drive and folder where your Project Files are stored, click Basketball-P, then click OK.
   c. In the Encrypt Database As dialog box, click **Basketball-P**, then click Save.
   d. Click Yes when asked to replace the existing Basketball-P file.
   e. To decrypt the database, click Tools on the menu bar, point to Security, then click Encrypt/Decrypt Database.
   f. In the Encrypt/Decrypt Database dialog box, click **Basketball-P**, then click OK.
   g. In the Decrypt Database As dialog box, click **Basketball-P**, click Save, then click Yes.
   h. On a piece of paper, identify two database threats for which encryption could be used to protect the database.

Practice

5. Analyze performance.

- **a.** Open **Basketball-P**, then close the Player Entry Form.
- **b.** Click Tools on the menu bar, point to Analyze, then click Performance.
- **c.** Click the All Object Types tab, click Select All, then click OK.
- **d.** Click each of the Analysis Results, and read the Analysis notes.
- **e.** On a piece of paper, record the analysis results (there should be three entries), and identify whether they are recommendations, suggestions, ideas, or items that were fixed.
- **f.** Close the Performance Analyzer dialog box.

6. Split a database.

- **a.** Click Tools on the menu bar, point to Database Utilities, then click Database Splitter.
- **b.** Click Split Database, make sure that the Save in list shows the drive and folder where your Project Files are stored, then click Split to accept the default name of **Basketball-P_be** as the file name.
- **c.** Click OK when prompted that the database was successfully split.
- **d.** On a sheet of paper, identify two reasons for splitting a database.
- **e.** On the paper, identify the back-end and front-end database filenames, then explain what these databases contain.
- **f.** On the paper, explain what the table icons in the front-end database look like and what they represent.
- **g.** Close the Basketball-P database.

7. Replicate using the Briefcase.

- **a.** Copy the **Team-P** database from the drive and folder where your project files are stored, then paste it to the desktop of your computer.
- **b.** Copy the **Team-P** database from your desktop, then paste it to an empty Briefcase folder. Click Yes when asked to continue, click No when asked to make a back-up copy, then click OK to choose the Original Copy as the one that allows changes to the design of the database. (*Hint*: If you need to create a new Briefcase folder, right-click the desktop, point to New, then click Briefcase.)
- **c.** Double-click the Team-P database in the Briefcase window, double-click the Players table, then modify the record for PlayerNo 21 with your own first and last name.
- **d.** Close the Players table, close the Team-P Replica database, then exit Access. Close the Briefcase window.
- **e.** Open the **Team-P Design Master** database from your desktop, then open the Players table. PlayerNo 21 is not modified.
- **f.** Change PlayerNo 22 to that of a friend's first and last name.
- **g.** Close the Players table, then close the Team-P Design Master database and Access window.

8. Synchronize using the Briefcase.

- **a.** Open the Briefcase on the desktop where the replicated Team-P database is stored, click the Update All button, then click the Update button to merge the databases.
- **b.** Double-click the **Team-P** entry in the Briefcase window to open the replica database, double-click the Players table, then print the Players datasheet. Both PlayerNo 21 and 22 should show the changes you made. Print the datasheet.
- **c.** Close the Players datasheet, close the Team-P Replica, and close the Briefcase window.
- **d.** Open the **Team-P Design Master** database, then open the Players table. Both PlayerNo 21 and 22 should show the changes you made.
- **e.** Close the Players table, then close the Team P-Design Master.
- **f.** Delete any files you created in the desktop.

▶ Independent Challenge 1

As the manager of a doctor's clinic, you have created an Access database called Patients-P to track insurance claims. You want to set a database password on this file, and also encrypt the database.

a. Start Access.
b. Click the Open button on the Standard toolbar, navigate to the drive and folder where your Project Files are stored, click **Patients-P**, click the Open list arrow, then click Open Exclusive.
c. Click Tools, point to Security, then click Set Database Password.
d. Enter **health** in the Password text box as well as the Verify text box, then click OK.
e. Close the Patients-P database, but leave Access running.
f. To encrypt the database, click Tools, point to Security, then click Encrypt/Decrypt Database.
g. In the Encrypt/Decrypt Database dialog box, click Patients-P, then click OK.
h. Enter **health** as the password, then click OK.
i. In the Encrypt Database As dialog box, click Patients-P, click Save, click Yes to replace the existing file, enter **health** when prompted, then click OK.
j. Exit Access.

▶ Independent Challenge 2

As the manager of a doctor's clinic, you have created an Access database called Patients-P to track insurance claims. You want to change the startup options.

a. Start Access, then open the database **Patients-P** from the drive and folder where your Project Files are located.
b. If prompted for a password (if you completed Independent Challenge 1, the file will be password protected), enter **health**, then click OK.
c. To set startup options, click Tools on the menu, then click Startup.
d. In the Startup dialog box, enter **Drs. Aaron and Kelsey** in the Application Title text box, choose the Claim Entry Form as the choice for the Display Form/Page option, clear the Allow Toolbar/Menu Changes check box, then click OK.
e. Close the Patients-P database.
f. Open the **Patients-P** database to test the Startup options. Enter **health** as the password if prompted, then click OK.
g. Close the Claim Entry Form, then right-click the toolbar to make sure that toolbars cannot be modified. Check to make sure that Drs. Aaron and Kelsey appears in the title bar of the Access window.
h. Close the Patients-P database, then exit Access.

▶ Independent Challenge 3

As the manager of a doctor's clinic, you have created an Access database called Patients-P to track insurance claims. You want to use the Briefcase to synchronize a replica set.

a. Open Windows Explorer, locate the **Patients-P** database from the drive and folder where your Project Files are located then copy the database to the desktop. Close Explorer.
b. Start Access, then open the **Patients-P** database stored on your desktop using the Open Exclusive option. If a password is set on the Patients-P database, you must remove it before you can use the database to create a replica set. If you were not prompted for a password, close the database, close Access, and skip the next step.
c. Enter **health** as the password, close the Claim Entry Form if it automatically opened, click Tools, point to Security, click Unset Database Password, enter **health**, click OK, then close the Patients-P database and close Access.
d. Copy the **Patients-P** database on your desktop, then paste it into an empty Briefcase. (*Hint*: If you need to create a new Briefcase folder, right-click the desktop, point to New, then click Briefcase.)

e. Click Yes to continue, click No when asked about making a back-up copy, then click OK to choose the Original Copy as the one that allows changes to the design of the database.
f. Double-click the **Patients-P** database in the Briefcase window, close the Claims Entry Form if it is opened, double-click the Doctors table, then enter your own information as a new record in the PodFirstName (your first name initial), PodLastName (your last name), and PodCode (your first and last name initials, which must be unique from the other records because it is the key field) fields.
g. Close the Doctors datasheet, then close the Patients-P Replica database.
h. Open the **Patients-P Design Master** stored on the desktop.
i. Close the Claim Entry Form if it is opened, then double-click the Doctors table to open its datasheet.
j. Add a friend's name as a new record in the table, making sure that you enter unique initials in the PodCode field.
k. Close the Doctors datasheet, then close the Patients-P Design Master.
l. Open the Briefcase folder that contains the Patients-P replica, click the Update All button, then click Update to merge the changes in the Replica and Design Master.
m. Double-click either the **Patients-P Replica** or **Patients-P Design Master** file to open it, close the Claim Entry Form if it opens, double-click the Doctors table, then print the datasheet. You should see both your name and your friend's name entered as records in the datasheet.
n. Close the Doctors datasheet, close the Patients-P database, then close Access.
o. Delete any files you created on the desktop.

Independent Challenge 4

Microsoft provides extra information, templates, files, and ideas at a Web site called Tools on the Web. In this exercise, you'll explore the Tools on the Web services.

a. Start Access, but do not open any databases.
b. Click Tools on the menu bar, then click Tools on the Web.
c. If prompted to identify the area of the world where you live, click the appropriate area.
d. Print the Tools on the Web home page.
e. Explore the site at your own pace. You may want to print some articles, but be careful as some articles are quite long.
f. Go back to the Tools on the Web home page, then click the Office Worldwide link.
g. Click the Canada (French) link. Notice that your browser is capable of displaying the characters in French words. Print the first page of the Canada (French) Web page, then click the Back button on your browser toolbar.
h. Click the China link. You may be prompted to install a language pack in order to display the Chinese language characters. Unless you are working on your own computer and have access to the Office XP CD, click Cancel. If you did not install the Chinese language pack, notice what characters your browser uses to represent the Chinese language.
i. Print the first page of the Chinese Web page (in whatever form it is in), then click the Back button on your browser toolbar.
j. Explore as many country sites as you like. Explore the More International Downloads link below the list of countries on the Welcome to Office Worldwide Web page.
k. Write a one-page, double-spaced paper describing some of the things you learned.

Visual Workshop

As the manager of a doctor's clinic, you have created an Access database called **Patients-P** to track insurance claims. Use the Performance Analyzer to generate the results shown in Figure P-18 by analyzing all object types.

FIGURE P-18

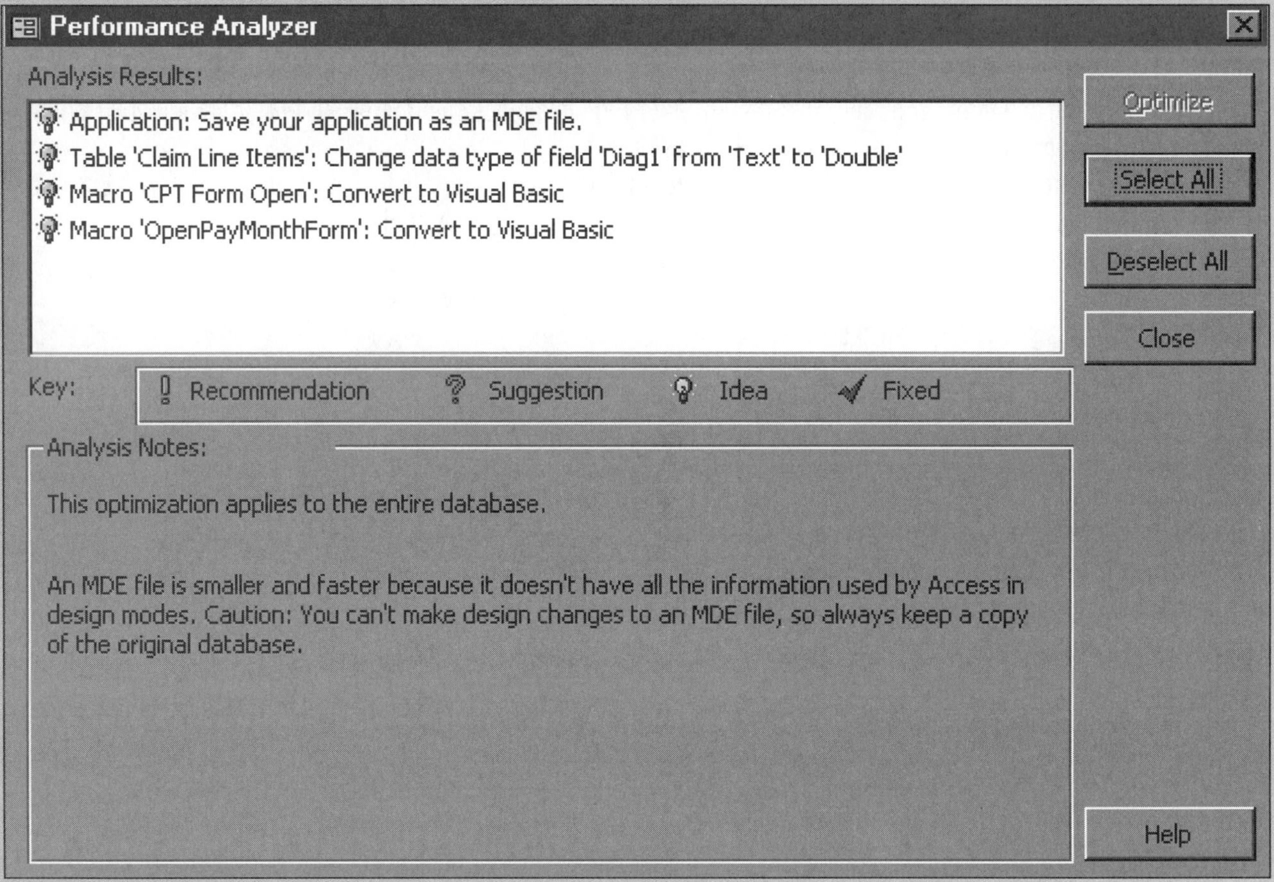

Performance Analyzer

Analysis Results:

Application: Save your application as an MDE file.
Table 'Claim Line Items': Change data type of field 'Diag1' from 'Text' to 'Double'
Macro 'CPT Form Open': Convert to Visual Basic
Macro 'OpenPayMonthForm': Convert to Visual Basic

Optimize | Select All | Deselect All | Close

Key: Recommendation | Suggestion | Idea | Fixed

Analysis Notes:

This optimization applies to the entire database.

An MDE file is smaller and faster because it doesn't have all the information used by Access in design modes. Caution: You can't make design changes to an MDE file, so always keep a copy of the original database.

Help

Formatting a Disk

A **disk** is a device on which you can store electronic data. Disks come in a variety of sizes and have varying storage capacities. Your computer's **hard disk**, one of its internal devices, can store large amounts of data. **Floppy disks**, on the other hand, are smaller, inexpensive, and portable. Most floppy disks that you buy today are 3½" (the diameter of the inside, circular part of the disk). Disks are sometimes called **drives**, but this term really refers to the name by which the operating system recognizes the disk (or a portion of the disk). The operating system typically assigns a drive letter to a drive (which you can reassign if you want). For example, on most computers the hard disk is identified by the drive letter "C" and the floppy drive by the drive letter "A." The amount of information a disk can hold is called its **capacity**, usually measured in megabytes (Mb). The most common floppy disk capacity is 1.44 Mb. Newer computers come with other disk drives, such as a **Zip drive**, a kind of disk drive made to handle **Zip disks**. These disks are portable like floppy disks, but they can contain 100 Mb, far more than regular floppy disks. In this appendix, you will prepare a floppy disk for use.

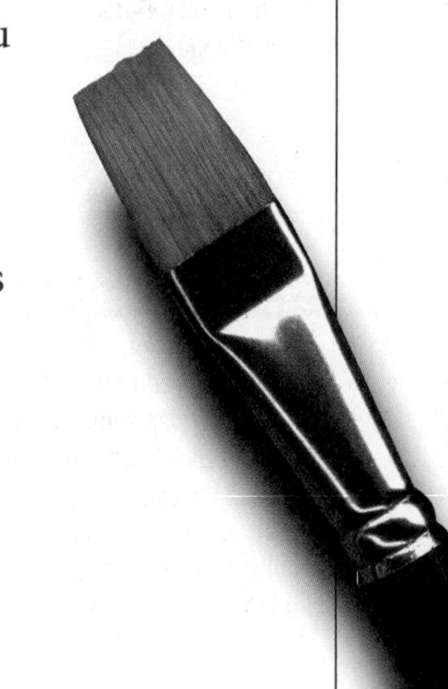

Windows 2000

Formatting a Disk

In order for an operating system to be able to store data on a disk, the disk must be formatted. **Formatting** prepares a disk so it can store information. Usually, floppy disks are formatted when you buy them, but if not, you can perform this function yourself using Windows 2000.

To complete the following steps, you need a blank floppy disk or a disk containing data you no longer need. Do not use your Project Disk for this lesson, as all information on the disk will be erased.

Steps

Trouble?

This unit assumes that the drive that will contain your floppy disks is drive A. If not, substitute the correct drive any time you are instructed to use the 3½ Floppy (A:) drive.

Trouble?

Windows cannot format a disk if it is write-protected; therefore, you may need to slide the write-protect tab over until it clicks to continue. See Figure AP-3 to locate the write-protect tab on your disk.

QuickTip

Once a disk is formatted, you do not need to format it again. However, some people use the Quick Format option to erase the contents of a disk quickly, rather than having to select the files and then delete them.

1. Start Windows if necessary, then place a 3½" floppy disk in drive A
2. Double-click the **My Computer icon** on the desktop
   My Computer opens, as shown in Figure AP-1. This window lists all the drives and printers that you can use on your computer. Because computers have different drives, printers, programs, and other devices installed, your window will probably look different.
3. Right-click the **3½ Floppy (A:) icon**
   When you click with the right mouse button, a pop-up menu of commands that apply to the item you right-clicked appears. Because you right-clicked a drive, the Format command is available.
4. Click **Format** on the pop-up menu
   The Format dialog box opens, as shown in Figure AP-2. In this dialog box, you specify the capacity of the disk you are formatting, the File system, the Allocation unit size, the kind of formatting you want to do, and if you want, a volume label. You are doing a standard format so you will accept the default settings.
5. Click **Start**, then, when you are warned that formatting will erase all data on the disk, click **OK** to continue
   Windows formats your disk. After the formatting is complete, you will probably see a summary about the size of the disk; it's okay if you don't.
6. Click **OK** when the message telling you that the format is complete appears, then click **Close** in the Format dialog box
7. Click the **Close button** in the My Computer window
   My Computer closes and you return to the desktop.

FIGURE AP-1: My Computer window

Drive containing your disk

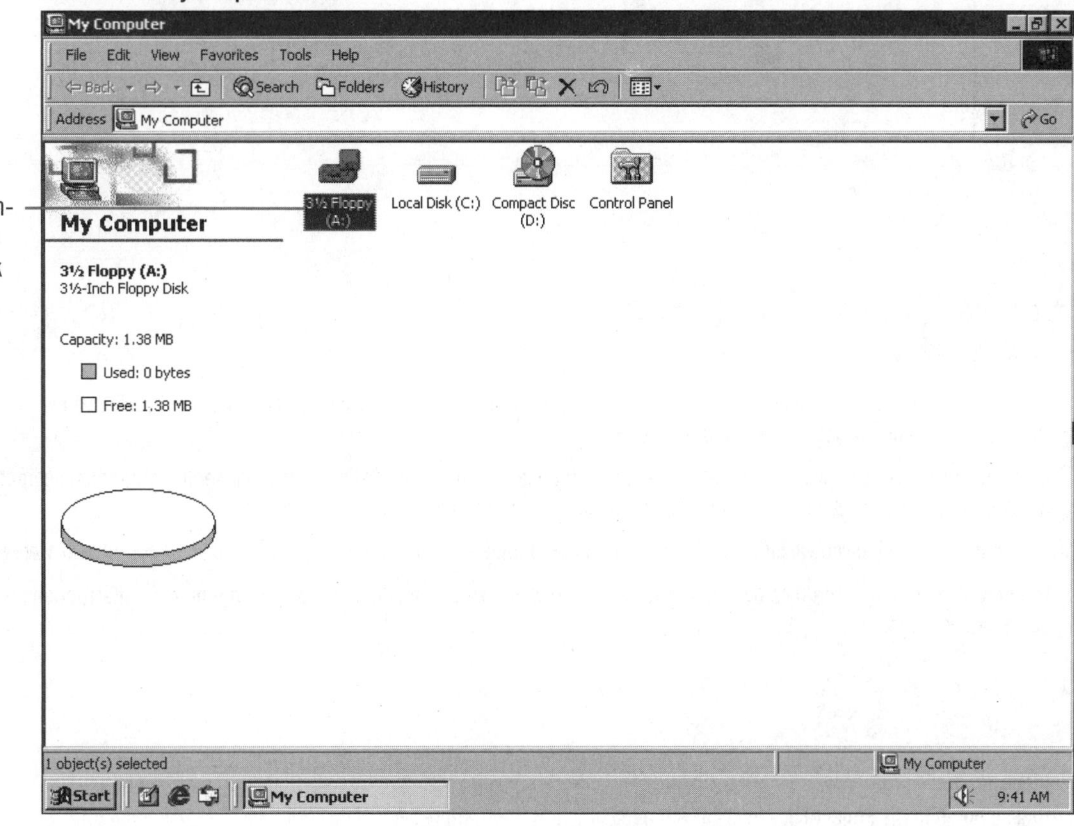

FIGURE AP-2: Format dialog box

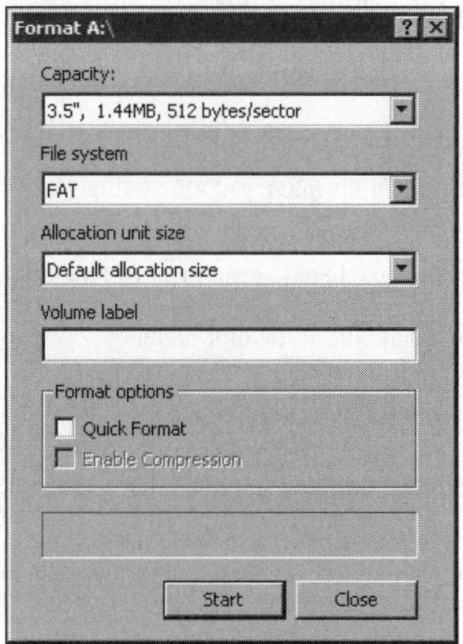

FIGURE AP-3: Write-protect tab

Move write-protect tab down to protect disk, or up to remove protection

3.5" disk

Access 2002

Project Files List

Read the following information carefully!!

Find out from your instructor the location of the Project Files you need and the location where you will store your files.

- To complete many of the units in this book, you need to use Project Files. Your instructor will either provide you with a copy of the Project Files or ask you to make your own copy.
- If you need to make a copy of the Project Files, you will need to copy a set of files from a file server, standalone computer, or the Web to the drive and location where you will be storing your Project Files.
- Your instructor will tell you which computer, drive letter, and folders contain the files you need, and where you will store your files.
- You can also download the files by going to *www.course.com*. See the inside back cover of the book for instructions to download your files.

Copy and organize your Project Files.

Floppy disk users

- If you are using floppy disks to store your Project Files, this list shows which files youíll need to copy onto your disk(s).
- Unless noted in the Project Files list, you will need one formatted, high-density disk for each unit. For each unit you are assigned, copy the files listed in the **Project File Supplied column** onto one disk.
- Make sure you label each disk clearly with the unit name (e.g., Access Unit I).
- When working through the unit, save all your files to this disk.

Users storing files in other locations

- If you are using a zip drive, network folder, hard drive, or other storage device, use the Project Files List to organize your files.
- Create a subfolder for each unit in the location where you are storing your files, and name it according to the unit title (e.g., Access Unit I).
- For each unit you are assigned, copy the files listed in the **Project File Supplied column** into that unitís folder.
- Store the files you modify or create in each unit in the unit folder.

Find and keep track of your Project Files and completed files.

- Use the **Project File Supplied column** to make sure you have the files you need before starting the unit or exercise indicated in the **Unit and Location column**.
- Use the **Student Creates File column** to find out the filename you use when saving your new file for the exercise.

Unit and Location	Project File Supplied	Student Creates File
Note: In Access, the original Project Files are used to complete the exercises. Therefore, it is a good practice to make a backup copy of the supplied Project Files before you use them, in case you need to go back and repeat any of the exercises.		
Windows 2000 Unit A	(No files provided or created)	
Windows 2000 Unit B		
DISK 1		
Lessons	Win_B-1.bmp	
DISK 2		
Skills Review	Win_B-2.bmp	
Access Unit A		
Lessons	MediaLoft-A.mdb	
Skills Review	Recycle-A.mdb	
Independent Challenge 1	(no files created or supplied)	
Independent Challenge 2	Recycle-A.mdb	
Independent Challenge 3	Recycle-A.mdb	
Independent Challenge 4	(no files created or supplied)	
Visual Workshop	Recycle-A.mdb	
Access Unit B*		
Disk 1		
Lessons	MediaLoft-B.mdb	MediaLoft.mdb
Skills Review	Doctors-B.mdb	Doctors.mdb
Independent Challenge 2	Doctors-B.mdb	
Visual Workshop	MediaLoft-B.mdb	
Disk 2		
Independent Challenge 1		Movies.mdb
Independent Challenge 3		People.mdb
Independent Challenge 4	Baltic-B.mdb	
*Because the files created in this unit are large, you will need to organize the files onto two floppy disks if you are using floppies and completing all the exercises. Copy the files as outlined above, and label each disk clearly (e.g., Access Unit B Disk 1).		
Access Unit C		
Lessons	MediaLoft-C.mdb Smallmedia.bmp	
Skills Review	Membership-C.mdb Hand.bmp	
Independent Challenge 1	Clinic-C.mdb	
Independent Challenge 2	Clinic-C.mdb	
Independent Challenge 3	Clinic-C.mdb Medical.bmp	
Independent Challenge 4	Baltic-C.bmp	
Visual Workshop	Clinic-C.mdb Medstaff.bmp	
Access Unit D		
Lessons	MediaLoft-D.mdb	
Skills Review	Club-D.mdb	
Independent Challenge 1	Therapy-D.mdb	

Unit and Location	Project File Supplied	Student Creates File
Independent Challenge 2	Therapy-D.mdb	
Independent Challenge 3		Colleges.mdb
Independent Challenge 4	Baltic-D.mdb	
Visual Workshop	Club-D.mdb	
Access Unit E		
Lessons	Training-E.mdb	
Skills Review		Membership-E.mdb
Independent Challenge 1		Music Store-E.mdb
Independent Challenge 2	(no files provided or created)	
Independent Challenge 3		Donations-E.mdb
Independent Challenge 4	Baltic-E.mdb	
Visual Workshop	Training-E.mdb	
Access Unit F		
Lessons	Training-F.mdb	
Skills Review	Membership-F.mdb	
Independent Challenge 1	Music Store-F.mdb	
Independent Challenge 2	Music Store-F.mdb	
Independent Challenge 3	Music Store-F.mdb	
Independent Challenge 4	Baltic-F.mdb	
Visual Workshop	Training-F.mdb	
Access Unit G		
Lessons	Training-G.mdb	
Skills Review	Membership-G.mdb	
Independent Challenge 1	Music Store-G.mdb	
Independent Challenge 2	Music Store-G.mdb	
Independent Challenge 3	Music Store-G.mdb	
Independent Challenge 4	(no files provided or created)	
Visual Workshop	Training-G.mdb	
Access Unit H*		
Disk 1		
Lessons	Training-H.mdb Deptcodes.xls	Accounting.mdb EmployeeData.xls edata.html einfo.htm
Visual Workshop	Training-H.mdb	
Disk 2		
Skills Review	Membership-H.mdb Prospects.xls	Contacts.mdb zip.htm list-yi.html (yi for your initials)
Disk 3		
Independent Challenge 1	Music Store-H.mdb	
Independent Challenge 2	Music Store-H.mdb	
Independent Challenge 3	Music Store-H.mdb	school.htm
Independent Challenge 4	(no files provided or created)	

*Because the files created in this unit are large, you will need to organize the files onto three floppy disks if you are using floppies and completing all the exercises. Copy the files as outlined above, and label each disk clearly (e.g., Access Unit H Disk 1).

Unit and Location	Project File Supplied	Student Creates File
Note: In Access, you do not save the database files with a different name. It is a good practice to make a backup copy of the files before you use them, in case you need to go back and repeat any of the exercises.		
Access Unit I		
Lessons	Training-I.mdb CourseMaterials.xls study.xml study.xsd	Access Courses Report.rtf Access Courses Report.xls acct.xml acct.xsd
Skills Review	Machinery-I.mdb Vendors.xls employ.xml employ.xsd	Every Product We Lease.rtf Products.xls prod.xml prod.xsd
Independent Challenge 1	Basketball-I.mdb	
Independent Challenge 2	Basketball-I.mdb	Player Statistics.rtf
Independent Challenge 3	Basketball-I.mdb	Games.xls
Independent Challenge 4	Languages-I.mdb	
Visual Workshop	Basketball-I.mdb	
Access Unit J		
Lessons	Training-J.mdb	dept.htm instruct.htm pivot.htm chart.htm
Skills Review	Machinery-J.mdb	garden.htm products.htm units.htm ucharts.htm
Independent Challenge 1	Basketball-J.mdb	pstats.htm
Independent Challenge 2	Basketball-J.mdb	games.htm
Independent Challenge 3	Basketball-J.mdb	gstats.htm
Independent Challenge 4	Languages-J.mdb	trans.htm
Visual Workshop	Basketball-J.mdb	scoring.htm
Access Unit K		
Lessons	Training-K.mdb	
Skills Review	Seminar-K.mdb	
Independent Challenge 1	Basketball-K.mdb	
Independent Challenge 2	Basketball-K.mdb	
Independent Challenge 3	Basketball-K.mdb	
Independent Challenge 4	Chocolate-K.mdb	
Visual Workshop	Basketball-K.mdb	
Access Unit L		
Lessons	Training-L.mdb	
Skills Review	Seminar-L.mdb	
Independent Challenge 1	Basketball-L.mdb	
Independent Challenge 2	Basketball-L.mdb	
Independent Challenge 3	Basketball-L.mdb	
Independent Challenge 4	(no files provided or created)	
Visual Workshop	Basketball-L.mdb	

Unit and Location	Project File Supplied	Student Creates File
Access Unit M		
Lessons	Technology-M.mdb	
Skills Review	Basketball-M.mdb	
Independent Challenge 1	Patients-M.mdb	
Independent Challenge 2	Patients-M.mdb	
Independent Challenge 3	Patients-M.mdb	
Independent Challenge 4	(no files provided or created)	
Visual Workshop	Patients-M.mdb	
Access Unit N		
Lessons	Technology-N.mdb	
Skills Review	Basketball-N.mdb	
Independent Challenge 1	Patients-N.mdb	
Independent Challenge 2	Patients-N.mdb	
Independent Challenge 3	Patients-N.mdb	
Independent Challenge 4	Chocolate-N.mdb	
Visual Workshop	Patients-N.mdb	
Access Unit O		
Lessons	Technology-O.mdb	
Skills Review	Basketball-O.mdb	
Independent Challenge 1	Patients-O.mdb	
Independent Challenge 2	Patients-O.mdb	
Independent Challenge 3	Patients-O.mdb	
Independent Challenge 4	(no files provided or created)	
Visual Workshop	Basketball-O.mdb	
Access Unit P		
Lessons	Technology-P.mdb	Technology-P_be.mdb Technology97.mdb
Skills Review	Basketball-P.mdb Team-P.mdb	Basketball-P_be.mdb Basketball97.mdb
Independent Challenge 1	Patients-P.mdb	
Independent Challenge 2	Patients-P.mdb	
Independent Challenge 3	Patients-P.mdb	
Independent Challenge 4	(no files provided or created)	
Visual Workshop	Patients-P.mdb	

Access 2002 Core MOUS Certification Objectives

Below is a list of the Microsoft Office User Specialist program objectives for Core Access 2002 skills, showing where each MOUS objective is covered in the Lessons and Practice.

MOUS standardized coding number	Activity	Lesson page where skill is covered	Location in lesson where skill is covered	Practice
AC2002-1	**Creating and Using Databases**			
AC2002-1-1	Create Access databases	ACCESS B-4	Steps 1–2	Skills Review Independent Challenges 1, 3
		ACCESS H-2	Steps 1–6	Skills Review
AC2002-1-2	Open database objects in multiple views	ACCESS A-4 ACCESS A-10 ACCESS A-16	Table A-2 Step 1 Step 1	Skills Review Independent Challenges 2, 3 Visual Workshop
		ACCESS B-6 ACCESS B-16	Step 7 Steps 5, 7	(Units B, C, D, F) Skills Review
		ACCESS C-6	Steps 1, 7	Independent Challenges 1, 2, 3
		ACCESS D-6	Steps 1, 7	Visual Workshop
		ACCESS F-4 ACCESS F-16 ACCESS H-12	Step 6 Steps 2, 7 Step 4	Skills Review Independent Challenges 1, 2, 3, 4 Visual Workshop
AC2002-1-3	Move among records	ACCESS A-10 ACCESS A-11	Steps 1–6 Table A-4	Skills Review Independent Challenge 2, 3 Visual Workshop
		ACCESS C-4 ACCESS C-12	Steps 5–6 Steps 5–7	Skills Review Independent Challenges 1, 2, 3, 4
AC2002-1-4	Format datasheets	ACCESS B-8	Steps 3–5	Skills Review Independent Challenges 2, 3
AC2002-2	**Creating and Modifying Tables**			
AC2002-2-1	Create and modify tables	ACCESS B-2 ACCESS B-3 ACCESS B-4 ACCESS B-6 ACCESS B-7	Clues to Use Table B-1 Steps 3–7 Steps 1–6 Clues to Use	Skills Review Independent Challenges 1, 3
		ACCESS E-6	Steps 2–7	Skills Review Independent Challenge 1 Visual Workshop
AC2002-2-2	Add a pre-defined input mask to a field	ACCESS E-8 ACCESS E-12	Step 5 Step 5	Skills Review
AC2002-2-3	Create Lookup fields	ACCESS E-4 ACCESS E-5 ACCESS E-18	Detail 5 Table E-2 Steps 1–8	Skills Review

MOUS standardized coding number	Activity	Lesson page where skill is covered	Location in lesson where skill is covered	Practice
AC2002-2-4	Modify field properties	ACCESS B-6 ACCESS B-7	Steps 2–6 Clues to Use	Skills Review Independent Challenges 1, 4
		ACCESS E-6 ACCESS E-8 ACCESS E-9 ACCESS E-10 ACCESS E-11 ACCESS E-12 ACCESS E-13	Steps 2–7 Steps 1–6 Table E-3 Steps 1–4 Table E-4 Steps 1–5 Steps 1–3	Skills Review Independent Challenges 1, 4 Visual Workshop
AC2002-3	**Creating and Modifying Queries**			
AC2002-3-1	Create and modify Select queries	ACCESS B-16 ACCESS B-18	Steps 1–7 Steps 1–8	Skills Review Independent Challenges 2, 3 Visual Workshop
		ACCESS F-2 ACCESS F-4 ACCESS F-6 ACCESS F-7 ACCESS F-8 ACCESS F-9	Steps 2–6 Steps 1–3 Steps 1–5 Table F-1 Steps 1–4 Clues to Use	Skills Review Independent Challenges 1, 2, 3, 4 Visual Workshop
AC2002-3-2	Add calculated fields to Select queries	ACCESS F-10	Steps 2–6	Skills Review
AC2002-4	**Creating and Modifying Forms**			
AC2002-4-1	Create and display forms	ACCESS C-4 ACCESS C-5 ACCESS C-5	Steps 2–4 Table C-2 Clues to Use	Skills Review Independent Challenges 1, 2, 3, 4 Visual Workshop
		ACCESS G-4 ACCESS G-5	Steps 2–6 Table G-1	
AC2002-4-2	Modify form properties	ACCESS C-2 ACCESS C-6 ACCESS C-7 ACCESS C-8 ACCESS C-9 ACCESS C-10 ACCESS C-12 ACCESS C-13 ACCESS C-16	Table C-1 Steps 1–6 Table C-3 Steps 1–6 Table C-4 Steps 1–7 Steps 2–4 Table C-5 Steps 1–5	Skills Review Independent Challenges 1, 2, 3 Visual Workshop
		ACCESS G-8 ACCESS G-10 ACCESS G-12 ACCESS G-14 ACCESS G-15 ACCESS G-16	Steps 1–7 Steps 1–7 Steps 1–8 Steps 1–7 Table G-3 Steps 1–8	Skills Review Independent Challenges 1, 2, 3, 4 Visual Workshop
AC2002-5	**Viewing and Organizing Information**			
AC2002-5-1	Enter, edit, and delete records	ACCESS A-12 ACCESS A-14 ACCESS A-15	Steps 2–5 Steps 1–9 Table A-5	Skills Review Independent Challenge 3 Visual Workshop
		ACCESS B-16	Step 4	Skills Review Independent Challenges 1, 2, 3, 4 Visual Workshop
		ACCESS C-12 ACCESS C-14 ACCESS C-16	Steps 1, 5–7 Steps 1–5 Step 6	Skills Review Independent Challenges 1, 2, 3, 4 Visual Workshop
AC2002-5-2	Create queries	ACCESS B-16 ACCESS B-18 ACCESS B-19	Steps 1–8 Steps 1–7 Clues to Use	Skills Review Independent Challenges 2, 3 Visual Workshop
		ACCESS F-2 ACCESS F-4 ACCESS F-6	Steps 2–6 Steps 1–3 Steps 1–5	Skills Review Independent Challenges 1, 2, 3, 4 Visual Workshop

MOUS standardized coding number	Activity	Lesson page where skill is covered	Location in lesson where skill is covered	Practice
		ACCESS F-7 ACCESS F-8 ACCESS F-9 ACCESS F-12 ACCESS F-13 ACCESS F-14	Table F-1 Steps 1–4 Clues to Use Steps 1–6 Table F-4 Steps 1–7	
AC2002-5-3	Sort records	ACCESS B-11 ACCESS B-12 ACCESS B-13 ACCESS B-18	Table B-2 Steps 1–3 Clues to Use Step 4	Skills Review Independent Challenges 2, 3 Visual Workshop
		ACCESS C-4	Step 5	Skills Review Independent Challenge 2
		ACCESS F-4	Steps 1–3	Skills Review Independent Challenges 1, 2, 3
AC2002-5-4	Filter records	ACCESS B-11 ACCESS B-14 ACCESS B-17	Table B-2 Steps 1–5 Table B-4	Skills Review Independent Challenge 2
		ACCESS C-4 ACCESS C-14	Step 7 Steps 6–8	Skills Review Independent Challenge 3
AC2002-6	**Defining Relationships**			
AC2002-6-1	Create one-to-many relationships	ACCESS E-2 ACCESS E-4 ACCESS E-16	Details 1–3 Details 1–4 Steps 1–5	Skills Review Independent Challenge 1
AC2002-6-2	Enforce referential integrity	ACCESS E-16 ACCESS E-17	Steps 3–4 Clues to Use	Skills Review Independent Challenge 1
AC2002-7	**Producing Reports**			
AC2002-7-1	Create and format reports	ACCESS D-3 ACCESS D-4 ACCESS D-14 ACCESS D-15 ACCESS D-16	Table D-1 Steps 2–6 Steps 1–6 Table D-3 Steps 1–7	Skills Review Independent Challenges 1, 2, 3, 4 Visual Workshop
		ACCESS H-6 ACCESS H-8 ACCESS H-10	Steps 1–8 Steps 1–7 Steps 1–8	Skills Review Independent Challenges 1, 2 Visual Workshop
AC2002-7-2	Add calculated controls to reports	ACCESS D-6 ACCESS D-10	Steps 4–6 Steps 1–3	Skills Review Independent Challenge 2 Visual Workshop
AC2002-7-3	Preview and print reports	ACCESS D-8 ACCESS D-14	Steps 3–5 Steps 6–7	Skills Review Independent Challenges 1, 2, 3, 4 Visual Workshop
AC2002-8	**Integrating with Other Applications**			
AC2002-8-1	Import data to Access	ACCESS H-4 ACCESS H-5	Steps 1–6 Table H-1	Skills Review
		ACCESS I-6	Steps 1–3	Skills Review
AC2002-8-2	Export data from Access	ACCESS H-14 ACCESS H-15	Steps 1, 5 Table H-2	Skills Review
		ACCESS I-10 ACCESS I-11 ACCESS I-12 ACCESS I-14 ACCESS I-16	Step 1 Table I-3 Step 1 Steps 1–6 Steps 1–3	Skills Review Independent Challenges 2, 3 Visual Workshop
AC2002-8-3	Create a simple data access page	ACCESS H-12	Steps 1–6	Skills Review Independent Challenge 3
		ACCESS J-6 ACCESS J-8	Steps 1–6 Steps 1–4	Skills Review Independent Challenges 1, 2, 4

Access 2002 Expert MOUS Certification Objectives

Below is a list of the Microsoft Office User Specialist program objectives for the Expert Access 2002 skills, showing where each MOUS objective is covered in the Lessons and Practice.

MOUS standardized coding number	Activity	Lesson page where skill is covered	Location in lesson where skill is covered	Practice
AC2002e-1	**Creating And Modifying Tables**			
AC2002e-1-1	Use data validation	ACCESS E-14 ACCESS E-15	Steps 1–2 Table E-5	Skills Review Independent Challenge 1
AC2002e-1-2	Link tables	ACCESS I-8	Steps 1–3	Skills Review
AC2002e-1-3	Create lookup fields and modify Lookup field properties	ACCESS E-4 ACCESS E-5 ACCESS E-18	Details Table E-2 Steps 1–7	Skills Review Independent Challenge 4 Skills Review
AC2002e-1-4	Create and modify input masks	ACCESS E-9 ACCESS E-12	Table E-3 Step 5	Skills Review
AC2002e-2	**Creating And Modifying Forms**			
AC2002e-2-1	Create a form in Design View	ACCESS L-2 ACCESS L-4 ACCESS L-8	Steps 1–8 Steps 1–4 Steps 1–5	Skills Review
		ACCESS M-10 ACCESS M-12	Steps 1–7 Steps 3–6	Skills Review Skills Review Independent Challenge 3
AC2002e-2-2	Create a Switchboard and set startup options	ACCESS M-14 ACCESS M-16	Steps 1–8 Steps 1–5	Skills Review Visual Workshop Skills Review Visual Workshop
		ACCESS P-6	Steps 1–5	Skills Review Independent Challenge 2
AC2002e-2-3	Add Subform controls to Access forms	ACCESS G-4 ACCESS G-6 ACCESS G-7	Steps 1–6 Steps 1–8 Clues to Use	Skills Review Independent Challenges 1, 2, 3 Visual Workshop
AC2002e-3	**Refining Queries**			
AC2002e-3-1	Specify multiple query criteria	ACCESS B-18 ACCESS B-19	Step 7 Clues to Use	Skills Review
		ACCESS F-6 ACCESS F-8	Steps 1–4 Steps 1–4	Skills Review Independent Challenge 2
AC2002e-3-2	Create and apply advanced filters	ACCESS B-14	Steps 1–5	Skills Review
AC2002e-3-3	Create and run parameter queries	ACCESS K-4	Steps 3–6	Skills Review Independent Challenge 1 Visual Workshop
AC2002e-3-4	Create and run action queries	ACCESS K-8 ACCESS K-9 ACCESS K-10 ACCESS K-12 ACCESS K-14	Steps 1–6 Table K-2 Steps 1–6 Steps 1–6 Steps 1–5	Skills Review Independent Challenge 2
AC2002e-3-5	Use aggregate functions in queries	ACCESS F-12 ACCESS F-13	Steps 1–5 Table F-4	Skills Review Independent Challenges 1, 3
AC2002e-4	**Producing Reports**			
AC2002e-4-1	Create and modify reports	ACCESS D-3	Table D-1	Skills Review

MOUS standardized coding number	Activity	Lesson page where skill is covered	Location in lesson where skill is covered	Practice
		ACCESS D-6 ACCESS D-8 ACCESS D-10 ACCESS D-12 ACCESS D-14	Steps 1–6 Steps 1–3 Steps 1–3 Steps 1–6 Steps 1–6	Independent Challenges 1, 2, 4 Visual Workshop
		ACCESS L-16	Steps 1–6	Skills Review
AC2002e-4-2	Add Subreport controls to Access reports	ACCESS L-14	Steps 1–4	Skills Review Independent Challenge 2
AC2002e-4-3	Sort and group data in reports	ACCESS D-6 ACCESS D-8	Steps 1–3 Steps 1–3	Skills Review Independent Challenges 2, 3 Visual Workshop
AC2002e-5	**Defining Relationships**			
AC2002e-5-1	Establish one-to-many relationships	ACCESS E-2	Table E-1	Skills Review Independent Challenge 1
		ACCESS I-4 ACCESS I-5	Steps 4–8 Table I-2	Skills Review Independent Challenges 1, 4
AC2002e-5-2	Establish many-to-many relationships	ACCESS E-3	Clues	Skills Review
		ACCESS I-4 ACCESS I-5	Steps 6–7 Table I-2	Skills Review Independent Challenges 1, 4
		ACCESS K-15	Clues	
AC2002e-6	**Operating Access on the Web**			
AC2002e-6-1	Create and Modify a Data Access Page	ACCESS J-10 ACCESS J-11 ACCESS J-12	Steps 1–4 Table J-4 Steps 1–7	Skills Review Independent Challenges 1, 2, 3, 4 Visual Workshop
AC2002e-6-2	Save PivotTables and PivotCharts views to Data Access Pages	ACCESS J-10 ACCESS J-12	Steps 1–6 Steps 1–7	Skills Review Independent Challenge 3 Visual Workshop
AC2002e-7	**Using Access tools**			
AC2002e-7-1	Import XML documents into Access	ACCESS I-6	Steps 1–3	Skills Review
AC2002e-7-2	Export Access data to XML documents	ACCESS I-16	Steps 1–2	Skills Review
AC2002e-7-3	Encrypt and decrypt databases	ACCESS P-8	Steps 1–3	Skills Review Independent Challenge 1
AC2002e-7-4	Compact and repair databases	ACCESS H-16	Steps 1–2	Skills Review
AC2002e-7-5	Assign database security	ACCESS P-4	Steps 1–9	Skills Review Independent Challenge 1
AC2002e-7-6	Replicate a database	ACCESS P-14 ACCESS P-16	Steps 1–5 Steps 1–2	Skills Review Independent Challenge 3
AC2002e-8	**Creating Database Applications**			
AC2002e-8-1	Create Access Modules	ACCESS O-6	Steps 1–7	Skills Review Independent Challenge 1 Visual Workshop
		ACCESS O-8 ACCESS O-10 ACCESS O-12 ACCESS O-14	Steps 1–9 Steps 1–8 Steps 1–6 Steps 1–6	
AC2002e-8-2	Use the Database Splitter	ACCESS P-12	Steps 1–8	Skills Review
AC2002e-8-3	Create an MDE file	ACCESS P-8	Clues to Use	

Glossary

Accessories Built-in programs that come with Windows 2000.

Active Desktop The screen that appears when you first start Windows 2000, providing access to your computer's programs and files and to the Internet. *See also* Desktop.

Active program The program that you are using, differentiated from other open programs by a highlighted program button on the taskbar and a differently colored title bar.

Active window The window that you are currently using, differentiated from other open windows by a differently colored title bar.

Address Bar The area below the toolbar in My Computer and Windows Explorer that you use to open and display a drive, folder, or Web page.

Back up To save files to another location in case you have computer trouble and lose files.

Browser A program, such as Microsoft Internet Explorer, designed to access the Internet.

Bullet mark A solid circle that indicates that an option is enabled.

Capacity The amount of information a disk can hold, usually measured in megabytes (Mb).

Cascading menu A list of commands from a menu item with an arrow next to it; pointing at the arrow displays a submenu from which you can choose additional commands.

Check box A square box in a dialog box that you click to turn an option on or off.

Check mark A mark that indicates that a feature is enabled.

Classic style A Windows 2000 setting in which you single-click to select items and double-click to open them.

Click To press and release the left mouse button once.

Clipboard Temporary storage space on your computer's hard disk containing information that has been cut or copied.

Close To quit a program or remove a window from the desktop. The Close button is usually located in the upper-right corner of a window.

Command A directive that provides access to a program's features.

Command button In a dialog box, a button that carries out an action. A command button usually has a label that describes its action, such as Cancel or Help. If the label is followed by an ellipses (…), clicking the button displays another dialog box.

Context-sensitive help Help that is specifically related to what you are doing.

Control Panel Used to change computer settings such as desktop colors or mouse settings.

Copy To place information onto the Clipboard in order to paste it in another location, but also leaving it in the original location.

Cut To remove information from a file and place it on the Clipboard, usually to be pasted into another location.

Default Settings preset by the operating system or program.

Delete To place a file or folder in the Recycle Bin, where you can either remove it from the disk permanently or restore it to its original location.

Desktop The screen that appears when you first start Windows 2000, providing access to your computer's programs and files and to the Internet. *See also* Active Desktop.

Dialog box A window that opens when more information is needed to carry out a command.

Document A file that you create using a program such as WordPad.

Double-click To press and release the left mouse button twice quickly.

Drag To move an item to a new location using the mouse.

Drive A device that reads and saves files on a disk and is also used to store files; floppy drives read and save files on floppy disks, whereas hard drives read and save files on your computer's built-in hard disk.

Edit To change the content or format of an existing file.

Explorer Bar The pane on the left side of the screen in Windows Explorer that lists all drives and folders on the computer.

File An electronic collection of information that has a unique name, distinguishing it from other files.

File hierarchy A logical structure for folders and files that mimics how you would organize files and folders in a filing cabinet.

File management The process of organizing and keeping track of files and folders.

Floppy disk A disk that you insert into a disk drive of your computer (usually drive A or B) to store files.

Folder A collection of files and/or other folders that helps you organize your disks.

Font The design of a set of characters (for example, Times New Roman).

Format To enhance the appearance of a document by, for example, changing the font or font size, adding borders and shading to a document.

Graphical user interface (GUI) An environment made up of meaningful symbols, words, and windows in which you can control the basic operation of a computer and the programs that run on it.

Hard disk A disk that is built into the computer (usually drive C) on which you store files and programs.

Highlighting When an icon is shaded differently, indicating it is selected. *See also* Select.

Icon Graphical representation of computer elements such as files and programs.

Inactive Refers to a window or program that is open but not currently in use.

Input device An item, such as a mouse or keyboard, that you use to interact with your computer.

Insertion point A blinking vertical line that indicates where text will appear when you type.

Internet A worldwide collection of over 40 million computers linked together to share information.

Internet style A Windows 2000 setting in which you point to select items and single-click to open them. *See also* Web style.

Keyboard shortcut A keyboard alternative for executing a menu command (for example, [Ctrl][X] for Cut).

List box A box in a dialog box containing a list of items; to choose an item, click the list arrow, then click the desired item.

Maximize To enlarge a window so it fills the entire screen. The Maximize button is usually located in the upper-right corner of a window.

Menu A list of related commands in a program (for example, the File menu).

Menu bar A bar near the top of the program window that provides access to most of a program's features through categories of related commands.

Minimize To reduce the size of a window. The Minimize button is usually located in the upper-right corner of a window.

Mouse A hand-held input device that you roll on your desk to position the mouse pointer on the Windows desktop. See also Mouse pointer.

Mouse buttons The two buttons on the mouse (right and left) that you use to make selections and issue commands.

Mouse pointer The arrow-shaped cursor on the screen that follows the movement of the mouse. The shape of the mouse pointer changes depending on the program and the task being executed. *See also* Mouse.

Multi-tasking Working with more than one window or program at a time.

My Computer A program that you use to manage the drives, folders, and files on your computer.

Open To start a program or open a window; also used to describe a program that is running but not active.

Operating system A computer program that controls the basic operation of your computer and the programs you run on it. Windows 2000 is an example of an operating system.

Option button A small circle in a dialog box that you click to select an option.

Paint A drawing program that comes with Windows 2000.

Pane A section of a divided window.

Point To position the mouse pointer over an item on your computer screen; also a unit of measurement (1/72nd inch) used to specify the size of text.

Pointer trail A shadow of the mouse pointer that appears when you move the mouse; helps you locate the pointer on your screen.

Pop-up menu A menu that appears when you right-click an item on the desktop.

Program Task-oriented software that you use for a particular kind of work, such as word processing or database management. Microsoft Access, Microsoft Excel, and Microsoft Word are all programs.

Program button A button on the taskbar that represents an open program or window.

Properties Characteristics of a specific computer element (such as the mouse, keyboard, or desktop display) that you can customize.

Quick Launch toolbar A toolbar located next to the Start button on the taskbar that contains buttons to start Internet-related programs and show the desktop.

Random access memory (RAM) The memory that programs use to perform necessary tasks while the computer is on. When you turn the computer off, all information in RAM is lost.

Recycle Bin An icon that appears on the desktop that represents a temporary storage area on your computer's hard disk for deleted files, which remain in the Recycle Bin until you empty it.

Restore To reduce the window to its previous size before it was maximized. The Restore button is usually located in the upper-right corner of a window.

Right-click To press and release the right mouse button once.

ScreenTip A description of a toolbar button that appears when you position the mouse pointer over the button.

Scroll bar A bar that appears at the bottom and/or right edge of a window whose contents are not entirely visible; you click the arrows or drag the box in the direction you want to move. *See also* Scroll box.

Scroll box A rectangle located in the vertical and horizontal scroll bars that indicates your relative position in a window. *See also* Scroll bar.

Select To click and highlight an item in order to perform some action on it. *See also* Highlighting.

Shortcut A link that you can place in any location that gives you instant access to a particular file, folder, or program on your hard disk or on a network.

Shut down The action you perform when you have finished working with Windows 2000; after you shut down it is safe to turn off your computer.

Slider An item in a dialog box that you drag to set the degree to which an option is in effect.

Spin box A box with two arrows and a text box; allows you to scroll in numerical increments or type a number.

Start button A button on the taskbar that you use to start programs, find and open files, access Windows Help and more.

Tab A place in a dialog box where related commands and options are organized.

Taskbar A strip at the bottom of the screen that contains the Start button, Quick Launch toolbar, and shows which programs are running.

Text box A rectangular area in a dialog box in which you type text.

Title bar The area along the top of the window that indicates the filename and program used to create it.

Toolbar A strip with buttons that allow you to activate a command quickly.

Web page A document that contains highlighted words, phrases, and graphics that link to other documents on the Internet.

Web site A computer on the Internet that contains Web pages.

Web style A Windows 2000 setting in which you point to select items and single-click to open them. *See also* Internet style.

Window A rectangular frame on a screen that can contain icons, the contents of a file, or other usable data.

Windows Explorer A program that you use to manage files, folders, and shortcuts; allows you to work with more than one computer, folder, or file at once.

Windows Help An online "book" stored on your computer, complete with an index and a table of contents, that contains information about Windows 2000.

WordPad A word processing program that comes with Windows 2000.

World Wide Web Part of the Internet that consists of Web sites located on different computers around the world.

Zip disk A portable disk that can contain 100 Mb, far more than a regular floppy disk.

Zip drive A drive that can handle Zip disks.

Glossary

.ldb The file extension for a temporary file that exists when an Access database is open that keeps track of record locking information when the database is opened.

.mdb The file extension for Access databases.

Action query A query that makes changes to underlying data. There are four types of action queries: delete, update, append, and make-table.

ActiveX control A control that follows ActiveX standards.

ActiveX standards Programming standards developed by Microsoft to allow developers to more easily share software components and functionality across multiple applications.

Aggregate function A special function used in a summary query that calculates information about a group of records rather than a new field of information about each record such as Sum, Avg, and Count.

Alignment Commands used in Form or Report Design View to either left-, center-, or right-align a value within its control, or to align the top, bottom, right, or left edge of the control with respect to other controls.

Analyze it with Microsoft Excel An OfficeLink feature that allows you to quickly copy Access data to Excel.

AND criteria Criteria placed in the same row of the query design grid. All criteria on the same row must be true for a record to appear on the resulting datasheet.

AND query A query that contains AND criteria (two or more criteria present on the same row of the query design grid. Both criteria must be true for the record to appear on the resulting datasheet).

Append query An action query that appends records to another table.

Argument Information that a function uses to create the final answer. In an expression, multiple arguments are separated by commas. All of the arguments are surrounded by a single set of parentheses.

Arguments The pieces of information a function needs to create the final answer.

Argument (macros) For a macro, arguments are additional information for each action of a macro that further clarifies how the action is to execute. For a module, arguments are constants, variables, or expressions that are passed to a procedure and are required for it to execute.

Argument (modules) The pieces of information a function needs to create the final answer. In an expression, multiple arguments are separated by commas. All of the arguments are surrounded by a single set of parentheses.

Arithmetic operator Plus (+), minus (–), multiply (*), divide (/), or exponentiation (^) character used in a mathematical calculation.

Ascending order A sequence in which information is placed in alphabetical order or arranged from smallest to largest.

Auto Center A form property that determines whether a form will be centered in the database window.

AutoFormat Predefined format that you can apply to a form or report to set the background picture, font, color, and alignment formatting choices.

AutoKeys A special name reserved for the macro group object that contains key combinations (such as Ctrl+L) that are used to run associated macros.

AutoNumber A field data type in which Access enters a sequential integer for each record added into the datasheet. Numbers cannot be reused even if the record is deleted.

AutoReport A tool used to quickly create a new report based on the selected table or query.

Back-end database When a database has been split using the Database Splitter, a back-end database is created which contains all of the data and is stored on a computer that is accessible by all users (which is usually the file server in a LAN).

Backup An up-to-date copy of data files.

Bang notation Syntax used to separate parts of an object (the parts are separated by an exclamation point, hence "bang") in the Visual Basic programming language.

Border Style A form property that determines the appearance of the borders around a form.

Bound control A control used in either a form or report to display data from the underlying record source; also used to edit and enter new data in a form.

Bound image control A bound control used to show OLE data such as a picture on a form or report.

Browser Software such as Microsoft Internet Explorer used to find, download, view, and use Web pages.

Breakpoint A bookmark set in VBA code that temporarily suspends execution of the procedure at that point in time so that the user can examine what is happening.

Briefcase A Windows program used to help synchronize two computers that regularly use the same files.

Calculated control A control that uses information from existing controls to calculate new data such as subtotals, dates, or page numbers; used in either a form or report.

Calculated field A field created in Query Design View that results from an expression of existing fields, Access functions, and arithmetic operators. For example the entry Profit: [RetailPrice]-[WholesalePrice] in the field cell of the query design grid creates a calculated field called Profit that is the difference between the values in the RetailPrice and WholesalePrice fields.

Calculation A new value that is created by entering an expression in a text box on a form or report.

Calendar control An ActiveX control that shows the current date selected on a small calendar. You can use this control to find or display a date in the past or future.

Caption A field property used to override the technical field name with an easy-to-read caption entry when the field name appears on datasheets, forms, and reports.

Caption property A field property used to override the technical field name with an easy-to-read caption when the field name appears on datasheets, forms, and reports.

Cascade Delete Related Records An option that can be applied to referential integrity that automatically deletes all records in the "many" table if the record with the matching key field in the "one" table is deleted.

Cascade Update Related Fields An option that can be applied to referential integrity that means that data in the foreign key field of the "many" table will automatically change when primary key fields values in the "one" table are changed.

Case In VBA, a group of statements.

Category axis On a PivotChart, the horizontal axis. Also called the x-axis.

Chart Graph. Visual representation of numeric data that helps a user see comparisons, patterns, and trends in data.

Chart Field List A list of the fields in the underlying record source for a PivotChart.

Chart Wizard Access Wizard that steps you through the process of creating charts within forms and reports.

Check box Bound control used to display "yes" or "no" answers for a field. If the box is "checked" it indicates "yes" information in a form or report.

Child record In a pair of tables that have a one-to-many relationship, the "many" table contains the child records.

Class module A module used only within a particular form or report object and therefore stored within the form or report object.

Client In Internet terminology, this would be your computer.

Client/server applications An application which uses both a server (typically used to manage data and communications process) and clients (typically used to manage the user interface such as forms) for one application.

Client/server computing Two or more information systems cooperatively processing to solve a problem.

Collapse button A button that looks like a "minus sign" to the left of a record displayed in a datasheet that when clicked, collapses the subdatasheet that is displayed.

Combo box A bound control used to display a list of possible entries for a field in which you can also type an entry from the keyboard. It is a "combination" of the list box and text box controls.

Command button An unbound control used to provide an easy way to initiate an action or run a macro.

Command Button Wizard A Wizard that steps you through the process of creating a command button.

Command-line option A special series of characters added to the end of the path to the database file that start with a forward slash and modify the way that the database is opened.

Comment line A VBA statement that does not execute any actions but is used to clarify or document other statements. Comment lines appear in green in the Code window and start with a single apostrophe.

Compacting Rearranging the data and objects on the storage medium so space formerly occupied by deleted objects is eliminated. Compacting a database doesn't change the data, but reduces the overall size of the database.

Comparison operators Characters such as > and < that allow you to find or filter data based on specific criteria.

Compile time The period during which source code is translated to executable code.

Compile time error A VBA error that occurs because of incorrectly constructed VBA code.

Conditional expression An expression that results in either a "true" or "false" answer that determines whether a macro action will execute or not.

Conditional formatting Formatting that is based on specified criteria. For example, a text box may be conditionally formatted to display its value in red if the value is a negative number.

Constant In VBA, a constant is an item that retains a constant value throughout the execution of the code.

Control Any element on a form or report such as a label, text box, line, or combo box. Controls can be bound, unbound, or calculated.

Control Source The most important property of a bound control on a form or report because it determines which field the bound control will display.

ControlTip Text property Property of a control that determines what text displays in tip that pops up when you point to that control with the mouse.

Convert To change a database file into one that can be opened by an earlier version of Access.

Criteria The entry that determines which records are displayed when finding or filtering records in a datasheet or form, or when building a query.

Crosstab query A query that presents data in a cross-tabular layout (fields are used for both column and row headings), similar to PivotTables in other database and spreadsheet products.

Crosstab Query Wizard A wizard used to create crosstab queries that helps identify which fields will be used for row and column headings, and which fields will be summarized within the datasheet.

Crosstab row A row in the query design grid used to specify the column and row headings and values for the crosstab query.

Currency A field data type used for monetary values.

Current record box *See* specific record box.

Current record symbol A black triangle symbol that appears in the record selector box to the left of the record that has the focus in either a datasheet or a form.

DAP *See* Data access page.

Data The unique information you enter into the fields of the records.

Data access page *See* page.

Database A collection of related information, such as a list of employees.

Database password A Password that is required to open a database.

Database software Software used to manage data that can be organized into lists of things such as customers, products, vendors, employees, projects, or sales.

Database Splitter An Access feature that improves the performance of a shared database by allowing you to split it into multiple files.

Database window The window that includes common elements such as the Access title bar, menu bar, and toolbar.

Database Wizard An Access wizard that creates a sample database file for a general purpose such as inventory control, event tracking, or expenses. The objects created by the Database Wizard can be used and modified.

Datasheet View A view that lists the records of the object in a datasheet. Table, query, and most form objects have a Datasheet View.

Data type A required property for each field that defines the type of data that can be entered in each field. Valid data types include AutoNumber, Text, Number, Currency, Date/Time, OLE Object, and Memo.

Date/Time A field data type used for date and time data.

Date function Access function that returns today's date.

Debug To determine why a macro doesn't run properly.

Decimal Places A field property that determines the number of digits that should be displayed to the right of the decimal point (for Number or Currency fields).

Declaration statement A VBA statement that precedes procedure statements and helps set rules for how the statements in the module are processed.

Decrypt To reverse the encryption process.

Default Switchboard When working with switchboards, the default switchboard is the first switchboard in the database, and the one used to link to additional switch board pages.

Default Value A field property that provides a default value, automatically entered for a given field when a new record is created.

Default View A form property that determines whether a subform automatically opens in Datasheet or Continuous Forms View.

Delete query An action query that deletes records based on an expression.

Delimited text file A file with only text (no formatting) that typically stores one record on each line with field values separated by a common character such as a comma, tab, or dash.

Design grid *See* query design grid.

Design View A view in which the structure of the object can be manipulated. Every Access object has a Design View.

Detail A section of the form or report that contains the controls that are printed for each record in the underlying query or table.

Detail section The section of a form or report that contains the controls that are printed for each record in the underlying query or table.

Dialer Software that helps you dial and connect to your Internet Service Provider.

Dialog box A special form that displays information or prompts a user for a choice.

Dialog property option An option for the Border Style form property that adds a thick border to the form, and prevents the form from being maximized, minimized, or resized.

Display Control A field property that determines how a Yes/No field appears in Datasheet View and Form View.

Display When A control property that determines whether the control will appear only on the screen, only when printed, or at all times.

Documenter An Access feature that creates reports on the properties and relationships between the objects in your database.

Domain name The middle part of a URL, such as www.course.com.

Drop area A position on a PivotChart or PivotTable where you can drag and place a field. Drop areas on a PivotTable include the Filter Field, Row Field, Column Field, and Totals or Detail Field. Drop areas on a PivotChart include the Filter Field, Category Field, Series Field, and Data Field.

Dynamic Web page A Web page automatically updated with the latest changes to the database each time it is opened. Web pages created by the page object are dynamic.

Dynaset A type of recordset displayed within a query's datasheet that allows you to update all fields except for those on the "one" side of a one-to-many relationship.

Edit mode The mode in which Access assumes you are trying to edit a particular field, so keystrokes such as [Ctrl][End], [Ctrl][Home], [←], and [→] move the insertion point within the field.

Edit record symbol A pencil-like symbol that appears in the record selector box to the left of the record that is currently being edited in either a datasheet or a form.

E-mail Electronic mail.

Enabled Control property that determines whether the control can have the focus in Form View.

Encrypt To make the database objects and data within the database indecipherable to other programs.

End tag In markup languages such as HTML and XML, an end tag is used to mark the end of data.

Enforce Referential Integrity An option that can be applied to a one-to-many relationship. When applied, it ensures that no orphan records are entered or created in the database by making sure that the "one" side of a linking relationship (CustomerNumber in a Customer table) is entered before that same value can be entered in the "many" side of the relationship (CustomerNumber in a Sales table).

Event Something that happens within a database (such as the click of a command button or the entry of a field) that can be used to initiate the execution of a macro. Events are associated with toolbars, objects, and controls, and can be viewed by examining that item's property sheet.

Expand button A button that looks like a "plus sign" to the left of a record displayed in datasheet view that when clicked, will show related records in a subdatasheet.

Exporting A process to quickly convert data from access to another file format such as an Excel workbook, a Word document, or a static Web page.

Expression A combination of values, functions, and operators that calculates to a single value. Access expressions start with an equal sign and are placed in a text box in either Form Design View or Report Design View.

Extensible Markup Language A set of tags and codes that allow one application to deliver data to another application using Web pages.

Extensible Schema Document A file format that stores structural information about a database. It accompanies and helps describe the data in an XML file.

Extensible Stylesheet Language A file format that stores presentation (formatting characteristics) about data. It accompanies and helps describe the data in an XML file.

Favorites group A group on the Groups bar that organizes frequently used objects.

Field The smallest piece of information in a database such as the customer's name, city, or phone number.

Field list A list of the available fields in the table or query that it represents.

Field names The names given to each field in Table Design or Table Datasheet View.

Field property *See* properties.

Field selector button The button to the left of a field in Table Design View that indicates which field is currently selected.

Field Size A field property that determines the largest number that can be entered in a field (for Number or Currency fields) or the number of characters that can be entered in a field (for Text fields).

Field Size property A field property that determines the number of characters or digits allowed for a field.

File transfer Uploading and downloading files containing anything from text to pictures to music to software programs.

Filter A temporary view of a subset of records. A filter can be saved as a query object if you wish to apply the same filter later without recreating it.

Filter window A window that appears when you click the Filter By Form button when viewing data in a datasheet or in a form window. The Filter window allows you to define the filter criteria.

Find A command used to locate specific data within a field or entire datasheet that the user specifies.

Find Duplicates Query Wizard A wizard used to create a query that determines whether a table contains duplicate values in one or more fields.

Find Unmatched Query Wizard A wizard used to create a query that finds records in one table that doesn't have related records in another table.

Fit (print option) An option that automatically adjusts a preview to display all pages in a report.

Foreign key field In a one-to-many relationship between two tables, the foreign key field is the field in the "many" table that links the table to the primary key field in the "one" table.

Focus The property that indicates which field would be edited if you were to start typing.

Form An Access object that provides an easy-to-use data entry screen that generally shows only one record at a time.

Form Design toolbar The toolbar that appears when working in Form Design View with buttons that help you modify a form's controls.

Form Design View The view of a form in which you add, delete, and modify the form's properties, sections, and controls.

Form Header A section that appears at the top of the screen in Form View for each record, but prints only once at the top of all records when the form is printed.

Form Footer A section that appears at the bottom of screen in Form View for each record, but prints only once at the end of all records when the form is printed.

Form Wizard An Access wizard that helps you create a form.

Format Painter A tool that you can use within Form Design View and Report Design View to copy formatting characteristic from one control, and paint them on another.

Format Field property that controls how information will be displayed and printed.

Front-end database When a database has been split using the Database Splitter, a front-end database is created which contains links back to the data stored in the back-end database as well as any objects needed by the user. The front-end database is stored on the user's computer, which is also called the client computer.

Function A special, predefined formula that provides a shortcut for a commonly used calculation, for example, SUM or COUNT.

Graphic *See* image.

Graphical user interface An interface that is comprised of buttons, lists, graphical elements, and other controls that can be controlled using the mouse rather than just the keyboard.

Group A collection of objects.

Groups bar Located just below the Objects bar in the database window, the Groups bar displays the Favorites and any user-created groups, which in turn contain shortcuts to objects. Groups are used to organize the database objects into logical sets.

Group Footer A section of the report that contains controls that print once at the end of each group of records.

Group Header A section of the report that contains controls that print once at the beginning of each group of records.

Grouping To sort records in a particular order plus provide a section before and after each group of records.

Grouping records In a report, to sort records based on the contents of a field, plus provide a group header section that precedes the group of records as well as a group footer section that follows the group of records.

Grouping controls Allows you to identify several controls as a group to quickly and easily apply the same formatting properties to them.

GUI *See* Graphical user interface

Handles *See* sizing handles.

Hide Duplicates Control property that when set to "Yes," hides duplicate values for the same field from record to record in the Detail section.

Home page The first page displayed when you enter a new URL in your browser.

HTML HyperText Markup Language, a set of codes inserted into a text file that browser software such as Internet Explorer can use to determine the way text, hyperlinks, images, and other elements appear on a Web page.

Hyperlink Address Property of an image on a Web page that stores address information so that if you click the image, it functions like a hyperlink.

HyperText Markup Language *See* HTML.

Hyperlink A field data type that stores World Wide Web addresses. A hyperlink can also be a control on a form that when clicked, opens another database object, external file, or external Web page.

If...Then...Else A series of VBA statements that allow you to test for a logical condition and execute one set of commands if the condition is true and another if the condition is false.

Image A nontextual piece of information such as a picture, piece of clip art, drawn object, or graph. Because images are graphical (not numbers or letters), they are sometimes referred to as graphical images.

Immediate window In the VBA Code window, the area where you can determine the value of any argument at the breakpoint.

Importing A process to quickly convert data from an external source, such as Excel or another database application, into an Access database.

Input Mask A field property that controls the type of data that can be entered into a field and also provides a visual guide as the data is entered.

Insert Merge Field A dialog box within Word that lists all of the fields you can use to merge into the main document to create a customized mass mailing.

Internet A worldwide network of computer networks that sends and receives information such as Web pages and e-mail through a common protocol called TCP/IP.

Internet Service Provider A company that connects your computer to the Internet.

Intranet A wide area network uses the same technologies as the Internet (TCP/IP protocol, e-mail, Web pages), but is built for the internal purposes of a company.

Is Not Null Criterion that finds all records in which any entry has been made in the field.

Is Null Criterion that finds all records in which no entry has been made in the field.

ISP *See* Internet Service Provider.

Junction table A table created for the purpose of establishing separate one-to-many relationships to two tables that have a many-to-many relationship.

Key field *See* primary key field.

Key field combination Two or more fields that as a group contains unique information for each record.

Key field symbol In Table Design View, the symbol that appears as a miniature key in the field indicator box to the left of the field name. It identifies the field that contains unique information for each record.

Key symbol In Table Design View, the symbol that appears as a miniature key in the field indicator box to the left of the field name. It identifies the field that contains unique information for each record.

Label An unbound control that displays static text on forms and reports.

Label Wizard A report-generation tool that helps you create mailing labels.

LAN *See* Local area network.

Layout The general arrangement in which a form will display the fields in the underlying recordset. Layout types include Columnar, Tabular, Datasheet, Chart, and PivotTable. Columnar is most popular for a form, and Datasheet is most popular for a subform.

Left function Access function that returns a specified number of characters starting with the left side of a value in a Text field.

Len function Access function that returns the count of the number of characters in a given field.

Like operator An Access comparison operator that allows queries to find records that match criteria that include a wildcard character.

Line control An unbound control used to draw lines on a form or report that divide it into logical groupings.

Linked table A table created in another database product or application such as Excel, that is stored outside an Access database, but which can still be used within an Access database.

Link Child Fields A subform property that determines which field will serve as the "many" link between the subform and main form.

Link Master Fields A subform property that determines which field will serve as the "one" link between the main form and the subform.

Linking Connects an Access database to an external file such as another Access, dBase, or Paradox database; an Excel spreadsheet, or a text file.

List box A bound control that displays a list of possible choices for the user. Used mainly on forms.

Local area network Connects local resources such as files servers, user computers, and printers by a direct cable.

Locked A control property that specifies whether you can edit data in a control in Form View.

Lookup A reference table or list of values used to populate the values of a field.

Lookup field A field that has lookup properties. Lookup properties are used to create a drop-down list of values to populate the field.

Lookup Wizard A wizard used in Table Design View that allows one field to "lookup" values from another table or entered list. For example, you might use the Lookup Wizard to specify that the CustomerNumber field in the Sales table display the CustomerName field entry from the Customers table.

Macro An Access object that stores a collection of keystrokes or commands such as those for printing several reports in a row or providing a toolbar when a form opens.

Macro Design View An Access view you use to create macros and list macro actions in the order you want them to run.

Macro Group An Access macro object that contains more than one macro.

Mail Merge toolbar Word toolbar that assists in the process of a mail merge.

Main document A Word document that contains the standard text that will be used for each letter in a mass mailing.

Main form A form that contains a subform control.

Main report A report that contains a subreport control is called the main report.

Make-table query An action query that creates a new table.

Many-to-many relationship The relationship between two tables in an Access database in which one record of one table relates to many records in the other table and vice versa. You cannot directly create a many-to-many relationship between two tables in Access. To relate two tables with such a relationship, you must establish a third table called a junction table that creates separate one-to-many relationships with the two original tables.

Master The original Access database file that is copied to the Briefcase.

Memo A field data type used for lengthy text such as comments or notes. It can hold up to 64,000 characters of information.

Merge fields The variable pieces of data that are merged from an Access database into a Word main document during a mail merge process.

Merge It with Microsoft Word An OfficeLink feature that allows you to quickly merge Access database records with a Word document for mass mailing purposes.

Method An action that an object can perform.

Modem Short for modulate-demodulate. Hardware that converts digital computer signals to analog telephone signals

Module An Access object that stores Visual Basic programming code that extends the functions an automated processes of Access.

MsgBox A macro action that displays an informational message.

Multi-user Access databases are inherently multi-user, so that many people can enter and update information at the same time.

Name property Property of a text box that gives the text box a meaningful name.

Named argument In VBA, a value that provides information to an action, event, method, procedure, property, or function.

Navigation buttons Buttons in the lower-left corner of a datasheet or form that allow you to quickly navigate between the records in the underlying object as well as add a new record.

Navigation mode A mode in which Access assumes that you are trying to move between the fields and records of the datasheet (rather than edit a specific field's contents), so keystrokes such as [Ctrl][Home] and [Ctrl][End] move you to the first and last field of the datasheet.

Navigation toolbar Toolbar at the bottom left corner of Datasheet View, Form View, or a Web page that helps you navigate between records.

Network administrator Person who builds and maintains a network.

Newsgroups SImilar to e-mail, but messages are posted in a "public mailbox" that is available to any subscriber, rather than sent to one individual.

Normalization The process of creating a relational database that involves determining the appropriate fields, tables, and table relationships.

NorthwindCS A sample Access database that illustrates how an Access database can connect to an SQL Server database.

Notepad A free Windows accessory text editing program.

Null The state of "nothingness" in a field. Any entry such as 0 in a numeric field or a space in a text field is not null. It is common to search for empty fields by using the Null criteria in a filter or query. Is Not Null criteria finds all records where there is an entry of any kind.

Number A field data type used for numeric information used in calculations, such as quantities.

Object A table, query, form, report, page, macro, or module in Access.

Object (VBA) An item that can be identified or manipulated, including the traditional Access objects, such as a table, query, or form, and smaller parts of these objects, such as controls, sections, and procedures.

Object list box In Form Design view and Report Design view, this box is located on the Formatting (Form/Report) toolbar and displays the name or caption for the currently selected control.

Objects bar In the opening database window, the toolbar that presents the seven Access objects and groups.

ODBC *See* Open Database Connectivity.

OfficeLinks Three tools within Access (Publish It with Microsoft Word, Publish It with Microsoft Excel, and Merge It with Microsoft Word) that allow you to quickly send data from an Access database to another Microsoft Office software product.

OLE Object A field data type that stores pointers that tie files created in other programs to a record such as pictures, sound clips, or spreadsheets.

On Click An event property that causes a macro to run when a command button is clicked.

One-to-many line The line that appears in the Relationships window that shows which field is duplicated between two tables to serve as the linking field. The one-to-many line displays a "1" next to the field that serves as the "one" side of the relationship and an infinity symbol next to the field that serves as the "many" side of the relationship when referential integrity is specified for the relationship. Also called one-to-many join line.

One-to-many relationship The relationship between two tables in an Access database in which a common field links the tables together. The linking field is called the primary key field in the "one" table of the relationship and the foreign key field in the "many" table of the relationship.

Open Database Connectivity Standards that allow data sources to share data with one another

Operators Symbols such as add (+), subtract (–), multiply (*), and divide (/) used in an expression.

Option button A bound control used to display a limited list of mutually exclusive choices for a field such as "female" or "male" for a gender field in a form or report.

Option group A bound control placed on a form that is used to group together several option buttons that provide a limited number of values for a field.

Option Group Wizard An Access wizard that guides the process of developing an option group with option buttons.

Option Value Property for each option button within an option group that identifies what value will be placed in the field when that option button is clicked.

OR criteria Criteria placed on different rows of the query design grid. A record will appear in the resulting datasheet if it is true for any single row.

OR query A query that contains OR criteria (two or more criteria present on different rows in the query design grid. A record will appear on the resulting datasheet if it is true for either criteria.)

Orphan record A record in a "many" table that doesn't have a linking field entry in the "one" table. Orphan records can be avoided by using referential integrity.

Page An Access object that creates Web pages from Access objects as well as provides Web page connectivity features to an Access database. Also called Data Access Page.

Page Design View A view that allows you to modify the structure of a data access page.

Page Footer A section of a form or report that contains controls that print once at the bottom of each page.

Page Header A section of a form or report that contains controls that print once at the top of each page. On the first page of the report, the Page Header section prints below the Report Header section.

Page View A view that allows you to see how your dynamic Web page will appear when opened in Internet Explorer.

Parameter query A query that displays a dialog box prompting you for criteria each time you run it.

Parent record In a pair of tables that have a one-to-many relationship, the "one" table contains the parent records.

Parent/Child relationship The relationship between the main form and subform. The main form acts as the parent, displaying the information about the "one" side of a one-to-many relationship between the forms. The subform acts as the "child" displaying as many records as exist in the "many" side of the one-to-many relationship.

Performance Analyzer An Access feature that studies the size and structure of your database and makes a variety of recommendations on how you could improve its performance.

PivotChart A graphical presentation of the data in a PivotTable.

PivotChart View The view in which you build a PivotChart.

PivotTable An arrangement of data that uses one field as acolumn heading, another as a row heading, and summarizes a third field, typically a Number field, in the body.

PivotTable An organization of data that groups and summarizes records according to a field that serves as a row heading, and another field that serves as a column heading.

PivotTable List A control on a Web page that summarizes data by columns and rows to make it easy to analyze.

PivotTable View The view in which you build a PivotTable.

Pixel One pixel is the measurement of one picture element on the screen.

PMT function Access function that returns the monthly payment for a loan.

Pop-up form A special type of form that stays on top of other open forms, even when another form is active.

Primary key field A field that contains unique information for each record. A primary key field cannot contain a null entry.

Primary sort field In a query grid, the left-most field that includes sort criteria. It determines the order in which the records will appear and can be specified "ascending" or "descending."

Procedure A series of VBA programming statements that perform an operation or calculate an answer. There are two types of procedures: functions and subs.

Project A special Access file that contains no data, but rather, form and report objects. The data for the database is typically located on a file/server to which the project file is linked to.

Properties Characteristics that further define the field (if field properties), control (if control properties), section (if section properties), or object (if object properties).

Property sheet A window that displays an exhaustive list of properties for the chosen control, section, or object within the Form Design View or Report Design View.

Publish It with Microsoft Excel An OfficeLink feature that allows you to quickly copy a query, form, or report object object to Excel.

Publish It with Microsoft Word An OfficeLink feature that allows you to quickly copy a query, form, or report object object to Word.

Publishing Saving Web files to Web folders on a server.

Query An Access object which provides a spreadsheet-like view of the data similar to tables. It may provide the user with a subset of fields and/or records from one or more tables. Queries are created when the user has a "question" about the data in the database.

Query design grid The bottom pane of the Query Design View window in which you specify the fields, sort order, and limiting criteria for the query.

Query Design View The window in which you develop queries by specifying the fields, sort order, and limiting criteria that determine which fields and records are displayed in the resulting datasheet.

Record A group of related fields, such as all demographic information for one customer.

Record locking A feature of Access databases that prevents two users from updating the same record at the same time.

Record selector box The small square to the left of a record in a datasheet that marks the current record or the edit record symbol when the record has the focus or is being edited.

Recordset Type A query property that determines if an how records displayed by a query are locked.

Record Source In a form or report, the property that determines which table or query object contains the fields and records that the form or report will display. It is the most important property of the form or report object. A bound control on a form or report also has a Record Source property. In this case, the Record Source property identifies the field to which the control is bound.

Recordset The value of the Record Source property.

Rectangle control An unbound control used to draw rectangles on the form that divide the other form controls into logical groupings.

Referential integrity Ensures that no orphan records are entered or created in the database by making sure that the "one" side of a linking relationship (CustomerNumber in a Customer table) is entered before that same value can be entered in the "many" side of the relationship (CustomerNumber in a Sales table).

Relational database A database in which more than one table, such as the customer, sales, and inventory tables, can share information. The term "relational database" comes from the fact that the tables are linked or "related" with a common field of information. An Access database is relational.

Replica The copy of the Access database file that is stored in the Briefcase.

Replica set Both the original (master) and replicated (replica) database file. There may be more than one replica in a replica set, but there is only one master.

Replication The process of making replicas of a master database file using the Briefcase.

Report An Access object that creates a professional printout of data that may contain such enhancements as headers, footers, and calculations on groups of records.

Report Design View View of a report in which you add, delete, and edit the report's properties, sections, and controls.

Report Footer On a report, a section that contains controls that print once at the end of the last page of the report.

Report Header On a report, a section that contains controls that print once at the top of the first page of the report.

Report section properties Properties that determine what information appears in different report sections, and how it is formatted.

Report Wizard An Access wizard that helps you create a report.

Required A field property that determines if an entry is required for a field.

Resize bar The bar that separates the upper and lower panes in Query Design View. You drag the resize bar up or down to provide more room for one of the panes.

Rich text format A file format that does not support all advanced Word features, but does support basic formatting embellishments such as font types and colors.

Right function Access function that returns a specified number of characters starting with the right side of a value in a Text field.

Row selector The small square to the left of a field in Table Design View.

Row Source A field Lookup property that provides values for the drop-down lookup list for that field.

RTF *See* Rich text format.

Schema A pictoral representation of how the tables of the database are related. Access presents the database schema in the Relationships window.

Section A location of a form or report that contains controls. The section in which a control is placed determines where and how often the control prints.

Secondary sort field In a query grid, the second field from the left that includes sort criteria. It determines the order in which the records will appear if there is a "tie" on the primary sort field. (For example, the primary sort field might be the State field. If two records both contained the data "IA" in that field, the secondary sort field, which might be the City field, would determine the order of the IA records in the resulting datasheet.)

Security account password A password applied to workgroups used to determine which objects each workgroup has access to and at what level.

Select query The most common type of query that retrieves data from one or more linked tables and displays the results in a datasheet.

Server In Internet terminology, this would be the computer that serves the information to you from the Internet such as a Web page or an e-mail message.

Simple Query Wizard A wizard used to create a select query.

Single step To run a macro one line at a time, and observing the effect of each line as it is executed.

Sizing handles Small squares at each corner of a selected control in Access. Dragging a handle resizes the control. Also known as handles.

Snapshot A type of recordset displayed within Query Datasheet View that does not allow you to update any field.

Sorting Reordering records in either ascending or descending order based on the values of a particular field.

Specific record box Part of a box in the lower-left corner in Datasheet view and Form view of the Navigation buttons that indicates the current record number. You can click in the specific record box, then type a record number to quickly move to that record. Also called the current record box or record number box.

Speech recognition A feature that allows you to speak directly to your computer and have it respond to your commands.

Spreadsheet control An ActiveX control that provides similar functionality.

SQL Server A database program provided by Microsoft for databases that are larger and more complex than those managed by Access.

Standard module A module stored as objects within the database window. Standard modules can be executed from anywhere within the database.

Start tag In markup languages such as HTML and XML, a start tag is used to mark the beginning of data.

Startup option A series of commands that execute when a database is opened.

Statement A line of VBA code.

Status bar The bar at the bottom of the Access window that provides informational messages and other status information (such as whether the Num Lock is active or not).

Status Bar Text property Property of a control that determines what text displays in the status bar when that control has the focus.

Structured Query Language (SQL) A standard programming language for selecting and manipulating data stored in a relational database.

Static Web page Web pages created by exporting a query or report to HTML from an Access database are static because they never change after they are created.

Structured query language *See* SQL.

Subdatasheet A datasheet that shows related records in the "many" table. It appears when the user clicks a record's expand button.

Sub A procedure that performs a series of VBA statements but does not return a value nor can it be used in an expression. You create subs to manipulate controls and objects.

Subform A form placed within a form that shows related records from another table or query. A subform generally displays many records at a time in a datasheet arrangement.

Sub procedure *See* Sub.

Subreport A report placed as a control within another report.

Summary query A query used to calculate and display information about records grouped together.

Switchboard A special type of form that uses command buttons to simplify and secure access to database objects.

Switchboard Manager An Access feature that simplifies the creation and maintenance of switchboard forms.

Synchronization The process of reconciling and updating changes between the master and replicas of a replica set.

Syntax The technical rules that govern a language or program.

Syntax error A VBA error which occurs because of a typing error or misspelling. Syntax errors are highlighted in the Code window in red.

Tab control An unbound control used to create a three-dimensional aspect to a form so that other controls can be organized and shown in Form View by clicking the "tabs."

Tab order The sequence in which the controls on the form receive the focus when the user presses [Tab] or [Enter] in Form view.

Table Datasheet toolbar The toolbar that appears when you are viewing a table's datasheet.

Table Design View The view in which you can add, delete, or modify fields and their associated properties.

Table Wizard An interactive tool used to create a new table from a list of sample tables and sample fields.

Target table A table to which an append query adds a record set.

Templates Sample databases that you can use and modify for your own purposes.

Text A field data type that allows text information or combinations of text and numbers such as a street address. By default, it is 50 characters but can be changed to 50 characters. The maximum length of a text field is 255 characters.

Text box A common control used on forms and reports to display data bound to an underlying field. A text box can also show calculated controls such as subtotals and dates.

Toggle button A bound control used to indicate "yes" or "no" answers for a field. If the button is "pressed" it displays "yes" information.

Toolbox toolbar The toolbar that has common controls that you can add to a report or form when working in Report Design View or Form Design View.

Top values A feature within Query Design View that allows you to limit the number of records in the resulting datasheet to a value or percentage of the total.

Unbound control A control that does not change from record to record and exist only to clarify or enhance the appearance of the form, such as labels, lines, and clip art.

Unbound image control An unbound control that is used to display clip art and that doesn't change as you navigate from record to record on a form or report.

UNC *See* Universal Naming Convention.

Uniform Resource Locator A Web page address that allows other computers to find that Web page.

Universal Naming Convention The address you give a file on a local area network.

Unmatched record *See* orphan record.

Update query An action query that updates data based on an expression.

Upsize Convert an Access database to an SQL Server database.

URL *See* Uniform Resource Locator.

Validation Rule A field property that helps eliminate unreasonable entries by establishing criteria for an entry before it is accepted into the database.

Validation Text A field property that determines what message will appear if a user attempts to make a field entry that does not pass the validation rule for that field.

Value axis On a PivotChart, the vertical axis. Also called the y-axis.

Variable A named storage location that can contain data that can be modified during program execution.

VBA (Visual Basic for Applications) The Access programming language that is very similar to Visual Basic and which is stored within module objects.

VBA password A password that prevents unauthorized users from modifying VBA code.

View buttons Four buttons in the database window that determines how the object icons are displayed (as Large Icons, Small Icons, List, and Details).

Visual Basic Editor Code window (Code window) The window you use to write Visual Basic programming code.

WAN *See* Wide area network.

Web folder Special folders dedicates to organizing Web pages.

Web page A file that is viewed using browser software such as Microsoft Internet Explorer.

Web server A computer that stores and serves Web pages to clients.

Webmaster Person who builds and maintains a Web server.

What-if analysis A reiterative analysis, usually performed in Excel, where you change values in a workbook and watch related calculated formuals update instantly.

Wide area network Created when a LAN is connected to an existing telecommunications network.

Wildcard characters Special characters used in criteria to find, filter, and query data. The asterisk (*) stands for any group of characters. For example, the criteria I* in a State field criteria cell would find all records where the state entry was IA, ID, IL, IN, or Iowa. The question mark (?) wildcard stands for only one character.

Word wrap A feature within Microsoft Word that determines when a line of text extends into the right margin of the page, and automatically forces text to the next line without you needing to press Enter.

Workgroup A description of users, objects, and permissions to which those users have access to the objects stored as a file.

World Wide Web A global network of networks that use Web servers, Web pages, browser software, and other common technologies to share documents across the world.

XML *See* Extensible Markup Language.

XML file A text file that contains Extensible Markup Language (XML) tags that identify fields and contain data.

XSD *See* Extensible Schema Document.

XSL *See* Extensible Stylesheet Language.

Yes/No A field data type that stores only one of two values, "Yes" or "No."

Zoom pointers Mouse pointers displayed in Print Preview that allow you to change the zoom magnification of a printout.

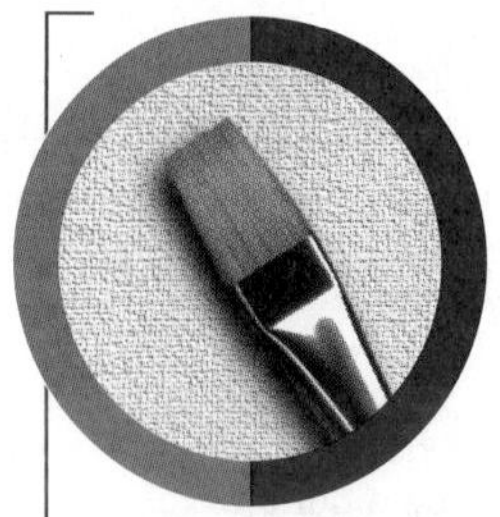

Index

▶D

Index

▶E

▶F

▶G

▶H

▶I

Index

Index

Q

R

Index